Ecuador
& the Galápagos Islands
a travel survival kit

Rob Rachowiecki

Ecuador & the Galápagos Islands – a travel survival kit

3rd edition

Published by
   Lonely Planet Publications
   Head Office: PO Box 617, Hawthorn, Vic 3122, Australia
   Branches: PO Box 2001A, Berkeley, CA 94702, USA and London, UK

Printed by
   Colorcraft, Hong Kong

Photographs by
   Rob Rachowiecki (RR)
   Tony Wheeler (TW)
   Jeff Williams (JW)
   Front cover: Red-billed tropicbird, Rob Rachowiecki
   Back cover: Red Sally Lightfoot crab, Rob Rachowiecki

First Published
   February 1986

This Edition
   August 1992

Although the authors and publisher have tried to make the information as accurate as possible, they accept no responsibility for any loss, injury or inconvenience sustained by any person using this book.

National Library of Australia Cataloguing in Publication Data

Rachowiecki, Rob, 1954 – .
   Ecuador & the Galápagos Islands.

   3rd ed.
   Includes index.
   ISBN 0 86442 148 6.

   1. Ecuador – Description and travel – 1981 – Guidebooks.
   2. Galápagos Islands – Description and travel – 1981 – Guidebooks.
   I. Title. (Series : Lonely Planet travel survival kit).

918.660474

Rob Rachowiecki

Rob Rachowiecki was born near London and became an avid traveller while still a teenager. In 1974, he left the UK to travel around the world – a goal which he finally accomplished ten years later. He spent several years in Latin America, travelling, mountaineering and teaching English, and he now works there part time for Wilderness Travel, an adventure tour company.

He has written many travel articles and guidebooks, including *Climbing & Hiking in Ecuador* (2nd edition 1991, Bradt Publications), and Lonely Planet travel survival kits for *Peru* and *Costa Rica*. When not travelling, Rob lives in Tucson, Arizona with his American wife, Cathy, and daughters Julia and Alison, four and two. He has a Masters Degree in Biology from the University of Arizona and considers the Galápagos Islands to be a fantastic destination for wildlife enthusiasts.

Dedication For Julia and her best friend, Tywannosaurus Wex.

From the Author

This edition has been completely revised and expanded following a recent 2½ month visit to Ecuador. The main changes are the inclusion of a comprehensive Wildlife Guide in the Galápagos section, and a particularly thorough revision of the coastal area which has now almost completely recovered from the disastrous El Niño floods of 1983.

In addition, the national parks and preserves throughout the country are covered in detail.

Many friends, travellers and residents of Ecuador helped me with information. I would particularly like to thank the following folks who shared information and travel experiences with me on the road: Andrea Heckman (shopping in Quito), Kaia Nielsen & Marion Collins (north coast travel), Jason Scholder in Vilcabamba, Sandra A van Dyk (coastal travel and boats to the Galápagos), Karen and Jo on the San Lorenzo train, Dana Burde (Quito nightlife) and Lynn Meisch (Otavalo).

In Quito, Peter and Judith Hurley shared both their knowledge of Ecuador and their apartment with me – many thanks for the hospitality and good times. Also in Quito, the wonderful people at the South American Explorers Club were a constant source of help and information and Oswaldo Muñoz of Nuevo Mundo Expeditions took me on a fascinating trip to the Equator.

I also wish to thank Laura Myers for her hospitality and restaurant information in Guayaquil and Lester 'Don Miguel' Meisenheimer in Borbón for an interesting perspective on the north coast.

Miguel Andrango, Luz María Andrango and Humberto Romero are always friendly and hospitable whenever I visit their Tahuantinsuyo Weaving Workshop in Agato. Randy Borman and Lorenzo Criollo have been especially informative on my various Río Aguarico jungle trips over the years.

Ingeniero Enrique Laso G of FEPROTUR and birding guide Antonio Torres both discussed ecotourism and conservation issues with me. I also received much useful information on these subjects from Rodrigo Ontaneda H of the Fundación Maquipucuna, Gregory A Miller, director of the Ecuador program of The Nature Conservancy, and the folks at Conservation International.

Thanks also to Bill Abbott of Wilderness Travel who sends me to Ecuador and the Galápagos every year and Miguel (Pepe) Salcedo of the *Sulidae* who has entertained me on many visits to the islands. Felipe Cruz, biologist from Isla Floreana, guided me in the Galápagos and contributed much useful background information on the islands.

David Horwell and Clive Green provided information and copies of their books on the Galápagos and birding in Ecuador and Juliana Diamond helped with airline information from the US.

Most of all, I thank Julia and Alison for allowing me to work peacefully in 'daddy's office' and my own Cathy June for her patience, love and understanding.

From the Publisher

Jeff Williams edited this revised edition and Tracey O'Mara was responsible for the maps, design, cover design and the illustrations. Thanks also to Michelle de Kretser, Greg Herriman and Tom Smallman for editorial and design guidance.

Warning & Request

Things change - prices go up, schedules change, good places go bad and bad places go bankrupt - nothing stays the same. So if you find things better or worse, recently opened or long since closed, please write and tell us about it.

Your letters will be used to help update future editions and, where possible, important changes will also be included as a Stop Press section in reprints.

All information is greatly appreciated and the best letters will receive a free copy of the next edition, or any other Lonely Planet book of your choice.

Contents

INTRODUCTION...9

FACTS ABOUT THE COUNTRY...11

History.............................11   Government...............................27   Arts.................................30
Geography.......................16   Economy....................................28   Culture............................32
Climate............................16   Population & People................28   Religion...........................33
Flora & Fauna.................17   Education..................................30   Language.........................33

FACTS FOR THE VISITOR..38

Visas & Embassies...................38   Time................................51   Dangers & Annoyances............65
Customs..................................40   Electricity.......................51   Work...67
Money....................................40   Laundry...........................51   Activities & Highlights............68
When to Go...........................43   Weights & Measures.......51   Accommodation........................69
What to Bring........................44   Books & Maps.................52   Food...72
Tourist Offices.......................45   Media..............................57   Drinks.....................................74
Useful Organisations.............46   Film & Photography.......57   Entertainment..........................76
Business Hours & Holidays......47   Health.............................58   Things to Buy..........................76
Post & Telecommunications......48   Women Travellers...........65

GETTING THERE & AWAY..79

Air...79   Land................................83   Sea...84

Getting Around..85

Air...85   Taxi................................90   Boat...92
Bus..87   Car.................................91   Tours..93
Train.......................................90   Hitching..........................92

QUITO...95

Quito.......................................95   Places to Stay..................116   Rumicucho...............................136
Orientation.............................95   Places to Eat...................121   Reserva Geobotánica
Information.............................95   Entertainment.................125   Pululahua................................136
Walking Tour.........................108   Things to Buy..................127   Pomasqui.................................137
Museums – New Town...........109   Getting There & Away.......128   Calderón..................................137
Museums – Old Town............110   Getting Around...............132   Sangolquí.................................137
Churches................................112   Around Quito..................133   Pasochoa Forest Reserve.........137
Other Sights...........................114   Mitad del Mundo..............135   Volcán Pichincha......................138

NORTH OF QUITO...140

North to Cayambe...................140   Cotacachi.......................155   La Esperanza...........................163
Cochasquí..............................140   Reserva Ecológica   North of Ibarra........................164
Cayambe................................141   Cotacachi-Cayapas...........155   San Gabriel..............................164
On to Otavalo........................141   Laguna de Cuicocha..........155   Tulcán......................................164
Otavalo..................................143   Apuela............................156   West of Tulcán..........................169
Around Otavalo......................152   Ibarra.............................156
Intag Cloud Forest Reserve.....154   San Antonio de Ibarra.......162

SOUTH OF QUITO...171

Machachi.................................171   Saquisilí.........................180   Salasaca...................................188
Ilinizas...................................171   Other Villages.................181   Pelileo.....................................189
La Ciénega.............................173   San Miguel de Salcedo......182   Baños.......................................189
Parque Nacional Cotopaxi......173   Ambato...........................182   Parque Nacional Sangay.........199
Latacunga..............................175   Nearby Villages...............188   Guaranda..................................201

Salinas	204	Guano & Santa Teresita	212	Alausí	213
Riobamba	205	South-West of Riobamba	212	Bucay	215
Chimborazo	211	Guamote	213	Achupallas	215

CUENCA & THE SOUTHERN HIGHLANDS 217

Cuenca	**217**	Area Nacional de Recreación		Oña	241
Information	219	Cajas	231	Saraguro	241
Things to See	222	Gualaceo, Chordeleg & Sígsig	234	Loja	242
Places to Stay	225	Paute	236	Parque Nacional Podocarpus	248
Places to Eat	228	**North of Cuenca**	**236**	Vilcabamba	250
Entertainment	229	Azogues	236	Zumba	251
Things to Buy	229	Cañar	239	Catamayo	251
Getting There & Around	230	Ingapirca	239	El Cisne	252
The Cuenca Area	**231**	**South of Cuenca**	**241**	Catacocha	253
Baños	231	The Road to Machala	241	Macará	253

THE SOUTHERN ORIENTE..256

Zamora	258	Limón	262	Macas	264
Parque Nacional Podocarpus	260	Méndez	262	Parque Nacional Sangay	266
Nambija	260	Morona	262	The Jungle from Macas	267
Yantzaza	261	Cueva de los Tayos	262		
Gualaquiza	261	Sucúa	263		

THE NORTHERN ORIENTE..268

The Road to Puyo	268	Hacienda Primavera	287	Zabalo	297
Shell	270	Pompeya & Limoncocha	288	Tarapoa	297
Puyo	271	La Selva Jungle Lodge	288	Reserva Producción Faunísta	
Puerto Napo	273	Pañacocha	289	Cuyabeno	298
Tena	275	Nuevo Rocafuerte	289	San Rafael Falls & Volcán	
Archidona	277	Parque Nacional Yasuní	290	Reventador	299
Misahuallí	277	Río Tiputini	291	Baeza	300
Ahuano	282	Lago Agrio	291	Papallacta	301
Jatun Sacha	284	Dureno	296		
Coca	284	Flotel Orellana	297		

THE WESTERN LOWLANDS 302

Mindo	302	The Main Road to Santo		Río Palenque Science Center	310
Reserva Biológica		Domingo	305	Quevedo	311
Maquipucuna	304	Tinalandia	306	South of Quevedo	314
The Old Road to Santo		Santo Domingo de los		Babahoyo	315
Domingo	305	Colorados	306		

THE NORTH COAST 318

San Lorenzo	318	Súa	333	Portoviejo	340
Limones	322	Same	334	Inland from Portoviejo	344
Borbón	322	Tonchigüe	334	Manta	344
San Miguel	324	Muisne	334	Bahía de Manta	349
Reserva Ecológica		South of Muisne	336	Montecristi	349
Cotacachi-Cayapas	324	Cojimíes	336	Jipijapa	350
La Tola	325	Pedernales	337	Parque Nacional Machalilla	351
The Road to Esmeraldas	326	Jama	337	Puerto López	353
Esmeraldas	326	Canoa	338	Machalilla	354
Tonsupa	331	San Vicente	338	Salango	354
Atacames	332	Bahía de Caráquez	338	Alandaluz	354

THE SOUTH COAST 356

Guayaquil **356**
Orientation.............................356
Information.............................358
Walking Tour 361
Places to Stay........................368
Places to Eat 371
Entertainment........................372
Getting There & Away 373
Getting Around 376
Durán.....................................377
West of Guayaquil 379

Progreso 379
Playas.....................................379
Punta Pelada 381
Posorja...................................381
Santa Elena Peninsula.............381
La Libertad 383
Punta Carnero 385
Salinas....................................385
North along the Coast..............386
South of Guayaquil..........387

Reserva Ecológica Manglares
Churute....................................387
Machala....................................387
Puerto Bolívar..........................391
Jambelí 392
Pasaje 392
Zaruma Area 392
Piñas..392
Puyango Petrified Forest 393
To the Peruvian Border............393
Huaquillas 394

THE GALÁPAGOS ISLANDS 397

**Introduction to the
Galápagos 397**
History.....................................397
Geography 398
Geology 398
Colonisation & Evolution 399

Wildlife 402
Conservation & Tourism 403
Visitor Sites.............................405
Activities.................................417
Visiting the Galápagos....418
Puerto Ayora 418

Puerto Baquerizo Moreno.......425
Puerto Velasco Ibarra..............426
Puerto Villamil 426
Tours & Charters.....................426

GALÁPAGOS WILDLIFE GUIDE..433

Birds....................................434
Penguins 434
Albatrosses 435
True Petrels & Shearwaters 435
Storm Petrels 436
Tropicbirds..............................437
Pelicans 437
Boobies 438
Cormorants 439
Frigatebirds.............................440
Herons & Egrets 441
Flamingos................................443
Ducks & Geese........................443
Hawks 443
Rails, Crakes & Gallinules 444

Oystercatchers 445
Plovers 445
Sandpipers 446
Stilts..447
Gulls, Terns & Skuas 447
Pigeons 448
Cuckoos & Anis.......................449
Owls..449
Tyrant Flycatchers 450
Swallows & Martins 451
Mockingbirds 451
Wood Warblers, Tanagers,
Blackbirds etc 452
Finches....................................452
Reptiles.............................454

Tortoises 454
Marine Turtles.........................455
Iguanas & Lizards....................456
Geckos....................................458
Snakes 458
Mammals..........................458
Plainnose Bats 458
Mice & Rats 459
Eared Seals..............................459
Whales & Dolphins..................460
Fish.....................................461
Invertebrates...................462
Plants................................464
Checklist 465

INDEX 467

Maps 467
Text 467

Map Legend

BOUNDARIES

— · — · — · — .... International Boundary
— · — · — · — .... Internal Boundary
+++++++++++ .... National Park or Reserve
- - - - - - - - - .... The Equator
.... The Tropics

SYMBOLS

⊙ NEW DELHI .... National Capital
● BOMBAY .... Provincial or State Capital
● Pune .... Major Town
• Barsi .... Minor Town
■ .... Places to Stay
▼ .... Places to Eat
≙ ....Post Office
✈ ✗ ....Airport, Airstrip
i ....Tourist Information
⊖ .... Bus Station or Terminal
66 .... Highway Route Number
☽ ✝ ✝ ...... Mosque, Church, Cathedral
∴ .... Temple or Ruin
✚ .... Hospital
✳ .... Lookout
⚑ .... Camping Area
⋏ .... Picnic Area
⌂ .... Hut or Chalet
▲ .... Mountain or Hill
.... Railway Station
.... Road Bridge
.... Railway Bridge
.... Road Tunnel
.... Railway Tunnel
.... Escarpment or Cliff
.... Pass
.... Ancient or Historic Wall

ROUTES

——————— ....Major Road or Highway
- - - - - - - - .... Unsealed Major Road
——————— .... Sealed Road
- - - - - - - ..... Unsealed Road or Track
═══════ .... City Street
+++++++++++ ....Railway
●━━●━━● .... Subway
....Walking Track
- - - - - - - .... Ferry Route
+++++++ .... Cable Car or Chair Lift

HYDROGRAPHIC FEATURES

.... River or Creek
.............Intermittent Stream
........Lake, Intermittent Lake
.... Coast Line
.... Spring
.... Waterfall
.... Swamp

.... Salt Lake or Reef

.... Glacier

OTHER FEATURES

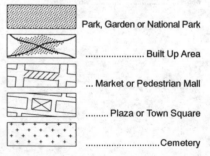

Park, Garden or National Park

.... Built Up Area

... Market or Pedestrian Mall

.... Plaza or Town Square

...........................Cemetery

Note: not all symbols displayed above appear in this book

Introduction

Ecuador is the smallest of the Andean countries, and in many ways it is the easiest and most pleasant to travel in.

From the beautifully preserved colonial capital of Quito, located in the highlands at 2850 metres (9300 feet) above sea level, you can travel by frequent buses to Andean Indian markets, remote jungle towns and warm Pacific beaches. In fact, starting from Quito, you can get to most points in this tropical country in less than a day by public transport.

The highlands have many colourful Indian markets, some world famous and deservedly so, and others which are rarely visited by foreigners but are no less interesting. Any journey in the highlands is dominated by magnificent volcanoes such as Cotopaxi – at 5897 metres (19,348 feet) one of the highest active volcanoes in the world – and many others.

Jungle travel in Ecuador is easier than in most other countries simply because the distances involved are far less, so you can be in the jungle after just a day of bus travel from Quito. There are many exciting opportunities to hire local guides or strike out on your own from jungle towns such as Misahuallí and Coca on the Río Napo, a tributary of the Amazon.

The coast, too, has much to offer. Go to a picturesque fishing village and watch the fishers expertly return their traditional balsawood rafts through the ocean breakers to the sandy shore, or help them pull in their nets in return for some of the catch. Laze on the beach in the equatorial sun, swim in the warm seas, and in the evening listen to salsa music in a local bar.

The Galápagos Islands, 1000 km off the Pacific coast of Ecuador, are high on the list of destinations for travellers interested in wildlife. Here you can swim with penguins and sea lions, or walk along beaches while pelicans flap by and huge land or marine iguanas scurry around your feet. The wildlife is so unafraid of humans that at times it's difficult to avoid stepping on the animals.

Ecuador – a travel survival kit tells you everything you'll need to know about travelling around this enchanting country. The most interesting sights, the best-value hotels and restaurants, details on taking all forms of public transport from cheap air flights to dugout canoes, and a host of background details will make this guide an indispensable part of your trip. And you can do it for as little as US$5 a day – or more if you want some comfort.

Facts about the Country

HISTORY

Most histories of Ecuador begin with the expansion of the Incas from Peru in the 1400s. Archaeological evidence, however, indicates the presence of people in Ecuador for many thousands of years before then. There are two theories explaining where the earliest inhabitants came from.

It is generally accepted that Asian nomads crossed what is now known as the Bering Strait some 25,000 years ago and began reaching the South American continent by about 12,000 BC. It is believed that several thousand years later, trans-Pacific colonisation by the island dwellers of Polynesia added to the population.

La Tolita gold mask

Although stone-age tools found in the Quito area have been dated to 9000 BC, the oldest signs of a more developed culture date back to 3200 BC. These belong to the Valdivia period and consist mainly of ceramics, especially small figurines, found in the central coastal area of Ecuador. Examples of these can be seen in the major museums of Quito and Guayaquil.

Early Tribes

The history of pre-Inca Ecuador is lost in a tangle of time and legend. Generally speaking, the main populations lived either on the coast or in the highlands. The earliest historical details we have date to the 11th century AD when there were two dominant tribes; the expansionist Caras in the coastal areas and the peaceful Quitus in the highlands.

The Caras, led by Shyri, conquered the Quitus but it seems to have been a peaceful expansion rather than bloody warfare. The Cara/Quitu peoples became collectively known as the Shyri nation and were the dominant force in the Ecuadorian highlands until about 1300 AD, by which time the Puruhá of the southern highlands had also risen to power under the Duchicela lineage.

Conflict was avoided by the marriage of a Shyri princess, the only child of a King Caran of the Shyris, to Duchicela, the eldest son of the king of the Puruhás. This Duchicela/Shyri alliance proved successful and the Duchicela line ruled more or less peacefully for about 150 years.

Strange deity image in clay

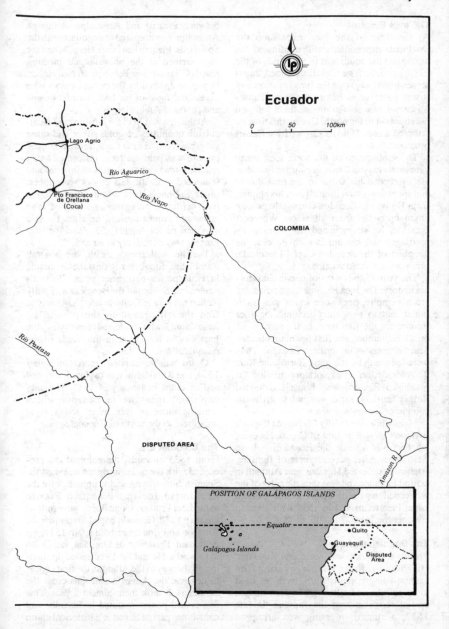

Ecuador

0   50   100km

COLOMBIA

Lago Agrio

Río Aguarico

Pto Francisco
de Orellana
(Coca)

Río Napo

Río Pastaza

Amazon R.

DISPUTED AREA

POSITION OF GALÁPAGOS ISLANDS

Equator

Galápagos Islands

Quito

Guayaquil

Disputed
Area

The Inca Empire

At the time of the Inca expansion the Duchicela descendants still dominated the north, and the south was in the hands of the Cañari people. The Cañari defended themselves bitterly against the Inca invaders and it was some years before the Inca, Tupac-Yupanqui, was able to subdue them and turn his attention to the north. During this time he fathered a son, Huayna Capac, by a Cañari princess.

The subjugation of the north took many years and Huayna Capac grew up in Ecuador. He succeeded his father to the Inca throne and spent years travelling all over his empire, from Bolivia to Ecuador, constantly putting down uprisings from all sides. Wherever possible, he strengthened his position by marriage; and his union with Paccha, the daughter of the defeated Cacha Duchicela, produced a son, Atahualpa.

The year 1526 is a major one in Ecuadorian history. The Inca Huayna Capac died and left his empire, not to one son as was traditional, but to two, thus dividing the Inca Empire for the first time. In the same year, on 21 September, the first Spaniards landed near Esmeraldas in northern Ecuador. They were led south by the pilot, Bartolomé Ruiz de Andrade, on an exploratory mission for Francisco Pizarro, who himself remained further north. Pizarro was not to arrive as conqueror for several years.

Meanwhile, the rivalry of Huayna Capac's two sons grew. The Inca of Cuzco, Huascar, went to war against the Ecuadorian Inca, Atahualpa. After several years of fighting, Atahualpa defeated Huascar near Ambato in central Ecuador and was thus the ruler of the weakened and still divided Inca Empire when Pizarro arrived in 1532 with plans to conquer the Incas.

The Spanish Conquest

Pizarro's advance was rapid and dramatic. His horse-riding, armour-wearing and cannon-firing conquistadors were believed to be godlike and, although few in number, spread terror among the Indians. In late 1532, a summit meeting was arranged between Pizarro and Atahualpa. Although Atahualpa was prepared to negotiate with the Spaniards, Pizarro had other ideas. When the Inca arrived at the pre-arranged meeting place (Cajamarca in Peru) on 16 November, he was ambushed by the conquistadors who massacred most of his badly-armed guards and captured Atahualpa.

Atahualpa was held for ransom, and incalculable quantities of gold, silver and other valuables poured in to Cajamarca. When the ransom was paid the Inca, instead of being released, was put through a sham trial and sentenced to death. His crimes were incest (marrying one's sister was traditional in the Inca heritage), polygamy, worship of false gods, and crimes against the king. He was executed on 29 August 1533, and the Inca Empire was effectively at an end.

Despite Atahualpa's death, his general, Rumiñahui, fought on against the Spaniards in Ecuador for two more years. Pizarro's lieutenant, Sebastián de Benalcázar, finally battled his way to Quito in late 1534, only to find the city razed to the ground by Rumiñahui, who preferred destroying the Inca city to leaving it in the hands of the conquistadors.

Quito was refounded on 6 December 1534, and Rumiñahui was captured, tortured and executed in January of 1535. The only important Inca site in Ecuador which remains more or less intact today is at Ingapirca, to the north of Cuenca.

The Colonial Era

From 1535 onwards, the colonial era proceeded with the usual intrigues amongst the Spanish but with no major uprisings by the Ecuadorian Indians. Francisco Pizarro named his brother, Gonzalo, as governor of Quito in 1540. Gonzalo hoped to conquer the Amazon and find more gold so, in 1541, his lieutenant, Francisco de Orellana, left Quito to prospect. He and his force ended up floating all the way to the Atlantic, the first people to descend the Amazon and thus cross the continent. It took them almost a year. This feat is still commemorated in Ecuador and constitutes part of Ecuador's historical claim to a greater part of the Amazon basin than they actually have.

Lima, Peru, was the seat of the political administration of Ecuador during the first centuries of colonial rule. Ecuador was first known as a *gobernación* (or province) but in 1563 became the *Audiencia de Quito*, a more important political division. In 1739 the *audiencia* was transferred from the viceroyalty of Peru, of which it was a part, to the viceroyalty of Colombia (then known as Nueva Grenada).

Ecuador remained a peaceful colony during these centuries, and agriculture and the arts flourished. Various new agricultural products were introduced from Europe, including cattle and bananas, which still remain important in Ecuador today. There was prolific construction of churches and monasteries which were decorated with unique carvings and paintings resulting from the blend of Spanish and Indian art influences. This so-called 'Quito School of Art' has left an indelible stamp on the colonial buildings of the time and is much admired by visitors today.

Life was comfortable for the ruling colonialists – but the Indians, and later *mestizos*, were treated abysmally under their rule. A system of forced labour was not only tolerated but encouraged, and it is no surprise that by the 18th century there were several uprisings of the Indians against the Spanish ruling classes. Both poor and rich died in violent fighting.

One of the best-remembered heroes of the early revolutionary period was Eugenio Espejo, born in Quito in 1747 of an Indian father and a mulatto mother. Espejo was a brilliant man who obtained his doctorate by the age of 20 and became a major literary voice for independence. He wrote political satire, founded a liberal newspaper and spoke out strongly against colonialism. He was imprisoned several times and died in jail in 1795.

Independence

The first serious attempt to liberate Ecuador from Spanish rule was by a partisan group led by Juan Pío Montúfar on 10 August 1809. The group managed to take Quito and install a government, but this lasted only 24 days before royalist troops (loyal to the King of Spain) were able to regain control.

Independence was finally achieved by Simón Bolívar, the Venezuelan liberator who marched southward from Caracas, freed Colombia in 1819, and supported the people of Guayaquil when they claimed independence on 9 October 1820. It took almost two years before Ecuador was entirely liberated from Spanish rule. The decisive battle was fought on 24 May 1822 when Field Marshal Sucre, one of Bolívar's best generals, defeated the royalists at the Battle of Pichincha and took Quito.

Bolívar's idealistic dream was to form a united South America and he began by amalgamating Venezuela, Colombia and Ecuador into the independent nation of Gran Colombia. This lasted only eight years and Ecuador became fully independent in 1830. In the same year a treaty was signed with Peru, drawing up a boundary between the two nations. This is the boundary that is marked on all Ecuadorian maps. In 1942, after a war between the two countries, the border was redrawn in Rio de Janeiro and it is this border that is found on non-Ecuadorian maps. However, it is not officially acknowledged by Ecuadorian authorities.

Independent Ecuador's internal history has been a typically Latin American turmoil of political and open warfare between liberals and conservatives. Quito emerged as the main centre for the church-backed conservatives and Guayaquil has traditionally been considered liberal and socialist. This rivalry continues on a social level today; Quiteños have nicknamed Guayaquileños as *monos* (monkeys) and the lively coastal people think of the highland inhabitants as very staid and dull.

The rivalry between the groups frequently escalated to extreme violence: conservative President García Moreno was shot and killed in 1875 and liberal President Eloy Alfaro was killed and burned by a mob in Quito in 1912. The military began to take control and the 20th century has seen more periods of military rule than of civilian.

Ecuador's most recent period of democracy began in 1979 when President Jaime Roldos Aguilera was elected. He was killed in an aeroplane crash in 1981 and his term of office was completed by his vice president, Osvaldo Hurtado Larrea.

In 1984 the conservative, León Febres Cordero, was elected to the presidency. Following the democratic elections of 10 August 1988, the social democrat, Rodrigo Borja, became president and the government leant to the left. The next elections are due in 1992. These, like previous elections, are not easy to follow – there are at least 13 political parties in Ecuador. There are also a number of communist, socialist, and revolutionary political movements which are not officially recognised. These do have a certain amount of political power which they exercise by forming alliances with one of the official parties.

Despite intense and bloody rivalry between liberals, conservatives and the military during the earlier part of this century, Ecuador has remained peaceful in recent years and is, at present, one of the safest countries to visit in South America.

GEOGRAPHY

Geographically, Ecuador is one of the world's most varied countries despite its small size, which at 283,520 sq km is about the size of either New Zealand or the US state of Nevada, or somewhat larger than either the UK or the Australian state of Victoria. Ecuador straddles the equator on the Pacific coast of South America and is bordered by only two countries, Colombia to the north and Peru to the south and east.

The country is divided into three regions. The backbone of Ecuador is the Andean range, with Chimborazo (6310 metres) its highest peak. The mountains run from north to south and split the country into the western coastal lowlands and the eastern jungles of the upper Amazonian basin, known in Ecuador as the Oriente. In only 200 km as the condor flies, you can climb from the coast to snowcaps over six km above sea level, and then descend down to the steaming rainforest on the eastern side.

The central highlands are composed of two volcanic mountain ranges, about 400 km long, with a valley nestled between them. This valley was appropriately dubbed 'The Avenue of the Volcanoes' by the German explorer, Alexander von Humboldt, who visited Ecuador in 1802. Within the valley are the capital, Quito – at 2850 metres above sea level the second highest capital in the world after La Paz, Bolivia – and many other towns and tiny villages often of great interest to the traveller for their Indian markets and fiestas. This is the region with the highest population density in the country.

The western coastal lowlands used to be heavily forested but most of the natural vegetation has now been destroyed for agriculture and the mangroves have been hacked out for shrimp ponds. The western provinces of Los Ríos, Manabí and El Oro are the most intensively farmed in Ecuador. The eastern lowlands of the Oriente still retain much of their virgin rainforest, but oil exploitation and colonisation are beginning to seriously threaten this habitat. The population of the Oriente has roughly tripled since the late 1970s.

CLIMATE

Ecuador's climate follows a pattern very different from the one travellers from temperate regions are used to. Instead of the four seasons, there are wet and dry seasons. The weather patterns also vary greatly depending on which geographical region you are in.

The Galápagos and coastal areas are influenced by ocean currents. The warm Ecuatorial countercurrent from the north causes a hot and rainy season from January through April. It doesn't rain all the time but you can expect torrential downpours which often disrupt communications. Daytime temperatures average about 31°C (88°F) but are often much higher, and this time of year is generally an unpleasant time to be travelling in the coastal regions. From May to December both the cool Humboldt and Peru currents from the south keep temperatures a few degrees lower and it rarely rains.

At irregular intervals of every few years, the warm currents of January through April are more pronounced and may flow for a longer period, causing the El Niño phenomenon. This is characterised by abnormally high oceanic temperatures during the coastal rainy season and much marine life (seaweeds, fishes) are unable to survive. This in turn creates problems for species ranging from marine iguanas to seabirds to human beings which rely on the marine life.

A particularly severe El Niño occurred in late 1982 and in to 1983, causing severe problems for the wildlife of the Galápagos Islands and for the coastal fishing industry. The climatological phenomenon is named El Niño (the baby boy) because it usually gets underway at year's end, or about the time the Christ child was born. Although very disruptive, it is still far from being fully understood by climatologists.

If you want to travel in the Oriente, bring your rain gear as it rains during most months. September to December are usually the driest, and June to August are the wettest – with regional variations. It's usually almost as hot as the coast.

The dry season in the highlands is from June through September and a short dry season also occurs during the month around Christmas. It doesn't rain daily in the wet season, however. April, the wettest month, averages one rainy day in two. Daytime temperatures average a high of 20°C to 22°C (68°F to 72°F) and a low of 7°C to 8°C (45°F to 48°F) year round, though you should expect more extreme variations on occasion. These figures are based on climatic data from Quito.

Despite all these statistics, you should remember the Ecuadorian adage that they can experience all four seasons in one day. Without a doubt, the most predictable aspect of Ecuador's weather is its unpredictability.

FLORA & FAUNA

Although Ecuador is a relatively small country, it has many more plant and animal species than do much larger countries. In fact, acre for acre, Ecuador is considered one of the most species-rich nations on the globe. Part of the reason for this is that Ecuador is a tropical country.

Scientists have, for many years, realised that the tropics harbour much greater biodiversity (numbers of different species) than do more temperate countries, but the reasons for this are still a matter of debate and research. The most commonly held belief is that the tropics acted as a refuge for plants and animals during the many ice ages affecting more temperate regions – the much longer and relatively stable climatic history of the tropics has enabled speciation to occur. This may be part of the answer, but ecologists offer various other more technical theories in addition to this one.

A better understood reason for Ecuador's biodiversity is simply that there are a great number of different habitats within the borders of this small country. Obviously, the cold, high Andes will support very different species from the low tropical rainforests, and when all the intermediate habitats are included and the coastal areas added the result is a wealth of habitats, ecosystems, and wildlife. Ecologists have labelled Ecuador as one of the world's 'megadiversity hotspots'. This has attracted increasing numbers of nature lovers from all over the world.

Habitats

Ecologists use a system called Holdridge Life Zones, presented by L R Holdridge in 1947, to classify the type of vegetation found in a given area. Climatic data such as temperature, rainfall, and their variation throughout the year is analysed and combined with information on latitudinal regions and altitudinal belts to give approximately 116 life zones on earth. Some two dozen tropical life zones are found in Ecuador. These are often named according to forest type and altitude and so there are dry, moist, wet, and rain forests in tropical, premontane, lower montane, montane, and subalpine areas. Within a life zone several types of habitat may occur. Thus Ecuador has a huge variety of habitats, each with particular associations of plants and animals. Some of the most important or interesting are described here.

The coastal lowlands have a variety of habitats, of which one of the most remarkable is mangrove swamp. Mangroves are trees which have evolved the remarkable ability of being able to grow in salt water. The red mangrove is the most common in Ecuador and, like other mangroves, has a broadly spreading system of intertwining stilt roots to support the tree in the unstable sandy or silty soils of the shoreline.

Mangroves form forests and are good colonising species – their stilt roots trap sediments and build up a rich organic soil which in turn supports other plants. In between the roots, a protected habitat is provided for many types of fish, as well as molluscs, crustaceans, and many other invertebrates. The branches provide nesting areas for a variety of seabirds such as pelicans, frigatebirds, and others. Mangroves are found primarily in the far northern and southern coastal regions of the country – the shrimp industry has extensively destroyed the mangroves on most of Ecuador's coastline, endangering the breeding grounds of many species.

Tropical dry forest is a fast disappearing habitat found in hot areas where there are well-defined wet and dry seasons, as on the coast. The trees lose their leaves during the dry season and tend to be more spaced out than in the rainforest, creating a more open habitat. It is estimated that only about 1% of tropical dry forest remains undisturbed. The best and only extensive example in Ecuador is found on the central Pacific coast in Parque Nacional Machalilla, and tropical dry forest is further described in that section.

In remote valleys at higher elevations, tropical cloud forests are found – one of the least known types of tropical forest. They are so named because they trap (and help create) clouds which drench the forest in a fine mist, allowing some particularly delicate forms of plant life to survive. Cloud forest trees are adapted to steep rocky soils and a harsh climate. They have a characteristic low gnarled growth, dense small-leaved canopies, and moss-covered branches supporting a host of plants such as orchids, ferns, bromeliads and many others. These aerial plants, which gather their moisture and some nutrients without ground roots, are collectively termed epiphytes.

The dense vegetation at all levels of this forest gives it a mysterious and delicate fairy-tale appearance. It is the home of such rare species as the woolly tapir, Andean spectacled bear, and puma. This habitat is particularly important as a source of fresh water and to control erosion.

Above these forests lies the *páramo*, or high altitude grassland and shrubland. This is the natural 'sponge' of the Andes – it catches and gradually releases much of the water that is eventually used by city dwellers in the highlands. The páramo covers over 10% of Ecuador's land area and is characterised by a harsh climate, high levels of ultra-violet light, and wet peaty soils. It is a highly specialised highland habitat unique to the neotropics (tropical America), and found only from the highlands of Costa Rica at 10°N to northern Peru at 10°S. Similarly elevated grasslands in other parts of the world differ in their climates and evolutionary history, and have different assemblages of plants and animals.

The páramo has a fairly limited flora dominated by hard grasses, cushion plants, and small herbaceous plants. These have adapted well to the harsh environment and consequently the vegetation looks strange and interesting. Major adaptations include the development of small, thick leaves which are less susceptible to frost; the development of curved leaves with heavy, waxy skins to reflect extreme solar radiation during cloudless days; the growth of a fine, hairy down as insulation on the plant's surface; the arrangement of leaves into a rosette to prevent them shading one another during photosynthesis and to protect the delicate centre of the plant; and the compacting of the plant so it grows close to the ground where the temperature is more constant and the wind less strong. Thus many páramo plants are characteristically small and compact, sometimes resembling a hard, waxy, green carpet.

Not all páramo plants are so compacted, however. The giant *Espeletia*, members of the daisy family, are a weird sight as their loosely arranged stands float into view in a typical páramo mist. They are as high as a person, hence the local nickname of *frailejones*, meaning 'grey friars'. They are an unmistakable feature of the northern Ecuadorian páramo, particularly in the El Angel region near Tulcán. Further south the páramo becomes rather drier and the bromeliads called *puyas* are found – plants with a rosette of spiky leaves growing out of a short trunk.

Another attractive plant of the central and southern Ecuadorian páramo is the *chuquiragua* which resembles a thistle topped with orange flower heads and with stems densely covered with tough spiky leaves. This plant has medicinal properties and is used locally to soothe coughs, and for liver and kidney infections.

The páramo is also characterised by dense thickets of small trees. These are often *Polylepsis* species, or *quinua* in Spanish, members of the rose family. With the Himalayan pines, they share the world altitudinal record for trees. They were once considerably more extensive but fire and grazing have pushed them back into small pockets. Instead, grasses are more common. A spiky, resistant tussock grass, locally called *ichu*, is commonly encountered. It grows in large clumps and makes walking uncomfortable.

Over half a million Ecuadorians live on the páramo, so it is of considerable importance to the inter-Andean economy. It has been used for growing a large variety of potatoes and other tubers for centuries, but the great increase in cattle grazing is a more recent phenomenon.

In order to manage the land for cattle, burning is carried out to encourage the growth of succulent young shoots. This does not favour older growth and, combined with erosion caused by overgrazing, poses considerable threats to this fragile habitat.

Of all the tropical habitats found in Ecuador, it is the rainforest which seems to attract the most attention from visitors.

A walk through a tropical forest shows that it is very different from the temperate forests that many North Americans or Europeans may be used to. Temperate forests, such as the coniferous forests of the far north or the deciduous woodlands of milder regions, tend to have little variety. It's pines, pines, and more pines, or interminable acres of oaks, beech, and birch. Tropical forests, on the other hand, have great variety. If you stand in one spot and look around, you see scores of different species of trees, but you often have to walk several hundred metres to find another example of any particular species.

Visitors to the rainforest are often bewildered by the huge variety of plants and animals found there. With the exception of mammals and birds, there are few useful field-guides to what there is to be seen. For this reason, it is worth investing in a guided tour if you are particularly interested in learning about the fantastic flora & fauna – not that any guide will be able to answer all your questions!

One thing which often astounds visitors is the sheer immensity of some trees. A good example is the ceiba tree (also called the kapok) which has huge flattened supports, or buttresses, around its base, which may easily reach five or more metres across. The smooth grey trunk often grows straight up for 50 metres before the branches are reached. These spread out into a huge crown with a slightly flattened appearance – the shape is distinctive and the tree is often the last to be logged in a ranching area. When you see a huge, buttressed, and flattened looking tree in a pasture in the Amazonian lowlands, it very often is a ceiba.

Some rainforest trees have strange roots looking like props or stilts supporting them. These trees are most frequently found in rainforest which is periodically flooded – the stilt roots are thought to play a role in keeping the tree upright during the inundations. Various types of trees use this technique – in the Oriente, palms are often supported by this kind of root system; on the coast look for mangroves with stilt roots.

In areas which have been cleared (often naturally, as by a flash flood which may remove the trees on the riverbanks, or simply by a gap created by an ancient forest giant falling during a storm) various fast-growing pioneer species appear. These may grow several metres a year in areas where abundant sunlight is suddenly available. Some of the most common and easily recognised of these are in the genus *Cecropia*, which has a number of species. Look for them in recently cleared areas, such as riverbanks. Their grey trunks are often circled by ridges at intervals of a few centimetres, but are otherwise fairly smooth, and their branches tend to form a canopy at the top of, rather than all along, the trunk. The leaves are very large and palmate (like a human hand with spread fingers), with the underside a much lighter green than the top surface. This is particularly noticeable when strong winds make the leaves display alternately light and dark green shades in a chaotic manner.

These are just a few of the most common sights in the forest. The incredible variety of plants is correlated with the high biodiversity of the animals which live within the forests. Terry Erwin of the Smithsonian Institution has spent much time in Amazonian rainforests and reports that 3000 species of beetles were found in five different areas of rainforest – but each area was only 12 metres square! Erwin estimates that each species of tree in the rainforest supports over 400 unique species of animals – given the thousands of known tree species, this means that there are millions of species of animals living in the rainforest, many of them insects and most unknown to science. These complex inter-relationships and high biodiversity are among the reasons why many people are calling for a halt to the destruction of tropical forests. Despite this, Ecuador currently has one of the highest rates of deforestation in South America.

Plants

There are over 20,000 species of vascular plants in Ecuador and new species are being discovered every year. It is likely that the final count will be in the region of 25,000 – this number is exceptionally high when compared to the 17,000 species found in the entire North American continent. An introduction to some of the most common plants of Ecuador can be found by reading Habitats earlier.

Birds

Birdwatchers from all over the world come to Ecuador because of the great number of species recorded here – about 1500, or approximately twice the number found in any one of the continents of North America, Europe, or Australia. The South American continent has almost 3000 species of birds, but it is impossible to give a precise number of bird species for either the continent or the countries within it. The noted ornithologist, Robert Ridgely, who is working on a fieldguide to Ecuadorian birds, estimates that several species are added to the Ecuadorian list every year. Paul Greenfield, an artist and ornithologist living in Quito and illustrating the forthcoming guide to the birds of Ecuador, recently reported 1550 species for the country.

Most of the birds being added to the Ecuadorian list are already known from other South American countries. Occasionally, however, a species new to science is discovered – a very rare event in the world of birds. The most recent Ecuadorian bird which has been discovered, described, scientifically named, and accepted by the ornithological community is the El Oro parakeet *(Pyrrhura orcesi)*. This bird was discovered west of Piñas in El Oro Province by Ridgely, Greenfield, and Rose Anne Rowlett in 1980 (it takes years for the full process from discovery to acceptance to occur).

Many visitors are less interested in observing a newly described species and are more interested in seeing the birds typical of Ecuador. One of these is the Andean condor, often called the largest flying bird in the world. With its three-metre wing span and 10-kg weight it is certainly magnificent. In 1880, the British mountaineer, Edward Whymper, noted that he commonly saw a dozen on the wing at the same time. Today, there are only a few hundred pairs left in the highlands. I have seen condors half a dozen times in several years of travel in Ecuador, so you shouldn't expect to see them very frequently. Condors are best recognised by their flat, gliding flight with fingered wing tips (formed by spread primary feathers), silvery patches on the upper wing surface (best seen when the bird wheels in the sun), and a white neck ruff and unfeathered, flesh-coloured head (binoculars help). Otherwise, the bird is black.

Other birds of the highlands include the carunculated caracara, a large member of the falcon family. It has bright orange-red facial skin, yellowish bill and legs, white thighs and underparts, and is otherwise black. This bird is often seen in the páramos of Parque Nacional Cotopaxi. Also frequently sighted here is the Andean lapwing, unmistakable with its harsh and noisy call, reddish eyes, legs, and bill, and brown/white/black striped wing pattern particularly noticeable in flight.

Most towns, both in the highlands and the lowlands, are host to the ubiquitous rufous-collared sparrow. The well-known house sparrow of Europe, Asia, Australia, and North America is not found in Ecuador – the similarly sized rufous-collared sparrow, readily identified by the chestnut collar on the back of the neck, replaces the house sparrow in Ecuador.

For many visitors, the diminutive hummingbirds are the most delightful birds to observe. About 120 species have been recorded from Ecuador, and their exquisite beauty is matched by extravagant names such as green-tailed goldenthroat, spangled coquette, fawn-breasted brilliant, and amethyst-throated sunangel, to name a few. Hummingbirds can beat their wings in a figure-of-eight pattern up to 80 times a second, thus producing the typical hum for which they are named. This exceptionally

rapid wingbeat enables them to hover in place when feeding on nectar, or even to fly backwards. These tiny birds must feed frequently to gain the energy needed to keep them flying. Species like the Andean hillstar, living in the páramo, have evolved an amazing strategy to survive a cold night. They go into a state of torpor, which is like a nightly hibernation, by lowering their body temperature by about 25°C, thus lowering their metabolism drastically.

For many visitors interested in birds, a trip to the Galápagos Islands is very rewarding. This is partly because about half of the 58 resident species are endemic to the Galápagos (they breed nowhere else in the world). Also, most of the Galápagos birds have either lost, or not evolved, a fear of human visitors. Therefore travellers can walk among colonies of blue-footed boobies or magnificent frigatebirds without causing the birds to fly off.

Other exciting birds (on the mainland) include brightly coloured blue-and-yellow macaws and 44 other parrot species; 19 different toucans with their incredibly large and hollow bills; the huge and very rare harpy eagle which is capable of snatching monkeys and sloths off branches as it flies past; and a large array of other tropical birds such as flycatchers (167 species), tanagers (133 species), antbirds (110 species), cotingas (43 species), and many others.

Mammals

Mammals, too, are well represented with some 300 species recorded in the country. These vary from monkeys in the Amazonian lowlands to the rare Andean spectacled bear in the highlands. The most diverse mammals are the bats – there are well over 100 species in Ecuador alone.

Visitors to protected areas of the Amazonian lowlands may see one or more of the several species of monkeys found in Ecuador, including the howler, spider, woolly, titi, capuchin, and squirrel monkeys, as well as tamarins and marmosets. The monkeys of the new world (the Platyrrhini) differ markedly from the monkeys of the old world, including ourselves (the Catarrhini). New world monkeys have, comparatively, been little studied and their names are still under constant study and revision.

The male howler monkeys are heard as often as they are seen; their eerie vocalisations carry long distances and have been likened to a baby crying or the wind moaning through the trees. Many visitors are unable to believe they are hearing a monkey when they first listen to the mournful sound.

Other tropical specialities include two species of sloths. The diurnal three-toed sloth is quite often sighted whereas the two-toed sloth is nocturnal and therefore rarely seen. Sloths are often found hanging motionless from tree limbs, or progressing at a painfully slow speed along a branch towards a particularly succulent bunch of leaves, which are their primary food source. Leaf digestion takes several days and sloths defecate about once a week.

They are most fastidious with their toilet habits, always climbing down from their tree to deposit their weekly bowel movement on the ground. Biologists do not know why sloths do this; one suggested hypothesis is that by consistently defecating at the base of a particular tree, the sloths provide a natural fertiliser which increases the quality of the leaves of that tree, thus improving the sloth's diet.

Mammals commonly seen in the highlands include deer, rabbits, and squirrels. Foxes are also occasionally sighted. There are far fewer species of mammals in the highlands than in the lowlands. The mammals most commonly associated with the Andes are the cameloids – the llamas, alpacas, guanacos, and vicuñas. Of these, only the llama lives in Ecuador, and in far fewer numbers than in Peru or Bolivia. Nevertheless, llamas can even be seen occasionally on the outskirts of Quito, and there is a huge experimental flock near the entrance of Parque Nacional Cotopaxi. Llamas are exclusively domesticated and are used primarily as pack animals, although their skin and meat is occasionally used in remote areas.

Other possible mammal sightings include anteaters agoutis (large rodents), armadillos, capybaras (even larger rodents, some weighing up to 65 kg), peccaries (wild pigs), and otters. River dolphins are occasionally sighted on Amazonian tributaries. Other exotic mammals such as ocelots, jaguars, tapirs, pumas, and spectacled bears are very rarely seen.

Insects

Many thousands of species of insects have been described from Ecuador, and many thousands more remain undiscovered.

Butterflies are among the first insects that the visitor to the tropics notices. Perhaps the most dazzling butterflies are the morphos. With their 15-cm wingspans and electric blue upper wings, they lazily flap and glide along tropical rivers in a shimmering display. When they land, however, their wings close and only the brown underwings are visible. In an instant they have changed from outrageous flaunting to a modest camouflage.

Camouflage plays an important part of many insects' lives. Some resting butterflies look exactly like green or brown leaves, others look like the scaly bark of the tree on which they are resting. Caterpillars are often masters of disguise. Some species mimic twigs, another is capable of constricting certain muscles to make itself look like the head of a viper, and yet another species looks so much like a bird dropping that it rarely gets attacked by predators.

Any walk through a tropical forest will almost invariably allow the observer to study many different types of ants. Among my favourites are the *Atta* leaf cutter ants, which can be seen marching in columns along the forest floor, carrying pieces of leaves like little parasols above their heads. The leaf segments are taken into the ants' underground colony and there the leaves are allowed to rot down into a mulch. The ants tend their mulch gardens carefully, and allow a certain species of fungus to grow there. The fruiting bodies of the fungus are then used to feed the colony, which can exceed a million ants.

Other insect species are so tiny as to be barely visible, yet their lifestyles are no less esoteric. The hummingbird flower mites are barely half a mm in length, and live in flowers visited by hummingbirds. When the flowers are visited by the hummers, the mites scuttle up into the birds' nostrils and use this novel form of air transport to disperse themselves to other plants. Smaller still are mites which live on the proboscis of the morpho butterflies.

From the largest to the smallest insects – there is a world of wonder in the tropical forests.

Other Animals

Amphibians and reptiles form a fascinating part of the Ecuadorian fauna. The approximately 400 species of amphibians include tree frogs who spend their entire life cycle in trees. Some of them have solved the problem of where to lay their eggs by doing so into the water trapped in cup-like plants called bromeliads, which live high up in the forest canopy.

Perhaps more bizarre still are the marsupial frogs. The females carry their eggs in pouches under their skins – sometimes 200 or more eggs may be carried. The eggs are pushed into the pouches by the male immediately after fertilisation. Hatching occurs in the pouches and the tadpoles eventually emerge from under their mother's skin.

Dendrobatids, better known by their colloquial name of poison-arrow frogs, are among the most brightly coloured of frogs. Some are bright red with black dots, others red with blue legs, and still others are bright green with black markings. Some species have skin glands exuding toxins which can cause paralysis and death in many animals, including humans. It is well known that dendrobatids have long been used by Latin American forest Indians to provide a poison with which to dip the tips of their hunting arrows. It should be mentioned that the toxins are most effective when introduced into the blood stream (as with arrows) but

have little effect when a frog is casually touched.

There are almost 400 species of reptiles recorded in Ecuador – about 100 more than in all of North America. Snakes make up roughly half of the Ecuadorian reptiles. They are much talked about but seldom seen – they usually slither away into the undergrowth when they hear people coming and only a lucky few visitors are able to catch sight of one. Perhaps the most feared is the fer-de-lance, which is very poisonous and sometimes fatal to humans. It often lives in overgrown, brushy fields. Agricultural workers clearing these fields are the most frequent victims but tourists are rarely bitten.

Recent inventories of Amazonian fish have shown surprisingly high biodiversity. There are about 2500 species in the whole Amazon basin, and roughly 1000 species in Ecuador. Some of these are fearsome and feared. The electric eel can produce shocks of 600 volts; schools of piranha can devour large animals in minutes; stingrays can deliver a crippling sting; and the tiny candirú catfish can swim up the human urethra and become lodged there by erecting its sharp spines. Despite these horror stories, most Amazonian rivers are safe to swim in – follow the example of the locals. Shuffle your feet as you enter the water – this scares off the bottom dwelling stingrays and stops you stepping on one. Wear a bathing suit to avoid having a candirú swim up your urethra. Don't swim with open, bleeding cuts or in areas where fish are being cleaned – piranhas are attracted to blood and guts.

National Parks

Ecuador's first *parque nacional* (national park) was the Galápagos, formed in 1959. But it was not until the mid to late 1970s that a comprehensive national park system began to be established on the mainland. The first mainland park was Cotopaxi, established in 1975, followed by Machalilla, Yasuní, and Sangay in 1979, and Podocarpus in 1982. Apart from these six national parks, there are six *reservas* (reserves) of various kinds, most created in 1979, and two national recreation areas. In addition, local conservation organisations such as the Fundación Natura and others have begun to set aside private nature reserves.

Together, these areas cover about 10% of the national territory. All of Ecuador's major ecosystems are partly protected in one (or more) of these areas.

The national parks do not have the tourist infrastructure which one may be used to in

least one park or reserve during their stay in Ecuador.

The national park system is administered by La División de Areas Naturales y Vida Silvestre (Division of Natural Areas and Wildlife), which is part of El Ministerio de Agricultura y Ganadería (the Ministry of Agriculture and Ranching). Unfortunately, MAG is unable to properly protect the national park system. Oil has been removed

Refuge, Area Nacional de Recreación Cajas

other parts of the world. There are almost no hostels, drive-in campgrounds, restaurants, ranger stations, museums, scenic overlooks, or information centres. Some of the parks or reserves are remote, difficult to get to, and lacking all facilities. Many are inhabited by native peoples who had been living in the area for generations before the area achieved park or reserve status.

All of these areas are susceptible to interests which are incompatible with full protection – oil drilling, logging, mining, ranching, and colonisation. Despite this, the national parks do preserve large tracts of pristine habitat and many travellers visit at

from the Reserva Producción Faunísta Cuyabeno for several years and, in 1991, the government gave permission to Conoco to begin oil exploration in Parque Nacional Yasuní.

Conservation

The loss of key habitats, particularly tropical forests, is a problem which has become extremely acute in recent years. Deforestation is happening at such a rate that most of the world's tropical forests will have disappeared by early in the 21st century; loss of other habitats is a less publicised but equally pressing concern. With this in mind, two important questions arise: why are habitats such as the tropical rainforests so important and what can be done to prevent their loss?

Much of Ecuador's remaining natural vegetation is tropical forest and there are many reasons why this particular ecosystem is important. Roughly half of the two million known species on earth live in tropical rainforests such as those found in Parque Nacional Yasuní. Scientists predict that millions more plant and animal species remain to be discovered, principally in the world's remaining rainforests which have the greatest biodiversity of all the habitats known on the planet. This incredible array of plants and animals cannot exist unless the rainforest that they inhabit is protected – deforestation will result not only in the loss of rainforest but in countless extinctions as well.

The value of tropical plants is more than simply providing habitat and food for animals; it is more than the aesthetic value of the plants themselves. Many types of medicines have been extracted from forest trees, shrubs, and flowers. These range from anaesthetics to antibiotics, from contraceptives to cures for heart diseases, malaria, and various other illnesses. Countless medicinal uses of plants are known only to the indigenous inhabitants of the forest. Much of this knowledge is being lost as the various indigenous cultures are assimilated into the Western way of life, or when tribal groups are destroyed by disease or genocide. Other pharmaceutical treasures remain locked up in tropical forests, unknown to anybody. They may never be discovered if the forests are destroyed.

Many tropical crops are monocultures which suffer from a lack of genetic diversity. In other words, all the plants are almost identical because agriculturalists have bred strains which are high yielding, easy to harvest, taste good etc. If these monocultures are attacked by a new disease or pest epidemic they could be wiped out because the resistant strains may have been bred out of the population. Plants such as bananas (Ecuador's most economically important agricultural product) are also found in the wild in tropical forests. In the event of an epidemic scientists could look for disease-resistant wild strains to breed into the commercially raised crops. Deforestation leads not only to species extinction, but also to loss of the genetic diversity which may help species adapt to a changing world.

Whilst biodiversity for aesthetic, medicinal, and genetic reasons may be important to us, it is even more important to the local indigenous peoples who still survive in tropical rainforests. In Ecuador there are Huoarani, Shuar, Cofan, Secoya, Cayapas and other Indian groups still living in the rainforest in a more or less traditional manner. They rely on the rainforest to maintain their cultural identity and a way of life that has lasted for centuries. The accelerated pace of deforestation leads to a loss of tribal groups who are as unable to survive in a Western world as we would be if forced to survive in the jungle.

Rainforests are important on a global scale because they moderate climatic patterns worldwide. Scientists have recently determined that destruction of the rainforests is a major contributing factor to global warming which would lead to disastrous changes to our world. These changes include melting of ice caps causing rising ocean levels and flooding of major coastal cities, many of which are only a scant few metres above present sea level. Global warming would also make many of the world's 'breadbasket' regions unsuitable for crop production.

All these are good reasons why the rainforest and other habitats should be preserved and protected, but the reality of the economic importance of forest exploitation by the developing nations which own tropical forests must also be considered. It is undeniably true that the rainforest provides resources in the way of lumber, pastureland, and possible mineral wealth, but this is a short-sighted view.

The long term importance of the rainforest both from a global view and as a resource of biodiversity, genetic variation, and pharmaceutical wealth is becoming recognised both by the countries that contain forest as well as the other nations of the world which will be affected by destruction of these rainforests. Efforts are now underway to show that the economic value of the standing rainforest is greater than wealth realised by deforestation.

One important way of making the tropical forest an economically productive resource without cutting it down is by protecting it in national parks and reserves and making it accessible to tourists and travellers from all over the world. This type of ecotourism is becoming increasingly important for the economy of Ecuador and other nations with similar natural resources.

More people are likely to visit Ecuador to see monkeys in the forest than to see cows on pasture. The visitors spend money on hotels, transport, tours, food, and souvenirs. In addition, many people who spend time in the tropics become more understanding of the natural beauty within the forests and of the importance of preserving them. As a result, visitors return home and become goodwill ambassadors for tropical forests.

Other innovative projects for sustainable development of tropical forests are being developed. Conservation International has developed the sustainable harvesting of the tagua nut – this rainforest product is as hard as ivory and is being used to carve ornaments (as souvenirs) and even to make buttons which are bought by North American clothing manufacturers.

Various international agencies such as Conservation International, The Nature Conservancy, Natural Resources Defense Council, and World Wildlife Fund have provided much needed expertise and economic support. They have developed programmes such as the 'debt for nature' swaps whereby parts of Ecuador's national debt was paid off in return for local groups receiving Ecuadorian funds for preserving crucial habitats.

Local conservation groups have blossomed in the late 1980s and early 1990s. In 1991 there was a real growth in groups on the coast. These are particularly concerned with the protection of the mangrove forests and have been forging cooperative links with shell and crab collectors who are being

affected by mangrove destruction. Some groups have been quite successful in providing legal protection for these forests. Other groups have concentrated on improving environmental data collection and training members in the disciplines needed to create a strong information base for national conservation research.

Several small groups have been established to protect specific natural areas. These groups then go on to involve communities around these reserves through environmental education, agroforestry, and community development projects. Such community involvement at the grass roots level is essential for viable conservation in Ecuador.

By far the biggest environmental NGO (non-government organisation) is the Fundación Natura. In the absence of a specific government department for the environment, the Fundación has been most involved in improving the system of protected areas in the country and has developed its own cloud forest reserve, Pasochoa, near Quito. The Fundación also has a large environmental education programme and arranges campaigns on specific conservation issues.

Perhaps the greatest focus for small groups in the early 1990s has been the Amazon. In a campaign called *Amazonia: Por la Vida* (Amazonia For Life), these groups have used street theatre, nonviolent direct action against petroleum companies, and public education campaigns to raise national consciousness and provoke debate on the cultural and ecological effects of oil-based development.

The role of indigenous organisations should also be recognised as an effective voice in environmental protection. The struggle they have been engaged in to secure land rights, particularly in the Amazon regions, has gone a long way to secure the future of the tropical forests in that area.

Most of these organisations rely on support from the public. Even large entities such as the World Wildlife Fund receive the bulk of their income not from government agencies or corporate contributions, but from individual members. In 1989, for example, fully 69% of the World Wildlife Fund's revenue came from its over half a million individual members worldwide. The Nature Conservancy reports that 78.7% of its 1990 revenue came from individual members. The vital work of these and other agencies requires every assistance possible. Ecuadorian conservation groups are particularly in need of assistance. If you visit Ecuador and would like to help conserve it, please obtain further information from and contribute whatever you can to the following addresses:

Fundación Natura
    Avenida América 5653 y Voz Andes, Quito, Ecuador
Fundación Maquipucuna
    PO Box 17-12-167, Quito, Ecuador
Campaña Amazonia: Por la Vida
    PO Box 246C, Quito, Ecuador
Conservation International
    1015 18th Street NW, Suite 1000, Washington DC 20036, USA
World Wildlife Fund
    1250 Twenty-Fourth Street, NW, Washington DC 20037, USA
    Panda House, Godalming, Surrey, GU7 1XR, United Kingdom
The Nature Conservancy
    Latin America Division, 1815 North Lynn Street, Arlington, VA 22209, USA
Rainforest Alliance
    295 Madison Avenue, Suite 1804, New York, NY 10017, USA
Natural Resources Defense Council
    40 West 20th St, New York, NY 10011, USA
International Union for the Conservation of Nature and Natural Resources
    Avenue Mont Blanc, 1196 Gland, Switzerland

An equally important way of contributing to the efforts of the Ecuadorian environmental movement is to be aware of some of the issues that lie behind conservation and to communicate your experiences to family, friends and policy-makers when back at home. Oil drilling in Ecuador's national parks occurs because we use gasoline (petrol) – the most effective remedy is to encourage use of fuel-efficient transport and to support research of alternative energy sources (solar energy is an excellent

example). Ecuador's debt problems must be solved so that it does not have to rely on unsustainable economic paths which ultimately are damaging to the world community.

GOVERNMENT

Ecuador is a republic with a democratic government headed by a president. The first constitution was written in 1830, but has had several changes since then, the most recent in 1978. Democratically elected governments have regularly been toppled by coups, often led by the military. Since 1979, however, all governments have been freely elected. All literate citizens over 18 have the vote and the president must receive over 50% of the vote to be elected. With at least 13 different political parties, 50% of the vote is rarely achieved, in which case there is a second round between the top two contenders. A president governs for a maximum of five years and cannot be re-elected.

The most recent elections were in 1988, with 10 candidates running for president. In the first round, held in January, Rodrigo Borja and Abdalá Bucaram respectively achieved 24.1% and 17.6% of the votes. In the August runoff, Borja of the Izquierda Democratica (Democratic Left) received a 52% majority and was elected.

The president is also the head of the armed

Ecuador's Coat of Arms

forces and appoints his own cabinet ministers. There are 12 ministries forming the executive branch of the government.

The legislative branch of government consists of a single Chamber of Representatives (or congress) which has 69 members. The congress appoints the justices of the Supreme Court.

There are 21 provinces, each with a governor appointed by the president and democratically elected prefects. The provinces are sub-divided into smaller political units called *cantones*; each cantón has a democratically elected *alcalde* or mayor.

ECONOMY

Until recently Ecuador was the archetypal 'banana republic' and, indeed, in the early 1970s, bananas were the single most important export; almost all other exports were agricultural. This changed very rapidly with the discovery of oil. Petroleum exports rose to first place in 1973 and by the early 1980s accounted for well over half of the total export earnings.

The new-found wealth produced by oil export improved the standards of living to some extent. Nevertheless, Ecuador remains a poor country. Distribution of wealth has been patchy, and much of the rural population continues to live at the same standards as it did in the 1970s. About 40% of the national income goes to the richest 5% of the population. However, education and medical services have improved.

Despite the new-found income from oil exports, the 1980s have been a difficult decade for the Ecuadorian economy. The El Niño floods of 1982/83 caused severe disruptions in agriculture, and exports of bananas and coffee were roughly halved. This was followed by a drop in world oil prices in 1986. In that year, oil exports dropped from about US$1820 million in 1985 to US$910 million in 1986. In 1987, a disastrous earthquake wiped out about 40 km of the oil pipeline, severely damaging both the environment and the economy. Oil exports in 1987 totalled only US$645 million.

After oil was discovered, Ecuador began borrowing money in the belief that profits from oil exports would enable the country to repay its foreign debts. This proved impossible in the mid 1980s with the sharp decline in Ecuador's oil exports. Although the pipeline has been repaired and oil imports have recovered to a certain extent (US$875 million in 1988, US$1030 million in 1989), they are still well short of the export levels of the early 1980s. Ecuador's foreign debt stands at about US$12,000 million, of which well over 60% is to foreign banks, almost 20% is to international agencies, and about 15% is to foreign governments. About 25% of the budget is used to pay for the foreign debt. Ecuador continues to rely on oil as its economic mainstay. Oil reserves are not as large as had been anticipated, however, and estimates range from 10 to 15 years for reserves remaining at the current rates of extraction.

According to the Banco Central del Ecuador, total exports in 1989 were US$2577 million, of which 40% was oil, 14% bananas, 13% shrimp, and 6% coffee. Manufactured goods such as textiles, wood products, processed foods, and other products accounted for 13% of exports. The main buyer is the USA, although the European Economic Community and Asia (particularly South Korea) are also important. Tourism is a rapidly developing new source of international income and is becoming more important than coffee. Imports for 1989 totalled US$1860 million.

Annual inflation had been about 20% in the early 1980s but reached nearly 100% in the problem years of the mid 1980s. The present government has managed to curb this somewhat, and by 1990 inflation was about 50%. One of the stated economic objectives of the present administration is to reduce inflation to less than 30%

Per capita GNP (Gross National Product) was US$1040 in 1989. This compares with US$14,400 for Australians, US$14,750 for British citizens, and US$21,100 for US citizens in the same year.

POPULATION & PEOPLE

The estimated population of Ecuador in 1991 was 10,800,000. This is approximately 10 times the number of Indians estimated to have been living in the area at the time of the Spanish conquest.

The population density of about 38 people per sq km is the highest of any South American nation. About 40% of this total are Indians and an equal number are *mestizos* or people of mixed Spanish/Indian stock. It is difficult to accurately quantify how many pure-blooded Indians and how many mestizos there are – some sources give figures of 25% Indian and 55% mestizo. About 10% are White and the remainder Black or Asian.

Of the Indians, the majority are Quechua-speaking descendants of the people of the Inca Empire and live mainly in the highlands. Various Quechua sub-groups have been isolated from one another for centuries and, consequently, the Quechua they speak varies markedly from province to province. Sometimes the Indians themselves have difficulty in understanding the dialect of a different region.

The Quechua Indians of each region also have distinctive differences in clothing – it is possible to tell where an Indian is from by the colour of his poncho or by the shape of her hat. Some of the best known highland groups are the Otavaleños, Salasacas, Cañaris, and Saraguros. Many Indians now live in towns and cities.

The province of Chimborazo has the largest population of rural Quechua Indians – some 250,000 living in 431 legally recognised communities and villages in the páramo.

A few other small groups live in the Amazonian lowlands. These groups include about 60,000 Quichuas (who are related to the highland Quechuas but who arrived in the Oriente around the time of the conquest), about 40,000 Shuar (formerly called Jivaro), about 1000 Huoaranis, and about 600 each of the Cofan and Siona-Secoya peoples. There are also about 5000 Cayapas Indians living near the coast in the rainforests of northern Esmeraldas Province, and about a thousand Colorado Indians living near Santo Domingo de los Colorados in the western lowlands.

All these groups have their own languages, often completely unrelated to one another.

Approximately 48% of the Ecuadorian population lives on the coast (and the Galápagos) and about 46% in the highlands. The remainder lives in the jungle region of the Oriente, and colonisation of this area is slowly increasing.

Colorado Indian woman

The birth rate is 31 per 1000 inhabitants and the annual population increase is 2.4%. This means that the population will double in 29 years. This is the third highest rate of population growth in South America (after Paraguay and Bolivia). Infant mortality is 58 per 1000 live births, and life expectancy is 66 years. Compare this to 7.7 per 1000, 76 years in Australia or 9.1 per 1000, 75 years in the US.

Over 40% of the population is under 15 (compared to 22% in Australia and the US, or 19% in Britain) and 4% is over 65 (compared with 11% in Australia, 12% in the US, and 16% in Britain).

The urban population is 55%. The remaining rural population is mainly indigenous and people living in the country are often referred to as *campesinos* (peasants or farmers). An indigenous person is called an *indigeno* but never *indio* which is considered extremely insulting.

EDUCATION

Elementary education (two years of kindergarten and six grades of school) is mandatory, although about 50% of children drop out of school before completing elementary education. Of those continuing on to the six grades of secondary education, about a further 50% drop out.

A student must satisfactorily complete a grade (normally taking a year) before being allowed to continue with the next grade. A high school diploma is issued to those students completing secondary education. The diploma is a basic requirement for higher education. There are about 20 universities and technical colleges in Ecuador.

In the highlands, the school year is from October to July. In the coast, however, the school year is from May to January.

Adult literacy rates are between 85% and 90%.

ARTS

A visit to any archaeology museum in Ecuador will testify to the artistic excellence of the pre-Columbian peoples. Their pottery showed fine painting and sculpture, and their metallurgy, particularly gold and silver work, was highly developed. Because the names of the artists have long been forgotten, their work is thought of as archaeology rather than fine art. Nevertheless, some of this archaeological work formed the basis of what became known as the Quito School of Art.

The Spaniards arriving in the 16th century brought their own artistic concepts with them. These often revolved around Catholic religious themes. The Spaniards soon began to train the local indigenous artists to produce the colonial religious art which can now be seen in many churches and art museums. Religious statues were first carved, then painted, then embellished with gold leaf — sculpture, painting, and gold work were all techniques with which the Indians had long been familiar. Paintings, too, had liberal amounts of gold leaf included. And so arose the Quito School of Art — Spanish religious concepts executed and heavily influenced by Indian artists.

The Quito School lasted through the 17th and 18th centuries. Some of the best known artists of this period include the sculptor Manuel Chili, better known by his Quechua nick-name 'Caspicara' which means pockmarked. Some of his work can be seen in the church of San Francisco in Quito. This church also contains a famous sculpture of the Virgin by Bernardo Legarda. Notable painters include Miguel de Santiago, whose huge canvases grace the walls of Quito's church of San Agustín, and Manuel Samaniego, Nicolás Goríbar and Bernardo Rodríguez.

Many of Quito's churches were built during this colonial period and the architects were also somewhat influenced by the Quito School. In addition, churches often had Moorish (Arab) influences (Spain had been under Arab rule for centuries). The overall appearance of the architecture of colonial churches is overpoweringly ornamental, and almost cloyingly rich — in short, baroque. The houses of the middle and upper class of that period were elegant and simple — the architecture often consisted of verandahed rooms around a central courtyard.

Many of the houses were two storied, with the upper floors bearing ornate balconies. The walls were whitewashed and the roofs were of red tile. Quito's colonial architecture has been well-preserved and led to UNESCO declaring old Quito *Patrimonio de Humanidad* (Patrimony of Humanity) in 1978. Several other towns, notably Cuenca, have attractive colonial architecture.

The Quito School died out with the coming of independence — the 19th century is called the Republican period and its art is characterised by formalism. Favourite subjects are heroes of the revolution or important members of high society in the new republic. Rather florid landscapes were another popular theme.

The 20th century saw the rise of the

indigenist school which is characterised by subject matter rather than style. The oppression and burdens of Ecuador's indigenous inhabitants are the unifying theme. Important indigenist artists include (among many others) Eduardo Kingman, Endara Crow, Camilo Egas, and Oswaldo Guayasamín. These and other artists have works in modern galleries and museums in Quito; Egas (died 1962) and Guayasamín (still alive) have museums in their homes.

Ecuador has not produced any writers which have become household names outside the country. Nevertheless, there are several notable literary figures.

Juan Montalvo (1832-89) from Ambato was a prolific essayist who frequently attacked the dictatorial political figures of the time, particularly President Gabriel García Moreno. His best known work is *Siete Tratados* (1882), or 'Seven Treatises', which includes a comparison between Simón Bolívar and George Washington. Juan León Mera (1832-94) was also from Ambato and is famous for his novel *Cumandá* describing Indian life in the 19th century.

Perhaps the most notable writer of the 20th century was the Quiteño, Jorge Icaza (1906-79). He was profoundly influenced by the indigenist school and his most famous novel is *Huasipingo* (1934), translated as *The Villagers* (1973). This is a brutal story about Indians – how their land is seized and the savage massacre of those who protested. The book is made all the more horrifying by the knowledge that the story is based on the real problems facing the Indians. Icaza was also known as a playwright, actor, and writer of short stories.

There are many contemporary writers. A good introduction is *Diez Cuentistas Ecuatorianas*, a book of short stories. Also well recommended is Pablo Cuvi's *In the Eyes of My People* (see Books & Maps in Facts for the Visitor for further information).

The performing arts are important in Ecuador although, as with literature, there are no artists whose names are known to most visitors. There are several theatres, especially in Quito, where performances range from street theatre to mime to political satire to more traditional plays. There are occasional symphony concerts, but it is the more traditional music, with pre-Columbian influences, which is of the greatest interest to many visitors.

Traditional Andean music has a distinctive and haunting sound which has been popularised in western culture by songs like Paul Simon's version of *El Condor Pasa* and the score of the excellent TV natural history series *The Flight of the Condor*.

Two main reasons contribute to the otherworldly quality of traditional music. The first is the scale: it is pentatonic, or consisting of five notes, compared to the eight note octaves we are used to. The second is the fact that string and brass instruments were imported by the Spanish – pre-Columbian instruments consisted of wind and percussion which effectively portrayed the windswept quality of páramo life.

The most ancient traditional instruments include the *rondador* or bamboo panpipe, the *quenua* and *pingullo* or large and small bamboo flutes, *conchas* or sea-conches played like a horn, as well as a variety of drums, rattles, and bells.

The Spanish brought string instruments (guitars, harps, and violins). Some of these were incorporated into Andean music and others were modified to produce the typical *charango*, a very small instrument with five double strings. The sounding box was often made of an armadillo shell, but fortunately wood is being increasingly used.

Most traditional music is a blend of pre-Columbian and Spanish influences. It is best heard in a *peña*, or a folkmusic club (see Entertainment in Facts for the Visitor). Traditional music can also be heard on the streets during fiestas, but increasingly often fiesta ensembles are cacophonous brass bands.

In Ecuador, indeed in much of Latin America, there is a bridge between fine arts and crafts – *artesanía*. This literally means artisanship and refers to textile crafts ranging from finely woven ponchos to hammocks, as well as well-made panama hats, basketwork, leatherwork, woodcarving, jewellery, and ceramics.

These items are discussed in more detail under Things to Buy in the Facts for the Visitor chapter.

CULTURE

By 'culture' here, I refer to some of the habits, attitudes and values of Ecuadorian society, particularly as they may apply to foreign travellers who may not be aware of what may be considered appropriate behaviour by Ecuadorians. I do not mean culture in the sense of intellectual and artistic pursuits, which are discussed in the earlier Arts section.

Greetings are important to Ecuadorians, especially in the highlands. Strangers conducting business will, at the minimum, exchange a cordial 'Buenos días, como esta?' before launching in to whatever they are doing. Male friends and casual acquaintances meeting one another in the street shake hands at the beginning and end of even a short meeting; women kiss one another on the cheek in greeting and farewell. Men often kiss women decorously on the cheek, except in a business setting where a handshake is more appropriate. Close male friends hug one another in the traditional *abrazo*.

Clothing is important to Ecuadorians – even poor people will try and dress in their best. The casually unkempt look is out; the well-pressed suit or attractive skirt and blouse are in. That is not to say that Ecuadorians don't like to dress informally – they do – but a neat and conservative turnout is usually strived for, especially in the highlands. Shorts are not worn in the highlands except by athletes and extremely gauche travellers. Wear long pants or a skirt.

Public lavatories are almost unknown, except in major bus terminals and airports. Lavatories are called *Servicios Hygienicos* and are usually marked 'SS.HH' – a little confusing until you learn the abbreviation. People needing to use the lavatory will often go into a restaurant and ask to use the *baño* – toilet paper is not always available, so carry a supply with you. Used toilet paper is

usually placed in a waste basket because the water pressure is often too poor to properly flush the toilet. Travellers are urged to follow suit – a basket of used toilet paper is a lot less unpleasant than an overflowing toilet.

Because of the lack of public lavatories, men tend to urinate outdoors much more than we may be used to, particularly in areas lacking restaurants or similar facilities. Behind trees, against walls, behind buses, up alleys – it is a common, discreet but unremarkable sight. However, belching or burping in public is considered the absolute height of bad manners. So, boys, urinate against a wall if you have to go, but hold that belch in.

Begging is a fact of life in Ecuador. If you drive on the back roads in the highlands at certain times, you may see campesinos literally lined up along the roads with their hands out in supplication. This is particularly true on Sunday and the period around Christmas. At those times, it's considered OK to give the people something but, please, do so in a manner which shows some basic human respect. I once saw a bus load of French tourists throw candy through the windows of the bus and onto the ground – they then filmed the ensuing scramble and roared off without any interaction with the people begging. It is difficult to say which were the more pathetic – the tourists or the beggars.

Begging children are becoming more common in the cities. Particularly sad is the sight of little girls, of only four or five years of age, walking the main drag of Quito (Avenida Amazonas) trying to sell roses to tourists at all hours of the night. These kids are often forced to work the streets until the early hours of the morning. Whilst giving them money may help them on an immediate level, the long term problem of homeless kids working the streets and not receiving an education is exacerbated. I suggest donations to one of the many charities, like Save the Children, which work at helping homeless children all over the world. You can specify that you wish the money to be spent in Ecuador. In Quito, you can make donations to *Centro del Muchacho Trabajador*

Top: Giant Tropical Snail, Western Lowlands (RR)
Left: Scarlet Macaw (RR)
Right: Lorenzo Criollo in traditional Cofan regalia (RR)

Top: Miguel Andrango of Tahuantinsuyo Weaving Workshop, Agato, near Otavalo (RR)
Bottom: Beads for sale at Otavalo Market (RR)

(Working Boy's Centre) on the Plaza San Martín at the intersection of Pichincha and Chile in La Marín. People interested in the work being done to help and educate shoeshine boys and other homeless kids can arrange a tour – this is free but a donation of several dollars would be appreciated.

Legally and morally, everyone is equal in Ecuador, irrespective of race or gender. In reality, Blacks and indigenous people are discriminated against and treated as second class citizens – this is particularly true of indigenous people. The term Indian, whilst having few negative connotations in English, is considered an insult in Spanish.

The Indian population frequently protests about their unfair and inhumane treatment – the most recent uprising was in June 1990. Then, Indians barricaded themselves into a church (Santo Domingo) and demanded their rights. Their demands ranged from autonomy of Indian groups to providing basic services, such as running water, to indigenous communities.

At one stage a large number of them symbolically marched from the forests to the capital gathering more supporters in each town that they passed through. Whilst autonomy could be considered a debatable issue, the right to running water seems basic. On the surface then, there is no discrimination. In reality, discrimination is very deep.

Graffiti of the *Vayase Yanqui* (Yankee, go home) type is frequently seen in Ecuador. Whilst many Ecuadorians have an anti-American sentiment, this is directed against the interventionist policy of the USA in Latin America, and not against the individual US traveller.

Indeed, US citizens often remark on how friendly the Ecuadorian people are. This is partly because of Ecuadorians' inherent politeness, and partly because US travellers are the second most frequent visitors (after neighbouring Colombians) to Ecuador, and thus contribute an important amount to the nation's economy.

RELIGION

As is common with other Latin American countries, the predominant religion is Roman Catholicism. Some of the older towns have splendid 16th and 17th-century Catholic churches. Although churches of other faiths can be found, they form only a very small minority. The Indians, while outwardly Roman Catholic, tend to blend Catholicism with their traditional beliefs.

LANGUAGE

For the traveller, Spanish is the main language. Most Indians are bilingual, with Quechua being their preferred language and Spanish their second tongue. As well as the Quechua-speaking Indians of the highlands, there are several small lowland groups speaking their own languages. It is rare to encounter Indians who understand no Spanish at all, although they certainly exist in the remoter communities. Although English is understood in the best hotels, airline offices and tourist agencies, it is of little use elsewhere.

If you don't speak Spanish, take heart. It is an easy language to learn. Courses are available in Quito (see the Quito chapter) or you can study books, records and tapes while you are still at home and planning your trip. These study aids are often available for free from many public libraries or you might want to consider taking an evening or college course. Once you have learned the basics, you'll find that you'll be able to travel all over Latin America because, apart from Brazil which is Portuguese-speaking, most of the countries use Spanish.

Spanish is easy to learn for several reasons. First, it uses Roman script, and secondly, with few exceptions, it is spoken as it is written and vice versa. Imagine trying to explain to someone learning English that there are seven different ways of pronouncing 'ough'. This isn't a problem in Spanish. Thirdly, many words are similar enough to English that you can figure them out by guesswork. *Instituto Geográfico Militar* means the Military Geographical Institute, for example.

Even if you don't have time to take a course, at least bring your phrasebook and dictionary. A good phrasebook is *Latin American Spanish Phrasebook* by Anna Cody (Lonely Planet). Don't dispense with the dictionary, because the phrasebook limits you to asking where the bus station is and won't help you translate the local newspaper. My favourite dictionary is the paperback *University of Chicago Spanish Dictionary*. It has both Spanish-English and English-Spanish sections, is small enough to travel with, yet has many more entries than most pocket dictionaries and also contains words used in Latin America but not in Spain.

Although the Spanish alphabet looks like the English one, it is in fact different. 'Ch' is considered a separate letter, for example, so *champù* (which simply means 'shampoo') will be listed in a dictionary after all the words beginning with just 'c'. Similarly, 'll' is a separate letter, so *llama* is listed after all the words beginning with a single 'l'. The letter 'ñ' is listed after the ordinary 'n'. Vowels with an accent are accented for stress and are not considered separate letters.

Pronunciation is generally more straightforward than it is in English, and if you say a word the way it looks like it should be said, the chances are that it will be close enough to be understood. You will get better with practice of course. A few notable exceptions are 'll' which is always pronounced 'y' as in 'yacht,' the 'j' which is pronounced 'h' as in 'happy,' and the 'h' which isn't pronounced at all. Thus the phrase *hojas en la calle* (leaves in the street) would be pronounced 'o-has en la ka-yea.' Finally, the letter 'ñ' is pronounced as the 'ny' sound in 'canyon'.

Grammar

Articles, adjectives and demonstrative pronouns must agree with the noun in both gender and number. Nouns ending in *a* are generally feminine and the corresponding articles are *la* (singular) and *las* (plural). Those ending in *o* are usually masculine and require the articles *el* (singular) and *los* (plural). Plurals are formed by adding *s* to words ending in a vowel and *es* to those ending in a consonant. There are, however, hundreds of exceptions to these guidelines which can only be memorised or deduced by the meaning of the word.

In addition to using all the familiar English tenses, Spanish also uses the imperfect tense and two subjunctive tenses (past and present). Tenses are formed either by adding lots of endings to the root verb or preceding the participle form by some variation of the verb *haber* (to have/to exist).

There are verb endings for first, second and third person singular and plural. Second person singular and plural are divided into formal and familiar modes. If that's not enough, there are three types of verbs – those ending in 'ar', 'er' and 'ir' – which are all conjugated differently. There are also a whole slough of stem-changing rules and irregularities which must be memorised. This sounds a lot more complicated than it really is – you'll be surprised at how quickly you'll pick it up.

Common Courtesies

good morning
buenos días
good afternoon (or good evening)
buenas tardes
yes
sí
no
no
hello
hola
See you later
Hasta luego
How are you?
Cómo estás? (familiar) or
Cómo está? (formal)
please
por favor
thank you
gracias
It's a pleasure
Con mucho gusto
Excuse me !
Perdone !
You're welcome
De nada

Some Useful Phrases

Do you speak Spanish (English)?
Habla usted español (inglés)?
Where do you come from?
De donde es usted?
Where are you staying?
Donde estás alojado?
What is your profession?
Cuál es su profesión?
Don't you have smaller change?
No tiene sencillo?
Do you understand? (casual)
Me entiende?
I don't understand
No entiendo
Where can I change money/travellers' cheques?
Donde se cambia dinero/cheques de viajeros?
Where is the ... ?
Donde está el/la ... ?
How much is this?
(There are fortunately several variations on this well-worn phrase.)
A cómo?, Cuanto cuesta esto?, Cuanto vale esto?
too expensive
muy caro
cheaper
más barato
I'll take it
Lo llevo
to the right
a la derecha
to the left
a la izquierda
Continue straight ahead
Siga derecho
more or less
más o menos
when?
cuando?
how?
cómo?
How's that again?
Cómo?
why?
por que?
where?
donde?

What time does the next plane/bus/train leave for ... ?
A qué hora sale el próximo avión/bús/tren para ... ?
where from?
de donde?
around there
por allá
around here
por acá
It's hot/cold
Hace calor/frío

Some Useful Words

airport
aeropuerto
bank
banco
block (in a city)
cuadra
bus station
terminal terrestre
cathedral/church
catedral/ iglesia
city
ciudad
downhill
para abajo
exchange house
casa de cambio
friend
amigo/a
here
aquí
husband/wife
marido/esposa
Indian/peasant
Indigeno/campesino (never *indio*)
mother/father
madre/padre
people
la gente
police
policía
post office
correo
rain
lluvia
snow
nieve

there
allí, allá
town square
plaza or *parque*
train station
estación de trenes
uphill
para arriba
wind
viento

Time & Dates
What time is it?
Qué hora es? or *Qué horas son?*
It is one o'clock
Es la una
It is two o'clock
Son las dos
midnight
medianoche
noon
mediodía
in the afternoon
de la tarde
in the morning
de la mañana
at night
de la noche
half past two
dos y media
quarter past two
dos y cuarto
two twenty-five
dos con veinticinco minutos
twenty to two
veinte para las dos

Sunday
Domingo
Monday
Lunes
Tuesday
Martes
Wednesday
Miércoles
Thursday
Jueves
Friday
Viernes

Saturday
Sábado

spring
la primavera
summer (dry season)
el verano
winter (wet season)
el invierno

today
hoy
tomorrow
mañana
yesterday
ayer

Numbers

1	*uno, una*
2	*dos*
3	*tres*
4	*cuatro*
5	*cinco*
6	*seis*
7	*siete*
8	*ocho*
9	*nueve*
10	*diez*
11	*once*
12	*doce*
13	*trece*
14	*catorce*
15	*quince*
16	*dieciseis*
17	*diecisiete*
18	*dieciocho*
19	*diecinueve*
20	*veinte*
21	*veintiuno*
30	*treinta*
40	*cuarenta*
50	*cincuenta*
60	*sesenta*
70	*setenta*
80	*ochenta*
90	*noventa*
100	*cien(to)*
101	*ciento uno*
200	*doscientos*
201	*doscientos uno*

300	*trescientos*	800	*ochocientos*
400	*cuatrocientos*	900	*novecientos*
500	*quinientos*	1000	*mil*
600	*seiscientos*	100,000	*cien mil*
700	*setecientos*	1,000,000	*un millón*

Facts for the Visitor

VISAS & EMBASSIES

Most travellers entering Ecuador as tourists do not require visas. Several guide books report that Australians, New Zealanders, and French require a tourist visa – when I called the Ecuadorian Consulate in Los Angeles, they assured me this was not true. Only citizens of Cuba and a few Asian countries (eg China, Taiwan, North and South Korea, Vietnam) and some middle Eastern countries currently require a tourist visa. Regulations change, so it is worth checking with an Ecuadorian consular office for current requirements.

All nationals entering as tourists need a passport (valid for six months or more) and a T-3 tourist card which is obtainable on arrival in Ecuador. There is no charge for this card, but don't lose it as you will need it for stay extensions, passport checks and leaving the country. If you should lose it, you can get another at the immigration office in Quito or Guayaquil, or at the exit point from the country.

All travellers who do not wish to enter as tourists require visas. Non-immigrant visas are available for diplomats, refugees, students, workers, religious workers, business people, and cultural exchange visitors. Various immigrant visas are also available. Obtaining a visa (with the exception of a tourist visa) is time consuming so commence the process as long ahead of your visit as possible.

On arrival, you are normally asked how long you want to stay. If you show your outbound ticket, you should get as many days as you need. You are given an identical *Entrada* stamp on both your passport and T-3 tourist card which indicates how long you can stay. The maximum is 90 days, but usually less is given. There is no set pattern in this; sometimes there are periods when everyone got 30 days irrespective of whether they wanted to stay for three days or three months. Whatever happens, keep cool. If you argue with the official who gave you only 30 days when you wanted 45, he could hassle you further. It's easy and quick to get a stay extension in Quito at Avenida Amazonas 2639 – allow a few hours for this.

Check your immigration stamp carefully before you leave the immigration area. Make sure it is properly dated. I know of one case when a person had a stamp for *1 JUN*, when in fact they arrived on 1 July. Also make sure your stamp is legible to avoid problems when you leave.

There are also T-1 and T-2 tourist cards. These are for short visits only and may be issued to travellers in transit through the country, or who are staying for less than 72 hours.

The main problem with staying in Ecuador is undoubtedly the 90-day rule. This means that you can't stay in the country for more than 90 days in any 12-month period. Ecuador isn't a large country and 90 days is more than enough for most people. A longer stay with a tourist card is flatly refused and the only official way to stay on is with an appropriate non-immigrant or immigrant visa. Obtaining one in Ecuador is often a time-consuming, frustrating and costly process, and it's usually better to apply for a visa at your nearest Ecuadorian consulate if you are a bona fide businessperson or whatever.

One traveller reports that he tried to obtain a six-month visa to teach English – the consul in San Francisco made this difficult by requiring police records and various other

official letters and documents. He tried again at the Los Angeles consulate and was able to obtain a visa with no problem just by presenting his airline ticket home and a valid passport. Obviously, the situation varies from consulate to consulate, so if at first you don't succeed, try again elsewhere. A list of Ecuadorian consulates is given at the end of this section.

If you are a tourist and want to stay longer than 90 days, simply leaving the country (across to Peru, for example) and returning a few days later doesn't work. The officials check your passport for entry and exit dates and are quick to notice if your 90 days have been used up. Should you go to Peru and get a new passport at your embassy because your previous one was lost, severely damaged, stolen or expired, then returning to Ecuador is another story. With no Ecuadorian stamps in your brand-new passport you have no problem. If you leave Ecuador with, say only 60 of your 90 days used, you will receive your balance of 30 days upon re-entry with no problem.

In addition to your passport and tourist card, you officially need a ticket out of the country and evidence of sufficient funds for your stay (US$20 per day). This is the law and if you turn up at the border stoned or looking as if you haven't washed or eaten for a week, the law will be enforced. However, during my many trips to Ecuador, I was never asked for an onward ticket and was only asked to show sufficient funds once. They didn't count it too carefully – I just waved a bunch of travellers' cheques.

I have heard a story of passengers on an Ecuatoriana flight from Miami to Quito being refused entry without an onward ticket – I don't know the details. If you're flying in, it's safest to buy an onward ticket. It can be refunded if you don't use it. In Ecuador this can take a couple of weeks but they'll give you the money in dollars. Don't worry about an onward ticket at the land borders; it's very unlikely that the rule will be mentioned if you arrive looking reasonably respectable.

You should always carry your passport as

there are occasional document checks on public transport. You can be arrested if you don't have identification. Immigration checks go through periodic swings. You can be in Ecuador for three months without anyone asking to see your passport or you can be stopped in the street for no reason and asked for your documents twice in one week. Failure to produce a visa or tourist card can result in deportation.

Leaving the Country

If you have a valid T-3 tourist card and leave overland, you need to turn in your T-3 card and receive a *Salida* exit stamp in your passport – this is done at the border. If you leave by air, the same applies and, in addition, you must pay a US$25 airport departure tax. Make sure you have both Entrada and Salida stamps in your passport when you leave.

If you have some other kind of visa, you need to get an exit permit from the immigration authorities in Quito, before you leave the country. Travellers with a visa also need to pay an exit tax and obtain police clearance.

Colombian Visas

Ecuador is bordered only by Colombia to the north and Peru to the south. To enter Colombia, some nationalities need a visa. Nationals of the following countries do not: Argentina, Austria, Barbados, Belgium, Brazil, Britain, Costa Rica, Denmark, Ecuador, El Salvador, Finland, Germany, Holland, Ireland, Italy, Japan, Liechtenstein, Luxembourg, Norway, Peru, Portugal, South Korea, Spain, Sweden, Switzerland, Trinidad & Tobago, and Uruguay.

US citizens and Canadians require a tourist card which is issued by a Colombian consulate, tourist office, or airline before arriving in Colombia. Recent reports indicate that a tourist card can be obtained at the land border without difficulty.

All other nationalities require a visa, which costs anywhere from US$5 to US$30 depending on your nationality. If you don't already have your visa, go to the Colombian consulate which has offices in Guayaquil,

Quito and Tulcán (see these cities for more information).

Peruvian Visas

Most European nationalities do not require a visa to enter Peru. Most Latins, except Chileans and Venezuelans, do not require visas. Canadians and US citizens do not require visas. Travellers from most communist countries and some African and Asian countries (not Japan) do require visas. Australians and New Zealanders, for some perverse reason, also require visas.

If you need a Peruvian visa, you can get one at the consulate in Quito, Guayaquil, Macará and Machala. (see these cities for more information.)

Other Paperwork

International vaccination certificates are not required by law, but vaccinations are advisable. See the Health section in this chapter.

Student cards are of little use, as the number of places that give discounts for students are very limited. There is no Youth Hostel system in Ecuador.

Ecuadorian Embassies

The following countries have Ecuadorian embassies or consular representation; their addresses and telephone numbers are too numerous to list here but can be found in telephone directories.

Argentina: Buenos Aires, Córdova, La Plata, Mar del Plata, Mendoza
Australia: Melbourne, Sydney
Austria: Vienna
Barbados: St Michael
Belgium: Antwerp, Brussels, Liége
Bolivia: La Paz
Brazil: Brasilia, Manaus, Porto Alegre, Recife, Río de Janeiro, São Paulo
Britain: London
Canada: Montreal, Ottawa, Toronto
Colombia: Barranquilla, Bogotá, Cali, Ipiales
Chile: Concepción, Santiago
Costa Rica: San José
Cyprus: Nicosia
Czechoslovakia: Prague
France: Marseilles, Paris
French West Indies, Guadeloupe: Pointe-á-Pitre

Germany: Berlin, Bonn, Frankfurt, Hamburg, Munich
Holland: Amsterdam, The Hague
Hong Kong: Kowloon
Italy: Florence, Genoa, Milan, Naples, Rome, Turin
Japan: Nagoya, Tokyo
Mexico: Guadalajara, Mexico City, Monterrey
New Zealand: Auckland
Panama: Colón, Panama City
Peru: Lima, Piura, Sullana, Tumbes
Poland: Warsaw
Portugal: Lisbon
Puerto Rico: San Juan
South Korea: Seoul
Spain: Barcelona, Bilbao. Madrid, Málaga
Sweden: Stockholm
Switzerland: Zurich
United States: Atlanta (Georgia), Baltimore (Maryland), Boston (Massachusetts), Chicago (Illinois), Columbia (S Carolina), Coral Gables (Florida), Dallas (Texas), Fort Lauderdale (Florida), Georgetown (S Carolina), Houston (Texas), Kansas City (Missouri), Las Vegas (Nevada), Los Angeles (California), Miami (Florida), Nashville (Tennessee), New Orleans (Louisiana), New York (New York), Palm Beach (Florida), San Francisco (California), Seattle (Washington), Washington DC
Venezuela: Caracas, Maracaibo

Foreign Embassies in Ecuador

Many countries have embassies or consulates in Quito, Guayaquil, or both. These are listed under the appropriate city.

CUSTOMS

Each traveller is allowed to import a litre of spirits, 300 cigarettes and an unspecified 'reasonable' amount of perfume into Ecuador, duty free. There is no problem in bringing in the usual personal belongings, but if you plan on bringing in several cameras or a computer or something which could be construed as not being 'usual personal belongings' you should check with an Ecuadorian consulate.

Pre-Columbian artefacts are not allowed to be taken out of Ecuador.

MONEY
Currency

The currency in Ecuador is the sucre, usually written as S/. It has nothing to do with sugar; in fact it is named after General Sucre, who defeated the Spanish colonialists at the Battle of Pichincha on 24 May 1824, thus opening the way to independence for Ecuador. There are bills of 5000, 1000, 500, 100, 50, 20, 10 and 5 sucres and coins of 50, 20, 10, five and one sucres.

Exchange Rates

There are two rates of exchange; the lower one is used in international business transactions and is of no concern to the traveller. The higher rate is available at all exchange houses. The sucre is frequently devalued, so it is impossible to give accurate exchange rates. The following table gives some idea:

1981	30 sucres per US dollar
1985	120 sucres per US dollar
1988	515 sucres per US dollar
1992	1230 sucres per US dollar

By far the easiest currency to exchange is the US dollar. Although hard currencies such as other dollars, pounds sterling, French and Swiss francs and German marks are exchangeable in Quito, Guayaquil and, perhaps, Cuenca, outside of these cities you should try to travel with US dollars. Therefore, recent exchange rates for other countries are not given, but they are loosely pegged to the US dollar.

Changing Money

It is best to try to exchange as much money as you need in the major cities, as exchange rates are lower in the smaller towns. In some places, notably the Oriente, it is very difficult to exchange any money at all. Quito, Guayaquil, and Cuenca are the best places to exchange money – Quito is the easiest but Cuenca has (marginally) the best rates.

If you are stuck in a small town and are out of sucres, try the banks. Even if they don't officially do foreign exchange, the bank manager may be persuaded to change a small amount of US cash dollars from his personal account, or he may know of someone who will do so. Also ask at the best hotels, restaurants and stores in town. Peace

Corps volunteers, missionaries and other travellers may help you exchange dollars.

Where you should exchange your money varies from month to month. On a visit to Ecuador in the mid 1980s, I found there was an embargo on foreign exchange at all banks so I had to change at *casas de cambio* (exchange houses). Now, banks are once again dealing in foreign currency, but you'll have to check the latest situation upon your arrival. Casas de cambio usually involve less paperwork and are quicker than banks.

Normally, all exchange rates are within 2% of one another, so it's not worth hassling all day for the best deal unless you're changing a sizable sum. Good places to change money are indicated under each town. There are street changers at the land borders and, when leaving or arriving overland, street changers are usually the best way to buy or sell sucres. Recently, there have also been street changers outside the main exchange houses of Quito and Guayaquil – their operation is supposedly illegal but authorities have been turning a blind eye. Street rates were not any better than bank or exchange house rates, although this may change in future.

There is not very much difference between exchange rates for cash and travellers' cheques. Occasionally, US$100 bills are looked upon with suspicion, because these have been counterfeited the most often. Once in a while, you are asked to produce proof of purchase (ie a receipt) when cashing travellers' cheques. These hassles are rarely major problems – if it happens you can always try somewhere else.

There isn't much advantage in carrying all your money in cash. Travellers' cheques are much safer because they are refunded if they are lost or stolen. I've had no difficulty in exchanging major brands of travellers' cheques in Ecuador. However, I definitely do not recommend using First National Citibank cheques. They took over a year to reimburse me for US$200 in stolen cheques and had the gall to charge me about US$20 for handling (the theft, I should add, occurred in Peru). Don't bring all your money in travellers' cheques; it's always useful to have a supply of cash dollars for the occasions when only cash is accepted.

Should you change more money than is actually necessary, you can buy back dollars at international airports when leaving the country. The loss depends on fluctuations of the dollar; rarely you get back more than you paid but usually you lose a few percent. If you aren't flying out, you can change money at the major land borders.

Credit Cards

Credit cards are also useful and most major cards are widely accepted, particularly in first class restaurants, hotels, gift shops, and travel agencies. Cheaper hotels, restaurants and stores don't want to deal with credit cards. Even if an establishment has a credit card sticker in the window, don't assume that they will accept that card. The sticker may be for embellishment only – ask.

Some transactions are classified as 'business' and you get the lower exchange rate, so check exchange rates carefully – paying cash is often better value. A good use for credit cards is buying dollars from a bank. Visa Card, MasterCard, Diners Club and American Express are the most widely accepted. All have representatives in Quito; some also have representatives in Guayaquil and Cuenca (see those sections for further information).

Transferring Money

Credit cards can get you instant cash – see under the major cities for the best places to go for this. Check about commissions for cash advances against credit cards. They should be nominal but I have heard of 15% commission being charged – this is very high.

If you run out of money, it is a simple matter to have more sent to you assuming, of course, that there's someone at home kind enough to send you some. A bank transfer is most quickly done by telex, although this will take at least three days. All you need to do is pick an Ecuadorian bank which will cooperate with your bank at home (eg Bank of America, Bank of London & South America, Banco del Pacífico) and telex your family, friend or bank manager to deposit the money in your name at the bank of your choice.

Unlike many Latin American countries, Ecuador allows you to receive the money in the currency of your choice (US dollars). If you are planning on travelling throughout Latin America, you'll find that Ecuador is one of the best countries to have money sent to.

Banking Hours

Banks are open for business from 9 am to 1 pm Monday to Friday. In some cities banks may stay open later or are open on Saturday, mainly if Saturday happens to be market day. Casas de cambio are usually open from 9 am to 6 pm Monday to Friday and until 12 noon on Saturday. There is usually a lunch hour, which varies from place to place.

In Quito and Guayaquil, the international airport and major hotels have exchange facilities outside of the usual hours.

Costs

Costs in Ecuador are among the lowest in Latin America. In a decade of travelling in Ecuador, I've noticed that the price of travel basics such as hotels, meals and transportation can almost double or halve (in US$ terms) from year to year, but are still cheap by western standards. Because prices tend to vary even more in terms of sucres than in US dollars, I've used the latter in all my price quotes in this book.

If you're on a very tight budget, you'll find that you can manage on the classic bare-bones budget of US$5 per day, including the occasional luxury such as a bottle of beer or a movie. If you're really economical, you could manage on less than US$5 per day if you stay in the cheapest US$1 hotels and eat the meal of the day in restaurants.

If you can afford to spend a little more, however, you'll probably enjoy yourself more. The luxury of a simple room with a private hot shower and a table and chair on which to write letters home can be had for as little as US$2.50 per person if you know where to go – this book will show you where.

Saving time and energy by flying back from a remote destination which took you several days of land travel to reach is also recommended. At present, the most expensive internal flight on the Ecuadorian mainland is about US$20 and most flights are much cheaper. A taxi, particularly when you're in a group, isn't expensive and usually costs less than a dollar for short but convenient rides.

Travelling hard, flying occasionally, eating well, staying in rooms with a private bath, writing an average of one letter each day to friends/family, buying a daily newspaper, seeing a movie once in a while, and drinking a couple of beers with dinner most nights sounds expensive – almost decadent – to the 'purist' budget traveller. I did that for months while researching this book, and averaged about US$13 a day. Even if you demand the best available, in most parts of Ecuador it will cost much less than wherever home may be.

I sometimes meet travellers who spend most of their time worrying how to make their every penny stretch further. It seems to me that they spend more time looking at their finances than looking at the places they're visiting. Of course many travellers are on a grand tour of South America and want to make their money last, but you can get so burned out on squalid hotels and bad food that the grand tour becomes an endurance test. I'd rather spend eight months travelling comfortably and enjoyably than a full year of strain and sacrifice.

There is one major stumbling block for budget travellers and that is the Galápagos Archipelago. Getting there is very expensive and staying there isn't particularly cheap. I suggest you read the chapter on the Galápagos before you decide whether you want to go.

Tipping

Better restaurants add 10% tax and 10% service charge to the bill – if the service has been satisfactory, you can add another 5% for the waiter (there are few waitresses). Cheaper restaurants don't include tax or service charge – if you want to tip your server, do so directly – don't just leave the money on the table.

Tip porters at the airport about US$0.25 per bag, bell-boys at a first class hotel about US$0.50 per bag. Hairdressers receive about US$0.25 or more for special services. Taxi drivers are not normally tipped, though you can leave them the small change from a metered ride.

If you go on a guided tour a tip is expected. Unfortunately, Ecuadorian tour companies pay their guides abysmally, and they make much more in tips than in wages. If you are in a group, tip a top-notch guide about US$2 per person per day – less for a half-day tour. Tip the driver about half as much as the guide. If you engage a private guide, think about US$10 per day. These suggestions are for professional, bilingual guides – tip more if you feel your guide is exceptional, less if they aren't that great.

If going on a long tour which involves guides, cooks, crew (eg in the Galápagos), tip about US$25 to US$50 per client per week, distributed among all the personnel.

If you are driving, and park your car on the street, boys or men will offer to look after your car. Give them about US$0.20 for several hours, a few cents for a short time.

WHEN TO GO

Travellers can visit Ecuador year-round. Certain areas are better at certain times of year, but there are no general cut and dried rules. If visiting the Galápagos, you'll find the warm rainy season, from January to April, has the warmest water for snorkelling, but the waved albatrosses are out at sea. During the rest of the year, the water is cooler (typically around 20°C), and the weather drier, but mistier. The roughest water for sailing seems to be around August and September – though it's not too bad. The busiest seasons in the Galápagos are around Christmas and June to August, coinciding with North American and European vacation time.

The coast has a similar weather pattern – hot and wet from January to May (when tropical rainstorms may make some of the poorer roads impassable) and drier and cooler during the rest of the year. The dry season in the highlands is normally June to August – but this coincides with the wettest months in the Oriente, when roads may be closed. So there is no perfect time for a general tour of the country.

WHAT TO BRING

As an inveterate traveller and guidebook writer, I've naturally read many guidebooks. I always find the What to Bring section depressing, as I'm always told to bring as little as possible; I look around at my huge backpack, my two beat-up duffel bags bursting at the seams, and I wonder sadly where I went wrong. I enjoy camping and climbing, so I carry tent, ice axe, heavy boots and so on. I'm an avid birdwatcher, and I'd feel naked without my binoculars and field guides. And of course I want to photograph these mountains and birds, which adds a camera, lenses, tripod, and other paraphernalia. In addition, I enjoy relaxing just as much as leaping around mountains taking photographs of birds so I always have at least two books to read as well as all my indispensable guides and maps. Luckily, I'm not a music addict so I'm able to live without a guitar, a portable tape player or a shortwave radio.

It appears that I'm not the only one afflicted with the kitchen-sink disease. In Latin America alone, I've met an Australian surfer who travelled the length of the Pacific coast with his board looking for the world's longest left-handed wave; a couple of Canadian skiers complete with those skinny boards; a black man from Chicago who travelled with a pair of three-foot-high bongo drums; an Italian with a saxophone (a memorable night when those two got together); a Danish journalist with a portable typewriter; a French freak with a ghetto blaster and (by my count) 32 tapes; and an American woman with several hundred weavings which she was planning on selling. All of these were budget travellers staying for at least 1½ months and using public transport.

After confessing to the amount of stuff I travel with, I can't very well give the time-honoured advice of 'travel as lightly as possible.' I suggest you bring anything that is important to you; if you're interested in photography, you'll only curse every time you see a good shot (if only you'd brought your telephoto lens), and if you're a musician you won't enjoy the trip if you constantly worry about how out of practice your fingers are getting.

A good idea once you're in Quito is to divide your gear into two piles. One is what you need for the next section of your trip, the rest you can stash in the storage room at your hotel (most hotels have one). Ecuador is a small country so you can use Quito as a base and divide your travelling into, say, coastal, highland and jungle portions, easily returning to Quito between sections and picking up the gear you need for the next.

There's no denying, however, that travelling light is much less of a hassle, so don't bring things you can do without. Travelling on buses and trains is bound to make you slightly grubby, so bring one change of dark clothes that don't show the dirt, rather than seven changes of nice clothes for a six-week trip. Many people go overboard with changes of clothes, but one change to wash and the other to wear is the best idea. Bring clothes that wash and dry easily (jeans take forever to dry).

Remember that clothes can be bought cheaply in Ecuador. T-shirts are popular and inexpensive souvenirs, and heavy wool sweaters and long-sleeved cotton shirts can be bought inexpensively at Indian markets such as Otavalo. A shopping mall will yield underwear and socks – in fact, you could outfit yourself quite well in Ecuador. This is very useful if you are arriving in the country on a cheap air-courier ticket, when you are allowed only carry-on luggage. You can buy clothes of almost any size if you need them, but shoes are limited to size 43 Ecuadorian, which is about 10½ North American. Suffice it to say that I have US size 12 feet (don't laugh, they're not that big!) and I can't buy any footwear at all in Ecuador. This is also true of most Latin American countries, so bring a spare pair of shoes if you're planning a long trip.

The highlands are often cold, so bring a wind-proof jacket and a warm layer to wear beneath, or plan on buying a thick sweater in Otavalo. A hat is indispensable; it'll keep you warm when it's cold, shade your eyes when it's sunny, and keep your head dry when it rains (a great deal!). A collapsible umbrella is great protection against sun and rain as well. Cheap highland hotels often lack heat in their rooms – usually, they will provide extra blankets on request, but a sleeping bag is very useful, though not essential.

I believe clothing is a personal thing and what works for one person is unsuitable for another. Therefore, I don't provide an exhaustive clothing list. The following is a checklist of small items you will find useful and probably need:

- Pocket torch (flashlight) with spare bulb and batteries
- Travel alarm clock
- Swiss Army-style penknife
- Sewing and repairs kit (dental floss makes excellent, strong and colourless emergency thread)
- A few metres of cord (also useful for clothesline and spare shoelaces)
- Sunglasses
- Plastic bags
- Soap and dish, shampoo, tooth brush and paste, shaving gear, towel
- Toilet paper (rarely found in cheaper hotels and restaurants)
- Ear plugs for sleeping in noisy hotels or buses
- Insect repellent (containing a high concentration of Deet)
- Suntan lotion (strong blocking lotions are expensive and hard to find in Ecuador)
- Address book
- Notebook
- Pens and pencils
- Paperback book (easily exchanged with other travellers when you've finished)
- Water bottle
- First-aid kit (see Health section)

Optional items include:

- Camera and film

- Spanish-English dictionary
- Small padlock
- Large folding nylon bag to leave things in storage
- Snorkelling gear (for the Galápagos)
- Water purification tablets or filter
- Binoculars and field-guides

Tampons are available in Ecuador, but only in the major cities and in regular sizes, so make sure you stock up with an adequate supply before visiting smaller towns, the jungle or the Galápagos. Tampons are relatively expensive – sanitary pads are cheaper. If you use contraceptives, then you'll also find them available in the major cities. Condoms are widely sold, but spermicidal jelly for diaphragms is hard to find. The choice of oral contraceptives is limited, so if you use a preferred brand, you should bring it from home.

You need something to carry everything around in. A backpack is recommended because carrying your baggage on your back is less exhausting than carrying it in your hands, which are left free. On the other hand, it's often more difficult to get at things inside a pack, so some travellers prefer a duffel bag with a full-length zipper.

Whichever you choose, ensure that it is a good, strongly made piece of luggage, or you'll find that you spend much of your trip replacing zippers, straps and buckles. Hard travelling is notoriously hard on your luggage, and if you bring a backpack, I suggest one with an internal frame. External frames snag on bus doors, luggage racks and airline baggage belts, and are liable to be twisted, cracked or broken.

TOURIST OFFICES

The government tourist information agency is called CETUR and they have offices in the major cities; the location of each of these is listed under the appropriate towns. CETUR seem mostly geared to affluent tourists wishing to see the standard tourist sights and I rarely found them of much help when it came to information about budget hotels, buses to remote villages, or inexpensive nightclubs where the locals go. English was spoken sometimes, but not always. Usually they were friendly and tried to help as much as their limited resources allowed, but at other times I found them uninterested and bored.

It's still worth trying them if you have a problem, because at times they really do go out of their way to be of assistance. I remember complaining to a man at the Esmeraldas tourist office that I couldn't find a bank that would change money for me. He took me to a bank and personally introduced me to a sub-manager he knew, told him I was a personal friend of his, and made sure that I got some dollars changed. I've never been elevated from the status of complete stranger to personal friend so quickly!

There are no CETUR tourist information offices outside of Ecuador. Your local Ecuadorian consulate will have some basic information. In the USA, the offices of Ecuatoriana and SAETA airlines (see Getting There & Away chapter) can also provide useful information.

The Fundación Ecuatoriana de Promoción Turística (FEPROTUR) was formed in 1989 and has offices in Ecuador and the USA. It is a private non-profit organisation whose function is to promote and develop tourism in Ecuador at both the national and international level. FEPROTUR works closely with the National Park Service, travel agents, scientists, indigenous people etc in an effort to develop socially and environmentally sound ecotourism practices. The organisation has organised seminars and prepared training courses for guides, and is publishing a series of useful booklets and field guides (see Books & maps later in this chapter). Information is available from:

Ecuador Tourist & Information Office
    7270 NW 12 St, Suite 400, Miami, FL 33126 or mail to PO Box 526532, Miami, FL 33152-6532, USA (☎ 1-800 553 6673, (305) 477 0041)
FEPROTUR
    Tamayo 935 and Foch, Quito or mail to PO Box 873, Sucursal 12, Quito, Ecuador (☎ 520 737, 524 301)

USEFUL ORGANISATIONS
South American Explorers Club
This club was founded in 1977 in Lima, Peru, by Don Montague and Linda Rojas, and a Quito office was founded by Betsy Wagenhauser in 1989. There is a US office in Ithaca, NY (☎ (607) 277 0488). The club functions as an information centre for travellers, adventurers, scientific expeditions etc and provides a wealth of advice about travelling anywhere in Latin America. Anyone considering a trip to Ecuador would do well to join this organisation.

Both the Quito and Lima clubhouses have an extensive library of books, maps, and trip reports left by other travellers. Many maps and books are for sale. Useful current advice can be obtained about travel conditions, currency regulations, weather conditions and so on.

The club is an entirely member-supported, nonprofit organisation. Membership costs US$30 per individual (US$40 per couple) and lasts for four quarterly issues of their informative and enjoyable *South American Explorer* magazine (add US$6 for mailing outside the USA).

In addition, members receive full use of both Quito and Lima clubhouses with the following facilities: an information service and library; introductions to other travellers and notification of expedition opportunities; storage of excess luggage (anything ranging from small valuables to a kayak); storage or forwarding of mail addressed to you at the club; a relaxing place in which to read and research, or just to have a cup of tea and a chat with the friendly staff; a book exchange; buying and selling of used equipment; a notice-board; discounts on the books, maps and gear sold at the club and other services. The storage facilities are particularly useful if you plan on returning to Ecuador – I leave heavy camping/climbing gear here from year to year.

Nonmembers are welcome to visit the club but are asked to limit their visit to about half an hour and are not eligible for membership privileges until they cough up their US$30. Paid-up members can hang out all day – the club is highly recommended. You can join when you get to Ecuador, or you can join in advance by writing to the US office.

NY
    126 Indian Creek Rd, Ithaca, NY 14650
    (☎ (607) 277 0488).
Quito
    Toledo 1254 y Cordero, La Floresta, Quito; mail to Apartado 21-431, Quito, Ecuador. (☎ 566 076)
Lima
    Avenida Portugal 145, Breña, Lima; mail to Casilla 3714, Lima 100, Peru. (☎ 314 480)

Fundación Natura

This is Ecuador's leading non-government organisation (NGO) dedicated to conservation, environmental advocacy and environmental education. They also manage the protected Pasochoa Forest Reserve, which is one of the few remaining inter-Andean humid forests left in the country. The reserve is described at the end of the Quito chapter.

Fundación Natura
    Avenida América 5663 and Voz Andes, Quito
    (☎ 447 342/343/344)

Studying in Ecuador

Various colleges and organisations in the USA can provide you with information on studying in Ecuador. Most of these courses are available for academic credit. You have to pay for tuition and room and board, but student grants, awards, and other financial aid can often be arranged. Students should talk to their own college advisors to see if their own institution has further contact.

Brethren Colleges Abroad
    Box 184, Manchester College, North Manchester, IN 46962-0365, USA (☎ (219) 982 5238 or 982 5000)
College Consortium for International Studies
    301 Oxford Valley Road, Suite 203 B, Yardley, PA 19067, USA (☎ (215) 493 4224)
University of Illinois
    Study Abroad Office, 115 International Studies Building, 910 South Fifth Street, Champaign, IL 61820, USA (☎ (217) 333 6322)

Indigenous Issues

The year 1992 marks the 500th anniversary of Columbus's arrival in the Americas. For native peoples from Alaska to Argentina, this is not an anniversary to celebrate. There are various organisations supporting indigenous rights throughout the Americas. More information (in Spanish) on the indigenous point of view is available from:

CONAIE (Confederación Nacional Indígena del Ecuador)
    Los Granados 2553 & 6 de Diciembre, El Batan, Quito or mail to Casilla 92-C, Sucursal 15, El Batan, Quito, Ecuador.

BUSINESS HOURS & HOLIDAYS
Business Hours

Banks are open from 9 am to 1 pm, Monday to Friday.

In Quito and Guayaquil, most stores, businesses, exchange houses and government offices are open from about 9 am to 5.30 pm, Monday to Friday, with an hour off for lunch. In smaller towns, lunch breaks of two (or even three) hours are not uncommon. On Saturday, many stores and some businesses are open from 9 am to 12 noon.

Restaurants tend to remain open late in the big cities, where 10 pm is not an unusual time to eat an evening meal. In smaller towns, restaurants often close by 9 pm or much earlier in villages. Restaurants often close on Sunday, when the selection of available eating places can be quite limited.

National Holidays

Many of the major festivals are oriented to the Roman Catholic liturgical calendar. These are often celebrated with great pageantry, especially in highland Indian villages where a Catholic feast day is often the excuse for a traditional Indian fiesta with much drinking, dancing, rituals and processions. Other holidays are of historical or political interest, for example Columbus Day on 12 October. On the days of the major holidays, banks, offices and other services are closed and transportation is often very crowded, so book ahead if possible.

The following list describes the major holidays, but they may well be celebrated for several days around the actual date.

1 January
New Year's Day
6 January
Epiphany
March or April
Carnival (Usually held the last few days before Lent, the Carnival is celebrated with water fights. Ambato has its fruit and flowers festival.)
Easter (Palm Sunday, Holy Thursday, Good Friday, Holy Saturday and Easter Sunday are celebrated with religious processions.)
1 May
Labour Day (workers' parades)
24 May
Battle of Pichincha (National holiday celebrates the decisive battle of independence from the Spanish in 1822.)
24 July
Simón Bolívar's Birthday (National holiday to celebrate the liberator's birthday.)
10 August
Independence Day
12 October
Columbus Day (National holiday to celebrate the 'discovery' of America, also known as Americas Day.)
1 November
All Saints' Day
2 November
All Souls' Day (Celebrated by flower-laying ceremonies in the cemeteries. Especially colourful in rural areas, where entire Indian families show up at the cemeteries to eat, drink, and leave offerings in memory of their departed relatives. The atmosphere often becomes festive rather than sombre.)
24 December
Christmas Eve
25 December
Christmas Day

Other Holidays

The following events, whilst not national public holidays, are often celebrated just as vigorously as national holidays.

June
Corpus Christi (A movable religious feast day combined with traditional harvest fiesta in many highland towns. Usually the 9th Thursday after Easter. Processions, street dancing.)
24 June
Saint John the Baptist (Fiestas in Otavalo area.)

29 June
Saints Peter & Paul (Fiestas in Otavalo area and other northern highland towns.)
25 July
Founding of Guayaquil (A major festival for the city of Guayaquil – it combines with the national holiday of 24 July and the city closes down and parties.)
1-15 September
Fiesta del Yamor (Otavalo's annual festival.)
9 October
Guayaquil's Independence Day (This combines with the 12 October national holiday and is an important festival in Guayaquil.)
3 November
Cuenca's Independence Day (This combines with the national holidays of 1 & 2 November to give Cuenca its most important fiesta of the year.)
6 December
Founding of Quito (Celebrated in Quito throughout the first week of December with bullfights, parades and street dances.)
28-31 December
End-of-year Celebrations (Parades and dances culminate in the burning of life-size effigies in the streets on New Year's Eve.)

In addition to these major festivals, there are many smaller ones. Most towns and villages have their own special day. In addition, many towns and villages have important weekly market days – these are listed under the Things to Buy section in this chapter.

POST & TELECOMMUNICATIONS

Post offices often have a number of kiosks next to them. These are often good places to buy postcards, aerogrammes, envelopes etc.

Sending Mail

Most of the letters which I've sent from Ecuador have arrived at their destinations, sometimes in as little as a week to the USA or Europe, though closer to two weeks is normal.

I like to use aerogrammes because they contain no enclosure and are more likely to arrive safely. For a few cents extra, you can send mail *certificado*, and although I haven't experienced a loss this way, there isn't much you can do if it doesn't arrive. You'll get some peace of mind, if nothing else.

I suggest that you ask each letter to be franked at the post office. I once left a pile of

unfranked, stamped postcards with the clerk at the Puerto Ayora post office in the Galápagos – not one of the postcards arrived! Dishonest postal workers will sometimes steam off the stamps to resell, and throw away your mail.

The post office in each town is marked on the town maps. In some smaller towns it is often just part of a house or a corner of a municipal office. In Quito and Guayaquil there are several post offices dotted around town. The hours are usually 9 am to 5 pm Monday to Friday. In the bigger cities they're open a half day on Saturday.

For reasons I don't understand, letters to the same destinations but mailed from different towns are often charged different postage. It appears that some post offices aren't sure what the correct postage is, or perhaps they don't have the correct denomination stamps. As a general rule, however, postage costs about two-thirds of what you'd expect to pay in Europe or North America.

Sending Parcels

Ecuadorian air-mail rates for parcels are cheaper than in most other Latin American countries, and many travellers report that they have successfully mailed parcels home, thus eliminating the need to lug souvenirs and presents around. Quito is definitely the best place from which to do this.

Parcels weighing less than 2 kg can be sent from most post offices. Heavier parcels should be mailed from the post office at Ulloa and Dávalos, in Quito. Regulations change, so you should check in advance whether the parcel should be sealed or unsealed (for customs inspection) when you bring it to the post office. Recently, parcels had to be open, and you had to seal it up in front of the postal official, so bring tape or strong string. The South American Explorers Club in Quito is usually up to date on this.

The large grain sacks available from many hardware stores or in public markets are good for mailing clothes and weavings. Cardboard boxes are often available from SuperMaxi supermarkets first thing in the morning. Box dimensions must be less than 70 x 30 x 30 cm; bags can be a little bigger. The maximum weight is 20 kg. You should bring a list of the contents and your passport to the post office. On the customs slip, tick the box for 'Gifts' rather than 'Samples' to minimise customs duties.

Recent (approximate) postal rates for airmail parcels under 10 kg were US$12 to the USA and US$22 to the rest of the world; parcels under 15 kg were US$19 to the USA and US$32 to the rest; parcels under 20 kg were US$26 to the USA and US$43 to the rest. Sea mail was available for *Impresos* (books or printed matter) – very slow but very cheap.

Courier companies in Quito and Guayaquil can send important parcels quickly to major airports in the world, but the addressee must come to the airport to pick up the parcel. This is a fast, reliable, but expensive service – about US$50 to the USA for a parcel weighing under 11 kg.

Receiving Mail

Incoming mail is somewhat less reliable. A few letters may take as long as two months to arrive and occasionally never make it. Ask your friends to photocopy important letters and to send two copies.

Most travellers use either the post office's poste restante (general delivery) or American Express for receiving mail. Sometimes embassies will hold mail for you, but some embassies refuse to do so and will return it to the sender. Ask before using your embassy. You can also have mail sent c/o your hotel, but it's liable to get lost. The best place for travellers to receive mail is c/o South American Explorers Club (for members only).

If you have mail sent to the post office, you should know that letters are filed alphabetically; so if it's addressed to John Gillis Payson, Esq it could well be filed under 'G' or 'E' instead of the correct 'P.' It should be addressed to John PAYSON, Lista de Correos, Correos Central, Quito (or town and province of your choice), Ecuador. Ask your loved ones to clearly print your last name and avoid having witticisms such as 'World Traveller Extraordinaire' appended to your name.

American Express will also hold mail for their clients if addressed in the following way: John PAYSON, c/o American Express, Aptdo 2605, Quito, Ecuador. Their street address is Avenida Amazonas 339 and they are open from 9.30 am to 12.30 pm and 2.30 to 6 pm Monday to Friday and 9 am to 12 noon on Saturday.

Receiving small packages is usually no problem. If the package weighs more than 2 kg, however, you will have to go to customs to retrieve it and perhaps pay duty.

Telephone

Telephone service is rather erratic, although it has improved somewhat since Christopher Isherwood described the Quito telephone service as 'about as reliable as roulette' (The Condor and the Cows, 1949). With a little patience, you can usually place calls to anywhere, although long-distance and international calls from small or remote towns can be problematical. There is a phone service on the Galápagos, but this almost never works.

IETEL is the place to go for long-distance national and international telephone, telex and telegram services. The IETEL offices are required by law to be open from 8 am to 10 pm on a daily basis, except in the case of offices in small and remote towns where they can keep shorter hours if they have a dispensation from the government. In a few places, IETEL offices are open before 8 am.

I checked on the IETEL office in every town I visited and found that in places of any size, they were indeed open during the specified hours. Calls must be placed by 9.30 pm. You will find the IETEL office locations marked on all the street plans in this book. The bigger towns have telex and telegram services; the smaller towns have only the phone.

Local Calls There are few public phone booths, except in IETEL offices and on a few major city streets. For local calls within a city, you can often borrow a phone in a store – they will dial the call for you (to make sure you are not calling your mum in London) and will charge you a few cents for the call. All but the most basic hotels will allow you to make local city calls.

Intercity calls can be dialled through the operator at IETEL offices. Some IETEL offices sell fichas (tokens) with which you can direct dial to other parts of the country.

If you need a national operator, dial 105. If you need information, dial 104.

Ecuador is divided into three area codes. The northern area (Quito and the provinces of Bolívar, Carchi, Cotopaxi, Chimborazo, Esmeraldas, Imbabura, Napo, Pastaza, Pichincha, Sucumbíos, Tungurahua) is area code 2. The southern coastal area (Guayaquil and the provinces of El Oro, Guayas, Los Ríos, Manabí) is area code 4. The southern inland area (Cuenca and the provinces of Azuay, Cañar, Loja, Morono-Santiago, Zamora-Chinchipe) is area code 7. These area codes are undergoing reorganisation (Loja and Zamora-Chinchipe were (4) until 1990, for example) so you may need to check these area codes. Don't use area codes unless calling a number outside of the area you are calling from. If you need to dial an area code, you normally have to dial a 0 first, unless you are calling from abroad.

International Calls Even the most remote villages can often communicate with Quito and connect you into an international call. These cost about US$9 for three minutes to the US, and about US$12 to Europe if you call from an IETEL office. Waiting time can sometimes be as short as 10 minutes, though it can also take an hour or more to get through. Rates are 20% cheaper on Sunday and from after 7 pm on other days.

The best hotels can connect international calls to your room at almost any time – these are often heavily surcharged by the hotel. Collect or reverse-charge phone calls are possible to a few countries which have reciprocal agreements with Ecuador – these agreements vary from year to year so you should ask at the nearest IETEL office.

If you are calling from a private phone, you can call the international operator (☎ 116) to place a call. After you have given the operator the number you want to call, hang up. They will call you back when the call gets through – anywhere from five minutes to over an hour. They will also call you back and tell you the charges. These operator-assisted calls are the most expensive.

The country code for Ecuador is 593. To call a number in Ecuador from abroad, call the international access code (011 from North America, 010 from Britain, 0011 from Australia), the country code (593), the area code (2, 4, or 7, depending on the area), and the six-digit local telephone number.

Telegrams & Telex
These can be sent from IETEL offices or from better hotels.

Fax
Major cities have private companies which will send and receive faxes for you. This service is also available in the best hotels.

TIME
The Ecuadorian mainland is five hours behind Greenwich Mean Time and the Galápagos are six hours behind. Mainland time is equivalent to Eastern Standard Time in North America. Because of Ecuador's location on the equator, days and nights are of equal length year round and there is no 'daylight saving time'.

It is appropriate to mention here that punctuality is not one of the things that Latin Americans are famous for.

ELECTRICITY
Ecuador uses 110 volts, 60 cycles, AC (the same as in North America, but not compatible with Britain and Australia). Plugs have two flat prongs, as in North America.

LAUNDRY
There are no self-service laundry machines in Ecuador. This means that you have to find someone to wash your clothes for you or wash them yourself. Many hotels will have someone to do your laundry; this can cost very little in the cheaper hotels (under a dollar for a full change of clothes). The major problem is that you might not see your clothes again for two or three days, particularly if it is raining and they can't be dried. There are laundromats *(lavanderías)* in Quito and Guayaquil but you still have to leave the clothes for at least 24 hours. Most of these lavanderías only do dry cleaning anyway.

If you wash the clothes yourself, ask the hotel staff where to do this. Most cheaper hotels will show you a huge cement sink and scrubbing board which is much easier to use than a bathroom washbasin. Often there is a well-like section next to the scrubbing board and it is full of clean water. Don't dunk your clothes in this water as it is often used as an emergency water supply in the case of water failure. Use a bowl or bucket to scoop water out instead, or run water from a tap.

WEIGHTS & MEASURES
Ecuador uses the metric system, and I have done so throughout this book. For travellers

who still use miles, ounces, bushels, leagues, rods, magnums, stones and other quaint and arcane expressions, there is a metric conversion table at the back of this book.

BOOKS & MAPS
Ecuador Travel Guides

There are few comprehensive guidebooks on Ecuador. *The Budget Travellers No Frills Guide to Ecuador* by John Forrest (1989, Bradt Publications) is a slim volume which is useful if you want the most basic of budget travel information – there are numerous maps.

Ecuador, the Galápagos & Colombia by John Paul Rathbone (1991, Cadogan Books, London and Globe Pequot Press, Connecticut) has about 130 pages on Ecuador and is a pretty-looking book. Unfortunately, the Ecuador section is neither very thorough nor very well researched, and it is riddled with irritating errors – I can't speak for the Colombia section. *Michael's Guide to Ecuador, Colombia, Venezuela* (1988) is even more sketchy and getting increasingly out of date.

Insight Guides Ecuador edited by Tony Perrottet (1991, APA Publications, Hong Kong) considers itself to be the first 'comprehensive guide' to Ecuador. It makes excellent background reading and is illustrated with beautiful photographs, but the travel guide section is extremely brief and limited to four cities plus the Galápagos. Read it at home.

Various other guidebooks are available in Ecuador. One is Arthur Weilbauer's booklet *A Guide for Excursions by Car in Ecuador* (3rd edition, 1985, Libri Mundi). This is available in Spanish, German and English although the English translation is entertainingly garbled – 'There are hotels of all denominations, but luckily no high-rise damage the aspect'. Only the Spanish version has maps.

Another useful book is *Quito – In the Pathway of the Sun* by Catalina Sosa (1990, Imprenta Mariscal, Quito). This slim volume has detailed descriptions of Quito's most interesting sights, but has little information

on the rest of the country. Most of the other books available are of the coffee-table variety – fun to look through in the store and suitable as a souvenir or present rather than as a travel guide.

Regional Travel Guides

There are some good general books on South America which have a chapter on Ecuador, and are mainly recommended for the traveller who wants one book for a 'grand tour' of Latin America.

South America on a shoestring by Geoff Crowther, Rob Rachowiecki & Krzystof Dydynski (4th edition, 1990, Lonely Planet) is recommended to the budget traveller for its many maps, detailed travel information and money-saving information. It is updated regularly.

A broader approach is available in *The South American Handbook* edited by Ben Box (68th edition, 1992, Trade & Travel Publications, Bath, UK). It has been referred to as the 'South American Bible' by some travellers – it weighs about as much as one and is quite pricey. It is suitable for everyone from penurious budget travellers to expense-accounted business people, so there is a lot of extraneous information for most readers. Nevertheless, it is the best general guide to the continent.

Another book which I enjoyed is Lynn Meisch's *A Traveler's Guide to El Dorado & the Inca Empire* (1984, Penguin Books). It's full of interesting details on the crafts, cultures, markets, fiestas and archaeology of Colombia, Ecuador, Peru and Bolivia, and has good background information for the traveller. However, it doesn't set out to help with specific information on hotels, restaurants or transport.

There are also 'mainstream' guides by Birnbaum, Fodor and others, which seem to cater to the 'today's Tuesday, so it must be Rio' crowd, and are fine if that's what you're looking for.

The Outdoors

My first two years in Ecuador were spent trying to climb as many of its mountains as

I could. At that time, there was only one climbers' guide available: *The Fool's Climbing Guide to Ecuador & Peru* by Michael Koerner, Buzzard Mountaineering, USA – now out of print although the South American Explorers Club has a few copies left. It's a whimsical little booklet from which I derived a great deal of pleasure, and although its mountain descriptions are not very detailed it remains a great favourite of mine.

More favourite still (though I must admit to a certain bias) is *Climbing & Hiking in Ecuador* by Rob Rachowiecki and Betsy Wagenhauser (2nd ed., 1991, Bradt Publications). It is a detailed guide to climbing Ecuador's mountains and also describes many beautiful hikes, some of which are simple day hikes suitable for the beginner.

My favourite of all is Edward Whymper's *Travels Amongst the Great Andes of the Equator*, first published in Britain in 1891 and now reprinted (1987, Gibbs M Smith, Utah and 1990, Peregrine Books, UK). This exceptional book describes an 1880 mountaineering expedition which made eight first ascents of Ecuadorian peaks, including the highest, Chimborazo. There are also fascinating descriptions of travel in Ecuador a century ago and the woodcut engravings are pure delight.

There is a series of climbing guides to Ecuador's more popular mountains by the guide, Jorge Anhalzer. These four-page guides have a sketch map of the 'ruta normal' on the back page – lightweight, if nothing else.

If the Pacific coast intrigues you as much as Andean mountains, read *Walking the Beaches of Ecuador* by José-Germán Cárdenas & Karen Marie Greiner (1988, Quito). The authors walked or jogged the entire length of Ecuador's coastline.

Natural History

Books on Ecuador's wildlife are sadly few. *Birds of Ecuador* by Crespo, Greenfield & Matheus (1990, FEPROTUR, Quito) is a locational checklist.

Birding Ecuador by Clive Green (1991, from the South American Explorers Club) is a handmade book detailing the author's two month birding trip to Ecuador – the sketch maps, practical birding information and checklist are very useful to birders.

Aves del valle de Quito y sus alrededores (Birds of the valley of Quito and environs) by Juan Manuel Carrión (1986, Fundación Natura, Quito) is a useful introductory book which illustrates 40 of the most common species.

A proper field guide by Ridgely and Greenfield will be available in the mid 1990s; meanwhile ornithologists have to avail themselves of either guides to the whole continent, or to nearby countries. The best of these is Hilty and Brown's *A Guide to the Birds of Colombia* (1986, Princeton University Press) which covers most of Ecuador's species.

A new series of pocket field guides and booklets on natural history is being produced by FEPROTUR (see Tourist Offices earlier). Apart from the *Birds of Ecuador* checklist, they have published *Conozca Las Aves del Bosque Petrificado de Puyango* by Deirdre Platt, 1991. An English translation ('Know the Birds of the Petrified Forest of Puyango') is being planned.

Other booklets planned for the early 1990s include *Common Birds of Guayas Province*; *Common Orchids of Loja and Zamora Chinchipe*; *Common Páramo Plants and Animals*; *Mangroves of Ecuador*; *Natural History of the Upper Napo*; *Ecuadorian National Parks and Equivalent Reserves* as well as tourist brochures and maps.

Neotropical Rainforest Mammals – A Field Guide by Louise H Emmons (1990, University of Chicago Press) is indispensable to those seriously interested in tropical mammals. The book is detailed and portable, with almost 300 species described and illustrated. Although some of the mammals included are found only in other neotropical countries, many of Ecuador's mammals, and certainly all the rainforest inhabitants, are found within the book's pages.

The only other books on Ecuadorian plants and animals I know of are *Flora de Ecuador* (Quito, 1985) and *Fauna del*

Ecuador (Quito, 1989) both by Erwin Patzelt, in Spanish. The Flora is now out of print (though there is talk of a new edition). The Fauna is a heavy encyclopaedic volume covering everything from mammals to molluscs and hence individual descriptions are not as detailed as Emmons' guide.

There are several excellent books on South American natural history which contain some information on Ecuador. One of my favourites is Michael Andrews' *Flight of the Condor* (1982, Little, Brown & Co.).

For the layperson interested in biology, particularly of the rainforest, I recommend the entertaining and readable *Tropical Nature* by Adrian Forsyth & Ken Miyata (1984, Scribner's & Sons, New York). Forsyth is also the author of a children's book *Journey Through a Tropical Jungle* (1988, Simon & Schuster, New York).

Other books of a general nature which have been well received include *A Neotropical Companion* by John C Kricher, (1989, Princeton University Press). This book is subtitled 'An Introduction to the Animals, Plants, and Ecosystems of the New World Tropics'. Another good choice is Catherine Caulfield's *In the Rainforest* (1989, University of Chicago Press), which emphasises the problems of the loss of the rainforest.

Recent awareness of the importance of the forest canopy as a 'new frontier' in biological discovery has prompted several excellent books such as *The Enchanted Canopy* by Andrew W Mitchell (1986, Macmillan, New York).

An interesting new book is *Rainforests – A Guide to Research and Tourist Facilities at Selected Tropical Forest Sites in Central and South America* by James L Castner (1990, Feline Press, Florida). This is a good source book particularly for those people wishing to visit rainforests in a variety of neotropical countries. A total of 39 sites in seven countries are described and much useful background information is given.

Galápagos Islands

The excellent *A Traveler's Guide to the Galápagos Islands* by Barry Boyce (1990,

Galápagos Travel, 2674 North First Street, San José, CA 95134, USA (☎ 1 800 223 3767) is written by an expert tour operator to the islands. It has detailed and lengthy listings of boats and tour agencies.

The best general guide to the history, geology and plant and animal life of these islands is the thorough and highly recommended *Galápagos: A Natural History Guide* by Michael H Jackson, himself a Galápagos guide (1985, University of Calgary Press). No trip to the Galápagos is complete without this guide.

Avid birders will want *A Field Guide to the Birds of the Galápagos* by Michael Harris (1982, Collins). This excellent handbook illustrates and fully describes every Galápagos bird species.

Amateur botanists will want Eileen Schofield's booklet *Plants of the Galápagos Islands* (1984, Universe Books, New York). This describes 87 common plants and is much more convenient than the classic, but encyclopaedic, *Flora of the Galápagos Islands* by Wiggins and Porter (1971, Stanford University Press).

Snorkellers and divers should look for *A Field Guide to the Fishes of Galapagos* by Godfrey Merlen (1988, Libri Mundi, Quito). About 300 fish are found in the Galápagos – this slim and portable book illustrates 107 of them. A dedicated ichthyologist may prefer *Galápagos Fishes: A Comprehensive Guide to Their Identification* by Jack S Grove & Robert S Lavenberg (due early 1990s, Stanford University Press). This book reportedly has 2,300 illustrations!

Divers will also like *Subtidal Galápagos* by James Cribb (1986, Camden House, Canada). This is too big a book to comfortably take with you, but the superb illustrations are the best underwater Galápagos photos I've seen, and the text is good as well.

In addition to these guides, there are several good books of a general nature about the Galápagos. The following are particularly recommended: *Islands Lost in Time* by Tui de Roy Moore (1980, Viking Press, New York) is a beautiful book illustrated by

Galápagos' premier photographer, Tui de Roy. *Galápagos – Islands of Birds* by Bryan Nelson (1968, William Morrow, New York) has superb descriptions of bird behaviour. *Darwin's Islands: A Natural History of the Galápagos* by Ian Thornton (1971, Natural History Press, New York) is one of the earliest natural history guides – I remember reading it as a teenager when it first appeared and wanting to go immediately to the islands.

The most famous of the visitors to the Galápagos was Charles Darwin who was there in 1835. You can read his *On the Origin of Species by Means of Natural Selection* or his accounts of *The Voyage of the Beagle.* These 19th-century books are rather dated and make heavy reading today. You may prefer one of the various modern biographies such as Irving Stone's excellent *The Origin* (1980, Doubleday) or Alan Moorehead's illustrated *Darwin & the Beagle* (1969, Harper & Row). Readers interested in a layperson's introduction to evolutionary theory can try the amusingly written but accurate *Darwin for Beginners* by Jonathan Miller and Borin Van Loon (1982, Pantheon Books, New York).

A book written for 12 to 16-year-old children is *Galapagos: the enchanted isles* by David Horwell, (1988, Dryad Press, London). This 64-page book will teach the young visitor about the Galápagos – parents will find it is a good introduction too.

Indigenous People

Various good books are available about the Indian populations of Ecuador. *The Awakening Valley* by Collier and Buitron (1949, University of Chicago Press) is a photographic anthropological study of the people of the Otavalo region. The Shuar are studied by Michael Harner using their old name, *The Jivaro: People of the Sacred Waterfall* (1973, Doubleday/Anchor). A well-illustrated multilingual book available in Quito is *The Lost World of the Aucas* by K D Gertelmann. *Otavalo: Weaving, Costume and the Market* by renowned textile expert, Lynn Meisch (1987, Libri Mundi, Quito) is informatively illustrated and written. Other books about Ecuador's and South America's Indian peoples are available at Libri Mundi.

History & Archaeology

Going back to the arrival of the Spanish conquistadors, the best book is undoubtedly John Hemming's excellent *The Conquest of the Incas* (1970, Harvest/HBJ). Although this mainly deals with Peru (the heart of the Inca Empire) there are several sections on Ecuador.

Four Years Among the Ecuadorians by Friedrich Hassaurek was originally published in 1867 (republished 1967, Southern Illinois University Press). The author was a US diplomat who travelled widely in the country and vividly reported what he saw.

If archaeology is your interest, look for Karl Dieter's *Digging up Prehistory: the Archaeology of Ecuador* (1989, Libri Mundi, Quito).

Politics

Ecuador – Fragile Democracy by David Corkill & David Cubitt (1988, Latin American Bureau, London) is a recent look at historical patterns and current trends in Ecuadorian politics.

Inside the Company: CIA Diary written by former CIA agent Philip Agee and published in 1975, gives a chilling look at US intervention in Ecuador's political affairs. The diary may be difficult to get hold of – Corkill & Cubitt's book has a few excerpts.

Political Power in Ecuador (1980, University of New Mexico Press) is written by former Ecuadorian president, Osvaldo Hurtado.

Amazon Crude (1991, Natural Resources Defense Council, USA) is an environmental look at some of the impacts and problems caused by oil drilling in the Amazon. They don't pull any punches.

Miscellaneous

One of my favourite books about travel in Ecuador is Henri Michaux' prose/poetry account of his 1928 visit. Michaux was a Belgian poet and mystic and his *Ecuador – A Travel Journal* (republished 1970, Peter

Owen, London) is an intriguing look at his impressions of the country more than half a century ago.

Another personal favourite is Tom Miller's *The Panama Hat Trail* (1988, Vintage Departures, New York). If reading about some guy going to Ecuador to find some Panama hats doesn't sound like your cup of tea – think again. This book is well written, fun to read, and very informative about Ecuadorian life.

Two Wheels & a Taxi by Virginia Urrutia (1987, The Mountaineers, Seattle) is the author's story of her bicycling trip around Ecuador, accompanied by a local cab driver for logistical support. Ms Urrutia was 70 when she did the trip – an inspiration to us all.

There are many contemporary Ecuadorian writers. A good introduction to Ecuadorian literature is *Diez Cuentistas Ecuatorianas* (1990, Libri Mundi, Quito), a book of short stories by 10 Ecuadorian writers born in the 1940s. The stories are in Spanish with English translations. My favourite recent book by an Ecuadorian is Pablo Cuvi's *In the Eyes of My People* (1988, Dinediciones, Quito). The book is illustrated with 121 superb colour photographs, most by the author, and is available in Spanish or English. It is an informed and informal travelogue of Ecuador, written in a distinctive and evocative style which reminded me of a cross between Kerouac's *On the Road* and Steinbeck's *Travel's with Charley*.

Magazines

There are several good magazines dealing with budget travel or Latin America, though none of them deal with Ecuador exclusively.

The quarterly *South American Explorer* published by the South American Explorers Club is a great source of information about the continent. *Great Expeditions* published in Canada at PO Box 8000-411, Abbotsford BC V2S 6H1 (☎ (604) 652 6170) is a very useful and entertaining magazine for independent and budget travellers. It is published five times a year, subscriptions are US$18 per year in Canada and the USA, US$23

elsewhere. *Transitions Abroad*, Dept TRA, Box 3000, Denville, NJ 07834, USA, is an independent resource guide to living, learning, employment, and educational travel abroad. It is published six times a year, subscriptions are US$18 per year in the USA, US$24 in Canada, and US$36 elsewhere.

Bookshops

There are two particularly well-known and very good bookshops in Ecuador which sell a wide selection of books in English (French and German too). In Guayaquil go to the Librería Científica on Luque 223. In Quito there is Libri Mundi, the best-known bookshop in Ecuador. It is at Juan León Mera 851, with branches at Hotel Colón and Hotel Oro Verde. Both shops also have a good selection of Spanish books.

Perhaps the best source of books about Latin America is the South American Explorers Club – stop by their Quito clubhouse or write to their US office for a catalogue. In Europe, an excellent source of books is Bradt Publications, 41 Nortoft Road, Chalfont St Peter, Bucks SL9 0LA, UK (☎ (02) 407 3478). They also have a catalogue. Bradt books are available in the USA from Hunter Publishing, 300 Raritan Center Parkway, CN 94 Edison, NJ 08810.

Maps

The bookstores have a limited selection of Ecuadorian maps. The best selection is to be had from the Instituto Geográfico Militar (IGM), which is on top of a hill on Avenida T Paz y Miño, off Avenida Colombia in Quito. The building can be recognised by a map of Ecuador painted on one of its outside walls. There are no buses; walk (maybe after a few days) or take a taxi (about a dollar). Permission to enter the building is given to you at the main gate in exchange for your passport. Opening hours are from 8 am to 3 pm Monday to Thursday and 8 am to 12 noon on Friday.

Few city maps are published, and except for detailed maps of the whole of Quito, Guayaquil and Cuenca, you'll find the city maps in this book are generally the best available. The IGM does have some excellent large-scale maps of the whole country, ranging from a 1:1,000,000 one-sheet Ecuador map to 1:50,000 topographical maps. These occasionally go out of print, but most maps are freely available for reference. Some areas, especially the Oriente and parts of the western lowlands, are inadequately mapped. Bradt Publications has Ecuadorian maps for sale.

MEDIA
Newspapers & Magazines

Although Ecuador is a small country, there are literally dozens of newspapers available. Most towns of any size publish a local newspaper which is useful for finding out what's screening in the town cinemas or catching up on the local gossip, but has little national news and even less international news. The best newspapers are available in Quito and Guayaquil.

The best newspapers are *El Comercio* and *Hoy* published in Quito and *El Telégrafo* and *El Universo* in Guayaquil. These are about US$0.20 each in the city of publication. The further away from the city you are, the more you pay. For example, a day-old *El Comercio* in a small jungle town will be about 50% more expensive.

The above are morning papers – *Ultimas Noticias* and *La Hora* are afternoon tabloids which allow readers to catch up with the latest news. There are also a few sensationalist rags which luridly portray traffic-accident victims on the front page while relegating world affairs to a few columns behind the sports section.

Ecuador's weekly news magazine is *Vistazo*. It is popular, widely read and covers most of what is going on in Ecuador – politics, sport, economy etc. Generally, most papers and magazines tend to report local political stories with the same slant.

Foreign newspapers and magazines are available at Libri Mundi bookstore, the reading rooms of the luxury hotels in Quito and Guayaquil, and at the international airports. The foreign edition of the *Miami Herald* is often available in the evening of the day it is published but costs about US$2. Other newspapers are usually a few days late. Latin American editions of *Time* and *Newsweek* are also readily available at about US$2 each. All foreign editions are in English, but have more space devoted to Latin American news.

Radio & TV

Quito has seven television channels, and Guayaquil has four. The programming leaves much to be desired. I remember one evening when Ecuador was playing Peru in a soccer match; every channel was carrying coverage of the match. If you're not much interested in sports, you can watch very bad Latin American soap operas or re-runs of old and equally bad North American sitcoms. The news broadcasts every evening are quite good, especially for local news. Occasionally, a National Geographic special makes its way to the screen. These kinds of programmes are advertised days ahead in the better newspapers.

There is a cable network which offers about 15 US satellite stations such as CNN, ABC, NBC, CBS etc.

If you carry a portable radio when you travel, you'll find plenty of stations to choose from. There is more variety on radio than TV, and you can listen to programmes in Quechua as well as Spanish. HCJB (89.1 and 98.3 FM) is run by the World Radio Missionary Fellowship – it has programming in English and a nightly world news roundup at 6.45 pm. Owners of portable shortwave radios can easily pick up BBC World Service, Voice of America and Radio Australia.

FILM & PHOTOGRAPHY

Definitely bring everything you'll need. Camera gear is very expensive in Ecuador and film choice is limited. Some good films are unavailable, such as Kodachrome slide film. Others are kept in hot storage cabinets and are sometimes sold outdated, so if you do buy any film in Ecuador, check its expiry date. Ordinary print film, such as Kodacolor, is the most widely available, reasonably priced (about the same as in the US) and is usually the best buy. Slide film is more expensive. Film is hard to find in small towns – buy it in the big cities.

Don't have film developed in Ecuador if you can help it, as processing is mediocre (though amateur photographers find the prints to be OK). On the other hand, carrying around exposed film for months is asking for washed-out results. It is best to send it home as soon after it's exposed as possible.

To avoid problems with the mail service, send film home with a friend. You'll often meet people heading back to whichever continent you're from and they can usually be persuaded to do you this favour, particularly if you offer to take them out to dinner. I always buy either process-paid film or prepaid film mailers so I can place the exposed film in the mailer and not worry about the costs. The last thing you want to do on your return from a trip is worry about how you're going to find the money to develop a few dozen rolls of film.

Equatorial shadows are very strong and come out almost black on photographs. Often a bright but hazy day makes for better photographs than a very sunny one. Photography in open shade or using fill-in flash will help. The best time for shooting is when the sun is low – the first and last two hours of the day. If you are heading into the Oriente you will need high-speed film, flash, a tripod, or a combination of these if you want to take photographs within the jungle. The amount of light penetrating the layers of vegetation is surprisingly very low.

The Ecuadorian people make wonderful subjects for photos. From an Indian child to the handsomely uniformed presidential guard – the possibilities of 'people pictures' are endless. However, most people resent having a camera thrust in their faces and people in markets will often proudly turn their backs on pushy photographers. Ask for permission with a smile or a joke and if this is refused don't become offended. Some people believe that bad luck can be brought upon them by the eye of the camera. Others, more sophisticated, are just fed up with

seeing their pictures used in books, magazines and postcards. Somebody is making money at their expense. Sometimes a 'tip' is asked. Be aware and sensitive of people's feelings – it is not worth upsetting someone to get your photograph.

It is worth bringing some photographs from home – your family, home, place where you live, work, or go to school etc. They will be of interest to the Ecuadorian friends you make – and a great ice-breaker if your Spanish is limited.

HEALTH

It's true that most people travelling for any length of time in South America are likely to have an occasional mild stomach upset. It's also true that if you take the appropriate precautions before, during and after your trip, it's unlikely that you will become seriously ill. In almost a decade of living and travelling in Latin America, I'm happy to report that I've picked up no major illnesses.

Vaccinations

Vaccinations are the most important of your pre-departure health preparations. Although the Ecuadorian authorities do not, at present, require anyone to have an up-to-date international vaccination card to enter the country, you are strongly advised to read the following list and receive the ones appropriate for your trip. Pregnant women should consult with their doctor before taking these vaccinations.

Yellow fever vaccination is very important if you are planning a trip to the jungles of the Oriente, but not necessary if you intend to avoid the Oriente altogether. This vaccination lasts 10 years.

Typhoid vaccination consists of two injections taken four weeks apart, so you have to think ahead for this one. This vaccine makes some people feel unwell and often gives you a sore arm, so try not to schedule the last shot for the day you're packing. You should get a booster shot every three years, but this doesn't normally feel so bad.

Most people in developed countries get a diphtheria-tetanus injection and oral polio vaccine while they are at school. You should get boosters for these every 10 years.

Research is currently underway to find a 100% effective prophylactic for hepatitis; meanwhile you are advised to get a gamma globulin shot as close to departure as possible. Although it is not 100% effective, your chances of getting hepatitis A are minimised. The shot should be repeated every six months, although some authorities recommend more frequent shots.

Since the outbreak of cholera in Latin America in 1990, many travellers have expressed interest in a cholera vaccine. These are available but are not very good. Protection is estimated as about 50% to 80% efficient and only lasts for a maximum of six months. The disease is best prevented by clean eating habits – see Cholera in this chapter.

Smallpox was eradicated worldwide in 1978 and protection is no longer necessary.

Travel Insurance

However fit and healthy you are, *do* take out medical insurance, preferably one with provisions for flying you home in the event of a medical emergency. Even if you don't get sick, you might be involved in an accident. Shop around for the best policy and read the fine print – some policies will not cover 'dangerous activities' such as diving, climbing or motorbike riding.

First-Aid Kit

How large or small your first-aid kit should be depends on your knowledge of first-aid procedures, where and how far off the beaten track you are going, how long you will need the kit for, and how many people will be sharing it. The following is a suggested checklist which you should amend as you require:

- Your own prescription medications
- Antiseptic cream
- Antihistamine or anti-itch cream for insect bites
- Aspirin
- Pepto-Bismol and/or Lomotil for diarrhoea
- Antibiotics such as ampicillin and tetracycline
- Water purification tablets or iodine

- Powdered rehydration mixture for severe diarrhoea – particularly useful if travelling with children
- Throat lozenges
- Ear and eye drops
- Antacid tablets
- Motion-sickness medication
- Alcohol swabs
- Lip salve
- Foot and groin (antifungal) powder
- Thermometer in a case
- Surgical tape, assorted sticky plasters (band-aids), gauze, bandages, butterfly closures
- Scissors
- First-aid booklet

A convenient way of carrying your first-aid kit so that it doesn't get crushed is in a small plastic container with a sealing lid, such as Tupperware.

Don't use these medications indiscriminately and be aware of their side effects. A few of the most common side effects follow. Some people may be allergic to things as simple as aspirin. Antibiotics such as tetracycline can make you extra sensitive to the sun, thus increasing the chance of severe sunburn. Antibiotics are not recommended for prophylactic use – they destroy the body's natural resistance to diarrhoea and other diseases. Lomotil will temporarily stop the symptoms of diarrhoea, but will not cure the problem. Motion sickness or antihistamine medications can make you very drowsy.

Although many drugs can be easily bought in Ecuadorian pharmacies, you should be aware that some drugs which have been banned in North America or Europe are still sold in third world countries (including Ecuador), where regulations are lax. Make sure you buy the drug you need and not some strange mixture which may not be good for you. Check expiry dates on over the counter medicines.

Health Precautions

Several other things must be thought about before leaving home. If you wear prescription glasses, make sure you have a spare pair and the prescription. The tropical sun is strong, so you may want to have a prescription pair of sunglasses made.

Also buy sunblock lotion, as the lotions available in Ecuador are not very effective. A minimum sunblocking factor of 10 is recommended, or 15 if you are fair or burn easily.

Ensure that you have an adequate supply of the prescription medicines you use on a regular basis.

If you haven't had a dental examination for a long time, you should have one rather than risk a dental problem in Ecuador.

Water Purification

If you use tap water for drinking or washing fruits and vegetables, you should purify it first. The most effective method is to boil it continuously for 20 minutes, which is obviously inconvenient.

Various water-purifying tablets are available but most of them aren't wholly effective – the hepatitis virus may survive. Also, they make the water taste strange and are not recommended for frequent and long-term use.

The most effective method is to use iodine. Some water-purifying tablets have iodine as their active ingredient – check the label. You can use a few drops of prepared iodine solution but the problem is that it's difficult to know exactly how strong the solution is in the first place and how many drops you should use. The South American Explorers Club can often advise you. I suggest buying a supply of iodine tablets at home before you leave for your trip – only use them when you have to. Drink bottled water or beverages instead of always purifying possibly contaminated water.

A variety of portable filters have recently come on the market. They are available from camping stores and tend to be expensive. The cheaper ones are fiddly to use and have low yields. I find iodine tablets more convenient.

Tooth-brushing and iced drinks are frequent subjects of debate. The safest way is to use bottled or purified water for brushing teeth and to avoid drinks with ice in them. However, if you are on an extended trip, you will tend to build up resistance over the months and the minute amount of tap water ingested in tooth-brushing becomes increasingly less likely to hurt you. In first-class hotels and restaurants, the waiter may tell you that the water used for ice has been purified. This may be true, but you can never really be sure. It's a risk you either decide to take or not – depending on how much you want a piece of ice in your drink.

Finally, frequent hand-washing with soap goes a long way to preventing the spread of infections and diseases.

Diarrhoea

The drastic change in diet experienced by travellers means that they are often susceptible to minor stomach ailments, such as diarrhoea. After you've been travelling in South America for a while you seem to build up some sort of immunity, which just goes to show that most of the stomach problems you get when you first arrive aren't serious.

The major problem when you have diarrhoea is fluid loss leading to severe dehydration – you can actually dry out to the point of death if you go for several days without replacing the fluids you're losing – so drink plenty of liquids. Caffeine is a stomach irritant and a diuretic, so the best drinks are weak herbal tea, mineral water and caffeine-free soft drinks. Avoid milk and, if you can, fast. If you are hungry, stick to a light, bland diet such as crackers, toast, and yoghurt. Cultured yoghurt helps repopulate your intestine with beneficial organisms – other dairy products are not recommended. By giving your body plenty of fluids and little food, you can often get rid of diarrhoea naturally in about 24 to 36 hours. Rest as much as you can.

If you need to make a long journey you can stop the symptoms of diarrhoea by taking Lomotil or Imodium. These pills will not cure you, however, and it is likely that your diarrhoea will recur after the drug wears off. Pepto-Bismol is also effective. Rest, fast and drinking plenty of fluids is the most benign treatment.

Most people get diarrhoea during a trip but, in most cases, it lasts only a few hours or a day and is a mild inconvenience rather than a major problem. You never know when it may hit you though, so it's worth carrying some toilet paper with you – many Ecuadorian toilets lack TP just when you need it the most.

If you have recurring diarrhoea, a course of antibiotics may help – but get a stool sample checked and talk to a doctor first.

Dysentery

If your diarrhoea continues for several days and is accompanied by nausea, severe abdominal pain and fever, and you find blood in your stool, it's likely that you have contracted dysentery. Although many travellers suffer from an occasional bout of diarrhoea, dysentery is fortunately not very common. There are two types: amoebic and bacillary. It is not always obvious which kind you have. Although bacillary responds well to antibiotics, amoebic – which is rarer – involves more complex treatment. If you contract dysentery, you should seek medical advice.

Hepatitis

Most serious diseases are relatively uncommon. A depressingly common disease is hepatitis A, which is caused by ingesting contaminated food or water. Salads, uncooked or unpeeled fruit, unboiled drinks, and dirty syringes (even in hospitals) are the worst offenders. Infection risks are minimised by using bottled drinks, washing your own salads with purified water, and paying scrupulous attention to your toilet habits.

If you get the disease you'll know it. Your skin and especially the whites of your eyes turn yellow, and you literally feel so tired that it takes all your effort to go to the toilet. There is no cure except bed rest. If you're lucky, you'll be on your feet in a couple of weeks; if you're not, expect to stay in bed for a couple of months.

If you do get hepatitis A, it's not the end of the world. You may feel deathly ill but people almost never suffer from permanent ill effects. If you're on a long trip, you don't have to give up and go home. Find a hotel

that has a decent restaurant and get a room which isn't two flights of stairs and three hallways away from the nearest bathroom. Arrange with the hotel staff to bring you meals and drinks as you need them, and go to bed. Chances are that you'll be fit enough to travel again within a month.

Cholera

Cholera is transmitted orally, by the ingestion of impure water or contaminated food. It is suggested that drinking only bottled drinks or purified water and avoiding all uncooked food is the best prevention – better than taking vaccinations. Talk to your physician if you are concerned about this. The bacteria which causes cholera is easily killed by boiling.

Cholera symptoms appear one to three days after infection – the symptoms are an extremely sudden and explosive onset of diarrhoea which rapidly empties the gastrointestinal tract. The patient continues to produce a watery, mucus-like diarrhoea and this is often accompanied by severe bouts of vomiting. Blood is not normally found in the stool. The main problem is rapid dehydration which, if left untreated, can lead to death in a few days. Treatment is by oral or intravenous replacement of fluids and is simple and very effective.

Although thousands of cholera victims have died in Latin America during the recent outbreak, they were generally extremely poor people who either could not afford or were too far away from medical treatment. Very few cases of cholera have been reported in travellers, and I have not heard of any deaths resulting from these cases. If you maintain clean toilet and eating habits, you are more likely to get killed in a transport accident than die from cholera.

Malaria

This is another disease to think about before leaving. Malarial mosquitoes don't live above 2500 metres, so if you plan on staying in the highlands you needn't worry about malaria. If you plan on visiting the lowlands, you should purchase anti-malarial pills in advance because they have to be taken from two weeks before until six weeks after your visit. Dosage and frequency of pill-taking varies from brand to brand, so check this carefully.

Chloroquine (called Aralen in Ecuador) is recommended for short term protection. Long term use of chloroquine *may* cause side effects and travellers planning a long trip into the lowlands should discuss this risk against the value of protection with their doctor. Recently, chloroquine-resistant strains of malaria have been found in Ecuador – the new recommended drug is now Mefloquine (Lariam) but this is less widely available and more expensive than chloroquine. Pregnant women are at a higher risk when taking anti-malarials. Fansidar is now known to cause sometimes fatal side effects and use of this drug should be only under medical supervision.

Protection Against Mosquitoes People who are going to spend a great deal of time in tropical lowlands and prefer not to take anti-malarial pills on a semi-permanent basis should remember that malarial mosquitoes bite at night. You should wear long-sleeved shirts and long trousers from dusk till dawn, use frequent applications of an insect repellent, and sleep under a good mosquito net. Sleeping under a fan is also effective; mosquitoes don't like wind.

A woman traveller suggests that getting changed or dressed for dinner is not a good idea in mosquito-prone areas, because dusk is a particularly bad time for mosquitoes and that dressy skirt does little to keep the insects away. Keep the long pants and bug repellent on!

The most effective ingredient in insect repellents. is *diethyl-metatoluamide*, also known as 'Deet.' You can buy repellent with 90% or more of this ingredient; many brands, including those available in Ecuador, contain less than 15%, so buy it ahead of time. I find that the rub-on lotions are the most effective, and pump sprays are good for spraying clothes, especially at the neck, wrist, waist and ankle openings.

Some people find that Deet is irritating to the skin – they should use lower strengths. Everyone should avoid getting Deet in the eyes, on the lips, and in other sensitive regions – this stuff can dissolve plastic, so keep it off plastic lenses etc. Deet is toxic to children and shouldn't be used on their skin. Instead, try 'Skin So Soft' which is made by Avon, has insect repellent properties and is not toxic – get the oil, not the lotion. Camping stores sometimes sell insect repellents with names such as 'Green Ban' – these are made with natural products, are not toxic, but I find them less effective than repellents with Deet.

Mosquito spirals (coils) can sometimes be bought in Ecuador. They work like incense sticks and are fairly effective at keeping mosquitoes away.

Sexually Transmitted Diseases (STDs)
Heterosexual, homosexual, and transvestite prostitutes are quite active in the major cities. The incidence of sexually transmitted diseases (including AIDS) is increasing in Ecuadorian prostitutes. There are two effective ways of avoiding contracting an STD: have a monogamous relationship with a healthy partner or abstain from sexual encounters.

Abstinence is easy to recommend but tough to practice. Travellers who have no sexual partner and who are unwilling to abstain are strongly advised against using prostitutes. Having sex with a person other than a prostitute is somewhat safer, but still far from risk-free. The use of condoms minimises, but does not eliminate, the chances of contracting a STD. Condoms are widely available in Ecuadorian pharmacies.

Diseases such as syphilis and gonorrhoea are marked by rashes or sores in the genital area and burning pain during urination. Women's symptoms may be less obvious than men's. These diseases can be cured relatively straightforwardly by antibiotics. If not treated they can become dormant, only to emerge in much more difficult to treat forms a few months or years later. Ecuadorian doctors know how to treat most STDs –

if you have a rash, discharge, or pain go see a doctor.

Diseases such as herpes and AIDS are incurable, as of this writing. Herpes is not fatal. AIDS, whilst not fatal in itself, leads to a loss of immunity to other diseases, a combination of which is fatal within a few years of contracting AIDS.

AIDS can also be contracted through the use of infected syringes or through transfusions of infected blood. If you need to have an injection in Ecuador, make sure that the needle is a new, unused one. Because of economic necessity, some hospitals will reuse needles. If you have any doubt, buy your own needle from a pharmacy. If you are ill enough to require a blood transfusion, go to the best hospital in Quito or Guayaquil. If you can fly home, so much the better – blood screening techniques do exist in Ecuador, but are better in most First-World countries.

Altitude Sickness

This occurs when you ascend to high altitude quickly, for example if you fly into Quito (2850 metres) from sea level. The best way to prevent altitude sickness is to spend a day or two travelling slowly to high altitudes, thus allowing your body time to adjust. Even if you don't do this, it is unlikely that you will suffer greatly in Quito because it is still relatively low. A very few people do become seriously ill, but most travellers experience no more than some shortness of breath and headache. If, however, you travel higher than Quito you may experience more severe symptoms, including vomiting, fatigue, insomnia, loss of appetite, a rapid pulse and irregular or Cheyne-Stokes breathing during sleep.

The best thing you can do upon arriving at high altitude is to take it easy for the first day, and to avoid cigarettes and alcohol. This will go a long way to helping you acclimatise. If you feel sick, the best treatment is rest, deep breathing, an adequate fluid intake and a mild pain killer such as Tylenol to alleviate headaches. If symptoms are very severe, the only effective cure is oxygen. The best way

to obtain more oxygen is to descend to a lower elevation.

Heat & Sun

The heat and humidity of the tropics make you sweat profusely and can also make you feel apathetic. It is important to maintain a high fluid intake and to ensure that your food is well salted. If fluids and salts lost through perspiration are not replaced, heat exhaustion and cramps frequently result. The feeling of apathy that some people experience usually fades after a week or two.

If you're arriving in the tropics with a great desire to improve your tan, you've certainly come to the right place. The tropical sun will not only improve your tan, it will also burn you to a crisp. I know several travellers who have enjoyed themselves in the sun for an afternoon, and then spent the next couple of days with severe sunburn. An effective way of immobilising yourself is to cover yourself with suntan lotion, walk down to the beach, remove your shoes and badly burn your feet, which you forgot to put lotion on and which are especially untanned.

The power of the tropical sun cannot be overemphasised. Don't spoil your trip by trying to tan too quickly; use strong suntan lotion frequently and put it on all exposed skin. It is hard to find strong suntan lotion – bring it from home. Wearing a wide-brimmed sun hat is also a good idea.

Insect Problems

Insect repellents go a long way in preventing bites but if you do get bitten, avoid scratching. Unfortunately this is easier said than done. To alleviate itching, try applying Hydrocortisone cream, Calamine lotion, or soaking in baking soda. Scratching will quickly open bites and cause them to become infected. Skin infections are slow to heal in the heat of the tropics and all infected bites as well as cuts and grazes should be kept scrupulously clean, treated with antiseptic creams, and covered with dressings on a daily basis.

Another insect problem is infestation by lice (including crabs) and scabies. Lice or crabs crawl around in your body hair and make you itch. To get rid of them, wash with a shampoo which contains benzene hexachloride, or shave the affected area. To avoid being re-infected, wash all your clothes and bedding in hot water and the shampoo. It's probably best to just throw away your underwear if you had body lice or crabs. Lice thrive on body warmth; clothing which isn't worn will cause the beasties lurking within to die in about 72 hours.

Scabies are mites which burrow into your skin and cause it to become red and itchy. To kill scabies, wash yourself with a benzene benzoate solution, and wash your clothes too. Both benzene hexachloride and benzoate are obtainable from pharmacies in Ecuador.

Scorpions and spiders can give severely painful – but rarely fatal – stings or bites. A common way to get bitten is to put on your clothes and shoes in the morning without checking them first. Develop the habit of shaking out your clothing before putting it on, especially in the lowlands. Check your bedding before going to sleep. Don't walk barefoot, and look where you place your hands when reaching to a shelf or branch. It's extremely unlikely that you will get stung, so don't worry too much about it.

Snakebite

This is also extremely unlikely. Should you be bitten, the snake may be a non-venomous one. In any event, follow this procedure: first, try and kill the offending creature for identification. Second, don't try the slash-and-suck routine. One of the world's deadliest snakes is the fer-de-lance, and it has an anti-coagulating agent in its venom. If you're bitten by a fer-de-lance, your blood coagulates twice as slowly as the average haemophiliac's and so slashing at the wound with a razor is a good way to help you bleed to death. The slash-and-suck routine does work in some cases, but this should be done only by someone who knows what they are doing. Third, get the victim to a doctor as soon as possible. Fourth, reassure the victim and keep calm. Even the deadly fer-de-lance

only succeeds in killing a small percentage of its victims. Fifth, while reassuring and evacuating the victim, apply a tourniquet just above the bite if it is on a limb. Release pressure for 90 seconds every 10 minutes, and make sure that the tourniquet is never so tight that you can't slide a finger underneath it. If circulation is cut off completely, worse damage will result.

In Australia, which has a fair amount of snakebite experience, a new method of treatment is now recommended. This is to simply immobilise the limb where the bite took place and bandage it tightly (but not like a tourniquet) and completely. Then, with the minimum of disturbance, particularly of the bound limb, quickly get the victim to medical attention.

Rabies

Rabid dogs are more common in Latin America than in more developed nations. If you are bitten by a dog, try and have it captured for tests. If you are unable to test the dog, you must assume that you have rabies, which is invariably fatal (if untreated) so you cannot take the risk of hoping that the dog was not infected. Treatment consists of a long series of injections which used to be painful but modern techniques are quicker and less painful. Rabies doesn't develop for several weeks, so if you are bitten, don't panic. You've got plenty of time to get treated.

Rabies is also carried by vampire bats, who actually prefer to bite the toes of their sleeping human victims rather than necks as in popular folklore. So don't stick your toes out from your mosquito net or blanket if you're sleeping in an area where there are bats.

Medical Attention

If you've taken the precautions mentioned in the previous sections you can look forward to a generally healthy trip. Should something go wrong, however, you can get good medical advice and treatment in the major cities – addresses and directions are given in the appropriate city sections. Guayaquil and

Top: Basketware, Saquisili (RR)
Left: Animal Market, Otavalo (RR)
Right: Inspecting weavings in Otavalo Market (RR)

Top: Río Cuchipamba raft ferry near Gualaquiza (RR)
Bottom: Disembarking from the panga, Galápagos (RR)

Quito have the most comprehensive medical facilities in Ecuador.

WOMEN TRAVELLERS

Generally, women travellers will find Ecuador safe and pleasant to visit.

That is not to say, however, that machismo is a thing of the past. On the contrary, it is very much alive and practised. Ecuadorian men generally consider *gringas* to be more liberated (and therefore to be easier sexual conquests) than their Ecuadorian counterparts. Local men will often make flirtatious comments, whistles, and hisses to single women – both Ecuadorian and foreign. Women travelling with another woman are not exempt from this attention. Ecuadorian women usually deal with this by looking away and completely ignoring the man – this works reasonably well for gringas too. Women who firmly ignore unwanted verbal advances are normally treated with respect.

Travelling with another woman gives you some measure of psychological support. Travelling with a man tends to minimise the attention that Ecuadorian men may direct towards women travellers. Increasing numbers of Ecuadorian men are becoming sensitive to the issue of machismo – they may practise it with their buddies, but won't hassle every gringa they see.

Occasionally, you hear of a woman traveller being raped. A rape prevention counsellor who works with women in the US Peace Corps suggests that a lone woman should never wander around poorly lit areas at night or remote places (empty looking beaches) at any time. Don't assume that a deserted tropical beach is really deserted – walk with friends. Other suggestions include carrying a metal whistle (in your hand – not in your backpack). This produces a piercing blast and will startle off most would-be rapists long enough for a woman to get away.

I have met many women who have travelled safely, and alone, throughout Ecuador. Many have made friends with Ecuadorian men and found them charming and friendly. Just because machismo exists does not mean that all single women travellers are going to have their entire trip ruined by unwanted advances or worse.

There are a handful of women's centres in Quito, but there is not much in the way of local resources for women travellers. The South American Explorers Club in Quito and Lima is usually staffed by women – these friendly and wonderful people can tell you like it is.

Two books which I have seen and which appear to be useful are *Women Travel – Adventures, Advice & Experience* by Natania Jansz & Miranda Davies (Prentice Hall) and *Handbook for Women Travellers* by Maggie & Jemma Moss (Piatkus Publishers).

I would be very pleased to receive practical advice for women from women travellers – Lonely Planet sends the best letter writers a copy of the guidebook of your choice.

DANGERS & ANNOYANCES

Although rip-offs are a fact of life in Latin America, you'll find Ecuador is safer than the worst offenders, Peru and Colombia. Unfortunately, Ecuador is not as safe to travel in as when I first visited it, over a decade ago. This is probably related to the recently depressed economic situation (see Economy in the Facts about the Country chapter) combined with the increase in tourism to Ecuador over the past decade. You should, therefore , take some simple precautions to avoid being robbed.

Armed robbery is still rare in Ecuador, although parts of Quito, Guayaquil and some coastal areas do have a reputation for being dangerous. Sneak theft is more common, and you should remember that crowded places are the haunts of pickpockets. This means badly lit bus stations, crowded city streets or bustling markets. What often happens is that travellers are so involved in their new surroundings and experiences that they forget to stay alert and that's when something is stolen. It could happen in New York City or London as well.

Thieves look for easy targets. Tourists who carry a wallet or passport in a hip pocket are asking for trouble. Leave your wallet at home; it's an easy mark for a pickpocket. Carrying a roll of bills loosely wadded under a handkerchief in your front pocket is as safe a way as any of carrying your daily spending money. The rest should be hidden. Always use at least an inside pocket or preferably a body pouch, money belt or leg pouch to protect your money and passport.

Thieves often work in pairs or groups and whilst your attention is being distracted, one thief is robbing you. This can happen in a variety of ways – a bunch of kids fighting in front of you, an old lady 'accidentally' bumping into you, someone dropping something in your path or spilling something on your clothes, several people closing in around you on a crowded city bus, the possibilities go on and on. The only thing you can do is to try, as much as possible, to avoid very tight crowds and to stay alert, especially when something out of the ordinary happens.

To worry you further, there are the razor blade artists. No, they don't wave a blade in your face and demand 'Your money or your life!'. They simply slit open your luggage with a razor when you're not looking. This includes a pack on your back or luggage in the rack of a bus or train, or even your trouser pocket.

Many travellers carry their day packs in front of them to avoid having them slashed during trips to markets etc. Some travellers buy large grain sacks from hardware stores or markets and put their packs or luggage in them when they travel. This makes their bag look less obviously a tourist's bag – many locals use grain sacks to transport their belongings. Also, the sacks will keep your luggage clean and more protected.

When walking with my large pack, I move fast and avoid stopping which makes it difficult for anyone intent on cutting the pack. If I have to stop, at a street crossing for example, I tend to gently swing from side to side and I look around a lot. I don't feel paranoid – walking fast and looking around as I walk from bus station to hotel has become second nature to me. Taking a taxi from the bus station to a hotel is a safer alternative in some cities (this is mentioned in the text under the appropriate city). I never put my bag down unless I have my foot firmly on it.

One of the best solutions to the rip-off problem is to travel with a friend and to watch out for one another. An extra pair of eyes makes a lot of difference. I often see shifty-eyed looking types eyeing baggage at bus stations or pockets in busy markets, but they notice if you are alert and are far less likely to bother you. They'd rather pick the wallet from some gawker who isn't paying attention.

Definitely avoid any conversation with someone who offers you drugs. In fact, talking to any stranger on the street can hold risks. It has happened that travellers who have talked to strangers have been stopped soon after by plain-clothes 'police officers' and accused of talking to a drug dealer. In such a situation, never get into a vehicle with the 'police', but insist on going to a bona fide police station on foot.

Be wary of false or crooked police who prey on tourists. On the other hand, a uniformed official who asks to see your passport in broad daylight in the middle of a busy street is probably just doing a job – a few friendly words and a compliment on how you are enjoying this beautiful country will usually ensure that your passport will be examined quickly and returned politely.

A recent report indicates that there are false policemen around who will stop you and claim that they are narcotics officers and that there is a drug tax that foreigners must pay to help eliminate the drug trade. An official-looking document is produced listing different countries and how much their citizens are required to pay. This is a complete scam – ignore it and walk away.

Don't accept food from strangers. I know of one person who ate some cookies given him by some smooth-talking 'friends' on a bus – he woke up two days later in an alley with just his shirt and trousers. I've heard of several reports of this; Ecuadorian authorities claim that it's Colombians who do it. Unopened packages of cookies and other foods are injected with horse tranquillisers using hypodermic syringes. I know it sounds weird, but it's true.

Every year or so, you hear of a couple of night bus robberies in the Guayaquil area. Night buses are simply held up at a road block and robbed by armed men. These are always long-distance buses, so you should avoid taking night buses that go through Guayas Province unless you have to. It happens to one bus in many thousands so don't get paranoid if your schedule demands a night bus through the area.

If you are driving a car, never park it unattended. Never leave any valuables in sight in the car – even attended cars will have their windows smashed by hit-and-run merchants.

You should carry the greater proportion of your money in the form of travellers' cheques. These can be refunded if lost or stolen. Some airlines will also reissue your ticket if it is lost. You have to give them details such as where and when you got it, the ticket number and which flight was involved. Sometimes a reissuing fee – about US$20 – is charged, but that's much better than buying a new ticket.

It is a good idea to carry an emergency packet somewhere separate from all your other valuables. This emergency packet could be sewn into a jacket (don't lose the jacket!) or even carried in your shoe. It should contain a photocopy of the important pages of your passport in case it is lost or stolen. On the back of the photocopy you should list important numbers such as all your travellers' cheques serial numbers, airline ticket numbers, credit card or bank account numbers, telephone numbers. Also keep one high-denomination bill in with this emergency stash. You will probably never have to use it, but it's a good idea not to put all your eggs into one basket. Divide the rest of your money – some in an inside pocket and some in a money pouch, for example. In most decent hotels, you can leave money and valuables in a safe deposit box – this is not very reliable in the most basic hotels.

There has been a rash of recent problems for climbers and hikers. Armed gangs have robbed tourists hiking up Quito's backyard volcano, Pichincha. A rapist with a gap in his teeth, surrounded by two gold teeth, has recently robbed and raped small groups staying in some of the more remote mountain huts, such as on Iliniza and Tungurahua. Never leave gear unattended in a mountain hut whilst you are hiking. Some huts, eg on Cotopaxi or Chimborazo, have guardians and a place to lock up gear when you climb and are relatively safe. I suggest enquiring at the South American Explorers Club for up-to-date information on these problems (perhaps the gold-toothed rapist is now in prison). Also, climb and hike in a sizable group in questionable areas.

Take out travellers' insurance if you're carrying really valuable gear such as a good camera. But don't get paranoid; Ecuador is not an extremely dangerous country and in dozens of trips during the past decade, I have yet to be robbed.

If you are robbed, you should get a police report as soon as possible. This is a requirement for any insurance claims, although it is unlikely that the police will be able to recover the property. In Quito you should go to *Servicio de Investigaciones Criminales de Pichincha* (SICP) which is at the intersection of Montúfar and Esmeraldas in the old town. In other towns go to the main police headquarters.

WORK

Officially you need a workers visa to be allowed to work in Ecuador. Tourists have, however, obtained jobs teaching English in language schools, usually in Quito. Schools often advertise for teachers on the bulletin boards of travellers' hotels and restaurants. You are expected to be a native English speaker, but I know of one Dutchman fluent in English who got a job. Pay is low but enough to live on if you're broke. It's best to start looking soon after you arrive, because it's not easy to get a work visa and you may have to leave in 90 days.

If, in addition to speaking English like a native, you actually have a bona fide teaching credential, so much the better. Schools such as the American School in Quito will often hire teachers of mathematics, biology and other subjects, and may often help you get a work visa if you want to stay on. They also pay much better than the language schools. I don't know of other jobs which are readily available without a working visa.

If you want to arrange a teaching job in advance, try the following organisations:

European Council of International Schools
    21 B, Lavant Street, Petersfield, Hampshire G432 3EL, England (☎ (730) 68244)
The International Educator
    PO Box 103, West Bridgewater, MA 02379, USA (☎ (508) 580 1880). *The International Educator* is a quarterly newspaper listing teaching jobs and information worldwide. Annual subscriptions are US$25 in the USA, US$35 elsewhere.
Overseas Placement Services for Educators
    University of Northern Iowa, Cedar Falls, Iowa 50614-0390, USA.

The following schools may employ qualified teachers:

Academia Cotopaxi
    De las Higuerillas & Alondras, Monteserrín, Quito (☎ 433 602)
Albert Einstein School
    ·Carcelén, Quito Norte (☎ 569 695)
American School of Quito
    Carcelén, Quito Norte (☎ 472 975)
British Council
    Amazonas 1615 and Orellana, Quito; PO Box 1197, Quito (☎ 236 144)
Colegio Americano de Guayaquil
    Avenida Juan Tanca Marengo, Km 6.5, Guayaquil (☎ 255 506/9)
German School
    Avenida 6 de Diciembre & J Moreno, Quito (☎ 240 488)

Another way of making money, if you're in that unfortunate position of needing it, is by selling good-quality equipment such as camping or camera items. Good used gear can be sold for about 50% to 60% of its new price.

ACTIVITIES & HIGHLIGHTS

Where to begin? There are so many exciting things to do, see and experience in Ecuador that any list of suggestions will certainly be inadequate. In this section, I try to outline the main reasons that the majority of travellers come to Ecuador – I apologise to those travellers (philatelists and numismatists, athletes and Zen Buddhists, cyclists and boaters, and many others) whose varied and worthwhile interests are not discussed here. You should still come!

Where I mention a place name, you should see that section for further information.

Indigenous Markets These are often a success story for everyone – gringos go home with beautiful souvenirs, artisans make a living selling their crafts, and local buses, hotels, and restaurants benefit as well. There are plenty of great markets – Otavalo is the most famous, but markets at Saquisilí and many other highland towns and villages are well worth visiting.

Climbing & Hiking Tents, sleeping bags, and other gear can be rented in Quito and some other towns. Adventures in Parque Nacional Cotopaxi, the Baños area, Area Nacional de Recreación Las Cajas (near Cuenca) and around Chimborazo (Ecuador's highest mountain) are all worthwhile and described in this book. For dedicated outdoor adventurers, I recommend *Climbing & Hiking in Ecuador* by Rob Rachowiecki & Betsy Wagenhauser.

Wildlife The first thought here is **birds**. Half of the birds in South America are found in Ecuador – and little Ecuador has twice as many birds as all of North America. See the Books & Maps section in this chapter for listings of bird guides. Pasochoa Forest Preserve near Quito, operated by the Fundación Natura, is one of the best places in the highlands to see many species of hummingbirds.

The second thought here is the **Galápagos Islands**. I place them second because they are becoming increasingly over-visited by curiosity seekers and are becoming prohibitively expensive to visit – go if you are really interested, don't bother if wildlife is not your thing. The Galápagos are a bunch of relatively recent volcanic rocks stuck in the middle of the Pacific; many of the plants and animals on them are endemic to the islands. If you don't know what endemic means, perhaps you should go elsewhere.

Thirdly, think **Amazon**. Various trips can be taken into the rainforest. I remember talking to a traveller who thought the Amazon would be a cross between Hawaii and the African plains – she was disappointed not to see more wildlife in a luxuriantly tropical setting. The wildlife is there – but the luxuriant vegetation masks much of it. Many areas of the Ecuadorian rainforest have been colonised and you won't see jaguars in these areas (which are, of course, the easiest to get to). Having said this, I recommend Ecuador as being as good a country as any to visit the rainforest – see the Oriente chapters for more information.

Finally, don't neglect the wildlife of the **highlands** – the páramo habitats of the Tulcán area, Parque Nacional Cotopaxi, and Area Nacional de Recreación Las Cajas are all recommended.

History Many highland towns have Spanish colonial architecture dominating their city centres. Quito's old town has been designated Patrimonio de Humanidad by UNESCO. Flying from Quito to Cuenca gives an unforgettable aerial glimpse of the beautiful colonial centre of Cuenca. Many other highland towns have interesting colonial architecture.

Fiestas From the capital's annual fiesta during the first week in December to the local festivities in small towns and villages – these are a chance to mingle with local people and have fun. All Souls' Day (2 November) is particularly recommended in the highlands; Bolívar's Birthday (24 July) and the Founding of Guayaquil (25 July) are particularly recommended in Guayaquil. Carnival time (the weekend preceding Ash Wednesday) is celebrated all over Latin America – in Ecuador, it takes the form of water throwing in most areas and a fruit and flowers festival in Ambato.

Hang Out Travellers needing a place to relax and hang out for a week or two will find several good spots. Vilcabamba in the Southern Highlands and Alandaluz on the central coast are both very laid back. Otavalo in the highlands, Baños on the edge of the highlands/jungle, Misahuallí in the jungle, and Atacames on the coast are all popular travellers' destinations, all accompanied by a certain amount of hype and frenzied activity – but if you want to meet people on the gringo trail, these are the places to go. Cuenca is the big city to quietly hang out in – the third largest Ecuadorian town, it is nevertheless very traditional and attractive. Quito is a better capital city to spend time in than many other capitals.

Learn Spanish Quito has a plethora of schools which will teach you Spanish at any level. You can learn in a class, a small group or receive individual 'one-to-one' tuition. Accommodation with an Ecuadorian family can also be arranged so that you can practice your newly acquired linguistic skills.

Travel There are numerous interesting, unusual and fun ways to travel – though I can't guarantee luxurious comfort! Ride on the roof of an old steam train as it zigzags down *El Nariz del Diablo* (the devil's nose) – a dizzying descent from Alausí in the highlands to Guayaquil on the coast. Voyage along a tropical river in a dugout canoe from Borbón on the coast or Misahuallí in the Oriente. Pack yourself into a bus full of locals and take the high road around Chimborazo. Take a flight along the Andes in a TAME jet or fly along the coast or over the Oriente in a light aircraft – don't forget your camera. You can also cross the Río Guayas by passenger ferry to see the busy traffic on Ecuador's widest river. Amble around the Vilcabamba or Baños area by horseback.

ACCOMMODATION
Youth Hostels & Camping
Youth hostels as we know them in other parts of the world aren't found in Ecuador. The

cheaper hotels make up for this lack anyway. There are climbers' refuges (*refugios*) on some of the major mountains and you can camp in the countryside. If you're carrying a tent or want to hike up to a mountaineering refugio, I suggest you get a copy of *Climbing & Hiking in Ecuador*. There are rarely camp sites in the towns; again, the constant availability of cheap hotels makes town camp sites redundant.

Hotels

There is much variety and no shortage of places to stay in Ecuador. It is almost unheard of to arrive in a town and not be able to find somewhere to sleep, but during major fiestas or the night before market day, accommodation can be rather tight. For this reason, I have marked as many hotels as possible on the town maps. Most of the time, many of these hotels will be superfluous, but once in a while you'll be glad to have the option of as many hotels as possible.

Hotels go by a variety of names. A *pensión* or a *hospedaje* is usually an inexpensive boarding-house or place of lodging, often family run. A *hostal* can vary from inexpensive to moderately priced, depending on whether the owner thinks of the place as a cheap hostel or an up-market inn. A *hostería* tends to be a mid-priced comfortable country inn. *Cabañas* are cabins found in both the coast and the Oriente – they can range from basic and cheap little boxes to pleasant mid-priced bungalows. *Hotel* is a catch-all phrase for anywhere from a flea-bitten whorehouse to the most luxurious place in town.

Budget travellers

The fact that a hotel is marked on a city map does not necessarily imply that I recommend it – read the Places to Stay sections for each town or area for descriptions of the hotels. If you are going to a town specifically for a market or fiesta, try and arrive a day early if possible, or at least arrive by early afternoon of the day before the market. I give telephone numbers for many hotels, but the cheaper ones may not want to take phone reservations or, if they take them, they may not honour them if you arrive late in the day. The use of the telephone in these cases is to call from the bus station to see if they have a room available and if you then intend to head over right away.

Sometimes it's a little difficult to find single rooms, and you may get a room with two or even three beds. In most cases, though, you are only charged for one bed and don't have to share, unless the hotel is full. You should ensure in advance that you won't be asked to pay for all the beds or share with a stranger if you don't want to. This is no problem 90% of the time. Some of the cheapest hotels will ask you to take a bed in a room with other travellers – this 'dormitory-style' accommodation may save you a little money, but don't think that every other traveller is as honest as you are and don't leave your valuables lying around unattended.

If you are travelling as a couple, or in a group, you can't automatically assume that a room with two or three beds will be cheaper per person than a room with one bed. Sometimes it is and sometimes it isn't. If I give a price per person, then usually a double or triple room will cost two or three times a single. If more than one price is given, this indicates that double and triples are cheaper per person than singles.

Couples sharing one bed (*cama matrimonial*) are usually, though not always, charged the same as a double room with people in separate beds. To avoid making my figures instantly obsolete because of inflation, I have used US dollars for costs.

Look around the hotel if possible. The same prices are often charged for rooms of widely differing quality. Even in the dollar-a-night cheapies, it's worth looking around. If you get shown into a horrible airless box with just a bed and a bare light bulb, you can ask to see a better room without giving offence simply by asking if they have a room with a window, or explaining that you have to write some letters home and is there a room with a table and chair. You'll often be amazed at the results.

Never rent a room without looking at it first. In most hotels, even the cheapest, they'll be happy to let you see the room. If they aren't, then it usually means that the room is filthy anyway. Also ask to see the bathroom and make sure that the toilet flushes and the water runs if you want a wash. If the shower looks and smells as if someone threw up in it, the staff obviously don't do a very good job of looking after the place. There's probably a better hotel at the same price a few blocks away.

Bathroom Facilities These are rarely what you may be used to at home. The cheapest hotels don't always have hot water. Even if they do, it might not work or it may only be turned on at certain hours of the day. Ask about this if you're planning on a hot shower before going out to dinner – often there's hot water only in the morning.

Another intriguing device you should know about is the electric shower. This consists of a single cold-water shower head hooked up to an electric heating element which is switched on when you want a hot (more likely tepid) shower. Don't touch anything metal while you're in the shower or you may discover what an electric shock feels like. The power is never high enough to actually throw you across the room, but it's unpleasant nevertheless. I managed to shock myself by simply picking up the soap which I had balanced on a horizontal water pipe (there wasn't a soap dish).

Some hotels charge extra for hot showers and some simply don't have any showers at all. You can always use the public hot baths – there's one in every town.

As you have probably gathered by now, Ecuadorian plumbing leaves something to be desired. Flushing a toilet creates another hazard – overflow. Putting toilet paper into the bowl seems to clog up the system, so a waste receptacle is often provided for the paper. This may not seem particularly sanitary, but it is much better than clogged bowls and water on the floor. A well-run hotel, even if it is cheap, will ensure that the receptacle is emptied and the toilet cleaned every day.

Security Most hotels will give you a key to lock your room, and theft from your hotel room is not as frequent as it is in some other countries. Nevertheless, carrying your own padlock is a good idea if you plan on staying in the cheapest hotels. Once in a while you'll find that a room doesn't look very secure – perhaps there's a window that doesn't close or the wall doesn't come to the ceiling and can be climbed over. It's worth finding another room. This is another reason why it's good to look at a room before you rent it.

You should never leave valuables lying around the room. It's just too tempting for a maid who makes US$2 a day for her work. Money and passport should be in a secure body pouch; other valuables can usually be kept in the hotel strongbox. (Some cheaper hotels might not want to take this responsibility.) Don't get paranoid though. I haven't had anything stolen from my room in years of travelling in Ecuador, and rarely hear of people who have.

Many small hotels lock their door at night, which may make it difficult for late night revellers to return to their rooms. Usually, there is a doorbell but this is often located in some not very obvious position. Normally, there is a night guard who will let you in, but if the guard is asleep it may take several minutes of ringing, knocking or yelling to get attention. It's worth asking about when the hotel locks up if you are planning on a night out – then at least someone might expect you.

Pricing In smaller towns, I usually lump the accommodation together in one section. In larger towns, however, I separate them into groups.

Bottom-end hotels are the cheapest, but not necessarily the worst. Although rooms are usually basic, with just a bed and four walls, they can nevertheless be well looked after, very clean, and amazing value for money. They are often good places to meet other travellers, both Ecuadorian and foreign. Prices in this category range from US$1 to about US$3 per person. Every town has hotels in this price range and in smaller towns there aren't any more expensive hotels. Although you'll usually have to use communal bathrooms in the cheapest hotels, you can sometimes find rooms with a private bathroom for as little as US$2 per person. In large cities, which are generally more expensive, rooms included in this category may be up to US$10 for a double.

Middle category hotels usually cost from about US$3 to US$10 per person, but are not always better than the best hotels in the bottom-end price range. On the whole, however, you can find some very good bargains here. My wife and I stayed in some really pleasant places in this range. For example, a huge carpeted room with a beautiful countryside view, large and comfortable bed, plenty of furniture, and a clean private bathroom (with twin sinks!) cost a princely US$16 for the two of us. Even if you're travelling on a budget, there are always special occasions (your birthday?) when you can indulge in comparative luxury for a day or two. In the major cities, hotels included in this category may go as high as US$40 a double.

Top-end hotels are absent from many towns. In major cities, hotels in this price category may be luxurious and have a two-tiered pricing system. In Guayaquil and Quito, for example, a luxury hotel may charge a foreigner over US$100 for a double, but an Ecuadorian gets the room for half the price or less. This system stinks, but is legal and there's not much you can do about it other than avoid staying in luxury hotels. Apart from the expensive luxury hotels, I include some very good hotels in this category where rates are still very cheap by western standards – from about US$20 a double and up.

Staying in Villages

If you're really travelling far off the beaten track, you may end up in a village that doesn't have even a basic pensión. You can usually find somewhere to sleep by asking around, but it might be just a roof over your head rather than a bed, so carry a sleeping bag or at least a blanket.

The place to ask at first would probably be a village store – the store owner usually knows everyone in the village and would know who is in the habit of renting rooms or floor space. If that fails, you can ask for the *alcalde* (mayor) or at the *policía*. You may end up sleeping on the floor of the schoolhouse, the jail or the village community centre, but you'll probably find somewhere if you persevere. People in remote areas are generally hospitable.

FOOD

If you're on a tight budget, food is the most important part of your trip expenses. You can stay in rock-bottom hotels, travel 2nd class, and never consider buying a souvenir, but you've got to eat well. This doesn't mean expensively, but it does mean that you want to avoid spending half your trip sitting on the toilet.

The worst culprits for making you sick are salads and unpeeled fruit. With the fruit, stick to bananas, oranges, pineapples and other fruit that you can peel yourself. With unpeeled fruit or salads, wash them yourself in water which you can trust (see Health in this chapter). It actually can be a lot of fun getting a group of you together and heading out to the market to buy salad vegetables and preparing a huge salad. You can often persuade someone in the hotel to lend you a suitable bowl, or you could buy a large plastic bowl quite inexpensively and sell or give it away afterwards.

As long as you take heed of the salad warning, you'll find plenty of good things to eat at reasonable prices. You certainly don't have to eat at a fancy restaurant; their kitchen facilities may not be as clean as their white tablecloths. A good sign for any restaurant is if the locals eat there – restaurants aren't empty if the food is delicious and healthy.

If you're on a tight budget you can eat from street and market stalls if the food looks freshly cooked, though watch to see if your plate is going to be 'washed' in a bowl of cold, greasy water and wiped with a filthy rag (it's worth carrying your own bowl and spoon). Alternatively, try food that can be wrapped in paper, such as pancakes.

Comedores are literally dining rooms – the name is often applied to a cheap restaurant where the locals eat. A comedor is a good place for a cheap meal.

Local Dishes

Good local dishes to try at markets, street stands and restaurants, are the following:

Caldo
Soups and stews are very popular and are often served in markets for breakfasts. Soups are known as *caldos, sopas,* or *locros.* Chicken soup, or *caldo de gallina,* is the most popular. *Caldo de patas* is soup made by boiling cattle hooves and, to my taste, is as bad as it sounds.

Cuy
Whole roasted guinea pig. This is a traditional food dating back to Inca times. It tastes rather like a cross between rabbit and chicken. The sight of the little paws and teeth sticking out and eyes tightly closed is a little unnerving, but cuy is supposed to be a delicacy and some people love it.

Lechón
Suckling pig. Pigs are often roasted whole and are a common sight at Ecuadorian food markets. Pork is also called *chancho.*

Llapingachos
Mashed-potato-and-cheese pancakes that are fried – these are my favourite. They are often served with *fritada* – scraps of fried or roast pork.

Seco
Stew. The word literally means 'dry' (as opposed to a 'wet' soup). The stew is usually meat served with rice and can be *seco de gallina* (chicken stew), *de res* (beef), *de chivo* (goat), or *de cordero* (lamb).

Tostadas de maíz
Tasty fried corn pancakes.

Yaguarlocro
Potato soup with chunks of barely congealed blood sausage floating in it. I happen to like blood sausage and find this soup very tasty; many people prefer just

straight *locro* which usually has potatoes, corn and an avocado or cheese topping.

Restaurants

In a restaurant, there'll be other dishes to choose from. For breakfast, the usual eggs and bread rolls or toast are available. *Huevos fritos* are fried eggs, *revueltos* are scrambled, and *pasados* or *a la copa* are boiled or poached. These last two are usually semi-raw, so ask for *bien cocidos* (well cooked) or *duros* (hard) if you don't like your eggs too runny. *Tostadas* are toast and *panes* are bread rolls which you can have with butter and jam (*mantequilla y mermelada*). A good local change from eggs are sweet corn tamales called *humitas*, often served for breakfast with coffee.

Lunch is the biggest meal of the day for many Ecuadorians. If you walk into a cheap restaurant and ask for the *almuerzo* or lunch of the day, you'll get a decent meal for under a dollar – highly recommended for the economy minded. An almuerzo always consists of a *sopa* and a *segundo* or 'second dish,' which is usually a seco (stew) with plenty of rice. Sometimes the segundo is *pescado* (fish) or a kind of lentil or pea stew (*lenteja, arveja*), but there's always rice. Many, but not all, restaurants will give you a salad (often cooked), juice and *postre* (dessert) as well as the two main courses.

The supper of the day is usually similar to lunch. Ask for the *merienda.* If you don't want the almuerzo or merienda, you can choose from the menu, but this is always more expensive. However, the set meals do tend to get a little repetitive after a while and most people try out other dishes – which can still cost little over a dollar.

A *churrasco* is a hearty plate with a slice of fried beef, one or two fried eggs, vegetables (usually boiled beet slices, carrots and beans), fried potatoes, a slice of avocado and tomato, and the inevitable rice. If you get *arroz con pollo* then you'll be served a mountain of rice with little bits of chicken mixed in. If you're fed up with rice, go to a *Pollo a la Brasa* restaurant where you can get fried chicken, often with fried potatoes on the side. *Gallina* is usually boiled chicken as in soups, and *pollo* is more often spit-roasted or fried. Pollo tends to be underdone but you can always send it back to get it cooked longer.

Parrilladas are steak houses or grills. These are recommended places to eat if you like meat and a complete loss if you don't. Steaks, pork chops, chicken breasts, blood sausages, liver and tripe are all served on a grill which is placed on the table. Every time I order a parrillada for two people, I find there's enough for three but they'll give you a plastic bag for the leftovers. If you don't want the whole thing you can choose just a chop or a steak. Although parrilladas aren't particularly cheap, they are reasonably priced and very good value.

Seafood is very good, even in the highlands, as it is brought in fresh from the coast and iced. The most common types of fish are a white sea bass called *corvina* and trout (*trucha*). *Ceviche* is popular throughout Ecuador; this is seafood marinated in lemon and served with popcorn and sliced onions, and it's delicious. Unfortunately, improperly prepared ceviche has recently been identified as a source of the cholera bacteria, so you may want to avoid the dish until the disease is fully under control. Ceviches in better hotels and restaurants are probably safer. Ceviche can be *de pescado* (fish), *de camarones* (shrimp) or *de concha* (shellfish, such as clams or mussels). A *langosta* (lobster dinner) costs about US$8 – a bargain by western standards.

Most Ecuadorian meals come with *arroz* (rice), and some travellers get fed up with it. Surprisingly, one of the best places to go for a change from rice is a Chinese restaurant. These are known as *chifas* and are generally inexpensive and good value. Apart from rice, they serve *tallarines*, which are noodles mixed with your choice of pork, chicken, beef or vegetables (*legumbres, verduras*). Portions tend to be filling.

Vegetarians will find that chifas offer the best choice for non-meat dishes, or you can go to a *cevicherta* if you don't consider seafood to be meat. Vegetarian restaurants are rare in Ecuador. If you have any kind of strict diet, you would be advised to bring a camping stove with you and cook your own. Most hotels don't mind this, especially the cheapest ones. Just don't burn the place down.

If you want inexpensive luxury, go for breakfast at the fanciest hotel in town (assuming they have a restaurant or cafeteria). You can relax with coffee and rolls and the morning paper, or get a window seat and watch the world go by. Despite the elegant surroundings and the bow-tied waiter, you are only charged an extra few cents for your coffee. Makes a nice change and the coffee is often very good.

Cities big enough to have first-class hotels also have good but expensive (by Ecuadorian standards) international restaurants, often right in the hotels themselves.

DRINKS
Water
I don't recommend drinking tap water anywhere in Latin America. *Agua potable* means that the water comes from the tap but it's not necessarily healthy. Even if it comes from a chlorination or filtration plant, the plumbing is often old, cracked and full of crud. Salads washed in this water aren't necessarily clean. One suggestion is to carry a water bottle and purify your own water (for more about this see the Health section in this chapter).

If you don't want to go through the hassle of constantly purifying water, you can buy bottled mineral water very cheaply. Don't ask for mineral water, ask for *Güitig* (pronounced Weetig) which is the best known brand. Another brand is *Manantial* but everyone still asks for Güitig. A large 650 ml bottle costs about US$0.25 in most restaurants and less in a store. Güitig and Manantial are usually highly carbonated and rather salty. Some people prefer *Orangine* or *Agua Linda* which are less fizzy and salty. These last two often come in large two-litre plastic bottles which are disposable but can be reused for your own purified water.

Buying water in a glass bottle means you have to pay a deposit on the bottle.

Soft Drinks

The advantage of buying a bottled drink in a store is that it is very cheap; the disadvantage is that you have to drink it at the store because the bottle is usually worth more than the drink inside (canned drinks cost up to three times more than bottles). You can pay a deposit, but you have to return the bottle to the store you bought it from; a different store won't give you any money for it. What many travellers do is pay a deposit on, or effectively buy, a bottle of pop, beer or mineral water and then trade it in every time they want to buy a drink in a different place.

All the usual soft drinks are available, as are some local ones with such endearing names as Bimbo or Lulu. Soft drinks are collectively known as *colas* and the local brands are very sweet. 7-Up is simply called *seven*, so don't try calling it 'siete arriba' as no one will have any idea what you're talking about. You can also buy Coca Cola, Pepsi Cola, Orange Fanta or Crush (called *croosh*) and Sprite – the latter pronounced *essprite*! Diet soft drinks are becoming available in the fancier hotels, restaurants and supermarkets.

Ask for your drink *helada* if you want it out of the refrigerator or *al clima* if you don't. Remember to say *sin hielo* (without ice) unless you really trust the water supply.

Fruit Juices

Juices *(jugos)* are available everywhere and are usually better than colas to my taste, but they cost more. Make sure you get *jugo puro* and not *con agua*. The most common kinds are *mora* (blackberry), *naranja* (orange), *toronja* (grapefruit), *piña* (pineapple), *maracuya* (passion fruit), *sandía* (watermelon), *naranjilla* (a local fruit tasting like bitter orange), or papaya.

Coffee & Tea

Coffee is available almost everywhere but is often disappointing. A favourite Ecuadorian way of making coffee is to boil it for hours until only a thick syrup remains. This is then poured into cruets and diluted down with milk or water. It doesn't taste that great and it looks very much like soy sauce, so always check before pouring it into your milk (or over your rice)! Instant coffee is also served. 'Real' filtered coffee is becoming more available. Expresso is available only in the better restaurants. *Café con leche* is milk with coffee, and *café con agua* or *café negro* is black coffee.

Tea, or *té*, is served black with lemon and sugar. If you ask for tea with milk, British style, you'll get a cup of hot milk with a tea bag to dunk in it. Hot chocolate is also popular.

Alcohol

Finally we come to those beverages which can loosely be labelled 'libations'. The selection of beers is limited, but they are quite palatable and inexpensive. Pilsener usually comes in large 650 ml bottles and is my drink of choice. Club is slightly more expensive, has a slightly higher alcohol content (3.9% as opposed to 3.5% if you're interested), and comes in small 330 ml bottles. Other beers are imported and available only in the more expensive restaurants or at speciality liquor stores.

Local wines are truly terrible and should not be experimented with. Imported wines from Chile, Argentina or Peru are good but cost much more than they do in their country of origin – nevertheless, these are the best deals for wine drinkers. Californian and European wines are available but are more expensive still, and Australian wines haven't made it to Ecuador yet.

Spirits are expensive if imported and not very good if made locally, with some notable exceptions. Rum is cheap and good. The local firewater, *aguardiente* or sugar cane alcohol, is an acquired taste but is also good. It's very cheap; you can get a half bottle of Cristal aguardiente for about US$0.75. A popular fiesta drink which is made and sold on the streets is a *canelita* or *canelazo* – a hot toddy made with hot water, aguardiente, lemon, and *canela* (cinnamon). If you're desperate for gin, vodka or whisky, try the Larios brand – probably the best of a bad bunch.

ENTERTAINMENT
Nightlife
The most typical nightlife is a peña, or Ecuadorian folkloric music club (see Culture in Facts about the Country for a description of traditional folkloric music). This is a popular form of entertainment for all levels of Ecuadorians, from cabinet ministers to campesinos. Concerts are informal affairs, usually held late of a weekend night, and accompanied by plenty of drinking. They are not held everywhere – Quito and Otavalo often have good ones.

Apart from peñas, there are the usual night time activities. Cinemas are popular and cheap, with shows for well under a dollar. There is theatre and symphony in the main cities. Discotheques are popular in the main cities too. In the smaller towns, there isn't much to do apart from go to the local cinema, except when it is the annual fiesta.

Sports
The national sport is *futbol* (soccer) which is played in every city, town, and village. Major league professional soccer games are played in Quito and Guayaquil on Saturday afternoons and Sunday mornings.

Volleyball is popular – but more as an amateur game played in parks than as a professional sport. Golf and tennis is becoming increasingly popular – Ecuadorian tennis player Andres Gomez won the US Open Men's Doubles (with Slobodan Zivojinovic) in 1986, and the French Open in 1990.

Typically Latin sports activities such as bullfighting and cockfighting are very popular. The main bullfighting season is during the first week in December in Quito when bullfighters from Mexico and Spain may take part. Other highland towns have occasional bullfights, but this sport is less popular in the lowlands. Cockfighting is popular nation-wide, and most towns of any size will have a *Coliseo de Gallos* or cockfighting coliseum. A variety of strange

ballgames are also played. These include a sort of paddle-ball where a rubber ball is hit with large spiked paddles, and marbles games played with giant steel ball-bearings.

THINGS TO BUY
Souvenirs are good, varied and cheap. Although going to villages and markets is fun, you won't necessarily save a great deal of money. Similar items for sale in the main cities are often not much more expensive, so if you're limited on time you can shop in Quito or Guayaquil. If you only have the time or inclination to go on one big shopping expedition, you'll find the Saturday market at Otavalo has a wide variety and is convenient – this makes it very popular. Many other markets are colourful events for locals rather than tourists.

In markets and smaller stores, bargaining is acceptable, indeed expected, though don't expect to reduce the price by more than about 20%. In 'tourist stores' in Quito, prices are usually fixed. Some of the best stores are quite expensive; on the other hand, the quality of their products is often superior. Shopping in markets is more traditional and fun – though remember to watch your pockets.

Main Market Days
The more important markets are asterisked*.

Saturday
   Otavalo*, Latacunga*, Riobamba*, Cotacachi, Guano, Azoguez
Sunday
   Sangolquí*, Machachi*, Pujilí*, Cuenca, Peguche, Santo Domingo de los Colorados, Salcedo, Tulcán
Monday
   Ambato*
Tuesday
   Latacunga, Riobamba, Guano
Wednesday
   Pujilí
Thursday
   Saquisilí*, Cuenca, Riobamba, Tulcán

Clothing

Woollen goods are popular and are often made of a pleasantly coarse homespun wool. Otavalo is good for these and you can find sweaters, scarves, hats, gloves and vests. The price of a thick sweater will begin at well under US$10 (depending on size and quality) so if you're planning trips high into the mountains you can get some good warm clothes in Ecuador. Wool is also spun into a much finer and tighter textile which is used for making ponchos. Otavaleño Indian ponchos are amongst the best anywhere.

Clothing made from orlon is also to be found. It's cheaper than wool but looks garish and unattractive. It's easy to tell the difference just by looking at it, but if you're not sure, you can try the match trick. Take a tiny piece of lint from the material and set light to it. If it melts, it's orlon; if it burns, it's wool (perhaps trying the match trick is not such a brilliant idea – the store-keeper may not appreciate it). Many people think that only woollen items are traditional, earthy,

cool, ethnic, etc. While that may be true, if you see an orlon sweater that you like, there's nothing to stop you buying it and it'll be one of the cheapest sweaters you've ever bought.

Hand-embroidered clothes are also attractive but it's worth getting them from a reputable shop; otherwise they may shrink or run. Cotton blouses, shirts, skirts, dresses and shawls are available.

Ecuadorian T-shirts are among the best I've seen anywhere. If you're a T-shirt collector you'll find all sizes and colours to choose from. The most popular designs are of Galápagos animals, but many others are available. The best designs are by Peter Mussfeldt and the shirts cost about US$5 to US$6 each.

Panama hats are worth buying. A good panama is so finely made that it can be rolled up and passed through a man's ring, though it's unlikely that you'll find many of that quality. They are made from a palmlike bush which grows abundantly in the coastal province of Manabí. Montecristi and Jipijapa are

Weaving panama hats

major centres. The hats' name dates back to the 1849 Californian gold rush, when prospectors travelling from the eastern US to California through the Isthmus of Panama bought the hats, but they are originally Ecuadorian.

Weavings

A large variety of mainly woollen weavings are to be found all over the country, with Otavalo as usual having a good selection. They range from foot-square weavings which can be sewn together to make throw cushions or shoulder bags, to weavings large enough to be used as floor rugs or wall hangings. Designs range from traditional to modern; Escher styles are popular.

Bags

Apart from bags made from two small weavings stitched together, you can buy *shigras* or shoulder bags made from agave fibre that are strong, colourful and eminently practical. They come in a variety of sizes and are expandable. Agave fibre is also used to make macramé bags.

Leather

A famous centre for leatherwork is Cotacachi, north of Otavalo. Prices are cheap in comparison to those in more developed countries, but quality is very variable, so examine possible purchases carefully. Although the best leatherwork in Ecuador is supposedly done in the Ambato area, it's much easier to find leather goods for sale in Cotacachi. Leatherwork items range from full suits to coin purses, and wide-brimmed hats to luggage bags.

Woodwork

The major woodworking centre of Ecuador is San Antonio de Ibarra, and any items bought elsewhere are likely to have been carved there. Items range from the utilitarian (bowls, salad utensils, chess sets, candlesticks) to the decorative (crucifixes, statues, wall plaques). Again, prices are very low, but quality varies.

Balsa wood models are also popular. They are made in the jungles of the Oriente and sold in many of Quito's gift stores. Brightly painted birds are the most frequently seen items, but other animals and boxes are also sold.

Tagua nut carvings are typical of Ecuador. The tagua nut is actually the seed of a coastal palm. The egg-sized seed is carved into a variety of novelty items such as napkin rings, egg cups and chess pieces.

Jewellery

Ecuador isn't famous for its gemstones but it does have good silver work. Chordeleg near Cuenca is a major jewellery centre. Beautifully filigreed silver items can be obtained here.

Other

Baskets made of straw, reeds, or agave fibres are common everywhere. Painted and varnished ornaments made of bread dough are unique to Ecuador and are best obtained in Calderón, a village just north of Quito.

Onyx (a pale, translucent quartz with parallel layers of different colours) is carved into chess sets and other objects.

Getting There & Away

There are three ways of getting to Ecuador: air, land and sea. However, very few people even consider the ocean route these days as it is more expensive and less convenient than flying.

AIR

There are two international airports serving Ecuador – Guayaquil on the coast and Quito in the highlands. Remember that an internal flight between these two cities only costs about US$17 if you buy the internal ticket in Ecuador.

If you fly to Ecuador, bear in mind that the main hub for flights to and from western South America is Lima, Peru. You may be able to fly more cheaply to Lima and finish your journey to Ecuador by land. Bus travel from Lima to the Ecuadorian border takes about 24 hours and costs about US$20. If you prefer to travel direct to Ecuador, frequent international flights arrive and depart from either Quito or Guayaquil.

The ordinary tourist or economy-class fare is not the most economical way to go. It is convenient, however, because it enables you to fly on the next plane out and your ticket is valid for 12 months. If you want to economise further, there are several options. Students and people under 26 qualify for discounts with most airlines.

Whatever age you are, if you can purchase your ticket well in advance and stay a minimum length of time, you can buy a ticket which is usually about 30% or 40% cheaper than the full economy fare. These are often called APEX, excursion or promotional fares depending on the country you are flying from and the rules and fare structures that apply there.

Normally the following restrictions apply. You must purchase your ticket at least 21 days (sometimes more) in advance and you must stay away a minimum period (about 14 days on average) and return within 180 days (sometimes less). Individual airlines have different requirements and these change from time to time. Most of these tickets do not allow stopovers and there are extra charges (penalties) if you change your dates of travel or destinations. These tickets are often sold out well in advance of departure so try and book early if possible.

Stand-by fares are another possibility from some countries, such as the USA. Some airlines will let you travel at the last minute if they have available seats just before the flight. These stand-by tickets cost less than an economy fare but are not usually as cheap as other discounted tickets.

It is worth bearing in mind that round-trip fares are always much cheaper than two one-way tickets. They are also cheaper than 'open jaws' fares – these enable you to fly into one city (say Quito) and leave via another (say Lima).

If, because of a late flight (but not a rescheduled one) you lose a connection or are forced to overnight, the carrier is responsible for providing you with help in making the earliest possible connection and paying for a room in a hotel of their choice. They should also provide you with meal vouchers. If you are seriously delayed on an international flight, ask for these services.

The cheapest way to go is via the so-called 'bucket shops' which are legally allowed to sell discounted tickets to help airlines fill their flights. These tickets are usually the cheapest of all, particularly in the low seasons, but they often sell out fast and you may be limited to only a few available dates.

While discounted tickets, economy and student flights are available direct from the airlines or from a travel agency (there is no extra charge for any of these flights if you buy them from an agent rather than direct from the airline), discount bucket shop tickets are available only from the bucket shops themselves. Most of them are good and reputable companies, but once in a while a fly-by-night operator comes along and takes your money for a super-cheap flight and gives you an invalid or unusable ticket, so check what you are buying carefully before handing over your money.

Bucket shops often advertise in newspapers and magazines; there is much competition and a variety of fares and schedules are available. Fares to South America have traditionally been relatively expensive, but bucket shops have recently been able to offer increasingly economical fares to that continent.

If you are travelling with minimal luggage, you can fly to Ecuador as a 'courier', especially from the USA. Couriers are hired by companies who need to have packages delivered to Ecuador (and other countries) and will give the courier exceptionally cheap tickets in return for using his or her baggage allowance. You can bring carry-on luggage only. These are legitimate operations – all baggage that you are to deliver is completely legal. More details are given in To/From the USA in this chapter.

To/From the USA

Generally speaking, the USA does not have as strong a bucket shop tradition as Europe or Asia, so it's harder getting cheap flights from the USA to South America. Sometimes the Sunday travel sections in the major newspapers (*The Los Angeles Times* on the west coast and *The New York Times* on the east coast) advertise cheap fares to South America although these are sometimes no cheaper than the APEX fares with one of the several airlines serving Ecuador.

Council Travel and STA Travel are two recommended travel agencies in the USA (and worldwide) which are helpful in finding the best deal to Ecuador (and anywhere else in the world). They work with consolidators which buy discounted tickets in bulk and sell them to travel agents. This is all completely legal and reliable but the pricing system is a grey area – a good deal may be available one month and not the next. These agencies will often be able to quote cheaper fares than the airlines will quote you themselves.

Council Travel is affiliated with the Council on International Educational Exchange (CIEE). You can find their addresses and telephone numbers in the telephone directories of Tempe (Arizona), Berkeley, La Jolla, Long Beach, Los Angeles, San Diego and San Francisco (all in California), Boulder (Colorado), New Haven (Connecticut), Washington (DC), Atlanta (Georgia), Chicago and Evanston (Illinois), New Orleans (Louisiana), Amherst, Boston and Cambridge (Massachusetts), Ann Arbor (Michigan), Minneapolis (Minnesota), New York City (New York), Durham (N Carolina), Portland (Oregon), Providence (Rhode Island), Austin and Dallas (Texas), Seattle (Washington) and Milwaukee (Wisconsin).

STA has a toll-free number in the USA (☎ 1 (800) 777 0112) and has local offices in Los Angeles, Santa Monica, San Diego, Berkeley, and San Francisco (California), Boston and Cambridge (Massachusetts) and New York.

There are flights to Ecuador from Los Angeles, Houston, and Miami. Flights from other cities connect with one of these, usually Miami. Prices depend mainly on two things: when you go and how long you want to stay for. The low season is 16 August to 30 November and 1 January to 30 June. December, July and the first half of August are the high season. Fares for short visits (up to 21 days) are the cheapest; fares for longer visits are more expensive. If you are planning on spending several months in South America, and want to visit several countries, Caracas, Venezuela, is usually the cheapest to fly to from the USA. Then you could travel overland via Colombia, Ecuador, Peru, Brazil, and back to Venezuela, for example.

Recent best low season fares from Miami have been US$430 for stays of less than 21 days, US$510 (up to 30 days), US$515 (up to 60 days), and US$670 (up to 150 days). High season fares were US$545 (21 days) or US$615 (60 days). From New York, add about US$120 to each Miami fare. From Los Angeles for up to 21 days, low season fares were US$705 and high season fares were US$820. Fares for up to 60 days were

US$950 any time. All prices above include an obligatory US$18 tax and are liable to change – downwards as well as up. People are often surprised that fares from Los Angeles in southern California are so much higher than from northerly New York. A glance at the world map soon shows why. New York at 74° west is almost due north of Miami at 80° and Quito at 78°. Thus planes can fly a shorter, faster and cheaper north-south route. Los Angeles, on the other hand, is 118° west and therefore much further away from Quito than New York is.

Another possibility, for travellers wishing to visit several Latin American countries, is to fly with AeroPeru (☎ 1 (800) 777 7717). They offer 'Around South America Airpasses' from Miami to Peru plus any two other countries from the following list: Ecuador, Argentina, Chile, Brazil, Mexico and Panama. Tickets are valid for 45 days and cost US$999. This is cheaper than buying individual portions separately. The same airpass has recently sold for US$759 with more stopovers allowed – I was quoted US$999, but obviously there is some flexibility with the details.

Courier travel is another possibility – if you are flexible with dates and can manage with only carry-on luggage. Recently, Line-haul Services (☎ (305) 477 0651) in Miami required couriers for flights from from Miami to Ecuador. Round-trip tickets cost about US$200 and were good for 30 days. Travel Unlimited, PO Box 1058, Allston, MA 02134 publishes monthly listings of courier and cheap flights to Ecuador and many other countries – this newsletter is recommended for cheap fare hunters. A year's subscription costs US$25 in the USA, US$35 elsewhere. You can get a single issue for US$5. Another source is the *Courier Air Travel Handbook* by Mark Field (Thunderbird Press, Glendale, Arizona).

Travellers wishing to visit the Galápagos will find that Ecuatoriana and Saeta will both sell 'tied-in' tickets from Miami to Quito (or Guayaquil) and on to the Galápagos. These fares are about US$100 cheaper than buying your Galápagos portion in Ecuador. The problem is, however, that you need to make your arrangements in advance because the tickets are valid for only certain dates. It may be possible to change the dates, but check first. Unless you are going on a first class tour with reliable boat departures, these 'tied-in' tickets may be more hassle than they are worth. Ecuatoriana uses TAME airline to Baltra (for Santa Cruz) and Saeta uses SAN airline to San Cristobal. The two islands are half a day's boat ride apart, there is no regular ferry service, and the two airlines will not honour one another's tickets, so you are stuck on whichever island you fly to. If you do book a tour in advance, make sure that it begins and ends at the right island.

To/From Canada

There are no direct flights from Canada to Ecuador; travellers must connect through one of the gateway cities in the USA. Particularly recommended Canadian travel agencies include Travel CUTS with the main office in Toronto (☎ (416) 977 3703, 979 2406) and other offices in Vancouver, Victoria, Edmonton, Saskatoon, Ottawa, Montreal and Halifax. Also recommended is Adventure Centre with offices in Vancouver, Edmonton, Calgary and Toronto.

To/From the UK & Europe

Bucket shops generally provide the cheapest fares from Europe to Latin America. Fares from London are often cheaper than from other European cities and there are also more bucket shops. For this reason some European budget travellers buy their tickets from London bucket shops. This is especially true of travellers from Scandinavian countries, where cheap fares are difficult to find.

In London competition for selling air tickets is fierce. Bucket shops advertise in the classifieds of newspapers ranging from *The Times* to *Time Out*. I have heard consistently good reports about Journey Latin America (☎ (01) 747 3108), 16 Devonshire Rd., Chiswick, London W4 2HD, who specialise in cheap fares to the entire continent as well as arranging itineraries for both independent and escorted travel. They will make arrangements for you over the phone. Another reputable budget travel agency is Trailfinders (☎ (01) 938 3366), 42-48 Earl's Court Rd, London W8 6EJ. The useful travel newspaper *Trailfinder* is available from them for free. Typical round trip fares from London begin around £500. Fare prices depend on how long you want to stay (longer

STA Travel has offices in London, Manchester, Bristol, Leeds, Oxford and Cambridge (UK) and Frankfurt, Germany. STA has agents with NBBS, Amsterdam, Holland; DIS REJSER, Copenhagen, Denmark; USIT, Dublin, Ireland; CTS, Milan and Rome, Italy; Travela, Helsinki, Finland; Univers Reiser, Oslo, Norway;

stays are more expensive), which airline you choose, and when you travel. The (expensive) high seasons are December, early January, July and August.

Most airlines from Europe will take you to Miami, Colombia, Venezuela, or the Caribbean where you connect with other flights to Ecuador. Air France flies non-stop to Quito from Paris. Note that fares, routes, and low/high seasons change frequently and that the best information is to be had from travel professionals.

Courier flights are also possible from Europe. Look in the classifieds of Sunday newspapers.

European agents selling cheap flights to South America from outside of the UK include: Sindbad Travel, 3 Schoffelgasse, Zurich 8025, Switzerland, and Uniclam, 63 Rue Monsieur Le Prince, Paris 75006, France. Council Travel has offices in London, Dusseldorf, and Paris. The cheapest fares, however, are usually to be had in London. The British agencies will sell tickets to other European nationals but you often have to pick them up in person in London (or have them mailed to a UK address).

SSTS, Paris, France; SFS-Resor, Stockholm, Sweden; SSR, Zurich, Switzerland; SSTS, Madrid, Spain; SSTS, Lisbon, Portugal; ISSTA, Tel Aviv, Israel.

To/From Central America

If you are travelling overland through Central America you will probably have to fly over the Darien Gap – the roadless region between Panama and Colombia. There aren't any bucket shops or other really cheap options. From most Central American countries, the cheapest route is to fly to San Andrés Island in the Caribbean (part of Colombia) and continue from there on a domestic Colombian flight to Cartagena. From there it's buses south to Ecuador. From Panama, it's cheapest to fly to Medellín (about US$100) and then take buses south.

There are direct flights from Mexico City, Panama City, and San José, Costa Rica to Ecuador. Other Central American countries have connecting flights from their capitals via San José or Panama on to Ecuador. There are no particularly cheap deals here – you pay whatever the going economy rate is. This is about US$260 one way from Panama or US$300 from San José.

To/From South America

Again, there are no bucket shops or particularly cheap deals. One-way economy class fares to Ecuador are about US$150 from Bogotá, Colombia; US$300 from Caracas, Venezuela; US$180 from Lima, Peru; US$450 from Santiago, Chile; US$340 from La Paz, Bolivia; US$580 from Buenos Aires, Argentina; and US$730 from Río de Janeiro, Brazil.

If you want to fly and are not in a desperate hurry, you can often go somewhat cheaper by taking internal flights. For example, you could fly Guayaquil-Machala for US$10, take a bus across the border to Tumbes, Peru (about four hours and a couple of dollars), then take internal Peruvian flights Tumbes-Lima and Lima-Tacna (about US$80 each leg), take a bus from Tacna across the border to Arica, Chile (a couple of hours), and fly Arica-Santiago (about US$110). The combined cost of under US$300 is better than the direct fare of US$450 – but expect to travel for about three days to make all connections.

To/From Australia & New Zealand

There is little choice of routes between Australia and South America and there are certainly no bargain fares available. For travellers going on to Europe or Asia, Round-the-World (RTW) tickets probably work out better value for money. Many travellers fly to the west coast of the USA and then overland through Mexico and Central America, returning to the USA to pick up their RTW flight. Alternatively, they can continue on to Miami and then take a return flight to their desired South American destination from there. Miami-Quito-Lima then Lima-Miami is one route that has been used. There are usually strict conditions – such as a five-month limit – applying to discount tickets, so be careful.

Aerolíneas Argentinas offer a special 'Circle Americas Fare' which would be suitable for those also wishing to visit the southern part of the continent, say Argentina and Chile. It has a 90-day restriction and costs $2950 but allows four free stopovers. A suggested route could be Sydney-Buenos Aires-Río de Janeiro-Guayaquil (not Quito) to Houston or Los Angeles and return to Sydney.

Check the ads in the travel pages of papers like the Melbourne *Age* or the *Sydney Morning Herald* for other possibilities.

STA Travel has offices in Adelaide, Brisbane, Cairns, Canberra, Darwin, Melbourne, Perth, Sydney, and Townsville (Australia). STA also has offices in Auckland, Christchurch, Dunedin, and Wellington (New Zealand).

To/From Asia

There is also very little choice of direct flights between Asia and South America apart from Japan and there certainly won't be any bargains there. Council Travel has an office in Tokyo, Japan. STA Travel has offices in Bangkok, Thailand; Kuala Lumpur, Malaysia; Singapore; Tokyo and Osaka, Japan. The cheapest way will be to fly to the US west coast and connect from there.

Departing Ecuador

There is a hefty US$25 departure tax on international flights from Ecuador. This is payable in cash dollars or sucres at the exchange rate of the day.

There is a 10% tax on all international flights originating in Ecuador. This has to be paid before you can board the aircraft. If, for example, you buy a ticket Miami-Caracas and Quito-Miami, with the intention of travelling overland from Caracas to Quito, you will be charged 10% of the Quito-Miami ticket value at the airport, because this flight originates in Ecuador. This does not apply to the return portion of a Miami-Quito-Miami ticket, because it does not originate in Ecuador. Check this carefully if you are buying a ticket originating in Ecuador.

LAND

If you live in the Americas, it is possible to travel overland. However, if you start from

North or Central America, the Panamerican Highway stops in Panama and begins again in Colombia, leaving a 200-km roadless section of jungle known as the Darien Gap. This takes about a week to cross on foot and by canoe in the dry season (January to mid-April) but is much heavier going in the wet season. Most travellers going by land fly around the Darien Gap.

From South America it is straightforward to travel by public transport to Peru or Colombia which are the only two countries having land borders with Ecuador.

SEA

It is occasionally possible to find a ship going to Guayaquil, Ecuador's main port, but this is a very unusual way to arrive in Ecuador. It is certainly cheaper and more convenient to fly, but some people simply hate flying or prefer the 'romance' of crossing the world the old way.

Very few cruise ships have Guayaquil as a port of call as they head down the Pacific coast of South America. A few cargo lines will carry passengers. The Polish Ocean Line has passages from several European ports to many South American ones – prices vary depending on the destination but expect to pay roughly US$2000 from Europe to Ecuador. The Chilean Ocean Line has passages from several US ports to Chile stopping at Guayaquil en route. Lykes Line and Egon Oldendorff also carry passengers from the USA to Guayaquil and other South American ports. Fares are very roughly US$1500 from the USA to Ecuador. These

are all one way – most shipping lines prefer to sell round trips, however.

It is possible to arrive in Ecuador on your own sailing boat, or, if you don't happen to have one, as a crew member. Crew don't have to be experienced because many long ocean passages involve standing watch and keeping your eyes open. You should be able to get along with people in close quarters for extended periods of time – this is the most difficult aspect of the trip. If you get fed up with someone, there is nowhere else to go. Crew members are often (but not always) asked to contribute towards expenses, especially food. This is usually much cheaper than travelling overland, however.

Atulyo and Preyasi, owners of the sailing vessel S/V *Wailana*, recently sailed from Sausalito, California to Ecuador. They report that the following are good places to hang out and meet 'yachties'. In Mexico, Papi's Deli, Cabo San Lucas, Baja California; Phil's Restaurant, Melaque, Bahía Navidada, near Manzanillo; La Sirena Gorda Restaurant, Zihuatenango; Acapulco Yacht Club, Acapulco. In Costa Rica, Playa de Cocos, Bahía Ballena (near Montezuma), Puntarenas, and Golfito are all good. The Jungle Club or Captain Tom's Place, on an island opposite Golfito, is one of the best places. The Balboa Yacht Club is a good place in Panama. In Ecuador, Salinas is the port most frequented by international yachts.

A possible source of informations is *The Hitchhikers Guide to the Oceans* by Alison Muir Bennett & Clare Davis (1990, Seven Seas Press, Maine, USA).

Getting Around

Ecuador has a more efficient transport system than most Andean countries. Also, it is a small country, which means you can usually get anywhere and everywhere quickly and easily. The bus is the most frequently used method of transportation; you can take buses from the Colombian border to the Peruvian border in 18 hours if you want to. Aeroplanes and boats (especially in the Oriente) are also frequently used, but trains less so.

Whichever form of transport you use, remember to have your passport with you and not leave it in the hotel safe or packed in your luggage. To board most planes and boats, you need to show your passport.

Buses often have to go through a transit police check upon entering any town and although your passport is not frequently asked for, it's as well to have it handy for those times that you are asked to show it. Passport controls are more frequent when travelling by bus in the Oriente. If your passport is in order, these procedures are no more than cursory. If you're travelling anywhere near the borders or in the Oriente, you can expect more frequent passport checks.

AIR

Even the budget traveller should consider the occasional internal flight. With the exception of flying to the Galápagos, internal flights are comparatively cheap, and even the most expensive flight is currently only US$20. Almost all flights originate or terminate in Quito or Guayaquil, so the most useful way for the traveller to utilise these services is by taking a long overland journey from one of these cities and then returning quickly by air.

Ecuador's most important domestic airline is TAME, which flies to almost all the destinations in the country. Their competitors are SAN and Saeta who have flights between Quito, Guayaquil and Cuenca. Prices are the same for all companies so, if

travelling between these major cities, use the one whose schedule most closely matches yours.

There are various small airlines like TAO, which flies small aircraft between Puyo and Macas in the Oriente, and AECA which flies on the coast. There are others. The military have been known to provide flights, as have the missions and the oil companies, however, you hear about this less and less. These days, with improving air services, it's usually easier to pay a few extra dollars for a scheduled flight than to spend several days lining up a flight with someone else.

TAME flies from Quito to and from Guayaquil, Cuenca, Loja, Macas, Coca, Tarapoa, Lago Agrio, Tulcán, Esmeraldas, Manta, Portoviejo and Baltra, Galápagos. TAME also flies from Guayaquil to and from Quito, Cuenca, Loja, Machala, and Baltra, Galápagos. There are seasonal TAME flights from Guayaquil to Salinas. In the past TAME has flown from Guayaquil to Macará and from Cuenca to Loja and Macas, but these flights have been suspended for some time because of lack of aircraft. For the same reason, flights are frequently suspended – if an airplane needs maintenance, flights to places like Machala and Tulcán (which are relatively easy to reach by bus) are the first to be suspended.

SAN schedules flights between Quito and Guayaquil, Quito and Cuenca, and to San

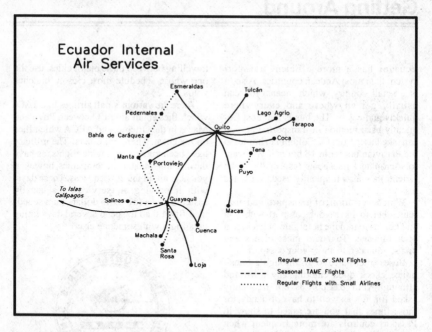

Ecuador Internal Air Services

Esmeraldas
Tulcán
Pedernales
Lago Agrio
Quito
Tarapoa
Bahía de Caráquez
Coca
Tena
Manta
Portoviejo
Puyo
To Islas Galápagos
Salinas
Guayaquil
Macas
Machala
Cuenca
Santa Rosa
Loja

——————— Regular TAME or SAN Flights
– – – – – Seasonal TAME Flights
·········· Regular Flights with Small Airlines

Cristóbal, Galápagos. Saeta has flights between Quito and Guayaquil. Between them, the airlines provide about between eight and 11 flights a day between Quito and Guayaquil. Except for the major cities, flights usually operate several times a week but not on a daily basis. For more details, see the Air sections under the appropriate cities.

Flights are frequently late, but not very much so. Flights first thing in the morning are more likely to be on time but by the afternoon things tend to have slid half an hour behind schedule. You should show up about an hour early for domestic flights, as baggage handling and check-in procedures tend to be rather chaotic. After one particularly bad overbooking incident where the plane 'grew smaller' a frustrated foreigner quipped that TAME stood for 'Try Again Mañana, Extranjera'.

If you show up early for your flight between Quito and Guayaquil, you can often get on the earlier flight if there is room. If you paid for your ticket with cash (not credit

card) then TAME will accept your SAN or Saeta ticket and vice versa.

There are no seating assignments on domestic flights so you choose your seat aboard on a first-come, first-served basis. There are no separate sections for smokers and nonsmokers. Many of the flights give extraordinarily good views of the snow-capped Andes and it is worth getting a window seat even if the weather is bad because the plane often rises above the clouds, giving spectacular views of volcanoes riding on a sea of cloud.

Once in a while you may get treated to a special mountain fly-by. This happened to me on the flight from Macas to Quito. We flew by Cotopaxi and the pilot decided to give us a closer look – he banked sharply and did a complete circuit of the volcano. For over a minute we were able to have wonderful views of the top of the mountain with a rare look directly down into the crater. TAME scored a lot of points that day! .

I also remember a most spectacular Quito-

Cuenca flight which I chanced to take one morning in June. As we took off, Cayambe (Ecuador's third highest peak) was briefly visible behind the aircraft and, almost immediately, the majestic bulk of Antisana (fourth highest) with it's four lumpy peaks rising up from the edge of the Amazon basin. After a few minutes of flight, we passed the ice cream cone of Cotopaxi (second highest) and then Tungurahua (10th highest) with the town of Baños nestling in a valley to the north of the mountain (to the left as we looked at it). Soon after, on this cloudless day, we saw the rarely clear, jagged peaks of El Altar (fifth highest) with the famous sulphur yellow lagoon in the middle of its blown-away crater, followed by the smoking volcano, Sangay (seventh highest).

Finally, after a most wonderful 40 minute flight, we descended, flying low over the red-tiled colonial roofs of Cuenca, with a good look at the blue-domed cathedral in the central plaza. The view I describe was from the left of the aircraft; on the right passengers could see Iliniza Norte and Iliniza Sur (eighth and sixth highest) followed by the highest mountain in Ecuador, Chimborazo, and the nearby Carihuairazo (ninth highest). This flight cost US$17.50 – if the weather looks really clear it's worth heading down to the airport just to joy-ride.

Flying from Quito to Guayaquil, you will get the most spectacular mountain views on the left-hand side; flying to Macas the view is on the right-hand side. Many of the other flights have mountains on either side. You should decide which specific peaks you would prefer to have a good look at and also consider the time of day so that you won't be looking into the sun. Make an effort to study a topographical map to see which side of the plane will be best for you and try to get on the plane early.

Flights on the mainland cost the same whether you're an Ecuadorian or foreigner. Flights to the Galápagos are a different matter, however. Although Ecuadorians pay only about US$40 for the round trip from Guayaquil, all foreigners have to pay about US$324 for the same flight, and they are not treated to better in-flight service. There is little you can do about this except be thankful that the rest of the internal flights cost the same for all nationalities (see the Galápagos chapter for some ideas about getting to the islands a little more cheaply).

Wherever you want to fly, don't despair if you can't get a ticket. It's always worth going to the airport in the hope of someone not turning up for the flight. Make sure that you're there early and get yourself on a waiting list if there is one. If you do have a reservation, make sure you confirm it. And reconfirm it. And reconfirm it again. As a general rule, I would confirm flights both 72 and 24 hours in advance, as well as when you arrive in Ecuador. Ecuadorians are notorious for bumping you off your flight if you don't reconfirm. Since the first edition of this book, the situation has improved somewhat – but still – reconfirm. If it's impossible for you to reconfirm because you're in the middle of nowhere, tell them so that they know. Try to have it on the computer if possible. And try to find someone to reconfirm for you.

A final point about air travel from Ecuador. You can't buy international charter or other economy flights in Ecuador. You have to pay full first-class or full tourist-class fare. In addition to the fare you must pay a 10% tax. There is a US$25 international departure tax but no taxes for domestic flights.

BUS

Long Distance

Ecuador is developing a system of central bus terminals in each city – especially in the highlands and increasingly in the lowlands – which means that if you have to change buses you don't have to go looking for different terminals. All buses arrive and depart from the same place. Once you have located the central bus terminal, often referred to as the *Terminal Terrestre*, it is a simple matter to find a bus to take you where you want to go. Some towns still haven't completed their main bus terminals, and may still have several smaller ones.

COOPERATIVA DE TRANSPORTES
"RIOBAMBA"

Riobamba Teléfonos: 961583 - 960766 - Sto. Domingo Telf. 750718
el Puyo Telf 885479 - Guayaquil Terminal Terrestre Oficina 2
Quito Term. Terrestre - Baños Term. Terrestre - Tena Term. Terrestre

Carro No. _____ Valor S/. _____
de _____ a _____
Asientos: _____
Hora de Salida _____
Fecha _____ de 19__

Throughout this book, I have indicated
where the bus terminals are located on the
city maps. The accompanying text will tell
you the most important destinations served
by the terminal, the approximate cost of the
journey, about how long it will take to get
there, and how frequently buses leave.

I have refrained from giving exact schedules, as that is a sure way of making this book
obsolete before it is published. Timetables
change frequently and are not necessarily
adhered to. If a bus is full, it might leave
early. Conversely, an almost-empty bus will
usually spend half an hour giving *vueltas* or
just driving from the terminal to the main
plaza and back again with the driver's assistant yelling out of the door in the hopes of
attracting more passengers. This is less likely
to happen in cities – but is the norm in
smaller towns.

Various types of buses are used; they can
be roughly grouped into two types. *Busetas*
(small buses) usually hold 22 passengers and
are fast and efficient. Although standing passengers are not normally allowed, the seats
can be rather cramped. Larger coaches have
more space, but they often allow standing
passengers and so can get rather crowded.
They are generally slower than the busetas
and at times can take almost twice as long to
reach their destinations because they drop off
and pick up so many standing passengers.

Although they're slow, the big old
coaches are sometimes more fun because
there's more activity going on with passengers getting on and off all the time, perhaps
accompanied by chickens or a couple of

hundredweight of potatoes. If you're in any
hurry, make sure that you get a buseta. The
approximate times given for most of the
journeys in this book tend to lean towards the
faster times.

Getting around Ecuador by bus is easy, but
here are some tips to make your travels more
enjoyable. If you go to the terminal the day
before your bus trip, you can usually buy
tickets in advance. This means you can
choose your approximate time of departure,
and often you can choose your seat number
too. I'm over six feet tall, and one of my pet
hates is being squished in the tiny back seat
of a bus. I think it's worth buying tickets in
advance so that I can get a front-row seat,
which generally means more leg room, much
better views and a more exciting trip.

Some people prefer second-row seats, to
avoid being jostled by passengers getting on
and off. Try to avoid those rows over the
wheels – usually the third row from the front
and the third from the back in the busetas,
and the fourth or fifth rows from the front
and back in larger buses. Ask about the position of the wheels when buying your ticket.
Also remember that the suspension at the
back of a bus is usually far worse than anywhere else, so try and avoid the back rows.

Some bus companies don't sell tickets in
advance. This is usually when they have
frequent departures (about twice an hour or
even more often). You just arrive and get on
the next bus that's going your way. If the next
bus out has only uncomfortable seats, you
can miss it and be first on the next one out
(assuming the wait is not too long).

If travelling during long holiday weekends or special fiestas, you may find that
buses are booked up for several days in
advance, so book early if you can.

If you're travelling very light, it's best to
keep your luggage inside the bus with you.
If I'm off on a trip for a few days, I often
leave much of my luggage at the South
American Explorers Club (or in a hotel
storage room) and travel with a bag small
enough to fit under the seat. Local people get
away with taking fairly large pieces of
luggage aboard so you don't have to put

yours on the outside luggage rack, even if the driver tells you to.

If your luggage is too big to fit under the seat, it will have to go on top or in a luggage compartment. Sometimes the top is covered with a tarpaulin, but not always, so pack your gear in large plastic bags (garbage bags are good) to avoid getting everything wet if it rains. The luggage compartment is sometimes filthy, and your luggage can get covered with grease or mud. Placing your luggage in a large protective sack is a good idea. Most of the Indians use grain sacks as luggage; you can buy them for a few cents in general stores or markets.

Often when a bus stops on the main routes, vendors selling fruit, rolls, ice cream or drinks suddenly appear – so you won't starve. Long-distance buses usually stop for a 20-minute meal break at the appropriate times. The food in the terminal restaurants may be somewhat basic, so if you're a picky eater you should bring food with you on longer trips.

Fares for tickets bought in bus terminals are a set price. The larger terminals often have traveller information booths which can advise you about this, but normally I find that you get charged the correct fare. The booths can give you information on all the routes available from the larger terminals.

If you're only going part of the way, or you get on a bus in a small town as it comes by between larger towns, the bus driver will charge you appropriately. About 90% of the time you are charged honestly, although once in a while they try and overcharge you.

Once I was charged US$0.50 for a ride that I paid US$0.20 for going the other way. I pointed this out to the driver who was adamant that the fare was US$0.50. The Latin American machismo meant that he didn't want to admit that he was wrong. Although there's little point in getting uptight about a few cents, this particular example was too blatant for me to ignore. I told him he could have US$0.20 or we could go talk to the transit police; he didn't want to talk to the transit police.

This sort of thing doesn't happen very

often; however, the only way to guard against it is to know roughly the correct fare beforehand.

If you want to travel somewhere immediately, just go to the terminal and you'll usually find the driver's assistant running around trying to hustle up some passengers for his bus. Often you'll be on a bus going your way within a few minutes of arriving at the terminal. Before boarding a bus, make sure it's going where you want to go.

Occasionally drivers will say that they are going where you want to go and then take you only part of the way and expect you to change buses. If you want a direct bus, make sure you ask for it. Also make sure that it is leaving soon, and not in two hours.

Finally, if the bus looks too slow, or too fast, or too old, or too cramped, or you just don't like it for some reason, you can usually find another bus leaving soon if you're going to a major destination. Most places are served by several bus companies and you can make the choice that's best for you.

One last word about Ecuadorian buses: toilets – there aren't any. Long-distance buses have rest stops every three or four hours – try not to get onto a bus with a full bladder or you may join the famous traveller who had to pee in his boot. A reader wrote to encourage me to state that children may piss or vomit on you on buses. I get some off-beat letters from people on the road...

Local

These are usually slow and crowded, but very cheap. You can get around most towns for about US$0.05. Local buses often go out to a nearby village and this is a good way to see an area. Just stay on the bus to the end of the line, pay another US$0.05, and head back again, usually sitting in the best seat on the bus. If you make friends with the driver, you may end up with an entertaining tour as he points out the local sights in between collecting other passengers' fares.

When you want to get off a local bus, yell *Baja!*, which means 'Down!' Telling the driver to stop will make him think you're trying to be a back-seat driver, and you will be ignored. He's only interested if you're getting off, or down from the bus. Another way of getting him to stop is to yell *Esquina!*, which means 'Corner!' He'll stop at the next one.

Trucks

In remote areas, trucks often double as buses. Sometimes they are flatbed trucks with a tin roof, open sides and uncomfortable wooden plank seats. These curious-looking buses are called *rancheros* and are especially common on the coast.

In the remoter parts of the highlands, ordinary trucks are used to carry passengers; you just climb in the back. If the weather is OK, you get fabulous views and can feel the wind blow refreshingly by (dress warmly). If the weather is bad you hunker down underneath a dark tarpaulin with the other passengers. It certainly isn't the height of luxury, but it may be the only way of getting to some areas, and if you're open-minded about the minor discomforts, you may find that these rides are among the most interesting you have in Ecuador.

Payment for these rides is usually determined by the driver and is a standard fare depending on the distance. You can ask other passengers how much they are paying; usually you'll find that the trucks double as buses and charge almost as much.

TRAIN

Ecuador's rail system was severely damaged by landslides and flooding during the extremely heavy rains of the 1982/83 El Niño wet season. Many km of track were totally destroyed. Roads and bridges were also badly damaged so available repair money has been channelled into the more important road network; the railway system has to wait until funds become available.

After the 1982/83 disaster (when thousands of families had their homes and fields flooded) Ecuador noticed a decline in the amount of tourist revenue entering the country. This was partly attributed to the loss of the Quito-Guayaquil railway line, which is one of the most spectacular train rides in the world and was one of the main reasons some tourists visited Guayaquil. The section from Alausí in the mountains to Guayaquil on the coast is a dramatic descent which has been made famous in a British TV series on the world's greatest train journeys. Fortunately, this fantastic trip is once again running – but the section from Riobamba to Alausí is still closed. The Quito-Riobamba section has run intermittently – check in Quito about this.

There are also trains running from Cuenca to Sibambe (on the Alausí-Durán line) but it is difficult to make convenient connections. In the north, there is an *autoferro* running most days between Ibarra and San Lorenzo, and sometimes between Otavalo and Ibarra as well.

Ordinary trains are not always used. Instead, an autoferro, which is like a bus mounted on a railway chassis, is used. Space is limited, so you are advised to buy tickets ahead of time if you wish to travel by autoferro. It is not as comfortable as a normal train. Departure times and other details are given under the appropriate town headings.

TAXI

Ecuador is an oil-producing country and it keeps down the price of gasoline (petrol) for domestic consumption. It's approximately a low US$0.50 a gallon (for some reason gas is not dispensed in litres). This price combined with low wages means that taxis in Ecuador are very cheap.

Ecuadorian taxis are a variety of shapes and sizes, but they are all yellow. Most have a lit sign on top reading 'Taxi' – those that don't have a taxi sticker in the windshield. Taxis often belong to cooperatives – the name and telephone number of the cooperative is usually on the door.

The main rule for taking taxis is to ask the fare beforehand, or you'll be overcharged more often than not. A long ride in a large city (Quito or Guayaquil) shouldn't go over US$3 and short hops can cost as little as US$0.50. In smaller towns fares vary from US$0.30 to about US$1. Meters are rarely seen, with the exception of in Quito where they are obligatory. Even if there is a meter, the driver may not want to use it. This can be to your advantage, because with the meter off the driver can avoid interminable downtown traffic jams by taking a longer route. This saves both you and him time and the extra cost in gas is negligible. Fares from international airports (Quito and Guayaquil) are exorbitantly high – see those towns for tips on how to avoid getting gouged. At weekends and at night fares are always about 25-50% higher. Taxis can be hard to flag down during rush hours.

You can hire a taxi for several hours. A half day might cost about US$10 to US$15 if you bargain. You can also hire pickup trucks which act as taxis to take you to remote areas (such as a refugio). If you hire a taxi to take you to another town, a rough rule of thumb is about US$1 for every 10 km. Remember to count the driver's return trip, even if you're not returning. A longer trip may average a little less. If you split the cost between four passengers, you'll each be paying between two and three times the bus fare for a round trip.

CAR
Rental

This is as expensive as full-price car rental in Europe or the US. Cheap car rentals aren't found. If the price seems reasonable, check to see for what extras you have to pay; often there is a per km charge and you have to buy insurance. Some cars are not in very good condition.

It is difficult to find any kind of car rental outside of Guayaquil, Quito, Cuenca and a few other towns. I checked several places in Quito and was told that I had to have a credit card to be able to rent, as they wouldn't accept a cash deposit. Renters normally have to be 25 years old (a few companies may accept 21-year-old drivers). A valid drivers licence from your home country is normally accepted if it is of the type that has a photograph on it. Some companies want an international drivers licence and so if you know that you will be driving, it's best to

apply for one in your home country before you leave. This is normally straightforward if you already have a drivers licence.

Typical rates start around US$30 per day. The best deals are for a weekly rental. Recent rates for one week, including insurance, tax, and 1200 'free' km, ranged from US$175 for a small Chevy Luv pickup truck, to US$195 for a two-door Fiat, to US$340 for a four-door Chevrolet Gemini saloon, to US$440 for a top of the line four-door Chevy Trooper with 4WD. Two-door Troopers with 4WD are about US$300. Extra distance beyond the 1200 km was from US$0.10 to US$0.29 per km, depending on the car. These prices include the 11.5% tax and US$8.50 daily insurance which is mandatory. The insurance policy has a hefty deductible – as much as US$1000 depending on the company. Some international agencies (Budget, Avis, Hertz) will make reservations for you from home ahead of time.

Generally, car rental places are honest, but I have received a few warnings and complaints. It is recommended that you have everything in writing to avoid confusion or misunderstandings. This document should include prices, free mileage (kilometraje), any applicable discounts, taxes, or surcharges, and place and time of vehicle return. Make sure any damage to the vehicle (scratches etc) are noted on the rental form. Rental cars are reasonably well-serviced, but you should check that there is a spare tyre and jack (if only to know where they are stored in case of a flat tyre).

If you are driving, bear in mind that the road sign system is very poor. A sign may point left to your destination a few km before the turn-off, but when you reach the actual turn-off, there may be no sign at all. Many roads are not signed. Public transport is cheap – renting a car is an expensive adventure, though it does give you the freedom to go where you want (if you can figure out how to get there)!

Rental cars are targets for thieves. Don't leave your car parked with bags or other valuables in sight. When leaving your car for any period, park in a guarded lot.

Your Own Vehicle

Few travellers arrive with their own vehicle because it is impossible to drive across the Darien Gap and shipping even a motorbike from Panama is expensive and time-consuming to arrange. About US$500 seems to be the cheapest shipping charge for a car from Panama to Colombia or Ecuador – though it can be much higher, especially for a large vehicle. Security is lax, items such as outside mirrors are normally stolen, and it is difficult to arrange a passage for the driver with the vehicle.

I have recently talked to someone who bought a motorbike in Santiago, Chile and he tells me that it is the best place in South America to buy your own vehicle, be it motorbike or car, new or used. People who would prefer to drive their own vehicle might consider buying it in Santiago and driving on from there.

HITCHING

As mentioned earlier, trucks are used as public transport in remote areas, so trying to hitch a free ride on one is the same as trying to hitch a free ride on a bus. Private cars are not as common in Ecuador as in more developed nations, so hitchhiking generally is not as easy or successful. It can be done, however.

I have hitched several times on secondary roads in Ecuador and generally I offer to pay the driver. If the driver is stopping to drop off and pick up other passengers, then you can assume that he will expect payment. Talk to other passengers to find out what the going rate is. If you are the only passenger, the driver may have picked you up just to talk to a foreigner, and he may wave aside your offer of payment. This was the case in almost half my rides. I have never hitched on roads with good bus services, however, because buses are so cheap. Hitchhiking isn't normally done and if you want to try, make sure in advance of your ride that you and the driver agree on the subject of payment.

BOAT

Boat transportation is commonly used in Ecuador and can be divided into four different types.

The most commonly used is the motorised dugout canoe, which acts as a water taxi or bus on the major rivers of the Oriente and parts of the coast. In the Galápagos you find medium-sized motor cruisers or motor sailboats which are used by small groups to visit the different islands of the archipelago, either on day trips or for trips of several days duration. Thirdly, there are large vessels used either for carrying cargo and a few passengers or as cruise ships for many passengers.

Finally, many rivers are crossed by ferries which vary from a paddled dugout taking one passenger at a time to a car ferry capable of taking half a dozen vehicles across the river. These are sometimes makeshift transportation to replace a bridge which has been washed out, is being repaired or is still in the planning stages.

Dugout Canoes

Dugout canoes often carry as many as three dozen passengers and are the only way to get around many roadless areas. You can hire one yourself to take you anywhere, but this is expensive. If you take a regularly scheduled one with other passengers, however, it is quite affordable, though not as cheap as a bus for a similar distance. This is simply because an outboard engine uses more fuel per km than a bus engine, and because a dugout travels more slowly than a bus.

The most likely places that you will travel any distance in dugouts are from Misahuallí or Coca in the jungles of the Oriente and San Lorenzo to La Tola on the north-west coast.

Most of the boats used are literally dugouts, with maybe a splashboard added to the gunwales. They are long in shape and short on comfort. Seating is normally on hard, low, uncomfortable wooden benches which accommodate two people each. Luggage is stashed forward under a tarpaulin, so carry hand baggage containing essentials for the journey. You will be miserable for hours if you don't take the following advice, which is worth the cost of this book! *Bring seat padding.* A folded sweater or towel will make a world of difference on the trip.

Pelting rain or glaring sun are major hazards and an umbrella is excellent defence against both. Bring suntan cream or wear long sleeves, long pants and a sun hat – I have seen people literally unable to walk because of second-degree burns on their legs from a six-hour exposure to the tropical sun. The breeze as the boat motors along tends to keep insects away, and it also tends to cool you so you don't notice the burning effect of the sun. If the sun should disappear or the rain begin, you can get quite chilled, so bring a light jacket.

Insect repellent is useful during stops along the river. A water bottle and food will complete your hand baggage. Remember to stash your spare clothes in plastic bags or they'll get soaked by rain or spray.

A final word about dugout canoes: they feel very unstable! Until you get used to the motion of them, you might worry about the whole thing just rolling over and tipping everybody into the shark, piranha or boa constrictor-infested waters. Desperately gripping the side of the canoe and wondering what madness possessed you to board the flimsy contraption in the first place doesn't seem to help. I've ridden many dugouts and never had a problem, even in rapids and ocean waves. Nor have I met anyone who was actually dunked in. Dugouts feel much more unstable than they really are, so don't worry about a disaster; it almost never happens.

Other Boats

In the Galápagos, you have the choice of travelling in anything from a small sailboat taking four passengers to a large cruise ship complete with 48 air-conditioned double cabins with private baths. The choice is yours. More information on these boats is given in the chapter on the Galápagos.

In addition to the dugout canoes of the Oriente, there is one cruise ship which makes relatively luxurious passages down the Río Aguarico. This is the *Flotel Orellana* – more

information about it is given in The Northern Oriente chapter.

There are a few ratty steamers plying coastal routes. These are mainly cargo boats and are rarely used by travellers. A few boats go out to the Galápagos from Guayaquil, but it's easier to fly there and sail around the islands themselves. Otherwise you could get stuck in Guayaquil for weeks. Again, there is more information under the appropriate coastal towns.

Your Own Boat

The idea of sailing your own yacht to the Galápagos sounds romantic. Unfortunately, to sail in the Galápagos you need a licence and these are all limited to Galápagos boats. If you arrive in the islands in your own boat, you will have to moor the boat in Puerto Ayora and hire one of the local boats to take you around. The Ecuadorian authorities give transit permits of only 72 hours for sailors on their own boats (though you can stay for longer if you are moored and not sailing).

TOURS

Many kinds of tours are available. These range from hotel-based visits of the highlands to strenuous mountaineering expeditions, from camping in the rainforest to staying at a luxurious jungle lodge, and, of course, tours to the Galápagos.

Many tours can be arranged within Ecuador and are described in the main body of the book. Others can be arranged in advance from home (especially if you live in the USA) or, to a lesser extent, Europe.

Responsible Tourism

Whether you go with a tour or arrange a trip for yourself, you are encouraged to travel in a culturally and environmentally sensitive manner. Try to be a positive force rather than a drain on the resources of the country you are visiting.

Some suggestions: talk and listen to and interact with local people – don't just take photos and run and don't make promises that you cannot keep. Accept and respect local customs and lifestyles rather than imposing

your own. Don't buy (illegal) pre-Columbian artefacts or items made from
endangered animals, such as sea turtle and
black coral ornaments and jewellery or
jaguar skins. Support local people by buying
locally made handicrafts and artwork. Learn
a few words of Spanish, try local food and
stay in small locally-run hotels.

For further information about these
matters, contact the following:

Center for Responsible Tourism
   2 Kensington Rd, San Anselmo, CA 94960, USA
   (☎ (415) 843 5506)
The Earth Preservation Fund
   3516 NE 155th, Seattle, WA 98155, USA
   (☎ (206) 365 0686)
Tourism Concern
   Froebel College, Roehampton Lane, London
   SW15 5PU, UK (☎ (081) 878 9053)

Quito

Quito is my favourite Latin American capital. At about 2850 metres above sea level it has a wonderful spring-like climate despite the fact that it is only 22 km south of the equator. It is in a valley flanked by mountains and, on a clear day, several snow-capped volcanoes are visible from the capital. As well as being in a beautiful location, it is rich in history and much of the old colonial town is well preserved.

The site of the capital dates from pre-Columbian times. Early inhabitants of the area were the peaceful Quitu people, who gave their name to the capital. The Quitus integrated with the expansionist coastal Caras to give rise to the Indian group known as the Shyris. About 1300 AD the Shyris joined with the Puruhás through marriage, and their descendants fought against the Incas in the late 1400s.

By the time of the Spanish arrival, Quito was a major Inca city but it was totally destroyed by Atahualpa's general, Rumiñahui, shortly before the arrival of the Spanish conquerors in Quito. There are no Inca remains. The present capital was founded on top of the ruins of the Inca city by Sebastián de Benalcázar on 6 December 1534, and many old colonial buildings survive in the old town.

In 1978 UNESCO declared Quito's colonial centre as one of the world's cultural heritage sites. Now, development and other changes in Quito's old town are strictly controlled. This does not mean that progress has stopped. On the contrary, the old centre is extremely bustling and full of traffic. The buildings haven't changed, however, and a walk down colonial Quito's streets late at night, after the rush hour traffic has finished, is a step into a past era. There are no modern buildings discordantly built next to centuries-old architecture and no flashing neon signs to disrupt the ambience of the past.

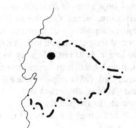

Orientation

Quito has a population of about 1,200,000 and is thus the second largest city in Ecuador (Guayaquil is the largest). It is located along the central valley in a roughly north-south direction and is approximately 17 km long and four km wide. It can conveniently be divided into three segments.

The centre (*el centro*) is the site of the old town with its whitewashed and red-tiled houses and colonial churches; this is the area of greatest interest to the traveller. The north is modern Quito (the new town) with its major businesses, airline offices, embassies, shopping centres and banks. The best hotels are found here. It also contains the airport and middle and upper-class residential areas. This area is of importance to the traveller who needs to get some business done. Finally, the south consists mainly of working-class housing areas and is of less interest.

Addresses in Quito, and throughout Ecuador, are given by placing the building number after the street name. Often, the nearest intersecting street name is also added, eg: Toledo 1254 and Cordero.

Map books of Quito are available – see Bookshops later in this chapter.

Information

Tourist Office CETUR runs three tourist information offices. The main one is in the new town at Calle Reina Victoria 514 and Roca (☎ 527 074/002). They can provide you with brochures, maps and tourist information, and there is often someone available who speaks English. (The availability of maps and brochures is sporadic and travellers have complained that the staff are not very knowledgeable – it depends on how experienced the person you talk to is.) Hours are 8.30 am to 4.30 pm, Monday to Friday. There is also a branch in the old town, in the Municipalidad (Municipal Palace) on the south-east side of the Plaza Independencia. This branch is frequently closed. Finally, there is a branch at the airport but it keeps irregular hours.

The CETUR tourist information office told me that churches are open from 9 to 11 am and 3 to 5 pm daily except Sunday, and that museums are open from 9 am to 5 pm daily except Monday. This is not true. Hours are haphazard to say the least. Museums can change hours for reasons varying from a national holiday to staff sickness, so the opening hours in the following sections are meant only as guidelines. If possible, call ahead to verify hours. Generally speaking, however, Monday is the worst day to visit museums, as many of them are closed.

Churches are open every day but are crowded with worshippers on Sunday. Hours are variable and changeable. The earthquake of 1987 damaged and closed several churches – most are open as of 1991, but hours seem to be different every time I go. Early morning seems to be a good time to visit churches. They are usually closed for a long lunch hour and in the afternoon sometimes remain open until after 6 pm. It's unpredictable. Good luck!

Useful Organisations The clubhouse of the South American Explorers Club (☎ 566 076) is at Calle Toledo 1254 and Cordero in the La Floresta district. Hours are 9 am to 5 pm, Monday to Friday. The mailing address is Apartado 21-431, Eloy Alfaro, Quito.

A recently-opened outfit is Ecuadorian Contact (☎ 548 408, fax 568 664), Avenida 10 de Agosto 1831 and Calle San Gregorio, office 602, Quito, mail to PO Box 17-03-00602, Quito. They will help with information about Spanish schools, visa extensions, obtaining an international student card, renting and repairing climbing equipment, staying with Ecuadorian families, and they will let you use their fax. They are open from 8.30 am to 6 pm, Monday to Friday.

The British Council (☎ 236 144) at Amazonas 1615 and Orellana has a library open 8 am to 12.45 pm and 3 to 7.15 pm. There are British newspapers to read and books (in English) may be borrowed for a small annual fee. There is also a café on the premises.

Money Banks are open from 9 am to 1.30 pm. They will handle money wired from your home bank and pay you in US dollars. Most bank offices are on Avenida Amazonas. Recent reports are that banks have been paying slightly better rates than casas de cambio, but the latter are open longer, require less paper work and are more convenient. Rates shouldn't vary by more than two or three per cent – shop around if you are trying to make your money stretch. Exchange rates for the previous day are usually in the newspaper but rates can change from hour to hour.

Rodrigo Paz is the best-known casa de cambio with branches at Amazonas 370 and Robles (☎ 563 900, 564 500) in the new town and at Calle Venezuela 659 and Sucre (☎ 511 222/551) in the old town. M M Jaramillo Arteaga is also good, with an office at the north-west corner of Amazonas and Colón (☎ 516 844) in the new town and at Mejía 401 and Venezuela (☎ 210 881) in the old town. There are a number of other exchange houses. Their offices are normally open from 9.30 am to 12.30 pm and 3 to 6 pm Monday to Friday, and mornings only on Saturday.

If you want to change money on Sunday, you will find the Rodrigo Paz airport office open. Also, the office at the Hotel Colón is open on Sunday and they are often open until 7 pm on weekdays.

If you change more money than you need, it is easy to buy back dollars at a rate about 2% below what you sold them for.

Credit cards are widely accepted in first-class restaurants, hotels, travel agents and stores. Make sure you are getting a good exchange rate. You can receive cash with your credit card – commissions vary depending on the card.

American Express
    Ecuadorian Tours, Avenida Amazonas 339 and Jorge Washington (☎ 560 488)
Diners Club
    Avenida República and Eloy Alfaro (☎ 553 211)
MasterCard
    Amazonas 720 and Veintimilla (☎ 542 566)
Visa
    Banco de Guayaquil, Avenida Colón and Reina Victoria (☎ 566 824)

Post & Telecommunications The main post office (☎ 519 875) is in the old town on Calle Benalcázar and Chile, behind the Plaza Independencia. They are open from 9 am to 5 pm on weekdays and booths selling stamps are usually open from about 8 am to 6 pm. There is a branch post office (☎ 523 787) in the new town at Avenida Colón and Reina Victoria. If you want to mail a package of over two kg, use the office at Calle Ulloa and Dávalos (☎ 546 917).

If you are an American Express client you can receive mail sent to you c/o Amex, Aptdo 2605, Quito, Ecuador. Their street address is Avenida Amazonas 339 at the Ecuadorian Tours office, which is open from 9.30 am to 12.30 pm and 2.30 to 6 pm Monday through Friday and in the morning only on Saturday.

There are several air courier services: DHL (☎ 554 177, 565 059), Reina Victoria and 18 de Septiembre; IML (☎ 567 112), Robles 954 and Paéz; MACOB (☎ 549 200), 10 de Agosto 639. There are others.

The central IETEL office (☎ 580 283/975) is a block away from the main post office on Benalcázar and Mejía in the old town. Other IETEL offices are on Avenida 6 de Diciembre near Avenida Colón (☎ 553 350) and at the Cumandá Terminal Terrestre de Buses (☎ 580 582). These offices are open from 8 am to 10 pm (last call at 9.30 pm) daily. Cheap rates for international calls are after 7 pm.

There are both IETEL and post offices at the airport. The airport IETEL (☎ 454 278) is open from 7 am to 8 pm daily.

Embassies & Consulates Many nationalities require visas to enter the neighbouring countries of Colombia and some to enter Peru (see the Facts for the Visitor chapter). A US embassy official suggests that if you plan on travelling to the USA you would find it easier to obtain a tourist visa in your home country. According to my nameless source, 'young, single, rootless people, such as the travellers who would normally be expected to use the book, might get turned down'. Don't ask me why this embassy official expects my readers to be 'young, single, rootless'.

Most consular offices don't work all day – you should call ahead for hours. Also check the address and how to get there – many of these consulates change addresses every year or two but often keep the same phone number. Many countries also have consular representation in Guayaquil.

Edificio in the following addresses means 'Building'.

Argentina
    Amazonas 477 and Robles, 5th floor (☎ 562 292)
Belgium
    J L Mera and Wilson
Bolivia
    Dávalos 258 and Páez (☎ 231 352)
Brazil
    Edificio España, Colón 1222 and Amazonas, 9th & 10th floors (☎ 563 086)
Britain
    González Suárez 111 and 12 de Octubre (☎ 560 670)
Canada
    6 de Diciembre 2816 and J Orton, office 4N (☎ 543 214)
Chile
    Edificio Xerox, Amazonas and Juan Pablo Sáenz, 3rd floor (☎ 247 802)
Colombia
    Colón 1133 and Amazonas, 7th floor (☎ 524 632)
Costa Rica
    Roca 538 and Reina Victoria (☎ 527 392)
Denmark
    Edificio Gabriela III, República de El Salvador 733 and Portugal, 3rd floor (☎ 437 163)
France
    General Plaza 107 and Patria (☎ 560 789)

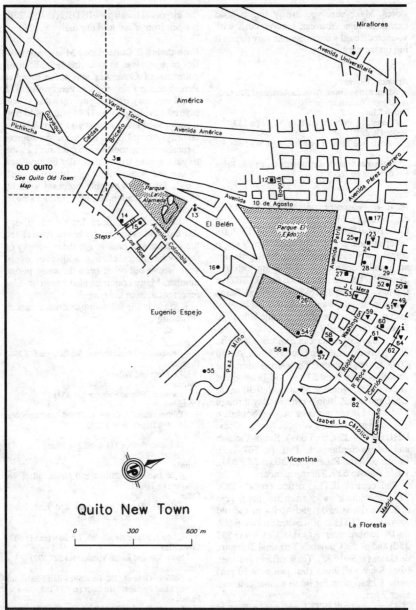

Quito New Town

0   300   600 m

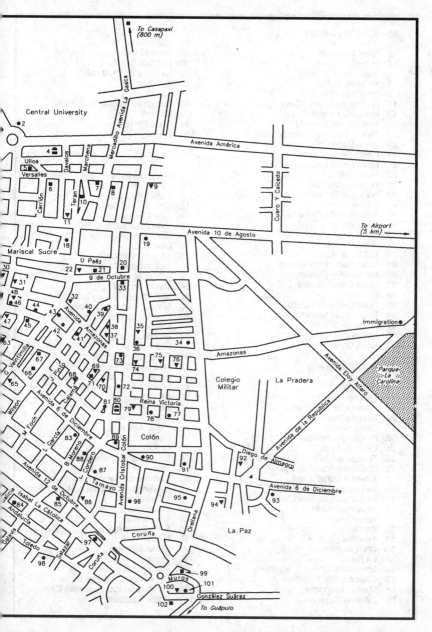

■ PLACES TO STAY

3   Hotel Embassy
5   Hotel St James
6   Residencial Carrión
7   Hotel Versalles
8   Hotel Majestic
10   Residencial Santa Clara
12   Hotel Inca Imperial
14   Residencial Marsella
17   Residencial 18 de Septiembre
20   Hotel Nueve de Octubre
21   Hostal Palm Garten
24   Residencial Italia
27   Hotel Colón
33   Hotel Ambassador
39   Albergue El Taxo
41   Pickett Hotel
45   Residencial Karol Jennifer
50   Hotel Alameda Real
56   Hotel Tambo Real
58   Hostal Los Alpes
60   Hotel Camila's
61   Hotel Seis de Diciembre
67   Residencial Cumbres
71   Hotel Chalet Suisse
84   La Casona
85   Hotel Oro Verde Quito
88   Residencial Los Angeles
97   La Casa de la Feliz Eliza
99   Hostal Los Andes
102   Hotel Quito

▼ PLACES TO EAT

9   Govinda
11   La Chiminea Inn
22   Cevichería Don José
23   Bailey's Restaurant
25   Costa Vasca
30   Rincón del Francia
31   Chantilly Café
32   Terraza del Tartaro & Las Redes
35   Columbus Steak House
37   Taberna Quiteña
38   La Cabaña
47   La Trattoria de Veneziano
48   Pavement café's
49   Adam's Rib
51   Bentley's
53   Tex-Mex
59   Chifa Mayflower
63   La Reina Victoria
64   Macrobiotico
65   Churrascaría Tropeiro
68   Mama Chlorindas
69   Taberna Bavaria
70   Vitalcentro
74   Chifa El Pino
75   La Vieja Castilla
76   La Casa de Mi Abuela
79   La Jaiba
86   La Choza
92   Rincón La Ronda & Le Péché Mignon
94   Chifa Pekin
100   El Pub

OTHER

1   Ñucanchi Peña
2   Cine Universitario
4   Parcel Post Office
13   Church of El Belén
15   Cine Capitol
16   Palacio Legislativo
18   Children's Playground
19   Cine Colón
26   Teatro Promoteo
28   Metropolitan Touring
29   American Express
34   British Council
36   MM Arteaga Money Exchange
40   Galasam Economic Tours
42   Libri Mundi Bookshop & Galería Latina
43   Rincón Andino Peña
44   Rumors Bar
46   Dayumak Peña Bar
52   Rodrigo Paz Money Exchange
54   Casa de la Cultura Ecuatoriana
55   Instituto Geográfico Militar
57   US Embassy
62   CETUR Tourist Information
72   TAME Airline
73   TAME Airline
77   Cowboy Bar
78   El Papillón Bar
80   Ecuatoriana Airline & Branch Post Office
81   Children's Playground
82   Universidad Católica & Museo Jijón y Caamaño
83   Cine Fénix
87   Lava Seco
89   SAN-Saeta Airline
90   IETEL
91   CC Multicentro
93   Canadian Consulate
95   Junior's Laundry
96   Olga Fisch's Folklore Store
98   South American Explorers Club
101   British Embassy

Germany
　Edificio Eteco, Patria and 9 de Octubre, 6th floor (☎ 232 660)
Holland
　Edificio Banco BHU, Buenos Aires 136 and 10 de Agosto, 4th floor (☎ 567 606)
Ireland
　Montes 577 and Las Casas (☎ 503 674)
Israel
　Eloy Alfaro 969 and Amazonas (☎ 565 509)
Italy
　La Isla 111 and Humberto Albornoz (☎ 561 074)
Japan
　J L Mera 130 and Patria (☎ 561 899)
Mexico
　6 de Diciembre 4843 and Naciones Unidas (☎ 457 820)
Norway
　Edificio Proinco, Robles 653 and Amazonas, 13th floor (☎ 526 564)
Panama
　Diego de Almagro 1550 and Pradera (☎ 565 234)
Paraguay
　Gaspar de Villaroel 2013 and Amazonas (☎ 245 871)
Peru
　Edificio España, Colón 1222 and Amazonas, 2nd floor (☎ 520 134)
Sweden
　Edificio Las Cámaras, Avenida República and Amazonas, 2nd floor (☎ 454 872)
Switzerland
　Edificio Xerox, Amazonas and Juan Pablo Sáenz, 2nd floor (☎ 434 113)
United States of America
　Patria and 12 de Octubre (☎ 562 890)
Uruguay
　Edificio Invescor, Tamayo 1025 and L García, 5th floor (☎ 541 968)
USSR
　Reina Victoria 462 and Roca (☎ 526 361)
Venezuela
　Coruña 1733 and Belo Horizonte (☎ 564 626)

Immigration There are two offices. One is for tourist card extensions and the other is for visas. Most travellers will only need the tourist card extension but if you want to stay longer than 90 days you will need a student, business, work or residence visa. Visas are usually expensive and complicated, while the tourist card extension is free and straightforward as long as you haven't used up your 90 days.

Tourist card extensions can be obtained from Migraciónes (☎ 454 122/099), Avenida Amazonas 2639 (also numbered 3149 for some strange reason) and República, from 8 am to 12 noon and 3 to 6 pm Monday to Friday. It takes anywhere from 10 minutes to two hours depending on how busy they are on the day you go. Although onward tickets out of Ecuador and 'sufficient funds' are legally required, they are rarely asked for. It's still worth bringing any airline tickets or travellers' cheques you may have, just in case. I have received a report that women in shorts are not allowed into the building.

For visas go to the Extranjería at Calle Reina Victoria and Colón. They are open mornings only, Monday to Thursday. I have received a recent report that this office has now moved to Carrión and Páez.

Jungle Permits To travel to some remote parts of the Oriente close to the Peruvian border, a permit is required from the *Ministerio de Defensa* (Ministry of Defense) on Avenida Pedro Maldonado, about one km south of the Plaza Santo Domingo in the old town. The Ministry is open from 8 am to 4 pm, Monday to Friday.

To obtain a permit you must provide a letter from your embassy stating that you are a citizen of that country. US citizens can get the letter for free in a few hours at their embassy; British citizens are charged £15 and are told to wait four days; some nationalities, such as Australians, are unable to obtain a letter because there is no embassy. In that case, bring an official looking letter from a government agency at home if you know you will need a permit or, if you are already in Quito, get a letter authorised by a notary public. In addition, you need two passport-sized photos of yourself, two photocopies of the page of your passport which has the number, and a letter stating which area you plan on visiting and when you are going.

Take these items to the Ministry as early as possible and ask to go to the *Comandancia del Ejercito* (Army Command). At the Command, explain what you need at the information desk and you will be attended to.

The procedure may take a couple of days and it is extremely useful if you speak Spanish.

Travel Agencies & Guides Most travel agents in Quito will sell you both domestic and international airline tickets (adding the obligatory 10% tax), make hotel reservations, and arrange guided trips to hike in the mountains, climb the snow-capped volcanoes, explore the jungle or visit the Galápagos – but be warned that most guide services are not cheap. It is usually better to deal directly with the agency supplying the services you want. The following is a list of agencies and the particular services which they provide. Most companies will provide city tours and standard excursions to Otavalo, Cotopaxi etc.

Many travellers believe that it is cheapest to arrange a tour in the Galápagos and the Oriente after you get there. This is probably true – but there are several problems. During the high season (December, January, June to August in the Galápagos) many boats are full and it may be difficult to find one available. During the low season, and anytime in the Oriente, it may take several days to get a group of people together who are all interested in doing the same thing. That's OK if you have a week or two to kill, but if you want to be sure of leaving on a trip soon after you arrive, you should book in advance, especially for the Galápagos.

For trips to the Oriente, it's a good idea to organise a group of budget travellers by advertising in your hotel or at the South American Explorers Club. Then go to the Oriente in that small group to look for a guide.

I do not give prices for Galápagos trips, because they are not fixed. As a rough guide, the cheapest trips are around US$450 per person per week, medium-priced trips are around US$800 and luxury trips can reach US$2000 per person per week.

Ecuadorian Tours (☎ 560 488), Amazonas 339 and Jorge Washington, is the American Express agent and is a good all-purpose travel agent.

The biggest and best known travel agency is Metropolitan Touring (☎ 560 550), Amazonas 239 (mail to PO Box 17-12-031), Quito. They run medium-priced to luxury tours in the Galápagos, on both yachts and cruise ships. Their naturalist guides are very good. They operate the *Flotel Orellana* in the Oriente (see The Northern Oriente chapter), run expensive but luxurious train trips in their own specially modified coaches, and hire Ecuador's best known mountaineer, Marco Cruz, to run their climbing programme.

Nuevo Mundo Expeditions (☎ 552 617/839), Amazonas 2468 y Mariana de Jesús, mail to PO Box 402-A, Quito, are a small but very professional outfit with strong conservation interests and excellent guides. Their tours and prices are nearer the top end of the market. They are the only company to visit the unique and fascinating Solar Museum during their equator tour. They also organise Galápagos tours, visit the Reserva Producción Faunísta Cuyabeno in the Oriente, and do a variety of Andean trekking and horseback trips.

Two companies which do expensive but very good luxury yacht trips in the Galápagos, for passengers willing to pay for them, are Quasar Nautica (☎ 439 734/5), Naciones Unidas 685 (mail to PO Box 69), Quito and Nixe Cruises (☎ 434 311), Eloy Alfaro 2013 and Suiza (mail to PO Box 6646), CCI, Quito. Slightly cheaper, but still at the top end of the market, are Angermeyer's Enchanted Excursions (☎ 569 960), Foch 769 and Amazonas. They run two of the best and most popular boats in the Galápagos – if you can get on them. Angermeyer's also arrange excursions to the Oriente and Andes.

Coltur (☎ 545 777), Paéz 370 and Robles (mail to PO Box 2771), Quito, does well-organised medium priced tours to the Galápagos. Some of their tours are land based for those who can't stand the thought of sleeping on a yacht every night. Somewhat more expensive trips are available with Turismo Galápagos (☎ 433 802), Reina Victoria 100, 3rd floor (write to PO Box 8989),

Sucursal 7, Quito. Quite often these trips are captained by Rolf Wittmer, who was the first person to be born in the islands (in 1933).

Galasam Economic Tours (☎ 550 094), Pinto 523 and Amazonas (head office in Guayaquil) has a variety of boats ranging from inexpensive to fairly expensive. Their inexpensive boats are among the cheapest Galápagos tours available. The cheapest of all are arranged by César Gavela Jr of the Hotel Gran Casino Internacional (☎ 514 905), Avenida 24 de Mayo and Bahía de Caráquez in the old town. These trips are the cheapest available and you cannot expect much comfort. I have received several reports stating that these trips are good value. On the other hand, I also have received several letters from travellers complaining that the trips were very poor, that the itinerary was not as advertised, and that the guides were unknowledgeable. This is what happens when you are at the very bottom end of the price market in the Galápagos. The Gran Casino also has information about cheap tours to the jungle.

There are several agencies offering rental equipment and guiding services for ascents of Ecuador's snow peaks. These mountains are well in excess of 5000 metres and require some basic mountaineering skill. The weather can turn bad quickly in the Andes, and inexperienced climbers have been killed. Some 'guides' have climbed a mountain a couple of times and then offer their services as a guide for very low prices – these people are not listed here. I recommend you hire an experienced climbing guide and climb in safety. Expect to pay very roughly US$100 per person to climb a major peak – this is for a group of three climbers with one guide. Climbs of minor peaks not requiring technical equipment are cheaper partly because the climb is easier and partly because a guide can take a larger group and the cost can be split more ways. The following are reputable agencies (many will also arrange trips to the Oriente):

Adventure Travels
    J L Mera 741 and Veintimilla, PO Box 17-16-190
    CEQ, Quito (☎ 322 331)
Agama Expediciones
    Venezuela 1163 and Manabí (contact Eduardo
    Agama)
Altamontaña Expediciones
    Avenida Universitaria 464 and Armero
    (☎ 520 592)
Campo Abierto
    Next to Sierra Nevada (see Sierra Nevada which
    follows)
Equipos Cotopaxi
    6 de Diciembre 929 and Patria (☎ 526 725)
Sierra Nevada
    6 de Diciembre 1329 and Roca (☎ 232 149,
    544 936)

Climbers should read *Climbing & Hiking in Ecuador*, 2nd edition, by Rob Rachowiecki & Betsy Wagenhauser, 1991, Bradt Publications.

Bookshops Libri Mundi is the best bookshop, with a good selection of books in English, German, French and Spanish. They have books about Ecuador as well as books of a more general nature. Their main shop (☎ 234 791) is at Calle J L Mera 851 near Veintimilla and is open from 9 am to 7 pm Monday to Friday, and 9 am to 1 pm on Saturday. A smaller branch is open until 8 pm in the Hotel Colón shopping mall (☎ 550 455) and at the Hotel Oro Verde (☎ 566 497, ext 3566). LibroExpress, on Amazonas 816 and Veintimilla, is good for maps, magazines, and some books. The other bookshops in Quito mainly sell books in Spanish.

You can read British newspapers and magazines at the British Council (☎ 236 144), Amazonas 1615 and Orellana. They also have a lending library for members – membership is US$4 per year. Hours are 8 am to 1 pm, Monday to Saturday, and 3 to 7 pm, Monday to Friday.

The best maps are available from the Instituto Geográfico Militar (IGM), which is on top of a hill at the end of Calle T Paz y Miño. This small street is off Avenida Colombia a few blocks south-east of Parque El Ejido in the new town. There are no buses, so walk or take a taxi. The IGM is open from

8 am to 3 pm Monday through Friday. You need to leave your passport at the gate to be allowed in.

They have a good selection of country and topographical maps to look at or buy, but their selection of city maps is very limited and you'll be better off with the city maps in this book. Country maps are also available from street vendors and the Libri Mundi bookstore, but they are more expensive than at the IGM.

The best map of Quito is the *Guia Informativa de Quito* by Nelson Gómez, published by Ediguias every few years. This is a slim blue book with about a dozen fold out maps covering Quito and an alphabetical index of avenidas and calles. It is available at most bookstores and is recommended for anyone wishing to spend time beyond the centre of Quito.

Medical Services An American-run hospital with an outpatient department and emergency room is Hospital Voz Andes, Juan Villalengua 263 (☎ 241 540) near the intersection of Avenidas América and 10 de Agosto. The No 1 Iñaquito bus passes close by. Fees are about US$4. A newer hospital which has been recommended is the Metropolitano (☎ 431 457/520), Avenida Mariana de Jesús and Occidental. A private clinic specialising in women's medical problems is Clínica de la Mujer (☎ 454 058), Amazonas and Gaspar de Villarroel.

There are many dentists in Quito. Some recommended dental clinics include the Clínica de Especialides Odontológicas (☎ 521 383, 237 562), Orellana 1782 and 10 de Agosto; Clínica Dental Arias Salazar (☎ 524 582), Amazonas 239 and 18 de Septiembre; and Clínica Dental' Dr Pedro Herrera (☎ 554 361), Amazonas 353 and Jorge Washington.

Emergency Police (☎ 101); Fire department (☎ 102); Red Cross ambulance (☎ 214 977/966, 210 567).

Spanish Courses There are many schools which will teach you Spanish. Classes are available at various levels; courses are offered for almost any length of time you want; classes can be individual or group; accommodation with local families can be arranged. With so many possibilities, it is easy to arrange classes once you arrive in Quito. Make sure you get what you want – talk to several schools to see what is best for you. Some people find that seven hours of one-on-one tuition is too demanding – others think this total immersion system is great. Choose what is best for you. Rates vary from a little over US$1 per hour to over US$3 per hour. The South American Explorers Club is a good source of recent recommendations. The following schools have been recommended – the cheapest ones may be noisy or cramped, but the teachers are OK:

Academia de Español Quito
  Marchena 130 and 10 de Agosto, PO Box 39-C, Quito (☎ 553 647) – expensive, good, accommodation with local families included.
Israel Spanish School
  Olmedo 552 and Flores, 2nd floor – inexpensive and enthusiastic.
La Casa
  Ulloa 650, 3rd floor (☎ 541 691) – economical accommodation included – good, friendly, Chilean-run.
Los Andes
  Perez Guerrero 441 and Versalles (☎ 565 856) – mid-priced, good, discounts for South American Explorers Club members.
Nueva Escuela de Español
  Benalcazar 934 and Olmedo, office 3 – one of the cheapest.
Nuevo Mundo
  Amazonas 662 and Carrion, 5th floor (☎ 236 129) – fairly inexpensive.
South American Spanish Institute
  Italia 169 and Eloy Alfaro (☎ 545 818) – expensive, very good, helpful, can help with visa extensions.
Superior
  Versalles 1009 and Carrion, 2nd floor (☎ 230 701) – mid-priced, friendly, discount for South American Explorers Club members.
Vida Nueva (New Life)
  Venezuela 1389 and Oriente (☎ 216 986) – cheap, with friendly instructors.

If you prefer group classes and providing your own accommodation, then try the Catholic University (Universidad Católica) at

Avenida 12 de Octubre and Robles. They have six-week classes for about US$100. The university also has classes in Quechua. The best time for classes is August and September – they don't always have them at other times of year.

Signing up for these classes may be a way of helping you get a student visa.

Student Cards If you sign up for a Spanish course at the university you can get a student card there. Otherwise, you can try Ecuadorian Tours where there is a US$15 fee – they verify your student status unless you look very young and obviously are a student. Ecuadorian Contact may also be able to help. Students can get a discount of up to 25% with TAME flying from Quito to the Galápagos. Otherwise, a student card does not save you much money in Ecuador, but if you're heading south to Peru you'll find it entitles you to substantial discounts there.

Teaching English This is the most usual way in which travellers are able to earn money in Ecuador. The best jobs are for bona-fide teachers who obtain work in advance – see the Facts for the Visitor chapter. If you have no job lined up, the best bet is at one of the local 'English as a second language' schools. These occasionally advertise in the 'gringo' hotels or in the newspapers when they need teachers.

Laundry There are no laundromats where you can wash and dry your own clothes. Instead, clothes must be left with a *lavandería* and picked up later, usually the following day. Most hotels will wash and dry your clothes – this gets quite expensive in the first-class hotels but is less expensive in the more modest establishments. Most of the cheaper hotels provide facilities for hand washing laundry. There are not many public lavanderías and many of those that are available are for dry cleaning only. The following will wash, dry, and fold your clothes in 24 to 48 hours:

Lava Seco
    Cordero 614 and Tamayo (☎ 529 009)
Junior's (they plan a name change soon)
    San Javier 232 and Orellana, a block uphill from 6 de Diciembre (☎ 527 551)
Lavanderías Modernas
    6 de Diciembre 2400 and Orellana

Photography Cameras are expensive in Quito. If yours breaks down, a recommended camera repairman is Gustavo Gómez (☎ 230 855), Edificio Molino, Asunción 130 and 10 de Agosto, office 1.

There are several places along Amazonas in the new town and around Plaza Santo Domingo in the old town where print film is processed within a day. The results are usually satisfactory but not top quality. The Kodak lab at Orellana 476 near 6 de Diciembre has been recommended for good quality processing.

For Women There is a women's coffee house called La Pajara Pinta at Avenida 9 de Octubre 1540 and Orellana. It is open from 4 to 9 pm most evenings. There is another women's café on the south side of Colón near Tamayo.

La Casa de Mujer (☎ 230 844), Los Ríos 2238 and Gándara, is a block south-west of the Isidro Ayora Maternity Hospital near La Parque Alameda. This provides emergency beds, showers and kitchen facilities for women for about US$1 per night. This is geared towards Ecuadorian women but might be of some assistance to other women in an emergency.

I would be pleased to hear about other women's centres from travellers who encounter them.

Dangers & Annoyances The elevation of about 2850 metres will make you feel somewhat breathless when you first arrive from sea level. This is a mild symptom of altitude sickness and will disappear after a day or two. It is best to take things easy on arrival. Don't over-exert yourself, eat lightly and cut back on cigarettes and alcohol to minimise altitude-sickness symptoms.

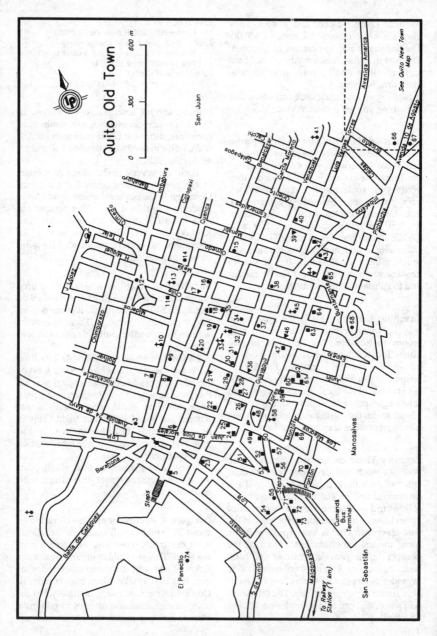

Quito Old Town

■ PLACES TO STAY

4	Hotel Gran Casino Internacional	36	Pollo Broaster
5	Hotel Gran Casino	39	Govinda Vegetarian Restaurant
7	Hotel Sucre	44	El Criollo
8	Hotel Benalcázar	46	Restaurant Oasis
11	Ecuahotel	47	Pizza Hut
22	Hotel Venecia		
23	Pensión Astoria & Hotel Minerva		OTHER
24	Hotel Felix		
25	Caspicara Hotel	1	Monastery of San Diego
27	Hotel Real Audiencia	2	Mitad del Mundo Bus Stop
30	Auca Hotel	3	Indian Market Area
42	Hotel Plaza del Teatro	9	Plaza San Francisco
47	Residencial Quitumbe	10	Monastery of San Francisco
49	Hotels Roma & Santo Domingo	12	Ipiales Market Area
50	Hotel Juana del Arco	13	Church of La Merced
51	Residencial Los Shyris	14	Museo de Arte Colonial
52	Hotel Interamericano	15	Casa de Benalcázar
53	Hotels Capitalino & Zulia	16	IETEL
54	Hotel Colonial	18	Central Post Office
56	Hotel Ingatur	19	Museo de Arte y Historia
57	Hotel Guayaquil	20	Church of La Compañía
59	Hotel Huasi Continental	28	Cine Atahualpa
60	Hostal Montúfar	29	Casa de Sucre
61	Hostal Rumiñahui	31	Rodrigo Paz Money Exchange &
62	Hotel Italia		Cine Metro
63	Hotel Viena	32	Cathedral
64	Hotels Viena Internacional & San	33	Church of El Sagrario
	Agustín	34	Plaza de la Independencia
65	Hotel Los Canarios	35	Palacio de Gobierno
69	Hotel Hogar	37	Municipalidad & Tourist Office
70	Hotel Grand	38	M M Arteaga Money Exchange
71	Hotel Indoamericano & Residencial	40	Museo Camilo Egas
	Los Andes	41	Church of La Basílica
72	Hostal Cumandá	43	Plaza del Teatro & Teatro Sucre
73	Hotels Los Andes & Caribe	45	Monastery of San Agustín
		47	Teatro Bolívar
▼	PLACES TO EAT	48	Plaza Santo Domingo
		55	Cine Cumandá
6	Pollo Gus	58	Church of Santo Domingo
17	Las Cuevas de Luis Candela	66	Museo del Banco Central
21	Restaurant Royal	67	Simón Bolívar Monument
25	Restaurant Los Olivos and others	68	Plaza La Marín
26	Chifa El Chino	74	La Virgen de Quito

Quito is a safer city than the neighbouring capitals of Bogotá or Lima but, unfortunately, crime has been on the increase over the last few years. You should be aware that pickpockets work crowded areas such as public buses, markets and church plazas. Thieves often work in groups to distract your attention – see the Facts for the Visitor chapter for more details. Keep money and other valuables in inside pockets and cameras firmly strapped across your body to minimise problems. Razor blade artists who slash camera straps or backpacks are becoming more common.

The old town, where there are plenty of sightseeing, camera-laden tourists, is becoming increasingly attractive to groups of thieves. Plaza San Francisco in particular has recently had a rash of thefts, and the old town as a whole is a place to be careful in. I suggest going on a tour or in a group to take photographs – and keep alert. If you dress inconspicuously and don't carry a valuable camera, you can wander around freely. After you have identified the areas you want to photograph, return with some friends and your camera.

One place you should definitely avoid is the climb up the steps of García Moreno heading from Ambato to the top of the El Panecillo hill. I have received repeated reports of armed thieves on this climb. Take a taxi or a tour to the top and, once there, stay in the paved area around the statue of the Virgin. You won't have any problem there and can take good photos of Quito and the surrounding mountains – but don't wander off down the grassy slopes or you stand a high chance of being robbed.

Generally, the new town is safer than the old town, but you should still stay alert, especially at night. The area bounded by Avenidas Patria, Amazonas, Colón and 12 de Octubre contains many of the better hotels, restaurants, gift shops and travel agencies – it is, therefore, popular with tourists and is also becoming the haunt of pickpockets, particularly at night. I hang out here at night and have never had a problem – but I dress casually and don't carry valuables to avoid attracting the attention of potential thieves.

Watch your belongings when travelling – be it by bus or by plane. Snatch theft of poorly attended luggage will occur at the bus terminal and at the airport. Watch your luggage like a hawk.

Should you be unfortunate enough to be robbed, you should file a police report, particularly if you wish to make an insurance claim. The place to go is the SICP (El Servicio de Investigacion Criminal de Pichincha) at the intersection of Montufar and Esmeraldas in the old town.

Despite the above warnings, I don't think that Quito is particularly dangerous. If you avoid attracting undue attention to yourself it is very unlikely that you'll have many problems at all.

Walking Tour
All sights mentioned in this section are described more fully later in this chapter.

The area of the old town bounded by the streets (calles) of Flores, Rocafuerte, Cuenca and Manabí has most of the colonial churches and major plazas, including the Plaza de la Independencia with the Presidential Palace and Cathedral. There is no set route that I especially recommend, but if you are short on time see at least the Plaza de Independencia and continue south-west on Calle García Moreno two blocks to the church of La Compañía. From here it is one block to the north-west (right) along Sucre to the Plaza and Monastery of San Francisco – a wonderful area but watch for pickpockets. Two blocks to the south-east (left) of La Compañía brings you to Calle Guayaquil; turn south-west (right) for one block to see the Plaza and Church of Santo Domingo.

Walk the old town streets and you'll pass an interesting sight on almost every block – but watch your bags and pockets. This is a historic area and well worth spending several hours walking around, if not several days. It is also a very busy commercial area, full of yelling street vendors and ambling pedestrians, tooting taxis and belching buses, and whistle-blowing policemen trying to direct traffic in the narrow and congested one-way streets. Sunday is therefore a good day to walk around the old centre if you'd like some peace and quiet.

From the old town, head north-west along Calle Guayaquil towards the new town. Guayaquil runs into the important Avenida 10 de Agosto – turn left and you will pass the Banco Central (with museums) on your left. Opposite the Banco Central is an impressive monument to Simón Bolívar; the monument is at the southernmost point of the triangular Parque La Alameda. As you head north through the park you pass the astronomical observatory. As you leave the park, continue northward on the important street of Avenida 6 de Diciembre.

After three blocks you pass the modern legislative congress building on your right on Calle Montalvo. Continuing on 6 de Diciembre takes you past the popular Parque El Ejido on your left and past the huge, circular, mirrored-wall Casa de Cultura building on your right. Past the Casa de Cultura, turn left for three blocks along Avenida Patria, with Parque El Ejido to your left, and you reach the a small stone arch opposite which is the beginning of Quito's most famous modern street, Avenida Amazonas.

It is about three km from the heart of the old town to the beginning of Amazonas. Walk along Amazonas for banks, boutiques, souvenir stands and sidewalk cafés. On the parallel street of J L Mera you'll find the best bookshops and craft stores. Almost 1½ km away from Parque El Ejido, Amazonas crosses Calamá which has several of Quito's best restaurants (to the right or south-east). There is much more to see outside of the old town, but it is scattered around Quito – you can walk but many people take buses or taxis to the places they are most interested in.

Museums – new town

Museo del Banco Central (☎ 510 302) The best archaeology museum is that of the Banco Central on Avenida 10 de Agosto and Briceño (opposite the Bolívar Monument at the apex of the Parque La Alameda), 5th floor. It houses well-displayed pottery, gold ornaments (including the gold mask that is the symbol of the Museo del Banco Central), skulls showing deformities and early surgical methods, a mummy and many other objects of interest. On the floor above is a display of colonial furniture and religious art and carving.

Entrance is about US$0.50 – tours in English can be arranged in advance for free. Hours are from 10.30 am to 6 pm, Tuesday through Friday, and 10.30 am to 3 pm on Saturday and Sunday. Outside of working hours, the entrance is through the gate to the right of the bank and then through a side door. There is an elevator.

Casa de Cultura Ecuatoriana (☎ 565 808, 522 410) This large circular glass building at the corner of Avenidas Patria and 12 de Octubre, to the east of the Parque El Ejido, has several collections. They are open from 10 am to 6 pm Tuesday to Friday and 9 am to 5 pm on Saturday, and admission is free.

There is a fascinating display of traditional musical instruments, many several centuries old. The instruments are mainly Ecuadorian, but there are also Asian, African and European oddities. Also on display are examples of traditional Ecuadorian regional dress. The large art collection contains both contemporary Ecuadorian work and 19th-century pieces. The contemporary work includes canvases by Ecuador's most famous artists, Guayasamín and Kingman among others.

There is also a movie theatre which often shows international movies of note and an auditorium where classical and other music is performed – check the newspapers or posters up in front of the building.

Museo de Jacinto Jijón y Caamaño (☎ 521 834, 529 240) Across the traffic circle from the Casa de Cultura and north-east along Avenida 12 de Octubre is the Catholic University, which has an interesting private archaeology museum on the 3rd floor of the library. The museum is named after an Ecuadorian archaeologist and much of the collection was donated by his family after his death. The entrance to the Museo Jijón y Caamaño is on 12 de Octubre near the intersection with Calle J Carrión.

Hours are from 9 am to 4 pm Monday through Friday (although they have, in the past, closed for lengthy lunch breaks). Admission is US$0.20 and you can get a guided tour (sometimes available in English) of the small archaeological collection. There is also a collection of colonial art exhibiting some of the masters of the Quito School.

Museo Amazonico Formerly the Museo Shuar, this museum run by the Salesian Mission has a small collection of jungle Indian artefacts. The museum is at 12 de

Octubre 1430. Hours are from 8.30 am to 12 noon and 2.30 to 6.30 pm from Monday to Friday and 9 am to 12 noon on Saturday. Admission is US$0.50.

Instituto Geográfico Militar (☎ 522 066) Apart from selling maps to the public, the IGM has a geographical museum and planetarium open to the public. The IGM is at the end of the steep climb up Calle Paz y Miño, to the south-east of the Parque El Ejido.

Hours are 8 am to 12 noon and 2 to 5 pm on Tuesday to Friday, and 10 am to 12 noon and 2 to 5 pm at weekends. Shows in the planetarium last 30 minutes and are at 9 am on Tuesday to Friday and at 11 am, 2.30 and 4.30 pm on Tuesday to Sunday. There are often more frequent shows for school groups during the school year. Admission is about US$0.30. You have to leave your passport at the IGM entrance gate to be allowed in.

Museo de Ciencias Naturales (☎ 449 824) This new museum houses a natural history collection which has previously been exhibited in a military college and at the Casa de Cultura. The current display is at Parque La Carolina, on the Avenida Los Shyris side, opposite Avenida República de El Salvador. This is the best natural history museum in Ecuador and worth a visit if you want to acquaint yourself with Ecuador's flora & fauna.

Hours are 9 am to 4.30 pm, Monday to Friday, and 9 am to 1 pm on Saturday. Admission is about US$0.10.

Vivarium (☎ 432 915) This museum was recently opened by the Gustavo Orces Herpetological Foundation, which itself was created in 1989 to study and teach about Ecuadorian reptiles and amphibians. The vivarium has a number of live animals including the highly poisonous fer-de-lance snake, boa constrictors, turtles and tortoises, lizards and iguanas etc. The address is Shyris 1130, opposite Portugal in the Parque La Carolina. Call ahead to arrange a tour. Admission is about US$0.50 – donations to

support this research and educational institution are gratefully accepted.

Museo Guayasamín (☎ 242 779, 244 373) Modern art can be seen at the Museo Guayasamín, the home of Oswaldo Guayasamín, an Ecuadorian Indian painter born in 1919 and now famous throughout the world. Guayasamín's collection of pre-Columbian and colonial pieces can also be seen.

The museum is at Calle José Bosmediano 543 in the residential district of Bellavista to the north-east of Quito. It's an uphill walk and the No 3 Colmena-Batan bus goes near the museum. Make sure the bus has a Bellavista placard, or ask the driver. Hours are from 9 am to 12.30 pm and 3 to 6 pm Monday to Friday and 9 am to 12.30 pm on Saturday, and entrance is free. You can buy original artwork here – beautiful and not cheap. Posters etc are available at a reasonable cost.

Museums – old town
Museo de Arte y Historia (☎ 214 018, 210 863) This museum, at Espejo 1147 and Benalcázar, is in an old building in the centre – it's also called Museo Municipal Albert Mena Caameño. It used to be a Jesuit house until 1767, when it became an army barracks. The present museum contains a wealth of early colonial art dating from the 16th and 17th centuries, as well as more modern art. The basement has gory waxworks showing the assassination of local patriots who were killed by royalist forces in 1810 – this was over a decade before independence was achieved.

The building is just off the Plaza Independencia, and is a little difficult to find because the sign is not obvious. As I went to press I received a report that the art collection is not available for viewing although the historical waxworks are. The museum is open from 8.30 am to 6.30 pm Tuesday to Friday and 10 am to 3 pm on Sunday. Admission is US$0.10.

Casa de Sucre (☎ 512 860, 218 102) Several historical buildings in the centre are

Casa de Sucre

now museums. A good one to visit is Casa de Sucre, which is well restored and contains period (1820s) furniture and a small museum. Mariscal (Field Marshal) Antonio José de Sucre, the hero of Ecuadorian independence (and the man after whom Ecuadorian currency is named) lived here.

The house is on Calle Venezuela 573 and Sucre. Hours are from 9 am to 3.30 pm Tuesday to Friday, 9 am to 11.30 am on Saturday and 10 am to 1 pm on Sunday – but they change frequently. Admission is free. They have a small gift shop with books about Ecuador.

Casa de Benalcázar (☎ 218 102) An older house is the Casa de Benalcázar, dating from 1534. It was restored by Spain in 1967 and entrance here is also free. It's on Calle Olmedo 962 and Benalcázar. There are sometimes classical piano recitals here and it is a delightful site for such entertainment. Check the newspapers or inquire at the house, which is closed on Saturday and Monday.

Museo de Arte Colonial (☎ 212 297) This museum is on the corner of Calle Cuenca and Mejía and reopened in the late 1980s after a long period of restoration. The colonial building dates from the 17th century and houses what many consider to be Quito's best collection of colonial art from the 16th to the 18th centuries. Many famous sculptors and painters are represented, and there is also a collection of period furniture. Hours are from 8.30 am to 4.30 pm Tuesday to Friday, and from 10 am to 2.30 pm on Saturday and Sunday. Admission is about US$0.25.

Museo Camilo Egas (☎ 514 511) Another Ecuadorian painter who has a museum in his name is Camilo Egas (1889-1962). Some 40 of his works are displayed in the Museo Camilo Egas, now under the auspices of the Banco Central. The collection has been recently restored. The museum is open 10 am to 1 pm and 3 to 5.30 pm Tuesday to Friday, and 10 am to 2.30 pm on Sunday. Hours are subject to frequent change and the museum may be closed when they are setting up a special exhibition; admission is free. The address is Calle Venezuela 1302 and Esmeraldas.

La Cima de la Libertad This museum is housed in a modern building on the flanks of Volcán Pichincha, west of the old town. It is best reached by taxi. The museum was built on the hill where Marshal Sucre fought the historical and decisive battle of Independence on 24 May 1822. There is a collection of historical and military artefacts and a huge and impressive mural by Kingman. Upon surrender of one's passport, a soldier will guide you around. Photography is prohibited inside the museum. Outside the museum, however, photography is recommended – great views of the city below. I forgot my camera and regretted it.

Hours are from 9 am to 12 noon and 3 to 6 pm daily except Monday; admission is free.

Churches

There is a wealth of churches, chapels, convents, monasteries, cathedrals and basilicas in Quito. The old town especially has so many of them that you can hardly walk two blocks without passing a church. Photography is not normally permitted because the intensity of the flash has a detrimental effect on the pigment in the many valuable religious paintings. Slides and postcards can be bought at the post office. There are signs asking tourists not to wander around during religious services – at such times you can enter and sit in a pew.

Monastery of San Francisco Ecuador's oldest church is the Monastery of San Francisco, on the plaza of the same name. Construction began only a few weeks after the founding of Quito in 1534, but the building was not finished until 70 years later. It is the largest colonial structure in Quito. The founder is commemorated by a statue at the far right of the raised terrace in front of the church. He is the Franciscan missionary Joedco Ricke, who is also credited with being the first man to sow wheat in Ecuador.

Although much of the church has been rebuilt because of earthquake damage, some of it is still original. Go to the chapel of Señor Jesus de Gran Poder to the right of the main altar to see original tilework. The main altar itself is a spectacular example of baroque carving, and the roof and walls are also wonderfully carved and richly covered in gold leaf. Much of the roof shows Moorish influence.

The church contains excellent examples of early religious art and sculpture; unfortunately it is often too dark to see them properly. Tour guides turn lights on periodically so keep your eyes open for this. The bells are rung every hour, and often on the quarter hour. You can see the bell-ringer at work in his cubbyhole just to the right of the main door. To the left of the monastery is the Cantuña chapel which houses an excellent collection of Quiteño art. Visiting hours recently were from 7 am to 11 am daily, and from 3 to 6 pm Monday to Thursday; admission is free.

To the right of the main entrance is the Franciscan Museum (☎ 211 124) which contains some of the monastery's finest artwork. Here you can see paintings, sculpture and furniture dating back to the 16th century. One of the oldest signed paintings is a Mateo Mejía canvas dated 1615. Some of the woodcarvings are even older and are covered with gold leaf, paint, period clothing or a fine porcelain flesh finish. Some of the furniture is fantastically wrought and inlaid with literally thousands of pieces of mother-of-pearl.

The museum costs US$0.50 to visit, and Spanish-speaking guides are available. Hours are from 9 to 11 am and from 3 to 6 pm Monday to Saturday.

La Compañía Looking out across the plain, cobblestoned plaza of San Francisco, you see the ornate green and gold domes of the church of La Compañía de Jesus, just two blocks away. The construction of this Jesuit church began in 1605, the year that San Francisco was completed, and it took 163 years to build. The church is famous as the most ornate in Ecuador; it has been claimed that seven tons of gold were used to gild the walls, ceilings and altars. Quiteños call La Compañía the most beautiful church in the country, although some visitors find its splendour a little too rich. Note the Arab (Moorish) influence in the intricate designs carved on the magnificent red-and-gold columns and ceilings. There is a beautiful cupola over the main altar. The remains of the Quiteño saint, Mariana de Jesús, who died in 1645, are kept here.

This church has suffered some settling of the foundations and was one of the most severely damaged in the 1987 earthquake. Restoration work continues but opening hours are changeable. A sign just inside the door gives visiting hours as 9.30 to 11 am and 4 to 6 pm on weekdays; 9.30 to 11 am and 4 to 5 pm on Saturday and Sunday – but don't rely on it. The church is normally open for services at 7 am.

The Cathedral One block away from the ornate Jesuit church is the Plaza de la Independencia with the stark cathedral. Although not as rich in decoration as some of the other churches, the cathedral has several points of historical interest. Plaques on the outside walls commemorate Quito's founders and Marshal Sucre, the leading figure of Quito's independence, is buried in the cathedral. To the left of the main altar is a statue of Juan José Flores, Ecuador's first president. Behind the main altar is the smaller altar of Nuestra Señora de los Dolores; the plaque there shows where President Gabriel García Moreno died on 6 August 1875. He was shot outside the Presidential Palace (just across the plaza) and was carried, dying, to the cathedral. The cathedral contains paintings by several notable artists of the Quito School. Visiting hours are among the most erratic of any church in Quito.

El Sagrario The main chapel of the cathedral was begun in 1657 and was finished 49 years later, but it is now a separate church, El Sagrario. This church was being renovated by Poland's University of Warsaw before the 1987 earthquake and was damaged during that quake. It is interesting to visit if you want to see how restoration work is done. El Sagrario is on García Moreno, next to the cathedral.

San Agustín Two blocks away from the Plaza de la Independencia (at Chile and Guayaquil) is the church where many of the heroes of the battles for Ecuador's independence are buried. This is the church of San Agustín, site of the signing of Ecuador's declaration of independence on 10 August 1809. The church is another fine example of 17th century architecture.

The Museo de San Agustín (☎ 515 525, 580 263) is in the convent to the right of the church (at Chile and Flores). It houses many canvases of the Quito School including a series depicting the life of Saint Augustine painted by Miguel de Santiago. The museum was recently being restored – call for hours.

Santo Domingo The church of Santo Domingo, on the plaza at the south-west end of Flores, is especially attractive in the evening, when its domes are floodlit. It too dates back to early Quito. Construction began in 1581 and continued until 1650. An exquisite statue of the Virgen del Rosario, a gift from King Charles V of Spain, is now one of the church's main showpieces. The statue is in an ornately carved baroque-style side chapel. In the busy Plaza Santo Domingo in front of the church is a statue of Marshal Sucre pointing in the direction of Pichincha, where he won the decisive battle for independence on 24 May 1822.

La Merced One of colonial Quito's most recent churches is that of La Merced (at Cuenca and Chile), which was begun in 1700 and completed in 1742. Its tower has the distinction of being the highest (47 metres) in colonial Quito and it contains the largest bell of Quito's churches.

The church has a wealth of fascinating art. Paintings show volcanoes glowing and erupting over the church roofs of colonial Quito, the capital covered with ashes, Marshal Sucre going into battle, and many other scenes. The stained-glass windows also show various scenes of colonial life such as early priests and conquistadors among the Indians of the Oriente. It is a surprising and intriguing collection.

San Diego This monastery, museum and cemetery are to the east of the Panecillo hill, between Calicuchima and Farfán. The monastery is an excellent example of 17th-century colonial architecture and the building (including the monk's living areas) can be toured. There is a treasure of colonial art, including a pulpit by the notable Indian wood-carver, Juan Bautista Menacho, which is considered one of the country's finest pulpits. The cemetery, with it's numerous tombs, mausoleums and other memorials, is also worth a visit. The monastery should be visited with a guide, available daily except Monday from 9 am to 12 noon and 3 to 5 pm – ring the doorbell. A tour costs about US$0.80.

Other Churches Moving out of the old town, you can still find several interesting churches. High on a hill on Calle Venezuela is the new basilica, which is still unfinished though work on it began in 1926. Obviously, the tradition of taking decades to construct a church is still alive. At the north end of the Parque La Alameda is the small church of El Belén, which was built on the site of the first Catholic mass to be held in Quito.

Finally, in a precipitous valley on the east side of town, is the Sanctuary of Guápulo, built between 1644 and 1693. The best views of this delightful-looking colonial church are from behind the Hotel Quito at the end of Avenida 12 de Octubre. Here, there is a statue of Francisco de Orellana looking down into the valley that was the beginning of his epic journey from Quito to the Atlantic – the first descent of the Amazon by a European. From the statue there is a steep footpath that leads down to Guápulo and it's a pleasant walk, though somewhat strenuous coming back. The local No 21 Santo Domingo-Guápulo bus goes there. The church is sometimes closed, though you can ask at the caretaker's house next to the church to have it opened up. There is an excellent collection of Quiteño colonial art and sculpture, and the pulpit, carved by Juan Bautista Menacho in the early 1700s, is particularly noteworthy.

This is just a selection of Quito's most interesting and frequently visited churches. There are dozens more.

Other Sights
Virgin of Quito The small, rounded hill which dominates the old town is called El Panecillo or 'the little bread loaf' and is a major Quito landmark. It is topped by a huge statue of the Virgin of Quito with a crown of stars, eagle's wings, and a chained dragon

atop the world. Read the Bible (Revelations, Chapter 12) for some ideas about why the Virgin was built as she is.

From the summit, there are marvellous views of the whole city stretching out below, as well as views of the surrounding volcanoes. The best time for volcano views, particularly in the rainy season, is early morning before the clouds roll in.

You can get there from the old town by climbing the stairs at the end of Calle García Moreno – it takes about half an hour. Unfortunately, I have received numerous reports of travellers being robbed on the climb and I can no longer recommend it. The thieves may work in gangs and are sometimes armed. If you do want to climb El Panecillo, go with a large group of people. A taxi from the old town costs about US$2 and they will wait and bring you back.

Markets At the bottom of El Panecillo is Avenida 24 de Mayo. This used to be a major open-air Indian market. An indoor market was opened in 1981 at the upper end of 24 de Mayo. Nonetheless, some outdoor selling still takes place, especially on Calle Cuenca and the streets to the north-west of it and the intersection with 24 de Mayo. Saturday and Wednesday are the main market days, but the area is busy on other days as well. Nearby is the so-called Ipiales Market, up the hill from Imbabura along Chile. Anything from stolen cameras to smuggled Colombian goods to underwear can be bought here. This is a fascinating area to visit, but there are many pickpockets and bag/camera snatchers, so go to look rather than photograph.

The most popular produce market in the new town is the Santa Clara market on Ulloa and Versalles, just south of Colón.

La Ronda Just off Avenida 24 de Mayo between Calles García Moreno and Venezuela and on to Maldonado is the historic alley now called Calle Juan de Dios Morales, but known to most people by its traditional name of La Ronda. This street is perhaps the best preserved in colonial Quito and is narrow enough so cars rarely drive along it, which adds to its charm. It is full of old, balconied houses and you can enter several of them. Just walk along the street and you'll see which ones are open to visitors; they usually have handicrafts for sale.

Plaza de la Independencia While wandering around the churches of colonial Quito you'll probably pass through the Plaza de la Independencia several times. Apart from the cathedral you can visit the Palacio de Gobierno, also known as the Palacio Presidencial. It is the low white building on the north-west side of the plaza and has the national flag flying atop it. The entrance is flanked by a pair of handsomely uniformed presidential guards.

Inside you can see a mural depicting Francisco de Orellana's descent of the Amazon. The president does indeed carry out business in this building, so sightseeing is limited to the mural and lower courtyard – if you are allowed in at all. Ask the guard at the gate for permission to view the mural.

The Archbishop's Palace, now a colonnaded row of small shops, can be seen on the north-east side of the Plaza. The interior patios can be visited.

Plaza del Teatro At the junction of Calles Guayaquil and Flores is the tiny Plaza del Teatro, where you'll find Teatro Sucre, built in 1878. This is Quito's most sophisticated theatre with frequent concerts and plays.

Parque La Alameda Leaving the old town, you'll see the long, triangular Parque La Alameda with an impressive monument of Simón Bolívar at the apex. There are several other interesting monuments in the park. On the south-east side there is a relief map of Ecuador and further in toward the centre there are statues of the members of the 1736-1744 French Académie des Sciences expedition which surveyed Ecuador and made the equatorial measurements which gave rise to the metric system of weights and measures. Look for the statues of the leader, the Frenchman Charles-Marie de La Condamine, and for one of the Ecuadorian

expedition members, Pedro Vicente Maldonado, who travelled to Europe after the expedition and died in London in 1748 at the age of 44. Quite by chance, I found a plaque dedicated to Maldonado at the rear of the St James Church in Piccadilly when I was walking around London recently.

In the centre of the park is the Quito Observatory, which was opened by President García Moreno in 1864 and is the oldest in the continent. It is used both for meteorology and astronomy and can be visited on Saturday morning.

At the north end of the park are a pair of ornamental lakes where rowboats can be hired for a few sucres. Nearby is a small monument with a spiral staircase and a view of the church of El Belén, site of the first mass in Quito. This part of the park is filled with picnicking families on weekends.

Palacio Legislativo The legislative palace is the equivalent of the Houses of Parliament or Congress. This is where the elected members of congress carry out the nation's affairs. A huge sculpted panel stretching across the north side of the building on Calle Montalvo, just off 6 de Diciembre, represents the history of Ecuador and is worth seeing.

Parque El Ejido A few blocks beyond Parque La Alameda is the biggest park in downtown Quito, the pleasant, tree-filled Parque El Ejido. This is a popular venue for ball games and you can usually see impromptu games of soccer and volleyball, as well as a strange, giant marbles game typical to Ecuador. It is played with golf ball sized steel balls. At the north end of the park there are open-air art shows at weekends.

Avenida Amazonas From the centre of the north end of the park runs modern Quito's showpiece street, Avenida Amazonas. Here are modern hotels and airline offices, banks and restaurants. It is a wide avenue with plenty of room for pedestrians. Buses and trucks are prohibited (except for blue double-decker London buses and a few others bound for the north end of the city). There are a great number of outdoor pavement restaurants where you can have a coffee or a snack and watch modern Quito go by.

Places to Stay

As befits a capital city, Quito has well over a hundred hotels and it would be pointless to list every one. The following selection will give you plenty of choice. As a general guideline, hotels in the old town tend to be less comfortable, older and much cheaper than those in the new town. That is not to say that there are no cheap hotels in the new town. The more expensive hotels add a 10% or 20% tax – my quotes below include taxes but ask the better hotels whether the tax is included in the rates they give you.

December is a busy month in Quito. The founding of Quito is celebrated on the 6th, and the Christmas-New Year period is also busy. Try not to arrive in the evening without a reservation if you wish to stay in a particular hotel.

Places to Stay – bottom end

Old Town When I first arrived in Quito in 1981 with a backpack full of climbing gear, no ticket home and about US$150 in my pocket, I stayed at the legendary *Hotel Gran Casino* (☎ 516 368) at Calle García Moreno 330 and Ambato. A classic backpackers' dive in a poor area of town, it is nicknamed the 'Gran Gringo' and is full of budget travellers – a good place to pick up on the latest travel news. There is a cheap restaurant, notice board, laundry facilities, left-luggage room (ensure luggage is clearly labelled and locked), and a good view from the roof. The rooms are very basic, although a few have nice views. The reason to stay here is to meet other budget travellers. Singles cost about US$1.80 and go fast. Rooms with two to six beds are about US$1.40 per person. Communal showers with hot water are available from 7 am to 3 pm only. A few rooms with a private shower are US$2 per person. Next door to the hotel are Turkish baths and sauna where you can soak away your travel grime and tensions for about US$1.

Two blocks away is the *Gran Casino Internacional* (☎ 514 905, 216 595) at 24 de Mayo and Bahía de Caráquez. They have much nicer rooms with private bath and hot water for about US$3 per person (few singles).

Nearby, on Calle Loja near Venezuela, is a small red-light district with some very cheap hotels. Several travellers have stayed here and reported the hotels as being OK. The *Pensión Astoria* at Loja 630 and the *Hotel Minerva* at Loja 656 charge about US$1 per person.

Better cheap hotels are found in the Plaza Santo Domingo area, especially on Calle Rocafuerte, Avenida Maldonado and Calle Flores running off the plaza, and on La Ronda (also called Juan de Dios Morales) south of the plaza. Here you'll find a score or more of cheap hotels within a few blocks of one another but some of them are not very good. The Terminal Terrestre de Cumandá is nearby.

There are several cheap and basic hotels on La Ronda of which one of the best is *Residencial Los Shyris* near the intersection with Avenida 24 de Mayo. They charge US$1.40 or US$2 per person depending on whether you have a private bath; hot water is available. There are other cheaper but worse places on the same block.

On the Plaza Santo Domingo is the *Hotel Roma* at Rocafuerte 1331 and the *Hotel Santo Domingo* next door. At the corner of the plaza is the *Caspicara Hotel* at Rocafuerte 1415. All three charge about US$1.70 per person, are basic but clean, and have hot water. The attractive *Hotel Juana del Arco* (☎ 214 175, 511 417), Rocafuerte 1311, has hot water and pleasant but noisy rooms (good views of the plaza) for US$2.40 per person or US$4.50 per person with private bath. The quieter rooms at the back lack windows. Just off the plaza at Guayaquil 431 is the *Hotel Felix*, which has pretty flowers on the balconies though the rooms are still basic. It has hot water and is secure – ring the bell to get in. The nearby *Hotel Venecia* at Rocafuerte and Venezuela is basic but clean – the electric showers, however, have warm water. These hotels charge about US$1.50 per person and are often full. Two blocks south-east of the plaza is the *Hotel Grand* (☎ 210 192, 519 411) at Rocafuerte 1001 and Pontón. This hotel is popular with budget travellers and has been well recommended. Rooms are about US$2 per person or US$3 per person with private bath. There are few singles. The hotel is family run and friendly, there is hot water, and a cheap restaurant downstairs.

As you head down Avenida Maldonado you'll encounter many hotels. In the first block on the right are the *Interamericano*, *Capitalino* and *Zulia*. The Interamericano (☎ 214 320) at Maldonado 3263, charges US$2 to US$4 single depending on whether or not you have a bathroom, telephone, or TV in your room. The Capitalino is US$1.80 each and looks basic but clean. They have hot water all day long. The Zulia is a basic cold-water hotel charging US$1 each.

On the left side of the first block of Maldonado are the basic but safe hotels *Guayaquil* (☎ 211 520) and *Ingatur*. The Guayaquil at Maldonado 3248 charges US$1.50 or US$3 per person depending on whether you have a bathroom or not. There is hot water and the rooms vary; some are good and spacious, others less so. The Ingatur at Maldonado 3226 has hot water, is clean and charges US$1.50 per person but has few singles. It's simple restaurant serves cheap almuerzos and meriendas.

There are several more cheap hotels further down Maldonado. One of the best is the *Hotel Colonial* (☎ 510 338) which is down an alley from Maldonado 3035, is quiet and has hot water. Basic but clean rooms are US$1.20 per person; or if you want a private bath the rooms are US$2.75 single and US$5 double.

On the other side of Maldonado are several more hotels which cost about US$1.40 per person but look grimy and have only cold water. These include the *Hotel Caribe* (☎ 212 966) at Maldonado 2852, and the nearby *Hotel Los Andes* and *Residencial Los Andes*. A little better is the cleaner *Hotel Indoamericano* (☎ 515 094) at Maldonado

3022, which charges US$1.50 per person and has hot water in the mornings.

Going in the opposite direction from Plaza Santo Domingo along Calle Flores, you'll find some more hotels to choose from. *Huasi Continental* (☎ 517 327) at Flores 330 and Sucre is quiet, friendly and recommended. Ask for a rooms away from the street. Spartan but clean rooms with private bathrooms and hot water are US$3.25/5.50 for singles/doubles; rooms with shared bathrooms are US$3.50 a double. The nearby *Hotel Montúfar* at Sucre 160 and Flores is also recommended. It is quiet, clean, has hot water and is very good value for US$1.50 per person. The *Residencial Quitumbe* at Espejo 815 and Flores is very clean and secure and has hot water but no private bathrooms. They charge US$3.50 per person in spacious rooms. The *Hotel Viena* (☎ 213 132) at Flores 562 and Chile charges US$1.50 per person and has hot water – there has been a report of petty theft from the rooms. The nearby *Hotel Viena Internacional* is in the middle-price category below.

Further down is the *Hotel San Agustín* (☎ 216 051, 212 847) at Flores 626 and the *Hotel Los Canarios* at Flores 856. Both charge about US$4.50/7 for clean singles/doubles with private bath and hot water. The San Agustín also has cheaper rooms with shared baths for US$3.40/4.75.

There are two cheap hotels on Calle Montúfar, which parallels Flores to the south-east. The *Hotel Hogar* (☎ 218 183) at Montúfar 208 and Calle de los Milagros charges US$2.25 per person in rooms with private baths; they have hot water in the mornings. The *Hostal Rumiñahui* (☎ 211 407) at Montúfar 449 and Junín charges US$3.50/6 for singles/doubles or US$4.50/7 for rooms with private bath. The hotel is clean, has hot water, and is recommended. Nearby is the *Hotel Italia* on Junín between Montúfar and Flores. Clean but basic rooms are about US$1.50 per person and hot water is available.

Other budget hotels in the old town include the *Hotel Sucre* at Cuenca and Bolívar on the corner of Plaza San Francisco.

The hotel is attractive from the outside, but has only basic rooms inside although some have good views. Warm water is available on request and rooms are only US$1.10 per person. Also on this plaza is the *Hotel Benalcázar* (☎ 518 302) at Benalcázar 388 and Bolívar. They charge about US$2.40 for a double with private bath and have been recommended by budget travellers. The *Ecuahotel* (☎ 515 984) at Chile 1427 near Cuenca has a few rooms with good views and charges US$5 for a double room with a bath or US$3.50 for a double with communal bathrooms.

The *Hotel Plaza del Teatro* is on Guayaquil at the theatre plaza and charges about US$4 per person.

New Town A popular budget hotel closer to the new part of town is the *Residencial Marsella* at Los Ríos and Castro just east of the Parque La Alameda. It charges about US$4 for a double room with bath, is clean, has hot water, a roof with a view, is family run, and is well recommended. Rooms vary quite widely in quality. A few singles are available. The manager has big extensions underway here.

Near the main drag of Amazonas you can stay at the *Residencial Italia* at 9 de Octubre 237 and 18 de Septiembre. This is one of the best budget places in the business area. They charge about US$2 for basic single rooms or US$5 for doubles with a bath, are family run, small, and often full. (As we go to press there is a recent unconfirmed report that it has closed.)

Around the corner is the very basic *Residencial 18 de Septiembre* on the street of the same name – they charge only about US$1.50 per person but aren't up to much. Another reasonable choice for budget accommodation in the new town is the *Residencial Los Angeles* (☎ 238 290) at Cordero 779 and 6 de Diciembre. They charge about US$2.50 per person and are often full.

Most of the cheaper hotels in the new town start at about US$4 or US$5 per person and are described under the 'middle' price range below.

Places to Stay – middle
Old Town The best hotel near the Terminal Terrestre de Cumandá is the *Hostal Cumandá* (☎ 516 984, 513 592) at Morales 449, right behind the bus terminal. Clean, carpeted rooms with bathrooms and hot water are US$5.50/8.50 for singles/doubles. TV and telephone are available in some rooms. Avoid the rooms on the terminal side as they can be noisy – otherwise it's value.

The *Hotel Viena Internacional* (☎ 213 605, 211 329) at Flores 600 and Chile is popular with travellers wishing reasonably priced comfort in the old town. They have large carpeted rooms, some with balconies, all with telephones, bathrooms and hot water. There is a book exchange and restaurant. Rooms are US$8/15 for singles/doubles.

The *Auca Hotel* (☎ 512 240) at Sucre and Venezuela looks spartan but has clean, small rooms with bathrooms for US$8/11. The nearby *Hotel Real Audiencia* (☎ 512 711) on the corner of the Plaza Santo Domingo at Bolívar 220 and Guayaquil is the best hotel in the old town. It has clean rooms with bath, phone and TV for US$12/16. There is a bar and restaurant.

New Town The best choice of mid-range hotels is in the new town. Many of them will provide full board if you ask them to.

Several small family-run hostales have recently opened – they cater especially to backpackers and students. Hot showers, kitchen and laundry facilities, luggage storage, living room, notice board and information are available in a friendly and relaxed environment. These are good places to meet travellers interested in hiking or off-the-beaten-track travel. Because they are small hostales, it is best to phone ahead for availability. They normally have a few small (single, double) rooms and a larger dormitory style room. *Casapaxi* (☎ 525 331) is at Pasaje Navarro 326 and Avenida La Gasca –

about one km north and uphill of Avenida América. The No 19 bus passes by. It is run by a friendly Ecuadorian woman, Martha, who charges US$4 per person and includes a 'tropical' breakfast of fruit and juice. *La Casa de la Feliz Eliza* (☎ 233 602) at Isabel La Católica 1559 (near the east end of Avenida Colón) is run by (who else?) a happy woman named Eliza. She charges US$4 per person. Very close by is *La Casona* (☎ 230 129, 544 036) at Andalucia 213 and Galicia – they charge US$5 per person including breakfast. Nearer the business centre is *Albergue El Taxo* (☎ 232 593) at Foch 909 and Cordero. They charge about US$5 per person and have information about mountaineering and guides.

There are several good small hotels in the area between Avenida 10 de Agosto and the university. One of the cheapest is the *Hotel Versalles* (☎ 547 321) at Versalles 1442 and Marchena. They charge US$7/9 for singles/doubles with a bathroom. It's OK but nothing fancy. The *Residencial Santa Clara* (☎ 541 472) at Darquea Teran 1578 and 10 de Agosto has recently enjoyed a great deal of popularity among travellers and is often full. The residencial is a pleasant-looking house and it's clean, comfortable and friendly. Rooms are available both with (US$5.60 per person) and without (US$4.70 per person) bathrooms. Meals are available. The clean *Hotel St James* (☎ 565 972, 567 972) at Versalles 1075 and Carrión is excellent value at US$7/9.50 in rooms with bath. Pleasant cheaper rooms with shared bath are also available. There is a cafeteria. Around the corner is the similarly priced and recommended *Residencial Carrión* (☎ 234 620, 548 256) at Carrión 1250 and Versalles. This residencial is popular, geared to long-staying guests and is often full. *Hotel Majestic* (☎ 543 182) at Mercadillo 366 and Versalles has pleasant, clean rooms with private baths, TV and telephone for US$9/13. They have friendly staff but their hot water supply is sometimes erratic. (Isn't it everywhere?) Most of the hotels in this section are excellent value and highly popular. They are often full so try early in the day.

Hotel Nueve de Octubre (☎ 552 424/524) at 9 de Octubre 1047 and Colón has simple rooms with bath for US$5/8.50 a single/ double. Better rooms with carpeting and telephone are US$5.50/10. There is a restaurant and they are friendly and recommended. The *Hotel Pickett* (☎ 541 453, 551 205) at Presidente Wilson 712 and J L Mera charges US$5.50/10 for rooms with telephone and bath with plenty of hot water. This is a centrally located and reasonable place to stay. The *Residencial Karol Jennifer* (☎ 230 777) is centrally located at Carrión 584 and J L Mera. They have no singles and charge US$11/16 for doubles/triples with bath and hot water. The *Posada Real Residencial* (☎ 231 162) at Plácido Caamaño 213 near the north end of Avenida Coruña is quiet and charges US$6.50/12 for rooms with bathroom and telephone. The *Hostal Los Andes* (☎ 550 839) at Muros 146 and González Suárez is in an upper-class residential area of town near the British Embassy. It is recommended, has English speaking staff and is good value for US$10.50/15.

Opposite the Quito Airport is the *Hotel Aeropuerto* (☎ 458 708) at Amazonas 7955 (the north end of the Avenida) which charges US$17/22 for singles/doubles with bath, hot water, and telephone. Some rooms have kitchenettes but otherwise there is little to recommend it other than its proximity to the airport (other hotels are seven to 11 km away from the airport). The *Savoy Inn* (☎ 246 263) at Yasuní 304 and El Inca is a little over 2 km from the airport and is a much better hotel, although prices are only a little higher.

Between the old and new towns, a couple of blocks west of Parque El Ejido, is the *Hotel Inca Imperial* (☎ 524 800) at Bogotá 219. This hotel is recommended for friendly and helpful English-speaking management and there is a restaurant. Rooms are US$12/20 for singles/doubles with private bath and hot water.

The *Hotel Embassy* (☎ 561 990) in the heart of a quiet residential district at Presidente Wilson 441 and 6 de Diciembre, is highly recommended as being very good value – it could almost be called a top-end hotel. It is motel-like and rather lacks character, but the comfortable rooms are spotless and complete with carpeting, telephone and bathroom – some have a kitchenette. Their restaurant is recommended and they charge around US$20/23, although they do have a few smaller rooms, also with bathroom, for several dollars less. This hotel is used by some airlines and smaller tour agencies to accommodate groups and independent travellers have occasionally had problems with reservations. A few blocks away is *Hostal Camila's* (☎ 232 412, 546 880) at 6 de Diciembre 1329 and Roca. This small hostal is in a recently renovated Spanish-style house and has comfortable, spacious rooms with telephone, TV and bathroom for US$16/22/24 for singles/doubles/triples.

Opposite, at 6 de Diciembre 1230 and Roca, is the *Hotel Seis de Diciembre* (☎ 544 866, 565 682) which has clean rooms for about the same price.

The *Hotel Ambassador* (☎ 561 777, 562 054) at Calle 9 de Octubre 1052 and Colón was renovated in the late 1980s. Clean comfortable rooms, many with TV and telephone, go for US$20/24. Nearby, the small and pleasant *Hostal Palm Garten* (☎ 523 960) at 9 de Octubre 923 and Cordero has rooms with a double bed for US$28 (single or double occupancy) and rooms with two beds for US$34.

Places to Stay – top end

All top-end hotels are in the new town. These hotels are very good and compare well with similar first-class hotels anywhere in the world. Unfortunately, they all suffer from the habit of charging non-Ecuadorian guests approximately twice as much as residents of Ecuador. (I give the high rates below.) This makes the luxury hotels beyond the needs or pocket-books of most independent travellers. They are popular with business people and tour groups which arrange discounts for clients by buying accommodation in volume.

There are a couple of smaller first class hotels which are reasonably economical but are often booked up well ahead. One of the best is *Hostal Los Alpes* (☎ 561 110) in a beautiful old house at Tamayo 223 and Jorge Washington. Comfortable carpeted rooms with spotless bathrooms and a telephone are about US$30/39. Their restaurant is excellent. Also good and recommended is *Residencial Cumbres* (☎ 562 538, 560 850) at Baqueadano 148 near 6 de Diciembre. It has clean rooms with bathrooms for US$36/42. Breakfast is included. Both these hotels have friendly English speaking management.

The *Hotel Tambo Real* (☎ 563 822) at 12 de Octubre and Queseras del Medio (opposite the US Embassy) is one of the cheapest of the larger luxury hotels. They charge US$66 for a double room – some come with kitchenettes. The *Chalet Suisse* (☎ 562 700) at Reina Victoria 312 and Calamá has double rooms beginning at US$70. This hotel has a small casino, and a sauna and exercise room.

There are two luxury hotels on Amazonas in the heart of the new town. The *Hotel Alameda Real* (☎ 562 345) at Roca 653 and Amazonas has very large rooms, many with balconies, wet bars or kitchenettes, renting for US$75/90 for singles/doubles. They have a good restaurant, bar, coffee shop and casino.

The biggest hotel in town is the *Hotel Colón* (☎ 561 333, 560 666) at Amazonas and Patria. This hotel has everything you might need for a luxurious stay – pool, sauna, massage parlour, exercise room, discotheque, casino, barber and hairdressing salons, a small shopping mall, a 24-hour coffee shop, two restaurants, two bars and numerous meeting rooms etc. The Colón is one of the capital's main social centres and this is where many visiting dignitaries stay. Almost all of the 450 rooms have good views of Quito – head up to the 20th floor and walk out onto the roof for a really great view. Rooms here vary in size and range from US$115 to US$145 double. All rooms have cable TV.

If you want a luxury hotel away from the centre, try the *Hotel Quito* (☎ 230 300) at González Suárez 2500 and 12 de Octubre. They have a panoramic view of both Quito and the Guápulo valley and attractive gardens with a pool. This hotel features most of the facilities of the Colón but is more out of the way and quieter. Prices are about the same.

Newly opened in the early 1990s, the *Hotel Oro Verde Quito* (☎ 566 497) at 12 de Octubre 1820 and Cordero is the city's most expensive hotel. It too has all the amenities you could possibly want if you are paying US$180 for a double room. They also have suites for up to twice that price.

Places to Stay – apartments
Visitors wanting to stay for a longer time may want to rent an apartment or suite with a kitchen for self catering. Often, apartments require a one-month minimum stay and are often full. One of the least expensive is the *Apart Hotel Panorámico* (☎ 542 425) at San Ignacio 1188 and González Suárez. They charge US$70 per person per month. Similarly priced is the *Apartamentos Calima* (☎ 524 036) at Cordero 2028 and 10 de Agosto. *Apartamentos Colón* (☎ 230 360) at Leonidas Plaza 326 and Roca has double apartments for US$325 per month.

The *Apart Hotel Mariscal* (☎ 528 833) at Robles 958 and Valdivia charges about US$20 for a double with kitchenette per night and long term discounts can be arranged. The *Amaranta Apart Hotel* (☎ 527 191) at Leonidas Plaza 194 and Jorge Washington charges US$27 for a double or US$44 for a suite with kitchenette – again long term discounts can be arranged.

Places to Eat
If you are economising, it is best to stick to the almuerzos or meriendas (set lunches and dinners) which are sold in many restaurants, particularly those used by workers and business people. These set meals often cost as little as US$1 and may not be listed on the menu – ask. Almuerzos and meriendas are more difficult to find at weekends because these meals are aimed at working people. Many restaurants are closed on Sunday.

The fancier restaurants add 10% tax plus 10% service charge to the bill. This does not necessarily happen in the cheaper places. In even the most expensive restaurants, however, two people can dine well for about US$25 to US$30, not including wine, which adds from about US$8 a bottle.

Old Town There are few restaurants of note in the old town, although this is where the cheapest places are found. There are several cheap restaurants on the 1400 block of Rocafuerte near the Plaza Santa Domingo. The *Restaurant Los Olivos* (☎ 514 150) at Rocafuerte 1421 is one – big helpings for a little over US$1. That doesn't mean this is the best choice – there are equally good places within a block.

Other cheap places which I have had recommended include the *Restaurant Royal* at García Moreno 666, the *Restaurant Oasis* at Espejo 812 and the more expensive *El Criollo* (☎ 219 828) at Flores 825 – this last restaurant serves no beer.

Las Cuevas de Luis Candela is a Spanish restaurant at Benalcázar and Chile and is probably the best restaurant in the old town. It is rather more expensive than the other places. The *Govinda* is a cheap, Hare Krishna-run, vegetarian restaurant at Esmeraldas 853 and Venezuela. They are open only for lunch from Monday to Friday. A good chinese restaurant is *Chifa El Chino* on Bolívar near Guayaquil. A *Pizza Hut* on Espejo near the Cine Bolívar serves decent Italian food but is not very cheap. There are several chicken restaurants such as *Pollo Gus* at 24 de Mayo 1246 and García Moreno and *Pollo Broaster* at Sucre 258 and Venezuela. This restaurant also serves desserts such as cakes and ice cream. Also good for desserts, snacks and juices is *Pastelería El Torreón* on the Plaza del Teatro at Guayaquil and Manabí – a place for rest and refreshment during a busy sightseeing visit to the old town.

The *Restaurant El Panecillo* (☎ 517 277) is just below the summit of El Panecillo on the side of the hill overlooking the city. The food is quite good and with a distinct Ecuadorian taste, the service leisurely, but the view very good. Several people have written to tell me that this restaurant has closed – it is not obviously visible from the summit and they have erratic hours, but they were open the last time I was there. Call first.

The rest of the places to eat described below are all in the new town.

Budget Just because you are in the new town doesn't mean you can't eat economically if you want to. The trick to finding cheap meals in the new town is to avoid eating on Amazonas and Calamá where restaurants are excellent but not inexpensive.

I have eaten consistently well at Cevichería Don José at Veintimilla 1254 and Páez – just a block and a half from Amazonas. Despite the name, they serve meat dishes as well as seafood. The restaurant is run by people from the coastal province of Manabí, the service is friendly, they open every day, and you can get a decent meal for about US$1. The *La Finca* at the corner of 9 de Octubre and Cordero is another good budget choice, particularly for set meals which are well under US$1.

The *La Chiminea Inn* on Darquea Teran just off 10 de Agosto is a nice looking restaurant that serves good meals for about US$1.25. There are plenty of other inexpensive places to be found just by wandering around and seeing where the local office workers eat.

If you want inexpensive fast food walk down Calle Carrión, east of Amazonas. This block has earned the nickname of 'Hamburger Alley'and has about a dozen places serving burgers etc. It is very popular with students.

Ecuadorian Budget travellers should check out *Mama Chlorindas* (☎ 544 362) at Reina Victoria 1144 and Calamá. This is a good, cheap place to try local food, particularly at lunch time – meals are only about US$1.

Good, typical Ecuadorian food served in elegant surroundings can be eaten at *La Choza* (☎ 230 839) at 12 de Octubre 1821 and Cordero. You can eat well here for about US$4. They were closed when I tried to eat

there on a Saturday night so call ahead for hours and reservations. Slightly more expensive and well recommended for typical Ecuadorian dishes is *Rincón La Ronda* (☎ 454 176) at Belo Horizonte 400 and Almagro. They often have live music in the evenings. Another place to try 'safe' Ecuadorian food is the *Taberna Quiteña* (☎ 230 009) at Amazonas 1259 and Cordero. This is a low-roofed cellar bar with musicians wandering around at night – the food is OK but check the prices before you order. The Taberna Quiteña in the old town is not as good.

Seafood Ecuador is famous for its cebiches made of marinated seafood. One of the best *cebicherías* is *Las Redes* (☎ 525 691) at Amazonas 845 and Veintimilla. Have the cebiche mixta; it's huge and delicious and costs about US$4. There are cheaper dishes. Other excellent seafood restaurants are *El Cebiche* (☎ 526 380) at J L Mera 1232 and Calamá, and *La Jaiba Mariscos* (☎ 543 887) at Avenida Colón 870 and Reina Victoria. Expect to pay about US$4 or US$5 for a full meal. Most restaurants in Quito have at least some seafood on the menu.

Vegetarian Quito is probably the best place in Ecuador for a choice of vegetarian food. The best, and most expensive, vegetarian restaurant is *La Cabaña* (☎ 230 085) at Cordero 1489 and Amazonas. They are particularly popular at lunch time. Expect to pay about US$3 for a meal. Another popular place is *Vitalcentro* at Lizardo García 630 and Reina Victoria. Hearty vegetarian lunches are under US$2 and are served between 12 noon and 2 pm. A cafeteria and health food store is open from 10 am to 5 pm. The Hare Krishna people have inexpensive lunches in their *Govinda* restaurant in the old town and at Versalles 1738 and Colón in the new town. Another less expensive place is the *Restaurant Macrobioteca* at Carrión and 6 de Diciembre. Also try *Salud y Vigor* (☎ 540 600) at Reina Victoria 1138 for vegetarian products.

Ñucca Llacta at Veintimilla 1163 and

Amazonas serves both vegetarian and meat dishes. Vegetarians can find decent meals in many non-vegetarian restaurants. For example, the *El Toro Steak House* (☎ 236 551) at Amazonas 878 and Veintimilla and at Jorge Washington 885 and Páez have buffet-style salad bars – you can buy a 'salad only' meal if you don't want steak. Various Italian restaurants, such as the *Pizza Huts*, serve meatless meals and have salad bars. Many chifas (Chinese restaurants) also have vegetarian choices on their menus.

Cafés Avenida Amazonas is a good place to come and watch the world go by, to see and be seen. There are four or five popular *pavement cafés* on the 400 and 500 blocks of Amazonas (near Roca). They serve a decent cup of coffee and don't hassle you if you sit there for hours. These are extremely popular meeting places and are not very expensive.

The *Colón Coffee Shop* at Amazonas and Jorge Washington is reasonably priced considering that it is in one of the capital's most luxurious hotels. It is open 24 hours and serves meals as well as snacks. For delicious pastries and desserts, or for a light lunch, the elegant *Chantilly Café* (☎ 528 226) at Roca 736 and Amazonas is recommended. This place is very popular for business lunches. The café opposite the Libri Mundi bookstore on J L Mera and Presidente Wilson is recommended for a light snack out of doors, with less of the hustle and bustle of Amazonas.

Italian There are many Italian restaurants but they are not very cheap. There are three or four on the two blocks of Roca east of Amazonas – these are all good but rather pricey. They include *La Trattoria de Veneziano* (☎ 523 085) at Roca 562 and *Vecchia Roma* (☎ 230 876) at Roca 618. Another good choice is *Rincón de Sicilia* on J L Mera and Carrión. Meals here are about US$4 or US$5. *La Gritta* (☎ 567 628) at Santa María 246 and Reina Victoria is one of the best (and priciest) Italian restaurants in town.

Cheaper Italian food is available in the many pizza restaurants. *Pizza Hut* (☎ 526 453) at J L Mera and Carrión are among the

most expensive (over US$3 per person). There is also a *Pizza Hut* at Naciones Unidas and Amazonas and in the old town. *El Hornero* at Amazonas 854 and Veintimilla (☎ 231 274) and at González Suárez 1070 (☎ 563 377) have very good pizzas for between US$2 and US$3 per person and other Italian food as well. They stay open to midnight and beyond. If you need take out, this is the place to go. They'll even deliver to your house or hotel if you don't live too far away. For outdoor dining, try *Pizza Masters* on Amazonas between Robles and Roca – meals are around US$2 to US$3. Rather cheaper is the *Pizza en 3 Minutos* at 12 de Octubre and Presidente Wilson – this is a good place for a cheap lunch.

Chinese Chifas are popular in Ecuador and Quito has several Chinese restaurants. Most are good, medium-priced places. The *Chifa Mayflower* (☎ 540 510) at 6 de Diciembre 1149 and Robles is good and charges about US$3 for a meal. Another good choice is *Chifa Gran Pino* at Colón and J L Mera. The *Chifa Feliz* at Carrión 661 and Amazonas has recommended vegetarian dishes. Slightly more expensive, but recommended, is the *Casa China* (☎ 551 857) at 12 de Octubre 1262 and Cordero. Also very good is the *Chifa Pekin* (☎ 520 841) at Belo Horizonte 197 and 6 de Diciembre. The *Chifa Palacio* at Calamá 434 has been recommended for reasonably priced but large portions.

Steak Houses The *Churrasquería* on Amazonas and Veintimilla has a huge model of a cow outside – you can't miss it. They serve 'all-you-can-eat' meals for about US$3 or US$4. Another good place to go if you are hungry, especially for meat, is the Brazilian *Churrascaría Tropeiro* (☎ 548 012) at Veintimilla 546 and 6 de Diciembre. US$5 buys an 'all-you-can-eat' meal. Waiters keep coming round with steak, roast pork and lamb, chicken, and other goodies and there is a help yourself salad bar. The food is good.

The *Casa de Mi Abuela* (☎ 230 945) at J L Mera 1649 and La Pinta is excellent and popular. Steaks are huge and delicious – this is my favourite steak house. Cheaper and locally popular is the *Columbus Steak House* (☎ 231 811) at Avenida Colón 1262 and Amazonas. It's good, but don't expect anything but meat. Their parrilladas are recommended.

French There are several French restaurants, all of which are rather pricey but serve good French cuisine in elegant surroundings and are popular. Calling ahead for a reservation is a good idea. One of the best known and reasonably priced ones is the *Rincón de Francia* (☎ 554 668) at Roca 779 and 9 de Octubre – a full meal will cost less than US$10. Also good and similarly priced is *La Belle Epoque* (☎ 233 163) at Whimper 925 and 6 de Diciembre. Slightly more expensive places are the *Le Péché Mignon* (☎ 230 709) at Belo Horizonte 338 and Almagro and the nearby *La Marmite* (☎ 237 751) at Mariano Aguilera 287 and Almagro.

Spanish Excellent Spanish food is served in a number of restaurants – as with the French places they tend to be elegant, pricey and popular. One of the best is *La Vieja Castilla* (☎ 566 979) at La Pinta 435 and Amazonas. *Costa Vasca* (☎ 564 940) at 18 de Septiembre 553 and Páez is also excellent and has an intriguing and unusual decor – look around. Other good choices are *La Paella Valenciana* (☎ 239 681) at Almagro 1727 and República, the *El Hobo* at Amazonas 3837 near Naciones Unidas, and *La Rana Verde* (☎ 563 022) at J L Mera 639 and Veintimilla – this last one has tapas (Spanish snacks and hors d'oeuvres) and is slightly less expensive than the others.

German As with French and Spanish places, the German restaurants in town are good but not cheap. *Der Rhein* (☎ 242 597) at 6 de Diciembre and Bélgica has been recommended. Other choices include *El Ciervo* (☎ 543 116) at Dávalos 270 and Páez and the *Taberna Bavaria* (☎ 233 206) at J L Mera 1238 and García.

Mexican A couple of Mexican restaurants

have opened in recent years. One is *La Guarida del Coyote* at Carrión 619 and Amazonas and another is *TexMex* at Reina Victoria 235 and 18 de Septiembre. Meals here cost about US$3 each. Opposite the TexMex is another, somewhat pricier, Mexican restaurant whose name escapes me.

Calamá This street is known for the number and variety of restaurants found along it, particularly in the two or three blocks east of Amazonas. Here you'll find *La Creperie* (☎ 233 780) at Calamá 362 – they serve both dinner and dessert crepes as well as other dishes such as goulash and steak. Meals are around US$5. The *Scherezade* (☎ 520 117) at Calamá 329 is known for its excellent and medium-priced Arabian food. The *Excalibur* (☎ 541 272) at Calamá 380 is an elegant and cosy restaurant considered one of the best in Quito – but some readers tell me that the food is not as good as the ambience. *Pim's* (☎ 561 192) and *Dickens* are two bar/restaurants next to one another on the first block of Calamá and are popular places for well-off young Ecuadorians to hang out. They serve snacks, meals, and drinks. There are several other places to choose from.

Bars There are several bars which serve food. American-run *Adam's Rib* at J L Mera and Roca serves ribs and a variety of other American-style dishes at medium prices. They have a pool table and are popular with young travellers. Also good is the British-run *Bailey's* (☎ 232 508) at Páez 232 and 18 de Septiembre – they have a pleasant pub-like bar where you can sit while you wait for your meal. *El Pub* (☎ 523 589) at González Suárez 135 (opposite the Hotel Quito) serves pub food and is popular with Ecuadorians looking for a touch of something British. My favourite bar is the friendly American/British owned *La Reina Victoria* (☎ 233 369) at Reina Victoria 530 near Roca. They are only open in the evening from Monday to Friday and serve light meals (pizzas, sandwiches, chilli etc) and bar snacks except on Thursday night or special holidays when full meals are made. This place is popular with expats.

Others One of my favourite places is the *La Terraza del Tartaro* (☎ 527 987) on the top floor of the Edificio Amazonas building at Veintimilla 1106 and Amazonas. An elevator at the back of the lobby will take you up (press button 2 and you automatically get taken to the top floor). This is a classy place and you can expect to pay about US$10 each for a full meal with a great view of Quito. Steaks are the speciality, though they also serve good chicken and seafood. *Bentley's* (☎ 238 684) at J L Mera 404 and Robles, is also a good choice for steaks and seafood in elegant surroundings.

At 6 de Diciembre 1329 near Roca, *Super Papa* (☎ 232 412) serves hot baked potatoes in their skins stuffed with a variety of fillings – absolutely delicious. This small restaurant is popular with travellers and is a good meeting place – unfortunately the owner tells me his lease runs out in 1992 and the future of this popular spot is uncertain. I list it here in the hopes that Super Papa will remain open.

Hotels Quito's luxury hotels have excellent restaurants. Two of the very best are the *El Techo del Mundo* in the Hotel Quito (superb views) and the elegant and expensive *El Conquistador* at the Hotel Colón. The Colón serves a delicious and varied all-you-can-eat lunch buffet in the lobby every Sunday from 12 noon till 2.30 pm. It costs US$7 and is well worth it if you are looking for a luxurious splurge. They also have an excellent daily all-you-can-eat breakfast buffet for US$4.50.

Entertainment
Quito is not the world's most exciting capital for nightlife. Read the newspapers for exact details of what is going on. *El Comercio* has the most thorough coverage.

Fiestas Entertainment reaches its height during the various fiestas. The founding of Quito is celebrated throughout the first week

of December and there are bullfights at the Plaza de Toros, just beyond the intersection of Avenida América and 10 de Agosto. There is also street-dancing on the night of 6 December.

New Year's Eve is celebrated by erecting life-sized puppets in the streets and burning them at midnight. These puppets are often very elaborate and usually represent politicians. Carnival, which is a movable Catholic feast, is celebrated by intense water fights – no-one is spared. Colourful religious processions are held during Easter week.

Cinemas On a day-to-day basis, films provide cheap and good entertainment. There are some 20 cinemas and movies range from pornography to kung fu to terminally violent but at least some of them show good English-language films with Spanish subtitles. The best theatres for comfort or quality of films are the Colón, Fénix, República, San Gabriel and Universitario. In addition, good films are sometimes shown at the Casa de Cultura. Entrance is well under US$1 for any show – often as low as US$0.50. The following theatres advertise their films in the daily newspapers:

Aeropuerto
  Jaime Chiriboga and Juan Pazmiño (☎ 451 151)
Alameda
  Arenas 140 near La Parque Alameda (☎ 553 853)
Alhambra
  Guayaquil 1613 (☎ 214 261)
América
  América 648 (☎ 231 201)
Atahualpa
  Venezuela and Bolívar (☎ 212 557)
Bolívar
  Espejo 847 and Guayaquil (☎ 210 960, 215 778)
Capitol
  Colombia 338 on La Parque Alameda (☎ 231 121)
Central
  Esmeraldas 579 (☎ 211 080)
Colón
  10 de Agosto 2436 and Colón (☎ 231 081)
Cumandá
  Maldonado 3035 near 24 de Mayo (☎ 210 657)
Fénix
  6 de Diciembre and Baquerizo Moreno (☎ 235 720)

Gemelo 1 & 2
Avenida de la Prensa and Naula (☎ 244 569)
Granada
Chile and Cuenca (☎ 210 220)
Hollywood
Guayaquil 828 (☎ 211 308)
Iñaquito
Avenida Naciones Unidas, Edificio Casa del
Médico (☎ 452 660)
Metro
Venezuela and Sucre (Pasaje Royal) (☎ 213 034)
México
Tomebamba 463 (near 1000 block of
Maldonado) (☎ 266 140)
República
Avenida de La República 476 and Almagro
(☎ 547 725)
San Gabriel
América and Mariana de Jesús (☎ 453 587)
Universitario
Plaza Indoamérica, Universidad Central,
América and Perez Guerrero
Variedades
Flores 930 at Plaza del Teatro (☎ 211 060)

Plays, Dance & Concerts If your Spanish
is up to it, you can see a play at the Teatro
Nacional Sucre in the old town – this is the
oldest of Quito's cultural spots and part of
the fun is seeing the elegant building. Metropolitan Touring has organised a
spectacular Ballet Folklorico which is presented in the Sucre every Wednesday night.
Classical music concerts are also presented
at this theatre – sometimes the symphony
plays for no charge.

Other possibilities include the Teatro Pro-
meteo which is inexpensive and sometimes
has mime performances which anyone can
understand. The Patio de Comedias has also
been recommended for plays which are often
presented on Sunday nights. The Pichincha
Playhouse presents plays in English by an
expat theatre company – amateur, but of a
high standard. Sala Gonzalo Bonilla also has
plays. The two universities in Quito present
a variety of performances – political satire is
high on the list of Ecuadorian students'
theatre.

The Teatro Bolívar presents classical and
opera concerts every once in a while. The
Casa de la Cultura has concerts and, occasionally, plays. Concerts are also presented

in the Conservatorio Nacional de la Música,
the auditorium of the Corporación
Financiera Nacional, and in the basement
theatre of the Las Cameras Centro de Comercio y Industria. These last two often have
free concerts. Latin American rock concerts
are occasionally presented – the Plaza de
Toros (bull ring) is a popular venue.

These cultural events are advertised in the
daily newspapers and on posters at the
venues themselves. There is usually more
going on in the rainy season.

Casa de la Cultura Ecuatoriana
Patria and 12 de Octubre (☎ 565 808, 522 410)
Conservatorio Nacional de la Música
1159 Madrid (☎ 564 790)
Corporación Financiera Nacional
J L Mera and Patria (behind the Hotel Colón)
(☎ 561 026)
Las Cameras Centro de Comercio y Industria
República and Amazonas (☎ 453 142)
Patio de Comedias
18 de Septiembre 457 and Amazonas (☎ 561
902)
Pichincha Playhouse
Colón 758 (☎ 543 689, 213 321)
Sala Gonzalo Bonilla
Iñaquito and Joaquín Auz (☎ 248 099, 454 175)
Teatro Bolívar
Espejo 847 and Guayaquil (☎ 210 960, 215 778)
Teatro Nacional Sucre
Flores and Manabí (Plaza del Teatro) (☎ 216 668,
211 644)
Teatro Promoteo
6 de Diciembre 794 and Tarqui (behind the Casa
de la Cultura) (☎ 230 505, 565 808)
Universidad Católica
12 de Octubre and Robles (☎ 529 240, 521 834)
Universidad Central
América and Perez Guerrero (☎ 521 590, 236
988)

Nightlife Peñas have traditional folklorico
music shows and are very popular among
Ecuadorians. They are usually quite expensive. Often there is a cover charge (up to
US$5 per couple) or a minimum consump-
tion and you may be expected to wear a
jacket or skirt. They don't open until 9 pm
and entertainment might not begin till 10 or
11 pm – and continue till the early hours.
Friday and Saturday nights are the busiest
nights. Peñas serve drinks and often snacks.

The audience does not usually dance at peñas.

The Ñucanchi Peña (☎ 540 967) at Avenida Universitaria 496 and Armero in front of the Universidad Central is a fairly inexpensive place. *Nuestra América* at Iñaqito 149 and Amazonas has also been recommended. Some peñas are held in small and crowded bars such as the *Guayusas Bar* (☎ 553 274) at J L Mera 555 and *Dayumak* which appears to be the same place and is popular with young people. Other peñas are *El Chúcaro* (☎ 236 085) at Reina Victoria 1335 and Cordero, *Peña del Castillo* at Calamá 270 and Reina Victoria, the *Rincón Andino Peña* at Veintimilla and J L Mera, the expensive (overpriced?) *Paccha Mama* on Jorge Washington and J L Mera and the *Taberna Quiteña* (see under Places to Eat – Ecuadorian).

Dancing is also popular – again, there is often a cover charge or a drinks minimum. For dancing to Latin American salsa music go to one of the *salsatecas* which generally have a lower cover charge than the discotheques which play North American-style music. Salsatecas are friendly and lively; they are especially popular with Ecuadorians and Latin American tourists though there's usually a sprinkling of slightly more adventurous gringos. The discotheques tend to attract rich young Ecuadorians who dress up and think it's cool to disco – 'plasticos' is a slightly disparaging term occasionally heard to describe some of the clientele.

Good salsatecas include the *Seseribó* in Edificio El Girón at Veintimilla and 12 de Octubre and *Gato Son* at Aldana 307 and Carvajal have both been well recommended. Another salsa possibility is the *Son y Candela* at Carrión and Reina Victoria. Possible discotheques include *Blues* at La Granja and Amazonas, *Gasoline* at Santa María and J L Mera, and *Club 330* at Whimper and Coruña. The *Licorne* in the Hotel Colón has also been recommended – its popularity waxes and wanes. The *La Pirámide* (☎ 566 078) at La Niña 655 and Amazonas sometimes has live bands playing rock or jazz music.

If your idea of a night out is to hang out in a bar for a drink and a chat, you'll find plenty of good places. Several are British or American bars which have a pub-like atmosphere. They are not cheap by Ecuadorian standards. Some of these serve food and are described under Places to Eat – Bars. They are all good but my choice is *La Reina Victoria* (☎ 233 369) at Reina Victoria 530 and Roca. Owned and managed by a friendly US/British couple, Dorothy and Gary, this is a real home away from home for the homesick traveller. There is a fireplace, dart board, bumper pool and excellent pub ambience. Cheers!

Other bars worthy of note are the quiet little *Rumors Bar* on J L Mera and Veintimilla, the *Cowboy Bar* on the 1100 block of Almagro at La Pinta which plays exclusively Country & Western tapes, and the *Latin Jazz Bar* (locally known as *El Papillón*) at Almagro and Santa María. The Papillón was the 'in' place in 1991 and every night saw crowds of gringo travellers and young Ecuadorians filling the place to overflowing and yelling over the sounds of 'The Doors' – not a place for a quiet drink and a chat. These drinking holes come and go – ask around about the latest 'in' place.

Things to Buy

There are many good stores for souvenir hunters in the new town along and near Avenida Amazonas. If buying on the streets (there are street stalls and ambulatory vendors) you should bargain. In the fancier stores, prices are normally fixed, though bargaining is not out of the question, particularly if you are buying several things. The better stores are usually more expensive but not necessarily exorbitant, and the items for sale are often top quality.

Some store sell pre-Columbian ceramics and colonial antiques. It is legal for Ecuadorian residents only to buy these items. You are not allowed to export archaeological or antique items and they will be confiscated at the customs upon departure from Ecuador or arrival at your home country.

The following is a list of recommended stores selling a wide selection of goods at a variety of price levels. Folklore (☎ 563 085) at Colón 260 is the store of legendary designer Olga Fisch (who died in 1991). This is the place to go for the very best and the most expensive items. They have a branch at the Hotel Colón (☎ 541 315). The Productos Andinos Indian Co-operative (☎ 231 565) at Urbina 111 and Cordero (near the intersection of Avenidas Colón and 6 de Diciembre) has much cheaper but still highly recommended goods. They have a branch at Robles 800 and 9 de Octubre. Also relatively inexpensively priced are the government-run OCEPA stores at a variety of locations: Jorge Washington 252 and Amazonas (☎ 236 334), Carrión 1236 and Versalles (☎ 239 420), Coruña 1447 and Orellana (☎ 235 602), and next to the Municipalidad on the Plaza de la Independencia in the old town.

Most other stores won't be much more expensive than Folklore, nor much cheaper than OCEPA or Productos Andinos and yet maintain a decent quality. The following are all reliable. Galería Latina (☎ 230 896) at J L Mera 823 and Veintimilla next to the Libri Mundi bookshop (itself a great place to shop) has superb Andean textiles and other products. Opposite is Coosas, at J L Mera 838, which sells the colourful T-shirts popularly called 'Galápagos T-shirts' – but which are in fact decorated with various Ecuadorian motifs designed by well-known local artist Peter Mussfeldt. Towels, bags, and leisure wear bearing the designs are also available. Nearby is the Centro Artesanal (☎ 263 193), at J L Mera 804, which is known for canvases painted by local Indian artists, and for other products. A block away is La Bodega (☎ 232 844), at J L Mera 614, with a wide and wonderful selection of souvenirs.

Other places nearby which have been recommended include La Guaragua (☎ 520 347) at Jorge Washington 610 and J L Mera, El Aborigen at Jorge Washington 536 and J L Mera, and Ecuafolklore at Robles 609 and J L Mera. There are many other stores in the area. For expensive modern art, see the Museo Guayasamín described earlier under Museums. Note that souvenirs are a little cheaper outside of Quito if you have the time

and inclination to search them out – it is more convenient to shop in the capital.

For more ordinary shopping, to buy groceries, batteries, stationery, soap and other travellers' essentials, a number of places can be recommended. A cheap general store with a large selection is El Globo at 10 de Agosto and Roca.

There are many supermarkets. One of the best in the old town is La Feria at Bolívar and and Venezuela. In the new town, the Supermaxi is good – there are branches at several shopping centres, including Multicentro and Centro Comercial Iñaquito. Shopping centres are similar to North American shopping malls – many small stores selling all kinds of things. They are often called Centro Comercial, abbreviated to CC. The most important are:

Centro Comercial El Bosque
    Occidental and Carvajal (☎ 456 333/016, 547 817)
Centro Comercial Caracol
    Amazonas and Naciones Unidas (☎ 458 553, 456 776)
Centro Comercial El Espiral
    Amazonas and Jorge Washington (convenient to downtown, but with a limited selection of stores and products) (☎ 563 337)
Centro Comercial Iñaquito (CCI)
    Amazonas and Naciones Unidas (opposite the CC Caracol) (☎ 245 072/430)
Centro Comercial Multicentro
    6 de Diciembre and La Niña (☎ 237 949)
Centro Comercial Naciones Unidas (CCNU)
    Naciones Unidas and Japón (☎ 459 094/194)
Centro Comercial Quicentro
    6 de Diciembre and Naciones Unidas (☎ 248 365)

Note that most stores and shopping centres are closed on Sunday. One exception is the new CC El Bosque on the north-western outskirts of town. Also note that the CCI, CCNU and CC Caracol are all clustered together which may be convenient.

Getting There & Away
Air There is one airport with a domestic and international terminal side by side. You can walk from one to the other in about 60 seconds.

Services at the airport terminal include tourist information, money exchange, post office, cafeteria/bar, IETEL international telephone office and gift shops. For airport information ☎ 241 580.

The airport is about 10 km north of the city centre. See Getting Around for bus/taxi information.

Domestic There is no departure tax for internal flights, most of which are run by TAME. In addition SAN has flights to Guayaquil and Cuenca and Saeta has flights to Guayaquil. The airlines will accept one another's tickets for Guayaquil and Cuenca if their flights aren't full and if you paid for the ticket with cash. Internal flights (except for the Galápagos) are inexpensive – prices and schedules change frequently and the following are approximate. Flights to Guayaquil (US$16) leave from 11 times a day from Monday to Friday, nine times daily on Saturday and eight times on Sunday. If you don't have a ticket and are in a hurry, you can often just show up at the airport and get on the next available flight to Guayaquil. Flights to Cuenca (US$17) leave one to three times a day.

Only TAME operates services to the following cities: Tulcán (US$9) Monday to Friday at 12 noon; Esmeraldas (US$12) Monday to Saturday mornings; Portoviejo (US$16) Monday to Friday afternoons; Manta (US$16) Monday to Saturday mornings and Sunday afternoons; Macas (US$12) Monday and Friday afternoons; Coca (US$12) Monday to Saturday mornings and 12 noon on Monday, Wednesday and Friday; Lago Agrio (US$11) Monday to Saturday mornings; Tarapoa (US$13) Wednesday and Friday mornings; Loja (US$20) Monday to Saturday mornings. Machala (US$23) can be reached from Quito with connections at Guayaquil from Monday to Friday.

These schedules can change frequently – a broken-down aeroplane can cause a city simply to be removed from the itinerary for a week or more until a needed part is obtained and replaced. In mid 1991, TAME had four Boeing jets, a Fokker, two small Avros and a Twin-Otter – not many aeroplanes to fall back on if one is out of service. Lack of passenger demand often leads to cancelled flights, particularly the second and third flights from Quito to Cuenca with SAN. But, despite these frustrations, flying from Quito is generally straightforward and economical.

Baltra Island in the Galápagos is reached from Quito by TAME flights every morning. There is usually a change at Guayaquil but your luggage is transferred. The return cost is about US$374 for non-Ecuadorian residents. These flights to Baltra Airport are the normal way to go for travellers heading to the main port of Puerto Ayora on Isla Santa Cruz. SAN also has morning flights to Isla San Cristobal (changing at Guayaquil) daily except Thursday and Sunday (same price).

TAME has several ticket offices – unfortunately they seem to change address quite frequently so check before you go. In the old town TAME is at Manabí 635 and Venezuela (☎ 512 988) and in the new town at Avenida Colón 1001 and Rábida (☎ 554 905) and 10 de Agosto 239 and La Parque Alameda (☎ 512 910, 510 305). SAN-Saeta share an office at at Guayaquil 1228 and Olmedo in the old town (☎ 211 431). SAN has an office at Avenida Colón 535 and 6 de Diciembre (☎ 561 995) and at Avenida Colombia 610 (☎ 527 555). Saeta has an office at 10 de Agosto 2356 and Colón (☎ 551 782). In addition, you can buy domestic air tickets from most reputable travel agents at the same cost as direct from the airlines.

Finally, Icaro (Instituto Civil Aeronautico) (☎ 247 468, 439 867) sometimes has sightseeing flights or even flying lessons available. For about US$120 you can hire a five-passenger airplane for a sightseeing flight past the mountains around Quito. This is not easy to arrange because the company does not have very many aircraft available.

International Several international airlines have offices in Quito – almost all of them are on or near Avenida Amazonas. Ecuador's international airlines are Ecuatoriana and Saeta. TAME, supposedly, is planning to begin international flights to Cali – but who knows when this will become a reality. SAN flies only domestically.

There is an international airport departure tax of US$25 payable in either US dollars or sucres. If you are flying internationally, confirm 72 hours in advance, reconfirm 24 hours in advance, and arrive at the airport two hours before your flight. You will probably take off several hours late, but at least you'll be on the flight. The local representatives of international airlines are notorious for bumping you off their frequently overbooked flights – 'Sorry, señor, you're not on the computer'.

The following airlines have offices in Quito. Those marked with an asterisk * have direct flights into and out of Ecuador. Their country of origin follows in parentheses (where it isn't obvious). Some airlines fly only into and out of Guayaquil but it is a simple matter to connect to Quito with one of the many daily domestic flights.

Aeroflot (USSR)
    Robles 653 and Amazonas (☎ 524 243)
Aerolíneas Argentinas*
    J L Mera 453 and Robles (☎ 551 524)
AeroPerú*
    Reina Victoria and Calamá (☎ 534 601, 561 699)
Air France*
    18 de Septiembre 368 and Amazonas (☎ 541 441, 523 596)
Air Panamá
    Colón and Reina Victoria (☎ 541 695)
Alitalia (Italy)
    Ernesto Noboa 474 and 6 de Diciembre, office 202 (☎ 238 871, 231 899)
American Airlines* (USA)
    Amazonas 367 and Robles (☎ 561 144)
Avianca* (Colombia)
    Amazonas 360 and Robles (☎ 545 200)
British Airways
    Santa María and Amazonas (☎ 540 902)
Ecuatoriana*
    Colón and Reina Victoria (☎ 563 003)
Iberia* (Spain)
    Amazonas 239 and Jorge Washington (☎ 560 456)
Icelandair
    Almagro 1822 and Alpallana (☎ 561 820)
JAL Japan Airlines
    (☎ 550 308, 500 241)

KLM* (Holland)
    Amazonas 3623 and Catalina Herrera, Edificio Xerox (☎ 455 550/233)
Korean Air
    CC Multicentro (☎ 543 502, 542 527)
Ladeco (Chile)
    Pinto and Amazonas, Edificio Saldaña (☎ 522 590)
Lufthansa* (Germany)
    6 de Diciembre 955 and 18 de Septiembre (☎ 541 300)
Saeta Internacional* (Ecuador)
    Santa María and Amazonas (☎ 502 706/12)
Swissair
    10 de Agosto 6116 (☎ 241 555)
Varig* (Brazil)
    Amazonas 1037 and Pinto (☎ 561 584)
Viasa* (Venezuela)
    Amazonas 1188 and Calamá (☎ 543 257)

Bus The new modern bus station known as *Terminal Terrestre de Cumandá* became fully operational in 1987. There are several dozen bus companies with offices at the terminal which is at Maldonado 3077, a few hundred metres south of the Plaza Santo Domingo in the old town. The terminal is best reached by walking down the steps from Maldonado (see map). Buses will drop you off on Maldonado by the steps or you may prefer to walk down from Plaza Santo Domingo – the traffic along Maldonado is snail-paced. Taxi drivers often take an alternate route which enters the terminal from the south side.

The terminal serves most destinations from Quito. There is an information window (☎ 571 163, 570 670) where staff will tell you which company goes where, although it's fairly obvious. Walk around and compare departures.

Usually there are several companies serving the same destination at different times. For the most popular towns you'll find ticket sellers yelling out their destinations – though each window is clearly labelled. Only buses departing within a few minutes are allowed to park outside the terminal so you can often be on your way within minutes of arriving. Usually it is easy enough to get onto the bus you want, but if you plan on travelling during holiday periods and just before the weekend it's best to go to the terminal and book in advance. If you do find you have to wait, there are several snack bars. There is also a post office, IETEL office, banking machines, and small stores. Watch your luggage carefully inside the terminal if you don't want someone else to walk off with it.

With literally hundreds of buses departing during the day, it is impossible to give accurate timetables. There are several buses a day to most destinations, and some places – such as Ambato or Otavalo – may have several departures an hour.

Here is a list of the major destinations served and the approximate cost and length of a journey. US$0.05 is added to each ticket as a terminal departure tax. These fares are subject to change – but it gives an idea of the comparative costs of the trips. Fares tend to remain the same, in sucre terms, for a year or so. This means if they have just gone up, their cost in US dollar terms will be high – if they haven't gone up in a while, costs can be almost half the price they were a year ago. The prices below tend towards the high end.

to	cost (US$)	hours
Ambato	1.10	2½
Bahía de Caráquez	3.80	8
Baños	1.50	3½
Coca	3.30	13
Cuenca	3.00	10
Guaranda	1.70	5
Guayaquil	2.80	8
Ibarra	0.90	3
Lago Agrio	3.00	10
Latacunga	0.80	1½
Loja	4.90	18
Machala	3.70	11
Manta	3.90	8
Otavalo	0.75	2¼
Portoviejo	3.90	8
Puyo	2.00	8
Riobamba	1.60	4
Santo Domingo	1.10	2½
Tena	2.90	9
Tulcán	2.00	5½

For other destinations, you may have to go to the nearest major city and change. Enquire at the bus offices.

With several companies serving most destinations, you have a choice. If the first company you talk to doesn't have a bus leaving when you want, ask at the next counter. Companies serving the same destination tend to be clustered together in one part of the terminal. Also, you can find out whether the bus will be a slow old one which may give a more interesting ride or a newer fast one which may be small and cramped, but will get you there quickly. If the bus isn't almost full, the ticket seller will often show you which seats are available so you can choose where you sit.

There are companies (for example TEPSA) which will sell international bus tickets to Peru or Colombia. Avoid these. The tickets are very expensive and you still have to change buses at the border. Once across the border you often find that only one company will accept your ticket and you can wait for hours until they depart. It's much cheaper and far more convenient to buy tickets as you go.

Train The famous Quito-Guayaquil train has been suspended since the 1982/83 El Niño floods which destroyed about 80 km of track. It is not known when, if ever, services will resume. The daily *autoferro* to Riobamba was running from Monday to Saturday until recently – it has now been suspended and will possibly resume in 1992. Departure from Quito used to be at 3 pm and the journey was via Latacunga (US$0.40, two hours) and Ambato (US$0.60, 3½ hours), to Riobamba (US$0.90, five hours). The trains can get very crowded when they run. They are slightly cheaper but slower than the bus and bathroom facilities are primitive.

The train station (☎ 266 142/4) is on Avenida Sincholagua and Vicente Maldonado about two km south of the old town. The No 2 Colón – Camal bus from the Plaza Santo Domingo goes there. The train station booking office used to open at 11 am to sell tickets for the train. There is a railway booking office in the old town on Calle Bolívar 443 and Benalcázar, but it remains closed while the line to Guayaquil is down.

Metropolitan Touring operates a pricey tourist train trip which includes an overnight at a first-class Riobamba hotel. The specially renovated coach car is comfortably furnished with clean bathrooms, a bar and dining area. Some tours are done by autoferro which is also comfortable. Tours are one way by train, return by bus, with stops at markets, villages, and other sites of interest. Guides are bilingual. Two-day/one-night tours including meals and accommodation are about US$133 per person. Larger and more expensive train tours from Quito are also available.

Getting Around

To/From the Airport The Quito International Airport is named after the hero of Ecuadorian independence, Mariscal Sucre. The terminal is at the north end of Avenida Amazonas where it intercepts with Avenida de la Prensa, about 11 km north of the old town centre. The easiest way to get there by public transport is aboard the blue double-decker London buses which begin from the south end of the Parque El Ejido and run along Avenida Amazonas to the airport – large articulated or jointed buses also do this trip. The journey in either direction costs only US$0.10 but the bus does not run after dark.

Other buses which go to the airport tend to be more crowded. They are usually marked by an 'Aeropuerto' placard. The No 1 Villa Flora-Iñaquito bus runs from Plaza Santo Domingo in the old town to the airport. There are several other bus routes passing the airport – most of them go out along Avenida 10 de Agosto.

If you have any large luggage, I recommend a taxi which costs about US$2 to US$3 depending on where you start from.

If you are going from the airport into town, you will find bus stops on Avenida 10 de Agosto, about 150 metres away from the front entrance of the terminal. Buses are crowded – watch for pickpockets and bag slashers. If you have a pile of luggage, taxi drivers charge anything they can get away with (US$10!) from in front of the international terminal, a little less from in front of the national terminal. Bargain to get the fare down to US$4 to US$5 or walk out to Avenida 10 de Agosto and flag down a cab on the street for less.

Bus The crowded local buses have a flat fare of about US$0.05 which you pay as you board. They are safe enough and rather fun – but watch your bags and pockets. Generally speaking, buses run north-south and have a fixed route. The drivers are usually helpful and will tell you which bus to take if they are not going to your destination. Traffic in the old town is very heavy and you may often find it faster to walk than to take a bus, especially during the rush hours. Buses have both a name and a number, and although they usually have a fixed route, this may vary because of heavy traffic, road repair or the whim of the driver.

The narrow streets of downtown are usually one-way. Calles Guayaquil and Venezuela are one way into the old town towards El Panecillo, and calles García Moreno and Flores are one way out of the old town and away from El Panecillo. There are about 40 different routes. The IGM published a Quito Bus Routes map in 1976 – this has now been out of print for many years and there seems to be little interest in publishing a new one. If you have a specific place you want to get to by local bus, ask at your hotel, bus drivers or the tourist office. A selection of the ones you might use follows (routes are liable to change – ask the driver to make sure he is passing near your destination):

1 Iñaquito-Villa Flora
    Airport-10 de Agosto-Guayaquil-Santo Domingo-Maldonado-Villa Flora
2 Colón-Camal
    Coruña-Colón-10 de Agosto-Guayaquil-Santo Domingo-Maldonado-Terminal Terrestre
3 Colmena-Batán
    La Colmena-24 de Mayo-García Moreno-Vargas Torres-Manuel Larrea-Patria-J L Mera-Colón-6 de Diciembre-El Batán
7 Marín-Cotocollao
    Plaza La Marín-10 de Agosto-Airport-Cotocollao
9 Ermita-Las Casas
    Ermita-24 de Mayo-García Moreno-América-Universidad Central-La Gasca-Las Casas

10 San Bartolo-Miraflores
    San Bartolo-Maldonado-Santo Domingo-10 de
    Agosto-18 de Septiembre-Miraflores
11 El Tejar-El Inca
    El Tejar-Mejía-La Alameda-6 de Diciembre-El
    Inca (end of 6 de Diciembre)
15 Marín-Quito Norte
    Plaza La Marín-10 de Agosto-Airport-North
    Quito
19 Camal-La Gasca
    Patria-Pérez Guerrero-América-La Gasca
21 Dos Puentes-Guápulo
    Bahía de Caráquez (Dos Puentes)-Rocafuerte-
    Santo Domingo-Venezuela-Guayaquil-Colom-
    bia-12 de Octubre-Madrid-Guápulo
El Tejar-Mitad del Mundo
    El Tejar-América-10 de Agosto-La Prensa-Mitad
    del Mundo

Some of the main streets, especially 10 de Agosto, have minibuses which cost a few cents extra and are a little faster – though no less crowded. Minibuses tend to run later at night.

Taxi Taxi cabs are all yellow and have red taxi stickers in the window. Usually, there are plenty available, but rush hour can leave you waiting for 10 or 15 minutes for an empty cab.

A law was passed in 1984 requiring Quito cabs to have meters and almost all drivers now use them, although occasionally they will ask to arrange a price with you beforehand. Sometimes this is to your advantage as it enables the driver to take a roundabout route to avoid traffic, thus saving both of you time. Generally, though, you should have the driver use the meter. Late at night they will ask for a higher fare, which is fair enough, but it shouldn't be more than twice the metered rate. Some drivers will say the meter is broken – you can always flag down another cab.

Taxis can be hired for several hours or for a day. If you bargain hard, you could hire a cab for a day for about US$30 if you don't plan on going very far. A trip from the old town up to El Panecillo and back down again, with a long enough wait at the top for sightseeing and photography (say 15 minutes), costs about US$2. Short journeys

downtown cost from about US$0.50 to about US$3 for a long trip.

Car Rental Car rental in Quito, as elsewhere in Ecuador, is expensive. There are car rental offices at the airport. Expect to pay at least US$30 per day for a seven-day rental and make sure that mileage and adequate insurance are included. See the Getting Around chapter for more car rental information.

The following companies are found in Quito. Ecuacar has been recommended as reliable and competitively priced. Major international companies are also here. I do not recommend renting a car for getting around Quito because taxis and buses are much cheaper and more convenient. A rental car is a possibility for getting around the country. However, if you plan on visiting the main towns and travellers' destinations, you will find buses fast, efficient and reliable in most cases – and very cheap. Rental vehicles are useful for visiting some out-of-the-way areas which don't have frequent bus connections (in which case a more expensive 4WD vehicle is a good idea).

Avis
    Colón 1741 and 10 de Agosto (☎ 550 238/43)
    Airport (☎ 440 270)
Budget
    Colón and Amazonas (☎ 237 026)
    Airport (☎ 240 763, 459 052)
    Hotel Colón Branch (☎ 525 328)
Dollar
    Airport (☎ 249 490)
Ecuacar
    Colón 1280 and Amazonas (☎ 529 781, 540 000)
    Airport (☎ 247 978)
Hertz
    Veintimilla 928 and Amazonas (☎ 238 932)
    Airport (☎ 246 381)
Los Carritos Diligentes
    Airport (☎ 544 999)

Around Quito

Many excursions can be made from Quito using the city as a base. Here, I describe those

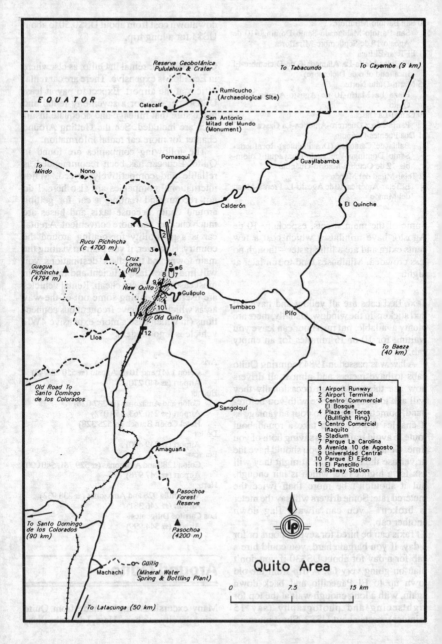

Reserva Geobotánica
Pululahua & Crater

To Tabacundo

To Cayembe (9 km)

EQUATOR

Rumicucho
(Archaeological Site)

Calacalí

San Antonio
Mitad del Mundo
(Monument)

To Mindo

Nono

Pomasqui

Guayllabamba

Calderón

El Quinche

Rucu Pichincha
(c 4700 m)

Cruz
Loma
(Hill)

Guagua
Pichincha
(4794 m)

New Quito

Guápulo

Tumbaco

Pifo

Old Quito

Lloa

To Baeza
(40 km)

Old Road To
Santo Domingo
de los Colorados

Sangolquí

Amaguaña

To Santo Domingo
de los Colorados
(90 km)

Pasochoa
Forest
Reserve

Pasochoa
(4200 m)

1 Airport Runway
2 Airport Terminal
3 Centro Commercial
   El Bosque
4 Plaza de Toros
   (Bullfight Ring)
5 Centro Commercial
   Iñaquito
6 Stadium
7 Parque La Carolina
8 Avenida 10 de Agosto
9 Universidad Central
10 Parque El Ejido
11 El Panecillo
12 Railway Station

Güitig
(Mineral Water
Spring & Bottling Plant)

Machachi

Quito Area

0   7.5   15 km

To Latacunga (50 km)

which are done from Quito as a day trip rather than as part of an overnight tour.

MITAD DEL MUNDO

The most famous excursion is to the equator at La Mitad del Mundo ('the middle of the world') in the village of San Antonio, about 22 km north of Quito. This is the place where, in 1736, Charles-Marie de la Condamine's expedition made the measurements which showed that this was, indeed, the equator. The measurements also gave rise to the metric system and proved that the world was not perfectly round, but bulged at the equator.

The centre of the Mitad del Mundo complex is a massive 30-metre-high **monument** topped by a brass globe, 4½ metres in diameter. The stone trapezoidal monument is built on the equator. Visitors take an elevator to the top, where there is a viewing platform, and then descend by stairs winding through the excellent **Museo Etnográfico** which is housed within the monument. The museum has interesting and well-displayed exhibits showing the many different Indian tribes which make up the indigenous population of the country. The museum and monument is open from 9 am to 3 pm on Tuesday to Friday and from 10 am to 4 pm on Saturday and Sunday. Admission is about US$0.50.

Also at Mitad del Mundo is a realistic looking 1:200 scale **model of colonial Quito**. This is housed in a building to the left (west) of the monument and costs US$0.20 to visit. It is worth the effort. Nearby, there is a **planetarium** run by the IGM with a variety of shows to do with astronomy. Shows are hourly from 11 am to 3 pm from Tuesday to Friday and till 4 pm on Saturday and Sunday. The 25-minute show costs US$0.30. To the south-east of the monument is a 'colonial village' which was recently built as part of the complex. There are plazas, buildings and a bull ring all of which are used occasionally, but are often closed and empty. There are plenty of giftshops for postcards and cheap souvenirs.

Outside of the Mitad del Mundo complex, on the other side of San Antonio, is a **solar museum** – a tiny, red brick construction with fascinating exhibits dedicated to astronomical geography and containing much data to enable the visitor to understand better the importance of Ecuador's geographical location. One of the highlights is the 'solar chronometer' – a unique instrument made in 1865 that shows precise astronomical and conventional time, as well as the month, day and season all by using the rays of the sun. This museum is not spectacular, it is small and special and opened only by appointment for those with a particular interest in astronomical geography. It was built by Ecuadorian scientist Luciano Andrade Marín in the 1950s and is currently curated by Oswaldo Muñoz of Nuevo Mundo Expeditions (☎ 552 839/617) who leads tours there on request.

Places to Stay & Eat

There is nowhere to stay – almost everybody returns to Quito. There are, however, several restaurants of which the recommended *Equinoccio* (☎ 533 741), near the entrance to the complex, is the best known (and most expensive). There are cheaper comedores in San Antonio on the road leading from Mitad del Mundo into the village centre.

Getting There & Away

To get there, take a No 22 Mitad del Mundo bus, which leaves about every 15 minutes from the El Tejar bus stop by the Ipiales street market in the old town. The bus stop is on the short street of José López, between Hermano Miguel and Mejía – it's not an easy-to-find bus stop so ask. Watch for pickpockets hanging out around the bus stop looking for tourists. I spotted several pickpockets – they can be pretty obvious sometimes! The journey takes about an hour and costs about US$0.15. The tourist office suggests catching the Mitad del Mundo bus on Avenida América anywhere between avenidas Peréz Guerrero and Mariana de Jesús, or along 10 de Agosto north of Mariana de Jesús, thus avoiding the old town altogether. This is a possibility, but I find that the buses come by very full and you often have to struggle to get on, particularly at weekends and rush hours.

A taxi, including waiting time at the monument, will cost about US$10, depending on how well you bargain. Taxis usually take a different route from the bus on a road which passes an intriguing highway art gallery. Famous Latin American artists have painted roadside billboards with weatherproof paint; the works, some two dozen of them, are stretched out along the highway. Ask your driver to go this way.

Tours, with bilingual guides, are available from most of the major travel agencies. They all go to the Mitad del Mundo complex except for Nuevo Mundo which will take you to the solar museum if you wish. Tours cost about US$20 per person (depending on your group size) and last about three hours.

RUMICUCHO

This is a small pre-Inca archaeological site about 3½ km north of San Antonio. Excavation is proceeding slowly under the auspices of the Banco Central. The site is open from 9 am to 3 pm from Monday to Friday and from 8 am to 4 pm on Saturday and Sunday. There is a small site museum nearby – entrance is about US$0.10.

Getting There & Away

Take a Mitad del Mundo bus to San Antonio (see the earlier reference) and walk north of the Solar Museum for about three km along Calle 13 de Junio. Taxis are available from San Antonio or Quito. Rumicucho is usually combined with a visit to Mitad del Mundo – several tour agencies will add the archaeological site to a tour for an extra fee.

RESERVA GEOBOTÁNICA PULULAHUA

This small 3,300-hectare reserve lies about four km north of San Antonio and is often visited in conjunction with a visit to Mitad del Mundo. The most interesting part of the reserve is the volcanic crater of the extinct Pululahua. This was apparently formed in ancient times when the cone of the volcano collapsed, leaving a huge crater some 300 metres deep and four km across (some guide-

books claim 500 metres deep and nine km in diameter – I think that is an exaggeration). The flat and fertile crater bottom is used for agriculture. Within the crater there are two small cones, the larger Loma Pondoña (2975 metres) and the smaller Loma El Chivo.

The crater is open to the west side through which winds from the Pacific, laden with clouds and moisture, blow dramatically. Sometimes it is difficult to see the crater because of the swirling mists. The moist winds, combined with the steep walls of the crater, create a variety of microclimates and the vegetation on the fertile volcanic slopes is rampant and diverse. Because the crater walls are much to steep to farm, the vegetation grows undisturbed and protected. There are many flowers and, of course, a variety of birds.

The crater can be entered on foot by a steep trail on its south-east side. There is also a rough track (suitable for 4WD vehicles) on the south-west side. The steep trail is the best way to see the birds and plants because most of the flat bottom is farmed. There is no fee or admission point to the reserve.

Getting There & Away

Take a Mitad del Mundo bus (see the earlier reference). From the monument, a paved road continues to the village of Calacalí, about 7½ km away. There are occasional buses from San Antonio to Calacalí, particularly at weekends. About four km beyond Mitad del Mundo on the road to Calacalí, there is a paved road to the right – the first one. Ask the driver to drop you off here. About one km along this road there is a small parking area – the crater is just beyond. The trail descends from the parking area to the crater bottom.

Alternatively, continue on the road to Calacalí for about a further 2½ km. A dirt road on your right leads into the crater. You can return the way you came, perhaps stopping at the picturesque little village of Calacalí (no facilities).

Taxis from San Antonio or Quito will take you to the rim and tours can be arranged from

Quito in combination with a visit to Mitad del Mundo.

POMASQUI

This village is passed about six km before reaching Mitad del Mundo on the way from Quito. It is worth a stop to see the two churches on the Plaza Yerovi (the main plaza) two blocks east of the petrol station on the main highway. On the south side of the plaza is the church of El Señor del Árbol (the Lord of the Tree) which has a noted sculpture of Christ in a tree – the branches of the tree look like Christ's arms raised above His head in a boxing champion's salute. Various miracles have been ascribed to this image by devotees. On the east side of the plaza is the parish church with a variety of religious paintings, some of which are slightly bizarre (the miraculous intervention of the Virgin to save a believer from certain death), and various statues including a carved and polychromed Santa Clara who is the patron saint of Pomasqui.

The Fiesta of El Señor del Árbol is normally the first Sunday in July. Santa Clara Day is 27 July and so the whole month is a busy one for the citizens of Pomasqui, who have processions, games, bull fights etc.

CALDERÓN

This village is about 10 km north-east of Quito on the Panamerican Highway (not the road to Mitad del Mundo). Calderón is a famous centre of a unique Ecuadorian folk art; here the people make bread-dough decorations ranging from small statuettes to colourful Christmas tree ornaments, such as stars, parrots, santas, tortoises, candles and tropical fish. The ornaments make practical gifts as they are small, unusual and cheap (about US$0.10 each). These are decorative figures and are inedible; preservatives are added to them and they'll last some years.

Some figurines are used for All Souls' Day (2 November) ceremonies in Calderón and many other Andean villages. It is thought that the figurines represented animal or human sacrifices in pre-conquest times. The cemetery here is a good place to visit from Quito on All Souls' Day.

Calderón is a small village so you won't have any difficulty finding stores on the one main street. There is nowhere to stay and only basic restaurants.

Getting There & Away

Buses run along 10 de Agosto toward Calderón and beyond. The corner with Avenida Colón is supposed to be a good place to flag one down. Buses going as far as Otavalo or beyond may possibly give you a ride if they aren't full (which they often are). Local city buses don't go as far as Calderón. Somewhere in between are buses that go there – keep trying and you'll eventually find one.

If you wanted to visit just Calderón from Quito, you could hire a cab for under US$10 including some waiting time for you to shop. Most tours to Otavalo stop at Calderón briefly.

SANGOLQUÍ

The Indian market nearest the capital is the Sangolquí Sunday morning market. There is a smaller market on Thursday. Frequent local buses go there from Plaza Marín at Calle Chile and M de Solanda in the old town. Sangolquí is about 15 km south-east of the old town.

PASOCHOA FOREST RESERVE

This is a private reserve operated by the Fundación Natura (☎ 447 341/342/343/344), Avenida América 5663, Ecuador's major non-governmental conservation organisation. The reserve is roughly 30 km south-east of Quito and has one of the last remaining stands of undisturbed humid Andean forest left in the Central Valley. Over 100 species of birds and many rare plants have been recorded here.

The forest is luxuriant and contains a wide range of highland trees and shrubs. These include the Podocarpaceae which are the only conifers native to the Ecuadorian Andes (the pines seen elsewhere are introduced), various species of mountain palm trees, the

Andean laurel, the huge-leaved *Gunnera* plant which has been nick-named 'the poor folks' umbrella' and many more. Bromeliads, orchids, lichens, ferns and other epiphytic plants contribute to the forest's attractions. The prolific birdlife includes hummingbirds, of which at least 11 species are present, and which are one of the main attractions. Various other tropical birds such as furnarids, tapaculos, honeycreepers and tanagers may be seen along the nature trails. Mammals such as rabbits, squirrels and deer are sometimes observed and, more rarely, foxes or even pumas. The reserve is very highly recommended to naturalists and birdwatchers.

The reserve is a small one, only 400 hectares in size, located on the northern flanks of the extinct volcano of Pasochoa at elevations of 2700 to 3800 metres. The area is within the collapsed volcanic caldera and there are good views of other peaks. There are several trails ranging from easy half-hour loops to fairly strenuous all-day hikes. The shorter trails are self-guiding; guides are available for the longer walks. One trail leads out of the reserve and to the summit of Pasochoa (4200 metres) – this takes about six hours.

Apart from protection and conservation of this unique habitat for recreational use, the Fundación Natura also encourages scientific research in the area and has set up an educational programme. This last is particularly designed to teach local schoolchildren about their environment – information that has hitherto been lacking for most students. These worthwhile programmes are funded, to a great extent, by contributions to the Fundación Natura, particularly the entrance fee which is charged to visitors.

Information

A daily entrance fee of US$7 is charged to foreign visitors. Overnight camping is permitted in designated areas – the fee for this is US$12 per person allowing the visitor to spend two days and a night within the reserve. Campers need to have all their own equipment including stoves. Fires are not allowed and no food is available. There are latrines, picnic areas, and water. There is also a simple building with bunk beds which is used by researchers and may be available to visitors if requested at the Fundación Natura offices. Bring your own sleeping bags. The reserve is open every day from dawn till dusk. The Fundación Natura asks visitors to check with their offices to obtain maps, information and camping permits, and pay fees. The number of visitors to the reserve is limited. Normally, however, the reserve is well-nigh empty, particularly mid-week, but on weekends it can be crowded.

Getting There & Away

Buses leave from Quito about twice an hour for the village of Amaguaña, about one hour away. These buses used to leave from the Villa Flora local bus stop at the south end of Quito but recently they have left from the Plaza La Marín in the old town. Check with the Fundación Natura about the current situation. Ask the driver to let you off near the 'El Ejido' and from the church nearby there is a signed road to the reserve, about six or seven km away. You have to walk this. Alternatively, go all the way into Amaguaña (about a km beyond El Ejido) and rent a truck to the reserve entrance and information centre for about US$4. The locals are used to people visiting the reserve and can help give directions – it's not hard to find.

Taxis from Quito can also get you there, but not all the drivers know where to go. If you can't find a driver who knows the way, ask at the Fundación Natura for help in finding a knowledgeable driver. You might want to arrange a driver on the day before you visit to get there early – the best birding is in the early hours.

VOLCÁN PICHINCHA

Quito's closest volcano is Pichincha, looming over the western side of the city. The volcano has two main summits, the closer Rucu Pichincha (about 4700 metres) and the higher Guagua Pichincha (4794 metres). Guagua is active and is being monitored by volcanologists. A major eruption in 1660 covered Quito in 40 cm of ash; there were three minor eruptions in the 1800s. The most recent bout of activity began in 1981 with a few puffs of smoke. It is unlikely that any serious activity will occur in the near future and the topography of the volcano is such that, even if a major eruption were to occur, lava flows would head into the almost unpopulated areas north, west and south of the volcano, sparing Quito which lies to the east.

Climbing either of the summits is strenuous but technically straightforward and no special equipment is required. By heading west on one of the streets leaving Quito and continuing upward, an ascent of Rucu Pichincha can be done in a long day, returning to the city by nightfall. Unfortunately, this is easier said than done. One main street of access, 24 de Mayo, has been the scene of frequent attacks and robberies of hikers, and this route is strongly discouraged. Another main access, through El Tejar, does not have robbery problems – instead, vicious dogs have often bitten hikers. Once out of the city, the route goes past the TV antennas on the hill named Cruz Loma – several attacks, robberies, and rapes have been reported in this area in recent years.

These warnings should not be taken lightly – walking through some of the poor suburbs on the western edges of the city is not a good idea if you are laden with good warm clothes and camera gear. The best solution is to go in a large group and check for the latest information before you go. The South American Explorers Club is always an

excellent source of up-to-date information. They can tell you the best route to take through the ever-changing and expanding western outskirts of town, and recommend a guide if you wish. The climbing guides listed in the Travel Agencies & Guides section listed earlier can also be of assistance. Guides will usually have a jeep available to drive you past all the problem areas to a point high up on the mountain (even so, the shortened climb to the summit is a strenuous affair taking most of a day). Many people continue to climb Pichincha because the views are superb, but get information before you go and and plan your trip with care to avoid having a problem.

Climbing smoking Guagua Pichincha is a longer trip, but less beset with non-mountainous hazards. A southbound No 8 Tola-Pintado bus will take you past Avenida Chilibulo shortly before the end of the run. Occasional buses head out along Avenida Chilibulo to the village of Lloa. From here, there is a track that takes about half a day of walking to reach a hut just below the crater summit of Guagua. This track can also be negotiated in a sturdy 4WD vehicle to just below the refugio. The refugio is very basic – a few bunks and, usually, a caretaker who can look after your gear and let you use the kitchen facilities. From the hut, reaching the crater rim and descending within takes about two to three hours. Again, check with the South American Explorers Club or a climbing guide for the latest information before you go.

North of Quito

The Andean highlands north of Quito are one of the most popular destinations in Ecuador. Few travellers spend any time in the country without visiting the famous Indian market at the small town of Otavalo, where you can buy a wide variety of weavings, clothing and handicrafts. Though many travellers limit their visit to just Otavalo, there is much more to see in the region.

The dramatic mountain scenery is dotted with shining white churches set in tiny villages, and includes views of Cayambe, the third highest peak in the country, as well as a beautiful lake district. Several small towns are noted for speciality handicrafts such as woodcarving or leatherwork.

Ibarra is a small, charmingly somnolent colonial city worth visiting, both in its own right and as the beginning of the Ibarra-San Lorenzo railway linking the northern highlands with the coast. If you are travelling overland to or from Colombia, it's almost impossible to avoid this region.

NORTH TO CAYAMBE

About 10 km north of Quito on the Panamerican Highway is the village of Calderón (see Around Quito in the Quito chapter). Beyond Calderón the road descends in a series of magnificent sweeps towards the village of **Guayllabamba**, in a fertile river valley of the same name and famous for its produce. Roadside stalls offer huge avocados and that strangely reptilian-looking Andean fruit, the *chirimoya*. It's a member of the custard apple family and perhaps the nearest translation is the 'sweetsop' – I prefer the Spanish name. Its knobbly green skin is discarded and you eat the white pulp inside. The chirimoya definitely tastes better than it looks or sounds.

Some three km beyond Guayllabamba, the road forks and you can take either fork as they both end at Cayambe. About 10 km along the right-hand road you pass a turn-off

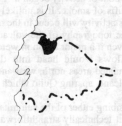

to the right which leads back to Quito via a roundabout route. This takes you through **Quinche**, famous for the Virgin and paintings inside the impressive church, and on through pretty countryside and tiny hamlets to Pifo. Here you turn right and return to Quito via Tumbaco.

A few km further you cross the equator, marked by a monument consisting of a large concrete globe which is much less visited than the ever popular Mitad del Mundo monument north of Quito. Soon you cross the railway tracks of the now defunct Quito-Ibarra train, and 60 km from Quito you reach Cayambe.

The left-hand route, although a little shorter, is somewhat more twisting and slower than the right-hand route and, therefore, some drivers avoid it. It also crosses the equator but there is no marker. It is generally less inhabited and has more barren countryside than the other road. I prefer it for the exciting drive and wild scenery. The only village of any size on this road is **Tabacundo**.

COCHASQUÍ

A few km before Tabacundo is a turn-off to the left which leads to Tocachi and the ruins of Cochasquí. These were built by the Cara Indians before the Inca conquest and had been largely forgotten until recently. The area was declared a national archaeological site in 1977 and is currently being excavated and investigated.

There are 15 pyramids, some of which are almost 100 metres long, and about 30 other mounds are also present. Because of the incredibly panoramic view from the site (you can see El Panecillo of Quito if you have good binoculars) it is assumed that Cochasquí was built for strategic purposes. Additionally, the alignments of the pyramids and some of the structures associated with them point to ceremonial and astronomical uses. There is a small on-site museum and local Spanish speaking guides will give you a tour of the museum and site. If you are pressed for time, ask for a short tour – longer tours may last a couple of hours. Although entrance to the site and tours are officially free, I encourage visitors to tip guides because their wages are inadequate.

The guides can also show you a couple of reconstructions demonstrating what the houses of the local indigenous people looked like in the past (and continue to look like in the more remote parts of the Sierra). These are built entirely from local materials using ancient methods – you won't see nails or electrical outlets! Inside, indigenous furnishings and cooking utensils can be seen, and guinea pigs (a traditional delicacy of the Incas) scurry around. Outside, there is a garden with a cornucopia of Andean plants used for food, medicinal, ceremonial and utilitarian purposes. Many of these plants and their uses are dying out in the highlands. The purpose of this project is to preserve traditional plant varieties and folk remedies in the face of today's monocultural agricultural practices and the ubiquitous panacea – aspirin.

Getting There & Away

There is no public transport. Some buses (not all, try Transportes Lagos) between Quito and Otavalo take the Tabacundo road and can drop you at the turn-off. There is a sign. From here, a dirt road climbs about eight or 10 km to the site. The site workers and guides usually drive up to the ruins about 9 am and can give you a lift – otherwise you have to walk. Hitching is poor because of lack of traffic. Taxis can be hired from Cayambe and will do the round trip (including waiting time) for about US$10.

CAYAMBE

Cayambe (population about 15,000) is the most important town on the way to Otavalo. It is famous for its dairy industry and there are many stores and restaurants selling a variety of local cheeses and cheese products. The local Salesian Monastery reportedly has an excellent library on indigenous cultures – I've never been there.

Places to Stay & Eat

Although this is the nearest town of any size to the equator, few people stay here, preferring instead to buy some cheese and continue to Otavalo. The *Pensión Cayambe* in the centre is the cheapest place to stay. The clean *Hostería Mitad del Mundo* (☎ 360 226) at the south end of town charges about US$4 per person.

The *Hostería Napoles* (☎ 360 231) is about one km north of town on the Panamerican Highway. They sell cheese products, have one of the best restaurants in Cayambe, and there is a garden with a miniature 'zoo' (a few caged parrots etc). Cabins with private bath, hot water and TV are US$7/12 for singles/doubles.

Getting There & Away

Any bus between Quito and Otavalo can drop you here.

Some buses run to places like Calderón, Guayllabamba, Tabacundo and Cayambe direct from Quito but they don't leave from the main bus terminal. It's best to catch one of these by standing on the side of the road. A good place to stand is on Avenida 10 de Agosto where it intersects with Avenida Juan de Ascaray near the bull ring in Quito. Flag down any bus that has a sign indicating it's going where you want to go or that looks like it could use some passengers. Start early enough in the day so that you won't get stuck somewhere at nightfall and you'll probably have plenty of adventures.

ON TO OTAVALO

It is a further 31 km along the Panamerican Highway to Otavalo. The snow-capped mountain to the right of the road is the extinct

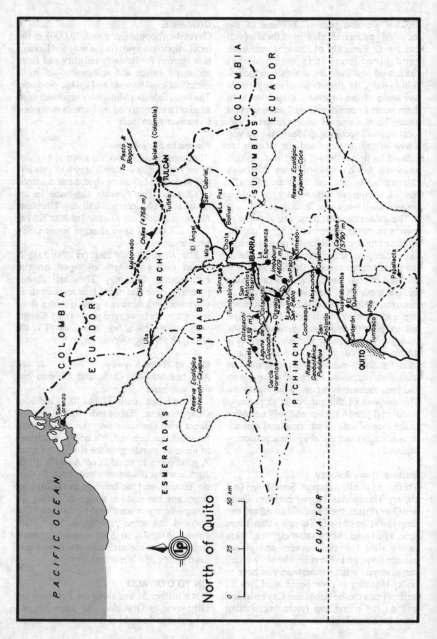

North of Quito

COLOMBIA

ECUADOR

To Pasto & Bogotá

Ipiales (Colombia)

TULCAN

Tufiño

Chiles (4768 m)

San Gabriel

La Paz

Bolívar

El Ángel

Chota

Maldonado

Chical

Mira

IBARRA

La Esperanza

Imbabura (4609 m)

San Pablo

Lita

Salinas

Tumbabiro

San Antonio de Ibarra

Cotacachi

Otavalo

Laguna de Cuicocha

Laguna San Pablo

Cayambe

Cayambe (5790 m)

Olmedo

Papallacta

Reserva Ecológica Cayambe-Coca

Tabacundo

Apuela

García Moreno

Cotacachi (4939 m)

Reserva Ecológica Cotacachi-Cayapas

Cochasquí

San Antonio

Guayllabamba

El Quinche

Reserva Geobotánica Pululahua

Calderón

Tumbaco

Pifo

QUITO

PICHINCHA

IMBABURA

CARCHI

SUCUMBÍOS

ESMERALDAS

COLOMBIA

ECUADOR

PACIFIC OCEAN

San Lorenzo

EQUATOR

50 km

0   25

Volcán Cayambe which, at 5790 metres, is Ecuador's third highest peak. For trivia buffs it is the highest point in the world through which the equator directly passes – at about 4600 metres on the south side. The road climbs and crosses the provincial line from Pichincha to Imbabura, a province known for its indigenous inhabitants and pretty lake district. Soon you see the largest of these lakes, Laguna San Pablo, stretching away to your right with the high peak of Imbabura (4609 metres) behind it. The area is dotted with many simple villages inhabited by the Otavaleño Indians.

OTAVALO

This small town of some 20,000 inhabitants is justly famous for its friendly people and their Saturday market. The market dates back to pre-Inca times when jungle products were brought up from the eastern lowlands and traded for highland goods. Today's market has two different functions: the local market for buying and bartering animals, food and other essentials, and the craft market for the tourists.

The story of the phenomenal success of the Otavaleño weavers is an intriguing one. The backstrap loom has been used in the area for some 4000 years. The Indians' ability as weavers was harshly exploited by the colonialists, beginning in 1555, and later the Ecuadorian landowners who forced them to labour in *obrajes* or sweatshops, often for 14 or more hours a day. Miserable though this was, it did have the effect of instilling a great knowledge of weaving in the Otavaleño people.

In 1917 a local weaver had the idea of copying the Scottish tweeds that were then in vogue and this was so successful that it led to recognition of the ability of the Otavaleño weavers. This ability, combined with the Agrarian Reform of 1964 and the people's shrewd business sense, has made the Otavaleños the most prosperous Indian group in Ecuador and perhaps on the continent. It is difficult to find a town of any size which does not have an Otavaleño store. They also make frequent business trips to

neighbouring countries and even to North America and Europe.

The goods they sell are undeniably oriented towards the tourist market and this has led to recent complaints from 'real travellers' that the market is too 'touristified'. This seems to me a kind of inverse snobbism that reveals a lack of concern for the well-being of the weavers. Their prosperity in a changing and difficult world is only to be applauded, but a truer measure of their success is perhaps not only their prosperity but their continuing sense of tribal identity and tradition.

One of the most evident features of the Otavaleños' cultural integrity is the traditional way of dress. This is not just put on specially for the tourists at the Saturday market, but is worn on normal workdays in their houses, villages and fields. The men are immediately noticeable because of their long single pigtails, calf-length white pants, rope sandals, reversible grey or blue ponchos and dark felt hats. The women are very striking with beautifully embroidered blouses, long black skirts and shawls, and interesting folded head cloths. The women also wear bright jewellery; the most obvious is the many strings of gold-coloured blown glass beads around their necks, and bracelets consisting of long strands of red beads.

Of the almost 20,000 inhabitants of Otavalo, the majority are whites or mestizos. There are about 40,000 Indians, most of whom live in the many nearby villages and come into Otavalo for market day. Quite a few Indians own stores in Otavalo, however, and you can buy most items here if you are unable to visit on market day.

For detailed cultural information, I recommend Lynn Meisch's *Otavalo: Weaving, Costume and the Market*, Libri Mundi, Quito, 1987.

Information

Money Bring as many sucres as you think you'll need from Quito because exchange in Otavalo is usually a little lower and less convenient than Quito. Banco del Pichincha on the main plaza usually accepts cash

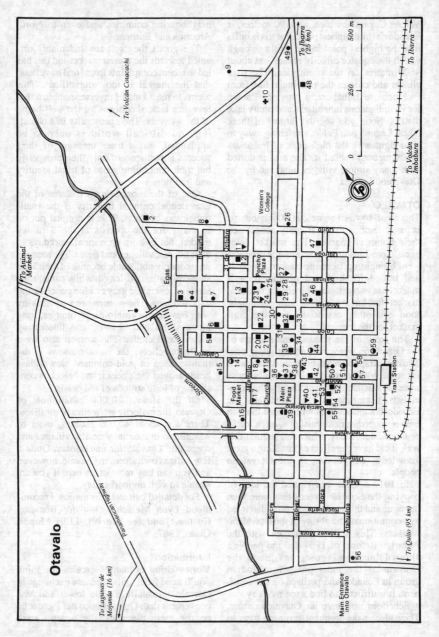

Otavalo

■ PLACES TO STAY		OTHER	
2	Hotel Ali Shungu	1	Stadium
3	Residencial El Rocío	4	Bar La Choza
5	Residencial Colón	7	Peña Tuparina - Centro de Difusion
6	Residencial Santa Martha		Andino
12	Residencial Centenario	8	Bahai Institute
13	Residencial Samar-Huasy	9	Instituto Otavaleño de Antropología
20	Residencial El Indio	10	Hospital
22	Pensión Imbabura	14	Buses to local villages
29	Hotel El Indio	15	Cockfight Stadium, Cine San Gabriel
32	Pensión Los Angeles		& Public Toilet
33	Residencial La Herradura	16	Police Station
35	Hotel Los Pendoneros	18	IETEL
42	Pensión Otavalo	21	Peña Oraibi
46	Hotel San Sebastian	23	Amauta Peña
47	Residencial Isabelita	24	Tucano Peña-Bar
48	Hotel Yamor Continental	26	Fire Station
52	Pensión Los Andes	28	Public Toilet
53	Hotel Otavalo	30	Several Tourist Agencies
54	Hotel Riviera-Sucre	31	Rodrigo Mora
		34	Cine Bolívar
▼ PLACES TO EAT		35	Lasso Turismo
		37	Banco del Pichincha
11	Ali Micui	39	Municipalidad & Post Office
17	Café El Triunfo	44	Transportes Otavalo (bus)
19	Mama Rosita's	45	Inti Peña Salsateca
21	El Mesón del Arrayan	49	Petrol (Gas) Station
24	Parenthese Pizza	50	Santo Domingo Church
25	Shenandoah Pie Shop & La Galería	51	Transportes Los Lagos (bus)
27	Tabascos	52	Museo Archaeológico
36	Royal Cafetería & Camba Huasy	55	Cine Apollo
	Fuente de Soda	56	Petrol (Gas) Station
38	Restaurant Copacabana	57	Buses to San Pablo
40	Chifa Tien An Men	58	Plaza Copacabana & New Covered
41	Chifa Casa de Korea		Market (under construction)
43	Camba Huasy Chicken Restaurant	59	Cooperativa Imbaburapac Churimi
			Canchic (buses to Agato)

dollars and travellers' cheques, but it's difficult to negotiate many other currencies (though Colombian pesos are accepted). Casas de cambio operate irregularly and there are street changers, particularly around the market on Saturday. Some of the better hotels will exchange dollars at an unfavourable rate but normally you have to stay there. You can sometimes buy souvenirs with cash dollars.

Post & Telecommunications The post office is in the Municipalidad on the García Moreno side of the main plaza. The IETEL office is at Calderón and Sucre.

Travel Agencies There is no tourist information office but there are several tourist agencies which are helpful with local information as well as providing excellent tours.

Zulaytur (☎ 921 176) at the east corner of Sucre and Colón, 2nd floor, is run by the friendly and knowledgeable Señor Rodrigo Mora – this agency has had many recommendations. Tourist information is given even if you don't want to go on one of his tours.

There are several other agencies on the same block – I keep getting letters from them telling me that they are the best and the others are all illegal! They all provide similar tours at competitive prices. *Intipungo* (☎ 920 037) has been recommended. *Lasso Turismo* (☎ 920 446) in the Hostal Los Pendoneros at Calderón and Bolívar has also been recommended by travellers. Visit the various agencies and choose the one that most appeals to you.

A variety of inexpensive guided tours are available which enable you to visit local Indian homes, learn about the entire weaving process, buy products off the loom, and take photographs. Rodrigo Mora's emphasis on anthropological and sociological background information makes his tours very worthwhile – most other agencies are following suit.

The most popular tour visits several local villages and takes all day. Transportation is included and a tour costs about US$7 per person with a maximum of ten passengers – more with fewer passengers. Lunch is extra. Other, more expensive, tours are available, for example to visit the beautiful Andean lakes around Otavalo or to trek in the local countryside. Some agencies have horses for rent – about US$15 for half a day. Ask at the tourist agencies for more information.

If you have a reasonably large-sized group, an informative slide presentation of the area can be arranged with Rodrigo Mora. At appropriate times of year, visits to some of the local fiestas may be possible (although not all fiestas are open to outsiders).

Mountains Two extinct volcanoes can be seen from Otavalo on clear days: the massive bulk of Volcán Imbabura (4609 metres) to the east and the sharper, more jagged Volcán Cotacachi (at 4939 metres, Ecuador's 11th highest mountain), to the north-west. The locals refer to these peaks as Taita Imbabura and Mama Cotacachi. Legend has it that when it's raining in Otavalo, Taita Imbabura is pissing in the valley.

Another legend suggests that when Mama Cotacachi awakes with a fresh covering of snow, she has been visited by Taita Imbabura during the night.

The Market

The main market day is Saturday. There are three main plazas, with the overflow spilling out onto the streets linking them. The Poncho Plaza is where the goods of most appeal to tourists are sold. Here you can buy woollen goods such as ponchos, blankets, scarves, sweaters, tapestries and gloves as well as a variety of embroidered blouses and shirts, shawls, string bags, rope sandals etc.

Bargaining for every purchase is expected. If you buy several items from the same person, you can expect a discount of 20% or even more if you are good at bargaining. Some people aren't good at it and feel uncomfortable trying to knock a few sucres off an already cheaply priced item. Just remember that it is expected and make an offer a little below the first asking price (assuming you want to buy the thing).

This market gets underway soon after dawn and continues until about 12 noon. You are advised to spend Friday night in Otavalo and get to the market early. It can get rather crowded in mid-morning when the big tour groups arrive and prices are higher. If you come in the early morning there's a greater selection at better prices. Note that there are increasing numbers of pickpockets and bag snatchers at the market – keep your eyes open and your valuables hidden.

The food market sells produce and household goods for the locals, and there is an animal market beginning in the pre-dawn hours (5 to 9 am) on the outskirts of town. These are not designed for tourists but you are welcome to visit them; many people find the sight of poncho-clad Indians quietly bartering for a string of screaming piglets much more interesting than the Poncho Plaza. The animal market is over by early morning, however, so you should plan on an early arrival. It lies over a km out of town – cross the bridge at the end of Morales and follow the crowds to get there.

The popularity of the market is such that there is a smaller market held on Wednesday (mainly for tourists) and selling goes on every day during the peak visitor months of June to August. Stores selling crafts are open daily year round.

Museums

The **Instituto Otavaleño de Antropología** houses a small archaeological museum of the area, a library and a bookshop selling books (in Spanish) about the anthropology and culture of Otavalo. The museum is just off the Panamerican Highway north of town, is free and is open from 8 am to 12 noon from Tuesday to Saturday, and from 2 to 6 pm from Tuesday to Friday.

There is a small **Museo Arqueológico** in the Pensión Los Andes on Montalvo near Roca. This is free for guests of the pensión and there is a modest admission charge for others.

Fiestas

Some small village fiestas date back to pre-Columbian rituals and can last as long as two weeks, with much drinking and dancing. They are not much visited by outsiders and, in some cases, it would be dangerous for tourists to just show up. One little-known annual event involves ritual battle between rival villages – locals may be killed – the authorities turn a blind eye and outsiders are not tolerated.

The 24 June is Saint John the Baptist Day, and 29 June is the Day of Saints Peter and Paul. These and the intervening days are an important fiesta for Otavalo and the surrounding villages. There is a bullfight in Otavalo and a boating regatta on Laguna San Pablo, as well as celebrations in nearby Ilumán.

A few km south-east of Otavalo, on the southern shores of Laguna San Pablo, in the villages around San Rafael, there is a fiesta called Corazas on 19 August. Also in some of the south shore villages is the Pendoneros Fiesta on 15 October.

Otavalo's best-known fiesta is held in the first two weeks of September. The Fiesta del Yamor, as it is known, consists of plenty of music, processions and dancing as well as firework displays, cockfights and election of the Queen of the Fiesta.

Precise dates of these can vary from year to year but they are usually well publicised

Rural scene near Otavalo

and you can find out what's going on from posters. In addition, there are the usual feast days celebrated throughout the land.

Places to Stay

Because Otavalo is such a popular destination, there are many more places to stay than in other, bigger, but less interesting towns. Despite this, it can get rather crowded on Friday night so arrive early for the best choice. Most places are quite cheap, and new hotels open regularly. If you arrive mid-week and plan to stay a few days, a cheaper price can often be negotiated – but late Friday night isn't a good time to expect any favours.

Note that the best hotels are in country haciendas out of town. A rented car is the most convenient way to get to these.

There have been several reports of theft from hotel rooms in Otavalo. Keep your room door locked, even if leaving for just a little while.

Places to Stay – bottom end

One of the most popular cheapies is the friendly *Residencial Santa Martha* (☎ 920 568), Colón 7-04 and 31 de Octubre. It is small and tends to fill up quickly. Beds are about US$1.25 each in quads, and a few cents more in the singles and doubles – but these go really fast. Most of the rooms are large, there's a pretty courtyard, but the showers are only tepid.

A rather larger and also friendly place is the *Pensión Otavalo* on Montalvo near Roca. Actually, it's not that much bigger but the rooms are smaller so there's more of them. There's hot water most of the time and prices are around US$1.50 per person, depending on the room and when you arrive.

The *Residencia Samar-Huasy* at Jaramillo 6-11 and Salinas is conveniently half a block from the Poncho Plaza and has many clean, though small, rooms. Hot showers are available at certain times of day. Rooms (shared showers) are US$1.50 per person.

The *Residencial La Herradura* on Bolívar near Morales has been described by one reader as 'dirty' and by another as 'pretty good, with clean rooms.' There are hot

showers and a restaurant. They tend to lock up early, so let them know if you are going to a peña. Rates are about US$1.80 per person.

If there's no room at any of these hotels you can try the *Pensión Los Andes* at Montalvo near Roca, the *Pensión Imbabura* at Colón near Sucre, the *Pensión Los Angeles* (☎ 920 058) at Colón 4-08 and Bolívar, or the *Residencial Colón* (☎ 920 022) at Colón 1-13 and Ricaurte. All of these are cheap and basic – I haven't heard any rave reviews about them.

The *Hotel Riviera-Sucre* (☎ 920 241) at Moreno 3-14 and Roca is good, clean and popular with budget travellers. It is run by a friendly Belgian-Ecuadorian couple who charge about US$4.50 for a double room. There are hot showers (ask for them), a nice courtyard, a noticeboard, and a map and information are available.

The clean and safe *Residencial Rocío* (☎ 920 584), Morales 11-70 and Egas, is also well recommended by budget travellers. They charge US$2 per person or US$3 per person in rooms with private bath. There is hot water and a nice view from the roof. The owner is friendly and has a van which you can hire for local trips.

The *Hostal San Sebastian* at Roca 9-05 and Morales is run by nice people and has large singles/doubles with bath for US$4/5.50. The *Hostal Los Pendoneros* at Calderón and Bolívar is clean and recommended. They charge US$3 per person and there are plenty of bathrooms with hot water. The restaurant downstairs is popular.

Other reasonable hotels in this price range which have been recommended are the *Residencial Isabelita* at Roca 11-07 and Quiroga; the *Residencial Centenario* (☎ 920 467) at Quiroga 7-03 and 31 de Octubre.

The *Hotel El Indio* (☎ 920 004) at Sucre 12-14 just off the Poncho Plaza is the most expensive of the budget hotels in town. It's clean, has hot water, and there's a restaurant. It is very popular and always full of gringos at weekends, and even mid-week rooms are often not available. Rooms vary in price from about US$5 a double with shared bath to US$10 for a double with private bath, TV and balcony. Don't confuse this hotel with the *Residencial El Indio* at Colón near Sucre. The residencial charges about US$2 per person and is OK but not as good as the hotel.

There are some reasonably priced hotels out of town. One of the best is the charming *Parador Santa Rosa de Molina* which is in the countryside about five or six km northeast of Otavalo. This is a beautiful old building with great views and a chance to get away from it all. Accommodation is about US$4.50 per person, breakfasts are US$1.50 and other meals are US$2.50. A couple of buses a day go by there but it is easier to get there by car. Information, reservations and transportation can be arranged through Rodrigo Mora at Zulaytur.

On the western shores of Laguna San Pablo is the *Hostal Chicapan* (☎ 920 331) which has rooms for about US$9 a double with bath.

Places to Stay – middle

The *Hotel Otavalo* (☎ 920 416) at Roca 5-04 and Montalvo (don't confuse it with the cheap *Pensión Otavalo*) is one of the best in the town centre. It's clean – in fact last time I was in there it smelt overpoweringly of wax polish – and has rooms with private baths and hot water for about US$8/12 for singles/doubles and somewhat less for rooms with shared baths. Breakfast is included. They recommend reservations for the weekend.

The *Hotel Yamor Continental* (☎ 920 451) has clean and spacious rooms in a hacienda-like building set in charming flower-filled gardens at the north-east end of town. There is a small pool and a games area with a miniature golf course and a tennis court. There's a pricey restaurant and bar. Rooms with private bath are about US$15/19 for singles/doubles. There are also family-sized cabins with up to eight beds for US$36. Hot water only runs in the evening and early mornings and you have to make sure that they turn it on; it can take half an hour to warm up. One traveller, however, reports that they had no hot water for four days.

Taxis from the bus station are about US$0.75 or you can walk in 20 minutes. The hotel is only 10 minutes from the Poncho Plaza.

The best hotel in town is the new *Hotel Ali Shungu* (☎ 920 750) which was opened in late 1991. The hotel is at the north-west end of Calle Quito and is owned and operated by a couple of long term US residents of Otavalo. There is a large and attractive patio and garden and the views of Volcán Imbabura are very fine. There are 16 large and comfortable rooms with private baths and plenty of hot water renting for US$17/24. A good restaurant serving vegetarian and meat dishes is on the premises. I have received several recommendations for this hotel.

Another possibility is the *Cabañas del Lago* whose main attraction is their location on the east side of Laguna San Pablo, two or three km north of the village of San Pablo. They have some 15 modern and comfortable cabins with private bath and a restaurant on the premises. Small boats are available for rides or hire. Rates are about US$16 for a double room. Reservations can be made in Quito (☎ 548 477).

Places to Stay – top end

The very popular *Hostería Cusín* is an excellent hotel on the southern outskirts of San Pablo (about 10 km to the south-east of Otavalo). It is a beautiful converted 17th-century hacienda with all the old trimmings. The oldest part of the hacienda dates to 1602 and it was completely remodelled in 1990. There is a cosy bar, a games room, beautiful gardens and horses and mountain bikes available for the guests' use. The Andrango family from Agato have an exclusive crafts shop on the premises.

The hostería is usually booked well ahead for weekends and may be closed midweek. It costs about US$35 per person per night in attractively furnished rooms with bath, some with fireplaces. Delicious home-cooked set meals are included in the price and discounts can be arranged for groups, families, longer stays, students or people wishing to eat elsewhere. Lunches are especially good with traditional soups and local dishes attracting day-trippers from Quito.

Reservations can be made in Quito at Latitud 0° (☎ 440 672) or in the US at Casamolina, 53 East 66th St, New York, NY 10021 (☎/fax (212) 988 4552). The owner, Nick Millhouse, is British and the manager, Marcia Simón, is Ecuadorian – one or the other is usually on the premises.

Places to Eat

There are several good places to eat, meet, and hang out on the Poncho Plaza. The good *Shenandoah* pie shop on the south-west side is OK for snacks and dessert – they have a wide selection of fruit pies and juices but they are not very cheap. There is a notice board and the place is very popular with travellers. Nearby, the Ecuadorian/Austrian-run *La Galería* has a wider range of meals and serves the best expresso in town. *Ali Micui's*, on the north corner of the Poncho Plaza, serves both vegetarian and non-vegetarian food at reasonable prices.

Half a block south-east of the plaza on Salinas is *Tabascos* which is run by an Ecuadorian/US couple. They serve good Mexican food, decent breakfasts, have music some evenings and have a rack of magazines in English to read. The US-run *Parenthese Pizza Restaurant* is on Morales and Sucre, one block from the Poncho Plaza. Apart from home-made vegetarian and meat pizzas, they serve snacks, sandwiches and salads – these last are made with vegetables disinfected in iodine, and can be eaten safely by travellers with sensitive stomachs. There is a notice board and the place is a popular travellers meeting place – except on Tuesday when they are closed.

If you're on a really tight budget, *Mama Rosita's* on Sucre near Montalvo (just off the Main Plaza) is basic and cheap and has been recommended for pancakes. They will reportedly prepare vegetarian meals if ordered in the morning. Another cheapie you might try is the *Copacabana* on the main plaza. If you just want a snack, there's *Chino's Fuente de Soda* on the Main Plaza for ice cream. Next door is the *Royal Cafetería* which is very clean and has good snacks and meals at reasonable prices. The *Café El Triunfo* by the food market on García Moreno and Jaramillo has been recommended for cheap meals and good early breakfasts. During the day the stalls at the food market are probably the cheapest of all.

The chifas are, as usual, good value and there are several in town. The best are the *Casa de Korea* on García Moreno and Roca and the *Tien An Men* on the same block. If you're after fried chicken, try the *Camba Huasy* at Bolívar and Calderón or the *Centro Latino* at Sucre and Calderón. There are several others – none of them seem especially noteworthy. Inexpensive vegetarian food is sold at *Jatun Pacha*, Morales 410 and Sucre, whilst pricier steaks and meat dishes are available at the more elegant *El Mesón del Arrayan*, Sucre and Colón, but it's not always open mid-week. The restaurants at the better hotels are also worth bearing in mind.

The popular and friendly *Restaurant Tuparina Encuentro* at Bolívar 815 and Calderón has been recommended for inexpensive meals and beer – they are affiliated with the Peña Tuparina described later. The *Restaurant Oraibi* is another possibility – see Peña Oraibi under Entertainment. A *Hard Rock Café* has reportedly opened on the Plaza de Ponchos – I haven't had the chance to check this out.

Entertainment

Otavalo is a quiet place during the week but gets livelier on the weekend. There are three cinemas (see map), and some screen English-language films.

On Friday and Saturday nights there's the popular *Amauta Peña* (☎ 920 967) at Jaramillo 6-14 and Salinas near the west corner of the Poncho Plaza. They open around 8 pm but music doesn't get under way until after 10 pm and costs about US$1 cover. The music and ambience can vary from abysmal to enjoyable – take your chances.

The newer *Peña Tuparina – Centro de Difusion Andino*, on Morales near 31 de Octubre, is similar and has received several recommendations from travellers – the cover here is about US$0.50. A third place which has received recommendations for weekend folkloric music is the *Peña Oraibi* (☎ 920 333) at Sucre 10-11 and Colón. They have a restaurant as well.

The *Tucano Peña-Bar* at Morales 5-10 and Sucre has both folkloric and salsa music and often has live or recorded music midweek as well as weekends. The place can get rather wild – machos and drunks may spoil a single woman's evening. Other places to check out include the *Inti Peña Salsateca* on Morales near Roca, and the *Bar La Choza* on Morales near Egas.

Finally, there's the weekly cockfight which costs about US$0.40 and is held in the ring at the west end of 31 de Octubre every Saturday afternoon about 3 pm.

Getting There & Away

Bus From Quito to Otavalo is totally straightforward. There are several companies at the Terminal Terrestre de Cumandá and the buses leave frequently. They all charge about US$0.75 for the two or three-hour ride. The best companies are Transportes Otavalo and Transportes Los Lagos, because they will take you into the town centre. The others tend to go on to Ibarra and will drop you off on the Panamerican Highway, forcing you to walk about a km into town.

From the northern towns of Ibarra or Tulcán you'll find buses leaving for Otavalo every hour or so from their respective terminal terrestres.

In Otavalo, the main bus terminal area is near the strangely named Plaza Copacabana, where you'll probably arrive from Quito on Transportes Los Lagos – a new market is being built here. There is a taxi rank if you need it; US$0.50 will take you to most hotels. This plaza is where you catch return buses to Quito and also old local buses to some of the villages south of Otavalo such as San Pablo del Lago. The deliciously sounding Cooperativa Imbaburapac Churimi Canchic has buses from here to Agato every hour or so.

A couple of blocks away, on Avenida Calderón, you'll find Transportes Otavalo, which has frequent buses to Ibarra (about US$0.20) where you change for buses further north. There are no buses direct to Tulcán at this time. Transportes Otavalo also has many Quito-bound buses. Ask here also for buses to Apuela and García Moreno (see the next paragraph also).

Further down Calderón, at the intersection with 31 de Octubre, you'll find a bunch of rather decrepit buses with people waiting hopefully in them. This is a good place to find out about bus services to Cotacachi, Apuela and many of the remoter towns and villages. Transportes Cotacachi and 6 de Julio go to Cotacachi – 6 de Julio is the faster and charges about US$0.15. Transportes Cotacachi has some buses continuing to Apuela and García Moreno. A truck leaves for these villages daily every morning except Tuesday at about 7 am. Transportes 8 de Septiembre goes to Ilumán. There is no strict schedule to any of these towns and prices are low. Adventurous travellers might just want to get aboard and see what happens – but leave yourself enough time to get back to a hotel, as most of these villages have no accommodation.

Reaching the villages of Calderón, Guayllabamba and Cayambe mentioned earlier in this section is not straightforward. The bus companies running between Otavalo and Quito normally don't sell tickets to intermediate points. You can buy a full-price ticket to Quito and get off where you want, discarding the rest of the ticket. Alternatively, if travelling midweek when there are fewer passengers, just board the bus as it leaves and pay the driver for where you want to go. You'll be dropped off at the turnoff from the main road and will have to walk several hundred metres to the village.

Train There is a railway station, though trains have not run to Quito for many years. Trains to Ibarra stopped running in 1986 but have started again since then and now run sporadically. The fare is marginally cheaper than the bus and you might want to ride the train just for the experience. Departures from Otavalo to Ibarra recently were at 7.30 and 11 am, 3 and 6 pm daily but this is more likely to change than not. It takes about one hour to Ibarra and you can get off in the villages of Peguche or Ilumán if you want.

Taxi You can always hire a taxi from Quito for a few hours and have them take you exactly where you want to go. A taxi for the day can easily be had for US$50 or less if you have any bargaining ability – not too bad if you split it three or four ways.

AROUND OTAVALO

Many of the Indians live and work in the nearby villages of Peguche, Ilumán and Agato (also known as Quinchuquí), which are loosely strung together on the east side of the Panamerican Highway a few km north-east from Otavalo. They can be reached on foot, by bus or taxi, or with a tour. There are many other Otavaleño villages in the area and a visit to the tourist agencies in Otavalo will yield much information. The villages to the south-west of Laguna San Pablo are known for the manufacture of fireworks and tortora reed mats and other reed objects.

Peguche

A popular walk is out of Otavalo to the north and then east off the main highway – you'll be in Peguche in about an hour. Some people go in the hopes of being invited into the Indians' houses and buying the best weavings direct from the loom at bargain prices. That's wishful thinking. Prices aren't much (if at all) lower than Otavalo's, and people have better things to do than invite curious gringos into their houses. On the other hand, the locals are friendly and you might be lucky – especially if you speak Spanish (or Quechua!). One place which may allow visits is Tejidos Mimahuasi, owned by weavers José María Cotacachi and Luz María Fichabamba. They are at stall 61 at the Saturday market in Otavalo.

Another way of reaching Peguche from Otavalo is simply by walking north-east along the railway tracks for about 4 km. Near the railway tracks is the *Cafetería Aya Huma* which serves snacks such as home-made pancakes. On the central plaza of Peguche is the Centro Pachacutic which sometimes has folkloric music concerts. The Cooperativa Imbaburapac Chirumi Canchic has some buses which go through Peguche en route to Agato.

You can continue north-east on foot to Ilumán, four or five km away, or east to Agato, three or four km from Peguche. About one or two km south-east of Peguche are some waterfalls, **Las Casacadas de Peguche**. A trail leads here from the railway line – ask locals for directions.

Agato

Another interesting village to visit is Agato, about four km north of Laguna San Pablo or three km east of Peguche. Here you can find the Tahuantinsuyo Weaving Workshop, run by master weaver Miguel Andrango in his house. He is assisted by his daughter, Luz María, who is an expert in embroidery and designs, and his son-in-law, Licenciado Humberto Romero, who is a specialist in compiling the traditional significance of the various designs used in Otavaleño weaving.

They make traditional weavings on back-strap looms and use handspun wool and natural dyes and products. Almost all other weavers use the upright Spanish loom and/or chemical dyes. Tahuatinsuyo's work is more expensive than the market weavings, however, and is mainly for those seriously interested in textiles. They are not normally sold in the Saturday market but can be bought direct from the weavers at the workshop. They have an outlet at the Hostería Cusín at weekends and orders can be placed by mail at PO Box 53, Otavalo. Visitors to the workshop are often able to see a demonstration of the weaving process. An excursion to Tahuantinsuyo is well recommended to people with knowledge and interest in weaving.

You can get there from Otavalo by

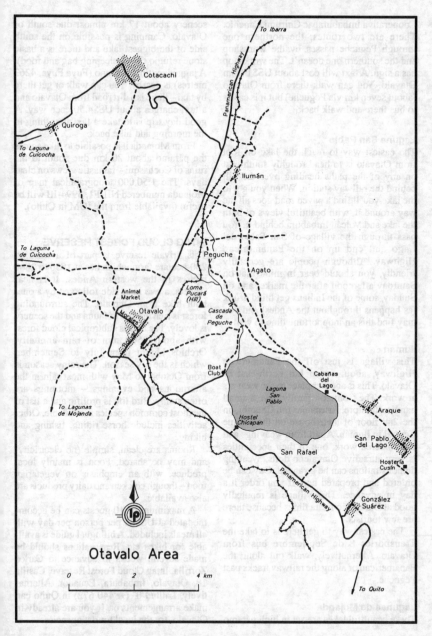

To Ibarra

Panamerican Highway

Cotacachi

Quiroga

To Laguna
de Cuicocha

To Laguna
de Cuicocha

Ilumán

Peguche

Agato

Animal
Market

Otavalo

Morales

Loma
Pucará
(Hill)

Cascada
de Peguche

Boat
Club

Cabañas
del Lago

Laguna
San Pablo

Araque

Hostel
Chicapan

To Lagunas
de Mojanda

San Rafael

San Pablo
del Lago

Hostería
Cusín

Panamerican Highway

González
Suárez

Otavalo Area

0   2   4 km

To Quito

Cooperativa Imbaburapac Chirumi Canchic. There are two routes; the northern one through Peguche passes by the workshop and the southern one doesn't. The workshop has a sign. A taxi will cost about US$1 from Otavalo. You can walk there from Otavalo (about seven km via Peguche) but it is easier to bus there and walk back.

Laguna San Pablo

The easiest way to reach the lake on foot from Otavalo is to head roughly south-east on any of the paths heading over the hill behind the railway station. When you get to the lake you'll find a paved road goes all the way around it, with beautiful views of both the lake and Volcán Imbabura behind it. You pass through the village of San Pablo del Lago and end up on the Panamerican Highway. Although people are generally friendly, you should bear in mind that on Saturday afternoon after the market and on Sunday, some of the Indians get blind drunk (as happens throughout the Andes) and you may find this an inopportune time to visit.

Ilumán

This village is just off the Panamerican Highway, about seven km north-east of Otavalo. This is another place to see weavers at work. The Conterón family have a small handicrafts store, Artesanías Inti Chumbi, on the 2nd floor of their house on the Parque Central in Ilumán. Apart from weavings and embroidered work, one of their specialities is very attractive Otavaleño dolls. Weaving demonstrations can be arranged. Cuy can be ordered and prepared here if you order it a day in advance. This village is reputedly good at Otavaleño fiesta times because there are few tourists.

The easiest way to get here is to take the Transportes 8 de Septiembre bus from Otavalo. Alternatively, walk out along the Panamerican or along the railway tracks past Peguche.

Lagunas de Mojanda

These beautiful lakes are set in high páramo scenery about 17 km almost due south of Otavalo. Camping is possible on the south side of the biggest lake and there is a basic stone refugio (bring sleeping bag and food). A jagged, extinct volcano (Fuya Fuya, 4263 metres) is nearby. You can walk or get there by taxi – there is a dirt road from Otavalo and a taxi charges about US$4.50 each way. A good day trip is to take a taxi first thing in the morning and hike back.

From Mojanda it is possible to hike across the páramo about 20 km due south to the ruins of Cochasqui – fantastic views on clear days. The 1:50,000 topographical map of Mojanda numbered ÑII-F1, 3994-III will be useful (available from the IGM in Quito).

INTAG CLOUD FOREST RESERVE

This private reserve is part of a working 200-hectare farm which lies at 1850 to 2800 metres in the western Andes. It is near Apuela, a two hour ride followed by a one-hour hike from Otavalo. The surrounding forest is rich in flora & fauna and the scenery is lovely. The area is subtropical cloud forest with about 2500 mm of rain annually. Orchids bloom from July to September, which is the dry season. The rainy season is from October to May with most rain in the afternoons and evenings – mornings are often sunny. Bird life is prolific and a list of the most common species is available. Other activities include horse riding, fishing and hiking.

Rooms are clean, simple (no electricity) and may be shared. Food is mainly local produce, with an emphasis on vegetarian food – though chicken and dairy products are also available.

A maximum of 10 guests can be accommodated at US$25 per person per day with all meals included. A bilingual guide is available for hikes etc. Reservations should be made several weeks in advance to Carlos Zorrilla, Intag Cloud Forest Reserve, Casilla 18, Otavalo, Imbabura, Ecuador. Alternatively, Latitud 0° (☎ 440 672) in Quito can make arrangements or, if you are already in Otavalo, try the local tourist agencies.

COTACACHI

This small village, some 15 km north of Otavalo, is famous for its leatherwork. Stores are strung out all along the main street and you can find almost anything you might want in the way of leather goods. Market day is Saturday. Most tourists just pay a quick visit to the stores and return to Ibarra or Otavalo but if you wander around to the right of the main street you'll find an attractive main plaza.

Places to Stay & Eat

The hotel *El Mesón de las Flores* (☎ 915 009, 952 270), at García Moreno and Sucre, is in a lovely building over two centuries old. They charge about US$15 for a double with private bath and there is a good bar/restaurant.

A newer hotel which opened in 1987 is the *Hostería La Mirage* (☎ 915 237), reservations at PO Box 11365, CCNU, Quito. It is an attractive country hotel with antique furniture, bar, restaurant, fireplace, sauna, tennis, horseriding, and tame birds. The hotel is in pleasant gardens almost a km out of town. There are only 12 rooms which cost US$15 for a single, US$22 a double and US$30 for a suite – it has been well recommended. The restaurant here is very good and it is very busy for lunch on Saturday with visitors and groups eating here after their visit to the Otavalo market.

There's also a cheaper restaurant at the corner of the small plaza on the main road. The *Restaurant La Estancia* is next to the hospital and open at weekends. You can eat cuy here. There are no cheap hotels.

Getting There & Away

From Otavalo there are buses about every hour. Camionetas can be hired from the market at the far end of town to take you to various local destinations such as Laguna Cuicocha (about US$2).

RESERVA ECOLÓGICA COTACACHI-CAYAPAS

This huge reserve protects western Andean habitats from Volcán Cotacachi down to the north-western coastal lowlands (see The North Coast chapter for more details). One cannot travel from the highland to lowland part of the reserve except by very difficult bushwhacking. Most visitors either visit the lowlands from San Miguel on the Río Cayapas or the highlands around Laguna de Cuicocha, described later.

LAGUNA DE CUICOCHA

Driving west some 18 km from the town of Cotacachi, you come to an ancient, eroded volcanic crater famous for the deep lake found within. The crater is on the lower southern flanks of Volcán Cotacachi. Just before arriving at the lake, the entrance to the Reserva Ecológica Cotacachi-Cayapas is passed and a US$0.15 entrance fee is paid.

At the lake, cheap boat rides (US$0.30) are available to take you on a half-hour trip around the islands in the middle. On sunny weekends it is often popular with the locals. Just watching everyone hanging around waiting for a boat can be more interesting than the ride itself. The view of the three-km-wide deep blue lake and the extinct Volcán Cotacachi behind it is quite impressive.

A path follows the edge of the lake, sometimes along the shore and often inland because of cliffs. A profusion of flowers attracts hummingbirds and there are orchids. Views of the lake and surrounding mountains are excellent when the weather is good. The trail begins near the reserve entrance booth and circles the lake counter-clockwise. Ask the guards at the booth for details. Allow about six hours for the complete circuit and bear in mind that the path becomes rather faint in places, particularly on the far side of the lake. Consider going as far as the trail is easy to follow and returning how you came.

Places to Stay & Eat

There is a *Parador Cuicocha* on the lakeshore. There is a nowhere to stay but a basic restaurant is open intermittently. Prices are medium to high. Camping is allowed by the lake – inquire at the guard booth for directions.

Getting There & Away

A group can hire a taxi or pickup from Cotacachi for about US$10, including waiting time at the lake and the return trip. One-way fares by taxi or truck are about US$2 from Cotacachi.

You can avoid the main roads (the Panamerican from Otavalo to the Cotacachi turn-off and then the paved road through Cotacachi to the lake) by hiking along the more direct, old, unpaved road between the lake and Cotacachi, or by taking the old road between the lake and Otavalo (a long day hike). The 1:50,000 Otavalo map numbered ÑII-F1, 3994-IV is recommended for this region.

APUELA

Soon after Laguna Cuicocha the road reaches its highest point and begins to drop down the western slopes of the Andes. The scenery is splendidly rugged and this is an opportunity to see some of the remoter and less-visited parts of the highlands. Some 40 km beyond Cuicocha you reach the village of Apuela set in sub-tropical forests at about 2000 metres above sea level. The people are very friendly and will direct you to thermal springs, about an hour's walk away from the village on the main road to the west.

Places to Stay & Eat

There are two cheap and very basic pensiones. The *Hostal Veritas* is on the plaza and the friendly *Residencial Don Luis* is a couple of blocks away up the hill. There is a simple *restaurant* opposite the Residencial Don Luis. There are also basic *cabañas* near the thermal springs, an hour's walk from town.

The Intag Cloud Forest Reserve (described earlier) is in the area before you get to Apuela from Otavalo.

Getting There & Away

There are two or three buses a day from Otavalo and more on Saturday. Buses are often crowded. Try Transportes Otavalo and Transportes Cotacachi. Beyond Apuela there are more remote villages – ask in Apuela about transportation.

IBARRA

Just 22 km north of Otavalo and 115 km north of Quito is the attractive colonial town of Ibarra (population about 80,000). It is the provincial capital of Imbabura. The elevation at the train station is 2210 metres which makes Ibarra several hundred metres lower than most highland cities and gives it a pleasant climate. One of the main reasons for coming here is to take the train from Ibarra to San Lorenzo on the coast.

There's not much to do in Ibarra but I enjoy it because it's so old-fashioned. Horse-drawn carts clatter along cobbled streets flanked by colonial buildings, dark-suited old gentlemen sit in the shady parks discussing the day's events, and most good folks are in bed by 10 pm. It's a relaxing sort of place. Many of Ibarra's houses are in colonial style – red-tiled and whitewashed, they have given Ibarra the nickname of *la ciudad blanca* (the white city).

Market day is Saturday and, because most tourists go to Otavalo on Saturday, the Ibarra market is full of locals. After the market, the local men play an Ecuadorian paddle-ball game near the railway station. It's a strange game played with a small soft ball and large spiked paddles that look like medieval torture implements. I couldn't figure it out.

Ibarra's annual fiesta is held during the last weekend in September when the hotels are often booked ahead.

Orientation & Information

Ibarra can be roughly divided into two areas. The south-east area around the railway station is the busiest and has the bulk of the cheap hotels, while to the west are the main plazas and the older buildings in a generally quieter and more pleasant area.

The CETUR information office is now at Colón 7-43 and Olmedo. The post office is on Flores, just south of the Parque Pedro Moncayo and the IETEL office is half a block west from the parque on Sucre. There is a casa de cambio (Polycambios) on Olmedo and Oviedo, and the Banco Continental on Olmedo and Colón will change money, but it's best to bring enough sucres with you.

Streets in Ibarra are both numbered and named. Roughly, north-south streets are numbered calles, and west-east streets are numbered carreteras. Both numbers and names are used on the street signs but names seem more widely accepted. I use names throughout this section.

Note that Ibarra is slowly going through the process of changing its telephone prefixes from 950 and 951 to 955 (and possibly 956). Some places are still using the old prefixes but may change by the time you read this. If you have problems with the 950 or 951 prefixes, try the others and see if that helps.

Things to See

The **Parque La Merced** (also known as Peñaherrera) has a small museum and a church with a famous image of the **Virgin of La Merced** – a huge statue on top of the building. Inside, there is an ornate altar. In the middle of the park there is a bust of Victor Manuel Peñaherrera (1865 – 1930), the Ibarra-born university professor who was Deacon of the Faculty of Law in the Central University and a judge on the Supreme Court during his lifetime.

The larger, tree-filled **Parque Pedro Moncayo** is dominated by the cathedral. Pedro Moncayo (1807-1888) was an Ibarra-born journalist and diplomat.

Out at the north end of Bolívar is the quaint little **Plazoleta Boyacá** with a monument to Simón Bolívar to commemorate his victory at the Battle of Ibarra on 17 July 1823 – it depicts the incongruous scene of an Andean condor attacking an African lion.

Behind the plazoleta is the modern concrete block church of **Santo Domingo** topped by a huge statue of Saint Dominic with a giant rosary swinging in the wind. Some people may enjoy viewing the paintings in the rather garish interior. A few of the paintings seem rather tongue-in-cheek: an old-fashioned representation of Jesus throwing the moneylenders out of the temple depicts one of the throng clutching a bag

marked '$1000 Petroleo'. The church also has a museum of religious art (open 9 am to 12 noon, 3 to 6 pm, Tuesday to Saturday – a small admission charge).

Also worth seeing is the ruined church of **La Dolorosa** on Sucre and Mosquera. This was built in 1928 but the domed roof collapsed during the earthquake of 1987. Now, closed and silent, the church and it's gaping roof are testimony to nature's forces.

Apart from visiting these plazas and churches, there's not much to do. The small, private **Museo Archaeológico** can be entered through the back of the La Estancia restaurant on the Plaza La Merced – it is closed on Sunday and Monday. There are a couple of cinemas. Ibarra is a good base from which to visit some of the nearby villages and to wait for the train to the coast.

Places to Stay – bottom end

There are many cheap hotels in Ibarra. The highest concentration of places to stay is near the railway station. Many cost only a dollar or so but are not particularly attractive – basic, noisy with train traffic, and usually with only cold water. There are a few decent budget hotels, however.

A popular place with budget travellers is *Hotel Imbabura* at Oviedo 9-33 and Narváez. It is friendly and has a delightful little courtyard with flowers, a fish pond and birds. The best rooms are on the quiet street, at US$1.40 per person. The rather dark inside rooms are US$1 per person. There's hot water.

Don't confuse this with the more basic *Residencial Imbabura*, at Flores 9-53 and Narváez, which is US$1 each and quite clean but has only cold water.

Almost next door to the Hotel Imbabura is the rather dark and uninviting-looking *Residencial Los Ceibos*, at Oviedo 9-53, which also charges US$1 and has only cold water. Another reasonably clean but basic cold-water cheapie is the *Residencial Imperial* (not to be confused with the Imperio) at Bolívar 6-22 and Flores. They charge about US$1.20 per person.

Also there are the similar *Residencial San*

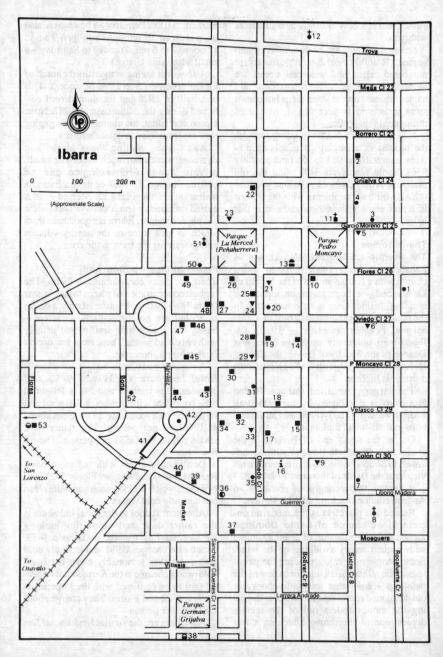

Ibarra

0   100   200 m

(Approximate Scale)

Troya

Mejía Cl 22

Borrero Cl 23

Grijalva Cl 24

Garció Moreno Cl 25

*Parque
La Merced
(Peñaherrera)*

*Parque
Pedro
Moncayo*

Flores Cl 26

Oviedo Cl 27

P Moncayo Cl 28

Velasco Cl 29

Colón Cl 30

Liborio Madera

Mosquera

Guerrero

Larrera Andrade

*Parque
German
Grijalva*

Villasis

Narvaez

Flores

Bolivar

Market

Olmedo Cr 10

Sanchez y Cifuentes Cr 11

Bolívar Cr 9

Sucre Cr 8

Rocafuerte Cr 7

To
San
Lorenzo

To
Otavalo

```
■  PLACES TO STAY

    2  Residencial Yahuarcocha        9  Crema Juguetaría
   10  Residencial Imperial          21  Restaurant La Chagra
   14  Residencial Vaca              23  Restaurant La Estancia
   15  Hostal El Ejecutivo           24  Café Pushkin
   17  Residencial San Lorenzo       29  Manolo's
   18  Residencial Los Alpes         32  Heladería La Nevada
   19  Residencial Imperio           33  Rincón Familiar
   22  Hotel Nueva Colonia
   25  Residencial Majestic              OTHER
   26  Hotel Berlin
   27  Residencial El Principe        1  Frederico Café Musical
   28  Residencial Madrid             3  Cine Grand Colombia
   30  Residencial Madrid             4  IETEL
   32  Pensión Olmedo 1               7  Public Hot Baths
   34  Residencial Atahualpa          8  Ruined Church of La Dolorosa
   37  Hotel Ibarra                  11  Cathedral
   39  Residencial Tahuando          12  Plazoleta Boyaca & Church of Santo
   40  Pensión Olmedo 2                  Domingo
   43  Pensión Varsovia              13  Post Office
   44  Residencial Colón             16  CETUR Tourist Information
   45  Residencial Guayas            20  Polycambios
   46  Hotel Imbabura                23  Museo Archaeológico
   47  Residencial Los Ceibos        31  El Encuentro Bar
   48  Residencial Primavera         35  Banco Continental
   49  Residencial Imbabura          36  Buses 28 de Septiembre & San
   53  To: Hotel Ajaví (600 metres), Hostal   Miguel de Ibarra
       Imbacocha, Hostería San Agustín,  38  Buses to La Esperanza
       Hostería Chorlavi             41  Railway Station
                                     42  Obelisk
▼  PLACES TO EAT                     50  Taxis Lagos
                                     51  Church of La Merced
    5  Luchino Pizza & Bar           52  Cine Popular
    6  Bar Restaurant El Dorado      53  To Terminal Terrestre (1200 metres),
                                         Otavalo (21 km)
```

Lorenzo at Olmedo 10-56 and Colón and *Residencial El Principe* (☎ 952 786) at Sánchez y Cifuentes 8-82 and Oviedo.

If you are really broke, try the *Residencial Guayas* at P Moncayo 8-54 and Narváez. They provide tolerable rooms for US$0.90 per person. If you stay in a place with cold water and want a hot shower you can always go to the public baths on Sucre and Guerrero which are open from 6 am to 9 pm daily.

There are plenty of other basic places with cold water which charge about US$0.90 to US$1.50 per person – none of them are particularly good and some are pretty bad. If you are desperate for cheap accommodation try

the following, arranged in roughly descending order of attractiveness: *Pensión Varsovia* and *Residencial Atahualpa* at Sánchez y Cifuentes and Velasco; *Residencial Primavera* at Sánchez y Cifuentes and Oviedo; *Residencial Yahuarcocha* at Sucre and Grijalva; *Pensión Olmedo 1* at Velasco 8-55 and Olmedo; *Pensión Olmedo 2* on Guerrero by the railway station; and on the same block the *Residencial Tahuando* which was described by one traveller as 'very poor and, literally, stinking'.

For a little more money you can do better. There are three simple hotels which all charge about US$1.75 to US$2 per person, are clean, and have hot (or at least tepid) water. All three have rooms with private baths and may have a few rooms with shared baths for a few cents less. The *Hotel Berlin*, at Flores 8-51 on the Parque La Merced, has spacious rooms and tepid showers. Some of the front rooms have little balconies and views of the park. The *Residencial Majestic* (☎ 950 052), at Olmedo 7-63 and Oviedo, has good hot water as does the *Residencial Vaca* (☎ 950 854) at Bolívar 7-53 and P Moncayo.

The popular *Residencial Colón* (☎ 950 093), at Narváez 8-62 and Velasco, is clean, friendly, pleasant and has warm showers. Rooms with a private bath are US$2.80 per person and with a shared bath about US$2.30 per person. They'll do your laundry for you. This hotel is often full by mid-afternoon. The *Residencial Los Alpes* at Velasco 7-32 and Olmedo is also in this price range and is OK.

There are several reasonably priced hotels which provide you with a little luxury if you're getting fed up with always slumming it. Most of these hotels are a good deal and would be priced at the mid-range category in other, more expensive towns. All have hot water. For example, the clean *Residencial Imperio* (not to be confused with the Imperial) (☎ 952 929), at Olmedo 8-54 and Oviedo, charges a reasonable US$3.50/5.50 for single/double rooms with a private bath and sometimes a TV!

For some reason there are two residenciales Madrid. The *Residencial Madrid* (☎ 951 760) on Olmedo 8-57 and Oviedo charges US$3.50/6.50 for singles/ doubles with private bath; many of the rooms are carpeted and have TV, but there are few singles available. Around the corner, *Residencial Madrid* (☎ 952 177) on P Moncayo 7-41 and Sánchez y Cifuentes offers phones in the rooms and charges US$5.50/8.50 for singles/doubles with bath or US$3 per person in rooms with shared bath.

The best hotels in the town centre include the nice-looking *Hotel Nueva Colonia* (☎ 952 918, 955 543), Olmedo 5-19 and Grijalva. They charge US$4.50 per person in carpeted rooms with private bath and telephone. There is a restaurant. The *Hostal El Ejecutivo* (☎ 956 575), Bolívar 9-69 and Velasco is quite good for US$7.50/9.50 for singles/doubles with bath, or between US$3.25 and US$4.75 per person in rooms with shared bath, depending on the room. Finally, the *Hotel Ibarra* (☎ 955 091, 953 475), Mosquera 6-158 and Sánchez y Cifuentes, has comfortable rooms with private bath and telephone for US$4.50/8 a single/double. They have a restaurant. One traveller complained, however, that they were charged US$14 for a double room in this hotel, which is too much and not worth the money.

Places to Stay – middle & top end

The better hotels are west of town, on or just off the Panamerican Highway heading to Otavalo. The first-class *Hotel Ajaví* (☎ 955 221/787) is halfway between town and the bus terminal, about one km west of the town centre. The hotel is modern and boasts a good restaurant and bar, swimming pool, sauna and relatively luxurious rooms for about US$18/23 for singles/doubles. In front of the Ajaví is the newly opened *Hostal Imbacocha* (☎ 950 800 or 955 800) which is comfortable but less fancy and about half the price. A km beyond the bus terminal is the *Hostería San Agustín* (☎ 951 888 or 955 888) in a pretty site 200 or 300 metres off the Panamerican Highway. They have a decent restaurant and pleasant rooms for about US$16/20 a single/double.

A km further is the best hotel in the Ibarra area, the *Hostería Chorlaví* (☎ 950 777 or 955 777; 522 703 in Quito). This has old-world charm; it is in a converted hacienda and has pretty gardens, a swimming pool and an excellent restaurant/bar. They have a famous buffet-style lunch with folk music on weekends, which is very popular with well-off Ecuadorians and tour groups after the Otavalo market – perhaps a bit too touristy for some travellers' tastes. There are both rooms in the old hacienda building and cabins in the grounds. Rates are about

Top: Monastery of San Francisco, Quito (RR)
Left: Presidential Palace guard, Quito (RR)
Right: Independence Plaza, Quito (RR)

Top: Climbing Cotopaxi (RR)
Left: Old Quito and Mt Cayambe (RR)
Right: Virgin of Quito, Panecillo (RR)

US$18/26 for singles/doubles depending on the room. Meals are about US$6.

The good hotels are often booked well in advance, particularly at weekends. Make reservations if possible.

Places to Eat

A good place to start the day off is *Café Pushkin*, on Olmedo 7-75 between Flores and Oviedo, which has decent breakfasts and fresh home-made bread. There are several other cafés on the same block serving breakfasts and snacks. There are also some good and inexpensive chifas and chicken restaurants on this block as well as the *Restaurant La Chagra*, Olmedo 7-48, which is low to medium priced, has big helpings, and is popular with the locals.

The *Luchino Pizza & Bar* on the Parque Pedro Moncayo is as much a bar as a restaurant, but they do serve pizza as advertised – it has been recommended. A new *pizzería* has opened at P Moncayo 630 and Bolívar – I haven't checked it out but it is reportedly good.

Also recommended is *Manolo's* at the corner of P Moncayo and Olmedo – it is popular with students and young people, serves snacks and beer, and has a friendly English-speaking owner. An inexpensive and clean restaurant is the *Rincón Familiar* on Olmedo near Velasco. For desserts, juices and ice cream, try the *Crema Juguetaría* at Colón 6-79 and Bolívar or the *Heladería Nevada* on Velasco near Olmedo.

The *Bar Restaurant El Dorado*, on Oviedo near Sucre, is trying to be the best place in town, judging by the white tablecloths and shining silverware. The meals, especially the seafood, are good and medium priced. Traditionally, the 'best' in town is the *Restaurant La Estancia* at García Moreno 7-66 on the Parque La Merced. It has old-world atmosphere and has medium-priced steaks, but has a hard time in competing with the El Dorado. The better hotels (out of town) serve excellent meals.

Entertainment

Ibarra is a quiet city and even on a Saturday night there is little going on. There are a couple of cinemas. A popular bar to hang out in is the *El Encuentro* at Olmedo 9-35 near Velasco. They have a rustic ambience (old leather saddles and strange implements hang from the walls) and music occasionally. A quieter bar is *Frederico Café Musical* at Rocafuerte 6-29 and Flores. Occasionally peñas are advertised .

Getting There & Away

Bus Buses from Quito leave from the Terminal Terrestre de Cumandá all day long, once or twice an hour. The trip can take from 2½ to four hours, depending on the company. The fastest is Transportes Andinos but the buses are small and uncomfortable and you feel like the driver has suicidal tendencies. Other companies will take you more slowly and safely. They all charge about US$1. There are also frequent buses from Otavalo and Tulcán.

In Ibarra, the main terminal terrestre for buses is on the Panamerican Highway about 1½ km west of the town centre. Buses from Quito and Otavalo will drop you here. If you are arriving from Tulcán you could get off before the terminal to save backtracking. There's little in the way of accommodation near the terminal. A taxi to the centre will cost well under a dollar. There are local buses for about US$0.05 which leave from outside the terminal. They all go within a couple of blocks of the railway station where there are plenty of hotels.

From the bus terminal there are frequent departures for Quito, Tulcán (US$1.10, 2½ hours) and Otavalo (US$0.20, 30 minutes). Two or three times a day there are buses direct to several other major towns – these trips usually involve a stop in Quito but save you having to look for another bus terminal in the capital.

There are four daily buses to Esmeraldas, for example, if you can't get on the train to San Lorenzo. There are also buses to less important towns such as Tumbabiro – ask at the terminal. Buses for Otavalo with Transportes Otavalo also leave from the left side of the Panamerican as you leave town, about ¾ km from the centre.

Rail It used to be that you could get from Quito to Ibarra by train, but this service has been discontinued for some years now. An autoferro runs irregularly between Ibarra and Otavalo – recently, there were four daily departures for the one-hour ride, but this is liable to change.

The train service of most interest is the Ibarra-San Lorenzo railway which links the highlands with the coast. The train is usually an autoferro (a converted school bus mounted onto a railway chassis). There is usually only one departure a day (6.30 am; US$0.90) so seats are limited, although a second and even a third train may sometimes be added. It is worth trying to make a reservation on the previous day, although normally you are told that you must buy tickets on the day of departure. This is notoriously difficult – huge crowds of people push and shove to try and get their money into the tiny opening in the ticket grille and you have to be pretty obnoxious to obtain a ticket. There are always thieves working the crowds – keep valuables well hidden on your body and luggage to a minimum.

The journey is scheduled to take about seven hours but in reality often takes twice as long. Delays caused by landslides, breakdowns and cows on the track are the norm. If there are two trains leaving, try and get on the first one because most of the line is single track and so a broken down train will block the train behind it. Every few weeks, a landslide will close the track for a few days and getting tickets for the next available train isn't easy. In short, it can be an exciting trip.

The scenery en route is quite spectacular. You drop from Ibarra at 2210 metres to San Lorenzo at sea level 193 km away. Thus you see a good cross-section of Ecuador. Most of the drop occurs during the first half of the trip as you descend along the Río Mira valley with good whitewater views on the right of the train. At several stops fruit and other food can be purchased but a water bottle and some emergency food is advised.

There is a passport check in Lita (see The North Coast chapter). Once in San Lorenzo you can return the way you came or continue along the north coast by boat – there are no roads.

If the weather looks at all reasonable, ride up on the roof of the train for excitement and great views – it can be a struggle to get on but try.

Recently, the track was closed, partly for repair and partly because of a road building project. In this case, trains may run only every other day or the train company may provide buses to a station a couple of hours drive down the line. This happened to me recently, but since then I have had reports both that the train goes daily, all the way, and that buses go all the way to Lita before the train is boarded.

Taxi If you are in a real hurry to get back to Quito you could use Taxis Lagos (☎ 951 150) on the Parque La Merced. They charge about US$3 and cram six passengers into a large taxi. The taxis leave five or six times a day for the 2¼-hour ride.

Getting Around
Bus Local buses leave for the main terminal three or four times an hour from near the railway station. They leave from Guerrero and Sánchez y Cifuentes and are usually marked for the terminal – if in doubt ask the driver. Two companies run this route: 28 de Septiembre and San Miguel de Ibarra. Some of their buses continue to San Antonio de Ibarra. Different buses leave from the same street for several other local destinations. An exception is the bus to La Esperanza, which leaves about once an hour from Parque German Grijalva near the east end of Avenida Sánchez y Cifuentes.

SAN ANTONIO DE IBARRA
This village, which is almost a suburb of Ibarra, is famous for its woodcarving. It has a pleasant main square around which are found a number of stores, poorly disguised as 'workshops'. The most famous is the

Galería Luís Potosí, which has some of the best carvings.

Señor Potosí is famous throughout Ecuador and sells his work all over the world. Some of his pieces are very well done and sell for hundreds of dollars – the best carvings are to be seen in the upstairs section of his gallery. The atmosphere is totally relaxed; there's no high-pressure salesperson breathing down your neck while you inspect the work.

A warning though – should you decide to purchase a large carving and have it shipped home, it's best to arrange for the shipping yourself. Some friends of mine bought a carving, left a deposit for it to be shipped back, and found out many months later that their carving had been sold to someone else a few days later. They received their deposit back but were very disappointed – their once-in-a-lifetime art investment had been sold to someone who paid cash and carried it out. That's Latin America!

There's little wood found in the Ibarra area so most of it comes from the Ecuadorian jungles. A type of cedar and walnut are among the more frequently used woods. Various subjects are depicted but the favourites seem to be beggars, religious statues and nude women – again, that's Latin America!

Not all the pieces are expensive and you can buy small, mass-produced carvings for a couple of dollars if you like that sort of thing. Some people recommend that the best deals and selections are to be found on the streets away from the main square. Frankly, I couldn't see any difference.

Places to Stay & Eat

The only place is the cheapish *Hostería Los Nogales* – most people stay in Ibarra or Otavalo. There are no proper restaurants in San Antonio de Ibarra – one place, a block off the main plaza, serves greasy hamburgers and hot dogs.

Getting There & Away

Transportation from Ibarra is frequent during day-light hours. Buses drop you off at the main plaza. The 15-minute ride costs just a few cents. Or you could walk the five km or so west on the Panamerican from Ibarra.

LA ESPERANZA

This is a pretty little village in the country six or seven km due south of Ibarra. It is a good place to stay for budget travellers looking for peace and quiet. There's nothing to do except talk to the locals and take walks in the surrounding countryside. It's supposed to be a good place to look for the San Pedro cactus.

Volcán Imbabura (4609 metres) is about nine km to the south-west as the crow flies. It is easier to climb this mountain from La Esperanza than from the Laguna San Pablo side. The nine km look deceptively close – remember that you are not a flying crow and that the summit is about 2000 metres higher than La Esperanza. There is a maze of tracks heading towards the summit but you'll have to scramble the last bit – ask the locals for directions. Allow about 10 hours for the round trip including time at the top for photographs of Laguna San Pablo way below you.

If Imbabura seems like too ambitious of a climb, try Loma Cubilche (3836 metres). This hill is about eight km almost due south of La Esperanza – easier and also with good views. If climbing doesn't appeal to you at all, you can take the cobbled road through pretty countryside to the south – buses go along here occasionally.

Places to Stay & Eat

There is only one very basic but friendly hotel which costs a little over US$1 per person – the *Casa Aida*. You can get good, simple and cheap meals here. This is a good place to get information and directions for local walks. There is also the small *Restaurant María* which can rent you a basic room.

Getting There & Away

Buses serve the village frequently along a cobbled country road from Ibarra (US$0.10) and irregularly continue further south through Olmedo to Cayambe.

NORTH OF IBARRA

As you drive north from Ibarra on the Panamerican Highway you soon pass the highly touted tourist site of Lago Yaguarcocha – Quechua for 'lake of blood'. It was so called after a battle between the Incas and the Caras, when the latter's bodies were supposedly thrown into the lake, turning the water red. There's not much to see except for a race track around the lake – it is used for auto racing during the annual fiesta at the end of September. You can walk there in a couple of hours from Ibarra (head east on Oviedo to the edge of town, cross the river, and head north) or take a taxi (about US$1). There is a good hotel on the edge of the lake, the *Cabañas Conquistador* (☎ 951 500 or 955 500). Rooms are about US$12 for a double with bath and there is a restaurant.

The Panamerican soon drops quite steeply to the Río Chota valley at about 1565 metres before beginning the long climb to San Gabriel at almost 2900 metres. The warm and dusty **Chota** area is inhabited by reserved but friendly Black people who make a living growing fruit – plenty for sale. The Blacks were originally slaves imported and bred by the Jesuits in the 17th century – I guess it wasn't considered immoral back then. Chota is less than an hour from Ibarra and can be visited on day trips. Fiestas and concerts in Chota may occasionally be advertised in Ibarra – the music is a weird and wonderful mix of plaintive Andean and driving African sounds. Worth hearing if you get the chance.

After leaving Chota, the Panamerican crosses the provincial line from Imbabura into Carchi. The little town of Bolívar, capital of the canton of the same name, is soon passed followed a few km later by the village of **La Paz**. Near La Paz are thermal springs and waterfalls as well as a grotto containing a famous statue of the Virgin and stalactites. There are buses to the springs from Tulcán or walk about five km southeast of the Panamerican Highway from La Paz on a signed road for the 'Grutas'. The complex (thermal springs, pool, and grotto) is open from Thursday to Sunday. There is reportedly a hotel open sporadically near the grotto, though I haven't checked it personally (send me a postcard if you go there). The road in this area is steep, winding and rather slow, and the scenery is wild.

SAN GABRIEL

This is the next town of any size north of Ibarra on the Panamerican Highway. It's almost 90 km away from Ibarra but only 38 km from the border town of Tulcán. It's not a particularly interesting place but I mention it here because Tulcán hotels can occasionally be full and this is the nearest place to stay. It's also a good place to go if you want to be the only gringo in town.

At San Gabriel there is a bus stop on the Panamerican Highway; many buses don't enter the town. Walk up the hill on Calle Montalvo for two blocks, then turn right onto Calle Bolívar, which is the main street. Walk three blocks, passing the church, until you reach the Plaza Central. Here there is a startling nude statue of Bolívar, the liberator – imagine a nude George Washington in a small US town.

Places to Stay & Eat

The *Residencial Montúfar* (☎ 990 385), which charges US$1.25 and doesn't have water (perhaps it has improved since I checked it), is on the plaza at Colón 03-44. Better is the *Residencial Ideal* (☎ 990 265), which costs about the same and has hot water in the mornings. It's on Calle Montúfar 08-26, half a block from the plaza. Also on the plaza are two or three simple restaurants, the IETEL office and a movie theatre.

Getting There & Away

The Ciudad de San Gabriel bus company is also on the plaza and has buses to Quito every 45 minutes from 3 am to 6.30 pm. The five-hour ride is about US$1.30. For buses to Tulcán it's best to wait on the Panamerican Highway.

TULCÁN

This small city of about 40,000 inhabitants is the provincial capital of Carchi. As you drive through this, the northernmost province of the Ecuadorian highlands, you see plenty of farms and ranches, particularly as you get close to Tulcán. It is therefore an important market town, but for most travellers its importance is mainly as the gateway city into Ecuador from Colombia, some seven km away.

With the present favourable rate of exchange of the Colombian peso against the Ecuadorian sucre, Tulcán has become very popular for Colombian weekend bargain hunters. There is a Sunday street market (few tourist items) and the hotels are often full of Colombian shoppers on Saturday night.

Tulcán lies almost 3000 metres above sea level and hence has a rather cold climate. It is the highest provincial capital or town of its size in the country.

Orientation & Information

There is no tourist information office in town (though basic information is available at the border crossing point, seven km away). In fact, Tulcán is not a particularly interesting town and most travellers continue on to Colombia or south into Ecuador. There are, however, some interesting trips in the vicinity, described at the end of this chapter.

The town is a long and narrow one with most things happening on or just off the parallel streets of Bolívar and Sucre, which run from the north-east to the south-west of Tulcán. There appear to be two numbering systems for street addresses – to avoid confusion I will not give street numbers in this section but will refer to the nearest street intersections instead.

The main IETEL telephone office is on Olmedo near Junín and there is also a branch at the bus terminal, south-west of town. The post office is on Bolívar near Junín. The Colombian Consulate (☎ 980 559) is on Bolívar between Junín and Ayacucho. They are supposedly open from 8.30 am to 12.30 pm and 2.30 to 4 pm Monday through Friday. Often it's difficult to find them open – it's better to check the consulate in Quito for visa requirements.

Money Money exchange is best in Tulcán rather than at the border, except at weekends when you are at the mercy of the street changers. The bus running between Tulcán and the border will accept both Colombian and Ecuadorian currency. Banco de los Andes, on Sucre and 10 de Agosto, is reputedly the only bank doing foreign exchange, but for some reason they are not always able to do so.

There are several exchange houses which pay about 4% less than you can get in Quito. The best known is Casa de Cambio Rodrigo Paz, on Ayacucho near Bolívar, which will exchange both pesos and dollars (including travellers' cheques at a 1% discount). There are several others nearby; most give rates within 1% of one another. The casas de cambio are closed from 12 noon to 2.30 pm for lunch.

There are also street changers with their little black attaché cases full of money. They hang out around the border, the banks and the bus terminal. Because there is no real black market, you won't get much better rates from them than from the exchange houses.

If leaving Ecuador, it is best to try and change sucres to dollars and then dollars to pesos when you get to Colombia. If arriving, cash dollars are your strongest currency.

Things to See

The big tourist attraction in town is the **topiary garden** in the cemetery. Topiary is a form of gardening where bushes and trees are trimmed into animal or geometrical shapes. The Tulcán cemetery is the most striking example of this work in Ecuador, and one of the best in Latin America. Behind the cemetery the locals play the strange Ecuadorian paddle-ball game (described briefly under Ibarra) at weekends.

Parque Isidro Ayora has a rather striking white **statue of Abdón Calderón** riding a horse. Calderón was a battle-hardened 18-year-old lieutenant fighting against the Spanish Royalists at the decisive Battle of Pichincha, which cemented Ecuador's independence on 24 May 1822. He is famous not

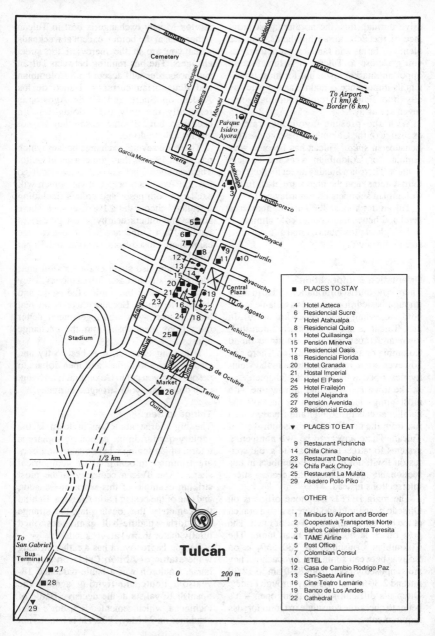

Cemetery

To Airport
(1 km) &
Border (6 km)

Parque
Isidro
Ayora

García Moreno

Central
Plaza

Stadium

Market

1/2 km

To
San Gabriel

Bus
Terminal

Tulcán

0   200 m

■ PLACES TO STAY

4   Hotel Azteca
6   Residencial Sucre
7   Hotel Atahualpa
8   Residencial Quito
11 Hotel Quillasinga
15 Pensión Minerva
17 Residencial Oasis
18 Residencial Florida
20 Hotel Granada
21 Hostal Imperial
24 Hotel El Paso
25 Hotel Frailejón
26 Hotel Alejandra
27 Pensión Avenida
28 Residencial Ecuador

▼ PLACES TO EAT

9   Restaurant Pichincha
14 Chifa China
23 Restaurant Danubio
24 Chifa Pack Choy
25 Restaurant La Mulata
29 Asadero Pollo Piko

OTHER

1   Minibus to Airport and Border
2   Cooperativa Transportes Norte
3   Baños Calientes Santa Teresita
4   TAME Airline
5   Post Office
7   Colombian Consul
10 IETEL
12 Casa de Cambio Rodrigo Paz
13 San-Saeta Airline
16 Cine Teatro Lemarie
19 Banco de Los Andes
22 Cathedral

only for his youthfulness, but for his tenacity during the battle. Historians report that he was shot in the right arm, causing him to wield his sword with his left hand. A second bullet in the left arm made him drop his sword, but he continued fighting after having one of his soldiers tie the sword to his arm. A third shot in the left leg didn't stop him either. Finally, a bullet tore apart his right leg just as the battle was ending victoriously. He died the next day, and was promoted to captain posthumously.

There's one movie theatre. If that's not enough to keep you enthralled, you can call your mother from the IETEL office or send your first/last postcards from Ecuador through the post office.

Places to Stay

The influx of Colombian visitors has led to an increase in the number of hotels – at least six have opened since the last edition of this book. There aren't any fancy hotels in Tulcán, however, and almost all are bottom end. Several lack hot water and others have hot showers only at certain times of day.

As usual in highland towns, there are public hot baths (*Baños Calientes Santa Teresita* on Atahualpa) which you can use if you can't face a freezing cold shower and the hot-water hotels are all full.

Saturday evening is a rotten time to arrive in Tulcán, as many hotels are completely full, mainly with Colombian visitors. The next town is San Gabriel, some 40 minutes away. There are two basic hotels there.

Places to Stay – bottom end

The *Residencial Quito* (☎ 980 541), on Ayacucho at Bolívar, is one of the better of the cheapest hotels – hot water is available at times. They charge about US$1.50 per person and rooms with private bath are a few cents more. Others at about this price include the *Pensión Minerva* at 10 de Agosto and Bolívar and the *Hotel Granada* on Bolívar near 10 de Agosto, both of which are basic and dingy cold water hotels. Some more recently opened cheap hotels which may have hot water are the *Residencial Florida*

on Sucre near 10 de Agosto, *Residencial Sucre* on Junín near Bolívar and *Hostal Imperial* on Bolívar and Pichincha.

There are two hotels out by the main bus terminal (just across the street). The *Pensión Avenida* is the cheapest place in town at US$1.20 each. Although it has only cold water, the staff are friendly. The *Residencial Ecuador* has quite nice rooms but a very erratic water supply. It costs US$1.50 and US$2.50 per person for rooms without and with private baths. There's supposed to be hot water but I once stayed there and they didn't even have cold, so check the water supply before accepting the room.

Several reasonably priced hotels have hot water (or are supposed to, at least some of the time). One of the best of these is the *Residencial Oasis* (☎ 980 342), on 10 de Agosto and Sucre, which costs just under US$3 per person in rooms with shared bathrooms. If you want a room with a bath you'll pay about US$1 extra. Another good place is the *Hotel El Paso* (☎ 981 094), on Sucre at Pichincha, which has good clean rooms for US$2 per person (shared baths) or US$3 (private baths). They have hot water and the hotel fills up very fast, especially at weekends.

Other reasonable hotels in the US$2 to US$3 per person range, all with hot water and with some rooms having a private bath, are the *Hotel Quillasinga* (☎ 981 892) on Sucre at Ayacucho, the *Hotel Alejandra* (☎ 981 784) on Sucre near Quito and the slightly cheaper *Hotel Atahualpa* on Bolívar near Junín.

The best hotel in the bottom-end category is the *Hotel Azteca* (☎ 981 447) on Bolívar near Atahualpa. They charge about US$5.50/8.50 for singles/doubles with bath and hot water.

Places to Stay – middle

The best hotel in Tulcán is currently the *Hotel Frailejón* (☎ 980 129, 981 149) on Sucre near Rocafuerte. Rooms with bath, hot water, and TV are US$7.50/12 for singles/doubles. There is a decent restaurant.

With the increase in the number of hotels

in recent years, I would not be surprised if another mid-range hotel opened in the near future.

Places to Stay – near the border

The best place to stay in the Tulcán area is near the border, six km away from town. The *Complejo Turistico Rumichaca* (☎ 980 276) is half a km away from the border and offers a swimming pool (US$0.50 for non-residents), restaurant, bar, discotheque and supposedly a casino if you can find someone to open it. Prices are US$10/$14 for singles/doubles with bath.

Places to Eat

Tulcán isn't one of this planet's culinary centres. Many restaurants only open for lunch and supper and close in mid-afternoon. Monday night is a particularly poor night to go out in search of gastronomic adventures as most of the restaurants are closed.

The best restaurant in town is the pricey *La Mulata* in the Hotel Frailejón. In the town centre there are the usual chifas, of which the *Chifa Pack Choy* beneath the Hotel El Paso isn't bad at all. Another is the *Chifa China* on 10 de Agosto near Sucre. For more Ecuadorian-style food, the cheap *Restaurant Danubio*, on Pichincha near Bolívar, is OK but has a limited menu. Another cheap and reasonable place is the *Restaurant Pichincha* on Sucre and Junín. The main bus terminal has a restaurant which is not always open and is nothing to write home about when it is, but at least it's cheap. Nearby is a basic chicken restaurant, the *Asadero Pollo Piko*.

Out by the border there are a bunch of stalls selling snacks, but no restaurants (except in Complejo Turistico Rumichaca).

Crossing the Colombian Border

You don't need to obtain an exit or entry stamp in the town of Tulcán. All formalities are taken care of at the Ecuador-Colombia border, 6½ km away at Rumichaca (a new highway is under construction which will shorten the drive by a couple of km). Fourteen-seater minibuses to the border leave all day long from Parque Isidro Ayora as soon as they are full. They cost about US$0.25 (Ecuadorian or Colombian currency).

Return buses from the border will charge the same to the town centre but you can usually persuade the driver to charge double and take you to the Tulcán bus terminal some 1½ km away if you are in a hurry to head south. Taxis between Tulcán and the border are about US$1.50.

The border is open daily from 6 am to 8 pm. It is closed for lunch from 12 noon to 2 pm. There is a lot of traffic from Colombia, and entrance formalities (into Ecuador) are usually no problem. Almost nobody needs a visa, and tourist cards (which you must keep until you leave) are issued at the border. An exit ticket or sufficient funds are rarely asked for unless you look like a bum. They often won't give you the full 90 days that you are allowed, but don't hassle over it – extensions in Quito are normally fast and straightforward. Make sure that both your tourist card and passport are correctly stamped and dated with an *Entrada*.

If leaving Ecuador, you have to get a *Salida* exit stamp in your passport and hand in your tourist card. If you've lost it they should give you another one free if your passport is in order but it's best not to lose it. Keep it tucked in your passport. If your documents aren't in order, several things could happen. If you've merely overstayed the time allowed by a few days you can pay a fine which is usually about US$10 – this really is a fine, not a bribe. If you've overstayed by several months you may well have to pay a hefty fine or get sent back to Quito. And if you don't have an *Entrada* stamp you also get sent back.

On the Colombian side, entrance formalities are straightforward, as long as your passport and visa are in order (see Visas which follows). From the border there is frequent transportation to Ipiales, two km away and the first town in Colombia. There are plenty of hotels and onward connections available here; see *Colombia – a travel survival kit* by Krzysztof Dydynski, published by Lonely Planet.

Visas Australians, New Zealanders and citizens of some 'socialist' Latin American countries need a visa for Colombia. Most western Europeans don't need visas and can enter with a tourist card available at the border. US and Canadian citizens used to need a visa but recently regulations have been relaxed and these citizens can enter Colombia with a tourist card obtainable at the border. Whichever category you fall into, you should check in case regulations have changed.

To get a Colombian visa you officially need a ticket out of Colombia, two photos and sufficient funds (US$10 per day for students, double for others) but this is not always asked for. Visas are not issued at the border – get one in Tulcán, Quito or your home country.

Getting There & Around

Air TAME (☎ 980 675) has an office in the Hotel Azteca. They operate flights from Quito to Tulcán at 12 noon, returning to Quito at 12.45 pm from Monday to Friday. This saves you five or six hours on the bus. The flight takes 30 minutes and costs US$9. That's not a misprint – internal flights are inexpensive in Ecuador.

SAN-Saeta used to operate flights into Tulcán but no longer do so. They maintain an office on Sucre near Ayacucho in Tulcán (☎ 980 368).

To get to the airport you can take the border-crossing bus, which will leave you there for the same price as going to the border. A taxi will cost about US$0.75. Or it's a two-km walk from the city centre. If flying into Tulcán, you have to take a taxi or walk because there are no airport buses.

Note that flights from Tulcán to Quito are often full and they are also among the first to get cancelled if TAME is having aircraft problems.

Bus Buses to and from Ibarra (two to three hours, US$1.10) and Quito (five to six hours, US$2.10) leave and arrive from the main terminal terrestre. There are frequent departures but there is a better selection of times in the mornings. There are also several daily departures direct for Santo Domingo de los Colorados or Guayaquil if you enjoy the slow form of torture provided by cramped Ecuadorian buses during journeys taking 10 hours or longer.

The main bus terminal is inconveniently located 1½ km uphill from the town centre. City buses (US$0.05) run south-west along Bolívar and will deposit you at the terminal. If arriving at Tulcán, you have to cross the street in front of the terminal and take the bus from the other side to get to the town centre.

If you wish to travel west of Tulcán along the border to Tufiño, Maldonado and Chical, take the Cooperativa Transportes Norte buses leaving from Sierra and Arellano near the town centre. There is a bus to Tufiño about every hour until mid-afternoon (one hour, US$0.25). There is also one daily bus which leaves about 11 am or 12 noon and continues on to Maldonado (four hours; US$1) and Chical. There may be more buses to Maldonado – check with Cooperativa Transportes Norte.

There are also weekend excursion buses with Cooperativa 11 de Abril leaving from a bus stop in front of the cathedral for day trips to nearby thermal springs. The La Paz hot springs, five km from the village of that name, are visited on a Saturday excursion leaving at 8 am for US$1 a return trip. The Aguas Hediondas (literally 'stinking waters') thermal baths, beyond Tufiño, are visited on the 8 am Sunday morning trip which costs US$0.50.

WEST OF TULCÁN

The small villages of **Tufiño, Maldonado** and **Chical** are right on the border to the west of Tulcán and are rarely visited by gringos. A road is planned, which will continue from Chical on to the coast at San Lorenzo, but this won't be completed for many years yet. Meanwhile, Chical is the end of the road and adventurous travellers may be intrigued to see what's there – it certainly is a remote area.

At **Tufiño** there are several thermal springs, most of them on the Colombian side of the border. It is easy enough to cross over to Colombia on a day pass to soak in the pools (US$0.30), but you are sent back to Tulcán if you want to enter Colombia properly. However, regulations may have changed.

There is a basic restaurant in the village but no hotels. If you ask around, you could probably find someone to rent you a bed or floor space, but it's probably easiest to visit Tufiño in the morning and return to Tulcán on an afternoon bus.

The drive beyond Tufiño takes you over the Páramos de El Ángel, famous for their strange highland vegetation, especially the giant frailejones. The dirt road climbs to well over 4000 metres as it crosses the wild country at the base of Volcán Chiles (4768 metres) which is an extinct volcano on the border. The summit is about three or four km away from the road and the mountain can be climbed in a day with no technical equipment. The bus drivers know where to drop you off and the mountain is the obvious volcano to the north.

From the high mountain pass it is a long descent down the western slopes of the Andes through wild and ever changing scenery into the cloud forests below. **Maldonado** is in the San Juan River valley at just over 2000 metres above sea level, and almost 90 km west of Tulcán by road. The climate is reportedly pleasant and swimming in the river invigorating, although I've never been there. There are a couple of small pensiónes. **Chical**, about 10 km beyond Maldonado, is the end of the road – one traveller reports that he camped here with no problems.

South of Quito

A glance at a relief map of Ecuador shows the Panamerican Highway heading almost due south of Quito along a long valley flanked by two parallel ranges of high mountains. These two ranges consist for the most part of volcanoes, and several of them are still active. It was this feature that prompted Alexander von Humboldt, the famous German explorer who visited the country in 1802, to name Ecuador's central valley 'The Avenue of the Volcanoes'. This name is still used today.

The central valley is only a tiny fraction of Ecuador's land surface, yet it contains almost half of its population. Traditionally Ecuador's Andean Indians farmed the relatively rich volcanic soils found here, and after the conquest the Spanish found that the central valley made a good communication route between north and south. Today the same route is used for the Panamerican Highway, and a string of towns stretches south from the capital to Ecuador's third largest city, Cuenca, some 300 km south of Quito by air or 442 km by road.

In between lies some of Ecuador's wildest scenery, with nine of the country's 10 highest peaks and scores of tiny villages of Andean Indians leading lives little changed in centuries. Many of these villages are so remote that access is only on foot; some are easier to get to and provide a fascinating glimpse of Andean life. The further south one gets, the larger and more remote are the Indian populations. In Chimborazo Province, for example, there are approximately 250,000 Indians living in 431 small legal communities and villages. Most villages have minor differences in dress which are immediately recognisable to the local people – the pattern, colour or shape of a poncho, hat, dress, blouse, trousers, or waist-band can all indicate where an Indian is from.

Most travellers, however, visit the larger towns which are well connected with one another by road, and travel is generally easy

with superb views along the road. Visiting smaller villages is possible, and details are given in the text. Villagers generally come into larger towns on market days, and their traditional and brightly dyed clothing adds splashes of colour to the market scenes.

MACHACHI

This small town of 7000 inhabitants is 35 km away from Quito and the first place you arrive at on the way south from the capital. Its main attraction is the Güitig mineral-water bottling plant which you can visit. It's a four-km walk or take a taxi – everyone knows where it is. There's not much else to do.

Places to Stay & Eat

There are two very basic hotels in the centre, both charging about US$2 per person. These are the *Hotel Residencial Mejía* and the *Pensión El Tiempo*. There is a simple restaurant nearby. Some travellers told me it was a quiet place in which to get away from Quito for a while without having to travel far.

Getting There & Away

Buses from the Terminal Terrestre de Cumandá in Quito go to Latacunga and can drop you in Machachi, although you will have to pay the full fare to Latacunga. Direct buses to Machachi leave from the small Villa Flora terminal in south Quito, reached by city buses for Villa Flora.

ILINIZAS

These are two mountains about 25 km south-

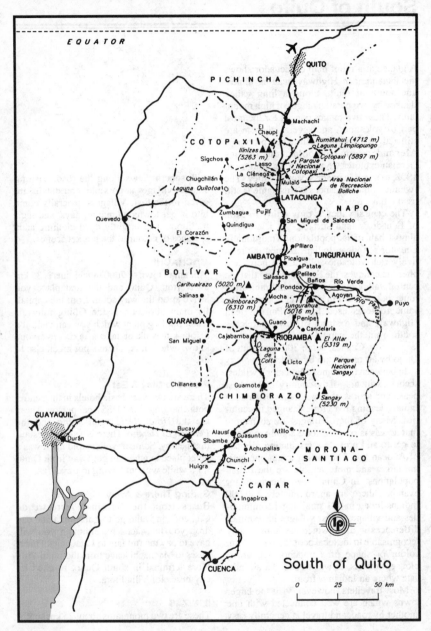

EQUATOR

QUITO

PICHINCHA

Machachi

El
Chaupi

COTOPAXI

Rumiñahui (4712 m)
Laguna Limpiopungo

Ilinizas
(5263 m)

Cotopaxi (5897 m)

Sigchos

Lasso

Parque
Nacional
Cotopaxi

Chugchilán

La Ciénega

Area Nacional
de Recreacion
Boliche

Laguna Quilotoa

Saquisilí

Mulaló

Zumbagua

Pujilí

LATACUNGA

NAPO

Quevedo

Quindigua

San Miguel de Salcedo

El Corazón

Píllaro

BOLÍVAR

AMBATO

Picaigua

TUNGURAHUA

Salasaca

Patate

Carihuairazo (5020 m)

Pelileo

Salinas

Mocha

Pondoa

Baños

Río Verde

Chimborazo
(6310 m)

Tungurahua
(5016 m)

Agoyan

Río Pastaza

Puyo

GUARANDA

Guano

Penipe

San Miguel

Cajabamba

Candelaria

RIOBAMBA

El Altar
(5319 m)

Laguna
de Colta

Chillanes

Licto

Parque
Nacional
Sangay

Guamote

Alao

CHIMBORAZO

Sangay
(5230 m)

GUAYAQUIL

Bucay

Alausí

Guasuntos

Atillo

Durán

Sibambe

Achupallas

MORONA–
SANTIAGO

Huigra

Chunchi

CAÑAR

Ingapirca

CUENCA

South of Quito

0   25   50 km

west of Machachi as the condor flies. Iliniza Sur (5263 metres) is Ecuador's sixth highest peak and a difficult ice climb for experienced mountaineers with technical equipment. Iliniza Norte (5126 metres) is Ecuador's eighth highest peak and is a rough scramble which can be accomplished by fit hikers.

To get there, take the unsigned turn-off from the Panamerican to El Chaupi. The turn-off is about eight km south of Machachi and taxi drivers know it. The road is cobbled for seven km to El Chaupi village, and continues a further nine km as a dirt road to a parking area (identified by a small shrine, 'La Virgen') which can be reached by hired pickups. From here, it is a three to four-hour climb to a refugio where you can spend the night. Part of the climb is up a steep ramp of volcanic scoria. The bulls you see along the way are those bred for the bull-ring – imagine their strength, living up here at 4200 metres! The locals all tell you 'Cuidado' or 'Beware'.

The refugio is in a saddle between the two mountains and has no facilities. Bring sleeping gear and food. From the refugio it is a two or three-hour climb to Iliniza Norte along a fairly well-defined trail. Don't leave gear in the refugio as it might well be stolen (stash it at an easily found spot well away from the hut). For further information, read *Climbing & Hiking in Ecuador* or ask at the South American Explorers Club.

LA CIÉNEGA

Some 30 km south of Machachi or 20 km north of Latacunga is the excellent *Hostería La Ciénega*. This is in a 400-year-old hacienda belonging to the Lasso family, whose land once spread from Quito to Ambato. The grounds are beautiful and you can go horse riding. The mansion was converted into a hotel in 1982 and it is marvellous, with most rooms having walls several feet thick as can be seen by looking through the windows. Furnishings are colonial or 19th century. There is a restaurant and bar – the restaurant is a popular stopping place for lunch.

The rates are about US$20/24 for singles/

doubles, all with private bath, hot water, and heater. There is a huge honeymoon suite for US$36. The hotel can be booked at Cordero 1442 and Amazonas in Quito (☎ 549 126, 541 337) or you can try calling the hotel direct (☎ 719 182, 801 622). You can risk just arriving, but they are often full, especially at weekends.

People in a hurry should note that service at the hotel is leisurely – it can take the receptionist up to half an hour to prepare your bill and the restaurant is not a fast-food joint. Early morning departures are difficult – if you want to leave earlier than 8 am, you should skip breakfast and try and settle your bill the day before.

The hotel is almost two km west of the Panamerican Highway, and a little south of the village of Lasso; there is a sign. Bus drivers can drop you at the sign and you have to walk, or you can hire a car or taxi from Quito or Latacunga.

PARQUE NACIONAL COTOPAXI

This 34,000-hectare park was established in 1975 and is mainland Ecuador's most popular and frequently visited national park. That is not to say it is crowded – indeed, it can be almost deserted midweek. Weekends can be crowded however, particularly with Ecuadorian visitors during the June to August dry season.

The centrepiece of the park is undoubtedly the beautifully cone-shaped and snow-capped Cotopaxi (5897 metres) which is the highest active volcano in the world and Ecuador's second highest peak. Present activity is limited to a few gently smoking fumaroles which cannot be seen except by experienced mountaineers who can climb up to the icy crater and peer within. There have been many violent eruptions in the past few centuries, however, with three of them literally wiping out the town of Latacunga.

There are also several other peaks within the park of which Rumiñahui (4712 metres) is the most important. The park gives you a good look at the páramo, as the typical high-altitude plateaus of Ecuador are called (see Habitats in the Facts about the Country chapter for more details). The forests of pines on the lower slopes are not Ecuadorian – they are imported trees grown for forestry purposes. They have been doing poorly in the last few years; disease seems to be taking its toll of the trees.

The wildlife is unusual and interesting. The Andean condor is present, though not often seen. The birds you are likely to see include the carunculated caracara (a falcon with a distinctive orange face), the Andean lapwing, the Andean gull (this 'seagull' is quite at home in the mountains, 4000 metres above sea level), various highland hummingbirds such as the Andean hillstar and sparkling violetear, the great thrush (a common black thrush with bright orange bill and feet, and yellow eyes), a number of duck and shorebird species, and birds which have names not immediately recognisable to most gringo visitors: cinclodes, solitaires, spinetails, canasteros and others.

The most frequently seen mammals in the park are white-tailed deer and rabbits. The tiny dwarf deer called the little red brocket and the southern pudú are also present – these deer are only about 35-cm high at the shoulder. Their predators are less often seen but if you are lucky you may catch a glimpse of the Andean fox (colpeo) or the mountain lion (puma). The rare Andean spectacled bear lives in the remote and infrequently visited eastern slopes of the park. Near the park entrance is a captive herd of llamas which is being studied to understand better how these animals should be managed. In the wetter areas keep your eyes open for the distinctive *Atelopus* frog which has an orange belly and black back – they are most likely to be seen near water during the wet season.

There are excellent hiking and mountaineering possibilities. A popular place to camp is near Limpiopungo, a large Andean lake at about 3800 metres above sea level, a few km beyond the information centre. There are simple cabins (roof and walls, no facilities) in the area between the information centre and the lake. Another popular camping place is in the **Area Nacional de Recreación**

Boliche which abuts the national park to the west. You can camp for a night, or bring plenty of food and hike all the way around Cotopaxi – this takes about a week. Information is available at the entrance booth and finding these places is straightforward.

Mountaineers and the curious like to go up to the José Ribas Refugio at about 4800 metres above sea level on the northern slopes of the mountain. Sleeping in the refugio costs about US$2 – bunk beds and cooking facilities are available, but bring a warm sleeping bag. There is a guardian on duty who can show you where you can leave your gear if you need to do so. Climbing beyond the refugio requires stamina, experience and snow and ice-climbing gear – it is definitely not a climb for the beginner although it is a relatively straightforward climb for those who know what they are doing. Mountaineering guides are available in Quito and Ambato (see also *Climbing & Hiking in Ecuador* for more details). There is also an abandoned refugio about 400 metres below the José Ribas Refugio – this could offer shelter in an emergency.

The park has a management plan which was organised with the technical and financial assistance of the World Wildlife Fund in 1983. It has the most well-developed infrastructure of the mainland parks. There are park rangers, a park centre (with an administrative building, a small museum and information centre), the domesticated llama herd, the refugio and camping and picnicking areas. Despite this list, facilities are very basic and most visitors either come on day trips or camp. A restaurant has been planned but was still under construction in 1991. Also in 1991, the museum and information centre were temporarily closed for rebuilding, although a large map was displayed outside. Meanwhile, ask for information at the entrance booth – they may be able to tell you that the information centre and museum have reopened.

The entrance fee to the park is only about US$0.20 and the combined fees collected from the approximately 35,000 annual visitors does not even begin to approach the costs of running the park. There has been talk for some years of raising the entrance fee to US$10 for foreign visitors, which would aid greatly in managing the park. The main problems facing the park at this time are quite simple – litter, poaching and lack of adequate staff for patrols, information and educational programmes. It is possible that an increased fee may be in effect by the time you go.

The entrance gate is open from 8 am to 6 pm on weekdays and from 7 am to 6.30 pm on weekends. If you are hiking, it is easy to get in or out anytime, because the 'gate' is a heavy padlocked chain which can be stepped over. Drivers can usually find a park guard in one of the nearby houses – the guard will be happy to let you through at odd hours for a tip.

Getting There & Around

You can walk or hitchhike into the park. There are two roads in from the Panamerican Highway roughly 20 and 26 km north of Latacunga respectively. You can ask any Latacunga-Quito bus driver to put you down at either entrance. The first entrance north of Latacunga has a national park sign and you follow the main dirt roads (also signed) through the entrance point (about eight or 10 km from the Panamerican) to the park centre about 15 km from the Panamerican.

The more northerly road also has a sign for the park and another sign for CLIRSEN. The road is paved as far as the CLIRSEN satellite tracking station (previously operated by NASA) and telecommunications towers, about two km from the Panamerican. The road then becomes dirt and soon passes the Río Daule campsite in the Boliche Recreation Area and eventually reaches the entrance station – this route is about three km shorter.

The Limpiopungo area for camping and picnicking is about four km beyond the park centre and the refugio about a further 12 km. The lake is at 3800 metres and the refugio is 1000 metres higher – it is very hard work walking at this altitude if you are not used to it.

Altitude sickness is a very real danger –

acclimatise for several days in Quito before attempting to walk in. Do not attempt to visit the park immediately after arriving in the highlands from a low elevation.

At weekends a fair number of local tourists visit the park and there is a very good chance of getting a lift. Mid-week the park is almost deserted and you'll probably end up walking.

Pickup trucks from Latacunga will cost about US$20 but you should bargain (I have heard that rates as cheap as US$7 can be obtained, but I have difficulty in believing this). Mountaineers wishing to reach the refugio must clearly specify that they want to go up the steep dirt road to the parking lot under the refugio at the end of the road. Most pickups will make it; a few can't. You can arrange for the pickup to return for you on a particular day – another US$20. It is almost an hour's walk uphill from the parking lot (at 4600 metres) to the refugio. Any car will get you into the park to visit the museum, see the llamas, and picnic by Limpiopungo from where excellent views of the mountain are obtained, weather permitting.

The major travel agencies in Quito can arrange tours to Cotopaxi. A day tour, including a picnic lunch, driver and bilingual guide, will visit the park as far as Limpiopungo but not necessarily as far as the parking lot below the refugio (ask about this). A two-day tour will combine a day trip to Cotopaxi with an overnight at La Ciénega and a visit to local Indian markets. Costs depend on the number of people in your group and the agency you book with. A day tour is roughly US$60 per person and a two-day tour costs about US$150 per person, both with a four person minimum.

LATACUNGA

It's worth coming here just for the drive from Quito, which is magnificent. Ice-cream cone-shaped Cotopaxi looms to the left of the Panamerican Highway and the two Ilinizas, also snow capped, are on your right. Several other peaks are visible during the 90-km drive.

About 50 km south of Quito the highway

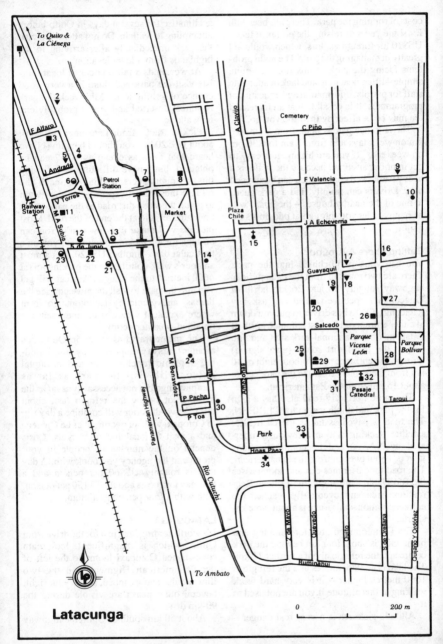

To Quito &
La Ciénega

Cemetery
C Piño

F Alfaro

J Andrade

Petrol
Station

Railway
Station

V Torres

A Subia

5 de Junio

Market

Plaza
Chile

F Valencia

J A Echeverria

Guayaquil

Salcedo

M Benavdez

Panamerican Highway

Amazonas

Parque
Vicente
León

Parque
Bolívar

Maldonado

Pasaje
Catedral

Tarqui

P Pacha

P Toa

Park

Hnas Paez

Río Cutuchi

2 de MAYO

Quevedo

Quito

Sta Oralina

Quijao Y Ordóñez

Rumiñahui

To Ambato

Latacunga

0   200 m

■ PLACES TO STAY

1 Hotel Latacunga
3 Residencial Los Andes
5 Hostal Quilotoa
8 Hostal Residencial Jackeline
11 Residencial La Estación
20 Hotel Estambul
22 Hotel Costa Azul
26 Hotel Cotopaxi

▼ PLACES TO EAT

2 Koko Riko
5 Pollos Gus
9 Restaurant El Mashca
17 Gran Pan Bakery
18 Pinguino Ice Cream
19 Restaurant La Carreta
22 Restaurant Costa Azul
27 Restaurant Los Alpes
31 Parrilladas Los Copihues

OTHER

4 Transportes Cotopaxi Ticket Office
6 Buses (Passing) to Ambato, Baños, Riobamba
7 Buses to Saquisilí
10 La Merced Market
12 Transportes Cotopaxi Buses to Zumbagua, Quevedo
13 Buses (Passing) to Quito
14 Several Cambios
15 Church
16 Bus Tickets to Guayaquil
21 Buses to Ambato
23 Buses to Pujilí
24 Molinos de Monserrat Museum
25 Teatro Vicente León
28 Town Hall
29 IETEL & Post Office
30 Cine Santiago
32 Cathedral
33 Old Hospital (Historic Landmark)
34 General Hospital

Latacunga (population about 40,000) is the capital of Cotopaxi Province. Although not a particularly exciting town, it has an interesting history and is a good base for several excellent excursions. It was an important centre for the Puruhá Indians who lived here before the Incas.

The town's name originates from the Indian words '*Llacta cunani*' which translate rather charmingly into 'land of my choice'. It became an important colonial centre immediately after the conquest but today there is little evidence of this long and varied history.

The reason is Cotopaxi, which dominates the town on a clear day. A major eruption in 1742 destroyed the town and it had to be rebuilt. Another eruption 26 years later wiped it out again but the indomitable (or foolhardy) survivors rebuilt it a second time. An immense eruption in 1877 destroyed it a third time – and yet again it was rebuilt on the same site. At present the volcano's activity is minor and it is extremely unlikely that an eruption will occur within the next several years.

Information
There is reportedly a tourist office on Quito just north of the Parque Vicente León, though I couldn't find it when I was there. OK, so I'm not perfect. The IETEL and post offices are on Quevedo near Maldonado. Banks are around Parque Vicente León but most don't change foreign currency, although the Banco de Pichincha might. Several cambios will change cash dollars at rates about 2% or 3% lower than Quito. Most cambios are on Vela on the block south of Plaza Chile. It is best to change money in Quito. The town closes down early – most restaurants stop serving by 8 or 9 pm.

Things to See
Latacunga is a good centre for several excursions: to Cotopaxi and to nearby villages which will be described at the end of this section. In the town itself, there's little to do. A small ethnography museum, the Molinos de Monserrat, is run by the Casa de Cultura

crosses a pass at over 3500 metres, and soon after there is an entrance road to Parque Nacional Cotopaxi. The road drops and crosses the railway at the small village of Lasso and then continues to Latacunga at about 2800 metres above sea level.

Ecuatoriana and is open from 10 am to 5 pm Tuesday through Saturday. They are on Vela near Maldonado.

There are several plazas, of which Parque Vicente León is the most attractive with a well-tended garden containing some topiary work. At the south-east corner of this plaza is the town hall topped by a pair of stone condors, and on the south side is the cathedral. Behind the cathedral is a little arcade (Pasaje Catedral) which includes an art gallery. Many of the buildings are light grey and have been built from the local volcanic rock.

Near the south end of town on Quevedo is an old hospital which is a historic landmark – though I couldn't find a way in to visit. The modern hospital is a block away. There is one tiny cinema which shows bad movies and a theatre which is usually closed.

Fiestas

Latacunga's major annual fiesta is La Virgen de las Mercedes, held 23-24 September. This is more popularly known as the Fiesta de la Mama Negra, and there are processions, costumes, streetdancing, Andean music and fireworks. This is one of those festivals which, although outwardly Christian, has much pagan Indian influence and is worth seeing. The Independence of Latacunga is celebrated on 11 November with parades and a bullfight.

There is also a weekly market on Saturday and a smaller one on Tuesday. The markets are colourful, but of no special interest although a few crafts are sold, especially the small string bags known as shigras.

Places to Stay

There are eight hotels open in Latacunga at this time, all of them fairly cheap. Many people stay in Latacunga on Wednesday nights for the Thursday morning Indian market at Saquisilí. Hotels are often full by mid afternoon so try and get there early if you're arriving on Wednesday.

A recommended budget-travellers' hotel which has large clean rooms and hot water in the communal showers is the friendly *Hotel Estambul* (☎ 800 354) on Quevedo and Salcedo. They charge about US$2.20 per person. There are two very basic hotels charging US$1.20 per person. The *Costa Azul* is over the restaurant of the same name, close to where you get off the bus on the Panamerican Highway. The *Residencial La Estación* is by the railway station. Neither of these two are very clean and the cold showers work only irregularly. The basic *Hostal Residencial Jackeline* (☎ 801 033), just across the river on Vela and Valencia, is friendlier, but the last time I was there the showers didn't work – though the manager will show you a place across the street where you can wash. They charge about US$1.50 per person.

The best hotel in the town centre is the *Hotel Cotopaxi* (☎ 801 310) on the north-eastern corner of Parque Vicente León. They charge US$4 per person in rooms with private bath and hot water. Some of the rooms have pretty views of the parque but they may be a little noisy. One reader wrote that she felt intimidated by the 'shady characters' hanging around in the little lobby – I've stayed here several times, however, and never had any problems.

The newest and probably best hotels are on the Panamerican Highway. Ask for rooms away from the highway to avoid street noise. The *Residencial Los Andes* (☎ 800 386) charges about US$3.50/6 for clean singles/doubles with private bathroom and hot water. The clean and friendly *Hotel Latacunga* (☎ 802 372) has good rooms with private bath and TV for US$6/10.50. Don't be put off by the fact that it's over a car dealership – they won't try and sell you a used car in the middle of the night. There is also the newly opened *Hostal Quilotoa* which I have not been able to price. People looking for some luxury often stay at the *La Ciénega*, about 20 km to the north.

Places to Eat

There are no particularly fine or expensive restaurants in Latacunga. The best are *Parrilladas Los Copihues* and *Restaurant La Carreta* both on Quito in the town centre, though neither are anything to get too excited about. Also on Quito, *Pinguino* is good for ice cream, snacks and coffee, and *Gran Pan* bakery is a good place to stock up on bread for picnics. *Restaurant Los Alpes* on Sanchez de Orellana is open fairly early for breakfasts (and all day) and is inexpensive. *El Mashca* on Valencia and Orellana is a reasonable chicken restaurant.

There is a cheap and simple restaurant which is open all day in the *Hotel Costa Azul* on 5 de Junio near the corner of the Panamerican Highway. Most restaurants close by about 8.30 pm. Two which stay open later are the *Pollos Gus* and *Koko Riko* on the Panamerican. They serve fast food-style hamburgers and roast chicken.

The Latacunga area is famous for its *allullas*, sold by local women at every bus stop or checkpoint. The women's high-pitched cries of '*aziuuuuzia*' become quite familiar. Allullas are rather dry biscuits made of flour, pork fat and a local unpasteurized cheese, and I'm afraid they taste no better than they sound.

Getting There & Away
Air There is a Latacunga airport but it is not used for regularly scheduled flights. On rare occasions a plane may be diverted here if it cannot land at Quito. You hear occasional discussion about expanding the airport into an international one for Quito traffic – I can't see it happening this century.

Bus – long distance There is no main bus terminal. Long-distance buses from Quito's terminal terrestre will usually drop you on the Panamerican Highway at the corner with Avenida 5 de Junio before continuing to Ambato. This corner is a good place to stand if you're wanting to catch any north or south-bound buses – they pass every few minutes. This may be difficult on holiday weekends, as many buses are full and tend to do the Quito-Ambato-Riobamba run without picking up passengers at Latacunga. Be patient or try to avoid leaving Latacunga on holiday weekends.

Slower buses leave from Quito's terminal

direct for Latacunga. The bus stop for Quito-bound buses originating in Latacunga is in the Plaza Chile (also popularly known as Plaza El Salto). There is also a bus stop on the Panamerican just south of 5 de Junio for buses originating in Latacunga and going to Ambato. Approximate fares and times: Quito, US$0.60, two hours; Ambato, US$0.40, one hour; Riobamba, US$1, 2¼ hours; and Baños, US$0.75, 1¾ hours.

Just half a block from the Panamerican Highway on Avenida 5 de Junio is the bus stop for westbound buses. The road is paved as far as Pujilí beyond which the road deteriorates. This is the roughest, least-travelled, and perhaps most spectacular bus route joining the highlands with the western lowlands. If you're not pressed for time and don't mind the discomfort, riding a beat-up crowded old bus on this dirt road may be the most interesting way of leaving the highlands. The bus climbs to Zumbagua at 3500 metres (US$0.60; two hours) and then drops to Quevedo at only 150 metres above sea level. Transportes Cotopaxi runs this route in six hours at an average speed of less than 30 km an hour and charges about US$1.60 for the ride. They have departures every two hours, all day long. Their ticket office is on the Panamerican just north of the petrol (gas) station, but the buses still seem to leave from 5 de Junio, a couple of blocks away. Ask carefully about where the bus leaves from when buying your ticket.

There is also a bus office on Sanchez de Orellana and Guayaquil which sells tickets for a daily departure to Guayaquil at 8.45 am. The fare is about US$1.40 and the buses leave from the Panamerican near the intersection with 5 de Junio. Ask carefully to ensure that the bus leaves from where you expect it to.

Bus – local villages The bus most frequently used by travellers is the one to Saquisilí, which charges US$0.15 for the half-hour ride. Departures are every few minutes on market-day mornings, and every hour or so at other times. The buses leave from Benavídez and Valencia, a block away from the Plaza Chile (El Salto). Buses departing for various other nearby villages leave from the Plaza Chile – destinations served by buses from this plaza include Sigchos, Chugchilán and Mulaló. Ask around for other villages. The bus for the village of Pujilí leaves at frequent intervals from M V Subia and 5 de Junio, a block west of the Panamerican.

Train The railway station is on the west side of the Panamerican Highway and a km from the town centre. At this time there is no Quito-Guayaquil train; the service goes only as far as Riobamba and this has recently been suspended as well. The autoferro train used to leave at 8 am for Quito (US$0.30; two hours) and at 5 pm for Riobamba (US$0.50; three hours). Perhaps the service will be reinstated by the time you get there. The train used to be very crowded and you should enquire and book in advance.

Taxi Plaza Chile (El Salto) is the place to go to hire taxis and pickup trucks for visits to Parque Nacional Cotopaxi and other remote villages (pickups double as taxis on many of the rough roads in the highlands). The manager of the Hotel Estambul will make arrangements for pickups to Cotopaxi. The fare is about US$20 one way – but you may have to bargain. A taxi (or pickup) to Zumbagua and Laguna Quilotoa costs about the same.

SAQUISILÍ

For many people, the Thursday morning market of Saquisilí is the main reason for coming to Latacunga. It is not a tourist-oriented market, though there are the usual few Otavaleño Indians selling their sweaters and weavings. This market is for the inhabitants of remote Indian villages who flood into town to buy (or sell) everything from bananas to homemade shotguns, and herbal remedies to strings of piglets. The majority of the Indians from the area are recognised by their little felt 'pork pie' hats and red ponchos.

There are eight different plazas, each of

which sell specific goods. One of my favourites is the animal market, a cacophonous affair with screaming pigs playing a major role. Cattle, sheep and a few llamas are also seen. The animal market is almost a km out of town – go early and ask for directions. Ecuadorian economists consider Saquisilí to have the most important Indian village market in the country and many travellers rate it as the best they've seen in Ecuador.

Along with the travellers, there are thieves – I saw two women with a small child expertly picking tourists' pockets. One woman and the child would stumble in front of an unsuspecting person and, in the ensuing apologies and confusion, the other woman lifted a wallet using her long poncho as a cover for her activities.

The bus from Latacunga drops you off near the Plaza La Concordia, which is recognised by its many trees surrounded by an iron railing. On Thursday this becomes the plaza selling clothes, hats, hardware and homemade shotguns.

Places to Stay

On the Plaza La Concordia at Bolívar 4-88 and Sucre is the *Pensión La Chabela* (also known as La Chabelita), which provides cheap and basic accommodation. There is no sign. A bed can also be found at *Salón Pichincha* a couple of blocks away at Bolívar 2-06 and Pichincha. They are likely to be full the night before the market and most travellers find it best to stay in Latacunga – the bus service begins at dawn and you don't miss anything.

Places to Eat

There are no restaurants but plenty of places to eat. I enjoyed breakfast in an unnamed place on the 700 block of Sucre and Bolívar. Inside there was a large smoky kitchen full of Indians and an Elvis Presley poster on the wall. A huge woman supervised the cooking of breakfast over a charcoal brazier and it was a good opportunity to try dishes such as llapingachos, fritada, caldo de gallina, tortillas de maíz and moté cooked in traditional style. Made a change from bacon and eggs!

There are similar places nearby and also plenty of street stands. One plaza seems to be nothing but food stalls – if you stick to cooked food and don't have a delicate stomach you'll enjoy it.

Getting There & Away

There are buses returning to Latacunga several times an hour after the market; there are also trucks and buses going to many of the remote villages in the interior such as Sigchos and Chugchilán. On market day, and sporadically on other days, there are slow and crowded old buses going direct to and from Quito (US$0.80; two to three hours). Buses leave from near Plaza La Concordia, more or less at where you arrived.

People unwilling to travel by public transport can hire a taxi in Quito (about US$30 for a half day, allowing a couple of hours at the market) or from Latacunga. The bigger tour companies organise one or two-day tours to Saquisilí and other places. Prices are about US$60/150 per person for one/two-days with a group of four. Overnights are usually at La Ciénega.

OTHER VILLAGES

Pujilí is 10 km west of Latacunga and can easily be visited. It has a basic unmarked pensión and a couple of simple restaurants on the main plaza. The main market day is Sunday with a smaller market on Wednesday. This is a good town for the All Souls Day festivities of 2 November.

Some 57 km further west is **Zumbagua**, a very small village which has an unspoilt and interesting local market on Saturday. The people of the region often use llamas to transport goods to and from the market. The drive there from Latacunga is through beautiful Andean scenery. Food is available but accommodation is extremely basic (one pensión, no water) and it is best to stay in Latacunga.

About 12 km north of Zumbagua is the famous volcanic lake of **Quilotoa** but transportation is both infrequent and irregular except after the Saturday market when vehicles crowded with market goers head that way. You could hire a taxi (in Latacunga) or walk there in three or four hours, but carry water – the lake is alkaline and the road dusty and fringed by cacti. The views from the lake are beautiful, but there have been reports of many beggars in the area.

North of the lake on a deteriorating road you can reach **Chugchilán**. This is five more hours on foot. The daily bus from Latacunga arrives via a different, more northerly road. At Chugchilán you can sleep in one of the houses on the square. North of Chugchilán is the bigger village of **Sigchos** on a better road and with two or three buses a day to Latacunga. There is a very basic place to stay and a small Sunday market here. These are all in a very remote area of the Ecuadorian highlands; still more remote communities can be found on foot.

South of Zumbagua is the **Río Tigua valley**. This area is known for the bright paintings of Andean life which are made on canvases of leather – the paintings can be seen for sale in Quito. The Tigua region is reached by taking the southbound road to the left, about five or six km beyond Zumbagua on the road to Quevedo. The poor road crosses the Tigua valley, goes past the tiny community of Quindigua and on to Angamarca beyond which the road swings west through the remote canton capital of El Corazón and, eventually, into Quevedo. This is one of the least accessible parts of the region and forays into here are not for the inexperienced traveller.

The scenery around all the areas described in this section is quite splendid and the Andean Indian inhabitants somewhat withdrawn and not used to seeing strangers. Travellers wishing to spend any time here should be self-sufficient and have some experience in rough travel in strange areas. Transportation cannot be relied upon, and you may have to walk for long distances or wait for hours. Hiring a car is an option, but limits your contact with the locals. Carry a sleeping bag or blanket, warm clothes, water and a snack. The area is photogenic but, please, don't be obnoxious with your camera. The people are not keen on being photographed by staring strangers who shoot and move on.

SAN MIGUEL DE SALCEDO

This small town is usually called Salcedo and is 14 km south of Latacunga on the Panamerican Highway. It has a Sunday market and a lesser one on Thursday. In mid-March they have an important Agricultural and Industrial Fair. Otherwise it's of little interest.

Places to Stay & Eat

There are a couple of basic hotels in the town centre. On the northern outskirts of the town is the *Hostería Rumibamba de las Rosas* (☎ 726 128, 800 550 or in Quito 233 715), a fairly modern hotel with 'log cabin' bungalows which are furnished and decorated with antiques. There is a small private zoo, duck pond, pony rides (and a saddled llama for children!), swimming pool, tennis courts, and games rooms. The whole place has a Disneyland atmosphere – rather corny but clean and well run and the management is very friendly and anxious to please.

There is a very good restaurant and bar on the premises and rooms start at about US$15. It is a popular place for Ecuadorians on family outings.

AMBATO

Some 47 km south of Latacunga (136 km south of Quito) is the important town of Ambato, the capital of Tungurahua Province. It was badly damaged in a 1949 earthquake but a modern city was soon rebuilt. It is prosperous and growing with a population of about 140,000. Its altitude is 2800 metres above sea level.

Ambato is famous for its annual flower festival (Fiesta de Frutas y Flores) which is supposed to coincide with Carnaval, but usually is held during the last two weeks in February. Hotels tend to be full at this time so plan ahead. 1991 marked the 40th anniversary of this festival which, apart from fruit and flower shows, includes bullfights, parades, late night street dancing and general fun. Travellers unable to find suitable accommodation during this time could try staying in Latacunga, Baños or Riobamba and take the one hour bus journey into Ambato.

It is worth noting that the Carnaval, held nationwide in the week before the beginning of Lent, is unique in Ambato in that the traditional 'sport' of water-throwing has been banned throughout the city. Hotels tend to be full at this time as well.

Apart from these festivals, most travellers just pass through Ambato on their way to Baños, which is one of the more popular destinations in the country. It is, however, worth staying in Ambato for a night to see the museum, which is little known but interesting, and a few other sights. The Monday market is a huge affair – the biggest in Ecuador.

Information

The CETUR tourist information office (☎ 821 800) has moved several times in the last few years. Their most recent location was in the Hotel Ambato on Guayaquil and Rocafuerte. They are open from 8.30 am to 12.30 pm and from 2.30 to 6 pm, Monday to Friday.

Money Cambiato (☎ 821 008), at Bolívar 686 and J L Mera, will change both US$ travellers' cheques and cash at rates a little below Quito's. Banks sometimes change foreign currency, but their regulations are much more liable to change than the exchange houses'.

Post & Telecommunications The IETEL and post office are on Castillo by the main plaza, called Parque Juan Montalvo.

Travel Agencies Travel and tour arrangements can be made at Metropolitan Touring (☎ 824 084), Bolívar 471 and Castillo or with Ecuadorian Tours (☎ 824 420), Bolívar 678 and J L Mera. Both have head offices in Quito.

A recommended adventure tour operator is Surtrek (☎ 827 349 821 353) at Avenida Los Shyris and Luis Cordero, just over two km south of the city centre. German, English and Spanish are spoken. They rent climbing equipment and provide mountaineering guides for climbing the local snow peaks and also arrange trips to the Oriente. Their mailing address is PO Box 865, Ambato, Ecuador.

Things to See

The **Museo de Ciencias Naturales** (☎ 821 958) in the Colegio Bolívar on Sucre and Lalama on the north-western side of the Parque Cevallos is well worth a visit. Entrance is US$0.25 and it's open from 8 am to 12.30 pm and 2 to 6 pm, Monday through Friday. It has a variety of exhibits. Primarily there are hundreds of stuffed birds, mammals and reptiles, some of which are quite well done and others rather ratty.

In the absence of comprehensive field guides to Ecuadorian wildlife, this is a good museum to visit if you wish to identify species you may have seen in the wild. There's also a rather gruesome display of freaks such as two-headed calves and six-legged lambs.

I particularly enjoyed the fine display of photographs taken around 1910 by the famous Ecuadorian mountaineer Nicolás Martínez who lived in Ambato. There are period street and countryside scenes, as well as photographs of early mountaineering expeditions and Cotopaxi in eruption. The museum curator, Señor Héctor Vásquez, is also a mountaineer with ascents of the highest peaks of Argentina, Peru and Ecuador to his credit. He is knowledgeable and helpful with the exhibits. There are also numismatic, geological, archaeological and other displays.

The most important plaza is the attractively laid out **Parque Juan Montalvo**, dedicated to the famous Ambateño writer Juan Montalvo (1832-89), of whom there is a statue (see Arts in the Facts about the Country chapter). On the north-western side of this plaza you can visit his house, **Casa de Montalvo** (☎ 821 024 for information); there is a small entrance fee. Next door is the **Casa de Cultura** (☎ 820 338, 824 248)

which has a small museum with displays labelled in Spanish of journalism, musical instruments, handicrafts, the history of Ambato and art. The museum is open from 8 am to 12 noon and from 2 to 5 pm; entrance is free. On the north-eastern side of this plaza is the modern and rather bleak **cathedral** with some good stained-glass windows.

Because of the recent reconstruction since the 1949 earthquake, most of the buildings in the centre are new and of no great interest. A recommended walk is along Bolívar, south-west of the centre, to the pleasant modern suburb of Miraflores on the banks of the Río Ambato (note that Calle Bolívar changes into Avenida Miraflores). The river can be crossed about two km away from town on Avenida Los Guaytambos which soon leads to the **Quinta de Montalvo** where that writer's country house stood. It can be visited from 9 am to 12 noon and 2 to 6 pm. This is in the suburb of Ficoa.

Several other famous Ambateños had country houses which survived the earthquake and are worth visiting (☎ 821 024 for information). **Quinta de Mera** belonged to the writer Juan León Mera and can be visited 9 am to 12 noon and 2 to 6 pm. The house is set in an attractive botanical garden on Avenida Los Capulíes in the suburb of Atocha. Close by is the **Quinta La Liria**, the country home of the mountaineer Nicolás Martinéz, and also set in a pleasant garden. Atocha is on the far side of the Río Ambato, about two km north-east of the city centre. It can be reached on foot by walking north-west out of town on Montalvo, which soon crosses the river, and then turning right on Capulíes about 200 metres beyond the river. Quinta de Mera is about 1½ km to the north-east, and the Quinta La Liria just beyond it. Local buses go to all these places.

The **market** is held on Monday, with smaller ones on Wednesday and Friday. The Monday market was established in 1861 and is the largest city market in the country. Although it has been modernised (buildings rather than outdoors) it is still a huge, bustling affair attracting Indians from many nearby communities. The main action for

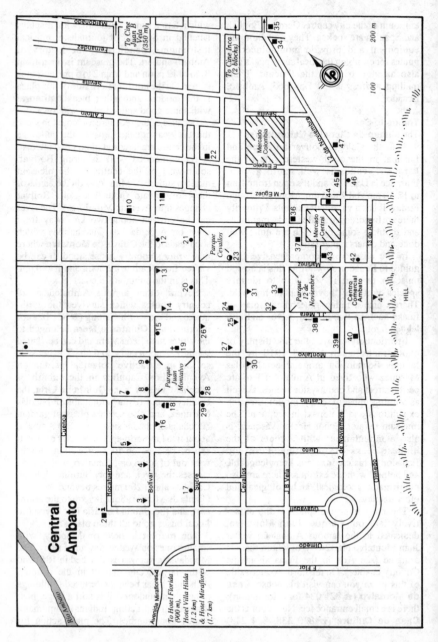

Central Ambato

■ PLACES TO STAY

2 Hotel Ambato & CETUR Tourist
  Information Office
10 Gran Hotel
11 Hotel Cumandá
22 Residencial Europa 2
24 Hotel Vivero
33 Residenciales América & Europa
34 Hotel San Ignacio
35 To Residencial Pichincha (600 m),
  Hotel Imperial (700 m),
  Hotel Carrillo (1200 m)
36 Hotel Nacional
37 Residencial Astoria
38 Residenciales Laurita & 9 de
  Octubre, Hotel Guayaquil
39 Residenciales San Andres & Napo
40 Residencial Orquidea
43 Residencial Ambato
44 Residencial Amazonas
45 Residencial La Unión
47 Hotel Ejecutivo

▼ PLACES TO EAT

3 El Coyote Cafetería
4 Pizzería La Cigarra
5 La Buena Mesa
6 Parrilladas El Gaucho
13 Chifa Nueva Hong Kong
14 Pastelería Quito
16 El Coyote Inn Restaurant

25 Kangaroo Bar
26 Restaurant El Alamo
27 Restaurant El Gran Alamo
30 El Alamo Junior Cafetería
31 Chifa Jao Fua
32 Panadería Enripan
35 To Restaurant La Paila (800 metres)
41 Mama Miche

OTHER

1 To Bridge Across Río Ambato (200 m)
2 CETUR Tourist Information Office
6 Cine Roxi & Metropolitan Touring
7 IETEL
8 Casa de Cultura Museums
9 Casa de Montalvo
12 Cine Lalama
15 Cambiato & Ecuadorian Tours
17 TAME Airline Office
18 Post Office
19 Cathedral
20 Cine Sucre
21 Museo de Ciencias Naturales
23 Local Buses
28 Banco Central
29 Government Office
35 To Terminal Terrestre (Buses) & Train
  Station (1200 m)
42 Peña Tungurahua Bar
46 Cine Bolívar & Taberna Disco Bar

produce is the modern Mercado Central at the south-eastern end of Lalama, but there are many other markets scattered around town and in the suburbs. Walking along Cevallos will bring you past Mercado Colombia (also called Modelo) and as you go further north-east along Cevallos you will pass many stalls selling local handicrafts – the best area is about 10 blocks from the centre. As always – watch for pickpockets.

Places to Stay – bottom end

The place for cheap hotels is in the Parque 12 de Noviembre area and Mercado Central area. These hotels are pretty basic. For about a dollar you can stay in the *Residencial*

América (☎ 821 092), J B Vela 737 and J L Mera, which has one of those showers that provides tepid water and electric shocks if you touch any of the pipes, but is probably the best of the super cheapies. Next door is the similarly priced *Residencial Europa* which claims to have hot water but often doesn't. Some way away, at E Espejo and Sucre, is the marginally better *Residencial Europa 2*. The *Hotel Nacional* (☎ 823 820), J B Vela and Lalama, charges US$1.25 and has hot water in the morning – sometimes. None of these places are particularly clean or recommended except for the penurious.

For US$1.60 you can stay at *Residencial Laurita* (☎ 821 377), J L Mera 333 and J B Vela, which is reasonably clean and friendly and has hot water, as does the similar *Hotel Guayaquil* (☎ 821 194, 823 886) a few doors away at J L Mera 311. The *Residencial 9 de Octubre* (☎ 820 018) on J L Mera at No 325 has cold water although they also charge about US$1.60.

Several other very basic and rather grungy-looking hotels in this price range are shown on the map. They include the residenciales *Orquidea, San Andres, Napo, La Unión, Ambato, Astoria* and *Amazonas*.

If you'd rather stay near the bus terminal, there is the *Hotel Carrillo* (☎ 827 200) right above the terminal for US$2 per person. They have hot showers but it's noisy. Walking right from the terminal along Avenida de las Américas to the traffic circle and left on Avenida 12 de Noviembre brings you to the friendly *Residencial Pichincha* on the right-hand side at No 2323 (five minutes from the terminal). They have clean rooms at US$1.60/2.80 for singles/doubles but only cold water. Just before Residencial Pichincha is the *Hotel Imperial* (☎ 824 837) at 12 de Noviembre 2494. They charge US$3 per person in rooms with private baths and hot water, though the water supply is erratic, as it is in many of the cheaper hotels in Ambato.

The *Hotel Ejecutivo* (☎ 820 370), 12 de Noviembre 1230 and E Espejo, has reasonable rooms with shared baths for about US$1.80 per person, or dark, small rooms with private bath and hot water at US$4/6 for singles/ doubles.

The *Gran Hotel* (☎ 824 235), at Lalama and Rocafuerte, has reasonable rooms with private bath and hot water for US$2.50 per person. The *Hotel Cumandá* (☎ 826 792), Egüez 837 and Bolívar, is a clean, good hotel charging US$3.25/6 for singles/doubles with private bath and hot water – there are some cheaper rooms with shared baths. Also good is the *Hotel Vivero* (☎ 820 088, 821 000), at J L Mera 504 and Cevallos, which charges US$5/7 for singles/doubles with shared bathrooms and US$7/9 for singles/doubles with private bathrooms and hot water. These could be middle-range rooms in other towns. Their rooms on the top floor are smaller and

not as good – but they are only half the price. These last three hotels are good value.

Finally, the five-story *Hotel San Ignacio* is under construction at 12 de Noviembre and Maldonado, but will probably be open by the time you get there.

Places to Stay – middle & top end

By far the best hotel in town is the *Hotel Ambato* (☎ 827 598/9), at Guayaquil and Rocafuerte. They have a casino, restaurant and bar, and rooms with private bath and hot water, telephone and TV. They charge US$28/34 for singles/doubles.

Out on Avenida Miraflores, in the suburb of the same name, are three quiet and pleasant hotels, all of which have been recommended. They all have restaurants (limited menus or set meals) and rooms with private baths and hot water for approximately US$12/16 for singles/doubles. The closest is the *Hotel Florida* (☎ 823 040/74) at Miraflores 1131. Further along Miraflores is the German-run *Hotel Villa Hilda* (☎ 824 065) which is set in pleasant gardens and has a pool. Finally, we come to the clean and modern *Hotel Miraflores* (☎ 824 395) at Miraflores 227.

Places to Eat

For budget travellers best value is the *Chifa Jao Fua* (☎ 829 306) at Cevallos and J L Mera where a good meal can be had for not much over US$1. Cheaper and almost as good is the *Chifa Nueva Hong Kong* at Bolívar 768 and Martínez. There are several other chifas. You can get super-cheap meals around the market. For breakfast the best bet is one of the cake shops for coffee, juice and rolls or sandwiches. Try the *Panadería Enripan* or the *Pastelería Quito*, both on J L Mera.

There are three good Swiss-run *El Alamo* restaurants. *Restaurant El Gran Alamo* (☎ 820 706), Montalvo 520 and Cevallos, is quite fancy and comparatively expensive. *Restaurant El Alamo* (☎ 821 710), Sucre 660 and J L Mera, is lower priced and good, and *El Alamo Junior*, Cevallos 612 and Montalvo, is a self-service-style cafeteria.

There are several good restaurants near the Hotel Ambato. If you're in the mood for steak, try the Argentine style *Parrilladas El Gaucho* (☎ 828 969), Bolívar and Quito, which is good and medium priced. The *La Buena Mesa* at Quito and Rocafuerte is a good French restaurant recommended for its very pleasant atmosphere. It is closed on Sunday. Nearby, the *Pizzería La Cigarra* (☎ 828 411), Bolívar 373 and Quito, does a reasonable pizza.

The *El Coyote Inn Restaurant* (☎ 822 424), Bolívar 432 and Castillo, sells a variety of good food – meals are about US$2 to US$3. Nearby, the *El Coyote Cafetería* (☎ 827 886), Bolívar 313 and Guayaquil, serves a variety of snacks as well as steaks and Mexican food – not bad. The *Kangaroo Bar*, Cevallos and J L Mera, also serves Mexican snacks, although it's primarily a bar and doesn't open until 3 pm; it's closed on Monday. *Mama Miche Restaurant* (☎ 822 913), on 13 de Abril behind the Centro Comercial Ambato, is quite good value considering it's open so late (supposedly 24 hours).

If you're staying near the bus terminal there's a basic restaurant in the terminal and food stalls outside. Also, at the traffic circle where 12 de Noviembre intersects with Avenida de las Américas, 300 metres to the west and slightly uphill from the terminal, is the *Restaurante La Paila* (☎ 824 844) which serves reasonably priced food and is the best in the terminal area.

All the best hotels have good restaurants, especially the Hotel Ambato.

Entertainment
There is some nightlife – but not much. The *Peña Tungurahua Bar* on Martínez and 13 de Abril has *música folklorica* evenings on some weekends but it doesn't get underway until about 11 pm. No cover is charged (they may have closed). Across the street, in the Centro Comercial Ambato building, there is a discotheque. You can try the *Taberna Disco Bar* in the Cine Bolívar building at 12 de Noviembre and E Espejo. There is a casino at the Hotel Ambato.

Ambato has six movie theatres, of which one may well be showing a decent film. Consult the map for locations and the local newspaper *El Heraldo* for what's playing.

Getting There & Away
Air There is a small airstrip nearby for emergency and military use only. TAME (☎ 826 601, 820 322, 822 595), Sucre 331 and Guayaquil, used to have a flight from and to Guayaquil early every morning, but these have now been suspended. They can make reservations for you from other cities.

Bus The terminal terrestre (☎ 821 481) is two km away from the town centre and buses to all destinations leave from here. The most frequent departures are for Quito (US$1.10; three hours), Baños (US$0.30; 45 minutes), Riobamba (US$0.50; one hour), and Guayaquil (US$2.40; six hours). There are several buses a day to Cuenca (US$4; seven hours) and also Guaranda (US$0.90; 2½ hours), some of which continue to Babahoyo and a couple to Chillanes. Several companies run a bus to Tena in the Oriente (US$2.25; six hours depending on road conditions).

For northern destinations it's usually best to take a bus to Quito and change at the terminal.

Train The train station is near the main bus terminal, two km away from the town centre. Services for Quito and Riobamba were suspended in 1991 but may restart in 1992. Enquire at the train station. Crowded autoferros used to leave for Quito at 6.30 am (US$0.40; 3½ hours) and at 5.30 pm for Riobamba (US$0.20; 1½ hours).

Getting Around
Bus The most important local bus service for the traveller is the route between the terminal terrestre and the town centre. From the terminal, climb the exit ramp to the Avenida de las Américas, which crosses the railway line on a bridge. On this bridge is a bus stop where a westbound (to your right) bus, often signed 'Centro', will take you to the Parque Cevallos for US$0.05.

Parque Cevallos is the centre for many buses out of town into the suburbs and is a good place to ask around if you need to get somewhere. Buses marked 'Terminal' leave from the Calle Martínez side of Parque Cevallos – if in doubt, ask. Buses to the suburb of Ficoa (for the Quinta de Montalvo) also leave from this park. A block away is Calle Bolívar, with buses to Miraflores running along it. Buses to the suburb of Atocha (more quintas) leave from 12 de Noviembre and Sevilla or E Espejo.

Taxi Taxis from the terminal terrestre to the centre will cost about US$0.50 and to Miraflores about US$1.

NEARBY VILLAGES

Salasaca and Pelileo (described later) are the most frequently visited nearby villages because they lie on the good main road to Baños. Other villages are off the main road but are interesting to visit on day trips. None of them have anywhere to stay and travellers are a rarity. Ask at the Parque Cevallos or the terminal terrestre about buses.

Píllaro, some 20 km to the north-east, is in a cereal and fruit growing area. It is known as a centre for making guitars and for carvings from animal horns. July to August are big months for fiestas with bullfights, typical highland food and parades. 15 July is the fiesta of Apostolo Santiago (Saint James) and 25 July is cantonisation day. 10 August, Quito's Independence Day, is also vigorously celebrated with a bullfight/bullrun in which the bulls charge through the streets and everybody participates.

This town is the entry point for the **Llanganates**, a very remote and difficult to reach mountain range in which Atahualpa's treasure is supposedly buried. Many bona-fide expeditions have searched for the treasure using ancient maps and documents from the time of the conquest, but nobody has found it yet!

Picaigua, some 10 km south-east of Ambato, is known for ropework and sandals made from the *cabuya* (agave) fibre. Nearby,

Pinllo is known for its leatherwork. **Patate**, 25 km from Ambato and 5km north-east of Pelileo, is known for its picturesque location on the Río Patate, the grapes grown in the region, and the production of some of the best aguardiente liquor in the highlands.

SALASACA

As you head south-east from Ambato on the Baños road, the first place of interest is Salasaca about 14 km away. The village and its environs are inhabited by some 2000 Salasaca Indians who are famous for their tapestries. They are less well known for their history, which is particularly interesting. Originally they came from Bolivia but were conquered by the Incas in the 1400s.

One of the ways in which the Incas controlled the peoples they had conquered was to move them en masse to an area which the Incas had long dominated and where there was less chance of an uprising. This is what apparently happened to the Salasacas. After the Spanish conquest, they remained where they were but retained an unusually high degree of independence and were almost unknown by outsiders until the middle of the 20th century.

The villagers are recognised by their typical dress, especially the men who are normally seen wearing broad-brimmed white hats, black ponchos, and white shirts and trousers. Traditionally they are farmers and raise their own sheep to obtain wool for their weavings which are a secondary source of income. Their tapestries are all made by hand and are different from work done by other Indian groups (though telling the difference may be difficult unless you have spent time examining Ecuadorian weaving).

There is no local produce market in Salasaca; the villagers use the nearby Pelileo Saturday market or go to Ambato. There is a craft market held every Sunday morning near the church on the Ambato-Baños road. Also along this road are several craft stores which are open daily. Salasacan tapestries are also sold in craft stores in Quito and Cuenca. There are no hotels – stay in Ambato or Baños.

There are many Indian fiestas in the Salasaca area which are worth looking out for. May and June are good months for fiestas all over the highlands. On the Sunday after Easter there is a street dance between Salasaca and Pelileo. On 15 June the Salasacas dress up in animal costumes for Santo Vintio. Corpus Christi (movable date in June) is celebrated in Salasaca and Pelileo. Saint Anthony is celebrated at the end of November.

All the usual dates (Christmas, Easter, etc) offer interesting fiesta possibilities.

the market town for nearby villages including Salasaca. Saturday is market day. Pelileo celebrates its cantonisation on 22 July with the usual highland festivities – bullfights, parades and plenty of typical food and drink.

Baños is only 24 km away but the road drops some 850 metres from Pelileo. The descent along the Pastaza River gorge is spectacular and some of the best views of the snow-capped volcano Tungurahua are to be seen on this drive. At 5016 metres, it is Ecuador's 10th highest peak and gives its name to the province.

PELILEO

Some six km beyond Salasaca on the Baños road is the rather bigger village of Pelileo. Despite its 400-year history, today's Pelileo is a very modern village. It was founded by the colonialist Antonio Clavijo in 1570 but destroyed by earthquakes in 1698, 1797, 1840 and 1949. The present site is about two km away from the ruins of the old town. It is

BAÑOS

The most recent census places the population of this small town at only some 16,000 people, yet there are about 50 hotels in Baños and its outskirts. It is one of the most important tourist spots in the country, popular with Ecuadorians and foreigners alike. Surprisingly, it is very pleasant and unspoilt and its popularity remains undiminished despite the

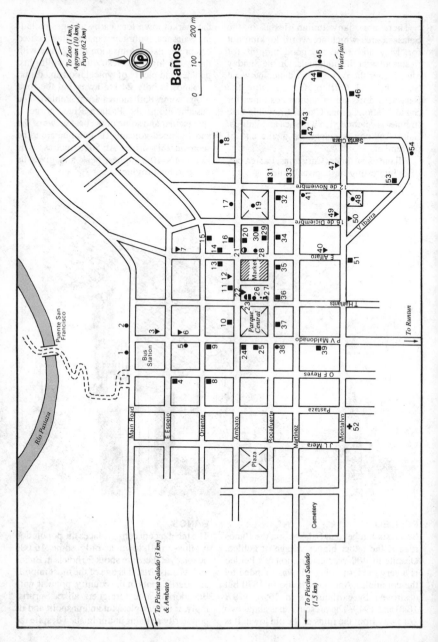

Baños

To Zoo (1 km),
Agoyan (10 km),
Puyo (62 km)

0   100   200 m

Waterfall

45
44
46

43
42

Santa Clara

18

54

31   33

47

12 de Noviembre

53

17   32
19   41

29
48

16 de Diciembre

49
50

Ibarra

15
14   16
20
21   30
28   34   40

E Alfaro

51

13
11   12   35
22   Market

26
23   27   36

T Halflants

To Runtun

10
Parque
Central   37

P V Maldonado

To Runtun →

3   6

2

5   9   24   25   38   39

O F Reyes

Bus
Station

1

4   8

Pastaza

Main Road

E Espejo

Oriente

Ambato

Rocafuerte

Martínez

J L Mera

Montalvo

52

Puente San
Francisco

Plaza

Río Pastaza

Cemetery

To Piscina Salado (3 km)
& Ambato

To Piscina Salado
(1.5 km)

■ PLACES TO STAY

4   Residencial Julia
8   Residencial El Rey
9   Residencial Charvic
10 Residencial La Delicia 1
11 Hotel Humboldt/Paraíso
13 Pensión Angela
14 Pensión Patty
15 Residencial Magdalena
16 Residencial Baños, Hostal Bolívar & others
20 Residencial Cordillera & others
24 Hostal Flor de Oriente
25 Residencial La Delicia 2
29 Residencial Lucy
30 Hotels Alborada & Achupallas
31 Residencial Teresita
32 Hotel Guayaquil, Hostal Agoyán, Residencial Acapulco
33 Hotel Americano
34 Residencial Anita
35 Hotel Danubio
36 Hostal Los Helechos/Las Orquideas
37 Residenciales Olguita & Los Piños
39 Residencial Timara
42 Hostal El Castillo
44 Hotel Sangay
46 Hotel Palace
51 Villa Gertrudis
53 Residencial Villa Santa Clara

▼ PLACES TO EAT

3   Cafeteria Chushi
6   El Eden
7   Restaurant Monica

10 Rico Pan
12 Chifa Central
16 Donde Marcelo
22 Chifa Oriental
29 Rincón de Suecia
30 Mi Pan
40 Le Petit
43 Restaurant El Paisano
47 Café Cultura
49 Regine Café Alemán
50 El Marqués & Restaurant Vegetariano y Carnes

OTHER

1   Sugar Cane Stalls
2   Peña
5   Backpacker's Store
10 Bus Stop for El Salado
13 Hard Rock Café & Video Cine
17 Basílica & Museum
18 La Burbuja Disco
19 Parque de la Basílica
21 Bus Stop for Zoo & Agoyán
23 Post Office
26 IETEL
27 Town Hall & Clocktower
28 America Nuestra Peña
37 Banco del Pacífico
38 Store & Book Exchange
41 Banco del Pacífico
45 Piscina de La Virgen (Hot Baths)
48 Children's Playground
52 Hospital
54 Santa Clara Swimming Pool

many thousands of visitors annually. Some people love it and spend a week or more; other travellers think the town too 'touristy' and pass on through. It is in a beautiful spot and there are many attractions in the area – it's certainly worth a visit so then decide for yourself whether to love it or leave it.

Unless you've only just arrived in Latin America, you'll know that Baños means 'baths' and that is precisely what the town is famous for. Some of them are fed by thermal springs from the base of the active volcano Tungurahua, which means 'little hell' in Quechua. Other baths have melt water running into them from Tungurahua's icy flanks. Locals swear that the baths are great for your health. While that is a debatable point, it is true that the casual atmosphere of this pretty resort town makes it an excellent place to unwind after some hard travelling, and few travellers can resist the opportunity to relax here for a while.

The baths are not the only attraction. Baños' elevation of 1800 metres gives it an extremely agreeable climate and the surroundings are green and attractive. There are good opportunities for both short walks and ambitious climbs of Volcán Tungurahua as well as El Altar, an even higher extinct volcano some 25 km south of Tungurahua. Both of these are in Parque Nacional Sangay which is described later.

Baños is also the gateway town into the jungle via Puyo and Misahuallí. East of Baños the road drops spectacularly and there are exceptional views of the upper Amazonian basin stretching away before you. In the town itself there are more attractions; an interesting basilica, a small museum, a little nightlife, and restaurants selling typical local food.

There is another, much smaller, Baños near Cuenca, also with thermal pools.

Information

There is no CETUR tourist office but information can be obtained from the town hall on the Parque Central. Several private tour agencies and guides will provide tourist information (see Tour Agencies & Guides which follows) and owners of hotels and restaurants are used to answering questions. There are always so many travellers in town that they are often your best source of up-to-date information.

Money The Banco del Pacífico (☎ 740 336/48), Martínez and 12 de Noviembre, changes both US cash dollars and travellers' cheques at rates about the same as Quito's. They are open from 11 am to 1 pm from Monday to Friday. Various stores, restaurants and hotels may also change US dollars.

Post & Telecommunications IETEL and the post office are both on the Parque Central. The IETEL sometimes has problems in making connections 'because of the surrounding mountains' and may close early because of this. The post office is open only from Tuesday to Saturday.

Tour Agencies & Guides There are many 'guides' to provide services for the large numbers of tourists passing through town. Some guides are bad, not very experienced or dishonest. If you hire a guide, make sure

that they have recommendations – listen to what other travellers have to say.

The Cafetería Chushi, on E Espejo and P V Maldonado by the bus terminal, has a library of guidebooks and provides information. A couple of doors down is a tourist information office (☎ 740 015/118/159) which has maps and information and can rent gear. The backpackers' store on P V Maldonado between E Espejo and Oriente has information and sells gear (backpacks, nylon jackets and sleeping bags).

For climbing Tungurahua, you need someone who knows what they are doing to prevent potentially fatal accidents. Carlos and José at the Pensión Patty (☎ 740 202) have been providing guiding services and renting equipment for years. They can also arrange for a vehicle to take you part of the way up the mountain and for mules to carry your gear. Gear (eg ice axe, crampons) can be rented for about US$1.50 per item per day. Guides charge roughly US$100 to take two people up Tungurahua – cheaper guides are available but may not have adequate experience.

For trips down to the Oriente, Tsantsa Tours, also based at the Pensión Patty, has been recommended. Guides are Shuar Indians (Sebastian Moya has been especially recommended) who are respectful and sensitive of the local people and environment – tours may involve flying in to remote areas and then hiking and canoeing. Marco Bermeo, based at the Residencial Timara (☎ 740 599), has also been recommended (although some of the guides who work for him are not as good). Bermeo is married to a Danish woman and they have a store on Maldonado and Rocafuerte where you can get information and also use their English book exchange. Fluvial Ayahuasca Tours has received several negative reports.

Tours into the jungle last about three to seven days and cost about US$25 to US$40 per person per day, depending on how remote an area you visit. A group of at least four or more is needed. Cheaper trips hiking around the Baños area are also available. Baños is always full of travellers and is a

Top: San Lorenzo Autoferro, Ibarra (RR)
Left: Church door in Otavalo (RR)
Right: Topiary at Tulcán Cemetery (RR)

Top: Town of Baños (TW)
Left: Aerial view of Cotopaxi crater (RR)
Right: Private Chapel at 400-year-old Hacienda La Cienga, Central Highlands (RR)

good town in which to organise a group if you are not already with one.

Various people rent horses for riding in the area. Price can vary from about US$15 to US$40 for two people for four to six hours – some horses are in much better shape than others and a guide usually accompanies you. Ask around. Outfitters which have been recommended include a German named Christian (☎ 746 690), Caballos José at Maldonado and Martínez, Julio Albán and Luis Sánchez at the tourist information office, and at the Restaurant Monica (which also has bicycles for hire).

Fiestas Baños became the seat of its canton on 16 December 1944, and an annual fiesta is celebrated on this and the preceding days. There are the usual processions, fireworks, music and a great deal of street dancing and drinking at night. Fun! Also, there are processions and fireworks during the entire month of October as the various barrios of Baños take turns to pay homage to the local icon, Nuestra Señora de Agua Santa.

Emergency The small local hospital (☎ 740 443/301) is on Montalvo and Pastaza. The police (☎ 740 251) are next to the town hall on the Parque Central. One of the biggest pharmacies is Farmacia La Salud (☎ 740 281) on Mera and Oriente. There are several others along Ambato.

Things to See
In the town itself the basilica with the **Santuario de Nuestra Señora de Agua Santa** is worth seeing. This Dominican church is dedicated to the Virgin of the Holy Water, who is credited with the performance of several miracles in the Baños area. The annual October celebration in her honour has much street music and many Indian bands playing, but generally she is the object of devout admiration, as exemplified by the many offerings to her and the paintings depicting her miracles.

These paintings are simple but charming, with explanations in Spanish along the lines of 'On 30 January, 1904, Sr X fell off his

horse as he was crossing the Río Pastaza bridge. As he fell 70 metres to the torrents below he yelled 'Holy Mother of the Holy Water' and was miraculously saved!' Other paintings show people being miraculously saved from exploding volcanoes, burning hotels, transit accidents and other misfortunes. Reading the explanations is amusing and a great way to practise your Spanish. Please remember however, that this is a place of worship and act accordingly.

Just above the church is a museum with an eclectic display of stuffed animals, religious paintings, church vestments and local handicrafts. It's open daily from 7.30 am to 4 pm and costs US$0.10. There is also a small gift shop.

Things to Do
First of all, relax. This is a laid-back town and most people take it slowly. You're on vacation in Baños.

Baths There are three baths, two in Baños and a third out of town. All have a modest entrance fee for which they provide changing rooms and a safe storage system for your clothes. Towels and bathing costumes may be available for rent and soap is for sale (nude bathing is prohibited).

The best-known bath is the Piscina de La Virgen, with hot showers and several pools of different temperatures. You can't miss them – they're right under the big waterfall at the south-east end of town. You can see the falls from most parts of Baños. They charge US$0.20, are open well before dawn and start getting quite busy soon after sunrise.

Nearby is a cold swimming pool at Santa Clara, which charges US$0.10. They have a sauna available for US$1 per person. Several of the better hotels have swimming pools or saunas.

If you walk up the hill past the cemetery on Martínez, you'll end up on a track which crosses a stream (Quebrada de Naguasco) on a small wooden footbridge. The track continues on the other side to a road in front of Cabañas Bascun, where you turn left to reach the Piscina El Salado. Here there are hot and cold showers, several pools of varying temperatures and an ice-cold waterfall to stand under if you're the masochistic sort. A real deal for US$0.25. Because these are two or three km of out of town, they're not quite so crowded. There are buses too.

Note that the locals use the pools for washing themselves and may enter the water with clothing on, especially on Friday which is traditionally washing day for the locals (to beat the out-of-town weekend crowds perhaps). The water is not particularly clean and you should avoid putting your head under or getting water in your mouth if you have a sensitive stomach. The baths are cleaned on Sunday evening (but the schedule is liable to change).

Despite this caveat, the waters of the baths are touted for their restorative and healthful properties. Chlorates, sulphates and magnesium are among the principal chemicals found in the baths. The Virgen and El Salado waters supposedly reach temperatures of over 50°C whilst the Santa Clara pool is normally about 24°C.

Walks Once you've visited all the pools, there are many walks to take. Plenty of information about these is available in Baños. The following are some suggestions.

The walk down to the Río Pastaza is easy and popular. Just behind the sugar cane stalls by the bus station is a short trail which leads to the **Puente San Francisco** (bridge) which crosses the river. You can continue on trails up the other side as far as you want.

Going south on Calle Maldonado takes you to a footpath which climbs to a building with a white cross high over Baños, and then continues to the tiny settlement of **Runtun** some two hours away. Great views!

At the police checkpoint at the west end of town, turn right by a religious shrine and walk down to the Puente San Martín and visit the impressive falls of **Cascada Ines María** a few hundred metres to the right of the bridge. You can also cross the bridge and continue to the village of **Lligua**, about three hours away. From this road, trails climb up the hills to your right.

You can walk out of town east on the main road to get to the **zoo** (☎ 740 552) a couple of km away. There is a bus as well. The zoo, although small, houses an interesting collection of Ecuadorian species, including tapir and the rare harpy eagle. Continue down to the river just beyond the zoo, cross it on the suspension bridge and follow the trail back round to Baños, crossing the Puente San Francisco. It takes an hour or two.

Six or seven km beyond the zoo are the famous **Agoyán Falls**, once the most impressive falls in the area but now turned to a mere trickle by the recent construction of the Agoyán Dam and hydroelectric project, in itself an impressive sight. Buses go here. Beyond Agoyán the road continues to the village of Agua Verde and on to the Amazonian lowlands, as described in The Northern Oriente chapter.

Hiking and climbing Tungurahua is described in the Parque Nacional Sangay section.

Places to Stay

There are literally dozens of hotels to choose from and obviously I couldn't spend a night in each! Therefore many of these descriptions are necessarily brief. Most of the hotels are bottom end in that they charge well under US$5 per person, but many are good value. Some of the cheap hotels have varying quality of rooms – check your rooms before accepting them. Others charge double rates for one night but will drop their prices if you spend more than one night. Usually there are plenty of rooms available but choice can become very limited and prices high if you arrive on a Friday night or if there is a fiesta underway. Try and arrive early in the day for best rooms. The prices given below assume that you are not arriving just before the annual fiestas.

Hotels in Baños can be noisy – it is a vacation town, after all. For quieter places check out the hotels at the El Salado Baths, listed at the end.

Places to Stay – bottom end

The block of Ambato west of the Parque de

la Basílica has about eight inexpensive hotels as well as several bars and restaurants – it's at the centre of things. The best of the hotels is probably the *Residencial Baños* (☎ 740 284) which is clean and good and charges about US$2 per person. They have hot water and some rooms with private bath. Also quite good are the *Hostal Bolívar* (☎ 740 497) and *Residencial Cordillera* (☎ 740 536). Other hotels in this block are cheaper and much more basic – they include *Pensión Luisita, Pensión San Martín, Pensión Ecuador, Residencial Irmita, Hostal Guayas* and *Residencial Guadalupe*. There are better cheap hotels nearby.

For many years the family-run *Pensión Patty* (☎ 740 202), E Alfaro 556 and Ambato, has been very popular with gringos, with basic but clean rooms, friendly management and information on trekking, climbing and horse riding in the area. Rooms are about US$1.80 the first night and US$1.25 for subsequent nights. The pensión has one hot and several cold showers, and a communal kitchen if you want to cook your own food. You sometimes meet a great group of people – everyone chips in with something to eat or drink, conversations flow, a rum bottle gets opened or a guitar appears. Opposite is the *Pensión Angela* which is also cheap and OK.

Other good cheap hotels include the basic but clean and friendly *Hotel Americano* (☎ 740 352), 12 de Noviembre and Martínez, with large rooms and a simple restaurant. They charge only about US$1 per person – a good deal. Nearby is the *Residencial Teresita* (☎ 740 471), 12 de Noviembre and Rocafuerte, with clean rooms, some of which overlook the Parque de la Basílica. They have hot water in the communal showers and charge between US$1.25 and US$2 per person depending on the room. These hotels will give you access to cooking facilities on request.

There are several other hotels on the Parque de la Basílica – they all have some rooms with views of the parque and basilica. Rooms with a view are attractive but are liable to suffer from street noise – ask for a room in the back if this is going to bother you. On the south side, the *Hostal Agoyán* charges about US$1.50 per person and has hot water. The similarly priced *Hotel Guayaquil* (☎ 740 434) has large rooms, hot showers and a restaurant. Both are OK but the *Residencial Acapulco* (☎ 740 457) on the same block is not as good, though still acceptable. On the west side of the parque is the new and modern *Hotel Alborada* (☎ 740 814) which has good clean rooms with private bath and hot water for US$3/5 for singles/doubles and a little less in rooms with shared baths. Next door is the *Hotel Achupallas* (☎ 740 422/389) which is also good and charges about US$3.50 per person in rooms with private bath and hot water.

Just west of the parque on Rocafuerte are more good hotels. The friendly *Residencial Lucy* (☎ 740 466) is very good value for US$1.60 per person in rooms with private bath and hot water, or a little less in rooms with shared bath. The equally friendly *Residencial Anita* (☎ 740 319) has small but spotless rooms and comfortable beds. They charge US$2.50 per person in rooms with private bath and hot water or about half that price in rooms with shared bath. They will let you use the kitchen on request. The *Hotel Danubio* (☎ 740 426), Rocafuerte and E Alfaro, is old and run down but has hot showers and large rooms for about US$1.50 per person.

The good and friendly *Residencial Timara* (☎ 740 599), P V Maldonado and Martínez, is about US$1.25 per person. They have hot water and jungle information and allow you to use their kitchen facilities. Also good is the *Residencial Villa Santa Clara* (☎ 740 349), 12 de Noviembre and V Ibarra, which offers kitchen facilities and hot showers and is set in a garden. They charge a little over US$1 per person. I've heard they have an 11 pm curfew – check if you are planning on a late night out.

On the Parque Central the *Residencial Olguita* (☎ 740 271) has front rooms with good views of the parque. They have hot showers and charge about US$1.25 per person. Next door is the better *Residencial Los Piños* (☎ 740 252) which also has some rooms with views of the parque at about US$2 per person. On the corner of the parque is the *Hostal Los Helechos* (☎ 740 387) which reportedly has been recently renamed *Las Orquideas* (helechos means ferns and orquideas means orchids – whatever the hotel's current name is, you will see plenty of potted plants in the lobby). They charge about US$3/5 for clean singles/doubles with private bath and hot water and have a café downstairs which serves vegetarian food (a recent report says it's closed, but some say it's open). Others on the Parque Central include the *Residencial La Delicia 1* (☎ 740 477) which is friendly but has only one hot shower for 22 rooms and the newer *Residencial La Delicia 2* (☎ 740 537). Both have some rooms overlooking the parque and are OK for about US$1.40 per person.

The friendly and pleasant *Hostal El Castillo* (☎ 740 285), Martínez 255 and Santa Clara, has received several recommendations. They provide home cooking in their dining room and charge US$5 per person in rooms with private shower and hot water and including three meals each day – a very good deal. Rooms without the meals are US$2.25 per person. The *Hotel Humboldt/Paraíso* (☎ 740 430/90), Ambato and T Halflants, also has clean rooms with private bathrooms and hot water for about the same price and can provide meals. Their breakfasts have been recommended. The Danish-run *Café Cultura* (☎ 740 419), Montalvo and Santa Clara, has three clean double rooms upstairs which share a bathroom with hot water. They charge US$4 per person including breakfast.

The *Residencial Charvic* (☎ 740 298/113), P V Maldonado and Oriente, is the best hotel within a block of the bus station. They charge US$3 per person but will give discounts for stays of more than one night. Rooms are clean with private bath, hot water and TV. Closer to the terminal are the cheaper and fairly basic *Residencial Julia* at E Espejo and O F Reyes and the *Residencial El Rey* (☎ 740 322) at Oriente and O F Reyes.

The good clean *Residencial Magdalena* (☎ 740 233/364), Oriente 1037 and 6 de Diciembre, charges about US$4 per person

in rooms with private bath and hot water. The *Hostal Flor de Oriente* (☎ 740 418/058), Ambato and P V Maldonado, has clean rooms with private bath, hot water and telephone for about US$4.50 per person. They have a decent restaurant downstairs and parking is available. These hotels would probably be priced in the middle range in a larger city.

Places to Stay – middle & top end

The *Hotel Palace* (☎ 740 470), Montalvo 2003 by the waterfall, is clean and pleasant with a good restaurant attached. There is a garden, games room, and the owners are friendly. Rooms with private baths are US$8/11/14 for singles/doubles/triples – suitable for families. They have rooms both in the old-fashioned house and in the annex which vary somewhat in quality.

The *Hotel Sangay* (☎ 740 490/056 or in Quito 432 066) is set in pleasant gardens opposite the Piscina de La Virgen baths. There are squash and tennis courts, a swimming pool, jacuzzi and sauna, and restaurant and bar. The (more expensive) rooms in the cabins have TV and are definitely better than rooms in the main building, where the rooms on the ground floor in particular have been criticised as damp and musty. All rooms have private bathroom and hot water. The hotel is popular with Ecuadorian tour groups. Rooms in the hotel building are US$11/15 for singles/doubles; rooms in the cabins are US$14/21 for singles/doubles. Rates include continental breakfast and use of the facilities. Non-guests can use the pool etc for a small fee.

The much quieter and lower key *Villa Gertrudis* (☎ 740 441), Montalvo and V Ibarra, is also set in pretty gardens and has a pool. They charge US$16 per person including two meals and have been recommended, but are often full. Non-guests can use the pool for about US$1.

Houses for Rent Ask at the *El Paisano* restaurant for simple houses to rent by the week or month.

Places to Stay – El Salado Baths

About two km from town by footpath or four km by road is the Piscina El Salado, with four hotels nearby which are quieter than most of the places in Baños. There are two basic US$1 residenciales right by the baths – *El Salado* and the *Puerto del Salado* with good views of Tungurahua.

About 10 minutes before getting to the baths are the *Cabañas Bascun* (☎ 740 334, in Quito at 552 637) which have a pool, sauna, tennis court and restaurant. Clean rooms in cabins are about US$12/18 for singles/doubles, including breakfast. Non-residents can use the pool and sauna for about US$1.50.

Between the Bascun and the pools is a recently opened bed & breakfast, the *Casa Nahuazo* (☎ 740 315) which is run by a friendly Hungarian/North American couple who arrived in Ecuador with the Peace Corps over a decade ago and somehow never left. The hotel is very quiet and is a good place to get travel information. There is an English book exchange. They have five clean and pleasant double rooms with private bath and hot water and charge about US$7.50 per person including continental breakfast.

Places to Eat

Several European-style restaurants have opened in Baños over the last few years and they tend to be popular with travellers. Among places which are currently enjoying favour are the following.

The *Rincón de Suecia* (☎ 740 365), Rocafuerte and 6 de Diciembre, bills itself as a 'pizzería' but also sells good steaks and seafood. The meals are good and reasonably priced and the place is often crowded with European travellers – it can get rather smoky.

Regine Cafe Alemán, Montalvo and 6 de Diciembre, has a German menu and is good for breakfast from 8 am onwards as well as for light meals, coffee and drinks. They serve (among other things) tasty potato pancakes and innovative concoctions of tea, coffee, hot chocolate etc laced with various alcoholic beverages. Prices are reasonable.

Le Petit, E Alfaro 246 and Montalvo, has a French menu and is not as cheap as the previous two recommendations. Nevertheless it's popular with travellers and the food is good – though portions are modest as is the way of most French restaurants. The service is leisurely and it's a place to hang out. They show video movies on some days.

The Danish-run *Café Cultura* (☎ 740 419), Montalvo and Santa Clara, features homemade breads, quiches, fruit pies, fresh fish, pastries, fruit juices and various other healthy and delectable items. English and Danish magazines are available to read.

The best Ecuadorian restaurant is probably the *El Marqués* (☎ 740 187), Montalvo and V Ibarra. They are particularly recommended for their steaks – about US$3. Also good is *Donde Marcelo*, Ambato and 6 de Diciembre, which has Ecuadorian food, friendly service, and a very popular bar upstairs. A reader recommends *Mario's*, Rocafuerte 275 and E Alfaro, for seafood.

There are several restaurants advertising vegetarian dishes (though most places have several vegetarian dishes on their menus). Travellers recommend the *Restaurant Vegetariano y Carnes*, Montalvo and V Ibarra, for friendly service and good food. Three course meals are under US$3. The simpler and cheaper *El Paisano* (☎ 740 207), Martínez and Santa Clara, has some vegetarian dishes but has received mixed reviews.

The *Chifa Oriental* and *Chifa Central* both on Ambato by the market are good for both Chinese and local food. There are several other cheap restaurants on Ambato and around the market. The bakery next to the market is one of the first places to have fresh bread in the mornings. Other bakers which have been recommended include *Rico Pan* on Ambato by the Parque Central – they have brown and rye bread, muesli, yoghurt and Beatles music on the stereo. Also try *Mi Pan* on the Parque de la Basílica, next to the Hotel Achupallas, for a fruit milkshake and croissant breakfast. *El Eden*, P V Maldonado and Oriente, has good pancake breakfasts, or try their muesli, yoghurt and fruit salad. Nearby is the *Café Chushi*, opposite the bus terminal, with a variety of snacks and an

English book exchange. The *Restaurant Monica*, E Alfaro and E Espejo, continues to be a gringo hang-out despite its slow and inefficient service. Menus in 12 languages hang on the wall but the menu prices and what you are charged may differ – ask.

On certain days (particularly during fiestas) you can buy cuy at some of the market restaurants. They are normally roasted whole and some people find the sight of their little roasted feet sticking up and their tiny teeth poking out a bit disconcerting. Don't say I didn't warn you! Surprisingly, they taste quite good, a little like a cross between a chicken and a rabbit. In fact the local nickname for them in some areas is *conejo*, which means rabbit.

Another local food popular in Baños is toffee. You can see people swinging it onto wooden pegs in the doorways of many of the town's shops – the idea is to blend and soften the toffee. You can try a fresh, soft piece for a few sucres or buy a box of hardened toffees as a souvenir of Baños.

Entertainment
Nightlife in Baños consists mainly of chatting with new friends in the restaurants after a strenuous day of soaking in the pools. Generally the town closes down early – many restaurants close by 9 pm. The cinema on the central plaza is closed, although the *Video Cine* opposite Pensión Patty has public screenings of their videos – ask what's available. They may play a movie on request. Other video 'cinemas' are opening.

There are several bars which are frequented by travellers but their popularity tends to wax and wane from year to year – new ones open and close frequently. Try the *Hard Rock Café* on E Alfaro and Ambato for inexpensive drinks and old rock classics. The somewhat pricier bar above *Donde Marcelo* is also popular and has rock music and a dance floor. Travellers hang out in the European restaurants mentioned above – they tend to stay open later than most. All of these are suitable for women. Less suitable for women are the many small pool halls (especially on the back streets) which are

frequented mainly by men – OK if you enjoy pool.

A couple of peñas with Ecuadorian folklorico music have recently opened – they are not as good as the peñas in towns with more Indian influence, such as Otavalo. Nevertheless, they make a change from rock and roll. They follow the usual pattern of being open only late on weekend nights – not much action before 10 pm. One place is *Peña América Nuestra* on Alfaro 420 and Ambato. Another place is the *Peña* a couple of blocks east of the bus terminal on the main road.

La Burbuja disco (☎ 740 520), on an alley off the east end of Ambato, is open nights from Tuesday to Saturday but there's rarely much happening except perhaps weekends after 10 pm (bring all your friends and make it happen). There's no cover but they get you for a minimum consumption of about US$4 per couple on Friday and Saturday nights (this may be waived if you show your passport). There is another disco out by the zoo, a couple of km east of town; this is *La Colita* (☎ 740 159).

Getting There & Away
Buses from Ambato's terminal terrestre leave about every half hour for Baños. The fare is US$0.30 and the ride is 45 minutes. From Quito and many other towns it's sometimes quicker to catch a bus to Ambato and change rather than wait for the less frequent direct buses.

The Baños terminal terrestre is within walking distance of most hotels – it's a small town. Buses for Quito (US$1.40; 3½ hours) leave almost every hour or you can take more frequent buses to Ambato and change for other destinations. There are frequent departures for Riobamba (US$0.40; one hour) but most of these buses go to Riobamba's Oriente bus terminal which is several km away from the main bus terminal (if you need to make a connection).

Ticket offices in the Baños bus terminal will sell you tickets for buses to the Oriente (Puyo or Tena) but usually won't guarantee you a seat nor give you a refund if the bus is full, except if the bus originates in Baños.

Therefore you should avoid buying a ticket for a bus originating in Quito, Riobamba or Ambato. You can, however, buy a ticket from the driver, so it's best to wait for a bus to pass by and then board if there's room. It's best to buy tickets in advance for buses starting at Baños.

During the rainiest months (July and August in the lowlands) there may be landslides blocking the road. In that case you take a bus to the closed area, drag your luggage across a km or more of churned-up mud, then catch another bus to your destination. This *trasbordo* (as the mud-slogging system is euphemistically called) is a frequent occurrence on roads in the Oriente during the rainy months, so be prepared. Assuming no problems with road conditions, the ride to Puyo costs US$1 and takes two to three hours. To Tena costs US$2 and takes five to six hours.

Getting Around
Eastbound local buses for the zoo and Agoyán Falls are marked 'Agoyán' and leave every few minutes during daylight hours from the corner of Ambato and E Alfaro. Westbound buses leave from the central plaza outside Residencial La Delicia 1. They are marked 'El Salado' and go to the baths of that name. Fares are about US$0.05. A taxi to these baths costs about US$0.40.

Buses to Río Verde leave from the bus terminal about once an hour.

PARQUE NACIONAL SANGAY
Stretching for about 70 km south and southeast of Baños, the 272,000-hectare Parque Nacional Sangay is one of the most remote and inaccessible areas in Ecuador. The park was established in 1979 and protects an incredible variety of terrain. Its western boundary is marked by the Eastern Cordillera and three of Ecuador's highest volcanoes are within the park. The most northerly of these, Tungurahua, can be accessed easily from Baños but the more southerly volcanoes of El Altar and Sangay require much greater effort to be reached. The area around the park's namesake Volcán Sangay, in particular, is very rugged and

remote and relatively few people have penetrated it. Nevertheless, the three volcanoes provide the most frequently used accesses to the park.

From the park's western areas, which climb to in excess of 5000 metres around each of the three volcanoes, the terrain plunges dizzyingly from the high páramos down the eastern slopes of the Andes to elevations barely in excess of 1000 metres at the park's eastern boundaries. In between is terrain so steep, rugged and wet (over 4000 mm annually in some eastern areas) that it remains a wilderness in the truest sense. There are a few small and remote Andean communities (not large enough to be graced by the title of villages) dotted around the páramos, but the tangled and thickly vegetated slopes east of the mountains are the haunt of very rarely seen mammals such as Andean spectacled bears, mountain tapirs, pumas, ocelots, jaguarundis and porcupines. Nobody lives there.

Only one road of any importance enters this national park, going from Riobamba to Alao (the main access point for Volcán Sangay) and petering out in the páramos to the east. Another road is still under construction. When this dirt road is completed it will link Guamote in the highlands with Macas in the southern Oriente, passing the southern extremities of the park. Colonisation following in the wake of these roads is the greatest threat to the park, but the inhospitability of the terrain will probably prevent severe damage to these wild areas and their scenic, biological and geological diversity.

Tungurahua
With an elevation of 5016 metres, Tungurahua is Ecuador's 10th highest peak. It is a beautiful cone-shaped volcano with a small cap of snow perched jauntily atop its lush green slopes. The volcano is active but has had no eruption since the beginning of this century. Fumaroles and steam vents can be seen in the crater. It is just within the northern boundaries of Parque Nacional Sangay and is the most frequent access point to at least a small part of the park.

Many travellers like to walk part of the way up the volcano, perhaps as far as the village of Pondoa or to the refugio at 3800 metres. Beyond the refugio the going gets steep and you should be careful on the slick grassy slopes – a tourist slipped on the grass in 1988 and fell 45 metres to his death. The final section on snow may or may not require crampons and ice axe, depending on the conditions. The summit is often very cloudy and climbers have become quite disoriented, which has led to other deaths as people lose the trail and head off in the wrong direction. The mountain is considered one of the easier ones to climb in Ecuador, but don't underestimate it. The 3200 metres of vertical ascent from Baños require plenty of endurance and the steep and misty upper slopes are not for novices.

From near the police checkpoint west of town there is a trail climbing to your left to the village of Pondoa (two hours), the climbers' refugio (four to six more hours), and the summit of Tungurahua. There is a dirt road that goes from Baños to Pondoa and then on to a point about half way to the refugio (the road does not, for the most part, follow the trail). Near this point there is a park entrance station where you pay a fee of about US$1 which allows use of the refugio.

A taxi can be hired from Baños to the end of the road for about US$6 and a pickup truck can be arranged from the Pensión Patty several times a week. This costs US$1 per person. The Pensión Patty has climbing information and can provide guides and rent equipment. Mules can be hired in Baños or in Pondoa (where there is a basic store).

The refugio is simply a roof over your head – bring food, cooking equipment, and sleeping bag. There is a stream for water. Do not leave anything in the refugio as it will probably disappear. The refugio can get very crowded at weekends. The mountain can be climbed at any time of year but December to March tend to be favoured. The wettest months in the Oriente (July and August) tend to influence Tungurahua's weather, often making it rainy and foggy at that time. There have been recent reports of armed robbery at the refugio (which has no guardian). Check in Baños or with the South American Explorer's Club in Quito for more information about this. For more information read *Climbing & Hiking in Ecuador*.

El Altar

This jagged and long-extinct volcano is 5319 metres high and is the fifth highest mountain in Ecuador. It is considered the most technically difficult of Ecuador's peaks and was not climbed until 1963. The wild páramo surrounding the mountain and the greenish lake (which is called Laguna Amarilla or Yellow Lagoon) within the blown away crater are targets for adventurous backpackers with complete camping gear. Although the area looks almost uninhabited, do not leave any gear unattended or it will disappear.

To get to El Altar, take a bus to Penipe, a village halfway between Baños and Riobamba. From here, go to Candelaria, about 15 km away. There is supposedly a daily bus between Penipe and Candelaria, trucks go there occasionally, or you can hire a pickup truck in Penipe. From Candelaria (which has a very simple store) it is about 2 km to the Hacienda Releche near which there is a Parque Nacional Sangay station. You pay the park fee (US$2) here and can stay the night for a further US$1. The station has cooking and washing facilities, but may be closed – check with the CETUR or MAG offices in Riobamba or with the climbing guides in Baños, Ambato or Riobamba.

From here it is a full-day hike to the crater. Guides and mules can be hired in Candelaria. There are many trails in the Candelaria and park station area and it is worth having a guide to show you the beginning of the main trail to El Altar, less than an hour away from the station. Once on the main trail the going is fairly obvious.

The best times to go are as for Tungurahua.

Sangay

This 5230-metre volcano is one of the most active in the Andes, constantly spewing out rocks, smoke and ash. The volcanological situation changes from hour to hour and year to year. The mountain is not technically difficult to climb but people attempting it run the risk of being killed by the explosions and therefore climbing attempts are rare. You can hike to the base if you wish, although the approach is long and tedious and the best views are from afar.

To get there take a bus south-east from Riobamba to the villages of Licto or Pungalá, which are next to one another. From there, occasional trucks go a further 20 km to the village of Alao where there is a national park ranger station. Here you pay the park fee, get information and may be allowed to sleep. There are a couple of simple stores in Alao. Guides are available in Alao for the three or four-day hike to base camp – you'll probably get hopelessly lost without a guide. Guides will watch you climb the mountain from the base camp – but they won't go up with you! Enough said.

Another approach is to take the incomplete highway from Guamote to Macas. The road goes south-west as far as the village of Atillo, then becomes a mule trail dropping down through the eastern Andes to the village of San Vicente, about two or three days away. En route, you pass through the southernmost extremity of the national park (see The Southern Oriente chapter). This long and ambitious hike is described in *Climbing & Hiking in Ecuador*, as are the approaches and climbs of Sangay and El Altar.

GUARANDA

Guaranda is the capital of the agricultural province of Bolívar but nevertheless is a small town (population about 15,000). Its name derives from that of the Indian chief Guarango. Guaranda is a quiet, provincial town which has been described as 'dismal'. I found it dignified rather than dismal, and it is pleasantly located with pretty hills all around – there are supposedly seven of these, which convinces the locals to call themselves 'the Rome of the Andes'. Ecuadorian guidebooks call it 'The authentic provincial city'. It certainly can't be described as exciting and the main reason you'd want to be here is probably for the bus rides, which are spectacular.

The road from Ambato is paved and comfortable (it was officially inaugurated in November 1980). The 99-km drive climbs from Ambato at 2800 metres to bleak páramo at well over 4000 metres before dropping to Guaranda at 2650 metres, making this the highest paved road in the country. It passes within 10 km of Chimborazo (6310 metres) and Carihuairazo (5020 metres), the highest and ninth highest peaks in Ecuador.

For the best views of these giants you should get seats on the left of the bus (if going to Guaranda). In addition to the mountains, you get a good look at the harsh and inhospitable Andean moorlands known as the páramo. The bus ride can get cold so remember to carry some warm clothes onto the bus with you.

When you leave Guaranda there are other equally exciting rides. You can continue on down the western slopes of the Andes to Babahoyo and the coast – a route which was once the most important connection between Quito and Guayaquil but which is now infrequently used. Or you can head due east to Riobamba on a dizzying dirt road which skirts the southern flanks of Chimborazo and gives fantastic views that are not for the faint-hearted (sit on the left side of the bus).

Information

Cash dollars can be changed (with difficulty) at the Banco de Pichincha (☎ 980 143), 7 de Mayo and 10 de Agosto, at 5% less than the Quito rate. The bank is open from 9 am to 1.30 pm daily except Sunday. Travellers' cheques are not changed – it's best to bring enough sucres with you.

Guaranda has an IETEL office on Rocafuerte near Pichincha and a post office on the corner of the Parque Simón Bolívar at García Moreno and Convención de 1884.

Things to See & Do

There is one movie theatre, which doesn't have shows every day. Off the map in the

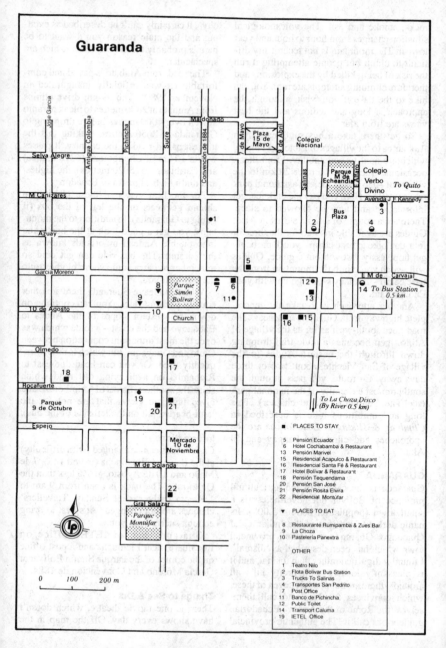

Guaranda

PLACES TO STAY

- 5 Pensión Ecuador
- 6 Hotel Cochabamba & Restaurant
- 13 Pensión Marivel
- 15 Residencial Acapulco & Restaurant
- 16 Residencial Santa Fé & Restaurant
- 17 Hotel Bolívar & Restaurant
- 18 Pensión Tequendama
- 20 Pensión San José
- 21 Pensión Rosita Elvira
- 22 Residencial Montúfar

PLACES TO EAT

- 8 Restaurante Rumipamba & Zues Bar
- 9 La Choza
- 10 Pastelería Panextra

OTHER

- 1 Teatro Nilo
- 2 Flota Bolívar Bus Station
- 3 Trucks To Salinas
- 4 Transportes San Pedrito
- 7 Post Office
- 11 Banco de Pichincha
- 12 Public Toilet
- 14 Transport Caluma
- 19 IETEL Office

0   100   200 m

To Quito

Avenida J F Kennedy

E M de Carvajal
14 *To Bus Station*
0.5 km

To La Choza Disco
(By River 0.5 km)

south end of town (which the locals call *abajo* or lower end) you'll find the *Disco La Choza* with a bar, restaurant, and music. Admission is US$0.75 and it's frequented by Peace Corps volunteers on their time off (or at least it used to be).

The main market day is Saturday with a smaller one on Wednesday. The best place for the market is Plaza 15 de Mayo – even on ordinary days it's worth visiting for its pleasantly quiet, forgotten colonial air (if you ignore the school on one side). The market at Mercado 10 de Noviembre is held in a modern but ugly concrete building.

If you've got nothing to do, go down to the Parque Montúfar and see if one of the statues there still has a bees' nest under its right armpit! (A reader of the 2nd edition of this book assures me it does, but please keep me informed.) Walk the streets for a few hours; you'll end up in the last century.

A favourite local activity is the evening *paseo* or stroll around the Parque Bolívar, from about 6 to 9 pm nightly. After meeting all your friends, stop into the *Zues* bar, on the Sucre side of the parque, for a beer.

The Carnaval is very popular with people streaming in from all over the province and beyond for such rural festivities as water fights, dances, parades, singing, eating and drinking.

About three km out of town is a five-metre-high monument called *El Indio de Guarango* from where you get a good view of Guaranda, Chimborazo and the surrounding countryside. There is a small museum here. A taxi will take you for about US$1 or you can walk north-west of town for about 30 minutes.

Places to Stay

Most of the hotels in town are basic cold-water cheapies. The water supply is erratic in most of them. *Pensión Tequendama*, Rocafuerte and José García, is US$1.50 per person and has a garage in case you happened to bring your own car.

For US$2 per person you can stay at the friendly *Pensión Ecuador*, 7 de Mayo and E M de Carvajal, which is run down but is

architecturally interesting, or at the marginally better *Pensión Marivel*, two blocks away. All have only cold water in the shared bathrooms.

The basic *Residencial Acapulco* (☎ 981 953), 10 de Agosto near 9 de Abril, US$1.25 per person (cold water) and has a few rooms for US$1.75 each with a hot water bathroom next door. The *Residencial Santa Fé* (☎ 981 526), 9 de Abril and 10 de Agosto, has a rather odd arrangement of rooms with communal hot showers for US$1.50 per person and rooms with private cold shower for US$2 per person. Other basic cold-water places priced at about US$1.50 per person include the *Pensión Rosita Elvira*, Sucre and Rocafuerte, the *Pensión San José*, opposite, and the *Pensión Montúfar*, Sucre and Salazar.

On the outskirts of town is the *Hotel Matiaví* at the bus terminal. It has clean rooms with private baths and hot water for about US$2 per person but can be noisy.

The *Hotel Bolívar* (☎ 980 547), Sucre and Olmedo, has been recommended for clean rooms and hot showers. Rooms with private bath are about US$3.50/4.50 for singles/doubles and rooms with shared bath are about US$1 less. The best place in town is reputedly the clean *Hotel Cochabamba* (☎ 819 583), García Moreno and 7 de Mayo. Spacious rooms with private bath, hot water and telephone are about US$6 per person and simpler rooms with shared showers are US$4 per person.

A 15-minute walk out of town on the Quito road is a 'tourist complex' called *Hotel La Colina* (☎ 980 666) which is often empty. Located on a hill, it has some rooms with good views, a restaurant, bar and small swimming pool. They charge US$11/16 for very comfortable singles/doubles with private bath and hot water.

Places to Eat

There are few restaurants and they close early – many by 7.30 pm. Several of the best places to eat are in hotels. The best in town is supposedly the pricey *Restaurant Cochabamba* under the hotel of that name, but they have been criticised for having only a few selections from the rather impressive-looking menu.

Progressively cheaper are the restaurants *Bolívar, Acapulco* and *Santa Fé* all in the hotels of the same name. The *Bolívar* has been recommended as having a better selection than the Cochabamba. The *Acapulco* has cheap food, especially the chaulafan (a rice dish).

On the west side of the Parque Bolívar you'll find the reasonably priced *Restaurante Rumipamba* which is one of the best places to eat. The local gringos (mainly Peace Corps volunteers) call it 'the chicken place' because of all the freshly killed chickens hanging in the refrigerator as you enter.

On the same block is the *Pastelería Panextra* which has good pastries. Around the corner on 10 de Agosto is the *La Choza* which serves tacos and other snacks. The *Disco La Choza* (mentioned earlier) also has a restaurant but I have no idea what it is like. There's a basic place to eat at the main bus terminal.

Getting There & Away

Bus Most buses now leave from the new bus terminal a km out of town. Just head east on García Moreno – you can't miss it. A few buses still leave from the bus plaza in town (locally known as Plaza Roja) and there are several bus company offices there. As a general rule, the old country buses may leave from the plaza, but the main buses for Riobamba, Ambato and Babahoyo will leave from the new terminal. Bus departures are from 4 am to 5 pm and no later. Afternoon buses can get booked up in advance so plan ahead.

The most frequent departures are for Ambato (US$0.90; 2½ hours) and Quito (US$1.70; five hours), with buses for these destinations leaving about once an hour with various companies. Almost as frequently there are buses for Babahoyo (US$1.40; four hours) and Guayaquil (US$1.80; five hours). There are about six daily buses on the spectacular but poor road to Riobamba (US$0.75; three hours).

There are also several buses a day to Chillanes, a small town at the end of the road some three hours south of Guaranda. I've never been there nor met anyone who has, but I'm told there's a basic pensión. It certainly would be getting off the beaten track if that's what you want. Chillanes is a coffee and aguardiente (sugar cane alcohol) producing area. En route to both Babahoyo and Chillanes, you pass through the old town of San Miguel, which still has wooden colonial buildings with carved balconies.

SALINAS

About 35 km north of Guaranda in wild and beautiful countryside is the peaceful community of Salinas. It is known for its excellent cheeses, homemade salamis and roughspun sweaters and you can visit the small 'factories' which produce them. The people are very friendly and not much used to seeing travellers. It's an interesting destination for people who enjoy off-the-beaten-track travel and seeing how people live in a remote rural Ecuadorian community. It is definitely very 'tranquilo'.

Information

There is a small store on the plaza which sells the naturally dyed roughspun sweaters for well under US$10. Prices are fixed and other woollen goods are available. There is also a small restaurant and you can buy cheese in 31 kilo balls! There is no telephone service and little electricity in town.

There are no hotels but you can probably find somewhere to stay if you ask around; most people come on day trips.

Getting There & Away

Trucks from near the bus plaza in Guaranda leave on Saturday (to coincide with Guaranda's market) and occasionally other days for Salinas. The fare is US$0.50.

Otherwise take a bus or truck from the bus plaza about 10 km north on the Guaranda-Ambato road and get off at Cuatro Esquinas. From here it is about 25 km to Salinas – wait for a passing truck to give you a ride for about US$0.50. In Salinas, hang out in the main plaza and flag down any vehicle. Most vehicles leaving town are going to Guaranda. The drive is a spectacular one.

RIOBAMBA

'All roads lead to Riobamba' proclaims a road sign as you enter this city, and it is indeed true that Riobamba is at the heart of an extensive and scenic road network. Whichever way you arrive or leave, you should try and plan your journey for daylight hours so as not to miss the great views.

The usual way to arrive is on the Panamerican Highway from Ambato, which is 52 km to the north. The road climbs over a 3600-metre-high pass which gives great views of Ecuador's highest peak (Chimborazo – 6310 metres) as well as the nearby Carihuairazo (5020 metres) before dropping to Riobamba at 2750 metres.

An even more spectacular route is the dirt road arriving from Guaranda. There is also a lower road from Baños which follows the Chambo River valley and passes through numerous small villages. One of these, Penipe, is the entrance to the dirt road climbing towards the rugged peak of El Altar. Looking back along this road will also give you views of Tungurahua.

Riobamba is fairly important and has a fast-growing population of over 100,000. It is the capital of Chimborazo Province, which is more or less the geographical centre of Ecuador. It has always been, and continues to be, an agriculturally important area which was inhabited long before the Spanish conquest. It was a Puruhá Indian centre before becoming part of the Inca Empire during the late 15th century.

The first Spanish colonialists built a city near present-day Cajabamba. This was destroyed in a 1797 earthquake and the survivors moved to the present site on a large plain surrounded by several snow-capped peaks. The flat terrain of Riobamba enabled it to be built in a regular chessboard pattern with wide avenues and imposing stone buildings. It has rather a sedate air and Ecuadorians call it the 'Sultan of the Andes'. The main street through town, with large plazas and government buildings, is called Primera Constituyente in commemoration of the fact that Ecuador's first constitution was written and signed here, in 1830.

Information

There is a CETUR tourist information office on the corner of Tarqui and Primera Constituyente. The staff is friendly and helpful and the office is open from 8 am to 12 noon and 2.30 to 6.30 pm from Tuesday to Friday and from 8.30 am to 2.30 pm on Saturday. There is also an information desk at the bus terminal which provides city maps.

Money The Banco Internacional on 10 de Agosto and García Moreno used to be the only place to change money, but recent reports indicate that it will no longer do so. Try the Banco Popular on España and Primera Constituyente or a recently opened casa de cambio nearby.

Post & Telecommunications There is an IETEL office downtown at Tarqui and Veloz and also at the bus terminal. The post office can be difficult to find as the sign is tiny and the office is on the 3rd floor of an office building on Primera Constituyente and García Moreno.

Climbing Guides Several guides are available for climbs or treks on or around any of the local mountains. The best known (and most expensive) is Marco Cruz who works for Metropolitan Touring in Quito. In Riobamba his office is at Expediciones Andinas (☎ 964 915, 962 845), Argentinos 38-60 and Zambrano.

Also very good, experienced and recommended is Marcelo Puruncajas of the Andes agency (☎ 966 344), E Espejo 24-43 and Orozco. Climbing gear is available for rent for about US$1.50 per item per day. He charges about US$240 to take two climbers to the summits of Cotopaxi or Chimborazo, everything provided. These trips last two days (one night) and there is no guarantee that the summit will be reached. Several other trips are offered.

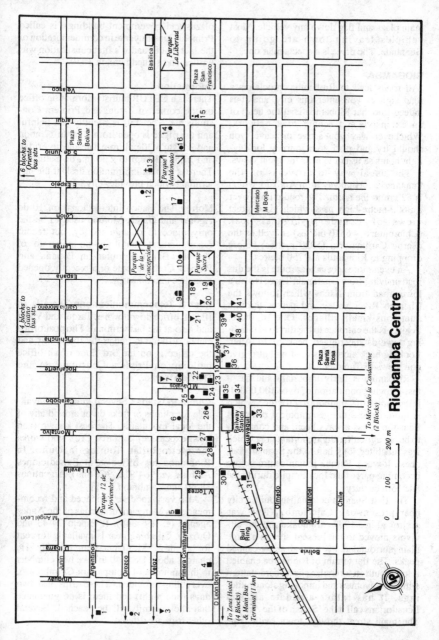

Riobamba Centre

■ PLACES TO STAY

1   To Hotels Chimborazo Internacional
    & El Galpón (5 Blocks)
4   Hotel Humboldt
5   Hotel Whymper
17 Hotel Segovia
22 Hotel Imperial
23 Residencial Ñuca Huasi
24 Residencial Venecia
27 Hotel Americano
28 Hotel Ecuador
30 Hotel Metro
31 Residenciales Villa Ester & Guayas
32 Residencial Chimborazo
34 Hotel Bolívar
35 Residencial Colonial
36 Hostal Los Shyris

▼ PLACES TO EAT

3   To Restaurant El Mesón (4 Blocks)
7   Steak House
20 Restaurant Kikirimiau
21 Restaurant León Rojo
29 Restaurant Los Alamos
33 Chifa Joy Sing
37 Restaurant Candilejas
38 Restaurant El Pailón
40 Chifa Pak Hao
41 La Cabaña Montecarlo

    OTHER

2   To Peña Taqui Huasi (4 Blocks)
6   Banco Central
8   Simón Bolívar stayed here
9   Post Office
10 Colegio, Museo & Teatro Maldonando
11 Museo de Arte Religioso
12 Andes Guides
13 Cathedral
14 IETEL
15 CETUR Tourist Information
16 Municipalidad (Town Hall)
18 Teatro T León
19 Consejo Provincial (Government
    Buildings)
25 Cine Fenix
26 Cine Imperial
39 Banco Internacional

Enrique Veloz of Riobamba is the president of the Asociación de Andinismo de Chimborazo (☎ 960 916), Chile 33-21 and Francia. He has climbed Chimborazo and the other peaks many times and may be able to guide you – he is experienced but I have received comments that some of the younger, less expensive guides which he knows are not very experienced. Make sure you get a good guide; your life depends on it. These trips are not recommended for the beginner mountaineer.

Fiesta Riobamba's annual fiesta celebrates the Battle of Tapi on 21 April. On and around that date there is a large agricultural fair with the usual highland events – street parades, dancing, and plenty of traditional food and drink. The city and hotels can be particularly crowded then.

Emergency The hospital (☎ 961 705) is at the east end of town at Olmedo 11-01. Contact the police on ☎ 961 913.

Other A reader writes that there is a British man named Jimmy in the Riobamba prison. He is interesting, likes visitors, makes tea, and will trade English books. A recent report is that he gets out in 1993.

Things to See & Do
Market Saturday is market day and there's much activity in the streets, especially around 5 de Junio and Argentinos, although almost every plaza and parque in the city seems to be busy. The market certainly is a colourful affair, with thousands of people from many surrounding villages flocking to market. It is rather incongruous to see a barefooted Indian woman leading a squealing piglet on a string through the streets of a major town.

New market buildings have been constructed which detract somewhat from the *ambiente*, and many market areas sell mainly food items and plastic consumer goods. Nevertheless, it is the shoppers rather than the shopping which are of interest to travellers. One plaza, however, has plenty of crafts for sale – this is the Parque de la Concepción at Orozco and Colón.

An interesting Riobambeño handicraft is tagua nut carving. These nuts are actually seeds from a type of rainforest palm. The seeds are fairly soft until they are carved, but when exposed to the sun and air they become very hard. They are the size of small chicken eggs and are carved into a variety of novelties such as statuettes, miniature cups and rings. This is starting to become an important industry to help preserve the rainforest by providing economically viable alternatives to cutting the forest down. Although the palm grows in many lowland areas, for some reason highland Riobamba has become a carving centre for the tagua nut.

Another interesting handicraft from the Riobamba area is the shigra, a tough woven bag made from *cabuya* – agave or century plant fibres. Their durability and practicality make shigras very popular souvenirs for many travellers, who often use them as day bags. Cabuya is also used for rope sandals and, simply, rope.

There are also baskets and mats made by the Colta Indians. They are woven from the reeds lining the shores of Lake Colta, a few km south of Riobamba. There are many clothing items such as woven belts, fine ponchos and embroidered shawls.

It should be mentioned that the Otavalo market is the most tourist-oriented and convenient place to shop for souvenirs. At the Riobamba market you'll have to do a lot of searching past stalls of potatoes, plastic buckets and polyester pants – less convenient but perhaps more fun! The tourist office will help pinpoint which of the many markets and plazas may be of interest to you (apart from the crafts at La Concepción).

Museo de Arte Religioso The museum in the old church of La Concepción (☎ 952 212), on Argentinos and Larrea, is famous and worth a visit. The building has been beautifully restored and there are many rooms with a good variety of paintings, sculptures and religious artefacts. Their major piece is a huge, gem-encrusted gold monstrance said to be priceless. Entrance is about US$1 from 9 am to 12 noon and 3 to

6 pm Tuesday through Saturday. On Sunday and on holidays it's open mornings only; it's closed on Monday.

Parque 21 de Abril There is an observation platform here, from which the city and surrounding countryside can be appreciated. There is also a tilework representation of the history of Ecuador. The view of snow-capped Tungurahua rising behind the church of San Antonio is especially impressive.

Parque La Libertad This is another quiet plaza. Its basilica is famous as the only round church in Ecuador. Begun in 1883, it took over 30 years to complete and was designed, built and decorated mainly by locals – a source of civic pride. It's often closed; try Sunday and evenings after 6 pm.

Parque Maldonado This is a pleasant park with trees, flowers, and birds. Riobamba's cathedral is on the north-eastern side. In the park is a statue of the Ecuadorian geographer, Pedro Maldonado (see Parque La Alameda in the Quito chapter).

Other There are several other plazas with impressive buildings and churches. A walk along Primera Constituente will take you past some of them.

On the corner of Primera Constituente and Rocafuerte there is a building in which Simón Bolívar stayed and, on 5 July 1822, wrote his famous epic poem about his attempted ascent of Chimborazo (he reached the snow line). During working hours you can read his poem and the story of his life (the building is now an office).

At Primera Constituyente and Carabobo is the Banco Central (☎ 963 153) which has an archaeology museum which is open occasionally . The Colegio Maldonado at Primera Constituyente and Larrea has a natural history museum which is occasionally open. Neither of these were open on my last visit.

Places to Stay – main bus terminal area
Most hotels are in the town centre a couple of km away from the main bus terminal. If

you prefer to stay near the terminal, you'll find a few inexpensive places nearby. Opposite the terminal is the friendly and clean *Residencial San Carlos* which charges about US$3 for a double room – they have hot water. Nearby is the *Hotel Monterrey* (☎ 962 421) which is similarly priced and also good. Across the street behind the terminal is the reasonably clean *Residencial Puruha*. They charge US$4.50 for a double room and have hot water.

In front of the terminal is the comfortable *Hotel Las Retamas* (☎ 965 004/5) which has a restaurant and charges US$5.50 per person in rooms with private baths, hot water and TV.

Places to Stay – bottom end

In the town centre, most of the cheap hotels are near the train station but many of them are very run down. The best of the cheapest is probably the *Residencial Colonial*, on Carabobo opposite the train station, which charges about US$1 per person and has hot water. Other hotels for about a dollar are less attractive. They include the residenciales *Villa Ester, Guayas* and the dirty *Chimborazo*, all on Guayaquil just west of the train station.

I prefer the *Residencial Ñuca Huasi* for US$1.30 per person. It is a block from the train station at 10 de Agosto 28-24 and Dávalos, and although it doesn't look up to much from the outside it has friendly staff, spacious rooms and hot showers. It is popular with backpackers and the owner will arrange transportation to the mountain refugios.

Other similarly priced places with hot water but facing the station are the hotels *Bolívar, Americano* and *Ecuador* (☎ 963 476), D León Borja 30-40, and the *Residencial Venecia* (☎ 961 809), Dávalos 22-21. Of these, the *Bolívar* (☎ 968 294), Carabobo 21-26, has been described by one budget traveller as 'old, colourful, cheap and good'.

The pleasant *Hotel Imperial* (☎ 960 429), Rocafuerte 22-15 and 10 de Agosto, is friendly, clean and recommended. It has an interesting glass ceiling/floor between the

2nd and 3rd-floor lobbies. They charge about US$3 per person in comfortable rooms with private bath and hot water and have some cheaper rooms with shared bath. The manager will arrange trips to Chimborazo. This is one of the best bottom-end hotels. They have recently opened the middle-range Riobamba Inn.

Other hotels charging about US$3 per person in rooms with private bath and hot water include the *Hotel Metro* (☎ 961 714), D León Borja and J Lavalle just west of the train station. This hotel has been described as old or traditional, depending on your point of view. They have some cheaper rooms with shared showers. The similarly priced *Hotel Segovia* (☎ 961 269), Primera Constituyente 22-26 and E Espejo, receives good recommendations in other guidebooks but had some robberies reported to me in 1991.

Places to Stay – middle & top end

Out on the way to the main bus terminal is the clean *Zeus Hotel* (☎ 962 292, 963 100, 968 036), D León Borja 41-29, which had good rooms with private bath, hot water, and TV for US$4/6.50 for singles/doubles – excellent value. Two reasonable hotels which have comfortable rooms with private baths for US$4 per person are the *Hotel Humboldt* (☎ 961 788), D León Borja 35-48 and Uruguay, and the newer *Hostal Los Shyris* (☎ 960 323), Rocafuerte 21-60 and 10 de Agosto. Both have cafeterias.

The clean and good *Hotel Whymper* (☎ 964 575, 968 137), M Angél León 23-10 and Primera Constituyente, has rooms with private bath and hot water for about US$10 a double (including breakfast). Some of the rooms have great views of the surrounding volcanoes. There is a jeep available for trips to the mountains. I have received several favourable reports about this hotel and one complaint – a couple of travellers were charged US$15 for a double room which they considered too high.

The *Hotel Riobamba Inn* (☎ 961 696), Carabobo 23-20 and Primera Constituyente is run by the folks who run the bottom-end Hotel Imperial. They have rooms with private bathroom, hot water, TV and telephone. The hotel is new and I have no prices but it should be good judging by the Hotel Imperial.

The two best hotels in town are within a block of one another on Avenida Argentinos some way west of the centre. The *Hotel Chimborazo Internacional* (☎ 963 473) is at Argentinos and Nogales and the *Hotel El Galpón* (☎ 960 981/2) is at Argentinos and Zambrano. Both have restaurants and bars. The Chimborazo charges US$24/28 for singles/doubles and, of the two hotels, is a better deal. The El Galpón is rather more expensive, has a swimming pool and sauna, but has been criticised by several travellers for being badly managed, not very clean and having a poor restaurant.

The best hotel in the Riobamba area is the *Hosteria El Troje* (☎ 960 826) which is 4½ km south-east of town on the minor road to Chambo. They have a pool and tennis court, restaurant and bar, and charge about US$28 for a double room.

Places to Eat

Most restaurants in Riobamba are fairly basic and cheap and there are many of them. Budget travellers are recommended to try the four-course lunch for less than US$1 at the simple and homely *Restaurant Kikirimiau*, García Moreno and 10 de Agosto. Other decent places for cheap set meals are the *Restaurant Los Alamos*, J Lavalle and D León Borja, and the *Restaurant El Pailón*, Pichincha and 10 de Agosto. There are several other cheap restaurants near the railway station.

As usual, there are several inexpensive chifas, of which the *Chifa Pak Hao*, García Moreno and 10 de Agosto, and *Chifa Joy Sing*, Guayaquil and Carabobo, have been recommended. There are many others.

For dining with a little style try the restaurants *Candilejas*, 10 de Agosto and Pichincha, or *La Cabaña Montecarlo*, García Moreno 24-10 and 10 de Agosto. They are less expensive than they look and even the most impoverished budget traveller

can afford a night out at a place with a clean tablecloth once in a while (both have received recommendations from readers of the last edition of this book). A new place that has been recommended as clean and inexpensive is the *El Delino Restaurant* on Primera Constituyente and Rocafuerte – I haven't tried it.

The *Steak House*, Dávalos and Veloz, is good for steaks and other food but is not particularly cheap. Somewhat out of the centre is the *El Mesón*, Veloz 41-99 and Los Sauces, which serves very good food but, again, is not particularly cheap. One of the fanciest places in town, not cheap but very good value, is the good German-run *Restaurant León Rojo*, Primera Constituyente 26-25 and García Moreno. (I recently received an unconfirmed report that this Riobamba mainstay has closed.)

Entertainment

Nightlife is limited. The *Peña Taqui Huasi* is on Orozco near Los Cipresses. There is a *Peña Bar* just off the west end of the map a D León Borja 37-47. There is a discotheque at the Hotel Chimborazo Internacional. These places are open late on weekend nights. Otherwise, I could find nothing except the movie theatres shown on the map. They advertise in *El Libertador*, the local daily paper.

Getting There & Away

Air There is a secondary airport which is used for military and emergency services only.

Bus There are two bus terminals. The main bus terminal is almost two km north-west of the town centre along D León Borja. Northbound buses for Quito (US$1.60; four hours) and intermediate points are frequent. Also frequent are buses for Guayaquil (US$1.95; five hours). There are two buses at 7 and 9 pm for Machala (US$3; 10 hours) and Huaquillas (US$3.50; 12 hours) if you're heading for Peru. There are six buses a day for Cuenca (US$2.50; six hours). Buses for

Alausí leave about every hour with CTA and cost US$0.80 for the 1½-hour ride. Buses for local towns leave from a smaller terminal to the south (see the Getting Around section).

For buses to Baños and the Oriente you have to go to the Oriente bus terminal on avenidas Espejo and Luz Elisa Borja almost four km away from the main bus terminal. There is no direct bus linking the two terminals – a taxi should be about US$0.50. You can walk to the Oriente bus terminal from downtown; it's a few blocks north of my map.

Once in a while there are buses leaving the main terminal for Baños – it's a matter of luck. If you're arriving in Riobamba from the Oriente, you may find that your bus makes a swing through the centre before ending up at the Oriente terminal.

Train The services to Guayaquil and Cuenca was disrupted by the 1982/83 El Niño floods which washed out over 80 km of the track beyond Riobamba. It is unlikely that services will resume for some years, if at all.

Until recently, there was one daily autoferro to Quito which left at 5 am, cost US$0.90 and took about five hours. It was usually full and it was best to buy tickets in advance. This service has been suspended but may start up again in 1992. Inquire at the train station (☎ 961 909).

Getting Around

Bus North of the main bus terminal, behind a church with a blue dome, is a local bus stop for the city centre nearly two km away. These buses run along D León Borga, which turns into 10 de Agosto near the railway station. Here there is a good selection of hotels. To return to the main terminal, take any bus marked 'Terminal' on Primera Constituyente. The fare is US$0.05.

Three long blocks south of the main bus terminal (turn left out of the front entrance) is a smaller terminal with frequent local buses for Cajabamba, Laguna de Colta and Balbanera; the fare is US$0.15. Buses for Guamote also leave from here.

To visit the villages of Guano and Santa Teresita, take a US$0.10 local bus ride from the stop at Avenidas Pichincha and New York (four blocks north of my map).

CHIMBORAZO

The 6310-metre extinct Volcán Chimborazo is not only the highest mountain in Ecuador, it is also the farthest point from the centre of the earth (due to the earth's equatorial bulge), and, for insatiable trivia buffs, it is higher than any other mountain in the Americas north of it. Nearby is the ninth highest mountain in Ecuador, the 5020-metre-high Carihuairazo. Climbing either mountain is an adventure only for experienced mountaineers with snow and ice-climbing gear (see *Climbing & Hiking in Ecuador* or contact a local guide) but reaching the refugio on Chimborazo is as simple as hiring a car. The area around these mountains is also suitable for backpacking trips – the walk from Mocha (on the Panamerican Highway north of Riobamba) over the pass between the two mountains and emerging at the Ambato-Guaranda road is particularly recommended. Allow three days for this hike and bring plenty of warm clothes. June to September is the dry season in this region.

There are two refugios. Most vehicles reach the lower one where you can sometimes buy drinks and sweets. You can sleep at the upper refugio (about a half hour walk uphill) for US$6 per night; there is a fireplace and cooking facilities but bring your own sleeping bag. Refugio guardians are on duty. The refugio is named after Edward Whymper, the British climber who in 1880 made the first ascent of Chimborazo with the Swiss guides, the Carrels.

At 5000 metres this is Ecuador's highest refugio, and altitude sickness is a very real danger. It is essential that you spend several days acclimatising at the elevation of Riobamba or higher before going to the refugio.

At Riobamba's Residencial Ñuca Huasi you can hire a pickup for about US$25 for a day trip to the refugios on Chimborazo. The manager of the Hotel Imperial, Señor Carlos Morales, has a 4WD jeep and will take you to the refugio for about US$33. He will also drive you to Ingapirca and other small villages for US$50 for the entire day. The manager of the Hotel Whymper also provides rides to the refugio.

If you can bargain hard, you can try hiring a pickup truck from near the Riobamba railway station – about US$15-20 depending on the vehicle and your bargaining abilities. Pickups are also available from the Plaza Simón Bolívar (Junín and 5 de Junio). If the road is in reasonable shape you could even get there in an ordinary car. It is also possible to get a truck to the village of San Juan (US$0.30) and from this village hire a pickup for about US$7 to the refugio – assuming that all the vehicles in San Juan haven't gone somewhere else!

GUANO & SANTA TERESITA
These small villages are a few km north of Riobamba and make an ideal day trip. Guano is an important carpet-making centre and although it's unlikely that many travellers will have room in their luggage for a couple of souvenir carpets, it is nevertheless interesting to see this cottage industry. In Guano you should get off the bus at the central plaza, where there are several carpet stores, and then continue down Avenida García Moreno which will take you past several more. There are no hotels or restaurants. Look for the topiary garden with El Altar in the background – a pretty sight.

From the main plaza you can continue with a US$0.05 bus ride to Santa Teresita a few km away. The bus terminates at the end of the road and you turn right and head down the hill for about 20 minutes to the Balneario. Here there are swimming pools fed by natural springs. The water is quite cool (22°C or 71°F) but the views of Tungurahua and El Altar are marvellous. There is a basic cafeteria, and camping is permitted. The baths were recently closed for repair but should have reopened by the time you read this.

The round trip from Riobamba will take about six hours if you take it leisurely and have a swim in the pool. There are frequent buses during daylight hours and it's a good

chance to see some of the local countryside. A taxi from Riobamba will cost about US$2.

SOUTH-WEST OF RIOBAMBA
The southbound Panamerican Highway actually heads west out of Riobamba until it reaches a cement factory 10 km away. Here the road forks, with the west fork continuing to Guaranda and the main highway heading south-west to **Cajabamba** about seven km further.

Cajabamba was founded in 1534 and was historically important until it was devastated by the 1797 earthquake which killed several thousands of its inhabitants. Most of the survivors founded nearby Riobamba, but a few remained and their descendants still live here. As you arrive, look up to your right and you'll see a huge scar on the hillside – the only sign of the landslide which caused much of the damage in 1797.

Most of the buses from Riobamba continue down the Panamerican Highway beyond Cajabamba; if you want to see some of the old town you should get off at the entrance which is at the junction of the main highway and Avenida 2 de Agosto on the right. Most bus drivers stop here. There's little to see; if you head down 2 de Agosto you'll soon come to the History Museum on your right, which contains about a dozen fragments of carved rock dating from before the earthquake. It's not worth seeing, but maybe in the future the museum will have a proper exhibit. Continuing down the road, you come to the earthquake-damaged town church on your left. There are no hotels.

Returning to the Panamerican, you'll see a few food stalls and very basic restaurants. Heading south on the main highway, you soon pass open fields which are the site of the interesting weekly market. There are no permanent buildings; the Indians just lay out their wares in neat rows. Every Sunday morning the bare fields are transformed by a bustling but surprisingly orderly throng who buy, sell and barter produce. Quechua rather than Spanish is spoken and there are no tourist items; this is one of the more traditional markets in the Ecuadorian highlands.

Amazingly, it takes place right by the side of the Panamerican Highway – a measure of just how rural this part of Ecuador is.

Most buses from Riobamba continue about four km beyond Cajabamba to **Laguna de Colta** – an interesting place. The road climbs gently to a notch in the hill to the south and the little chapel of **La Balbanera**. It is built on the site of the earliest church in Ecuador, which dates from 15 August 1534, though only a few stones at the front survived the devastating earthquake of 1797. The church has been almost completely rebuilt and the curious traveller can enter to inspect its simple interior and look at the usual disaster paintings.

In La Balbanera one painting carries the explanation: 'On the 17th of May, 1959, the train derailed, setting the whole convoy on fire. Sr Juan Peñafiel, the brakeman, prayed to the Divine Lady of La Balbanera and her miracle saved the train near Alausí'.

Looking almost due north of the chapel, you can see Chimborazo looming up from 30 km away. Next to the chapel are a few basic restaurants and the more elaborate *La Balbanera* tourist restaurant where you can sample local dishes – tasty and recommended. A little to the south of the chapel there is a road fork. This is where the decision must be made whether to continue south on the Panamerican or take the 100-km detour to the right via the junction of El Triunfo and then return to the Panamerican at Cañar. Occasional road closures caused by landslides might make the detour impossible to avoid.

Opposite the road fork is Laguna de Colta. Its blue expanse is often choked up by reeds, which form an important crop for the local Colta Indians. Sometimes you can see the Coltas' rafts on the lake; the Indians cut the reeds for use as cattle fodder or for the reed mats and baskets for which they are famous.

Some of the more traditional Colta Indian women can be easily identified, as they dye the fringes of their hair a startling golden colour. If you have the time or inclination you could walk around the lake in a couple of hours.

This area can be visited on a day excursion from Riobamba using local buses or hiring a taxi. The views of the volcanoes, especially Chimborazo, are particularly good as you return from Colta to Riobamba along the Panamerican – try to sit near the front of the bus.

GUAMOTE

From the Cajabamba region the southbound Panamerican Highway roughly follows the (now unused) railway and crosses the tracks quite often. Some 30 km beyond Cajabamba you reach the village of Guamote, which has an interesting and unspoilt Thursday market. Until 1982 it had some importance because of its railway station, but the trains haven't run for some years and it's rather a forgotten little place now. There is a basic pensión near the train tracks.

Guamote is the beginning of a new road being built to the south-east, over the Atillo Pass in the Eastern Cordillera, down the eastern slopes of the Andes, past the southern edge of Parque Nacional Sangay and on to Macas in the southern Oriente (see the earlier section on the Parque Nacional Sangay for more details). From Guamote, it is possible to hire a truck as far as Atillo, about 45 km away – there is no bus.

Note that Guamote is located almost one km off the Panamerican Highway in a valley – unless your bus is actually going to Guamote, you will be dropped off on the Panamerican and will have to walk in.

ALAUSÍ

Almost 50 km south of Guamote you reach Alausí, which is near the head of the Río Chanchán valley down which the railway runs to the coast. Just below Alausí begins the famous Nariz del Diablo, where a hair-raising series of railway switchbacks negotiate the steep descent towards the lowlands.

This is the area where the most damage was done by the landslides caused by the torrential rains of the 1982/83 El Niño. The tracks were finally repaired in the late 1980s and now the spectacular train ride between

Alausí and Guayaquil attracts many travellers. Alausí is also a popular highland resort for Guayaquileños wishing to get away from the unpleasant heat and humidity of the coast while experiencing one of the world's great feats of railway engineering.

In addition, there is a busy Sunday market and so, after several quiet years, Alausí has once again become an important, albeit brief, destination for travellers.

Orientation & Information

The main street is Avenida 5 de Junio which is about six blocks long. Buses arrive and depart from this street and most of the hotels are located along it. The train station is at the north end of 5 de Junio. There is an IETEL office one block to the west of 5 de Junio behind the fire station which is near the train station. From the train station, you can head east and wander around to find a plaza, church, cobbled streets and balconied buildings – tranqilissimo. There is one movie theatre.

Apart from the Sunday market, there is a smaller one on Thursday. The feast of San Pedro & Paulo (28 June) is one of Alausí's major fiestas and the town is very crowded then.

Places to Stay & Eat

Hotels are often full on Saturday night for the Sunday market and Ecuadorian weekend visitors. There are no first-class hotels and the 'best' seems to be the *Hotel Gampala* (☎ 930 138), which has hot water and charges about US$3 per person in rooms with private bath and a little less with shared bath. Their water supply can be erratic (as is true of anywhere in Alausí) so check the water before paying extra for a room with a shower.

For just under US$2 per person you can stay at the clean and friendly *Hotel Tequendama* (☎ 930 123) which also has hot water. This hotel is around a little courtyard and is family run. Similarly priced is the clean but basic *Hotel Panamericano* (☎ 930 156) which has electric showers and a basic restaurant below. Another possibility is the

Hotel Europa which also has a restaurant and can provide hot showers if you ask in advance.

A block east of 5 de Junio near the train station there is an *American Ice Cream* place. I've just received a report of a new hotel opening above it – so new that it has no name as of this writing. They charge about US$4.50 per person with bath and hot water in the rooms. Write and tell me how it is.

Apart from the hotel restaurants, there are a couple of other basic places to eat along the main street, mostly serving meriendas. There's really not much choice but the food is quite adequate.

Getting There & Away

Bus Buses from Riobamba (US$0.90; 1½ hours) arrive every hour or so. Buses turn off the Panamerican Highway and drop down into town, where they normally stop near the Hotel Panamericano. Buses for Cuenca (US$1.50; four hours) also leave from here several times a day. Buses between Riobamba and Cuenca don't normally enter town and leave passengers on the Panamerican from which it is almost a one-km walk down into town.

Pick-up trucks act as buses for nearby destinations and leave from this street. Some of the rides can be quite spectacular, especially the one to Achupallas about 23 km to the south-east. Make sure that any sightseeing ride you take is coming back to Alausí, as there are few, if any, places to stay in these villages.

There are also buses and trucks to Chunchi, about 25 km further south on the Panamerican Highway. From Chunchi, there is a daily train south to Cuenca, described in the next chapter.

Train Alausí used to be a major railroad junction, with tracks heading north to Riobamba and Quito, south to Cuenca, and west to Guayaquil. Only the Alausí to Guayaquil section is running at this time. About 12 km beyond Alausí on the Guayaquil train line is the little station of **Sibambe**. This is where the track divides with the south branch going to Cuenca. Trains actually do run between Cuenca and Sibambe (see Cuenca), making connections for Guayaquil or Alausí technically possible, but there is nowhere to stay in Sibambe and connections require an overnight stop.

The most exciting part of the train ride to Guayaquil is the 66-km descent from Alausí to Bucay. According to one tourist brochure, Alausí is at 2607 metres above sea level; another guide book puts it at 2356 metres; a sign at the Alausí train station, however, puts it at 2347 metres. Whatever the height, the first few km are very steep. At the station of Huigra, about 26 km away, the elevation is given as only 1255 metres and at Bucay the elevation is considerably lower.

The steep descent is accomplished by switchbacking back and forth down the steep mountainside. Occasional rickety looking bridges cross steep ravines. To add to the excitement, you can ride on the flat roof of the train — thus there is nothing but empty space between you and the valleys far below. The local machos stand up on the roof, especially when going through the tunnels where there is barely enough clearance for the sombrero jammed jauntily on their heads. I was content with sitting on the roof and grinning like an idiot. Actually, the greatest hazard is probably the steam locomotive which will blow steam, soot and cinders during the ride, so wear clothes you don't mind getting dirty.

The train leaves Alausí daily at 9 am and tickets go on sale at 7.30 am. The train is usually quite full but ticket sales are orderly. The fare to Bucay is US$0.30 and to Durán (Guayaquil) is US$0.60. It takes three to four hours to Bucay and about eight to Guayaquil.

There was an (unconfirmed) rumour circulating in 1991 that the service was to be stopped by the end of 1992, or that the famous steam locomotive was going to be replaced by the less picturesque autoferro.

BUCAY

OK. I'll finally let you in on the secret – there is no place called Bucay on any map of Ecuador (at least none of the many I have examined). Bucay is the name of the train

station in the small town officially known as General Elizalde. Maps mark Gral Elizalde but, inexplicably, no one knows where Gral Elizalde is – it's Bucay to everybody except Ecuadorian map makers. It took me several years to figure this out – I used to think that Bucay was simply too small to put on the map.

Bucay is a small but bustling town. Many people get off the train here and continue by bus. It is two hours to Guayaquil by bus as opposed to four by train, and you end up in the Guayaquil bus terminal rather than Durán. Alternatively, you can catch a bus to Riobamba. There are plenty of buses leaving in the middle of the day when the train from Alausí arrives.

Usually, the train from Alausí arrives in Bucay before the train from Durán. In that case, you can get off the down train and catch the up one back to Alausí. You can't rely on this however – the last time I took the train from Alausí we didn't make it to Bucay before the train in the opposite direction left.

I don't particularly recommend staying in Bucay but if you get stuck here for some reason, there's the basic *Hotel California* for about US$2 per night and the even more basic *Hotel Central*. At least the people are friendly.

ACHUPALLAS

This village is the beginning of a three-day hike south along the old Inca road to Ingapirca, the most important Inca ruin in Ecuador (see the next chapter). Occasional trucks leave Alausí for Achupallas or you can hire a taxi (pickup) for about US$6. Alternatively, there is transport from Alausí to Guasuntos (La Moya) from where you can wait for trucks to Achupallas. It is about 10 km from Alausí to La Moya and a further 15 km to Achupallas. There is nowhere to stay at either place.

The hike from Achupallas to Ingapirca is a good one – a detailed description can be found in *Climbing & Hiking in Ecuador*. The Inca road is faint in places, but you could probably find your way to Ingapirca with a compass and map and asking the locals if you don't have the hiking book. Head south and pack some extra food in case you get temporarily lost. The area is covered by three 1:50,000 topographical maps available from the IGM in Quito. These are the Alausí CT-ÑV-A3, Juncal CT-ÑV-C1 and Cañar CT-ÑV-C3 sheets.

Cuenca & the Southern Highlands

The three southern Sierra provinces, Cañar, Azuay and Loja, are noticeably different from the seven highland provinces to the north. Geographically they are much lower, with very few peaks reaching 4000 metres. The topography is rugged nevertheless, and communications with the rest of Ecuador have been developed only relatively recently.

Cuenca, the major city of the region and Ecuador's third largest, didn't have paved highway connections with Guayaquil and Quito until the 1960s, and even today these highways are not in particularly good shape. The area is rich in history and the region has a strong flavour of the colonial past, due to its isolation until recent times.

The southern highlands had a colourful history even before the Spanish conquest. These were the lands of the Cañari Indians, an independent culture with exceptional skill in producing gold jewellery and other metal-work, fine weavings and ceramics.

In the late 15th century the Cañaris were conquered by the Incas, who built several major centres. These included the city of Tomebamba near present-day Cuenca, and the fortress of Ingapirca – the best-preserved pre-colonial ruin found in Ecuador today. The Inca influence was short lived, however, and the Spanish conquistadors under Pizarro were in control by the 1530s. Cuenca was (re)founded relatively late in 1557. Several other important towns of the region were founded earlier, such as Loja in 1548.

Remnants of the colonial era are more likely to be seen here than anywhere else in the country, except Quito. Although progress is slowly catching up with the southern Sierra, this area is still a long way behind the coast and northern highlands. Today travellers are struck by the paucity of large cities in the southern highlands.

Apart from Cuenca and Loja, there are no towns with a population of over 20,000 inhabitants. There are many villages with old balconied houses and cobbled streets, and there is a strong tradition of handicrafts ranging from jewellery-making to weaving. A journey through the provinces of Cañar, Azuay and Loja is a journey into the past.

CUENCA

Barely half a century before the arrival of the Spaniards, the powerful Inca Tupac (or Topa) Yupanqui was undertaking the difficult conquest of the Cañari Indians, who struggled bravely to stem the expansion of the Inca Empire. After several years of bitter fighting, Tupac Yupanqui's forces prevailed.

The Inca began the construction of a major city whose splendour and importance was to rival that of the imperial capital of Cuzco. The Indians told of sun temples covered with gold sheets and palaces built using the finest skill of Cuzqueño stonemasons, but what happened to Tomebamba, as the city was called, is shrouded in mystery.

By the time Spanish chronicler Cieza de León passed through in 1547, Tomebamba lay largely in ruins, although well-stocked storehouses indicated how great it recently had been. Today it is difficult to imagine Tomebamba's splendour, for all that remains are a few recently excavated Inca walls by the river.

This river bears the name of the Inca city and divides Cuenca in half. South of the river lie fairly recent suburbs and the modern university. To the north is the heart of the colonial city which is at about 2530 metres above sea level.

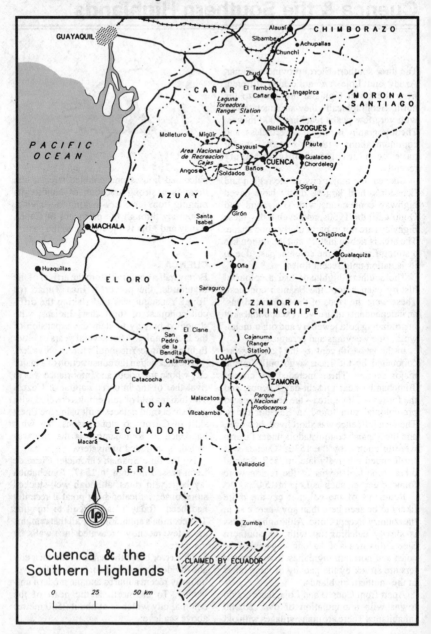

Cuenca & the
Southern Highlands

0   25   50 km

Although Cuenca has expanded to become Ecuador's third largest town with about 200,000 inhabitants, it still retains a pleasantly provincial air.

The old colonial centre has churches dating from the 16th and 17th centuries and is a delight to stroll around. The earliest building is the original cathedral, construction of which began in 1557, the year Cuenca was founded by the Spanish conquistador Gil Ramirez Dávalos.

There are cobbled streets and red-tiled roofs, art galleries and flower markets, shady plazas and museums.

The majority of the hotels, too, are near the centre, so the traveller can conveniently enjoy a relaxing few days in this colonial city.

Cuenca also makes a good base from which to take a railway trip, or to visit thermal baths, the Area Nacional de Recreación Cajas, villages and markets (described in Around Cuenca). The ruins of Ingapirca are described in the section North of Cuenca.

Information

The CETUR tourist information office (☎ 831 414) is at Hermano Miguel 6-86 and Córdova. They are friendly and they do try to help with city maps and information. They say that their hours are from 8 am to 4 pm, Monday to Friday, but they usually are closed around 1 pm for lunch.

The MAG information office (for Area Nacional de Recreación Cajas, described later) is behind the stadium on the south side of the Río Tomebamba off Avenida Vicente Solano. Cross the river on Benigno Malo; from the river walk about 500 metres south along Vicente Solano and turn left on Remigio Crespo Toral (behind the stadium). The MAG is on the second street on the right. The downtown MAG office, at Bolívar 5-32 and Hermano Miguel, will direct you there for permits, maps and information.

If you need a detailed city map, the booklet *Guia Informativa de Cuenca y su Región* by Nelson Gómez, Ediguias 1991, is available in bookshops in Cuenca and Quito. It costs about US$2.

Money Both banks and casas de cambio will change money at rates even better than Quito's – in fact, on my last visit, Cuenca had the most favourable exchange rate in Ecuador for US dollars.

Cambistral, next to the Hotel Internacional Paris on Sucre and Borrero, also accepted other currencies (German, French, Swiss). There are other casas de cambio around Borrero and Sucre and another on Cordero near Gran Colombia. Banks are variable – some will and some won't change foreign currency, but those that do may have rates as good as or even slightly better than the casas de cambio.

Post & Telecommunications The post office is on the corner of Gran Colombia and Presidente Borrero. The IETEL office is at Benigno Malo and Sucre.

Travel Agencies & Guides Several local agencies and guides have been recommended for tours to Ingapirca, Area Nacional de Recreación Cajas, nearby villages and markets and various other local attractions.

Excursiones Santa Ana (☎ 832 340, 831 120), Córdova and Borrero, has eight-hour tours to Ingapirca for about US$32 per person; four people minimum. Yroo Tours (☎ 835 533/888), Larga 8-90 and Benigno Malo, are slightly cheaper. Metrotours (☎ 834 057), Cordero 10-10 and Gran Colombia, have tours to Ingapirca by train (part of the way) on Tuesday, Thursday and Saturday. The cost is about US$46 per person.

English-speaking Eduardo Quito of Abitahua Tours (☎ 823 018) has been recommended. He charges about US$45 for a tour to Ingapirca. Similarly priced is Eduardo Astudillo, who works as a guide and also as a translator for Parlaphone (☎ 804 919). These guides can take three or four passengers for this price. They also do tours to Cajas and nearby villages.

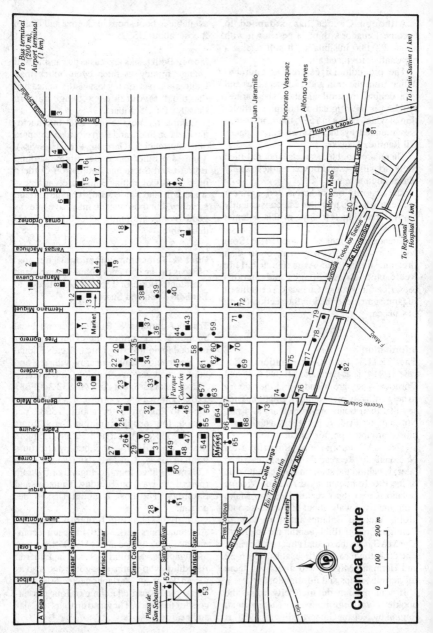

Cuenca Centre

0   100   200 m

■ PLACES TO STAY

1 Hotel Las Américas
2 Residencial Sánchez
3 Residencial La Alborada
4 Hotel Los Libertadores
5 Hostal Hurtado de Mendoza
6 Hostal El Galeon
7 Pensión Taiwan
8 Pensión Andaluz
9 Residencial Atenas
10 Hostal Paredes
12 Residencial La Ramada
13 Residenciales Norte & Colombia
15 Residencial Tito
16 Hotel España
19 Residencial Niza
20 Hotel Cuenca
24 Hotel Internacional
27 Residencial Paris
29 Hotel Emperador
31 Gran Hotel
34 Hotel El Dorado
37 Hotels El Conquistador & Presidente
38 Residencial Siberia
41 Hotel Atahualpa
43 Internacional Hotel Paris
47 Hotel Catedral
48 Hotel Inca Real
49 Hotel Pichincha
50 Tomebamba Hotel
54 Pensión Azuay
64 Hotel Alli Tiana
66 Hotel Milan
67 Hotel Cantabri
68 Hostal San Francisco
75 Hotel Crespo Annexe
77 Hotel Crespo

▼ PLACES TO EAT

11 El Balcón Quiteño
17 El Paraiso Vegetarian Restaurant
18 El Paraiso Vegetarian Restaurant
21 Los Pibes Pizzería
23 Pizzería La Tuna
28 Café Austria
30 El Pedregal Azteca
32 Heladería Holandesa
33 Pio Pio Chicken Restaurant
36 D'Bernardo's Restaurant

47 Govinda Vegetarian Restaurant
48 Restaurant El Túnel
56 Café El Carmen
60 La Cantina Bar & Restaurant
62 Chifa Pack How
70 Restaurant El Jardín
73 Panadería Centenario
76 La Napoletana Pizzería

OTHER

14 Cine 9 de Octubre
22 Metrotours & YAZ Casa de Cambio
25 Teatro Cuenca
26 Santo Domingo Church
35 Post Office
37 TAME Airline
38 Ecuatoriana Airline
39 MAG Office
40 SAN Airline
42 San Blas Church
43 Cambistral Casa de Cambio
44 Several Casas de Cambio
45 Old Cathedral
46 New Cathedral
51 San Cenáculo Church
52 San Sebastián Church
53 Museo de Arte Moderno
55 Plazoleta del Carmen & Flower Market
56 Casa de Cultura
57 Municipio
58 Teatro Sucre
59 Picadilly Bar
60 Excursiones Santa Ana
61 Teatro Casa de Cultura
63 IETEL
65 San Francisco Church
69 Mi Comisariato Supermercado
71 Museo de las Conceptas
72 CETUR Tourist Information
74 Yroo Tours
78 Museo Remigio Crespo Toral
79 Museo de Artes Populares
80 Inca Ruins
81 Museo del Banco Central
82 Museo de la Historia de la Medicina (Hospital Militar)

Juan Carrasco (☎ 831 976) is a bilingual guide who has been recommended for trekking and climbing trips. Vicente López (☎ 823 790) is a recommended Spanish speaking guide. Daniel Cooperman (☎ 811 216) is associated with the Hotel Crespo and offers trekking and Oriente excursions – the trips to the Oriente are sensitively organised. These are private guides who are best reached in the evening – they can tailor tours to suit you.

There is a US$2 entry fee into Ingapirca – check to see if this is included in tour prices.

Fiestas Cuenca's Independence Day is 3 November which combines with 1 and 2 November (All Saints' Day and All Souls' Day) to form an important holiday period for the city. The markets are in full swing and there is music and dancing, parades and drinking. Hotel rooms may be very difficult to find at this time and prices may rise.

Carnaval, as in other parts of Ecuador, is celebrated with boisterous water fights. No one is spared – I saw a whole bucket of water poured from a balcony over an old nun's head! Cuenca seems to be more enamoured of these soggy celebrations than the rest of the country; Easter and New Year's are also popular with water-throwers. Protect your camera gear. There is a colourful city parade on Christmas Eve starting in the suburbs in late morning and emerging, finally, near the cathedral in the afternoon.

Emergency The Regional Hospital (☎ 811 299) is on Avenida del Paraíso on the south-eastern outskirts of town. The Red Cross Ambulance is can be contacted on ☎ 822 520. The police (☎ 101 or 810 068) are at Cordero and Córdova.

Warning For some years, the *South American Handbook* has reported that a short, dark, pudgy man asks lone female travellers to write letters for him and then invites them out. He may claim to be a businessman travelling abroad and asks women to answer questions and then go with him to meet his female friends or relations by way of thanks. He is a known rapist and dangerous, but seems to have close relations with the police.

Travellers visiting Cuenca in 1991 have reported that this guy is still around.

Things to See
Tourism in Cuenca is not well developed and most sites of interest are closed at weekends or, in the cases of churches, are open at irregular hours.

The Río Tomebamba is attractively lined with old colonial buildings, and washerwomen still lay out their clothes to dry on its grassy banks. A pleasant walk is along Avenida 3 de Noviembre, which follows the north bank of the river. The following selection of places of interest to the visitor begins near the south-eastern end of the river, moves north-west into the town centre, and finally moves out to the west. All the sites are marked on the city map and the complete walk out along the river and back is about six km.

If you happen to like museums, the good news is that you'll find quite a selection in Cuenca, although they aren't as good as the museums in Quito or Guayaquil. The bad news is that the most famous Cuenca museum, the wonderful rambling collection of Padre Crespo, has been closed indefinitely since the Padre's death in 1982. The collection has been taken over by the Banco Central but it was not available for viewing when I was last in Cuenca. Padre Crespo was an eccentric local cleric who claimed that Ecuador was settled by the Phoenicians who sailed from the eastern Mediterranean, across the Atlantic and up the Amazon – 3000 years ago! The Crespo 'stones', described in Von Daniken's *Chariots of the Gods*, are now reported to be in a private collection.

Museo del Banco Central This museum is in the south-east part of town near the River Tomebamba and is not very obvious (no sign). The entrance gate is on Calle Larga (see map) and the building is across open grounds. The guard at the gate will indicate the way but you should have your passport.

Entrance is free and the museum is open from 9 am to 4 pm Tuesday to Friday. There is a permanent collection of old black-and-white photographs of Cuenca and a changing exhibit which is often very good. On one of my recent visits this was about the evolution of man and it was interesting to see this familiar subject explained from a distinctly Ecuadorian point of view which uses local examples. There is also a small exhibit of ancient musical instruments.

Behind the museum is an archaeological site, Pumapungo, which is currently being excavated. The ruins date to Inca times.

Inca Ruins Walking back along Calle Larga and along the river, you come to the ruins on Avenida Todos los Santos. There are some fine niches and walls but most of the stonework was destroyed to build colonial buildings. There are a few explanatory signs in Spanish. If you're coming from Peru the ruins will seem rather lacklustre. Admission to the site is free, but it can be seen quite well from the road. On the Calle Larga side of the ruins is a small site museum which was recently closed.

Museo de Artes Populares This small but worthwhile museum is run by the Centro Interamericano de Artesanías y Artes Populares, or CIDAP, (☎ 828 878) and is open from 8.30 am to 12.30 pm and from 2.30 to 6.30 pm, Monday through Friday. The address is Hermano Miguel 3-23 on the steps leading down to the river. Admission is free and there is a small but worthwhile exhibit of traditional musical instruments, native and regional costumes, and various handicrafts. There is also a changing exhibition of anything from Chinese porcelains to Cuencaño pottery.

Museo Remigio Crespo Toral (also known as the Museo Municipal). This museum is at Calle Larga 7-07 and Borrero and used to be open from 8 am to 1 pm and 3 to 5 pm, Monday to Friday, but is currently under restoration. This is probably just as well, because the creaking old building seemed positively dangerous last time I was in it. The collection contains religious sculptures, colonial furniture and paintings, a fine collection of Indian artefacts and relics of the local Saint Miguel who was canonised in

1984. It may have reopened by the time you get there.

Museo de las Conceptas This museum is housed in the Convent of the Immaculate Conception at Hermano Miguel 6-33, three blocks up from the river and opposite the tourist information office. The museum is in what used to be the old infirmary of the convent, which was founded on 13 June 1599. Parts of the building dates to the 17th century. The chapel of the infirmary has a display of crucifixes by the noted 19th century local sculptor, Gaspar Sangurima. Other parts of the building display a variety of religious art: paintings, carvings, statuettes, nativity scenes etc. There is also a display of photographs showing the austere daily life of the nuns. There is an audio-visual presentation at 11 am and 3 pm. Museum hours are 9 am to 4 pm, Tuesday to Friday, and 10 am to 1 pm on Saturday; admission is US$0.75.

Museo de la Historia de la Medicina This museum is open sporadically and has art shows and a small botanical garden as well as displays related to the history of medicine. It is in the grounds of the Military Hospital on 12 de Octubre on the south side of the Río Tomebamba, reached by crossing the river on the Hermano Miguel bridge.

Parque Calderón The main plaza, or Parque Calderón, is three blocks away from the Museo de las Conceptas. The dominant building is the **new Cathedral** with its huge blue domes. It is particularly attractive when illuminated, although the lighting hours are unpredictable. The marbled interior is rather stark. Construction began in 1885 and the cathedral was supposed to be much taller than it is – an error in design meant that the tall bell-towers could not be supported by the building and so it was not built as originally planned.

Almost unnoticed on the other side of the park is the squat but more interesting **old Cathedral** (also known as El Sagrario) which was renovated for the visit of Pope

John Paul II to Ecuador in 1985. Construction of this building began in 1557, the year that Cuenca was founded. In 1739 it was used as a triangulation point by La Condamine's expedition to measure the shape of the earth. It is open to the public but hours are variable.

Casa de Cultura At the south-west corner of Parque Calderón is the Casa de Cultura. There is a good art gallery here with frequently changing exhibits. Most paintings are by local artists and are for sale but there is absolutely no pressure to buy. In fact it's hard to find a salesperson if you should happen to see a work that you're seriously interested in. There's also a bookshop of art-oriented Spanish-language books and a coffee shop.

Plazoleta del Carmen A block from the Parque Calderón at the corner of Sucre and

Aguirre is the church of El Carmen de la Asunción, founded 1 August 1682. Although the church is open infrequently, there is a colourful and attractive daily flower market in the small plaza in front of the church. Turning left down Aguirre brings you to the **San Francisco** church and market, a block away.

Plaza de San Sebastián Continuing west along Sucre for six blocks brings you to this plaza, also known as the Parque Miguel León. This is a quiet and pleasant park with the interesting old Church of San Sebastián at the north end. The park seems to be developing into an 'artists' quarter', with a mural of infant art on one wall, a couple of art galleries, and the modern art museum.

Museo de Arte Moderno This is on Sucre and Talbot (☎ 830 499) and is open from 9 am to 1 pm and 3 to 6 pm Monday to Friday and on Saturday morning. They plan on opening on Sunday too; it's worth checking if that is your only free day. Admission is free. They have a small permanent collection and changing shows of (mainly) local artists and sculptors.

Back into the Centre Return into the centre along Bolívar and look into the colonial **Church of San Cenáculo** as you go. This has recently been cleaned and has had work done on it – it looks very bare in contrast to the opulent churches of Quito. After San Cenáculo, head north for one block and continue into the centre along Gran Colombia, the main handicraft and shopping shop street in Cuenca. Soon you pass the **Church of Santo Domingo** on your left, which has some fine carved wooden doors and colonial paintings inside. In the next few blocks you pass by many arts and crafts stores selling a variety of handicrafts. Parque Calderón is only a block to the south.

Markets Market day is Thursday, with a smaller market on Saturday. There are two main market areas: one around the Church of San Francisco and the other at the Plaza

Rotary by Avenidas Mariscal Lamar and Hermano Miguel. The San Francisco market is mainly for locals rather than tourists, and crafts shoppers will do better to look into the Plaza Rotary market or along Gran Colombia. The markets are lively and interesting but watch your belongings – pickpockets have been reported. The market continues on a smaller scale on other days of the week.

Places to Stay

Hotels are often full for the celebrations 1-3 November and your choice will be limited – though there are so many places listed that you're bound to find somewhere. Prices tend to rise during the fiestas.

For some reason, most hotels (except a few of the most desperately cheap) have hot or at least tepid water. There are, however, occasional problems with water supply in even the top-end hotels, so make sure the water is running before you pay extra for a room with private bath.

There are half a dozen hotels within a few hundred metres of the bus terminal, but most are a km or more away in the downtown area.

Places to Stay – bus terminal area

Directly opposite the front of the terminal is

the *Residencial Los Alamos*, which has a simple restaurant attached. They charge US$2 and US$4 per person for clean rooms with shared and private baths.

Turning right out of the terminal and heading down Avenida España for about five minutes, you reach the *Residencial La Alborada*, Olmedo 13-82 and España, which charges US$2 per person and has shared baths. A block further, by the traffic circle marking the intersection of España with Sangurima, is the fairly new *Hotel Los Libertadores* which has clean rooms with private bathroom and electric shower for about US$3.75 per person. Also by the traffic circle is the *Hostal Hurtado de Mendoza* (☎ 831 909, 827 909), Sangurima and Huayna Capac, which has a restaurant attached and clean rooms with private bath, carpet and phone for US$4.50 per person. Opposite is the friendly *Hotel España* (☎ 824 723), Sangurima 1-19, which is US$1.80 per person or US$2.70 with a private bath. Some rooms have TVs and there is a restaurant.

A block from the traffic circle is the *Residencial Tito* (☎ 829 734), Sangurima 1-49, which charges US$2.30 per person. The rooms are clean but mostly windowless; the

attached restaurant is inexpensive and good.
A few slightly more expensive rooms with a
private bath are available. Also recommended is the modern and clean *Hostal El
Galeon* (☎ 831 827), Sangurima 2-36. It has
spacious rooms with private bathrooms for
US$3.50/6.50 for singles/doubles. El Galeon
is about 700 metres from the bus terminal
and is the most distant from the terminal in
this section; all the other hotels described
below are a km or more from the terminal.

Places to Stay – bottom end

There are several budget hotels in the market
area by Mariano Cueva and Sangurima. Here
you will find the basic but adequate *Residencial Norte*, Mariano Cueva 11-63 and
Sangurima, which charges US$1.50 per
person or US$2 for a single with private bath.
Travellers told me that the showers were
good and hot. Next door is the basic *Residencial Colombia* (☎ 827 851), Mariano Cueva
11-61, which is OK and charges US$1.60 per
person in large rooms, some with balcony.

Around the corner is the basic but adequate *La Ramada*, Sangurima 5-51, which
charges from US$1.50 per person. Just over
a block away is the *Residencial Sánchez*
(☎ 831 519), A Vega Muñoz 4-28 and
Mariano Cueva, which is OK for about
US$1.40 per person. There are some other
similarly priced cheapies nearby but I
wouldn't recommend them unless you're
desperate. These include the pensiones
Andaluz and *Taiwan*.

The best budget hotel in this market area
is the *Residencial Niza* (☎ 823 284), Lamar
4-51 and M Cueva, which is clean and
friendly. The staff always chatted to me when
I went in and out and tried to answer my
questions when they could. They charge
US$2 each in rooms with shared baths or
US$3/5 for singles/doubles with a private
bath.

Going further into town, for US$1.40 per
person try the *Residencial Siberia*, Gran
Colombia 5-31 and Mariano Cueva, which
is old and basic but friendly, pleasant and
helpful. They have fairly reliable hot water
and lots of flowers at the entrance. The

extremely cheap and basic *Pensión Azuay,*
Hotel Cantabri and *Hostal San Francisco*
are by the San Francisco market. They have
nothing to recommend them except their
cheapness.

For US$2.25 per person you can stay in a
spacious room in the clean *Hotel Pichincha*
(☎ 823 868), Torres and Bolívar. The management is friendly. For US$2.75 per person
there is the clean *Hotel Emperador* (☎ 825
469), Gran Colombia 10-77 and Torres,
which is OK but the rooms are small.

If you are trying to economise but would
like a simple and clean room with a private
bath, try the following selection. The recommended and friendly *Hotel Milan* (☎ 835
351), Córdova 9-89 and Aguirre, is worth the
US$3/5 charged for singles/doubles with
bath (some slightly cheaper rooms with
shared bath are available). Some rooms have
balconies and great city views – but they tend
to be noisy from street noise – your choice.
There is a simple restaurant. The friendly
Gran Hotel (☎ 831 934, 835 154), Torres
9-70 and Bolívar, at US$3.25 per person with
bath has also been recommended. There is a
restaurant and an attractive courtyard – both
these last two have good luggage storage
facilities. Also good at this price is the
Residencial Paris (☎ 842 656, 827 257),
Torres 10-48 and Gran Colombia, which has
a helpful English-speaking manager.

The *Residencial Atenas*, Cordero 11-89
and Sangurima, charges US$3.50/6 for
singles/doubles with bath and US$2.75/5
without. The hotel is clean and the management friendly but their left-luggage facilities
have been criticised.

Places to Stay – middle

Cuenca has experienced a rash of hotel
'improvements' over the last two or three
years and a number of hotels have raised
their prices dramatically, by over 100% in
several cases. I give prices current at time of
writing but expect a few more of the hotels
in the following sections to do some price
raising during the life of this book. Many of
the hotels in this section add 20% tax – I

include this in the price but you should check the total rates before booking a room.

There are three hotels charging about US$6.50/10.50 for singles/doubles with private baths. The *Hotel Alli Tiana* (☎ 831 844), Córdova and Aguirre, has some rooms with balconies and good views but its water supply has been criticised. The *Hotel Las Américas* (☎ 831 160), Mariano Cueva 13-59 and A Vega Muñoz, has a friendly English-speaking manager and a good reasonably priced restaurant – both hotel and restaurant have been gaining popularity with budget travellers recently. The newly remodelled *Hostal Paredes* (☎ 835 674), Cordero 11-29 and Lamar, has spacious rooms and is OK.

The *Hotel Crespo Annexe* (☎ 829 989), Cordero 4-22 and Larga, has decent rooms with private bath for US$8.75/12 for singles/doubles (not to be confused with the top-end Hotel Crespo). Similarly priced is the new *Hotel Cuenca* (☎ 823 843), Borrero 10-69 and Gran Colombia, which is quiet, friendly and clean and has rooms with private bathroom, TV and telephone.

The new *Hotel Inca Real* (☎ 823 636, 825 571), Torres 8-40 and Bolívar, is in a traditional Cuencan building with a pleasant courtyard. It has been a hotel for 50 years, and until recently was a popular bottom-end hotel, the Residencial Inca. This was totally remodelled in 1991 and the new version has quaint carpeted rooms with private bathrooms, TV and telephone for US$9/15. Also at this price is the *Tomebamba Hotel* (☎ 823 797, 831 589), Bolívar 11-19 and Torres, and the *Hotel Atahualpa* (☎ 826 906, 831 841), Sucre 3-50 and Tomas Ordóñez. Both have pleasant clean rooms with telephone and TV.

For US$11/15 try the newly remodelled *Hotel Catedral* (☎ 823 204, 834 631), Aguirre 8-17 and Sucre. The friendly management readily gives discounts to Peace Corps workers and similar organisations – use your imagination and bargain. They have a good restaurant.

For about US$12/16 there are several good places with clean rooms containing telephones and TVs. The *Internacional*

Hotel Paris (☎ 827 118/525), Sucre 6-78 and Borrero, is good, modern, recommended and has a decent restaurant with a variety of good meals for about US$3 or US$4. The modern *Hotel El Conquistador* (☎ 831 788), Gran Colombia 6-65 and Hermano Miguel, has a sauna, restaurant and bar and seems like excellent value for the price.

Next door, the newer *Hotel Presidente* (☎ 831 979/066), Gran Colombia 6-59 and Borrero, is also good for the price. Apart from having all the usual amenities, it has a 9th-floor bar with a great view of the city. Any one of these hotels may decide to go 'top end' in the next few years.

The newly remodelled *Hotel Internacional* (831 348, 823 731), Benigno Malo 10-15 and Gran Colombia, in an elegant 19th-century mansion, charges US$18/23 in nice rooms with all the usual amenities.

Places to Stay – top end

Cuenca's top-end hotels charge foreigners twice the rate that residents pay. If you don't want to pay that much, stay in one of the better middle-priced hotels – there really isn't that much difference in quality.

The most worthwhile of the top-end hotels, in my mind, is the *Hotel Crespo* (☎ 831 837, 827 857, 835 984), Larga 7-93 and Cordero. It is in an attractive building overlooking the Río Tomebamba – the more expensive rooms have lovely river views. There is a good restaurant. River view rooms are US$35/45; rooms without a river view are US$4 less.

The fanciest hotel downtown is the modern *Hotel El Dorado* (☎ 831 390), Gran Colombia 7-87 and Cordero. It charges about US$50 for a double room. I'd rather spend US$50 on three nights somewhere else.

Finally, if you want luxury and prefer staying out of town, try the expensive, Swiss-run *Hotel La Laguna* (☎ 831 200) on Avenida Ordoñez Lazo, at the north-western edge of Cuenca, just over three km from the city centre. The hotel is currently popular with North Americans (US Embassy staff stay here on their jaunts down to Cuenca) and is set in pleasant gardens with a small pool, sauna, a little lake and an expensive restaurant. Rates are around US$60 for a double.

Places to Eat

Many restaurants are closed on Sunday and some also on Saturday. Several good new restaurants have opened recently and some are aimed at the traveller.

Budget travellers can find several cheap places along Sangurima. The restaurants at the *Hotel España* and *Residencial Tito* are good and there are several other places as you walk in to town. Turning right on Mariano Cueva brings you to the *Hotel Las Américas* which also has a good budget restaurant. The areas around the two markets have plenty of cheap restaurants. The *Balcón Quiteño* (☎ 824 281), Sangurima 6-49 and Hermano Miguel, is recommended. Local people eat here which is always a good sign. One of the cheapest near the San Francisco market is the restaurant under the *Hostal San Francisco*, where a set meal can cost as little as US$0.70.

There are several chifas of which the *Chifa Pak How*, Córdova and Cordero, is popular and one of the best. Meals are around US$1.50.

Vegetarians can try the Hare Krishna-run *Govinda* which has changed addresses a couple of times in the past few years. The latest reincarnation is at Aguirre 8-15 and Sucre, right next to the Hotel Catedral. There are two locations for the *Restaurant El Paraiso*; the first is at Tomas Ordoñez 10-19 and Gran Colombia and there is a branch at Lamar 1-82 and Manuel Vega. They are homey little places, usually closed at weekends and early in the evenings, which leads people to write me letters saying that these restaurants are out of business. Try a weekday lunch time – I recently had a very good lunch (at the Ordoñez location) of soup, salad, rice with vegetable stew, and juice all for a princely US$0.90.

On the north side of Parque Calderón is the *Pio Pio* chicken restaurant, which has your basic chicken. Also on the parque is the *Raymypampa* restaurant under the new cathedral. It looks quite nice but is fairly expensive, has mediocre food and very slow service.

There are several good cafés and snack bars. One of the best, and currently very popular as a gringo travellers' hang-out and meeting place, is the *Heladería Holandesa*, Benigno Malo 9-45 and Bolívar. This Dutch-Swiss run café has excellent ice cream, cakes, coffee, yoghurt and fruit salad. Another good place is the very small *Café Austria*, Bolívar and Juan Montalvo, which has delicious Austrian-style cakes and coffee. The *Café El Carmen*, next to the Casa de Cultura on the south-west corner of the Parque Calderón, has good snacks and inexpensive local dishes, many of which are not on the menu – ask.

There are plenty of bakeries for fresh bread to make your own sandwiches. Noteworthy is the *Panadería Centenario*, Benigno Malo and Juan Jaramillo, which sells fresh bread from 7 am till 10 pm.

Lovers of Italian food will find plenty to choose from. There are two pizzerías on Gran Colombia on either side of Cordero – the *Los Pibes* and the *La Tuna*. Both have been recommended. Also good is the small and homey *La Napoletana Pizzería*, Benigno Malo 4-104 and Larga. Get there early – the place is popular with locals and is often full. There are other Italian places.

El Pedregal Azteca restaurant and bar (☎ 823 652), Gran Colombia 10-33 and Aguirre, is Mexican-run and serves good and quite authentic Mexican food at medium prices. This place has been recommended by several travellers (including me – I do get to travel when I'm not glued to the word processor!) The building and ambience are as enjoyable as the food, but they are closed on Sunday and Monday. Another pleasant building with a nice atmosphere is *D'Bernardo's Restaurant*, Borrero 9-68 and Bolívar, which serves good and reasonably priced local dishes and rather more expensive international food.

The *La Cantina* bar and restaurant, Córdova and Borrero, has a pleasant and elegant patio and serves good meals. One traveller reports that this place is 'full of US tour groups'. Opposite, and also popular with tourists, is the *Restaurant El Jardín* (☎ 831 120, 824 882), at Córdova 7-23 and Borrero. This restaurant is reputedly the best in town (some say the country) and a meal will cost about US$25 for two – not bad. They are closed on Sunday. The *Restaurant El Túnel* (☎ 823 109), Torres 8-60 and Bolívar, is a small, intimate place with medium-priced local food.

The best hotels in town have good restaurants open to the general public; you can relax inexpensively with coffee and croissants in pleasant surroundings. The Internacional Hotel Paris has a good and moderately priced restaurant, *El Conquistador*, which has some of the best coffee in town. *El Dorado* can give you breakfast from 6.30 am, though it's somewhat expensive for other meals. Both the hotels Presidente and El Dorado have top floor restaurant/bars with good city views. You can just have a drink.

If you're leaving town – or arriving, for that matter – you can eat at the main bus terminal. They have a 24-hour snack bar and a decent restaurant open during the day.

Entertainment

Though Cuenca is Ecuador's third largest city, entertainment is minimal. *El Mercurio* is the Cuenca newspaper for listings of movies at the half dozen cinemas. The Teatro Casa de Cultura is not the same place as the Casa de Cultura, which occasionally also has movies or lectures – both are shown on the map.

There are two rather fancy and pricey bars where well-off locals and rich tourists like to hang out. One is the *La Cantina* bar and restaurant at Córdova and Borrero, and the other is the *Picadilly Bar*, across the street on Borrero. Neither of these places will sell you a bottle of beer. When I asked for a beer, I got a glass poured from an already opened Pilsener bottle behind the counter. When I said that I wanted my own bottle, they refused to give me one though they did offer to open a new bottle of Pilsener and pour about half of it into a glass, saving the other

half for the next customer. They also charged more for my small glass than I would have paid for the whole large bottle almost anywhere else. A very strange habit which I only found in these pretentious and overpriced bars in Cuenca. Go for the surroundings, not the drinks. I preferred a bottle of beer in one of the other restaurants, such as El Pedregal Azteca, D'Bernardo's or El Balcón Quiteño.

The expensive El Dorado Hotel has a nightclub and there's a discotheque weekends at the Hotel Alli Tiana and the Hotel El Conquistador. There are a couple of other disco or show possibilities on the same block as the Alli Tiana – irregular dates. The *Boogaloo Disco Club* (☎ 832 637, 823 256) is at Gran Colombia and Unidad Nacional, over the Pollos Gus, about 1½ km west of downtown. I have never tried boogalooing down there – let me know how groovy it is. I suggest you bring a good long novel if you need entertainment.

Things to Buy

Cuenca is the centre of the panama hat industry and is one of the best places to buy these hats anywhere in the world. A good place to start is near the tourist office – on the same block (Tarqui 6-93 and Córdova) is a hat shop run by the well known Ortega family.

Other crafts of the Cuenca area include *ikat* textiles which are made with threads that have been tie-dyed before weaving; this ancient method dates to pre-Columbian times. Traditional colours are indigo (a deep blue-violet) but red and black have appeared recently. Handmade ceramic tiles, plates, cups and bowls are also popular as are baskets. Typical Cuencaño baskets are huge and come with lids – few people can manage to take one of these home. Gold and silver filigreed jewellery from the nearby village of Chordeleg is for sale as are the usual weavings, carvings and leatherwork of Ecuador.

Wandering down Gran Colombia and the city blocks just north of the Parque Calderón will bring you to most of the best crafts stores. The Thursday market at Lamar and Hermano Miguel also has crafts for sale – watch your pockets.

For utilitarian shopping, try the Mi Comisariato Supermarket on Cordero at Córdova.

Getting There & Around

Air The Aeropuerto Mariscal Lamar passenger terminal is conveniently only two km from the heart of town, on Avenida España. Taxis are about US$0.50 and city buses pass the terminal frequently, although they tend to be rather full just after a plane arrives. Downtown, buses depart from the stop by the flower market on Aguirre – not all are marked so ask the drivers.

Flight schedules to and from Cuenca change several times a year so you should make local enquiries about these. At time of writing, TAME has flights to and from Guayaquil in the mid-morning from Monday to Friday. Fares are about US$13.50. From Monday to Friday there are three flights a day to and from Quito for US$17.50. There are two morning Quito flights on Saturday and one afternoon flight on Sunday. Both TAME and SAN service this route. There used to be flights to Macas and there is talk of flights to Loja – but nothing happening now. For flights to Loja and Machala and some coastal cities, fly to Guayaquil and change; for most other cities change in Quito.

TAME has an airport desk (☎ 800 193) and a downtown office (☎ 827 609) in the alley off Gran Colombia between the hotels Presidente and El Conquistador. Business hours are 9.30 am to 12.30 pm and 2 to 5 pm on weekdays, but are subject to change. Their airport desk is open for incoming and outgoing flights. SAN has an office at the Cuenca Airport (☎ 804 033) and downtown at Bolívar 5-39 and Mariano Cueva (☎ 823 403, 828 557, 800 239).

Ecuatoriana (☎ 830 611/287) has an office at Gran Colombia 5-20 and Mariano Cueva for information on international flights. All of these leave from either Guayaquil or Quito.

Bus A new and well-organised terminal terrestre was opened in November 1983 and most long-distance buses now arrive and leave from here. It is on Avenida España on the way to the airport and about 1½ km from the town centre. City buses leave from in front of the terminal for the centre (US$0.05) and buses for the terminal leave from the bus stop on Aguirre by the flower market. Most (but not all) buses are marked 'Terminal' so ask the driver to be sure.

There are literally dozens of different bus companies with offices in the terminal. Some run two or three buses every hour, others run two or three every week. Some run fast, small and cramped minibuses (or busetas) with guaranteed seating, others use huge but slow old coaches with more leg room but standing passengers as well. One reader suggests that the fast, small buses stop for longer meal stops than the slower coaches, making arrival times about the same. You should check out the various possibilities and find the one most convenient for you.

Buses leave for Guayaquil (US$2.50; five hours) many times daily. Buses for Azogues (US$0.25; 45 minutes) leave at least every hour, many continuing to Cañar (US$0.45; 1½ hours) and Alausí (US$1.50; four hours). For Quito (US$3; nine hours depending on route and road conditions) there are buses about every hour.

For destinations between Alausí and Quito there are several departures every day, eg Riobamba (six hours). Buses leave for Machala (US$2; five hours) about every hour; a few continue to Huaquillas but it's usually quicker to change buses in Machala. There are six or seven buses a day to Saraguro (US$1.90; 4½ hours) continuing to Loja (US$2.40; seven hours).

For destinations south of Loja it is best to change in Loja. There are three or four buses a day to Macas (US$2.40; 10 hours) and a couple of buses to Gualaquiza (US$2; seven hours) if you want to go into the southern Oriente. There is a passenger information desk at the terminal where you can ask about other unusual destinations.

Buses to Gualaceo for the Sunday market depart from the corner of Avenidas España and Benalcázar about 100 metres south-west of the main terminal. They leave every few minutes on market day and less frequently on weekdays for the 40-minute, US$0.25 ride. Ask in the main terminal for buses continuing to Sígsig; they leave almost hourly with CITES (US$0.40; 1½ hours).

Local buses (US$0.05) for Baños leave from Avenida Torres by the San Francisco market.

Train The railway station is on the southeastern outskirts of town, reached by following Avenida Huayna Capac south for about one km beyond Calle Larga, crossing both the Río Tomebamba and the Río Tarqui. A taxi will be about US$0.50 from down town.

There is a daily autoferro at 2 pm going to Sibambe (US$0.80; five hours). Here, you can catch the train as it passes from Alausí to Guayaquil the following morning, but there are no facilities at Sibambe (no hotels, no restaurants). The train returns from Sibambe to Cuenca the following morning. You can get off at Chunchi (4½ hours from Cuenca), where there is a basic pensión with cold water showers (US$2, or less if there are few guests and you bargain). There are a couple of basic restaurants here and you can get frequent buses on to Alausí, half an hour away.

On Sunday there is an old-fashioned steam train to Azogues at 9 am and 2 pm (US$0.40; 1½ hours). The train returns from Azogues to Cuenca or you can take a bus back. The carriages are open sided and this is a trip done for fun rather than to get anywhere. There is also a comfortable and expensive tourist autoferro run by Metrotours (see earlier information).

You can ride on the roof of these trains for good views. Times are most definitely liable to change so check at the train station first – the folks down there were helpful when I stopped by.

The Cuenca Area

BAÑOS

This is a much smaller version of the Baños in the South of Quito chapter. Here you'll find sulphurous hot springs with public pools and restaurants – a popular getaway for Cuencaños.

The village is about five km south-west of Cuenca. Local buses go there or a taxi will cost under US$2. Use of the thermal pools costs about US$0.40, or twice that in a private bathroom.

Places to Stay & Eat

There are a couple of basic residenciales by the baths, charging about US$2 per person in rooms with hot water. A short distance away is the comfortable *Hostería Durán* (☎ 810 064, 817 444) which has a private thermal pool, pleasant gardens, and the best restaurant in the area. A double room is about US$15.

Apart from the Durán, there are several simple restaurants in the area serving inexpensive Ecuadorian food.

AREA NACIONAL DE RECREACIÓN CAJAS

This 28,808-hectare recreation area lies about 30 km west of Cuenca and is famous for its many beautiful lakes – well over 200 have been named and there are countless smaller ponds, pools and puddles. There is trout in the lakes and fishing is permitted. The terrain is bleak and rough and the lakes set into the harsh countryside shine like jewels. It is rugged hiking and camping country, much of it páramo at around 4000 metres above sea level. None of the area is above 4500 metres so it doesn't snow, although the winds and rains can make it very cold. Hikers and campers should be well prepared with warm and windproof gear and have plenty of energy.

In sheltered hollows and natural depressions of the terrain, small forests of the quinua tree are seen. This tree grows at the

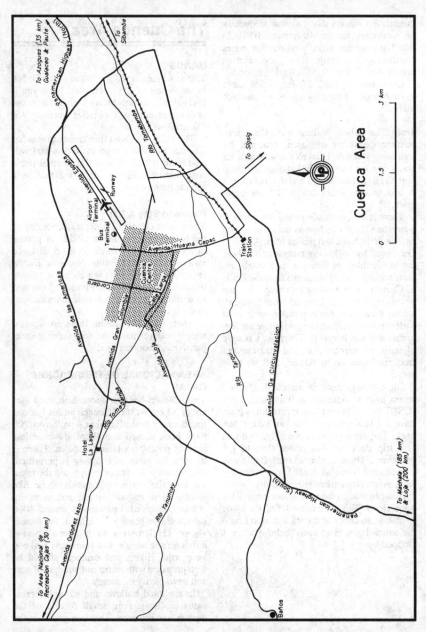

Cuenca Area

Area Nacional de Recreación Cajas landscape

highest altitudes of any tree in the world and the quinua thickets provide welcome protection from the elements for all kinds of unusual plants and animals. Everything is on a small, tightly-packed scale, and forcing one's way into one of these dense dwarf forests is like entering a scene from a Grimm's fairy tale.

Birdwatchers will have a great time looking for the many different species found on the lakes, in the quinua forests and in the surrounding páramo. The dwarf forests are the habitats of birds with such delicious names as giant conebill, tit-like dacnis and grey-breasted mountain toucan.

A variety of exotically named hummingbirds are present: rainbow-bearded thornbill, sapphire-vented puffleg and purple-throated sunangel are just a few of them. Raptors, including the Andean condor, come lazily flapping overhead. Even the LBBs (little brown birds) which hop unobtrusively through the thickets have interesting names like mouse-coloured thistletail. So bring your binoculars and bird book if you have them.

Information

Buses from Cuenca leave at 6.30 am (except Thursday) from the Church of San Sebastián for the cramped two-hour ride to the Laguna Toreadora ranger station on the northern side of Cajas, 34 km from Cuenca. There is a return bus in the afternoon at about 3 pm (check with the driver). The bus is often crowded and has been known to leave early – get to the bus stop by 6 am. It is particularly crowded at weekends with local fishing enthusiasts. Make sure the driver knows to drop you off at the park entrance – the bus continues 12 km beyond it to the village of Migüir and you'll miss the park otherwise.

There is a ranger station where you can usually sleep for a small fee (but don't rely on it – there are only four beds) and camping is allowed anywhere in the recreation area. The bus passes within a few hundred metres of the ranger station. A permit costs US$2 for overnight stays but is not needed for day trips. The park is administered by the MAG. The MAG offices in Cuenca can give you further information, maps and permits – but the maps are very sketchy. You can also obtain permits at the park station so there really is little reason to go to the MAG office, although the staff there are helpful.

There is also a southern road passing the park at the villages of Soldados and Angas. This road is in very poor shape but there are buses on Monday, Wednesday, Friday and Saturday leaving from El Vado and Loja in Cuenca at 6 am. It is 34 km to Soldados and 56 km to Angas and the bus takes about four hours. There are no ranger stations or facilities at either of these tiny and remote villages; Cajas lies to the north of you. Buses return to Cuenca in the afternoon.

Hikers may want to buy topographical maps from the IGM in Quito. Four 1:50,000 maps cover the area: Cuenca CT-NV-F4; Chaucha CT-NV-F3; San Felipe de Molleturo CT-NV-F1; and Chiquintad CT-NV-F2.

Apart from the bus, you can take a taxi (about US$20) or go on a day trip with one of the tour agencies with Cuenca. Hitchhiking is possible but difficult – there are very few vehicles.

The driest months are August to January but it can rain anytime – those hundreds of beautiful lakes need to be kept full! During the dry season, day-time temperatures can go into the high teens Centigrade; night temperatures can go well below zero. Wet season temperatures are less extreme. Annual rainfall is about 1200 m. Water temperatures are usually below 5°C – you can leave your swimming suit at home.

GUALACEO, CHORDELEG & SÍGSIG

These three villages are all famous for their Sunday markets. If you started from Cuenca early in the morning you could easily visit all three markets and be back in Cuenca in the afternoon. Buses leave Cuenca from south-west of the main terminal. The best-known markets are at Gualaceo and Chordeleg, which are within two or three km of one another.

Gualaceo has the biggest market and sells mainly produce, animals and household goods. Chordeleg's market is smaller but important for textiles and jewellery – it is one of Ecuador's most famous jewellery centres.

Sígsig market is further away from Cuenca and less visited by tourists. All three villages are good examples of colonial towns.

Gualaceo

In addition to being an important market town, Gualaceo has some importance as a tourist resort and has a pretty location by the Río Santa Barbara. It is 36 km from Cuenca at a pleasant elevation of about 2370 metres above sea level. There are several restaurants by the river and a stroll along the banks is pleasant. The town is quite progressive and has a large and spacious modern church with good stained-glass windows. There are several restaurants and places to stay as well as an IETEL office and a cinema.

Note that the Sunday market is several blocks from the bus station in Gualaceo, although there are some souvenir stands near the bus plaza which may fool you into thinking that was the market. There is also a colourful animal market across the covered bridge and on the east bank of the river.

The annual fiesta on 25 June celebrates the cantonisation of Gualaceo. There is also an annual peach festival on 4 March which goes on for about a week with an agricultural fair (flower and fruit shows, parades).

Places to Stay & Eat The best place to stay in the town centre is the *Gran Hostal Gualaceo*, which charges about US$2.75 per person for a room with a private bath and hot water (a recent report suggests that this place has closed). The *Residencial Gualaceo* charges about US$2 per person, has hot water sometimes and is OK. There is also the cheaper and more basic *Residencial Español*.

About 15 minutes south of town is the *Hostería La Ribera* (☎ 823 454) which is by the river and has a restaurant and small swimming pool. They charge US$8/12 for singles/doubles with private bath but are open to bargaining, especially for stays of more than one night.

The best place in the area is the pleasant *Parador Turistico Gualaceo* (☎ 255 110/26) about one km south of town and it is set in

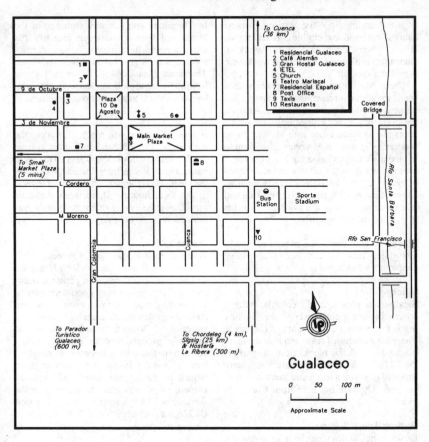

Gualaceo

1 Residencial Gualaceo
2 Café Alemán
3 Gran Hostal Gualaceo
4 IETEL
5 Church
6 Teatro Mariscal
7 Residencial Español
8 Post Office
9 Taxis
10 Restaurants

0   50   100 m

Approximate Scale

attractive gardens with flowers and birds. There is a swimming pool and horse riding can be arranged. They have a decent restaurant and bar with good meals for about US$4. There is a a discotheque which opens on demand (10 people paying a cover charge, usually at weekends). Clean, flower-filled rooms with private bath and hot water are US$16/20 for singles/doubles.

Gualaceo has a couple of basic restaurants just south of the bus plaza. The *Café Alemán*, on the other side of town, is good for snacks and desserts rather than meals. The stalls in the market on market day serve a variety of local dishes like whole roast pigs (you don't have to eat it all). The restaurants at the better hotels are another possibility.

Chordeleg
Chordeleg is about five km south of Gualaceo and has many stores selling a great variety of crafts – some people complain that it is too 'touristy'. Maybe it is; it's especially popular with Guayaquileños looking for highland bargains. On the other hand, if you're shopping for souvenirs or gifts you can choose from gold and silver filigree jewellery (the item of major interest) as well

as woodcarvings, pottery, textiles, panama hats and embroidered clothing. A reader who is a goldsmith writes that the walk to Chordeleg is pleasant but the gold work there is nothing special.

There is a pleasant central plaza with a small modern church containing simple but attractive stained-glass windows. Also on the plaza is a small village museum which manages to pack more into it than some bigger city museums. It's open from 8 am to 5 pm daily except Monday and is free. There are displays about the history and techniques of many of the local handicrafts such as filigreed metalwork, panama hat making and ikat weaving. Guides are available. It helps if you understand Spanish.

Places to Eat There is nowhere to stay in Chordeleg but you can find a couple of simple restaurants.

Sígsig

Sígsig is a pleasant, old colonial village where little happens except the Sunday market. It is about 25 km south of Gualaceo. There are a couple of restaurants on the main market plaza. A few blocks from the plaza is the CITES bus office. Opposite it is a store that will rent you a room and there is a basic pensión. The ride out here from Cuenca is nice.

Getting There & Away

Buses from Cuenca take about 45 minutes to reach Gualaceo and leave every few minutes on market day and about every hour on weekdays. You can continue the four or five km to Chordeleg on foot or take a local bus. Buses pass the Chordeleg plaza for Sígsig at least once an hour and charge US$0.20 for the 40-minute ride. Sit on the right-hand side of the bus for good views of the river canyon on the way to Sígsig. CITES buses return from Sígsig to Cuenca about every hour for US$0.40. Three buses a week (Monday, Wednesday and Saturday at 6 am) leave Sígsig for Gualaquiza if the road is passable. A new road to Gualaquiza is being built via **Chigüinda** – buses go there from Sígsig.

In Chigüinda you can stay with one of the locals and then continue on foot towards Gualaquiza via the remote villages of Aguacate and Río Negro. I read this in the *South American Handbook* – I haven't gone beyond Sígsig myself, nor know anyone who has. Good luck to adventurous travellers.

PAUTE

A few km before you reach Gualaceo, the road forks. The left-hand fork takes you up the Río Paute valley to the village of the same name, about 30 km from Cuenca. Nearby is the Distilería Uzhupud, which makes several of the local liquors. There is an attractive local flower festival to celebrate Paute's cantonisation on 26 February.

Places to Stay

There is one basic pensión in Paute.

Near the village is the *Hostería Uzhupud*, an excellent tourist resort in pleasant countryside. They have a very good restaurant, a swimming pool, tennis courts and an amazing garden which contains hundreds of varieties of flowers, including dozens of species of orchids. Birdlife is also prolific – you can see the world's largest hummingbird here. This is the 19-cm giant hummingbird, largest of the approximately 320 species known, all of which are found only in the Americas. The hostería charges about US$28 for a double room. Rooms vary in quality and price.

North of Cuenca

AZOGUES

About 35 km north of Cuenca on the Panamerican Highway lies Azogues. It is a quiet, small town of only some 25,000 inhabitants, yet it is the capital of the province of Cañar. 'Azogues' literally means 'quicksilver' and the name is derived from the mercury-rich ores supposedly found in the area; I could find no evidence of mercury extraction. The town is more important for its panama hat industry and Saturday market, and is worth visiting for its church. It is a possible alternative to Cuenca as a base for visiting Biblian, Cañar and Ingapirca to the north.

Information
The IETEL and post office are on the main plaza. Filanbanco will reluctantly exchange dollars at a bad rate – it's better to go to Cuenca. The provincial hospital is on the other side of the river west of town (though Cuenca has better facilities).

Things to See
The most interesting place to visit is the **Church of San Francisco**, which dominates the town from a hill to the south-east. You can't see it when you arrive at the bus terminal but if you head generally south-east and then climb up the Avenida de la Virgen, you'll reach it in about half an hour.

From the church there are sweeping views of the town, the surrounding countryside, and several other churches perched on the top of nearby hills. Hilltops seem to be the place to build churches in this region. Inside San Francisco there is a beautiful gilt altar. The building is sometimes illuminated at night and sitting on the dark hill it looks almost as if it were floating in mid-air.

Another church worth visiting is that of **Biblian**. This village is some nine km north of Azogues on the Panamerican; there are plenty of buses from the terminal. The **Santuario de la Virgen del Rocío** (or Sanctuary of the Virgin of the Dew) is highly visible to the right of the main highway on a steep hill dominating Biblian. It is one of the most attractive churches I've seen and looks more like a fairy-tale princess's palace than it does a church. Keep your eyes open for it even if you're just driving straight through Biblian. There is an annual pilgrimage here on 8 September. There's also a weekly market on Sunday.

Both these churches were renovated in late 1984 for the Pope's visit in 1985. The buildings on all the main streets in Azogues are whitewashed. Walking the streets of the town and admiring the colonial architecture is very pleasant.

As you stroll, keep your eyes open for signs of the panama hat industry. Avenida 3 de Noviembre is a good street to see hats being blocked and sold. The main market is on this street and is where the bustling Saturday morning market is held. There is also a smaller market on the Plaza San Francisco in front of the church – it's worth going to for the view.

If you spend the night and want something to do, try the movie theatre. There's only one.

Places to Stay
Despite its provincial capital status, Azogues does not yet have any particularly good hotels. The best place in town is the reasonably clean *Hotel Charles* at the corner of Rivera and Solano. They charge US$2.25 per person and have hot water in the showers. Nearby is the more basic *Pensión Tropical* at US$1.50 each.

The new *Hotel Playa* is under construction by the river, west of town, and will be by far the best place to stay. It may be open by the time you get there.

Places to Eat
There are a couple of simple but adequate restaurants by the bus plaza, the *Chifa La Florida* and the *Restaurant Anzuelo*.

Further into town, the *Restaurant Don Pancho* is small but friendly. The inexpensive *El Padrino* has meals for about US$1 and is OK. The *Restaurant Gran Manila* is also quite good – their lomito saltado has been recommended (this is a dish of chopped and fried beef mixed with vegetables such as onions, tomatoes and potatoes, served with rice). The *Pollería 87* is a clean and family-run chicken restaurant which opened, unsurprisingly, in 1987. They serve other dishes too and have been recommended by one traveller as the best place in town. Meals are about US$1.50. The *Chifa Familiar* is nearby.

Getting There & Away
Bus The main bus plaza is just off the

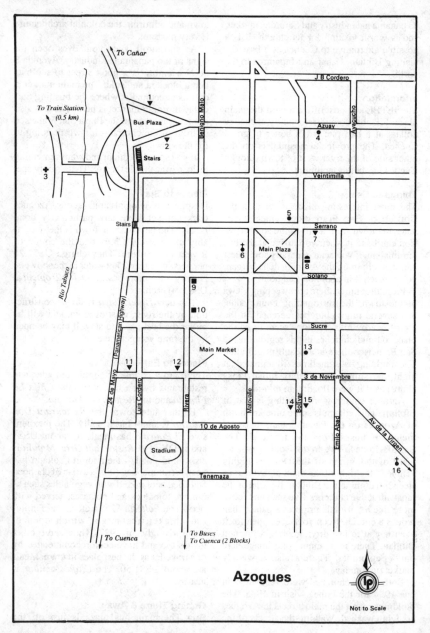

Azogues

Not to Scale

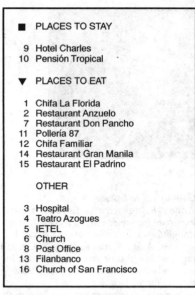

■ PLACES TO STAY

9 Hotel Charles
10 Pensión Tropical

▼ PLACES TO EAT

1 Chifa La Florida
2 Restaurant Anzuelo
7 Restaurant Don Pancho
11 Pollería 87
12 Chifa Familiar
14 Restaurant Gran Manila
15 Restaurant El Padrino

OTHER

3 Hospital
4 Teatro Azogues
5 IETEL
6 Church
8 Post Office
13 Filanbanco
16 Church of San Francisco

Panamerican Highway, which is renamed 24 de Mayo as it goes through Azogues. There are several departures a day for Quito, Guayaquil and Machala. For other destinations it is best to go to Cuenca and change buses.

For buses to Cañar it may be best to stand on the highway and wait for one to come by – often Cuenca-Cañar buses don't pull into the bus plaza (see what the locals are doing).

For Cuenca there is a local bus terminal on the east side of Matovalle at the south end of town. Buses for Cuenca leave as soon as they are full – several times an hour from dawn until about 6 or 7 pm. The fare to either Cuenca or Cañar shouldn't be more than about US$0.30.

Train The train station is across the river almost one km west of town.

There is a daily autoferro to Sibambe (US$0.60; 3½ hours) at 3.30 pm and to Cuenca (US$0.30; 1½ hours) at about 9 am. On Sunday, there is a steam train to Cuenca at 11 am and 4 pm (US$0.40). See under the

Cuenca Train section for more details. Departure times are liable to change so check at the train station.

CAÑAR
The small town of Cañar on the Panamerican is the nearest place to stay for travellers wishing to visit the Inca ruins of Ingapirca. At 66 km north of Cuenca and 3104 metres above sea level, it is a chilly place. There is a very colourful local market on Sunday which is visited by Cañari Indians coming down from the remote villages in the surrounding mountains.

Cañari men wear distinctive belts made by an unusual weaving method which gives rise to designs and motifs appearing on both sides of the belt. These may be available in the market – they are also woven by the local prisoners and if you head down to the jail, you will be allowed in to make purchases.

Places to Stay & Eat
Cañar has some simple places to stay. The basic *Pensión Guayaquil* on the street of the same name charges US$1.20 per person and US$0.30 extra for hot water. The friendly *Residencial Monica* is on the corner of the main plaza and charges US$1.50 per person. They have hot water. If these are all full you can find accommodation in unsigned private houses if you ask around. Places to eat are not particularly noteworthy and most close by about 7 pm.

Getting There & Away
Buses from Cuenca's terminal terrestre leave for Cañar (US$0.50; 1½ hours) every hour or so.

INGAPIRCA
Although Ingapirca (3230 metres above sea level) is the major Inca site in Ecuador it is difficult to get to and opinions are mixed about the importance or significance of the ruins. They have never been 'lost', as was Machu Picchu. As a matter of fact, the Frenchman Charles-Marie de La Condamine

Running Fox God

drew accurate plans of them as far back as 1739. The ruins are referred to as a fortress, but its garrison – if there was one – must have been quite small.

Archaeologists think that the main structure, an *usnu* elliptical platform known as the Temple of the Sun, had religious and ceremonial purposes. This building boasts some of the Inca's finest mortarless stonework and has several of the typical trapezoidal niches and doorways which are a hallmark of Inca construction. The less well-preserved buildings were probably storehouses and the complex may have been used as a *tambo* or stopping place for runners carrying imperial messages from Quito to Tomebamba.

At Ingapirca there is a small village with an several crafts stores and an occasionally open craft shop/museum by the church on the plaza. There are a few simple restaurants but no hotels. There is a weekly market on Friday.

The ruins are about a km away from the village. An interesting on-site museum was recently opened and is informative, particularly if you have a guide. Entrance to the site and museum is US$2. The museum is open from 9 am to 5 pm from Tuesday to Friday (a recent report says Saturday as well) and the ruins are open daily.

There is a shelter by the entrance with basic toilet facilities and benches. Officially, you can't sleep there but if you are stuck in Ingapirca you may be allowed to do so – you would need a sleeping bag.

Getting There & Away

Although Ingapirca is Ecuador's most important Inca ruin, visiting it cheaply is not straightforward as there are no direct bus services. A few tourist agencies in Cuenca organise day trips or you can rent a taxi for the day, which should cost about US$35 – bargain for the best rate.

To make an economical visit, you must first take a bus to Cañar (US$0.50; 1½ hours from Cuenca). About two km before Cañar there is a signed turnoff to Ingapirca on your right. You can wait here for a passing vehicle to take you the 15 km to the ruins; expect to pay about US$0.30 for the ride. You can walk or hitch but still are expected to pay if you get a ride. Vehicles pass by about once an hour. Leave early or you may get stuck without a ride back.

The bus from Cuenca usually continues through Cañar to **El Tambo.** From here there is a shorter (eight km) road to Ingapirca which is the shortest walk from the Panamerican. Pickup trucks travel the road several times a day and act as buses. This route is probably the fastest and most convenient. I'm told that there is a very basic place to stay in El Tambo but I've never tried it. There are plans to pave this road in 1992 – I'll believe it when I see it.

The San Pedro train station is about three or four km from Ingapirca – you could walk from there. Trains from Cuenca pass by around nightfall which is somewhat inconvenient. Supposedly there is somewhere to stay, but I would bring my sleeping bag if going this way. Metrotours in Cuenca organises private train trips to this station for Ingapirca visits.

Pickup trucks leave Cañar for Ingapirca when they have a load. There are no set departure times or places – ask around. You could probably hire a truck to take you there for about US$3.

South of Cuenca

About 20 km south of Cuenca, the road forks. The Panamerican Highway heads to the left and goes south to Loja via the towns of Oña and Saraguro. The right fork heads south-west to Machala

THE ROAD TO MACHALA

This road goes through impressive mountain scenery and is worth doing in daylight. Some 23 km from the Panamerican, the small town of **Girón** is passed. As one looks down on it from the road, one gets the impression of a neat-looking town of red-tiled roofs interspersed with brightly coloured red, blue, and green tin roofs.

At **Santa Isabel**, 37 km beyond Girón, buses may stop for a meal break. There are several restaurants in this bustling little community but I didn't see a hotel. The town is an agricultural centre for tropical fruits grown in this area, which is about 1600 metres above sea level. Banana and papaya plantations are seen interspersed among the corn-fields.

Just below Santa Isabela the scenery changes suddenly and dramatically as the road winds through completely barren mountains with no signs of life. Just as suddenly, a forest of columnar cacti appears and this vegetation soon gives way to cloud forest mixed with tropical agriculture.

About 35 km beyond Santa Isabel there is a military checkpoint – have your passport ready. Ten km beyond is the town of Pasaje,

and 25 km still further is Machala. Both are described in The South Coast chapter.

OÑA

The Panamerican Highway climbs steadily from Cuenca and there are good views of páramo moorlands and the southern Ecuadorian Andes. Oña, 105 km south of Cuenca, is reached after about three hours and the bus sometimes stops here to refuel. The interesting and ancient petrol pump is generator-driven. The attendant has to switch on the generator before he can deliver the fuel, and then he switches it off – a good measure of how frequently vehicles stop in Oña. It's a small town with a couple of simple restaurants and a basic pensión – there's not much reason to stop here.

SARAGURO

Just beyond Oña, the road crosses the provincial line into Loja and continues rising and falling through the eerie páramo scenery until it reaches Saraguro, 4½ hours, 165 km and US$1.80 south of Cuenca.

The town is named after the Saraguro Indians, who originally came from the Lake Titicaca region in Peru but became colonists in this region under the Incas. They are readily identifiable by their traditional dress. Both men and women (but especially the women) wear flat white felt hats with wide brims. The men sport a single pigtail and wear a black poncho but perhaps the most unusual part of their attire is their knee-length black or navy-blue shorts which are sometimes covered with an odd little white apron. They carry double shoulder bags with one pouch in front and one behind for a balanced load. The women wear heavy pleated black skirts and shawls fastened with ornate silver pins. The pins are known as *tupus* and are highly prized, often being passed down from mother to daughter as family heirlooms.

The Saraguros were well known for their jewellery but this craft seems to be dying out. Cattle-raising is their main occupation and they can be seen on foot driving their herds to tropical pastures in the 28 de Mayo area.

Wherever they go, they normally wear their traditional clothing and are the most successful Indian group of the southern Ecuadorian highlands. Their market day is Sunday when local Indians show up in their traditional black clothing.

Places to Stay & Eat
There are a few very basic places to stay, none with hot water or private bathrooms. Half a block north of the church is a *pensión* charging about US$1 per person. It's at number 03-5 – if there's nobody there ask at the store opposite. There are also rooms above the *Farmacia Nueva York* opposite the bus stop, but they are not always open. There is also the basic *Residencial Amigos* east of the church.

There are two or three basic restaurants, of which the 'best' is the *Salón Cristal* behind the church.

Getting There & Away
Loja, the provincial capital, is 62 km to the south and CTS buses leave Saraguro six or eight times a day for the two-hour ride, which costs US$0.60. The CTS bus office is a block from the main plaza. They also have buses leaving for various small villages in the area. For Cuenca, it is best to wait in the plaza for a northbound bus from Loja to pass by.

LOJA
From Saraguro the road continues to drop steadily to Loja at 2100 metres – a pleasant elevation which leads to a temperate climate. Loja was founded by the Spanish captain, Alonso de Mercadillo, on 8 December 1548 and so is one of the oldest towns in Ecuador. None of the earliest buildings survive, although houses from the 18th century can be found. With about 120,000 inhabitants (some local sources claim 160,000), Loja is both an important provincial capital and a college town, with two universities, a music conservatory and a law school. A small hydroelectric project became operational in 1897, at the base of Pedestal Hill a short distance west of the town centre. It generated

34 kilowatts, and gave Loja the distinction of being the first city in Ecuador to have electric energy.

Loja is very close to the Oriente and the surrounding countryside is green and pleasant. The people are proud of the great variety of plant species found in the region. They tell the story of the beautiful Countess of Chinchón, wife of an early 17th-century Peruvian viceroy, who was dying of malaria. A Franciscan monk cured her with quinine extracted from the bark of a tree found in the Loja area. After her recovery, fame of the 'miraculous' properties of the tree spread throughout the Spanish Empire and the world. Today the scientific name of the tree is *Chinchona succirubra* after the countess.

Alexander von Humboldt, the German scientist and explorer, visited the area in 1802 and called it 'the garden of Ecuador'. The British botanist Richard Spruce also mounted an expedition here in the mid-19th century. Recently, the area has been recognised for its biological value and the Parque Nacional Podocarpus was established in the nearby mountains in 1982 (see Parque Nacional Podocarpus later). The proximity of the Oriente influences Loja's climate; June and July are the wettest months (when roads into the Oriente may be closed by landslides caused by the torrential rains) and October through December are considered the most pleasant by local inhabitants.

Although the town itself is not particularly exciting, it is attractive and travellers on their way to Peru via the border town of Macará find this a convenient place to stop. The highland route to Peru through Loja and Macará is slower and rougher but much more scenic than the more travelled route through the coastal towns of Machala and Huaquillas. The road between Cuenca and Loja is being improved.

Information
The CETUR tourist information office (☎ 962 964) is on Bernardo Valdivieso just south of 10 de Agosto.

The MAG office (☎ 961 534), which is responsible for administering the Parque

Nacional Podocarpus, is at Miguel Riofrio 13-54 and Bolívar.

Two local newspapers, *El Mundo* and *El Siglo*, carry only local news, including movie listings. Guayaquil and Quito newspapers are available by about 8 am.

Money There are no exchange houses. Few of the banks change money. Two that do are Filanbanco on the Parque Central and Banco de Azuay (☎ 960 262) on the south-east corner of the parque. Various stores will change money – an ice cream heladería on Colón between Bolívar and Sucre and a gift shop in front of the Hotel Acapulco on Sucre were recently giving good rates. This is liable to change. Try and change money in Macará or Cuenca. Don't bring your Peruvian currency into Ecuador – get rid of it at the border.

Post & Telecommunications The post office (☎ 961 600) is in the municipal building on the north side of the Parque Central (main plaza). There is another post office at the corner of Colón and Sucre – it's not always open. The IETEL office is a block east of the Parque Central on Antonio Eguiguren.

Foreign Embassies The Peruvian Consulate (☎ 961 668) by the Univision TV towers near the UTPL (Universidad Tecnica Particular de Loja) on the outskirts of town is planning on moving into the town centre soon. Try calling or ask at the CETUR office for the current address.

Travel Agencies Hidaltur (☎ 963 378, 962 554), 10 de Agosto 15-34 and Sucre, is recommended for international travel services and local travel information. Franklin Hidalgo is the owner. They were recently selling three AeroPeru tickets for US$132 for use on any three flights within Peru – this is a good deal available only outside Peru and will save money if you plan on making flights in Peru.

Emergency The hospital (☎ 960 540) is at Kennedy and Quito. The Red Cross ambulance (☎ 960 200) is by the hospital.

Things to See & Do

A short but pleasant walk is east from the centre on Rocafuerte and across the Río Zamora, where washerwomen can sometimes be seen at work, and then up the small hill to the statue of the Virgin of Loja, which is protected by a caged (stone) lion. Here there is a rather damaged lookout with good city views. Another good lookout point is the hill and church of El Pedestal, west of the centre on 10 de Agosto – this area is known as 'El Balcón de Loja'.

In the centre, both the cathedral and the church of Santo Domingo have interesting painted interiors and elaborate statues. The cathedral is on the Parque Central and Santo Domingo is on a pretty and traditional little plaza at Bolívar and Rocafuerte. Also found on the Parque Central are government buildings and the Museo del Banco Central, which has a small archaeological collection and is open from 9 am to 5 pm, Monday to Friday. The Plaza of San Francisco, Bolívar and Colón, has a statue of the city's founder riding in on his horse – the monument is attractively framed by the trees growing around it.

From late August to the beginning of November the cathedral contains the miraculous Virgen del Cisne (Virgin of the Swan), carved in the late 1500s by Diego de Robles. During other months of the year the statue is kept at the village of El Cisne (described later in this chapter), some 70 km away. The day of the Virgen del Cisne is celebrated in Loja on 8 September with huge processions, and an annual international produce fair is held for about four or five days on either side of the 8th (the fair is called 'international' because Peruvians attend it).

Other important fiestas include 18 November which celebrates the Independence of Loja. Festivities may go on for a week and include parades and cultural events. The feast of San Sebastián, which coincides with the foundation of Loja, is celebrated every 8 December.

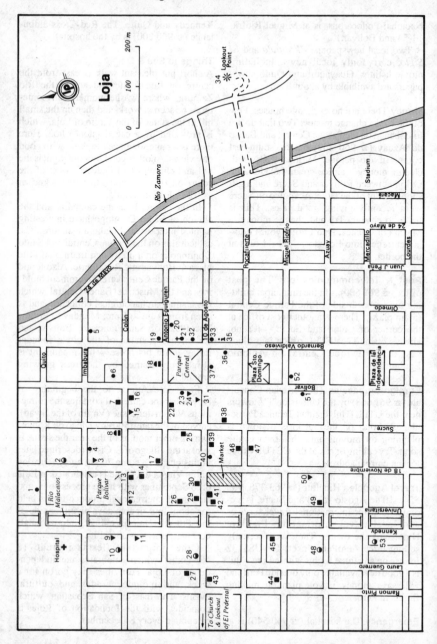

■ PLACES TO STAY

7	Hotel Ramses
13	Hostal Carrión & Residencial Primavera
14	Hotel Metropolitan
16	Hotel Libertador
17	Hotel Mexico
22	Residencial Pasaje
25	Hotels Acapulco, Londres & Cuxubamba
26	Hotel Saraguros Internacional
27	Hotel Hidalgo
28	Pensión (above Transportes Loja Bus Terminal)
29	Hotel Miraflores
30	Hotel Paris
38	Hotel Rocafuerte
39	Hotels Internacional & Paraiso
41	Hotel Americano
42	Hostal Quinara, Hotels Riviera & Inca
43	Residencial Macará
44	Residencial San Andres
45	Hotel Vilcabamba Internacional
46	Hotels Crystal & Loja
47	Hotel Caribe
49	Hotel Los Ejecutivos

▼ PLACES TO EAT

3	Restaurant La Tullpa
9	Pollos Gusy
11	Top Cream
15	Don Pepe's Restaurant
22	Casa China
24	Chifa 85 & Pescadería 200 Millas

30	Restaurant 85
31	Restaurant La Cordillera
45	Restaurant Kennedy
50	Pescadería Las Redes

OTHER

1	Las Ruedes Disco Club
2	Viajeros & Ejecutivo San Luis Buses
4	Peña Bar Don Pancho's
5	Latino's Discotheque
6	Plaza San Francisco
8	Branch Post Office
10	Transportes Saraguro Buses
12	Petrol (Gas) Station
18	Post Office & Government Buildings
19	TAME Airline
20	IETEL
21	Cathedral
23	Cine Velez & Unicornio Piano Bar
28	Transportes Loja Bus Terminal
32	Filanbanco
33	Banco de Azuay
34	Virgin of Loja Statue
35	CETUR Tourist Information
36	Cine El Dorado
37	Museo del Banco Central
40	Hidaltur
43	Transportes Yantzaza
44	Transportes Cariamanga Buses
48	Transportes Sur-Oriente Buses
51	Teatro Popular
52	MAG Office
53	Transportes Catamayo Buses

The weekly market is on Sunday, but Saturday and Monday also seem to be busy. The Plaza de la Independencia (also known as Plaza San Sebastián) is one of several places where market activities go on. This plaza also has 'Cultural Thursdays' when outdoor performances of dance or music may be given for free. It is a historic spot – this is where the Independence of Loja was declared on 18 November 1820. There are several colonial buildings around the plaza, and an incongruous 32-metre-high modern clocktower.

A couple of km north of the centre (head north on Universitario) are the parques de El Valle and de Jipiro. This is where the annual produce fair is held and there is also some Sunday market activity here. At other times, the suburban community of El Valle is worth a visit to see the old church and to try some of the typical food sold in comedores around the plaza. The nearby Parque de Jipiro has a small lake with a miniature island adorned by a white statue of a larger than life 'Venus'. This island is sometimes the scene of symphony performances. The musicians cluster around the statue and the audience must content itself with listening from the shores of the lake – the orchestra takes up the entire island.

At the south end of town is the Universidad Nacional (☎ 961 841), set in a large park containing a botanical garden which can be visited. Recent reports are that the gardens are not very well tended.

North-east of town is the UTPL (☎ 960 375) which sometimes has demonstrations of how ceramics are made. Items are for sale.

Places to Stay

Loja appears to have an excess of accommodation. I counted over two dozen hotels and many of them were nearly empty when I was there one July, admittedly not one of the best months for tourism. Maybe they fill up for the annual fiestas. Some of the hotels were closed and others were open but I couldn't find anyone to show me a room. The lack of guests may well mean that the owners will be willing to bargain during off-peak seasons, especially for two or more people sharing a room. The hotels are close together so wander around until you find one that appeals to you.

Places to Stay – bottom end

There is a basic pensión right above the *Transportes Loja Terminal*. It is cheap but very noisy. Across the street are the *Hotel Hidalgo* and *Residencial Macará* which both charge US$2 per person or US$2.50 in rooms with private bath and cold water. Two blocks away on Miguel Riofrio and Lauro Guerrero is the cheaper and more basic *Residencial San Andres*. These hotels are convenient for the bus but otherwise poor value – there are better and cheaper hotels in town across the river just a few minutes' walk away.

One of the cheapest places is the *Residencial Primavera*, Colón 16-44 and 18 de Noviembre, which is clean and secure but has only cold water. They charge about US$1 per person. On the same block is the *Hostal Carrión* (☎ 961 127), Colón 16-30, which is also basic, clean and safe and charges about US$1.50 per person.

Other basic cheapies charging under US$1.50 per person include the *Hotel Americano*, 10 de Agosto 16-62 and Universitaria,

and the *Hotel Mexico*, 18 de Noviembre and Antonio Eguiguren, which has hot water. The friendly *Hostal Pasaje*, Antonio Eguiguren and Bolívar, charges US$1.25 per person or US$11.75 with private bath and hot water.

Hotels charging about US$1.50 per person include the *Hotel Londres* and *Hotel Cuxubamba*, almost next to one another on Sucre and 10 de Agosto. The Londres has plenty of hot water and is clean, but there have been reports of thefts from rooms. The Cuxubamba has nice management and some rooms with bath and hot water for about US$2.50. On the same block is the *Hotel Acapulco* (☎ 960 651), Sucre 7-47, which is clean, safe, has hot water, and is fair value. They charge US$1.75 per person or US$2.25 in rooms with bath. A block away on Sucre is the *Hotel Rocafuerte*, also in this price range.

Around the corner is the *Hotel Internacional*, 10 de Agosto 15-28, which has plenty of hot water and is friendly. They charge US$1.70/2.30 per person depending on whether you have a private bath. A few doors away is the *Hotel Paraiso* which costs about the same.

There are several cheap hotels on Rocafuerte and Sucre. The *Hotel Caribe* (☎ 962 102), Rocafuerte 15-52, charges US$1.60 per person, is clean and has plenty of hot water. The *Hostal Crystal*, Rocafuerte 15-39, charges US$1.70 per person and has large rooms and hot water. The nearby *Hotel Loja* is similarly priced and friendly.

The friendly *Hotel Miraflores*, 10 de Agosto 16-65 and Universitaria, charges US$2/3 for singles/doubles or US$3/5 for singles/doubles with private bath. Rooms are large and clean. On the same block is the clean *Hotel Paris* (☎ 961 639), 10 de Agosto 16-37, which charges US$2 for a single or US$3.50 in singles with private bath, hot water and TV. The good *Hotel Metropolitan*, 18 de Noviembre and Colón, used to be similarly priced with helpful staff – the hotel is being remodelled and may raise its prices when it reopens.

The following hotels are reasonably

priced and would probably be middle range hotels in Quito or Guayaquil. The *Hotel Inca* (☎ 961 308, 962 478), Universitaria and 10 de Agosto, is OK and charges US$3.50 per person in rooms with private bath and hot water, or US$4 for the same with TV. Two other good hotels on the same block are the *Hotel Riviera* (☎ 962 863) which charges US$4.50/6.50 for singles/doubles with bath and hot water and the *Hostal Quinara* (☎ 960 785, 963 132) which charges US$4 per person in clean carpeted rooms with bathroom and TV.

A block away is the similar *Hotel Saraguros Internacional* (☎ 960 552), Universitaria 7-24. Nearby is the good *Hotel Los Ejecutivos* (☎ 960 004), Universitaria 10-76 and Azuay, which has similar rooms for US$4/6 for singles/doubles.

Places to Stay – middle
There are currently three very pleasant hotels in Loja which vie for the title of 'best in town'. They all charge about the same: US$10.50/14 for singles/doubles. They all offer comfortable rooms with private bath, TV and telephone.

The oldest of these hotels is the *Hotel Vilcabamba Internacional* (☎ 961 538, 962 362, 963 393), on Kennedy and Miguel Riofrio, overlooking the Río Zamora (the river is not very scenic here).

The other two hotels are newer and plusher, and may raise their prices once they get better known. Both have good restaurants, helpful staff and good service and are opposite one another – take your pick. The *Hotel Libertador* (☎ 962 119, 960 779, in Quito 544 249) is at Colón 14-30 and Bolívar and the *Hotel Ramses* (☎ 961 402, 960 868) is at Colón 14-31.

Places to Eat
Two very simple, cheap, but clean restaurants are *La Cordillera*, 10 de Agosto 14-19 and Bolívar, and *Don Pepes*, Colón and Sucre. On the west side of the Parque Central you have the choice of Chinese or seafood at the *Chifa 85* and the *Pescadería 200 Millas*. Both are OK, but opening hours are erratic,

particularly the pescadería. Just around the corner on Antonio Eguiguren is the *Chifa China*. The *Restaurant La Tullpa*, 18 de Noviembre 5-12 on Parque Bolívar, is also good for inexpensive Chinese and other food.

For chicken in a chain-restaurant setting, try *Pollos Gusy*, Kennedy 5-55 in front of the Parque Bolívar. The place is a popular hangout with local youngsters. A block away on Kennedy is the *Top Cream* which has been recommended as the best ice-cream place in town, though I think the *Heladería Sinai* under the Hotel Ramses is just as good. Further down by the Hotel Vilcabamba Internacional is the *Restaurant Kennedy*, which is a fairly inexpensive all-purpose restaurant. Also reasonably priced is the *Restaurant 85* next to the Hotel Paris.

My favourite inexpensive restaurant is the *Pescadería Las Redes*, 18 de Noviembre 10-41 and Azuay. They serve both seafood and other dishes in pleasant surroundings – almost any meal is well under US$2. The classic best place in town is the *Mesón Andaluz*, but it was closed and boarded up last time I went. Since then I've heard that they have reopened in a new location at Antonio Eguiguren and Juan J Peña (☎ 962 900) and are still very good.

The best hotels are also good for meals; the *Restaurant Faraon* in the Ramses and the *La Castellana* in the Libertador are recommended.

Entertainment
Though Lojanos are known as good singers and guitar players, nightlife is fairly low key. Places to try for a drink and possibly music at weekends are the *Unicornio Piano Bar* (☎ 964 083) on the west side of the Parque Central and *Peña Bar Don Pancho's*, Imbabura and 18 de Noviembre. For dancing, try *Latino's Discotheque* (☎ 960 069), Imbabura 12-76 and Bernardo Valdivieso, and the *Las Ruedes Disco Club*, Quito 16-33 and Universitaria.

There are a couple of movie theatres marked on the map. There is a military band which often plays in the Parque Central on

Sunday evening – the young population of the town comes to watch the band and each other. There are sometimes 'Cultural Thursdays' on the Plaza de la Independencia – free shows.

Getting There & Away

Air Loja is served by La Tola Airport, which is in Catamayo (described later in this chapter) some 30 km to the west. TAME has a plane leaving Quito at 6 am, continuing from Guayaquil to Loja (Catamayo) at 7 am, and returning from Loja (Catamayo) at 8 am via Guayaquil to Quito, daily except Sunday. The fare is US$12.50 to Guayaquil and US$20.50 to Quito. This service changes departure times frequently so check with TAME (☎ 963 030) on the north-east corner of the Parque Central in Loja. The office is open from 8 am to 5 pm, Monday to Friday.

Taxi drivers hang out in front of the TAME office and will arrange to pick you up from your hotel to take you to the airport for the flight. They charge about US$1.50 per person in a shared cab (five or six passengers). Alternatively, you can arrange transportation with the better hotels, or take a bus into Catamayo the night before the flight.

Bus There are several different bus terminals in Loja but the most important is the Transportes Loja Terminal on Avenida 10 dé Agosto and Lauro Guerrero. Their buses are often booked up several hours or a day in advance, so you should book early. The booking office is crowded, noisy and intimidating, so be prepared. There are two desks: one for same-day bookings and the other for departures on future dates. Once you've sorted out which is which, you can ask the clerk at what times buses are available and buy your ticket.

There are four daily buses to Quito (US$4.50; 18 hours); four buses to Macará (US$1.80; seven hours); eight buses to Zamora (US$0.80; three hours); six buses to Machala (US$2.10; eight hours); five buses to Guayaquil (US$3.20; 11 hours); two buses to Cuenca (US$2.40; eight hours); one night

bus at 10.30 pm to Huaquillas (US$2.90; 10 hours); and various other departures to intermediate points. It's a very busy terminal. Across the street is Transportes Yantzaza with four buses a day to El Pangui in the Southern Oriente.

There are other terminals near the Parque Bolívar. Co-op Viajeros has seven daily buses to Cuenca (US$2.40; eight hours) and Ejecutivo San Luis also has buses to Cuenca which are a little faster. Both these companies are on 18 de Noviembre a block north of Parque Bolívar. Transportes Saraguro on Colón and Kennedy has six or seven buses a day to – you guessed it – Saraguro (US$0.60; two hours). Some of these continue on to remote communities beyond Saraguro, such as Selva Alegre and Manú.

For buses to Vilcabamba (US$0.50; one hour) use Transportes Sur-Oriente, Azuay and Kennedy, which has several buses a day. A few of their buses continue south as far as Valladolid or Zumba.

Transportes Catamayo, just off Mercadillo in an alley behind Kennedy, has buses to Catamayo (US$0.40; 45 minutes) about every hour.

Transportes Cariamanga, Miguel Riofrio and Ramon Pinto, has buses to various outlying and remote towns in the province. There are a few other infrequent buses going to and from rarely visited villages in the surrounding mountains – ask around. These are most likely to run at weekends for the Loja Market.

Buses for the El Valle region run north along Universitaria.

There is talk of building a terminal terrestre about a km north of town – I don't know when this may happen, if at all.

PARQUE NACIONAL PODOCARPUS

This 146,280-hectare national park was created in 1982 and is the newest of Ecuador's six national parks. It is the only park in the southern Andes and protects a wide range of habitats at altitudes ranging from over 3600 metres in the páramo and lake covered mountains south-east of Loja to about 1000 metres in the rainforests south of

Zamora in the southern Oriente. In between there is wild and rugged countryside, haunt of many rare animal and plant species.

The biological diversity of the area has been remarked upon by a succession of travellers and explorers through the centuries (see Loja earlier). Currently, a Danish scientific team from the University of Aarhus is working with Ecuadorian biologists to classify the species present. They have found a high degree of endemism (species found nowhere else) apparently because the complex topography combines with the junction of Andean and Amazonian weather patterns to cause unique microclimates throughout the park. These microclimatic areas give rise to many unique habitats within the park.

Some of the most important plants here include the park's namesake genus *Podocarpus* which is Ecuador's only native Gymnosperm (the division of plants that includes all conifers and a few smaller classes of trees). There are three species of *Podocarpus* present here. Also of interest is *Chinchona succirubra*, locally called 'cascarilla', from which quinine, the drug that cures malaria, is extracted. Demand for this product has meant that few cascarillas exist outside of the park. Other plant species are being discovered that are new to science – always an exciting day in the life of a botanist studying a new area.

Animals include the Andean spectacled bear, mountain tapirs, puma, two species of deer, the Andean fox (locally called a wolf) and several other mammals. All of these animals are hard to see, but they are prized by local poachers who will sometimes burn habitat in an attempt to flush out animals for their 'sport'. Birds, too, are of great interest and more abundant and easy to see. Scores of species are known to be present but many more remain to be added to the list. They include the usual string of exotic sounding species such as lachrymose mountaintanager (and many other types of tanagers), streaked tuftedcheek, superciliaried hemispingus and pearled treerunner. (I swear I am not making these names up!)

Despite being a national park, Podocarpus faces huge problems in protecting the varied habitats within its boundaries. Not least of the problems is that these legal boundaries are not respected by local colonists – by 1990 approximately 800 people were logging and ranching in the north-western parts of the park, occupying about 5000 hectares. Cattle and horses are permitted within the park; hunting is not permitted but poaching is an ever-present problem.

The Nature Conservancy's Latin American Program reports that over 99% (!) of the park has been granted in mining concessions, with gold being the mineral of interest. Mining companies with armed guards work within the park – meanwhile, the park staff consists of a total of eight workers to try to protect the park, carry out local environmental education programmes, maintain trails and shelters, take park fees and provide visitor information.

In 1990 Parque Nacional Podocarpus was named as one of Ecuador's four most biologically significant and yet imperilled conservation areas. The Nature Conservancy-sponsored 'Parks in Peril' program provides financial support and ongoing management and training programs for Ecuadorians to work in the parks involved. This is an essential project which is well worth supporting. The Peace Corps is also involved in park projects.

Information

For the eastern part of the park, see under Zamora in The Southern Oriente chapter.

For the western and central parts of the park, information, maps and permits should be obtained from the MAG office in Loja. Admission to the park is US$2 and a basic map and verbal information is available.

If you are in Quito, you can get topographical maps at the IGM. The western side of the park is covered by two 1:50,000 maps: Río Sabanilla CT-ÑVII-B2 and Vilcabamba CT-NVII-B4. Alternatively the 1:100,000 Gonzanamá CT-ÑVII-B map covers the area in lesser detail. The eastern (Oriente) side of the park is covered by the 1:50,000 maps of

Zamora CT-ÑVII-A1 and Cordillera de Tzunantza CT-ÑVII-A3.

Podocarpus receives a lot of rainfall, so be prepared for it. October to December are the driest months on the west side of the park.

Getting There & Around

To get there, take a Vilcabamba-bound bus from Loja and get off at the Cajanuma park entrance about 10 km south of the city. There is a large sign on the left hand side of the road – the entrance building rarely has anybody in it. From the entrance, a driveable track leads 8½ km uphill to Cajanuma ranger station. There is no public transport here, though you could hire a taxi for about US$6 from Loja to the guard station and arrange to be picked up at a later time. Make sure you are clear with the driver about whether you want to go to the Cajanuma park entrance or the ranger station.

The ranger station may or may not have someone on duty – plans are to expand facilities here. Camping is allowed. From the station there are two trails heading up into the lake and páramo region – a full day of hiking is required to reach the lakes where you can camp. Birdlife is varied and interesting both on the dirt road up to the ranger station and around the station. How far you go depends on your equipment and how much food and energy you have. There are no facilities so you should be entirely self sufficient.

VILCABAMBA

The minor road from Loja passing Podocarpus continues due south and drops steadily through green mountainous scenery to Vilcabamba, some 45 km from Loja. En route you pass through the village of **Malacatos**, distinguished by a large church with its three blue domes, visible from a great distance. Malacatos has a Sunday market and there is a basic restaurant, *Salón Estrellita* behind the main plaza.

Vilcabamba has for many years been famous as 'the valley of longevity'. Inhabitants supposedly lived to be 100 or more, and some claimed to be 120 years old. This was attributed to their simple, hard-working lifestyle, non-fatty foods and the excellent local climate. Scientific investigation has been unable to substantiate these beliefs but the legend persists and gives rise to some minor local tourism. The climate certainly is very pleasant and the surrounding countryside offers lovely walks.

About 1½ km out of town (along the main southbound road) is the **Area Nacional de Recreación Yamburaro** which has a small zoo of local animals and a greenhouse with an excellent collection of orchids – some 30 species by one account.

Most of the town surrounds the main square, where there is a local tourist information office, a church, an IETEL office, a few simple stores and some simple accommodation. Many people stay in one of the excellent hotels out of town.

Places to Stay & Eat

On the main square there are a few basic restaurants and the clean and friendly *Hotel Valle Sagrado*, which charges US$1 per person.

About a km from the main plaza, on the very outskirts of town, is the modern *Parador Turistico Vilcabamba*, which has a restaurant, bar and rooms with private baths for about US$4 per person. On the northern side of town, just off the main road from Loja, is the new *Hostería de Vilcabamba* which has a pool, sauna and the best restaurant in town. Comfortable rooms with private bath and hot water are US$11/17.50 for singles/doubles – family rooms and cabins sleeping five to seven people rent for US$33 to US$38. Both the Parador Turistico and the hostería can be booked at Hidaltur Travel Agency in Loja.

The current favourite of travellers is the tranquil *Hostal Madre Tierra* (Mother Earth), about two km north of Vilcabamba. Bus drivers from Loja will drop you off at the lane leading up to the hostal, which has accommodation for about two dozen people. The Ecuadorian/Canadian couple running the place are friendly and informative about the area. They have organised a variety of activities for guests, ranging from directions about local hikes to saunas, a book exchange, table games, and a video room. Horses can be hired and there's a woman who does massages for about US$5.

Rooms are US$8 per person per day, including breakfast and dinner, and lunches can be served with advance request. All bathrooms are shared and hot water is available. Rooms vary from being inside the main house to being in rustic little cabins up on a hill several minutes' walk away – beautiful views. Reservations can be made by writing or telegraphing Jaime Mendoza, Hostal Madre Tierra, PO Box 354, Loja.

About five km south of Vilcabamba are the smaller and more remote *Cabañas Río Yambala*, located by a mountain stream. The two cabañas are run by a North American guy named Charlie who is very friendly and will help arrange guided trips into Podocarpus. There is a book exchange. Rooms in cabins are US$3 per person and hot water is available. Kitchen facilities are provided or you can buy vegetarian meals for about US$2 to US$3.

In Vilcabamba, the people at the tienda (store) de Señora Carmita on the main plaza, opposite the church, usually know if there is space available in the cabañas and can give you directions on how to get to Río Yambala.

Getting There & Away

Transportes Sur-Oriente has buses from Loja. There is a bus office on the main plaza and buses return to Loja every hour or so. Two buses a day continue south to Zumba.

If you are in a hurry to get here, take a taxi from the airport at Catamayo to Vilcabamba for approximately US$10, or from Loja to Vilcabamba for about US$7. Bargain hard for these rates, which are what the locals are charged.

ZUMBA

The all-weather road continues south of Vilcabamba through the village of Valladolid to the small town of Zumba, about 115 km south of Vilcabamba. The drive is through attractive countryside. Zumba is about 10 km north of the (disputed) border with Peru – there are no border crossing facilities and visitors must return the way they came. There is a basic pensión in Zumba and two buses a day from Loja.

CATAMAYO

The Panamerican Highway continues west of Loja, through Catamayo, Catacocha and on to the Peruvian border at Macará.

Loja was founded twice. The first time was in 1546, on what is now Catamayo; the second time on its present site two years later. Despite its long history, Catamayo is a totally unremarkable town except for its airport, La Tola, which serves Loja 30 km away.

Places to Stay & Eat

The best place in town is *Hostal El Vergel* which charges US$2.30 for singles with shared bath and cold water, or US$3.75/4.60 for better singles/doubles with bathroom and hot water. The *Hotel Granada* has basic rooms for US$1.80 per person, including a cold shower and TV (not that the local programming is very exciting). The *Hotel Turis* is similarly priced and has some cheaper rooms without the shower. Also at this price is the *Hotel San Marcos*. The cheapest is the *Residencial Maria Dolores* which is basic but adequate and charges just US$1 per person.

There are several simple restaurants on or near the plaza. I had a merienda washed down with a beer at a pavement table outside a place on the north side of the plaza – watching the activities in the plaza was the extent of the evening's entertainment.

Two or three km outside Catamayo to the west is the *Hostería Bellavista* (☎ in Loja 962 450/592). Reservations can be made at B Valdivieso 8-22 in Loja, next to the CETUR tourist information office. They have a pool, restaurant and bar, and can arrange airport transfers or local tours. Rooms are about US$4/7 with private bath. On Sunday they have a popular buffet lunch with traditional dishes such as caldo de patas (cow's hoof soup), seco de chivo (goat stew)

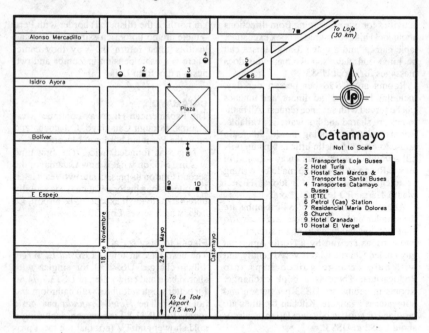

Catamayo
Not to Scale

1 Transportes Loja Buses
2 Hotel Turis
3 Hostal San Marcos &
  Transportes Santa Buses
4 Transportes Catamayo
  Buses
5 IETEL
6 Petrol (Gas) Station
7 Residencial Maria Dolores
8 Church
9 Hotel Granada
10 Hostal El Vergel

and cecina (smoked ham). The buffet is about US$2.50 per person.

Getting There & Away

Air The local La Tola Airport is about 1½ km south of town – a taxi will cost about US$0.50. Services are described under Loja.

Bus Transportes Catamayo, just north-east of the plaza, has frequent buses to (and from) Loja. Transportes Loja, half a block west of the plaza, has about eight buses a day to Machala (six hours), two night buses to Huaquillas, eight buses a day to Guayaquil (nine hours), four a day to Macará, and six a day to Quito. Local buses from here can take you to explore the small villages to the north and south of Catamayo. The long-distance buses may be full or have limited seating availability and better services are available from Loja. Transportes Santa, on the plaza, has a few buses to Quito.

About 25 km west of Catamayo the road

forks. The north-west fork goes to Machala and the south-west fork goes through Catacocha to the border town of Macará.

EL CISNE

About 15 km west of Catamayo, the Panamerican Highway passes through the village of San Pedro de la Bendita. From here, a road runs north for a further 22 km to the village of El Cisne, home of the famous sanctuary and miraculous Virgen del Cisne. The sanctuary is an enormous church in Gothic style surrounded by the unpretentious houses of the local campesinos.

According to local lore, it was the ancestors of these campesinos who made the long and difficult journey to Quito in the late 1500s in search of a fitting religious statue. They returned in 1594 with the carving of La Virgen del Cisne and installed it in a small shrine. Since that time, this icon has been the 'Queen' of the campesinos.

The major religious festivals in El Cisne

are on 30 May and 15 August. After the August festival, thousands of pilgrims from Ecuador and northern Peru carry the statue on their shoulders to Loja (70 km away). This is an impressive sight, with many of the pilgrims walking the entire way. The Virgin finally arrives in Loja on 20 August, when she is ceremoniously installed in the cathedral. On 1 November, the process is repeated in reverse, and the Virgin rests in El Cisne until the following August.

For most of the year, tours and buses go from Loja and Catamayo to the village on day trips to see the sanctuary and statue. But on procession days, forget it! You walk like everybody else – the road is so full of pilgrims that vehicles can't get through. This is a very moving religious festival for those who are so inclined.

CATACOCHA

It's a scenic but bumpy seven-hour ride from Loja to Macará. Catacocha is the halfway point and the only place after Catamayo where you could break the journey. Catacocha is the capital of the Canton of Paltas and is only about 1800 metres above sea level. From here, the Panamerican drops towards Macará and the Peruvian coast. It's a very rural village and on market day (Sunday) it seems as if there are almost as many horses as vehicles in town.

Places to Stay & Eat

There are four basic hotels, all a couple of blocks from the main plaza but in different directions. They are the *Pensión Guayaquil*, *Residencial Buena Esperanza*, *Hotel Turismo* and *Residencial Patense*. They charge between US$1 and US$1.50 per person – one traveller reports that the Guayaquil is friendly. There are a few basic restaurants.

MACARÁ

From Catacocha the road continues to drop steadily to Macará at a hot and dusty 450 metres above sea level. Macará is a small and not very important town on the Peruvian border. The faster and more convenient coastal route carries almost 100% of the international traffic. The main advantage to the Macará route is the scenic descent from Loja. There are two police checkpoints on this road – no problem if your passport is in order.

Information

Although there is a bank in Macará, it does not have foreign exchange facilities. Because of the low volume of border traffic, there are few people who will change money. If you ask around, however, you will invariably find someone. There are usually moneychangers hanging out around the market.

Rates for exchanging Peruvian currency into sucres and vice versa are inferior to using US cash dollars, so try to arrive at the border with as little local cash as possible. Exchange rates for cash dollars with Macará street changers were about as good as in Loja. If possible, try to ascertain exchange rates before arrival at the border by talking with travellers going the other way.

There is an IETEL office and a ratty movie theatre. There is supposedly a Peruvian Consulate but I couldn't find it when I was in town – most travellers don't need a visa anyway.

Places to Stay & Eat

There are some cheap and basic hotels in the town centre. They only have cold water but the weather is warm enough that it isn't a great hardship. The cheapest is the poor and dirty *Hotel Guayaquil* which is over a store – ask the store owners for rooms which are about US$1.25 per person. The *Hotel Internacional* and *Hotel Amazonas* are about the same price but better.

Two newer and nicer hotels are the *Hotel Paraiso* and *Hotel Espiga de Oro*. Both charge US$3.75/5.50 for clean singles/ doubles with private bath – still cold water though. The Paraiso also has rooms without private bath for US$2.25/3.75.

There are a few basic restaurants around the intersection of Bolívar and M Rengel –

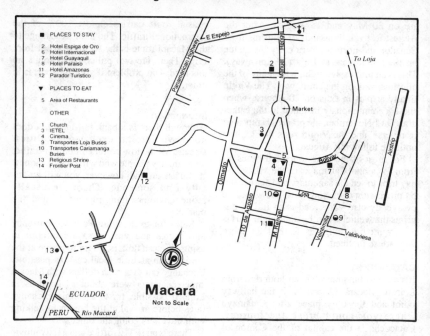

PLACES TO STAY
2 Hotel Espiga de Oro
6 Hotel Internacional
7 Hotel Guayaquil
8 Hotel Paraiso
11 Hotel Amazonas
12 Parador Turistico

PLACES TO EAT
5 Area of Restaurants

OTHER
1 Church
3 IETEL
4 Cinema
9 Transportes Loja Buses
10 Transportes Cariamanga Buses
13 Religious Shrine
14 Frontier Post

Macará
Not to Scale

ECUADOR
PERU   Río Macará

most are open only at meal times and have limited menus.

The best hotel and restaurant is the CETUR-run *Parador Turistico* on the outskirts of Macará on the way to the border. It has simple, clean rooms with private baths and hot water for US$10/13 for singles/doubles. There is a restaurant, which is by far the best (and most expensive) place to eat in Macará. There is also a swimming pool.

Getting There & Away
Air There is an airstrip which used to have flights to Guayaquil with TAME, using small aircraft such as Twin Otters or Avros. These flights have been suspended for some years now, but something may be available. There is no airline office; enquire at the airstrip a few minutes' walk from the town centre.

Bus Transportes Loja is the main bus company. Buses are available to Loja

(US$1.80; seven hours, five daily); Guayaquil (6 pm; US$4; 12 hours); Quito (10 am; US$5.20; 22 hours). There is also Transportes Cariamanga with three morning buses to Loja.

These times are rough estimates. The journeys are tiring and uncomfortable, and you are recommended to go to Loja and break up the journey.

Crossing the Peruvian Border
Macará is about an hour's walk away from the border at the Río Macará. Pickup trucks leave the market once or twice an hour and charge about US$0.10 (Peruvian or Ecuadorian currency). You can take a taxi for US$0.60. Vehicles wait at the border to pick up passengers from Peru.

At the border there are a couple of flyblown restaurants where you can get a cold drink. Border crossings are from 8 am to 6 pm daily with irregular lunch hours. The formalities are fairly relaxed as long as your documents are in order, but can take up to an hour or more.

Travellers entering Ecuador are rarely asked to show exit tickets or money, though a valid passport and tourist card are needed. If arriving, you will be given a tourist card at the border; if leaving, you will be expected to surrender the card you received on arrival to the border authorities.

Travellers entering Peru are occasionally asked for a ticket out of the country, especially those who require a visa. If you don't require a visa you probably won't be asked. If you are, and you don't have an airline ticket out of Lima, you can usually satisfy this requirement by buying a return bus ticket to Sullana, the nearest large town and about 150 km away. The unused portion of the ticket is non-refundable. Most nationalities, however, need only a valid passport and

tourist card which is obtainable from the border authorities. Gringo exceptions who require visas are Australians and New Zealanders.

Facilities for accommodation, transport and food are inferior on the Peruvian side and it is best to stay in Macará if possible. Trucks leave the border for the first Peruvian town of Las Lomas when there are enough passengers (usually about 10 am). The road is bad. From Las Lomas to the main town of Sullana the road is paved. A bus leaves the border for Sullana at 2 pm daily. It is difficult to get transport into Peru later in the afternoon and evening; therefore crossing the border in the morning is advisable.

Lonely Planet publishes *Peru – a travel survival kit* for travellers continuing to that country.

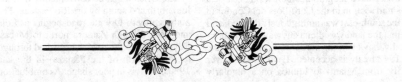

The Southern Oriente

Oriente literally means the orient, or east, and is the term used by Ecuadorians for all of their Amazon basin lowlands east of the Andes. The words *selva* or *jungla* are not used for the area as a whole, although selva can refer to a particular part of the forest of the Oriente. Even though the Amazon River itself does not flow through Ecuador, every one of Ecuador's rivers east of the Andean divide eventually empties into the Amazon and hence all of the Oriente can properly be referred to as being part of the upper Amazon basin. The correct term for most of the basin's vegetation is 'rainforest'; popular usage, however, refers to this lush tropical growth as jungle.

A glance at any Ecuadorian map will show Ecuador's claim to a large section of jungle extending beyond Iquitos. The basis of this claim has a long history. After independence in 1822, the new republic claimed lands as far as the Río Marañon to the south, and far eastwards into what is now Brazil. This remote and difficult-to-control area was slowly settled by increasing numbers of Peruvians (as well as a few Colombians and Brazilians). Ecuador gradually lost lands to these countries. In 1941 matters came to a head and war with Peru broke out. Each country accused the other of beginning the aggression. The following year a treaty at Rio de Janeiro ended the war and Peru was allotted a huge section of what had been Ecuador.

The Ecuadorians have never officially accepted the full terms of this treaty, claiming that it was bulldozed through when most of the world was occupied with WW II; that Peru invaded them; that the limits of the treaty were geographically invalid because a small section in the Cordillera del Cóndor in the south-east was ambiguously defined; and that the land was theirs anyway. Internationally, however, the border as drawn up by the 1942 treaty is accepted. If you should ever fly from Miami to Iquitos on a regularly scheduled jet service, rest assured that you will be landing in Peru!

This dispute affects the traveller in several ways. The south-eastern border region is still very sensitive and there are skirmishes every few years. The last major battles were in early 1981, when several soldiers were killed and aircraft shot down in an area only 20 km from the main road through the southern Oriente. Sabre-rattling continues intermittently. While journeying through the Oriente, even on the well-travelled tourist routes, you should always have documentation on hand, as passport checks at military checkpoints are not uncommon. These are usually quick and hassle-free, assuming your papers are in order.

The dispute also means that crossing the border into the Peruvian jungle is no longer possible for foreign travellers (though various Indian groups do so all the time). So if you were hoping to descend from Ecuador to the Amazon in river boats or canoes, forget it. Finally, try not to wave non-Ecuadorian maps of the region under peoples' noses. One friend had maps of Peru confiscated by customs officers at Quito Airport, because the Peruvian maps naturally didn't show the Ecuadorian claim. It should be emphasised that the area is safe to travel in at this time.

The Oriente can be conveniently divided into north and south by the Río Pastaza. The main southern Oriente road begins at Loja and goes through Zamora north to Macas. Beyond Macas the road was pushed through to Puyo (north of the Pastaza) in the late 1980s, but it is in poor shape. A combination

Top: Colonial Cuenca and Río Tomebamba (RR)
Bottom: Cofan Indian house (RR)

Top: Cofan Indian Children (RR)
Left: Oriente Boy (RR)
Right: Group of Cofan Indians passing under a breadfruit tree (RR)

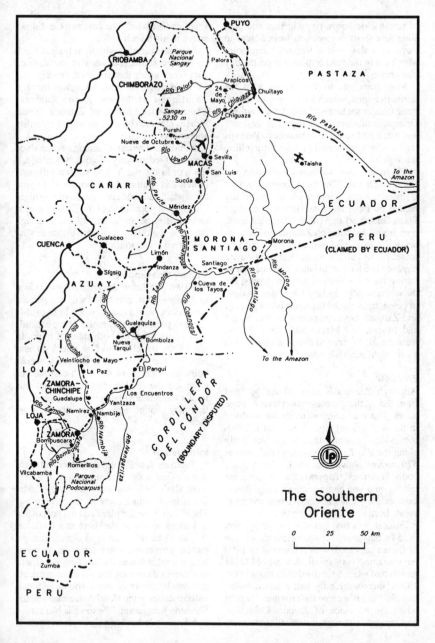

The Southern Oriente

0   25   50 km

of ramshackle buses, tippy ferries, and possible foot slogs can get you from Macas to Puyo in a day – if a torrential rainstorm hasn't made the road impassable on the day you chose.

Most travellers to the Oriente visit the northern region, which admittedly has much more to offer the tourist. Indeed, the southern Oriente is the least-visited part of Ecuador and has a real sense of remoteness. Perhaps that is why I particularly enjoyed travelling through it.

There are two surface routes into the southern Oriente. The most frequently used is from Cuenca through Limón (officially named on most maps as General Leonidas Plaza Gutiérrez) to Macas. The other route runs from Loja through Zamora and continues north to Limón, where it joins the first route. Almost all the roads in this region are unpaved and subject to landslides and delays during the rainy season. June to August are the worst months. In July 1991, several days of heavy rains closed the roads between Loja and Zamora, Gualaquiza and Limón, Sucúa and Macas, and Macas and Puyo. People were cut off for several days – so don't plan a very tight schedule here.

ZAMORA

Although Zamora is only 60 km by road from Loja, the journey takes about three hours. The road climbs dustily (or muddily in the wet season) from Loja over a 2500-metre-high pass and then drops tortuously along the Río Zamora valley to the town at 970 metres above sea level. The scenery soon becomes tropical, the vegetation thicker, and you begin seeing strange plants such as the giant tree fern. There are good views from both sides of the bus.

Zamora was first founded by the Spanish in 1549, but the colony soon died out because of Indian attacks. It was refounded in 1800 but remained very small. A local old-timer recalls that when he arrived in Zamora in the 1930s, there were only half a dozen buildings. In 1953 it became the provincial capital when the province of Zamora-Chinchipe was created, although it was still extremely

small and isolated. The first vehicle did not arrive in town until 1962.

Saraguro Indians, with their typical black shorts, are sometimes seen in the Zamora area. They arrive there on foot, driving their cattle on the trail from Saraguro, through Veintiocho de Mayo, to the Zamora-Yantzaza road. North of Zamora, Shuar Indians may also be seen, as well as colonists and miners.

Zamora is now experiencing a boom since the recent rediscovery of gold in Nambija, a few km to the north. The sudden influx of miners has strained the resources of the area somewhat, and food costs are relatively high. The present population of the Zamora area is estimated to be about 15,000 and although the town is growing it still retains somewhat of a frontier feel to it.

Military Checkpoint

The 1981 conflict with Peru took place close to Zamora. This, combined with the present gold boom, means that there is a high-profile military presence in Zamora. There are military checkpoints on both sides of town. In the 1980s travellers had to check in and register their passports at the main checkpoint three km from the north-east side of town, on the road to Gualaquiza, but this regulation has now been relaxed. The situation may change again by the time you get there.

Information

There are few foreign travellers and there is not much to do. The main plaza is a concrete affair with few trees and little shade, but is improving slowly as the trees grow. The IETEL is on the plaza and the post office is a block to the west. There is a bank but they can't be relied upon to change foreign currency, so come with sucres. The covered indoor market is near the bus terminal. There is a movie theatre on the northern outskirts of town by the river and a couple of small video theatres at the Hotel Amazonas and the Sheraton Restaurant. The town is planning a tree-lined, two-km long riverside avenue.

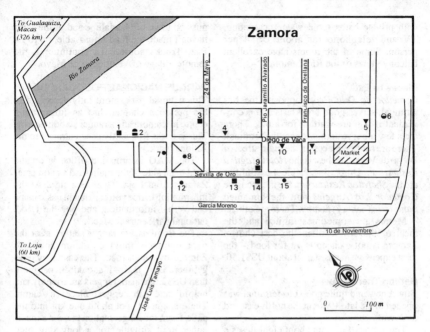

PLACES TO STAY
- 1 Hotel Maguna
- 3 Hostal Seyma
- 9 Hotel Zamora
- 13 Residencial Venecia
- 14 Hotel Amazonas

PLACES TO EAT
- 4 Sheraton Restaurant
- 5 Comedor de Don Pepe
- 10 Panadería
- 11 Comedor Los Angeles

OTHER
- 2 Post Office
- 6 Bus Terminal
- 7 IETEL
- 8 Main Plaza
- 12 School
- 15 Hospital

Most restaurants are closed by 8 pm, so eat early. The weather is not too hot, with day-time temperatures averaging about 20°C and pleasant evenings (with few insects).

Places to Stay

The three cheapest hotels are all clustered together on Sevilla de Oro, a block east from the plaza. The best and cleanest of these is the *Hotel Zamora*, which charges US$1.50 per person. They have some good balcony rooms which you should ask to see. *Hotel Amazonas* and *Residencia Venecia* are not as good and charge US$1.40. None of them have private bathrooms or hot water, but you have to start getting used to that in the Oriente. Anyway, cold showers are refreshing in the hot weather.

The newer *Hostal Seyma*, on 24 de Mayo a block north of the plaza, has rooms which are a little nicer than in the three cheapest hotels. They charge about US$2 per person.

The best place in town is the *Hotel Maguna* on Diego de Vaca, a couple of blocks west of the plaza. They have rooms with private baths (cold water), carpeting, TV and telephone for about US$4 per person. Some of the rooms have excellent balcony views of the Río Zamora.

Places to Eat

Comedor de Don Pepe, opposite the bus terminal, serves good breakfasts and is convenient if you are waiting for a bus. There are a few other restaurants near the terminal. There are several places on the main street of Diego de Vaca. The best is the *Hotel Maguna Restaurant*. Other reasonable possibilities are the *Sheraton Restaurant*, the inexpensive *Comedor Los Angeles* and the unnamed *panadería* (bakery) nearby. There are others.

Menus are sometimes limited and the meal of the day is often the best choice. Zamora is not a cheap town for food – the least expensive meals start at about US$1.50.

Getting There & Away

Bus A new and quite good bus terminal was opened in the late 1980s at the north-east end of downtown.

Transportes Loja run about eight buses a day to Loja (US$0.75; three hours). One bus a day continues through Loja to Cuenca (US$3.20; 11 hours).

Buses north to Gualaquiza and beyond usually originate in Loja and stop at the bus terminal in Zamora. Enough passengers normally get off at Zamora so that it's not very difficult to get a seat to continue north. Some of these buses go only as far as Yantzaza (US$0.50; 1½ hours); only two or three a day continue as far as Gualaquiza (US$1.30; 4½ hours).

Zamora-Chinchipe buses are often open-sided trucks with uncomfortable bench seats designed for midgets. They provide frequent services to nearby villages as far north as Yantzaza. To visit the wild gold-mining town of Nambija, go to Namirez (half way between Zamora and Yantzaza) and change there (US$1.00; three to four hours from Zamora). There are two daily buses to Romerillos leaving at dawn and early afternoon (US$0.50; two hours). Buses also go up the Río Yacuambi valley as far as the mission town of Guadalupe and, if the rains haven't made the road impassable, on to La Paz. Trucks sometimes continue to the remote village of Veintiocho de Mayo.

PARQUE NACIONAL PODOCARPUS

This national park, more fully described in the previous chapter, has an information centre in Zamora and a ranger station nearby. This is a less frequently used entrance to the national park.

The MAG information office is on the right hand side of the main road as you enter Zamora from Loja. There is a sign. At the information office you can obtain basic maps and verbal information, and pay the US$2 national park entrance fee.

The Bombuscara ranger station is at the park entrance about eight km south of Zamora by rough road. The easiest way to get there is by taxi – it shouldn't cost more than US$2. The park rangers are friendly and helpful and can suggest places to camp. There is a good spot about one km into the park. From the ranger station there is a maintained trail suitable for a long day hike through the cloud forest. The birding is reported to be excellent.

Another way into the park is to take a bus from Zamora to the tiny village of **Romerillos**, about 25 km south of Zamora (not the same road as the one going to Bombuscara). There is reportedly a park refugio here, but no ranger station. A rugged three-day loop trek leaves Romerillos, but is recommended for only the hardy, experienced, and properly equipped hiker. Be prepared for lots of mud. A mining company was given a concession to survey this part of the national park but their exploratory work was apparently unsuccessful (from the miners' point of view) and they have reportedly departed, leaving the area relatively unscathed. Again, the birding here is very good.

NAMBIJA

This mining village is on the banks of the Río Nambija where gold was discovered around 1980. This led to a gold rush to the area and

Nambija is now a wild mining town with heavy drinking, prostitution, smelly open sewers, very muddy streets, and constant frenzied mining action. Although Nambija itself is a new town, the area has been a source of gold for centuries. The Incas used to mine nearby, though few of the modern-day prospectors realise the historical significance of the area.

Few travellers go there. A couple of friends told me that it was an interesting place if you want to see what a gold-rush town is like, but they advised visitors to bring no valuables and to have a friendly and open disposition. The miners are a hard-bitten bunch but a pack of cigarettes will help in making friends.

There is a noisy and basic hotel, but you could go on a day trip from Zamora if you left first thing in the morning. All the locals wear rubber boots – this is the best footwear for the very muddy streets.

YANTZAZA

The northbound road to Yantzaza follows the left bank of the Río Zamora, so the best views are on the right of the bus. There is a passport checkpoint between Zamora and Yantzaza. There are beautiful vistas of open stretches of the river with heavily forested hills on either side, often with tropical trees flowering in bright reds, yellows and purples. The bus goes through many little Indian hamlets and *fincas* growing a variety of tropical produce such as coffee, sugar cane and citrus fruit. The road also goes near the Nambija mining area, so the journey is enlivened by the various interesting characters getting on and off the bus.

Yantzaza is the first village of any size on the road north of Zamora, 1½ hours away. In 1970 it was only a couple of shacks but since the Nambija gold boom it has become one of the fastest-growing towns in the province. Its population is now several thousand and there are restaurants and a couple of basic places to stay. The hotels *Amazonas* and *Central* are both just off the main square. These are likely to be full of miners, so it's probably best to continue to Gualaquiza.

GUALAQUIZA

North of Yantzaza the population thins and houses are seen infrequently. The road continues to follow the left bank of the gently dropping Río Zamora, and there are fine tropical views. Sit on the right of the bus. The road continues through the tiny village of Los Encuentros and on to **El Pangui**, where there is the basic *Hotel El Cóndor* on the one street. Just north of this village the road drops suddenly and a lovely jungle panorama stretches out below. Soon, the road crosses the provincial line into Morona-Santiago Province.

Several km before reaching Gualaquiza, a turn-off to the right leads to **Bomboiza** where a Salesian mission can be visited. A couple of km beyond the turn-off, the road to Gualaquiza crosses the Río Cuchipamba. A new steel bridge is under construction, but meanwhile all traffic must cross the river by a decrepit wooden raft capable of transporting only a single vehicle at a time. Most passengers get off the bus – you can cross on a footbridge.

Gualaquiza is a pretty little village of about 4,000 inhabitants. It is set at an altitude of about 950 metres and surrounded by forested hills. There are pleasant walks in the surrounding countryside. A rough road heads west out of town for about 15km to the village of Nueva Tarqui, where caves can be explored. There are reportedly some poorly explored Inca ruins in the Gualaquiza area – ask the locals for guidance.

The church on the main plaza looks like a toy building. There are cobbled streets and houses with attractive balconies, giving the town a Spanish colonial air. Gualaquiza closes down early and is definitely tranquilo. A new cinema has recently opened.

Places to Stay & Eat

Accommodation is limited as this is a little-visited town. On the main plaza is the simple *Residencial Amazonas*, which charges US$1.50 each. It is probably better than the *Pensión Oriental* on the main street. Recently opened on the main street is the clean *Hotel Turismo* which charges about

US$1.50 each. Also on this street is the *Bar Restaurant Gualaquiza*, as good as any of the few restaurants. There is a small market just off the main street.

Getting There & Away

There are several bus companies on the main street, Calle Gonzalo Pezantes Lefebre. Transportes Sucúa, El Cóndor and Oriental each have two or three departures a day for various destinations. Ask around. You can go south (Zamora and Loja), north (Limón, Sucúa and Macas) or west (Cuenca). The next town to the north is Limón (US$1.40; four hours). Buses to Cuenca go via Indanza (about 10 km before Limón) and take about seven hours, but a new, more direct road via Sígsig is under construction. To Macas it's US$2.80 and takes nine hours.

LIMÓN (General Leonidas Plaza Gutiérrez)

Limón (population 3000) is a totally unprepossessing town whose primary importance is that it lies near the junction of the roads to Cuenca, Macas and Zamora. From Gualaquiza the road passes through pretty but sparsely populated countryside until it reaches the missions of San Juan Bosco and Plan de Milagro (also known as Indanza), about an hour before Limón.

Places to Stay & Eat

Limón is a typical small Ecuadorian jungle town containing one main street (Calle Quito) with a few hotels, several simple restaurants and bus offices. Both the *Residencial Paraiso* and *Amazonas* are basic but clean and charge about US$1 each. The *Residencial Limón* has large clean rooms and is also cheap. Avoid getting rooms on the street as bus drivers park their buses with engines running while they have a midnight snack or early-morning breakfast. Exhaust fumes fill your room and the noise keeps you awake.

Getting There & Away

Buses from Limón are available to the north, south and west several times a day with various companies which have their offices along the main street. Few buses originate in Limón, however, so departure times are at best approximate. The road up to Cuenca climbs steeply from Limón at 1400 metres to a pass over 4000 metres in elevation – the ride is spectacular. If you are going to Macas, sit on the right-hand side of the bus, as there are good views of the Río Upano.

MÉNDEZ

This quiet little village of 2000 inhabitants is passed through on the way to Sucúa. It's official name is Santiago de Méndez. It is less than two hours from Limón and the fare is US$0.60. The houses have red-tiled roofs and flowery gardens. On the corner of its shady plaza are the very simple pensiones *Miranda* and *Medina*, both charging about US$1 per person. There are only a couple of restaurants here.

About 1½ hours away on foot, in the hills surrounding the town, is the Centro Kuchiankas – Escuela Kayap. This is a Shuar school and development centre and visitors are welcomed, although a donation to the school is asked for. Ask in Méndez for directions if you are interested.

MORONA

This remote settlement is on the Río Morona near where it crosses the border with Peru. This border is not recognised by Ecuador and therefore border crossing is not permitted.

Until the late 1980s, the only way in to Morona was to fly, but a newly constructed road know links the village with Méndez. The trip takes about 10 hours – ask around in Méndez for trucks going to Morona. There are no places to stay and not much in the way of places to eat, so bring a tent and food. This is a remote and poorly explored area – you are really off the beaten track.

CUEVA DE LOS TAYOS

About half way on the road between Méndez and Morona lies the settlement of Santiago on the Río Santiago. Here, one can hire dugout canoes to go upriver to the Río Coangos for about US$30. From the

Coangos there is a trail to the 'Cueva de los Tayos' (the Cave of the Oilbirds). The trail is in poor condition and you should hire a guide – it is about a two or three-hour hike. You should be self sufficient with sleeping gear and food for this expedition.

Oilbirds

There is only one species of oilbird and it is so unusual that it is placed in its own family, the Steatornithidae, related to the nightjars. Oilbirds are nocturnal, and spend most of the day roosting in caves in colonies which may number thousands of birds. The Cueva de los Tayos is one such cave. At dusk, huge numbers of oilbirds leave the cave to go in search of fruit, particularly that of palm trees. This makes oilbirds the world's only nocturnal fruit-eating birds.

Palm fruits are known for having a high fat content which gives the oilbirds a very fatty or oily flesh. In 1799, when oilbirds were first described in Venezuela by Alexander von Humboldt, the local people already knew about these birds. They were captured in their roosting colonies and boiled down into a valuable oil used in cooking and for lighting. This practice is now discouraged although it still occurs occasionally.

Oilbirds feed on the wing and their feet are poorly developed. They require caves with ledges upon which to build their cone-shaped nests, which are constructed of regurgitated fruit and are enlarged regularly. Two to four eggs are laid and incubation is a relatively long 32 to 35 days. After hatching, the young are fed regurgitated fruit for up to four months, and during this time a nestling can reach a weight of 1½ times that of an adult. It was these fat chicks which were most highly prized as a source of oil. Once the chicks leave the nest, they lose their accumulated baby fat. Adults weigh about 400 gm and reach a length of about 45 cm.

Oilbirds are adapted to their dark environment by having well-developed eyes and exceptional night vision. They also have a sensitive sense of smell which may help them detect the palm fruits, which have a distinctive fragrance. The caves they roost in are often pitch black. To avoid crashing into the cave walls (and into other birds) oilbirds emit audible, frequently repeated clicks which they use for echolocation, much as bats do. In addition they have a loud screaming call which they use for communication. The combination of screams and clicks made by thousands of birds within the confines of a cave can be deafening.

SUCÚA

Sucúa, population 6000, is one of the more interesting villages in the southern Oriente. It is the major centre of the Shuar Indians, who were formerly called the Jivaro and were infamous for shrinking the heads of their defeated enemies. This practice still occurred as recently as two generations ago and the *tsantsas*, or shrunken heads, can still be seen in various museums, notably the Municipal Museum in Guayaquil. Most of today's Shuar look very Ecuadorian in jeans and T-shirts, but you still see older Indians, especially women, with elaborate facial or body tattoos.

Information

There is a pleasant main plaza with shady trees, tropical flowers, cicadas and birds. From the plaza, walk down the main street (Avenida Francisco de Orellana) and you'll come to the Shuar Cultural Centre on your left, about a km away. Here you can buy booklets and obtain further information about the Shuar. The Shuar have become missionised, as have most of the surviving Oriente Indian groups, so you won't be shown tsantsas; other crafts are, however, on display and there is a small selection for sale. The cultural centre is oriented more to the proud preservation of the Shuar way of life rather than to tourists, but you can visit if you want to.

There is a small zoological garden with local animals; the entrance fee is US$0.20. There is also a mission hospital and a movie theatre. Market day is on Sunday.

Places to Stay & Eat

The *Hotel Oriente*, down the main street close to the Shuar Cultural Centre, costs about US$2 per person and has a restaurant. The basic *Hotel Colón*, just off the plaza on the main street, is cheaper. Another place to try is the *Hostal Alborada* which also has a restaurant. Perhaps the cheapest place in town is the *Residencial Cuenca*. The clean *Hotel Cumanda* on the corner of the plaza used to charge US$2 per person; I have received reports of it closing in 1990 and reopening in 1991.

There are several restaurants on the corner of the plaza with the main street, including the *Bar Restaurant Rincón Oriental*, which is probably the best restaurant in the southern Oriente. The waiters wear bow ties and charge about US$0.15 more than the basic places – definitely worth it. It may be possible to find somewhere to stay above the restaurant. The *Bar/Restaurant Alborada* is another possibility for eating. Typical dishes here feature rice and beans as the mainstay.

Getting There & Away
Air For several years, the airstrip at Sucúa provided regular service to Puyo with TAO. In mid-1984, however, the new airport at Macas was opened with a runway capable of taking large planes; that airport has now largely superseded the strip at Sucúa. Light aircraft might take passengers to Puyo on a semi-regular basis so ask at the office by the airstrip. It may be possible to charter aircraft for flights into the interior of the Oriente; ask at the Shuar Cultural Centre or the mission. Villages in the interior are for Indians and missionaries; tourists are not encouraged and there are no facilities for them

Bus Pickup trucks and minibuses for Macas (US$0.30; one hour) leave at frequent intervals from 6 am to 7 pm every day. Departures are from the corner of the main plaza near the Hotel Cumanda. The Thursday service is reported to be more irregular than the rest of the week.

Southbound buses pass by the restaurants on the main street at the corner of the plaza. Services are better from Macas.

MACAS
This small (population 12,000 and growing) but important town is the capital of the province of Morona-Santiago. It has four centuries of history as a Spanish trading and missionary outpost, and an old mule trail still joins Macas with the highlands near Riobamba. A road is planned which will follow this trail, and large segments of it have now been completed. A road north to Puyo has recently been completed but is subject to closure in the wet months and is a hard trip in the less wet months. The most reliable road link with Quito is via Cuenca.

Despite its history, Macas is essentially a modern and developing town. There is a new bus terminal and airport, and the main plaza was completed only in 1983. A new cathedral has been built on a small hill above the main plaza. Almost hidden behind the cathedral is a quaint and simple old wooden church containing some well-carved stations of the cross. From the cathedral hill there's a view of the town and, on a clear day, the often smoking Volcán Sangay some 40 km to the north-west. At 5230 metres, it is the seventh highest mountain in Ecuador and one of the most active volcanoes in the world.

Information
There are both IETEL and post offices. The first is new and the second is old. It is possible that a new post office will be built by the main plaza. Next to the IETEL office on 24 de Mayo and Sucre there is a movie theatre which shows films at weekends.

A jungle outfitter and guide has recently opened. This is Tuntiak Expediciones de la Selva (☎ 700 185/082) at 24 de Mayo 14-13 and Bolívar.

Places to Stay
Most hotels seem to charge about US$1.50 each. One of the better cheap hotels is the clean *Residencial Macas* on 24 de Mayo just south of Sucre. Others include the *Hotel Amazonas* which is quite good, the *Hotels Kiruba* and *Splendit,* the *Residenciales Elvira, Emperatriz* and *Upano* and the *Pensión Turismo.* None of these hotels have hot water or private bathrooms, although I hear that the Turismo may be installing hot showers.

The best in town at time of writing is the *Hotel Peñon del Oriente* at the corner of Amazonas and Domingo. This hotel was opened in the late 1980s and has rooms with private electric (warm) showers for about US$2 per person. There are good views from the roof.

About three km south of town, on the road to Sucúa, is the *Parador del Valle,* which has clean, bungalow-style accommodation for

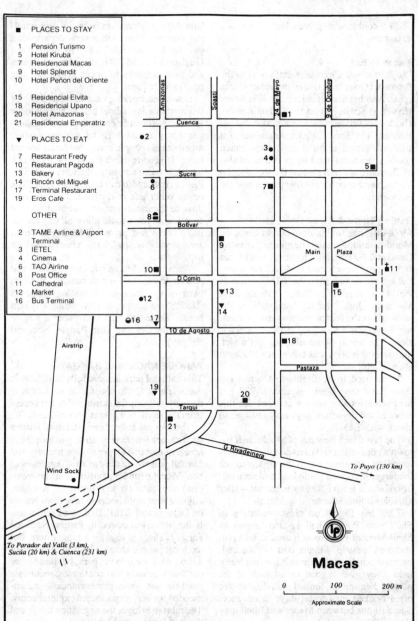

PLACES TO STAY

1 Pensión Turismo
5 Hotel Kiruba
7 Residencial Macas
9 Hotel Splendit
10 Hotel Peñon del Oriente

15 Residencial Elvita
18 Residencial Upano
20 Hotel Amazonas
21 Residencial Emperatriz

PLACES TO EAT

7 Restaurant Fredy
10 Restaurant Pagoda
13 Bakery
14 Rincón del Miguel
17 Terminal Restaurant
19 Eros Café

OTHER

2 TAME Airline & Airport Terminal
3 IETEL
4 Cinema
6 TAO Airline
8 Post Office
11 Cathedral
12 Market
16 Bus Terminal

Amazonas
Soasti
24 de Mayo
9 de Octubre

Cuenca
Sucre
Bolivar
D Comin
10 de Agosto
Pastaza
Targui
G Rivadeinera

Main Plaza

Airstrip

Wind Sock

To Puyo (130 km)

To Parador del Valle (3 km),
Sucúa (20 km) & Cuenca (231 km)

Macas

0   100   200 m

Approximate Scale

US$7 a double with private bath. There is a restaurant.

Places to Eat
The *Restaurant Pagoda*, a chifa next to the Peñon del Oriente, is one of the better places to eat. Another decent chifa is the *Rincón del Miguel* on Soasti just north of 10 de Agosto. The bakery on the same block is also recommended. The *Eros Cafe* on Amazonas just north of Tarqui is good for juices, baked goods, snacks and breakfasts. You could also try *Restaurant Fredy*, below the Residencial Macas, and a number of other places near the bus station.

Getting There & Away
Air TAME has flights from and to Quito on Monday and Friday afternoons, leaving Quito at 2.00 pm and returning from Macas at 3.15 pm. Tickets cost US$12.50 one way and are obtainable from the TAME office in the Macas Airport building. If flying from Macas to Quito, the left-hand side of the plane offers the best mountain views, including Sangay and Cotopaxi if the weather is clear. The aerial photo of Cotopaxi which illustrates this book was taken on a Macas to Quito flight.

There used to be flights to Cuenca but these have now been suspended. 727 jets have occasionally been scheduled for this service, and departure days may change, so check with TAME.

The last time I flew out of Macas, half the town's population and even people from surrounding villages came to the airport to see the large, four-prop plane land and take off. There was a festive feeling in the air – after all, there's little else to do in Macas.

TAO has flights on most weekdays to Shell near Puyo. Shell is also known as Shell-Mera or Pastazo as it used to be an oil company airstrip. Flights cost US$10 and, because small, light aircraft are normally used, they give a good aerial look at the jungle. Seating is limited and flights are often booked up several days in advance. Some flights between Macas and Shell may stop at Taisha.

Bus All departures are from the new terminal terrestre. There are several departures a day for Cuenca (US$2.40; 10 hours) and Gualaquiza (US$2.80; nine hours). Buses and pickup trucks to Sucúa (US$0.30; one hour) are frequent.

Buses and trucks go north to Puyo two or three times a day. About half way to Puyo the Río Pastaza must be crossed. A small passenger ferry consisting of canoes lashed together gets people across but buses are not taken. If you are driving a jeep, you can risk having it taken across on the ferry for US$5. Passengers have to catch another bus or truck on the other side of the river. The bus takes three to four hours and costs about US$1 for each leg so you should allow all day for the trip. There are plans of having a direct service via Puyo to Quito – about a 14-hour trip.

Transportes Macas runs small buses and pickup trucks to various remote, northern parts of the province, including Chiguaza (US$1; two hours), hourly during daylight hours. There are also two buses a day to Nueve de Octubre (for Parque Nacional Sangay).

PARQUE NACIONAL SANGAY
This national park is more fully described in the South of Quito chapter. Most access to the park is from the north and west; access from the south and east is very difficult.

You can get buses from Macas to **Nueve de Octubre** where you can stay in the school house or camp. The people are friendly and can tell you where the dirt road continues to San Vicente (under construction, no vehicles) and then on to **Purshi** by footpath. Allow about eight hours to hike from Nueve de Octubre to Purshi. This small settlement is the official entrance to Parque Nacional Sangay. There is usually a ranger here, but the local people are also helpful. Trails lead a short distance into the park, but these peter out fairly quickly and continuing requires a machete and great perseverance – recommended for very experienced explorers only. The rainfall is high, the vegetation thick, and the terrain steep and broken.

It is possible to continue on foot beyond Purshi to Atillo in the highlands, from where a dirt road eventually connects with the Panamerican Highway. This is a several-day trip and most people do it from the highlands down to the jungle. A road is under construction and will eventually link Macas with Cebadas and Guamote in the highlands.

THE JUNGLE FROM MACAS

There are various ways to see more of the Oriente from Macas. It should be mentioned, however, that the best centre for tourism in the jungle is Misahuallí in the northern Oriente.

Many Ecuadorian maps show tracks or trails leading from Macas into the interior. These often lead to the Shuar Indian villages and missions further into the Oriente. The trails are usually overgrown, however, because transportation is mainly by light aircraft these days. It is difficult but not impossible to visit some of these villages.

You can hire an *expreso* light aircraft to take you to some of the better-known centres such as **Taisha**, 70 km due east of Macas by air. There is a basic place to stay here. With luck or the right contacts, flights can be arranged with the Salesian mission aircraft, but flights are often full and inclement weather may cause days of delay. Hiring your own aircraft is subject to availability of planes and costs about US$60 for a five-seater. Flights between Macas and Shell sometimes stop in Taisha. A Shuar guide, Carlos Arcos, who can be found near the Macas Airport, is reportedly a good contact.

Visiting nearby Shuar centres on foot or bus is fairly straightforward. There are frequent buses to the mission of Sevilla (Don Bosco), about an hour's walk away on the other side of the Río Upano. A new bridge is being built; at present there is a rickety wooden suspension bridge which takes only one vehicle at a time. All the passengers disembark and walk across the bridge, and the bus follows.

From Sevilla you can head south on foot along a broad track to the village of San Luis, about four hours' walk away. This makes a good day trip and en route you'll pass cultivated areas and Indian huts, where you may be invited to try some *yucca chicha*. This traditional Shuar drink is made by the women, who grind up the yucca by chewing it and then spit it into a bowl where it is left to ferment. If this doesn't appeal to you, bring a water bottle. There are no facilities of any kind beyond Sevilla.

Buses go north along a fairly good gravel road to various destinations up to and including the Río Chiguaza, beyond which the road deteriorates as it heads to Puyo. The bus passes through Shuar territory and you can see a few of their oval-shaped, bamboo-caned, thatched huts on the sides of the road. Most of the Indians riding the bus look unremarkably Western, but occasionally a beautifully beaded bracelet or tattooed face is seen.

Most travellers now go to Puyo by road and the passenger ferry over the Río Pastaza. An alternate and much less frequently used route goes via the settlement of Chiguaza where you can hire a canoe to ferry you across the Río Chiguaza. Then you have to continue on foot. Ask the way to the villages of 24 de Mayo and Arapicos, where another canoe will ferry you across the Río Palora. There are no facilities at these villages although, if you're lucky, you may find a pickup truck going from Arapicos to Palora where there is a very basic pensión. You may have to walk as far as Palora, as the road is often impassable.

From Palora there are three buses a day to Puyo, in the northern Oriente. Locals say that if you take the first morning bus from Macas to Chiguaza, you can walk to Palora in one long day. I've never tried it. This route may be even less used now that the bus goes via the Río Pastaza ferry – ask before attempting the adventure.

The Northern Oriente

North of the Río Pastaza are the provinces of Pastaza, Napo and Sumbíos which together form the northern Oriente. Unlike the southern Oriente, the northern Oriente is well connected with two roads to Quito and hence this is the most visited part of Ecuador's jungle. In one long day of bus riding, you can go from Quito to the oil boom town of Lago Agrio in the far north-eastern jungle, or to the tourist centre of Misahuallí in the central Oriente.

Various round trips can be made by bus, boat and air. If your time is limited, the quickest of these is the bus journey from Quito through Ambato, Baños, Puyo, Tena, Baeza and back to Quito. This can be done in two long days and gives a good look at the jungle where it meets the eastern slopes of the Andes.

A longer trip can be made by omitting the Tena-Baeza section and going instead to Coca either on the new road from Tena or by canoe from Misahuallí down the Río Napo. From Coca one can continue by bus to Lago Agrio and back to Quito through Baeza.

Such a trip gives a good look at many facets of the Ecuadorian Oriente and is not beyond anyone's resources. It is feasible to do it in four days, but at least a week or more is recommended. The journey could be broken at either Coca or Lago Agrio, both of which have regular air services to Quito.

These areas have been colonised by farmers, ranchers, loggers, and oil workers. Therefore transportation is relatively straightforward on these circuits but one shouldn't expect to see much in the way of wildlife. For that one has to stop and take tours into the interior; Misahuallí, Coca, and Lago Agrio are all possible places from which to begin a more nature-oriented trip.

You should note that during the rainiest months of June to August, roads can be washed out, airports closed, and travel delays are common. Always allow a day or

two of leeway if you need to return and make important connections in Quito.

THE ROAD TO PUYO

If I were to choose just one stretch of road in Ecuador for the best views of the upper Amazon basin, I would have difficulty in improving upon the Baños to Puyo drive.

The road follows the Río Pastaza canyon as it drops steadily from Baños at 1800 metres to Puyo at 950 metres. This road has recently been rebuilt, and buses now regularly make the through journey. Just beyond the famous Agoyan Falls – now the site of a new hydroelectric project – the road passes through a tunnel. A few km further, a waterfall splashes from the overhanging cliff onto the road – quite a surprise if you're hitch-hiking in the back of a pickup truck.

Waterfalls frequently cascade into the canyon, and one of the most impressive is by the village of **Río Verde**, 20 km beyond Baños. You have to walk down a short trail to a suspension bridge to appreciate the waterfall properly. There is a sign at the beginning of the trail which reads 'Pailón del Diablo'. Ask at the village for directions.

As the road drops beyond Río Verde, the vegetation rapidly becomes more tropical and the walls of the Pastaza canyon are covered with bromeliads, giant tree ferns, orchids and flowering trees.

Near the small community of Mera the canyon walls spread apart, and you see a breathtaking view of the Río Pastaza meandering away to the south-east through the vast, rolling plains of the Amazon basin. The

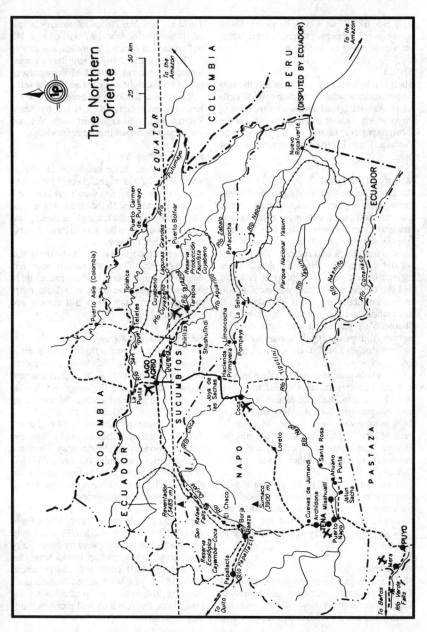

right side of the bus is best for views. There is no higher land between here and the Atlantic, almost 4000 km to the east.

SHELL

Shell is a few km beyond Mera and the two communities together are often called Shell-Mera. At Shell is the Pastaza airstrip, serving Puyo which is about 10 km away. This is the most important airstrip in the province of Pastaza. There is also a military checkpoint here.

Military Checkpoint

All foreign travellers arriving in the Oriente through Shell must register with the army. The registration procedure is efficient and straightforward. Buses on the way to Puyo stop by the checkpoint and wait while foreigners disembark and register. You have to fill out a form with the usual details (age, nationality, etc) and present your passport and the tourist card which you received on entry into Ecuador. You'll be asked your destination and the purpose of your visit. 'Turismo' is the safest and most obvious answer. Your passport will be stamped by the Brigada de Selva No 20 and you'll be free to go.

The whole procedure takes only a minute and the bus drivers are so used to it that they'll wait as a matter of course. The only possible problem is if you have only a few days left on your visa, as they like you to have at least 10 days before going into the Oriente. The stamp is important; it may be inspected in various other places in the Oriente.

If you arrive in Puyo by air you should also register. The checkpoint is a five-minute walk east of the airport on the one main street of town. If you are leaving the Oriente through Puyo, you may or may not have to register.

Information

Shell is a major US missionary centre and there are schools, churches and hospitals. The missions often have flights into the Oriente and can provide emergency services.

There is a new Voz Andes missionary hospital. It is reported that they will change US dollars as well as provide medical assistance.

There is a 'Cine Militar' (military cinema) where civilians are allowed. Military personnel sit on the right and civilians on the left.

There is a workshop where balsa wood birds are manufactured. It is run by Señor Fabio who is well known in town. You can visit and watch the birds being made.

Places to Stay & Eat

There are three basic hotels which charge about US$1.20 a night. There are a few simple restaurants. You won't get lost − it's a one-street town with the airport at the west end on the way to Baños, and the checkpoint near the east end on the way to Puyo. Everything else lies in between.

A reader reports that the old hospital Voz Andes (☎ 795 171) on the edge of town has been turned into a hostal, with a restaurant in the old surgical ward. It is a little more expensive to stay here but meals are included.

Getting There & Away

Air There are no regular flights from Shell to Quito. Flights with TAO leave most mornings for Macas aboard light aircraft and cost about US$10. Some flights go via Taisha. Seating is limited and tends to be booked up ahead. The TAO office is in the airport.

The Ecuadorian Air Force, FAE (Fuerza Aerea Ecuatoriana), has flights to Tena and Coca on Monday and Wednesday. There are various other companies (Condor, ATESA) in Shell which can provide light aircraft for chartered flights to other jungle strips. For all of these, inquire at the airport.

Bus Most people going through Shell will already be on a bus through to Puyo. Should you need a bus to Puyo, wait by the military checkpoint, where pickup trucks leave for Puyo every half hour and charge about US$0.15. If you want to go to Baños or Ambato, also wait by the checkpoint for buses from Puyo, which will pick you up if they have room.

PUYO

Puyo, with a growing population of about 20,000, is the provincial capital of Pastaza. Until the early 1970s it had a real 'frontier' atmosphere, and was the most important town in the Oriente. Since the discovery of oil, however, the frontier has been pushed deep into the jungle and now Lago Agrio vies for the claim of being Ecuador's most important Oriente town.

It is not a particularly attractive town, but it makes a good stopping point if you need a night's sleep before continuing into the Oriente or returning to the highlands.

Information

There are IETEL and post offices marked on the map. Three banks are also marked but they don't normally change money, though you can ask. Sometimes one of the bank managers will buy cash dollars as a 'favour' at unfavourable rates. Bank clerks can often direct you to store owners who will change money, or ask around. It is difficult to negotiate anything but cash US dollars. You are best off if you can bring plenty of sucres with you.

The hospital is west of town but the Voz Andes mission hospital in Shell is a better bet for medical emergencies.

Things to See

If you can get up at dawn you'll often see a spectacular view of jagged snow peaks rising up over a jungle covered with rolling morning mists. Later in the morning, the mountains usually disappear into the clouds. The jagged peaks belong to El Altar (5319 metres), the fifth highest mountain in Ecuador, about 50 km to the south-east. Sangay (5230 metres) is also occasionally seen. A good view can be had from the main plaza. On a clear day this is worth getting up early for.

During the day you can go swimming in the river. If you're a birdwatcher you'll see a variety of jungle species near the river. Alternatively, you can visit the La Libertad sports complex just north of the bus terminal. There is a swimming pool here open to the public, as well as tennis and volleyball courts. Hours are 10 am to 10 pm daily, except Tuesday, and they charge US$0.15 to get in.

There is not much nightlife. What there is tends to be short lived – here one year and gone the next. You can usually find the latest fad, video movie theatres. There is sometimes a disco – ask around.

Places to Stay

There's no shortage of accommodation in Puyo but there are frequent water shortages. During a recent visit, none of the cheaper hotels had any water at all and you had to swim in the river. The water system has been under repair for some years. If you need a shower, ensure that there is running water before renting a room.

Places to Stay – bottom end

Hotel Granada on 27 de Febrero by the market charges US$1.20 per person and has been recommended by budget travellers. The *Residencial Ecuador*, on 24 de Mayo, is old but well looked after, secure, and has pretty flowers in the balconies. The *Residencial Carmita* on 9 de Octubre and Atahualpa is basic but reasonably clean. Other places in this price range include the very basic *Pensión Georginita* and the marginally better *Residencial Santa* and *Pensión Tungurahua*. Closer to the centre of town are some cheap and run-down hotels such as the *Pensiones Guayaquil, Paris* and *Ambato* the *Residencial El Alamo*. I must confess to a no more than cursory examination of these – they don't look up to much.

If you want to be fairly sure of a constant water supply and reasonable comfort, try the *Hotel Europa* (☎ 885 220) on 9 de Octubre just north of Atahualpa. The *Hotel California* next door is also OK. They both charge US$2.40/3.60 for singles/doubles with a private bath. Rooms with communal bathrooms are cheaper. The Europa has hot water and a good view from the roof.

Places to Stay – middle

Hotel Europa Internacional on 9 de Octubre

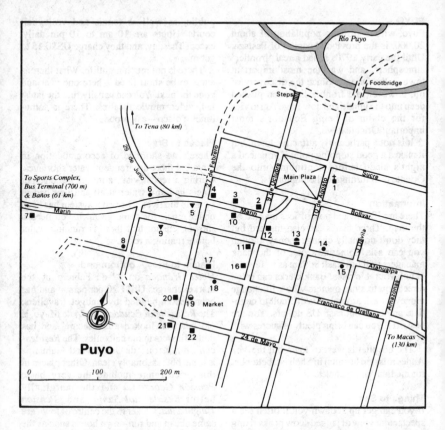

To Tena (80 km)

To Sports Complex,
Bus Terminal (700 m)
& Baños (61 km)

Río Puyo

Footbridge

Steps

Main Plaza

Sucre

Marin

Bolivar

Atahualpa

Francisco de Orellana

Amazonas

To Macas
(130 km)

Market

24 de Mayo

Puyo

0   100   200 m

and Orellana is a modern hotel in the town centre which charges about US$4.50 per person for rooms with a bath. The hotel is clean, friendly, and has hot water.

The *Hostería Turingia* (☎ 885 180/384) has been a Puyo institution for years and is the best hotel in town. It is on Marin on the outskirts of town on the road to Baños. They have accommodation in bungalows with private bath and hot water for US$7/11 for singles/doubles. Their comfortable bungalows are set in a tropical garden with orchids and other plants. The restaurant here is overpriced.

Also, a reasonable choice is the *Hostería Safari* (☎ 885465/6) about six km away on the road to Tena. They have a nice garden, a games area, and a simple restaurant and bar. Singles/doubles with private bath and hot water are US$8/12.

Places to Eat

Puyo cannot be recommended to gourmets. One of its better restaurants, and it's by no means fancy, is the *Restaurant El Ejecutivo* on Marin near 27 de Febrero. The better hotels have adequate restaurants, of which the *Europa Internacional* is the best downtown. The *Restaurant Su Casa* on Atahualpa between Villamil and 27 de Febrero is quite good for broasted chicken. There are several other places.

Top: Inca ruins of Ingapirca (RR)
Left: Guayaquil Cathedral and statue of Simon Bolívar (TW)
Right: All Saints Church, Tomebamba River, Cuenca (RR)

Top: Fishermen at work, Atacames (RR)
Left: Domes of La Compañía from Plaza San Francisco, Quito (RR)
Right: Fisherman Monument, Manta (RR)

■ PLACES TO STAY

2   Pensión Ambato
3   Pensión Paris
4   Residencial El Alamo
7   Hostería Turingia
10 Pensión Guayaquil
11 Pensión Carmita
12 Hotels Europa &
    California
16 Hotel Europa Internacional
17 Residencial Santa &
    Pensión Georginita
20 Hotel Granada
21 Pensión Tungurahua
22 Residencial Ecuador

▼ PLACES TO EAT

5   Restaurant El Ejecutivo
9   Restaurant Su Casa

    OTHER

1   Cathedral
6   Banco de Fomento
8   IETEL
13 Post Office
14 Banco Internacional
15 Banco Central
18 Town Hall
19 Buses to Shell

The *Rincón Ambateño* is out by the Río Puyo waterfront and has reasonable food and a swimming pool. To get there, head out on 29 de Julio, across a bridge, and start asking. It's about two km from downtown (taxi drivers know it). The *restaurant* in the Hostería Turingia is considered the best in Puyo and is used by occasional tour groups and foreign workers in the area. The food is good but I found it rather overpriced.

Getting There & Away

Air Small local buses providing service to Shell for the Pastaza airstrip leave from the west side of the market.

Bus The new terminal terrestre is to the south-west of town and became fully opera-

tional in 1990. There is a restaurant and most buses now leave from and arrive here. There are frequent buses to Baños (two hours) and Ambato (US$1.20; three hours). There are several buses a day to Quito (US$2; six to seven hours) and Riobamba (US$1.30; four hours). Buses to Tena (US$1; three hours) often originate in Ambato or Baños and may be full or standing room only when they pass through Puyo. Those buses which originate in Puyo should be booked a day ahead to ensure a seat.

Centinela del Oriente runs ancient buses to various small villages in the surrounding jungle. The most important of these is Palora, where there is a basic pensión and from where you can continue south by pickup truck (if you are lucky), foot and canoe ferry to Chiguaza near Macas in the southern Oriente (for more information about this journey, see Macas in The Southern Oriente chapter). Buses for Palora leave three times a day for the three-hour ride, which involves two river crossings.

Buses to Macas leave two or three times every morning. The bus goes as far as the Río Pastaza (US$1; three to four hours) where a passenger ferry (US$0.20) takes you across the river to meet another bus continuing to Macas (another US$1; three to four hours). Buses for Macas leave from Atahualpa near the intersection with Amazonas, though they may be leaving from the terminal terrestre by the time you read this.

PUERTO NAPO

The narrow, gravelled road from Puyo into the Oriente heads almost due north, passing small homesteads and occasional banana plantations until the road crosses the provincial line into Napo. About seven km from Tena, Puerto Napo is reached. There is a place to stay, the basic *Hotel Palandacocha*. A road fork to the right leads to Misahuallí, 17 km away, or you can continue north to Tena.

You can wait here for a vehicle to take you to Misahuallí. Many buses/trucks to Misahuallí come from Tena and there is often a scramble for seats. It is probably easier to

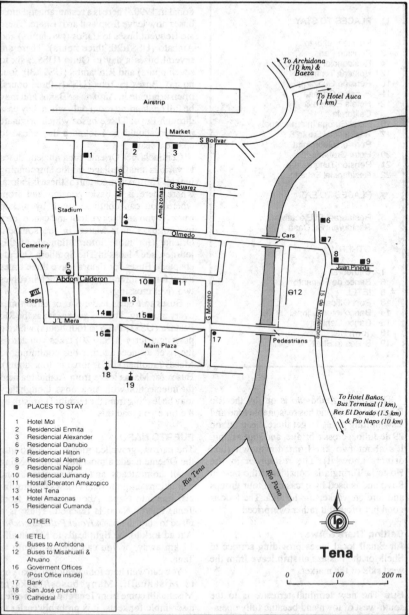

To Archidona
(10 km) &
Baeza

To Hotel Auca
(1 km)

Airstrip

Market

S Bolivar

■1   ■2   ■3

G Suarez

J Montalvo

Amazonas

Stadium

●4

Olmedo   Cars   ■6

                          ■7

Cemetery   ■8   ■9

                          Juan Pineda

●5

Abdon Calderon

Steps   ■10 ■11   ⊖12

                 ■13

■14 ■15   G Moreno   15 de Noviembre

J'L Mera

■16⬤   ●17

        Main Plaza   Pedestrians

†18

†19

                To Hotel Baños,
                Bus Terminal (1 km),
                Res El Dorado (1.5 km)
                & Pto Napo (10 km)

Rio Tena

Rio Pano

Tena

0   100   200 m

■ PLACES TO STAY
1   Hotel Mol
2   Residencial Enmita
3   Residencial Alexander
6   Residencial Danubio
7   Residencial Hilton
8   Residencial Alemán
9   Residencial Napoli
10 Residencial Jumandy
11 Hostal Sheraton Amazonico
13 Hotel Tena
14 Hotel Amazonas
15 Residencial Cumanda

    OTHER
4   IETEL
5   Buses to Archidona
12 Buses to Misahualli &
    Ahuano
16 Goverment Offices
    (Post Office inside)
17 Bank
18 San José church
19 Cathedral

get a seat, though slower, if you go into Tena and take a bus back to Misahuallí from there.

TENA

Tena, at about 600 metres above sea level, is the capital of the Napo Province. This province, with an area of 33,409 sq km – almost an eighth of the country – is the largest in Ecuador. Its capital, however, has a population of only about 12,000.

Tena was founded in 1560, and was the most easterly of Ecuador's early colonial missionary and trading outposts. There were several Indian uprisings in the early days, notably in 1578 when Jumandy, chief of the Quijos, led an unsuccessful revolt against the Spaniards. Tena survived, though many early Oriente towns were completely wiped out by other Indian attacks. Today the area is largely agricultural, with cattle ranches and coffee or banana plantations. It is at the junction of the Tena and Pano rivers and is a minor centre for Ecuadorian tourism. The average year-round temperature is 24°C, with the rivers having a moderating effect on the climate.

Information

There are the usual IETEL and post offices, the latter difficult to find as there are no signs. The post office is inside the provincial government offices at the west end of the main plaza. Moneychanging facilities are limited; the bank will sometimes change cash dollars but not travellers' cheques. The mission may be able to help.

Amaroncachi (☎ 886 372) is a tour company which opened in 1990 and has been well recommended. The people are friendly and take you to their house in the nearby jungle where you live like a member of the family, eat good local food, go for nature hikes in the forest, pan for gold and swim in the rivers, and get a look at the local (colonised) rainforest. It's a much lower key operation than those in Misahuallí, but don't expect a virgin jungle experience. Members of Amaroncachi often approach arriving travellers in the bus station. The company

has an office at Calle Tarqui 321, in the Bellavista Baja section of town (east of the river, ask). Rates are about US$25 per person per day and is all inclusive – no minimum number of people are needed.

Things to See & Do

There's not much to do in town – one couple wrote to say they didn't think it was worth staying. Most people visit the nearby village of Archidona and a few go on to the Cuevas de Jumandi (Caves of Jumandi). More often than not, Tena is just a resting-up place for a night or two.

If you're interested in looking for tropical birds, the steps leading down to the Río Tena near the cemetery are a good place for **birdwatching**.

On a clear day, visitors are sometimes puzzled by the sight of a volcano looming up out of the jungle, some 50 km away to the north-north-east. This is the 3900-metre-high cone of **Sumaco**, surrounded by rainforest, plagued by wet weather, and the most remote and least known of Ecuador's volcanoes. It is dormant at this time, though volcanologists believe it to be potentially active. It lies about 25 km north of the new Tena-Coca road, from which it can be climbed in about five days. A few km away from the junction of this road with the Tena-Baeza road, there is a hard-to-find trail to the village of Huamani (a long day's walk) from where a guide can be hired to chop through the jungle to the summit (several days).

The anniversary of Tena's foundation is celebrated on 15 November, and is the time for celebrations, colourful processions and other festivities.

While visiting the town during one of their fiestas, I had one of those unusual experiences which make travelling all the more fun. I was sitting quietly in my hotel room, making notes for the Tena city map, when there was a knock on the door. I opened up, and two officious-looking gentlemen in plain clothes walked in. Perhaps it's the sign of a guilty conscience, but my first thought was, 'Oh, no, what am I in for now?' The gentlemen introduced themselves as the organisers of the Tena beauty pageant which was being held that evening to elect 'Señorita Tena, 1984'. They had heard that a Spanish-speaking foreigner was in town and would I be kind enough to help judge the contest, as they wanted some non-biased judges for a fair vote!

I don't normally hold beauty contests in very high esteem, but I couldn't refuse. The evening turned out to be riotous fun, with each señorita having her own wildly cheering following of relatives, friends and neighbours, and a sound system which screeched maniacally at inopportune moments. Perhaps the most memorable segment of the evening's events was when the MC asked the contestants a question, taken out of a sealed envelope. One of the young ladies, flustered by the rapt attention of several thousand listeners, nervously began to pick her nose before she realised what she was doing. The crowd roared with a mixture of rage and delight. Although I enjoyed myself, I haven't noticed any recent change in my opinion of beauty contests.

Places to Stay – bottom end

The cheapest hotels are in the town centre but they all suffer from water shortages. Make sure there is running water if you don't want to bathe in the river. The cheapest place in town (and it looks it) is the *Hotel Tena* on J Montalvo and J L Mera. They charge about US$1.20 per person. The *Hotel Amazonas* across the street is better and cleaner and charges US$1.50 per person. They have communal showers only. The *Residenciales Jumandy* and *Cumanda*, both on Amazonas on the block north of the main plaza, are also in the US$1.50 price range and are basic but OK.

Accommodation away from the centre costs a little more, but is usually worth it. The *Residenciales Alexander* and *Enmita* are at the north end of town on S Bolívar. The clean Alexander has pleasant rooms with communal showers for US$1.80 per person and with private bathroom for US$2.50 each. The Enmita charges US$2.50 per person in basic rooms with a private bath – they have their own private water supply which usually (but not always) carries them through any water shortage. Rooms without private baths are cheaper. The Enmita is run by a friendly lady who also manages one of the best restaurants in town.

The *Residencial Hilton* across the bridge, at the north end of 15 de Noviembre in the Bellavista district, charges US$4 for a double room and won't give a lower price for singles. They have communal showers. The *Residencial Napoli* (☎ 886 194) is nearby and is one of the newer hotels in town. They charge US$2 per person. The *Residencial Danubio* is cheaper, but not as good. The clean and friendly *Residencial Alemán* (☎ 886 409) charges US$3/5 for singles/ doubles with a private bath and fans.

The *Hotel Baños* (☎ 886 477) at 15 de Noviembre 9-19 and *Residencial El Dorado* are close to the new bus terminal but are 1½ km from downtown. Singles/doubles are about US$3/5.

Places to Stay – middle

There are two better hotels near the town centre. The *Hotel Mol* at the north end of town charges US$7/11 for singles/doubles with private bath. It is modern and clean, but has been criticised for raising its prices during fiestas. The *Hostal Sheraton Amazonico* (☎ 886 436) is a block north of the main plaza and charges US$7 per person in rooms with private bath, TV and fridge.

The DITURIS-run *Hotel Auca* (☎ Tena 161), about two km north-east of the town centre, is also good. They have spacious grounds by the river, a restaurant and bar, a discotheque (which they'll open up, they told me, for a couple of paying guests) and a casino. They charge US$7/10 for singles/ doubles with private bathroom.

Places to Eat

There are a number of small and inexpensive restaurants but I always seem to end up eating at the *Residencial Enmita* – some Peace Corps volunteers told me it was the best place in town. It's not expensive.

Getting There & Away

Air There is an airstrip at the north end of town. The Ecuadorian Air Force (FAE) has flights to Shell and Coca on Monday and Wednesday. Fares are very cheap but seats are often booked well in advance – inquire at the airstrip.

Bus The main bus terminal is about 1½ km

away from the centre in the south-eastern outskirts of town on the Puerto Napo road. There are several departures a day for Quito (US$2; six hours) via Baeza; the southern route (via Puyo) is longer. Fares to Puyo or Baeza cost about US$0.80, and to Ambato US$1.60. Flota Jumandy run several buses a day to Lago Agrio (US$3.50; 10 hours). There are several buses a day to Coca (US$3; seven hours). These times are approximate, as bad roads, old buses and inclement weather make all journey times in the Oriente notoriously unreliable.

Getting Around
Local buses do not leave from the main terminal. For Archidona (US$0.10; 15 minutes), buses leave about every half hour during daylight hours from the west end of Abdon Calderon. Equally frequent services for Misahuallí (US$0.30; one hour) leave from the east side of the river by the bridge. There are several buses from this stop to Ahuano (US$0.50; 1½ hours).

ARCHIDONA
Archidona is a small mission village founded in 1560, the same year as Tena, which lies 10 km to the south. Although found on the earliest maps of Ecuador, Archidona has grown little in the intervening centuries and remains a village.

The main reason for visiting is to see the main plaza, which is a small but very well laid out forest of tropical palms, vines, ferns, flowers and trees. The plaza is crossed with paths from which you can admire the varied flora.

It comes as a real surprise to see such a beautiful plaza in so small a village; it is probably the mission's work. Their carefully but strangely painted concrete-block church is also very colourful. A good day to visit Archidona is on Sunday, when the local Quijos Indians come to their weekly market and to hear mass.

From the plaza you can take a bus to Cotundo and ask to be dropped at the entrance to the **Cuevas de Jumandi**, about

five km north of Archidona. There are three main branches in the cave system, which apparently has not yet been fully explored. There is a snack bar (not always open) by the caves but there are no other facilities. You must bring your own lights to see the stalagmites and other formations within.

The cave is muddy and rubber boots and old clothes are recommended. If you plan on going deep into the cave you should have a local guide and equipment; entry costs US$0.50.

The next town of any importance to the north is Baeza, about 100 km away. This is at the junction with the Lago Agrio-Quito road and will be described later in this chapter.

Places to Stay & Eat
There are a couple of cheap and basic hotels near the plaza. *Residencial Regina* has been recommended and there is also the *Residencial Carolina* which is OK. There are a few simple places to eat.

MISAHUALLÍ
This small village is marked on many maps as Puerto Misahuallí and is at the end of the road running from Puerto Napo along the north bank of the Río Napo. It is a popular place from which to see some of the Oriente because you can easily get here by bus from Quito in a day, so it is suitable for the traveller with a limited amount of time. Tours from Misahuallí are often cheaper than from many other parts of the Amazon.

However, before you grab your hammock and pith helmet and jump on the next bus, you should realise that this isn't virgin jungle. The area has been colonised for decades and most mammals (monkey, wild pig, jaguar, capybara) have been either hunted out or had their habitats encroached upon to the point where they cannot survive.

What you will see, if you keep your eyes open – or better still, with a local guide – is a variety of jungle birds, tropical flowers, army ants and other insects, and hundreds of dazzling butterflies.

In addition you will see the people living in the jungle – colonists, gold panners, oil workers, farmers, ranchers, military personnel, people in the tourism industry, and entrepreneurs. The remaining Indians tribes live deeper into the jungle and, for the most part, prefer to be left alone. Most of the Indians in the area are either transplanted highlanders or acculturated locals.

Buses can usually reach Misahuallí in any weather, but extremely high or low water levels can disrupt river services. The 'dry' season – though it can still rain – is November and December. The wettest period is June to August.

If you want an excursion deep into the jungle, it can be arranged in Misahuallí. This will require time, patience, flexibility and money – but still it is less expensive than jungle expeditions in other countries. Excursions can also be arranged in Coca, Baños, Dureno, Tena and Quito. Finally, if you want a reasonable amount of comfort – or even luxury – that is available further downriver, but not at Misahuallí.

Information

Money For most trips, both sucres and cash US dollars are accepted. US dollar travellers' cheques can sometimes be negotiated, but cash is better. There are no proper exchange facilities in Misahuallí, although locals may change small amounts of cash dollars.

Post & Telecommunications There is no post office as such in Misahuallí, and mail takes months to arrive. From Europe to Quito usually takes one to two weeks, and from Quito to Misahuallí takes one to two months. If you have the time, you can make postal enquiries and reservations with the guide of your choice by writing to Misahuallí, Provincia de Napo, Ecuador.

A few guides (see Jungle Tours later) now have telephone or fax facilities. Long tours can be arranged in advance in Quito or Baños, or go to Misahuallí at the beginning of your stay in Ecuador and make the arrangements in advance.

Jungle Tours The various restaurants in Misahuallí are good places to meet potential travelling companions for excursions, or to pick the brains of travellers returning from a trip. Any one of the several small restaurants on the plaza is a good place to start. Other places include Douglas Clarke's Restaurant Dayuma, just off the plaza, and the Hotel Albergue Español just beyond the Dayuma. The El Paisano restaurant is also popular with travellers.

It's a small village; you'll be able to 'cruise' the likely places in a few minutes. If you want to see some of the river without taking a tour, you can take a passenger boat trip as far as Coca. These go several times a week.

Even if you don't usually enjoy organised tours, you should consider joining one if you want to see some of the jungle, particularly if this is your first visit. There are many guides available in Misahuallí, and they offer a variety of tours ranging from one to 10 days in duration. Usually you have to get a group together to make it economical.

Travellers pass through Misahuallí every day and it's a small place; if you're alone you'll meet others very soon. Alternatively, get a group together in advance in Quito or Baños. Also, bear in mind that tourism is increasing in the Coca area, where tours are a little cheaper than from Misahuallí.

One of the best guide services is Douglas Clarke's Expediciones Dayuma, which has been offering guide services for many years. Douglas's son Wilfrid and his sister Billy often work for him but he also hires a variety of other guides as his operation expands. I have received generally favourable reports of Expediciones Dayuma – they are good, have been around for a long time, and so they charge a little more than other outfits.

They do a simple one-day walk as an introduction to the jungle; various plant and insect species are pointed out, and a swim under a hidden waterfall can be included. They also do four to eight-day trips, which include camping in their jungle camp where all necessary equipment is provided. Some canoeing in dugouts as well as hiking is involved.

Other trips go to the Coca region where there is a greater chance of seeing wildlife. These trips can all be organised to leave from Quito.

Finally, they will organise a 10-day trip which takes you far down the Río Napo and back up the Río Aguarico with a chance of seeing wildlife such as macaws, parrots, toucans and rarer bird species; and animals such as caymans, various monkey species and perhaps wild pigs, anteaters, or – with a great deal of luck – a jungle cat. This trip must be requested ahead of time. It is a rugged expedition and there is little comfort. It is not for the faint-hearted.

You can find Douglas Clarke at the Dayuma Lodge half a block from the plaza in Misahuallí. He speaks some English (few of the guides in Misahuallí are fluent English speakers), and he has a photo album which will give you a good idea of what to expect on his trips. Everything, except for bus or plane fares from Quito, is included in the cost.

He charges US$25 to US$30 per person per day and you normally need a minimum of four people at these prices. For the 10-day trip he charges US$30 to US$35 per person per day, with an eight-person minimum. If your party is smaller, the per-person costs go up proportionately, and with a bigger party you have to negotiate. Costs tend to vary with fluctuations of the dollar.

Reservations and information are obtainable from Expediciones Dayuma (☎ & fax 564 924), 10 de Agosto 38-15 and Mariana de Jesús, Edificio Villacis Pasos, Office 301, Quito, Ecuador. In Misahuallí (☎ 571 513) the address is Casilla 291, Tena, Provincia de Napo, Ecuador.

Douglas Clarke is but one example of the type of guide services available in Misahuallí. There are many others and you have to shop around to get exactly what you want. Douglas' prices are amongst the highest in Misahuallí and you can find similar tours starting at about US$20 per person per day.

On the other hand, by saving yourself money you may find that the standard of guide service, environmental concern, care for the 'client', or quality of the food is other than what you would have liked.

Another outfitter who has been around for a long time is Héctor Fiallos. He runs Fluvial River Tours (☎ 239 044 in Quito). There is a little office on the plaza and headquarters at the Residencial Sacha by the river. He is Douglas' main competitor and runs similar but cheaper tours.

I've heard very mixed reviews of his operation. Occasionally, I'm told that his guides are not very good or experienced and the food inadequate. Other times I receive glowing reports of an adventurous and enjoyable jungle trip for a reasonable price.

Various itineraries are available and they change from year to year. Discuss them thoroughly before making your choice. In addition to running the standard one to 10-day tours, trips are also made to visit the villages of 'primitive' Huoarani (Auca) Indians two or three days' walk into the jungle.

I feel strongly that these kind of tours are not to be encouraged. The guides are rarely sensitive to the needs of the Indians who are undergoing the painful process of integration into 20th-century life. Many guides are just inexperienced local youngsters trying to make a living, and through simple ignorance or sheer bravado the Indians are treated in a degrading or abusive manner.

As often as twice a week, groups of tourists are taken to gawk at 'real' Indians in the 'real' jungle. The Indians stare miserably and with little interest at the frequent hordes of tourists and the parade of goods that to us seems basic: backpacks, not one but two pairs of shoes and a change of clothing, sleeping bag, rain gear, sunglasses, cameras, penknives, cigarette lighters, plastic water bottles, canned food and so on.

The tourists expect and demand the basic necessities of water and a place to sleep, but the Indians' thoughts about the matter are ignored and little is given in return. I recently read an open letter to the public from Moi Vicente Enomenga, the coordinator of the 1st Huoarani National Assembly which was held in 1990. In his letter Enomega writes:

We don't want to see tour guides or tourists because they bring diseases that the Huoarani can't cure; tour guides and tourists enter our houses when we are working in the fields, they hunt and fish for the food we need, they leave garbage. Tourists are paying US$20 to $30 per day for this and we are being exploited and receive nothing.
Therefore we resist tourism and want the tours to leave us alone. If necessary, we will oppose tourism with our spears.

If you want to see the Indians it is best to wait until they come to you. A few of the more adventurous and acculturated Aucas usually come to trade in Misahuallí or Coca, where you can see them and they, in turn, can see you in an unstrained and uncompromising atmosphere.

There are many other guides apart from Douglas Clarke and Héctor Fiallos. Most of them started working with either Douglas or Héctor and decided to branch off on their own. Carlos Lastra Lasso is one such; he is very friendly and does a good job. I enjoyed being with him. He charges about US$20 per person per day with a five-person minimum.

Adonis Muñoz of Caiman Safaris, Casilla 255, Puerto Misahuallí, Tena, Ecuador speaks English and has been frequently recommended. Luis Alberto García of Emerald Forest Expeditions, Casilla 247, Puerto Misahuallí, Tena, Ecuador also speaks English and is a great cook. Although he has been generally recommended, some travellers write that he is not very environmentally aware, particularly with regard to the Indians. Talk to him about this!

Other outfitters whom I haven't met but who have been recommended are Carlos Santandar, Julio Angeles, Elias Arteaga and Mariana Ortiz of Ñuca Shasha Tours. I have received mixed reports about Carlos Sevilla. These and other guides usually have signs or booths up in the corner of the main square.

Make sure that whoever you choose gives you a good deal. Work the details out carefully beforehand to avoid confusion or disappointment. Common sense dictates making sure that costs, food, equipment, itinerary and group numbers are all discussed thoroughly before the tour.

The most important matter to settle is the guide; a good guide will be able to show you much you would have missed on your own, particularly if you convey your enthusiasm and interest by asking questions. An inadequate guide will spoil the trip. Guides should be able to produce a Tourist Guide Card on request.

A common problem is that a group makes arrangements with an outfitter and then an inferior guide is supplied at the last moment. All the outfitters are guilty of this to a greater or lesser extent and Fluvial River Tours in particular has built up quite a reputation for this. Douglas Clarke obviously can't join every group himself, but at least he tells you so from the beginning and tries to find a suitable guide for you. If you want a specific guide, you may have to wait until he is available.

Make sure you meet with your guide before you leave. Can you communicate adequately? Has he or she done this before? Can they show you the *achiote* plant (whose red berries are crushed to make decorative body paints)? Can he or she find the vine which, when cut, provides water fit to drink? Can you go for a swim by a waterfall, go fishing from a dugout canoe, go birdwatching or do whatever it is you want? What will be cooked for dinner and breakfast? Will game be hunted for the pot? – the area is overhunted and a no-hunting policy is encouraged. A few questions like these will soon tell you if you and the guide are going to have a good trip together. Most people have a great time, especially if they plan their excursion carefully.

Anyone heading downriver is required to register their passport number at the Port Captain's office by the waterfront.

There is not much in the way of equipment available in Misahuallí. Insect repellent, water purifying tablets and sun lotion are essential and should be brought with you. Sheets of plastic can be bought in Misahuallí and they make reasonable rain ponchos. Rubber boots in small and medium sizes and blankets are also available.

Guiding is a lucrative way of earning money and inevitably gives rise to inexperienced people who think 'I can take a bunch of gringos for a walk into the jungle and make good money'. Make sure you find a guide who knows what needs to be done and is experienced. I heard from one traveller who paid US$26 per day to go on a trip with Cruceros Fluvial Guacamayo Tours. He said that food was limited to two daily meals of rice and manioc, drink was untreated river water, and almost a day was wasted trying to get permits.

Obviously, I am unable to take trips with all the local outfitters or I would never have time to see the rest of the country and write the book. I would appreciate travellers sending me recommendations and criticisms of guides so that I can include them in the next edition.

Waterfall Walk This is a short trip which is offered by some guides as a one-day look at the local jungle. It is one that you can do yourself quite easily. First, take a Misahuallí-Puerto Napo bus and ask the driver to set you down at the Río Latas, about 15 or 20 minutes away from Misahuallí. All the drivers know *el camino a las cascadas* (the trail to the falls). Follow the river upstream to the falls, passing several swimming holes en route. Be prepared to wade. It takes about an hour to reach the falls, depending on how fast you walk. It's a nice place to swim and have a picnic.

Places to Stay & Eat
None of the accommodation in Misahuallí (with the possible exception of the *Hotel Albergue Español*) is expensive or particularly luxurious. Water and electricity failures are the rule rather than the exception in all these places.

On the plaza you'll find the *Residencial El Balcón de Napo* which has small concrete block rooms, some of them like jail cells. The rooms with a window are OK. The residencial is fairly clean by jungle standards, though the showers are a bit grungy. They charge just over a US$1, as does the rambling old *Residencial La Posada*, which has a hodgepodge arrangement of creaky wooden rooms and somewhat dubious bathroom facilities. Others on the plaza which cost between US$1 and US$2 per person and are just as 'good' are the *Hotel Etsa* which has a few rooms with private bath, the basic but friendly *Hotel 55* and the *Hotel Jennifer*.

Half a block from the plaza is Douglas Clarke's *Dayuma Lodge*, behind the restaurant. The lodge is a small, wooden, jungle-style building with four rooms. Two rooms have four bunks each and the other two have six bunks each, dorm style. One of each of these has a private bathroom and there is also a communal bathroom. If there's two or more of you, you can normally have a room to yourselves, but if you're alone you may have to share.

Prices vary from less than a dollar if you use your own sleeping bag in a room without a private shower, to US$2 each if you want bedding and a private shower.

Héctor Fiallos' *Residencial Sacha* is located down by the river. It has basic, jungle-cabin-style accommodation for US$1.50 each. During the wet season, especially June through August, the river can be high enough that guests have to wade to this hotel! A canoe is sometimes available.

The folks at *El Paisano* restaurant have a small hotel which is popular with travellers. Rooms are US$2 per person for clean, basic rooms or US$5.50 for a double with private bath. There is a garden with hammocks.

The Spanish-run *Hotel Albergue Español* charges US$3.50 per person in rooms with private bath – water is heated by solar energy. There is jazz music in the dining room. The hotel is about 200 metres off the plaza past the Dayuma Lodge.

All the hotels have some kind of restaurant. The *Dayuma*, *Albergue Español*, *55* and *El Paisano* are all good. El Paisano is 100 metres from the plaza on the road past the military post. Both the El Paisano and the 55 serve vegetarian fare. The *Sacha* has riverside dining but erratic service.

There are several comfortable and more expensive jungle lodges downriver from Misahuallí which are described under Ahuano.

Entertainment

Nightlife is rather limited. There is one video movie theatre. Otherwise, there are restaurant/bars to hang out with locals and other travellers, and usually a disco happening somewhere at weekends.

Getting There & Away

Bus Buses leave from the plaza at about 30-minute intervals during daylight hours. The only destination is Tena, where you can make connections to elsewhere. The ride costs US$0.30 and takes about one hour.

Boat Motorised dugout canoes leave from the port for various destinations downriver. The port is a block away from the plaza. Since the opening of the Tena-Coca road and the construction of roads east along the Río Napo, river traffic has dwindled. It is still possible, however, to travel downriver by occasional public canoes or by private charters. You are required to register with the Port Captain if heading downriver.

A passenger boat leaves most mornings for the villages or settlements of (in geographical order) Ahuano, Anaconda Island, Hotel Jaguar, Santa Rosa, and Bellavista. This last village is about half way to Coca.

On Monday, Wednesday, Friday, and Sunday a boat leaves for Coca if there is enough passenger demand. The fare is around US$10 per person with a 10-person minimum. If there are fewer people, the fare is US$100 split among the passengers. On other days, you can charter a canoe, but bargain hard. You may be asked for US$150 but should be able to get it down to around US$100. Ask around about what the going rate is. The journey to Coca takes about six hours if the river is running normally.

Ahuano is near several tourist lodges and the fare there is about US$1.50 if you go on a regular passenger boat. A charter is about US$25 one way or US$37 for a round trip.

Note that buses now go from Tena to both Ahuano and Coca and most of the locals go by bus because it is cheaper and more reliable. Often, boats for Coca are full of gringos wanting the experience of travelling by river.

The front seats give better forward views but are narrower, the middle seats are wider and more comfortable, the back seats are close to the noise and fumes of the engine. Read the section on dugout canoes in the Getting Around chapter for more information.

Even on the second half of the trip down to Coca you won't see much wildlife, as the area is heavily colonised. Little houses on stilts huddle on the bank, prospectors wash sand or pan for gold by the river's edge, colonists wave and whistle for a ride, and impossibly tiny dugout canoes, loaded to the gunwales with an Indian family perched on a pile of bananas, are steadily and gracefully poled upriver. A sudden rain shower can enhance the beauty of the river. The jungle glows greenly in the late afternoon sun, and a few pure white clouds suspended in a perfectly blue sky contrast dramatically with the muddy flowing river. The scenery is worth the discomfort.

AHUANO

This small mission village is about one hour downriver from Misahuallí. There is not much to do here. It is a departure point for several nearby jungle lodges.

Places to Stay

In the village itself, there is a basic pensión (no sign) run by a friendly lady who charges US$2 per person. Ask in the village.

On the outskirts of the village is the comfortable *Casa del Suizo* (☎ in Quito 524 616, 233 611), a Swiss-run jungle lodge. They have 22 double rooms with private bath, a restaurant and bar, and a pleasant location by the river. The place is clean, comfortable, and has been recommended by travellers.

There is a variety of tours available including river trips, jungle hikes, visits to missions and local communities, and wildlife walks. Rates depend on the number of people in a group, how long you stay and what you want to do. Single visitors pay an expensive surcharge. Sample prices are US$77 per person for three days and two nights, including all meals, for two visitors. Four visitors pay US$68 per person. If, additionally, you want to go on tours with a Spanish-speaking guide, the rate goes up US$10 per person for the above package. Bilingual guides are available but are extremely expensive. Extra nights are about US$20 per person (including meals) or US$30 per person (including meals and guided tours).

The *Aliñahui Cabins* (☎ in Quito 448 439, 479 831) is on the left-hand side of the Puerto Napo-Ahuano road, about 23 km from Puerto Napo and 5 km before reaching Ahuano. There are six cabins, each with two double rooms and a bathroom. There is a restaurant, bar, and gift shop. The site is on a bluff above the river and there are good views (hence the name of the cabins, which means 'good view' in Quechua). Horseback riding, jungle hikes, and boat trips can be arranged. The place is German-run, clean, and recommended by travellers. English is spoken. Rates are about US$16 per person per day and include all meals – a good deal. Reservations can be made by telephoning Quito or by writing to Cabañas Aliñahui, Apartado 5150 CCI, Quito, Ecuador.

There are two tourist lodges further down the Río Napo. The nearest is *Hotel Anaconda* (☎ in Quito 545 426) on Anaconda Island, about an hour from Misahuallí and just a few minutes from Ahuano. This is a fairly comfortable jungle-style lodge (bamboo walls and thatched roofs), but there is no electricity. Rooms come with private bathrooms and mosquito screens, and the meals (included in the price) are good. They charge about US$40 per person, per day. Canoe trips and jungle excursions from the island are available at extra cost, and are more expensive than from Misahuallí. You'll see pet animals such as monkeys and peccaries. I have

received reports that reservations made in Quito have not been honoured by the lodge for travellers arriving under their own steam. Occasionally, the lodge is full with tour groups.

Further downriver is the similarly priced *Hotel Jaguar* (☎ in Quito 239 400) about 1½ hours from Misahuallí. This is a comfortable modern hotel on the banks of the Río Napo. You can make reservations for it in Quito (the agency is at Dávalos 653) but usually this involves an all-inclusive jungle tour package from Quito lasting three or more days. It is possible to enquire in Misahuallí about shorter or cheaper stays.

Getting There & Away
Bus Buses from Tena run several times a day to Ahuano, which is about 28 km east of Puerto Napo. If you are driving, note that the road to Ahuano is on the south side of the Río Napo from Puerto Napo; the road on the north side of the river goes to Misahuallí; the roads are dirt. The bus can drop you off at the entrance to the Aliñahui Cabins, from where it is a one km walk to the cabins themselves. The bus goes as far as La Punta, on the south side of the Río Napo. From here, you have to cross to the north side of the river by boat to get to Ahuano and the other jungle lodges. Despite the fact that the bus doesn't actually go to Ahuano, it's still called the Ahuano bus locally because there isn't much happening at La Punta. There is little problem in crossing the Río Napo from La Punta to Ahuano.

Boat Dugout canoes wait at La Punta to take you across to Ahuano. The fare is about US$0.40 per person and there are frequent boats, particularly after a bus arrives. Chartering your own boat costs US$3. These boats can drop you off at La Casa del Suizo. Boats to the Hotel Anaconda and Hotel Jaguar can also be arranged but are more expensive, particularly to the Jaguar.

You can also get to Ahuano or any of the lodges by boat from Misahuallí. For more information, see under Misahuallí. Most people go via the bus to La Punta because there is more frequent and cheaper service.

JATUN SACHA

This is a biological station and rainforest preserve near Ahuano. It is run by an Ecuadorian non-profit organisation with the goals of promoting rainforest research, conservation, and education. Scientists are currently carrying out surveys of what species are present. This may appear simple, but is complicated by the fact that the Jatun Sacha area is one of the most species-rich regions on earth. Some of the plants and animals found here are unknown to science – exciting stuff. Herpetologists (scientists who study reptiles) claim that there are more different species of 'herps' here than almost anywhere on the globe. Botanists echo this with flowering plants. The preserve covers only about 300 hectares, of which most is virgin rainforest. There are several km of trails. Unfortunately, neighbouring areas are being rapidly cleared for logging and agriculture, and it is not known how long the incredible biodiversity of Jatun Sacha will remain intact.

Places to Stay & Eat

There are four unscreened buildings sleeping about two dozen people. Accommodation is primitive – bunk beds and outdoor showers and latrines. You need insect repellent or mosquito nets plus a sleeping bag or blankets – the beds only have a bare mattress. Cooking facilities are available but there is no restaurant so bring your own food.

Reservations can be made at Casilla 867, Sucursal 12, Quito, Ecuador or c/o Missouri Botanical Gardens, P O Box 299, St Louis, MO 63166-0299, USA (☎ in USA (314) 577 5100).

Occasionally, Jatun Sacha is full of researchers or students, but much of the time you can just show up and there is space available. Fees are US$5 per person per day.

If the facilities here are too primitive, you could stay (or eat) at the Aliñahui Cabins, which are about 3 km away to the east on the road towards Ahuano.

Getting There & Away

Bus The best way is to take the Tena-Ahuano bus (see Ahuano). Jatun Sacha is about 21 km east of Puerto Napo or seven km before you reach Ahuano.

COCA

All Ecuadorian maps show this town's official name of Puerto Francisco de Orellana, but I've never heard of it referred to by any name other than Coca. It is located at the junction of the Río Coca and the Río Napo (hence its popular name). Its official name derives from the fact that Francisco de Orellana came through here on his way to 'discover' the Amazon in 1542.

The Río Napo is Ecuador's major tributary into the Amazon. Indeed, it is at the point where Ecuador's Río Napo and Peru's Río Marañon meet that the Amazon continues as a single river.

The Coca of today is a sprawling oil town with little to recommend it. There are no street signs, and every road is unpaved and hence covered with dust, puddles or mud depending on the season. Most of the buildings are just shacks and the place has a real shanty-town appearance – they don't even have a town plaza. There's not much to do apart from drink beer or go to bed. The population is about 16,000 and growing and Coca can be expected to improve in the future. A local tourist industry is growing because Coca is closer to primary rainforest than Misahuallí.

Information

The IETEL office, unlike most of Ecuador, is open only from 9 am to 12 noon, 2 to 5 pm, and 7 to 9 pm Monday to Saturday. On Sunday it is open during the morning and evening hours only. There is a post office but service is very slow. There are no proper money exchange facilities; although dollars can be exchanged by asking around, your best bet is to bring plenty of sucres with you. The owner of the Comercial Londoño store is often able to change dollars.

All travellers arriving and departing by

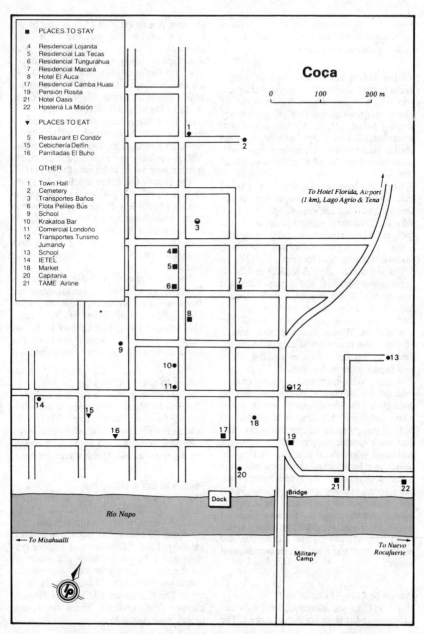

Coça

0   100   200 m

To Hotel Florida, Airport
(1 km), Lago Agrio & Tena

■ PLACES TO STAY

4   Residencial Lojanita
5   Residencial Las Tecas
6   Residencial Tungurahua
7   Residencial Macará
8   Hotel El Auca
17 Residencial Camba Huasi
19 Pensión Rosita
21 Hotel Oasis
22 Hostería La Misión

▼ PLACES TO EAT

5   Restaurant El Condór
15 Cebichería Delfín
16 Parrilladas El Buho

    OTHER

1   Town Hall
2   Cemetery
3   Transportes Baños
6   Flota Pelileo Bús
9   School
10 Krakatoa Bar
11 Comercial Londoño
12 Transportes Turismo
    Jumandy
13 School
14 IETEL
18 Market
20 Capitania
21 TAME Airline

Río Napo

Dock

Bridge

← To Misahualli

Military
Camp

To Nuevo
Rocafuerte

river must register with the Port Captain at the Capitanía by the landing dock. I was treated extremely courteously here.

Jungle Tours Read the section on Jungle Tours under Misahuallí for general information which is also useful for tours out of Coca. A growing number of guides are leaving Misahuallí to work out of Coca, where there is less competition. Some of the guides listed under Misahuallí may well have moved to Coca by the time you read this.

Coca is closer to the Huoarani (Auca) Indian villages than any major town in the Oriente and tours are available to visit these villages. These have a negative impact on the Indians, who themselves prefer to be left alone – I do not recommend any tour which involves visits to the Huoarani.

Guides charge around US$20 to US$30 per person per day and group sizes are usually four to six people. Smaller groups have to pay more per person. It is easier to find people to make up a group in Quito than it is in Coca. Trips are usually from three to 10 days. You may have to bargain to get the best rate, but make sure everything which you expect to be included is.

A guide who has been frequently recommended is Whymper Torres. He can be contacted at the Hotel Auca or you can make reservations with his sister in Quito (☎ 269 511). If you do make arrangements in Quito, you are expected to pay half in advance. Although Whymper doesn't speak English, he has been recommended as knowledgeable and experienced. Other guides which have been recommended include Walter Vasco and Edgar San Miguel; again, these people do not speak English. Braulio Llori of Indillama Tours (☎ 880 166) does speak some English, but I have received mixed reports about his trips. There are several others.

Places to Stay – bottom end

Hotels in Coca sometimes suffer from water shortages in the showers and lavatories. The

Pensión Rosita (☎ 880 167) is one of the hotels nearest to the port and so is often crowded and noisy. It has variously been described as musty, dirty, and barely habitable. It is also one of the cheapest at US$2.75 a double without a fan or US$3.60 a double with a fan. A better place is the *Hotel Oasis* (☎ 880 174) behind the TAME office on the river. They charge US$3 per person and have some rooms with private bath and some with air-conditioning. The *Hotel Florida* (☎ 880 177) is similarly priced and quite good, but is some way out of town near the airport.

The best of the cheap hotels is the *Hotel El Auca* (☎ 880 127), which is set in a garden and isn't bad. They charge US$2.50 each in rooms with communal bath or US$3.75/5.50 for singles/doubles with private bath, and they are often full before nightfall. I have received reports of overcharging in this hotel.

There are also three basic residenciales across the street a block from the Auca: the *Tungurahua, Las Tecas* and *Lojanita* (☎ 880 132), in descending order of appearance. They charge about US$1.50 to US$2 per person. Other cheapies include the *Residenciales Macará* and *Camba Huasi.*

Places to Stay – middle

The best place in town is the new and good *Hostería La Misión* with many rooms overlooking the river. They charge US$11/17 for singles/doubles with fan and cold water bathroom, or US$20/30 with air-conditioning and hot water. All rooms have fridges.

Places to Eat & Drink

The best place in town is the restaurant at the *Hostería La Misión*. The *Hotel Auca* has a halfway decent restaurant although the menu is limited. The best place outside of hotels is the *Parrilladas El Buho* which has big portions and is frequented by North American oil workers, among others. Around the corner the *Cebichería El Delfín* is also quite good. The *Restaurant El Condór* sells roast chicken (not condors). There are several others basic places to eat.

A good place for a beer is the *Krakatoa Bar* which has shaded ramadas outside. As with all bars in Coca, unaccompanied females may receive unwanted attention.

Getting There & Around

Air TAME has a regular service from and to Quito. Flights leave Quito at 9.45 am and return from Coca to Quito at 10.45 am daily, except Sunday. Additionally, there are flights from Quito at 1.00 pm, returning from Coca to Quito at 2.00 pm on Monday, Wednesday and Friday. Tickets cost about US$12 and are available from the TAME office at the Hotel Oasis, a short way east of the bridge. Tickets can be bought in Quito but TAME will only confirm reservations from Coca in Coca.

It is best to confirm as far in advance as possible and to reconfirm your flight the day before, if possible. Flights are not always full, however, and you can sometimes buy tickets at the airport before the flight if the TAME office is closed when you arrive. Even if there are seats available, TAME office personnel are often reluctant to sell seats until the very last minute – hang around the TAME office looking forlorn until they relent.

FAE (the air force) has cheap flights to Tena and Shell on Monday and Wednesday. Ask about these at the airport control tower. Small aircraft are used, so book as far in advance as possible to get a seat.

It is occasionally possible to fly with an oil company plane, which might be cheaper, or free. You need the usual combination of luck, contacts, and being at the right place at the right time.

The airport is almost two km north of town on the left hand side of the road to Lago Agrio.

Bus Transportes Baños has five daily buses to Quito (US$4; about 12 hours) and an overnight bus to both Ambato and Santo Domingo. Transportes Turismo Jumandy has four buses a day on the new road to Tena (US$3; seven hours). Both companies have buses to Lago Agrio (US$1; three hours). Flota Pelileo has a nightly bus to Ambato.

Open-sided trucks, called rancheros, leave from the market for various destinations between Coca and Lago Agrio, and to Río Tiputini to the south.

Boat Since the completion of the new Tena-Coca road, it is difficult to get boats to Misahuallí. Usually at least 10 passengers are required and the trip takes about 14 hours so you are advised to take the trip in the opposite direction, from Misahuallí to Coca, which takes only six hours. The upriver trip is sometimes broken and passengers camp out by the river – be prepared. The bus is much cheaper and quicker.

The Capitanía may be able to give you information about getting a boat further downriver. Destinations of interest downriver include the Hacienda Primavera, Pompeya, Limoncocha, the La Selva Jungle Lodge, Pañacocha, and Nuevo Rocafuerte on the Peruvian border, about 14 hours away from Coca (all these places are described later in this chapter).

Boat services to these destinations are irregular, infrequent and comparatively expensive. A weekly passenger boat leaves Coca for Nuevo Rocafuerte on Monday morning, returning on Thursday. The fare is US$7. Otherwise, you have to hire your own boat – expensive. Note that special (and difficult to obtain) permits are required for travel to Nuevo Rocafuerte.

HACIENDA PRIMAVERA

This small lodge is a two-hour trip downriver from Coca on the Río Napo. There are pleasant walks and lakes in the nearby jungle. The hotel and surrounding jungle have been recommended by travellers, though I have never been there. Tours are available to various local destinations: eg a two-day tour to Limoncocha, with a night trip to see caiman and canoe rides on the lake. A new company took over in 1991 and plans on expanding the operation – prices were not available. The company can be contacted in Quito for further information – Xetro (c/o Marvelandia), U Paéz 229 and 18 de

Septiembre or PO Box 653-A, Quito (☎ 541 599, 563 146).

The main problem with this place (and others further downriver) is getting there. Transport can be arranged in advance with Xetro in Quito, but it is more difficult to arrange for the independent traveller already in the Oriente. The Monday boat from Coca to Nuevo Rocafuerte may take you if there is room (they prefer long-distance passengers). Other boats leave at irregular intervals. The passenger fare is US$1.

To hire your own boat costs US$30 from Coca, but they can take several passengers for that price. Returning to Coca is more of a problem – either you have to rent your own boat or you may have to wait for some days for a passing passenger boat. Be prepared with either extra time or money.

POMPEYA & LIMONCOCHA

Pompeya is a Catholic mission about three or four hours downriver from Coca on the Río Napo. There is a school and small museum here, and basic food and lodging can be arranged. Opposite Pompeya is Monkey Island which can be reached by canoe in a few minutes. The troops of monkeys living on this island can be spotted relatively easily.

From Pompeya one can walk for one to two hours on a northbound trail to the ex-North American mission of Limoncocha where there is a beautiful lake. There is a store here where rooms can be rented inexpensively. There is also a small lodge. A new road from Limoncocha has reportedly been pushed through as far as the small oil town of Shushufindi. A truck is supposed to leave Limoncocha on Saturday for Shushufindi from where connections for Lago Agrio or Coca can be made.

The area south of Limoncocha is a biological reserve, where thousands of Huoarani people hunt and gather in a traditional manner. The reserve acts as a buffer zone for the nearby Parque Nacional Yasuní, which is largely uninhabited.

To get to Pompeya, take a boat from Coca (see under Hacienda Primavera for more information).

LA SELVA JUNGLE LODGE

This is the most expensive but also the most comfortable and well-run jungle lodge in Ecuador. If you can afford it, you'll enjoy it. I have heard reports ranging from positive to ravingly impressed – no negative reports have been received.

The lodge is run by a North American-Ecuadorian couple, Eric and Magdalena Schwartz, who are interested both in providing a first-class ecotourism experience and in responsible tourism. They hire as many local people as possible, offer excursions into the rainforest with informed and interested guides, incorporate local food into their cuisine, and avoid annoying visits to the unacculturated Indians living in the vicinity.

Accommodation is in 15 double cabins, each with private bath and mosquito screens. Lighting is by kerosene lanterns which avoids the noise of a generator outside your bedroom window. Meals are excellent by any standards, and absolutely outstanding for Oriente standards.

There is also a small research facility where scientists and students can work on their projects. Discounted accommodation is available for researchers if arranged well in advance – often, researchers pay off part of their expenses by giving guided jungle excursions to interested visitors.

Excursions are mainly by dugout canoe, although there are also a few km of trails. Birdwatching is a highlight – about 500 species have been recorded in the area. About half of Ecuador's 44 species of parrots have been recorded from La Selva, as well as a host of other exotic tropical birds: toucans and trogons, jacamars and tanagers, antbirds and fruitcrows just to name a few. Monkeys are frequently seen, and other mammals are occasionally sighted. Of course, there are tens of thousands of species of plants and insects.

The lodge is about five to six hours downriver from Coca by regular passenger canoe, but visitors usually pay for a complete package from Quito. This includes air transport to Coca and river transportation in La Selva's private launches which go twice as fast as the ordinary passenger boats. Visitors are required to spend a three-night minimum at the lodge. Prices include round air trip from Quito to Coca, river travel, accommodation, all meals, and all guide services. The bar tab is extra.

The short three-night package (Wednesday to Saturday) costs US$470 per person; the long four-night package (Saturday to Thursday) costs US$570 per person. You can combine any number of three and four day packages to make seven, 10, 11, or 14-day stays – these are discounted.

Visits can be made at any time of year. June and July are the wettest months. Information and reservations are available from La Selva (☎ 554 686, 550 995, fax 563 814), PO Box 635, Sucursal 12 de Octubre, Quito, Ecuador. The street address is 6 de Diciembre 2816 and James Orton, Quito.

PAÑACOCHA

Pañacocha is Quechua for 'the Lake of the Piranhas'. There is a small community near the lake where you can stay. Pañacocha is about seven hours downstream from Coca, or about halfway to Nuevo Rocafuerte.

Accommodation is available at *Cabañas Pañacocha* which are run by the same people that own the Hacienda Primavera – see that section for prices and information. The cabañas are right by the lake and away from the village.

A popular activity is to go piranha fishing – the fish are fairly easy to catch and make good eating, but don't let them get their razor sharp jaws around your finger or you might lose it.

NUEVO ROCAFUERTE

This small river town is on the Peruvian border, about 14 hours from Coca along the Río Napo. Entering Peru at this point is prohibited. Since the 1981 Peruvian/Ecuadorian war, you need a military permit to be allowed to travel to this area. This is not easy to arrange, but if you can get the permit it'll give you the opportunity to see life on the frontier of the Oriente.

One way to get the permit is to apply at the *Comandancia General del Ejercito* (the General Army Command) at the *Ministerio de Defensa* (Ministry of Defence) in Quito. If a permit is refused, you can try again at the Military Camp by the bridge in Coca, where you have to speak to the *commandante*. Being able to speak Spanish helps.

If you are a writer on assignment or are doing scientific research you may find it easier to get a permit, particularly if you have some kind of professional credentials and a letter from your embassy. If you are simply a tourist, you may be allowed to do the trip if you hire a local guide (expensive). Tourists travelling alone are generally refused permission – this is a remote and politically sensitive area. I have heard of travellers being accused of drug smuggling when they tried to go to Nuevo Rocafuerte. If you are allowed to go, you will have to leave your passport with the commandante in Coca.

Places to Stay & Eat

There is one basic pensión in Nuevo Rocafuerte. Rooms are about US$2.50 per person. There is a small store with basic supplies, but you should bring everything you need with you. There is no restaurant, but by asking around you can find someone to cook simple and inexpensive meals for you.

Getting There & Away

The weekly canoe from Coca leaves early on Monday morning, so you should be in Coca by Thursday night to allow time on Friday to try to get a permit. The 14-hour trip is usually broken at Pañacocha for a meal.

The return canoe leaves Nuevo Rocafuerte early on Thursday morning. Because travel is against the flow of the river, the return trip takes about 28 to 30 hours and an overnight stop is usually made at Pompeya. The fare is US$7 each way.

PARQUE NACIONAL YASUNÍ

Yasuní lies south of the Río Napo and includes most of the watersheds of the Río Yasuní and Río Nashiño, as well as substantial parts of the Río Tiputini. This 679,730-hectare national park is by far the largest in mainland Ecuador and was established in 1979 to conserve a wide variety of different rainforest habitats.

These can be divided into three major groups: 'terra firme' or forested hills which are never inundated by even the highest floods; 'varzea' or lowlands which are periodically inundated by flooding rivers; and 'igapó' which are lowlands which are inundated semi- permanently. Thus, Parque Nacional Yasuní has wetlands, marshes, swamps, lakes, river systems, and rainforest.

The biodiversity of this varied and remote tropical landscape is staggeringly high. Not many scientists have had the opportunity of visiting the park, but those that have report much higher species counts than they had expected, including many new species. The animals present include some of the rarer and more difficult to see jungle wildlife such as the jaguar, harpy eagle, puma, and tapir.

Because of the importance of the park's incredible biodiversity, UNESCO (United Nations Educational, Scientific, and Cultural Organisation) has declared Yasuní an international biosphere reserve.

The national park is almost uninhabited, except for about 20 Huoarani Indian families. Most Huoaranis live outside the park boundaries, especially in the Limoncocha Biological Reserve, which acts as an ecological buffer zone for the national park.

As we go to press I have read a report that a new Huoarani Ethnobotanical Reserve has been created in 1991, encompassing much of the western part of Yasuní and providing the Huoarani with a suitable area of rainforest in which to live in a traditional manner.

The southern border of Parque Nacional Yasuní has been extended to the Río Cururay, so that the size of the park remains about the same.

On the face of it, then, this huge, remote national park, surrounded by a buffer zone, is a modern conservation success story. Unfortunately, this is not the case. Oil has been discovered within the boundaries of the park. In 1991, despite Yasuní's protected status, the Ecuadorian government gave the US-based oil company, Conoco, the right to begin oil exploitation. It is understandable that the Ecuadorian government wants to make money from its oil reserves, but much of the profit will benefit foreign interests rather than Ecuador.

Where drilling begins, a road soon follows, thus opening up pristine rainforest to colonisation, deforestation, and degradation. It is the roads and the subsequent colonisation that cause greater long term damage than the oil drilling itself. Conoco has talked of low impact drilling, using helicopters to supply the oil wells, thus avoiding roads and subsequent deforestation.

However, at the same time, they are planning a US$22 million road into Yasuní – the road would be cheaper than the low impact method. Whichever method ends up being used, the degradation caused by the oil drilling process itself will still occur. This includes contamination of soil and drainage system by oil and the waste products associated with oil exploitation, as well as the noise pollution and destruction of vegetation causing the exodus of wildlife from the region.

It now seems unlikely that Yasuní's national park status will protect the area from oil drilling. Conoco's business is to recover the oil for the greatest possible profit and, if it is allowed to do so by building a road, it is likely that it will build the road.

Various international organisations, such as the Nature Conservancy, Conservation International and Natural Resources Defense Council, in coalition with Ecuadorian groups such as the Fundación Natura and local grass roots conservation groups, are working to minimise Conoco's impact in Yasuní.

As we go to press, I have received a report that Conoco has decided to pull out of Yasuní, because they were unable to extract oil as well as maintain the 'clean image' which they are now cultivating. A half-built road remains in the area and Conoco have sold their operation to Maxus, a division of the Diamond Shamrock Corporation. Therefore Parque Nacional Yasuní remains threatened by oil exploitation.

In common with the majority of Ecuador's preserved areas, Yasuní is woefully understaffed. In 1990, they had only one ranger. Poaching of game for sale to pet traders is a growing concern. Most of the organisations mentioned above are working to train and fund an Ecuadorian park staff consisting of administrators, rangers, and management technicians to combat the various threats facing Yasuní.

At present, the only ranger station is at Nuevo Rocafuerte, which is difficult to reach. La Selva Jungle Lodge lies at the north-western boundary of the park, and visitors to the lodge can make brief forays into the edges of the park. Some of the guides in Coca can take you on trips into the park – the Río Tiputini is a possible way of entering the park.

Annual rainfall is about 3500 mm depending on which part of the park one is in. May to July are the wettest months; January to March are the driest ones. This is one of the few remaining true wildernesses in Ecuador, but don't expect to see the shy wildlife like jaguars unless you are very lucky. One of the beauties of this area is its remoteness and inaccessibility which allows the wildlife to remain in the region, relatively undisturbed. I hope that it will be able to remain so.

RÍO TIPUTINI

A road from Coca crosses the Río Tiputini, about 2½ hours south of the Río Napo. There is a small community here with daily buses from Coca. There is a Shell oil camp nearby. In Tiputini, the Grefa family can provide basic accommodation and guide services for trips down the Río Tiputini and into Parque Nacional Yasuní.

LAGO AGRIO

Lago Agrio's official name is 'Nueva Loja', because many of the early Ecuadorians who colonised the area came from Loja. But US oil workers working for Texaco nicknamed the town 'Lago Agrio' after a small oil town in Texas called Sour Lake, and the nickname has stuck. Many locals simply call the town 'Lago'.

The bus ride from Coca to Lago Agrio gives an interesting look at how the discovery of oil has changed the Oriente. Barely 20 years ago, this was all virgin jungle and communications were limited to mission airstrips and river travel. Today there are roads and buses, and there are always signs of the oil industry – the pipelines, oil wells or trucks.

A short way north of Coca the bus heads east and passes the belching wells of the Sacha oil works. It continues through the small oil town of **La Joya de las Sachas**, where there are a few restaurants and two basic residenciales – the *Carmita* and *Zaruma*. The road is narrow but in good condition and almost entirely paved. It follows the oil pipeline for most of the way, and there are several stretches with fine scenery and vistas of the jungle.

You'll frequently see those tropical birds which have learnt to co-exist with people; one of the most common is the all-black ani with a long, drooping tail and extremely thick bill. The bus passes occasional small communities and reaches the Río Aguarico. Here a ferry takes the bus across the river, although a bridge is planned. The town of Lago Agrio is a few km beyond.

Lago Agrio is one of the fastest-growing towns in Ecuador. Since the discovery of oil, it has changed from literally virgin jungle to the most important of Ecuador's oil towns. It now has a growing population of about 20,000. A road has been built from Quito and there are daily flights. There are new road links with Colombia and a modern hotel has been opened.

Lago Agrio became the capital of its *cantón* in 1979. In the 1980s, it began lobbying to have the old province of Napo divided into two, with the southern half keeping the old capital of Tena and the northern half having Lago Agrio as its new capital. The

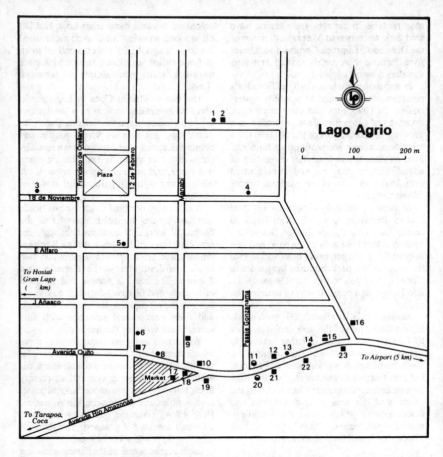

Lago Agrio

0   100   200 m

new province of Sucumbíos was created on 12 February 1989, with Lago Agrio as the provincial capital. The streets are beginning to be paved and a new town plaza has been laid out on the north-western edge of town. Avenida Quito is the main route from Quito to Coca and is still the main street and town centre, but the town is planning to spread around the plaza. It will be interesting to watch Lago Agrio's progress over the next decade.

Although it's the oldest, biggest and 'best' of Ecuador's oil towns, Lago Agrio is still just an oil town, and an oil town is an oil town

is an oil town. Most travellers spend as little time here as possible; it's simply a convenient overnight stop. The drive from the jungle up into the Andes is very beautiful and it's a good idea to rest in Lago Agrio and leave refreshed on a morning bus if you're headed to Quito, so that you can appreciate the scenery. Also, you can use Lago Agrio as a base for further excursions into the jungle on the road which is being pushed ever deeper into the Oriente.

Information
The post office (closed weekends) is up some

■ PLACES TO STAY

2   Hotel San Carlos
7   Hostal El Cofan
9   Residencial Chimborazo
10 Residencial Acapulco
12 Residencial Ecuador
16 Hostal Machala 2
17 Residencial Lago Agrio
18 Hotel Cabaña
19 Residencial El Dorado
    & Hotel Willigram
21 Residencial La Mexicana
    & Hotel Casablanca
22 Hotel Machala
23 Hotel Oriental &
    Transportes Jumandy

▼ PLACES TO EAT

7   Hostal El Cofan

OTHER

1   TAME Office
3   IETEL
4   Cine Oriente
5   Banco de Formento
6   Banco Internacional
8   Policine
10 Transportes Baños &
    Transportes Putumayo
11 Transportes Centinela
    del Norte
13 Colombian Consulate
14 Vaquero Bar
15 Post Office
20 Transportes Occidentales

rickety stairs near the east end of the Avenida Quito, and looks like it's in the front room of a private home. Nevertheless, a letter I mailed from there to the USA arrived safely.

The two cinemas sometimes show fairly good English-language films.

There is an IETEL office on 18 de Noviembre and Francisco de Orellana but it suffers from regular communication breakdowns.

There is a Colombian Consulate on Avenida Quito, although I suggest you check in Quito for entrance requirements into Colombia. There is also a migración office in the police station at Avenida Quito 111.

Money Lago Agrio is only 20 km south of the Colombian border and exchange facilities exist mainly to deal with Colombian pesos, though cash dollars can also be changed. There are several casas de cambio on Avenida Quito. Sometimes you may have to wait a few hours for 'authorisation' to change money. The Banco de Fomento normally deals only with pesos. The Banco Internacional sometimes will accept dollars. As usual, it's easiest to change money in the highlands.

Things to See

There's a Sunday-morning market which can be quite interesting when the local Cofan Indians come into town to buy staples and sell their handicrafts, such as necklaces made of seeds and iridescent beetle wings.

The men often wear a typical one-piece, knee-length smock called a *kushma*, along with a headband around their short hair. This latter may be made of porcupine quills.

The women wear very brightly patterned flounced skirts, short blouses which expose an inch of midriff, bright red lipstick, and have beautiful, long, dark hair.

The Cofan Indians are related to the Secoya people and there used to be tens of thousands of them before early contacts with whites decimated them, mainly by disease. This, unfortunately, is the history of most Amazonian Indian groups. Before the discovery of oil, most Cofans' exposure to non-Indian people was limited to the occasional missionary and they still remain quite shy, as opposed to the Otavaleño Indians for example. They live in several river villages near Lago Agrio but there are no restaurant or accommodation facilities there. Their main village is Dureno and jungle tours can be arranged.

Places to Stay

Lago Agrio is a fast-growing town and new hotels open every year. Some hotels are expanding upwards. The top floor has the advantage of being newer and hence cleaner, but then there's the disadvantage of being closer to the roof, the sun and the heat. It's worth looking at different rooms in the same hotel to see what's best for you.

Most hotels provide a fan or mosquito net with the bed. Although spraying keeps the mosquito population in Lago Agrio down to a minimum, you should look for rooms with fans or nets, especially if you're not taking malaria pills – fans keep the mosquitoes away because they don't like flying in wind.

Places to Stay – bottom end

There are plenty of budget hotels which are cheap, basic and usually look horrible because the rate of deterioration of cheap architecture in the humid jungle is very fast. Some of the oldest and cheapest places are getting a bit rank, so the sensitive might consider it worthwhile staying somewhere more expensive. Most of the hotels are on Avenida Quito.

The *Hotel Willigram* by the market looks like one of the best cheap and basic hotels; they charge US$4.50 for a double with a private bath and fan. *Residencial La Mexicana* (poorly signed) has some rooms for US$1.50 and others for US$3 per person. These have private baths and are fair value. If you stay here, have a good look around, as some of the rooms are definitely much worse than others.

Hotel Casablanca is basic but cleaner than most and charges US$2 each. *Hotel Cabaña* is similarly priced. The basic *Hotel Machala* charges US$1.50 per person and the newer *Hostal Machala 2* charges a little more. The *Hotel San Carlos* is by the TAME office, several blocks north of Avenida Quito, and looks quite good for about US$6 double.

The very basic *Residencial Chimborazo* on Manabí, half a block north of Avenida Quito, is one of the cheapest places in town. Other places which are recommended for their cheap price rather than anything else include the residenciales *Ecuador, Acapulco, El Dorado* and *Lago Agrio* and the *Hotel Oriental*, all on Avenida Quito.

Places to Stay – middle

There are two better hotels. The modern *Hostal El Cofan* (☎ 830 009/109) which is on Avenida Quito and 12 de Febrero charges about US$13/18.50 for singles/doubles with private bathrooms (cold water) and fan. Rooms with air-conditioning cost US$2 more. The hotel is often full, so get there early or call ahead.

The newer *Hostal Gran Lago* is almost a km west of downtown heading out along J Añasco. This place has bungalows set in pleasant surrounds, and there is a restaurant. Prices are about the same as the El Cofan.

Places to Eat & Drink

There are several chifas and some of the hotels have reasonable and cheap restaurants attached – try along Avenida Quito east of the market. The *Hostal El Cofan* restaurant is supposedly the best in town and is not too expensive. The *Hostal Gran Lago* also has a decent restaurant.

The *Vaquero Bar* may be the best bet for a beer in the evening, but it is not recommended for unaccompanied women.

Getting There & Around

Air TAME has a daily flight (except Sunday) from Quito at 10.15 am returning from Lago Agrio to Quito at 11 am. The fare is US$11 each way. Flights are often full but it's always worth getting on the waiting list and going to the airport in the hope of cancellations. Tour companies sometimes book up more seats than they can use. The TAME office (☎ 830 113) is next to the Hotel San Carlos in Lago Agrio. It is usually open on weekdays but their hours are quite erratic. Often everyone packs up and goes to the airport.

The airport is about five km east of town and there is a TAME pickup truck which may take people from the office to the airport for US$0.20 about an hour before the flight. Taxis (which are usually yellow pickup trucks) cost up to US$2 depending on how well you bargain.

If you are arriving in Lago Agrio by air, it's likely you'll see several buses waiting at the airstrip. Unfortunately, most of these are oil company vehicles picking up workers on the flight and they can't or won't give you a ride. If you ask around, however, you'll eventually find something. One of the buses is usually a public bus, and the TAME people often take passengers back in their truck. There are usually taxis hanging around – see if you can share with someone. The muggy or wet five-km walk is not recommended.

The airport is also used by the local oil companies, of which Texaco seems to be the biggest. They can occasionally be persuaded to give travellers a ride in an emergency.

I had an amusing experience once, flying from Quito to Lago Agrio. At the Quito airport I ran into an anthropologist I knew. She was accompanying a Cofan couple who had been in hospital in Quito and who were now returning home. She explained that it was the first flight for both of them and they spoke a lot of Cofan and very little Spanish – could I keep an eye on them? Of course; I was delighted to do so, though I couldn't imagine that there would be any problems. And so off I set with my new Cofan friends.

Our first little problem was with the X-ray machine. I convinced them that no harm would come to their little bundles, so they put them onto the conveyer belt and then walked to the waiting plane. They didn't realise that the X-ray machine didn't automatically deliver all hand luggage to the plane – and after all, with all the automated devices to be seen in Quito, why not? So I called the Cofans back for their bundles and they looked at me with some disgust; obviously this fancy machine was no good at all.

We clambered aboard the aircraft and the next thing to deal with were the seat belts. They couldn't quite understand why the stewardess was buckling them in and seemed rather worried when they couldn't unbuckle their belts. A quick demonstration of the fast release device on the seat belts seemed in order. Once we were airborne, they started to complain of an earache. I tried to show them how to equalise the pressure in their ears and there followed a hilarious episode as we held our noses and swallowed and blew and snorted and sprayed. Finally, through the giggles and general uproar, I managed to convey, in sign language, how to get rid of the pain in their ears.

It was a short flight, and soon we were preparing to land at Lago Agrio. I had made sure that the Cofans had gotten window seats, thinking that they would enjoy the views. Instead, as we came in to land, one of the Cofans firmly covered the window with a blanket and then took a couple of very quick, tentative peeks before closing her eyes tightly shut. We landed safely.

Bus There is no main bus terminal and most bus companies have their offices on or near the main street, Avenida Quito. Buses to Quito cost about US$4 and take eight to 11 hours. The following companies have buses to Quito: Transportes Occidentales, Transportes Jumandy, and Transportes Centinela del Norte.

Each company has a variety of buses ranging from slow, noisy old monsters to smaller and faster buses; they all seem to break down periodically so I can't recommend one in particular because you'll only blame me if your bus breaks down! Most of these companies also have services to either Coca (US$1; two to four hours) or Tena (US$3.50; nine to 10 hours).

You can continue further into the Oriente with Transportes Jumandy, which have a daily 1 pm bus to Tarapoa (US$1; 2½ hours). Transportes Putumayo also has buses to Tarapoa. Their rancheros (open-sided trucks with uncomfortable narrow bench seats) run three times every morning to La Punta on the the Río San Miguel, at the Colombian border (US$0.40; one hour). They have three buses every morning to Tipishca (five hours) also on the Río San Miguel near the Colombian border.

This route goes through the Reserva Producción Faunísta Cuyabeno. There is also a bus to Tetetes, also on the Río San Miguel. Buses to the oil town of Shushufindi are available. The roads into the Oriente from Lago Agrio are constantly being improved and expanded; ask at Transportes Putumayo for the most recent information.

Crossing the Colombian Border
It's certainly possible to enter Colombia from Lago Agrio; the border is less than 20 km to the north and there's always a few Colombians in town. However, gringos should be extremely careful entering or leaving Colombia via these border crossings. The area is notorious for smugglers, and the Colombian side has been called 'dangerous'

by Ecuadorian locals – I wonder if the same is said of Ecuador by the Colombians. I know of only one gringo who has crossed the border here and he writes that the towns on the Colombian side are so primitive in terms of law and order that it was like being a part of the Gold Rush days. At any rate, if you decide that this little adventure is for you, take care, guard your belongings, and I'd enjoy hearing about your experiences – if you survive!

Note that there are no Ecuadorian border crossing posts at border itself. If you are entering or leaving Ecuador, you should get your passport stamped at the migración office in Lago Agrio.

There are currently three routes which are regularly used from Lago Agrio. One way is to take a Transportes Putumayo bus to La Punta (called Puerto Colón on the Colombian side) on the Río San Miguel. Then take a dugout canoe for the short river crossing to the Colombian side. When you arrive in Puerto Colón, you'll find several buses each day to take you to Puerto Asis (about six hours) where there are places to stay and road, air and river transportation to other parts of Colombia.

An alternative route is to take a bus from Lago Agrio to Tetetes and cross the Río San Miguel to the Colombian village of San Miguel, where there are basic pensiones. From San Miguel there are also buses to Puerto Asis – this is a shorter trip on the Colombian side.

A third route is to take a bus from Lago Agrio to Tipishca. From here, you can find canoes to take you down the Río San Miguel to its confluence with the Río Putumayo at Puerto Carmen de Putumayo. The Río Putumayo is quite busy and boats go downriver to Puerto Leguizamo or upriver to Puerto Asis (both in Colombia). A road is planned from Tipishca all the way to Puerto Carmen de Putumayo.

DURENO

There are two Durenos. The Cofan village of Dureno (described in this section) lies on the south banks of the Río Aguarico about an hour east of Lago Agrio by bus or dugout canoe. The Cofan village is 23 km east of Lago Agrio; if you miss the turn-off for it you will end up at the colonists' village of Dureno, 27 km east of Lago Agrio. There are basic comedores here and you could find floor space to sleep on if you asked around.

River transportation is infrequent but Transportes Putumayo have several buses a day to Tarapoa or Tipishca which pass the Dureno (Cofan village) turn-off, 23 km from Lago Agrio. It is marked with a small sign which is not very obvious; it's best to ask the driver for the 'Comuna Cofan Dureno'. From the turn-off follow the path until you reach the Río Aguarico about 100 metres away. From the river bank yell and whistle to attract the attention of the villagers on the other side – somebody will come and get you in a dugout. It may take an hour or more before somebody comes over – keep whistling and yelling!

Crossing the river costs about US$0.30 per person with a US$0.60 minimum. In the village, you'll be given a roof over your head in an Indian-style hut for about US$0.60 each – bring a hammock or sleeping mat as there are no beds. Bring your own food and stove as supplies are not available in Dureno.

The Cofans are excellent wilderness guides and know much about medicinal and practical uses of jungle plants. You can hire a guide with a dugout canoe for about US$20 per day. Up to six people can be accommodated in a dugout so it's cheaper in a group. One of the best guides is Emerihildo Criollo. If he's not around ask for Elias Lucitante. They speak Cofan and Spanish is their second language, but English is not understood. This is off-the-beaten-path tourism and not for those expecting any comfort.

A good one-day trip is from Dureno to the Río Pisuri. Although you won't see much wildlife, jungle plants will be shown and explained to you. Ask questions! For a longer trip ask to be taken to the Río Cuyabeno where there is a wildlife reserve, although there has been some colonisation there, too.

An American missionary family work in

the village – although they don't arrange trips for travellers they can be of assistance in an emergency.

You can look for Cofans in Lago Agrio at weekends. They are there to sell their handicrafts and to do some shopping, so look for them around the market area. They often wear their distinctive traditional clothing (described under Lago Agrio) and are easy to spot. Ask them if you could join them after the Sunday morning market when they return to Dureno – they will then be able to show you where to get off the bus and you can cross the river with them.

FLOTEL ORELLANA

This large, flat-bottomed river boat has three decks and 20 double cabins, each with private bath and hot water. The *Flotel* cruises the Río Aguarico in the sections close to the Peruvian border and provides a comfortable base from which to tour the region. These tours are operated by Metropolitan Touring, Ecuador's biggest travel agency, and the prices are commensurate with this. Bilingual naturalist guides accompany the boat to explain the wildlife and surroundings. Day trips to shore are taken in dugout canoes and short nature hikes (often on boardwalks) and canoe rides on a lake are part of the adventure. An optional overnight in a rustic lakeside lodge can be arranged. Otherwise nights are spent in relative luxury aboard the *Flotel*, which provides good food, a bar and lectures about the jungle. Metropolitan Touring is taking an increasingly active role in promoting responsible ecotourism, using local guides, trying to minimise impact on the environment and culture of the region, and educating their passengers about the rainforest. I have heard good reports about the tours.

Voyages on the *Flotel* are for three or four nights and are all-inclusive from Quito (you arrive and leave by air via Tarapoa or Lago Agrio, included in the price). The three-night trip is from Tuesday to Friday and costs US$395 per person (double occupancy) or US$595 for a single. The four-night trip is from Friday to Tuesday and costs US$485 per person (double occupancy) or US$730 for a single.

Full information can be had from Metropolitan Touring (☎ 560 550/801, fax 564 655), PO Box 17-12-0310, Quito, Ecuador. The street address is Avenida Amazonas 239, Quito.

ZABALO

This is a small Cofan community on the Río Aguarico near the confluence of the Aguarico with the smaller Río Zabalo.

Randy Borman, born and raised in the Oriente as the son of American missionaries, lives at Zabalo with his Cofan wife and family. He speaks and lives as a Cofan and guides occasional groups on excursions into the jungle. Metropolitan Touring's *Flotel* sometimes makes a stop here. For an exceptional in-depth jungle expedition with the Cofans (where you sleep in Indian-style huts, bathe in the river, travel by foot or in dugout canoes) you can contact Randy through Wilderness Travel (☎ (415) 548 0420, or toll-free (800) 247 6700), 801 Allston Way, Berkeley, CA 94710, USA.

A 16-day tour of Ecuador, including nine days with the Cofans, costs about US$2100 and is limited to 10 participants.

TARAPOA

This oil centre, about 85 km by road east of Lago Agrio, is Ecuador's newest boom town. At this time there's nothing to do except see the nearby oil works, but Tarapoa is a possible jumping-off point for visiting the Reserva Producción Faunísta Cuyabeno, heading to the (rarely used) border crossing into Colombia, or joining a tour on the *Flotel*. There is a guard station for the Cuyabeno in Tarapoa. There are two basic places to stay.

Getting There & Away

Air Since the mid-1980s, TAME have had morning flights from Quito to Tarapoa on Wednesday and Friday. Since the *Flotel* began operating on the Río Aguarico in 1991, flights have been added on Tuesday. Whether the Wednesday flight will now be eliminated remains to be seen. Check with TAME. Flights leave Quito at 7.15 am and return from Tarapoa to Quito at 8.30 am. The fare is US$13.50 one way. If you are unable to fly to Lago Agrio, a flight to Tarapoa may be an alternative.

Bus There are several buses a day to Lago Agrio (US$1; 2½ hours).

RESERVA PRODUCCIÓN FAUNÍSTA CUYABENO

This reserve covers 254,760 hectares of rainforest around the Río Cuyabeno, between the Río Aguarico and the Río San Miguel in north-eastern Ecuador. The reserve was created in 1979 with the goals of protecting this area of rainforest, conserving its wildlife, and providing a sanctuary in which the traditional inhabitants of the area, the Siona and Secoya Indians, could lead their customary way of life. There are several lakes and swamps in Cuyabeno and some of the most interesting animals found here are aquatic species such as freshwater dolphins, manatees, caiman, and anaconda. Monkeys abound, and tapirs, peccaries, agoutis, and several cat species have been recorded. The birdlife is prolific.

Its protected status notwithstanding, Cuyabeno was opened to oil exploitation almost immediately after its creation. The new oil towns of Tarapoa and Cuyabeno have been built on tributaries of the Río Cuyabeno and both these towns and segments of the trans-Ecuadorian oil pipeline are within the reserve boundaries. Roads have been built, colonists have followed, and tens of thousands of hectares of the reserve have now been logged or degraded by spills of oil and toxic waste.

At least six oil spills were recorded between 1984 and 1989, and others went by unnoticed. Many of the spills find their way into the Río Cuyabeno itself, which is precisely the river basin that the preserve was supposed to protect.

Cuybeno and Yasuní are the only two legally protected areas of lowland rainforest in the Ecuadorian Oriente. Although Ecuador needs what revenue it can get from oil, it is very disturbing to think that both Cuyabeno and Yasuní are severely threatened by oil exploitation.

Various international and local agencies are working to protect these areas which, although legally protected, are in reality open to development. Conservation International is funding projects to establish more guard stations in Cuyabeno, to train local Siona and Secoya Indians to work in wildlife management, and to support CORDAVI, an Ecuadorian environmental law group which is challenging the legality of allowing oil exploitation in protected areas.

One effect of the building of a road through the reserve is that it has now become a tourist destination. It is quite easy to visit the reserve without being aware of the problems facing it. Some areas of the reserve remain relatively untouched, but with the fast rate of development in the region, it is difficult to foresee how long even parts of the reserve will remain protected.

It is interesting to see how MAG, which is the government body charged with overseeing the reserve, manages to remain apparently oblivious of the oil development in the midst of the protected area. An informative leaflet published in 1991 by MAG's Division of Natural Areas and Wildlife urges the visitor: 'We must contribute to a national ecological conscience!'

They list 10 rules for visiting Cuyabeno. The number one rule is 'Put litter in its place'. Other rules include: avoid getting lost, do not molest the wildlife, do not make unnecessary noise, do not damage the trees, and inform the authorities of any 'irregularities'. Yet the leaflet makes no mention whatsoever of the oil exploitation and colonisation within the reserve!

Several tour companies in Quito offer tours of Cuyabeno. These go beyond the colonised areas and do give a chance at seeing some of the wildlife, such as monkeys and freshwater dolphins.

One company is Nuevo Mundo Expeditions (☎ 552 617/816, fax 552 916), PO Box 402-A, Quito, Ecuador. Their street address is Amazonas 2468, Quito. Their tours are among the best, well-informed, with a conservationist attitude and professionally led by bilingual guides. They are not cheap, however – a five-day/four-night tour with three nights of camping in the reserve costs about US$700 per person (four minimum) all inclusive from Quito.

Etnotur (☎ 230 552, 564 465) at Luis Cordero 1313 and J L Mera, Quito, also arrange tours to Cuyabeno, and are not quite as expensive. Several other companies in Quito offer cheaper tours, but check carefully that they offer you the type of experience that you are after.

It is possible to visit Cuyabeno independently. Entry to the reserve costs US$10 per person (less for Ecuadorians). There is a guard post in Tarapoa where you can pay the fee and ask for information. There is also a post at the mouth of the Río Cuyabeno (where it flows into the Río Aguarico). The area known as Lagunas Grandes, in the middle of the reserve, is the most frequently visited. Here, there are two simple shelters built for overnight stays (bring a hammock or sleeping bag). An administration centre is planned (that may be years away).

From Tarapoa, a bus heading to Tipishca can drop you at the Río Tarapoa bridge, about two km north of the 'Y de Cuyabeno' which itself is a few km north of Tarapoa. Dugout canoes can be hired to take you along the Río Tarapoa to the lakes known as the Lagunas Grandes – about three to four hours of river travel. Ask in Tarapoa about this entry route, which is the most frequently used to visit the reserve.

An alternate route to the Lagunas Grandes is to go back from Tarapoa to Chiritza on the Río Aguarico. From here you can hire a dugout canoe down the Río Aguarico to the mouth of the Río Cuyabeno, about a day away depending on how fast your canoe goes. There is a military guard post here where you could sleep (make sure your papers are in order). Then head upriver to the

lagunas, several hours away. En route to the lagunas you pass through the Siona village of Puerto Bolívar. The Sionas are becoming increasingly involved in guiding visitors to the area.

In the mid to late 1980s, Cuyabeno received an average of about 150 registered visitors annually, according to MAG records. This included both Ecuadorian and foreign visitors travelling in organised groups or independently. Most visitors come during the wetter months of March to September. In the less rainy months, river levels may be too low to allow easy navigation. Annual rainfall is between 2000 and 4000 mm depending on location, humidity is often between 90 and 100%. Be prepared with sun protection, rain gear, insect repellent, water purification tablets and food. If travelling independently, don't expect anything to run on schedule!

As we go to press I am informed that, in late 1991, Cuyabeno's boundaries were extended westward almost to the Peruvian border and the reserve has increased in size by some 400,000 hectares. Ecotourism is becoming increasingly important and local native communities and agencies from Quito are competing keenly for a slice of the new tourist trade.

SAN RAFAEL FALLS & VOLCÁN REVENTADOR

The road west of Lago Agrio roughly follows the Río Aguarico for some 50 km before turning south-west and beginning the long climb up into the Andes by following the valley of the Río Quijos. There are two major landmarks on this ascent. On the left of the road, some 95 km from Lago Agrio, are the San Rafael Falls (also called the Coca Falls), about 145 metres high and the biggest in Ecuador.

To the right of the road is the 3485-metre Volcán Reventador, which means 'the exploder' and which had a period of major activity in the late 1970s. Unfortunately, it's obscured by cloud more often than not.

You can glimpse the San Rafael Falls briefly from the road. To see them properly, get off the bus just beyond the bridge crossing Río Reventador, at a concrete-block hut with an INECEL sign on the left of the road. Make sure you get off the bus at the Río Reventador and not at the bigger community of Reventador which is about 20 km away in the direction of Lago Agrio. A new metal bridge has been built by Río Reventador and a correspondent writes that the bridge has a plaque proclaiming *Obra de Norman* meaning 'Norman's Work'.

From the INECEL hut it's about 2½ km down a steep track to the falls. You pass through the INECEL (Ecuadorian Electric Company) camp near the top. There used to be a jeep track, but that was destroyed by the 1987 earthquake and now there is just a foot trail. You can camp within sight of the falls. The caretaker of the INECEL camp may allow you to sleep there if you get stuck – but don't rely on it. Once back on the road, flag a bus down when you want to go on, and be prepared to wait, as buses are sometimes full.

Just north of the Río Reventador bridge there are a couple of houses and just north of here there is a trail that climbs up Volcán Reventador, on the north-west side of the road. It is hard to find the beginning of the trail and there are various confusing little paths, so you should ask anyone you see (there are very few people around here). After a few minutes, the trail crosses the river and about half an hour later the trail goes through a grove of palm trees. Beyond that there is only one trail to the summit, but it is steep and slippery in places. There is almost no water and the climb takes two days – only for experienced hikers with plenty of extra water bottles and camping gear. Technical climbing is not involved.

This area is within the eastern boundaries of **Reserva Ecológica Cayambe-Coca**, described in the North of Quito chapter. There are no signs or entrance stations. There is reportedly a guard station in the village of **El Chaco** about 20 km beyond the Río Reventador bridge on the way to Baeza. In El Chaco there are a couple of very basic residenciales.

Bus drivers on the Lago Agrio-Quito run

usually know the San Rafael Falls, but few of them know about the Río Reventador bridge or climbing the volcano. So ask about the falls, even if you plan on climbing Reventador.

BAEZA

Beyond Río Reventador the road continues climbing, following the trans-Ecuadorian oil pipeline and the Río Quijos all the way. There are enchanting views of beautiful cloudforest full of strange species of birds and plants. Several small communities with little to recommend them are passed, and Baeza is reached after 170 km from Lago Agrio and six hours.

Baeza is on the junction with the road to Tena and is the most important village between Lago Agrio and Quito. It was an old Spanish missionary and trading outpost, having been first founded in 1548 and refounded three more times since. The pass from Baeza via Papallacta to the Quito valley was known well before the conquest, but the road from Baeza to Lago Agrio has been opened only by the oil boom, so Baeza is both a historical and geographical junction. It is also recommended as a good, quiet and inexpensive spot to stay for walks in the surrounding hills. The plants of the Andean foothills and the bird life are outstanding.

Places to Stay & Eat

Facilities are very limited. There is a petrol station, basic hotel, and restaurant in the *Oro Negro* complex at the junction of the road going to Tena. About two km away from the junction, heading towards Tena, the village of Baeza proper is reached. Here, there is the basic but clean *Hotel Samay* which charges about US$1 a night. The *Hostería El Nogal de Jumandy* is also clean, charges US$1 per night, and has hot showers for an extra US$0.25. There are a couple of simple restaurants. If the hotels are full (very unusual as Baeza is a small town) you can go down to the village of **Borja**, about four km from the Baeza junction towards Lago Agrio, which also has a basic pensión.

Getting There & Away

There are no bus stations in these villages. You must flag down passing buses and hope that they have room. Buses to and from Lago Agrio, Tena and Quito pass through regularly. If coming from one of these towns, you may find that bus companies will only sell you a ticket for the whole journey (eg Lago Agrio-Quito). If you don't want to pay full price, you have to jump on the bus just after it leaves the terminal, hope you can get a seat, and pay the driver a pro-rated fare.

PAPALLACTA

The westbound road from Baeza continues climbing steadily for some 40 km until the village of Papallacta. About 1½ km beyond the village, on the right as you head to Quito, are the Aguas Termales or natural hot springs of Papallacta. There is a pool but the springs are not overly developed and their setting is grand; on a clear day you can see the snow-capped Antisana (5704 metres) about 15 km to the south. The hottest spring is very hot, and there's a refreshing cold plunge pool. It costs about US$0.20 to get in, and changing rooms and toilet facilities are provided, but nothing else. There is a small café on the premises. The setting is beautiful, the pools are clean, and there are very few visitors midweek, although a few Quiteños may arrive at weekends. Papallacta is a nice place to relax and soak away the aches and pains of a jungle expedition.

Quito is only 60 km away, but the drive is difficult and spectacular. The road climbs over the Eastern Cordillera of the Andes via a pass which is nearly 4100 metres in height, and sometimes snow covered. This pass is literally the rim of the Amazon basin. If you're driving up from the Oriente, be prepared for the cold. Beyond the pass is the valley of Quito.

Places to Stay & Eat

It's possible to camp by the springs. Otherwise there is a small, basic, unsigned residencial (well, there is a 'Tome Coca Cola' sign) in Papallacta itself. The people are friendly and rooms are US$1.10 per night. The owners will cook for you on request, but there are also a couple of small restaurants in town.

Getting There & Away

To get to Papallacta from Quito isn't straightforward. Most bus companies going to Tena or Lago Agrio will sell tickets for the entire journey only. You have to wait until departure time and then hop onto the bus and buy a pro-rated ticket from the driver. Unfortunately, the buses are often full (that's why they didn't want to sell you a ticket for such a short distance in the first place) and even if they're not, some drivers will charge you the full price to Lago Agrio, because 'that's what this company does'. One company which can be persuaded to sell you tickets to Papallacta is Centinela del Norte.

There are four local buses a day leaving Papallacta for Quito (US$0.90).

The Western Lowlands

A physical map of Ecuador shows the country divided neatly into two by the massive range of the Andes. To the east lie the jungles of the upper Amazon basin, and to the west you find the coastal lowlands. The western drop of the Andes is dramatic and steeper than the eastern side. Lowlands of below 300 metres are soon reached; from Ecuador's highest peak (Chimborazo at 6310 metres) it is only 50 km due west to the 300-metre contour, a gradient of about 12%. It does not stay low all the way to the coast, however. After dropping to almost sea level, the land rises again in a barren, scrubby and almost uninhabited range of 700-metre-high hills before dropping to the coast. Thus the coastal lowlands are subdivided into the coast itself, west of the coastal hills, and the flat lowlands lying east of the hills and west of the Andes. It is the latter which are described in this chapter. In addition, the descent down the steep western slopes of the Andes is also described here.

The western lowlands were once forested, but well over 90% of these forests have now been cleared to develop banana plantations and other forms of agriculture, predominantly cacao and African oil palm. The forests that used to exist here were very different from those found in the Oriente – indeed, botanists estimate that about half the species which used to grow in these western Andean slopes and lowlands were found nowhere else! Almost no forest is left in the flat lowlands but, in the more difficult to reach areas of the steep western slopes of the Andes, a few areas have become belatedly protected, thus preserving small parts of a unique ecosystem which is on the verge of disappearing from the globe. The small Reserva Biológica Maquipucuna, the Río Palenque Science Center and a couple of other private reserves are included in this chapter. The much larger **Reserva Ecológica Cotacachi-Cayapas** protects some of the northern parts of the western

lowlands, but access is very difficult from here. Cotacachi-Cayapas can be more easily accessed from the area North of Quito and from the North Coast, and so it is described under those chapters.

Some travellers think of Ecuador as a 'banana republic' – one of those tropical countries that produce bananas and little else. Indeed, until the export of oil began in 1972, bananas were Ecuador's most important product and they remain the country's major agricultural export.

Fortunately for agriculturalists and the Ecuadorian economy, the western lowlands are fertile and huge banana and palm tree plantations are seen by travellers through this area. It has not been developed much for tourists, and many people rush through it on their way to the coast or highlands. If you're interested in seeing some of the tropical 'banana republic' Ecuador – the kind of countryside that was typically Ecuadorian before the recent oil boom – then it is worth taking a couple of days to travel slowly through this area instead of rushing through.

MINDO
This is a small and infrequently visited village about three or four hours drive west of Quito. It is at about 1300 metres elevation and has an area of premontane forest nearby. A local private group is trying to preserve the area, which is very beautiful and excellent for birdwatching. Beyond Mindo, the poor road drops further to San Miguel de los Bancos (locally called Los Bancos), shortly

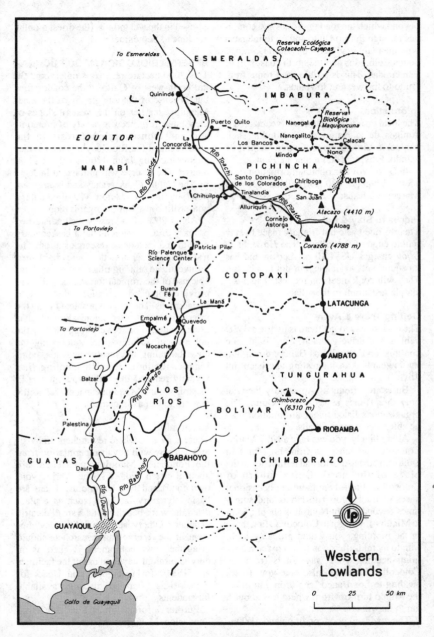

Western
Lowlands

0   25   50 km

beyond which the road improves and continues through Puerto Quito and on to intersect with the main road between Santo Domingo de los Colorados and the north coast port of Esmeraldas. This is a little used route from Quito to the western lowlands.

Information

The local group trying to preserve the area is Amigos de la Naturaleza – Mindo. Their contact is Vinicio Perez, Correo Central de Mindo, Provincia de Pichincha, Ecuador.

In Quito, you can obtain information from Tierra Viva (☎ 230 746), Italia 832 and Mariana de Jesús.

Places to Stay & Eat

There is one basic but friendly place to stay on the edge of the village. The *Hostería El Bijou* charges US$1.10 per person and has mosquito nets available, but not much else. They will cook meals on request. There is a simple restaurant in the village.

Getting There & Away

The easiest way to get there is to hire a 4WD vehicle and drive yourself. You could then continue on through Los Bancos down into the lowlands – an interesting and beautiful drive.

Buses are infrequent. Apparently, they run only three times a week from Quito. The organisations listed under information may be able to give more details.

Alternatively, you can take a No 7 Marin-Cotocollao which goes from La Marin in Quito, up 10 de Agosto, and terminates in the plaza of the north Quito suburb of Cotocollao. From here there are occasional buses or trucks going to Nono, and sometimes beyond. From Nono it is about 55 km to Mindo – if you got to Cotocollao first thing in the morning, you would probably be in Mindo by mid-afternoon if you rode on anything heading your way. Taxis from the Cotocollao Plaza can also take you. Buses heading to Los Bancos can drop you off at the Mindo turn-off from where it is about 8 km to the village.

The road is in poor condition and 4WD is advised in the wet months (the driest months are June to September).

RESERVA BIOLÓGICA MAQUIPUCUNA

This 3000-hectare reserve is only about 30 km north-west of Quito as the condor flies but, because of the topography of the land, Maquipucuna lies on the western slopes of the Andes. It protects a variety of premontane and montane cloudforests in the headwaters of the Río Guayllabamba at elevations ranging from 1200 to about 2800 metres. The reserve was purchased in 1987 by The Nature Conservancy and is administered by the Fundación Maquipucuna, a non-profit conservation organisation.

About 80% of the reserve is undisturbed primary forest – the remainder is secondary growth and includes a research station. The reserve and research station were established to investigate, among other things, sustainable use of the tropical forests, as well as to provide some conservation education to Ecuadorians. The biggest problem facing the reserve is uncontrolled colonisation which is often condoned or actively supported by the government. Colonists are deforesting the areas bounding the reserve and this, combined with indiscriminate hunting, has severely reduced the plants and animals in the area around Maquipucuna, as well as the western lowlands in general.

Information

There is a cabin where researchers and visitors can stay with advance permission from the Fundación Maquipucuna. There are about a dozen beds, a kitchen (bring your own food) and two bathrooms. There are basic laboratory facilities, such as a plant drier and work benches, and a small electric generator. Otherwise there is little development in the reserve and researchers should bring their own equipment. A guard is on duty. Overnight stays and use of the facilities are US$10 for foreigners and US$5 for Ecuadorians. There are discounts available for students.

Further information is available from Fundación Maquipucuna (☎ 235 736, fax

504 571), San Ignacio 739 and Orellana, Quito, or write to Casilla 17-12-167, Quito, Ecuador. Preliminary plant lists (about 2000 species) and bird lists (about 250 species) have been prepared by Ecuadorian, Latin American, North American, and British workers. A more complete plant inventory is currently being written. Several conservation workshops have been held, some in collaboration with the University of California Research Expeditions Program or with the US Peace Corps. These have been aimed particularly at the local people. This education, inventory, and research work is urgently in need of financial support – all contributions are welcomed at the address above.

Getting There & Away

A bus from Quito's Cotocollao Plaza leaves at 12.30 pm daily for Nanegalito and on to Nanegal (2½ hours). Shortly before Nanegal, at a place locally called 'Las Delicias', you get off the bus and walk on the road to your right for about 1½ hours to the reserve. At Las Delicias there is a country store and a 'Departamento Forestal' sign.

If you are driving, head west of Quito via the Mindo road. About 30 km past Nono, turn right to the village of Nanegalito about eight km away and continue about 12 km to Las Delicias. The reserve cabin is about 7 km away by very bad road, so 4WD is recommended.

You can also reach Nanegalito from the village of Calacalí, which is about eight km beyond the Mitad del Mundo monument. From Calacalí it is about 31 km to Nanegalito.

Hitchhiking is possible but there is very little traffic indeed.

THE OLD ROAD TO SANTO DOMINGO

This little used gravel road is an alternate route to Santo Domingo de los Colorados – one that is a favourite of birders who like to spend the entire day driving and birding the 55 or 60 km from Quito until the new main road to Santo Domingo is reached. The trans-Ecuadorian pipeline follows the old road and

thus it is kept in reasonably good shape. Few vehicles travel along it, however, and so it gives an easy look at relatively undisturbed premontane habitat as the road drops from over 3000 metres to 1200 metres above sea level. You have to have your own transport.

To get onto this road, head south on the highway on the west side of Quito, Avenida Occidental, continue under the tunnels, through the one-way system on the west side of the old town, and out on Avenida Vencedores de Pichincha. About half a km before the end of this road, just beyond a CEPE petrol station, the old road to Santo Domingo de los Colorados goes to the right.

There are a few villages along the road but nowhere to stay. You should bring some food. The first village to ask for is San Juan, about 10 km out of Quito. After this, ask for Chiriboga, the half way point on the road and the largest village. Once you are beyond San Juan, it's hard to get lost. A few km beyond Chiriboga, you cross the Río Guajalito. Reportedly, the **Reserva Río Guajalito** is near here – a small reserve with mixed pasture, secondary growth, and virgin forest. Dr Jaramillo of the botany department at the Catholic University in Quito is a contact for the area.

THE MAIN ROAD TO SANTO DOMINGO

The most frequently used route from the highlands to the western lowlands is the main road from Quito to Santo Domingo de los Colorados. From Santo Domingo you can head south, through Quevedo and Babahoyo in the lowland province of Los Ríos, to Guayaquil on the coast. This is the travellers' route I follow in the rest of this chapter.

From Quito, the bus heads south through the 'Avenue of the Volcanoes' to Aloag, where the road to Santo Domingo branches off from the Panamerican Highway. The bus often refuels here and is surrounded by hordes of snack sellers lustily hawking their delicacies. *Aziuuuzias!* is a frequently heard cry as these dry biscuits are usually sold here.

The descent into the lowlands is a spectacular and sometimes terrifying one. It is best to make the journey in the morning, as in the afternoon both the passengers' and the driver's views are often obscured by fog. Despite almost nonexistent visibility, the drivers hurtle down the western slopes of the Andes at breakneck speeds. Amazingly, accidents are very rare but near misses somewhat more common.

The road begins in high páramo, with views of the extinct volcanoes Atacazo and Corazón to the north and south. The tortuous descent follows the left bank of the Río Pilatón and occasionally waterfalls cascade into the narrow gorge. The road passes the village of Cornejo Astorga (also known as Tandapi) and follows the Río Toachi valley. The vegetation starts becoming increasingly tropical and if you're lucky you may see orchids growing on the side of the road. The higher temperatures are noticeable by the time you pull into the village of Alluriquín.

Both **Cornejo Astorga** and **Alluriquín** have basic hotels and restaurants; the best of these is the *Hotel Florida* in Alluriquín, but few travellers stay in these villages. They seem to be overnight stops for truck drivers doing the long slow haul from the lowlands up to Quito.

TINALANDIA

About 16 km before Santo Domingo is a famous hotel run by Señora Tina Garzón, who emigrated to Ecuador from Russia many years ago. The hotel is called, appropriately enough, *Tinalandia* and is the haunt of birdwatchers and naturalists. There is a nine-hole golf course next to the hotel, but otherwise the extensive grounds have been left largely undisturbed except for a few nature trails.

The birdwatching is excellent and Tinalandia boasts a list of more than 150 sub-tropical species. It is definitely worthwhile if you have an interest in ornithology. The vegetation is premontane wet forest at an elevation of about 600 metres.

The accommodation is in a number of bungalows and cabins and is comfortable with private baths and hot showers in all rooms. There is a restaurant serving meals which have been described as mediocre to excellent – but there is nowhere else to eat so you have to take what they give you. Rates are US$48/80 for singles/doubles including three meals. The hotel is sometimes booked by birdwatching groups so you have to take your chances. There is no telephone so to make a reservation write to Tinalandia, Santo Domingo de los Colorados, Provincia de Pichincha, Ecuador. Major travel agencies in Ecuador can make reservations for you and these are recommended in the driest months of May and June, which are particularly popular with birders. You can make day visits to the grounds for US$3.

Tinalandia is about 86 km after turning off the Panamerican Highway in Aloag. There is a small stone sign on the right side of the road as you drive from Quito, and the hotel itself is about half a km up a track on the left side of the road. If you are on a bus to Santo Domingo, ask the driver to let you off at Tinalandia – all the drivers know it.

Shortly before reaching Santo Domingo you pass an oil pressure station. The road has been following the trans-Ecuadorian oil pipeline for the last third of its distance. If your bus is continuing beyond Santo Domingo it may avoid the town altogether because there are a couple of bypasses; normally, however, even long-distance buses pull into the town for a break.

SANTO DOMINGO DE LOS COLORADOS

Santo Domingo de los Colorados, as the town is officially known, is one of the fastest growing cities in Ecuador and the population has surpassed 100,000. Santo Domingo is important as a road hub: major roads head north, south, east and west. At only 500 metres above sea level and just 130 km from Quito, this is the nearest lowland tropical town easily accessible from the capital and hence it is a popular weekend destination for Quiteños.

Colorado Indians

The town used to be famous for the Colorado Indians who painted their faces with black stripes and dyed their bowl-shaped haircuts

Colorado Indian Man

a brilliant red using achiote. You can buy postcards of them all over Ecuador, but the Indians are now fairly westernised and you are unlikely to see them in their traditional finery except by going to one of their nearby villages and paying them to dress up. Photographers are expected to give 'tips' but the Colorados are becoming increasingly unhappy with their role as models for foreign photographers. Please be sensitive to this.

The best known Colorado village is **Chihuilpe**, about seven km south of Santo Domingo on the road to Quevedo and then about three km east on a dirt road. Some of the older Indians, notably the headman Abraham Calazacon (who died in the 1980s) and his brother Gabriel, built up reputations as *curanderos* (medicine men) and people still come from all over Ecuador to be cured. The present *gobernador* (headman) is Abraham's son, Nicanor Calazacon, who continues the traditional work of a curandero. Nearby, the house of Augusto Calazacon is a tourist centre and Augusto will dress traditionally for photographers. He charges a US$4 fee.

There are other Colorado villages in the area south of Santo Domingo but, for the most part, the villagers prefer to be left alone. Apart from the tourist centre in Chihuilpe, I do not recommend visits to see the Colorados. A taxi from Santo Domingo to Chihuilpe will cost about US$15 for a two to three-hour trip.

Information
Because Sunday is the main market day, the town closes down on Monday. There are the usual IETEL and post offices, and the Banco Internacional (open Tuesday to Saturday) will exchange US dollars at rates surprisingly close to Quito's.

Things to See & Do
Santo Domingo is a convenient city in which to make bus connections or break a long journey. There are lively street markets (see map) and a busy Sunday market, but otherwise it's not a particularly interesting town. There are two cinemas.

The Río Toachi is nearby and city buses go there. Just across the river is a resort village with a few restaurants, a swimming pool (you may prefer to swim in the river), and some games courts.

Santo Domingo is the capital of its cantón and celebrates its cantonisation day on 3 July. There are street fairs and an Industrial & Agricultural Festival – the town and the hotels are quite crowded then.

Places to Stay
Apart from the 3 July celebrations, weekends are also crowded, both with shoppers at the Sunday market and with weekend visitors from Quito. You will have a better choice of hotels mid-week. Most of the cheaper hotels have only cold water in the showers and don't look up to much.

Places to Stay – bottom end
There are many extremely basic hotels near the main square and bus terminal areas. The *Residencial Astoria* (☎ 750 080) and the *Pensión Guayaquil*, on or near the plaza, are extremely basic and cheap – about US$1 per person. For about US$1.25 per person try the

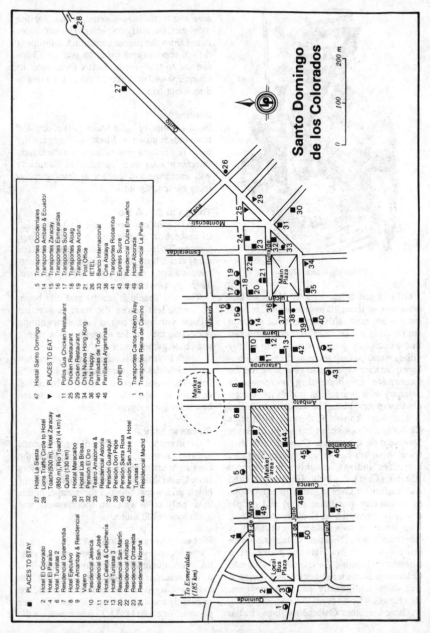

Santo Domingo de los Colorados

0   100   200 m

PLACES TO STAY

- 2 Hotel El Colorado
- 4 Hotel El Paraíso
- 6 Hotel Turistas 2
- 7 Residencial Groenlandia
- 8 Hotel Ejecutivo
- 9 Hotel Amanbay & Residencial Viajero
- 10 Residencial Jessica
- 11 Residencial San José
- 12 Hotel Caleta & Cebichería
- 13 Hotel Turistas 3
- 20 Residencial San Martín
- 22 Residencial Ambato
- 23 Residencial Ontaneda
- 24 Residencial Noroña
- 27 Hotel La Siesta
- 28 Lions Traffic Circle to Hotel Toachi (500 m), Hotel Zaracay (850 m), Río Toachi (4 km) & Quito (130 km)
- 30 Hostal Maracaibo
- 31 Hostal Las Brisas
- 32 Pensión El Oro
- 35 Teatro Amazonas & Residencial Astoria
- 37 Pensión Guayaquil
- 39 Pensión Don Pepe
- 40 Pensión Santa Rosa
- 42 Pensión San Jose & Hotel Turistas 1
- 44 Residencial Madrid
- 47 Hostal Santo Domingo

▼ PLACES TO EAT

- 11 Pollos Gus Chicken Restaurant
- 25 Chicken Restaurant
- 29 Chicken Restaurant
- 34 Chifa Nueva Hong Kong
- 36 Chifa Happy
- 45 Parrilladas de Toño
- 46 Parrilladas Argentinas

OTHER

- 1 Transportes Carlos Alberto Aray
- 3 Transportes Reina del Camino
- 5 Transportes Occidentales
- 14 Transportes Ambato & Ecuador
- 15 Transportes Zaracay
- 16 Transportes Esmeraldas
- 17 Transportes Sucre
- 18 Transportes Aloag
- 19 Transportes Andina
- 26 Post Office
- 33 Banco Internacional
- 38 Cine Atalaya
- 41 Transportes Riobamba
- 43 Express Sucre
- 48 Residencial Dulce Ensueños
- 49 Hotel Alborada
- 50 Residencial La Peria

To Esmeraldas (185 km)

Quito

slightly better *Pensión San José* or the *Residencial Noroña* which has good-sized, clean rooms close to the buses. The similarly priced *Residencial Ambato* around the corner is OK. Also at this price, the *Residencial San José* has some rooms with private bath.

The *Residencial Ontaneda* charges US$1.80 per person but is not much better than the cheaper places, though the 'matrimonial' rooms (US$3.60 double in one bed) boast a private shower. Right across from the bus offices is the clean and helpful *Residencial San Martín*, but make sure your room doesn't face the buses. They charge US$1.50 per person and this is a good budget choice. Other reasonable places in this price range are the *Hotel Ejecutivo* (☎ 751 943, 752 893) at US$1.25 per person or US$2.50 per person with private bathroom and the *Residencial La Perla* which charges US$1.80 per person with private bath. It is clean but often full. The *Hotel Turistas 1, 2, & 3* claim to have hot water but are fairly basic hotels at US$1.80 per person.

Other cheapies include the *Hotel El Paraíso, Hotel Amambay, Residencial Viajero, Pensión El Oro, Hostal Maracaibo, Pensión Don Pepe, Residencial Madrid, Pensión Santa Rosa, Residencial Groenlandia* and *Hotel Alborada*. No, I didn't check them out.

A little upmarket is the *Hostal Las Brisas* (☎ 750 560) at US$2 per person, or US$3.50 with private bath. *Hostal Santo Domingo* (☎ 754 078) at Avenida Quito 715 and Cuenca, is clean and charges US$2.50 per person with private bath. *Hotel Caleta* (☎ 750 277) at Ibarra 137 and 3 de Julio, is clean and pleasant and charges US$3.50 per person in rooms with private baths. They have a reasonable restaurant. *Hotel El Colorado* (☎ 750 226, 754 299) at 29 de Mayo and Quinindé, is huge and has simple clean rooms with private baths (cold water) for about US$3 per person. The new *Residencial Jessica* looks quite good for US$3.50/5.50 for singles/ doubles with bath. The *Residencial Dulce Ensueños* has hot water in its private bathrooms and charges US$4 per

person. The *Hotel La Siesta* (☎ 751 860/013, 750 013) at Quito 606 and Guayaquil on the outskirts of town has nice gardens. They charge a reasonable US$3 per person with bath.

Places to Stay – middle

Continuing out along Avenida Quito, you'll come to the two best hotels in town. First is the *Hotel Toachi* (☎ 750 316, 750 295), charging US$8/10/12 for spacious and clean singles/doubles/triples with private shower and hot water. There is a swimming pool and a restaurant.

Further out of town is the well-known *Hotel Zaracay* (☎ 750 316/023/429), which charges US$26 for a spacious double room with bath and balcony. The food is pricey but good and the rooms are in jungle-style cabins with thatched roofs. There are pleasant gardens and a swimming pool. They have a casino which is sometimes open.

Places to Eat

There are cheap and basic restaurants next to the bus offices but they don't have much except for the set meal – OK if you're in a hurry. There are plenty of inexpensive chifas; two good ones are on the main square (see the map). *Pollos Gus* is a plastic, clean, US-style fried chicken restaurant on Latacunga just off 29 de Mayo. At the east end of 29 de Mayo there are a couple of other cheap chicken places.

The *Hotel Caleta Cebichería* on Ibarra between 29 de Mayo and 3 de Julio has tables on the street – a good place for a snack and a cold beer as you watch the goings on. Meals are also available. *Parrilladas Argentinas* on Quito and Riobamba is a totally unpretentious steak house. There is no menu – it's a steak or nothing. The steaks are pretty good for about US$2 each. Just half a block away is the tonier *Parrilladas de Toño* with an upstairs dining balcony, good steaks and other food, a bar, and a live show and dancing at weekends – probably the best in town outside of the hotel restaurants.

Getting There & Around

Bus There is no central bus terminal. Several companies have offices around 29 de Mayo and Tulcán, and if you go to this area you'll find the drivers' assistants yelling out destinations and it's easy to find the bus you want. Quito (US$1.10; 2½ hours) and Guayaquil (US$1.90; five hours) are the most frequent destinations with buses leaving at least once an hour with various companies. Make sure you take a small buseta if you're in a hurry to get to Guayaquil, as the larger buses can take two hours longer. It's easy enough to get buses to intermediate points such as Quevedo or Daule, but if you want to go to Babahoyo you'll find fewer buses, as most southbound buses take the Daule road beyond Quevedo.

There are buses about every hour to Esmeraldas on the north coast (US$1.50; 3½ hours) with Transportes Esmeraldas and less frequently with Transportes Ambato. This journey could be broken at either **La Concordia** or **Quinindé** (officially Rosa Zárate), both of which have simple hotels but otherwise are of little interest.

If you're heading south to Peru and don't want to change at Guayaquil, try Transportes Occidentales at 29 de Mayo and Cuenca who have several departures a day to Machala (US$2.60; eight hours). Their buses are fairly slow but are large and reasonably comfortable.

Buses also go to the central coast but not as frequently as to Esmeraldas. Bahía de Caráquez (US$2.10; six hours) and Manta (US$2.30; seven hours) are both served by Transportes Reina del Camino, who have an office at the west end of town on 29 de Mayo and Quinindé. Across the street, Transportes Carlos Alberto Aray also have buses to Manta.

Express Sucre at Quito and Latacunga has five daily buses to Cuenca (US$3; 10 hours). Half a block away is Transportes Riobamba with 10 daily buses to Latacunga, Ambato and Riobamba (US$1.50; five hours).

There is a local bus plaza at the west end of Avenida 3 de Julio where you can find beat-up old bone-shakers to take you to nearby villages. It can be interesting to take one of these buses just to see the countryside, but make sure that there is a return bus, as these villages often don't have restaurants, let alone a place to stay. You can also find buses here returning to Quito via La Concordia and (San Miguel de) Los Bancos, an uncomfortable eight-hour ride, but with beautiful scenery.

Finally, the most useful city bus runs east along Avenida Quito and takes you past the hotels Toachi and Zaracay on the way to the Río Toachi swimming area. Take any bus marked 'Río Toachi'.

RÍO PALENQUE SCIENCE CENTER

This small preserve of 180 hectares contains about 100 hectares of primary rainforest. Although this is not a very large area, it is one of the largest tracts of western lowland forest left. It forms a habitat island and is surrounded by agricultural land. There are about 70 hectares of African oil palm plantation within the science center and more palm, banana, cacao and other crops are grown for many km around the center. The elevation is about 200 metres, and it is hot and humid for much of the year, particularly from December to July. It is drier for the rest of the year.

There are facilities for researchers within the center, which used to be operated by the University of Miami but is now privately owned. The center has a small library of books and papers relevant to the area and there are laboratory facilities. A flora checklist published in 1978 lists 1100 plants occurring at the center and of these about 100 species were new to science. This gives an indication of how important it is to preserve what little there is left of this unique habitat. Bird lists include over 360 species from the area and insect lists are equally impressive. Because of the small size of the preserve, however, there are no large mammals and few small ones present. Slowly, pressure from the surrounding agricultural lands is lowering the species counts for the science center – if a species dies out or leaves, it is unlikely to come back again.

There are about three km of trails at the center, and the birdwatching is excellent. A day use fee of US$3 is charged.

Places to Stay & Eat
The field station housing the laboratory and library also has six quadruple rooms, shower and toilet facilities, and an equipped kitchen. Accommodation is adequate but not luxurious. Rates are US$15 per person per night if you bring your own food or US$30 if you have the caretaker prepare meals for you. The nearest store is in the village of Patricia Pilar, about two km north of the entrance to the science center.

Reservations and information are available from Centro Científico Río Palenque (☎ 561 646), Casilla 95, Santo Domingo de los Colorados, Provincia de Pichincha, Ecuador. If the place is not full of researchers (which it usually isn't) you can just show up.

Getting There & Away
Río Palenque Research Center is just off the main Santo Domingo-Quevedo road, about 46 km south of Santo Domingo and 56 km north of Quevedo. If you are coming from Santo Domingo, you pass through the small village of Patricia Pilar about two km before reaching a sign 'Centro Científico Río Palenque' on the left. From here, there is a dirt road leading about 1½ km to the field station. The road is usually locked with a chain, but the caretaker has the key.

Any bus between Santo Domingo and Quevedo can drop you off or pick you up at the entrance road to the centre.

QUEVEDO
It's a little over 100 km from Santo Domingo to Quevedo on a gently dropping paved road. During the first 15 km you see frequent signs on the sides of the road advertising the homes of Colorado Indian curanderos (medicine men). This is where you go if you want to see them, but expect to pay for both cures and photography.

There are little villages about every 20 km along this road. The most important is the small market town of **Buena Fe**, about 15

km before Quevedo. Buena Fe has a couple of basic hotels on the main street. The land is agricultural with many banana plantations and, as you get closer to Quevedo, African palm and papaya groves. The palm is important for vegetable oil.

One of the first things I noticed in Quevedo was a strange smell, rather like stale beer. I thought there was a brewery in town but I was told that it was *tamarindo*, a brown, bean-like fruit popular in fruit juices. Quevedo, with about 80,000 inhabitants, is an important road hub and market town, and tamarindo and many other products pass through here. At only 145 metres above sea level, the town is hot but the mountains are not far away.

There are many hotels and it is a good place to break the journey from Latacunga to the coast, if you're going that way. For some reason, the Ecuadorian Chinese community has settled in this bustling and progressive town, so there are many good chifas and other Chinese-run businesses.

Information
There IETEL office is on 7 de Octubre at the south-east end of downtown. The post office is on the river side street, Malecón Eloy Alfaro, but it is poorly signposted and you can't tell it's there when it's closed. The Banco Internacional on 7 de Octubre and Quarta will change US dollars at a rate of some 3% less than Quito. Avenida 7 de Octubre is the main drag.

Things to See & Do
As you might expect in a growing market town, there are markets. The daily early morning produce market on the Malecón by the river is quite colourful and it's pleasant to walk along the river before it gets hot. The market at Septima and Progreso has plenty of plastic junk but also hammocks if you need one.

Quevedo is the capital of its cantón and celebrates its cantonisation on 7 October with street parades and a fair on the days preceding the 7th. Hotels are liable to be quite full then.

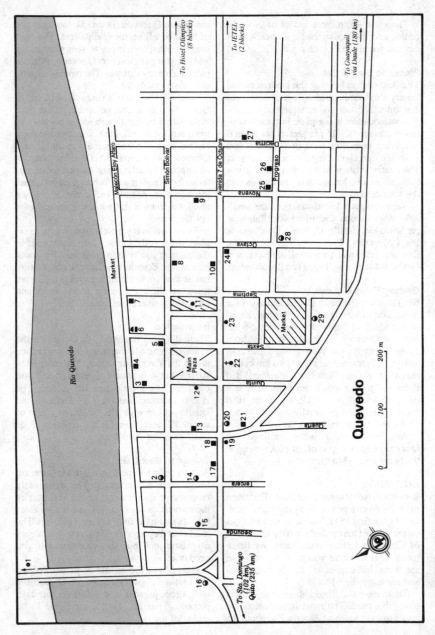

■ PLACES TO STAY

3 Pensión Patricia
4 Hotel El Condado
5 Residencial San Marcos
7 Hotel Imperial
8 Residencial Charito
9 Hotel Turistas
10 Hotel Continental
13 Hotel Guayaquil
17 Residencial Vilmita
18 Hotel Ejecutivo Continental
21 Residencial Mayrita
24 Pensión Azuay
25 Hotel Hilton
26 Pensíon Florida
27 Barra Bar & Residencial Familiar

OTHER

1 To Latacunga (177 km) &
  Guayaquil via Babahoyo
2 Flota Babahoyo Internacional
6 Post Office
11 Market
12 Cine Quevedo
14 Buses CIA to Guayaquil
15 Flota Bolívar (to Portoviejo)
16 Buses 'de paso' to Quito &
  Transportes Macuchi
18 Buses TIA to Guayaquil
19 Banco Internacional
20 Transportes Sucre (to Guayaquil &
  Santo Domingo)
22 Church
23 Cine Chan
28 Transportes Flor de Los Ríos
29 Transportes Cotopaxi (To Latacunga)

Places to Stay – bottom end

There are many cheap hotels in Quevedo but the half dozen or so I visited looked depressingly similar – peeling walls, a lumpy bed, a broken window or no window at all. Some of the rooms were marginally better than others, so it is worth asking to see another room if you don't like the first you look at. Many of the cheaper hotels suffer from water shortages so check that the water's running if you want to shower immediately. People often swim in the river.

For US$1.20 you can stay at the basic

Hotel Guayaquil, which also has some slightly more expensive rooms with private bath. For US$1.50 there is the *Residencial Vilmita* which is clean but nonetheless just your basic cell. The *Hotel Hilton* isn't bad for US$1.80 per person. Others in the US$1 to S$1.80 price range are the pensiones *Patricia, Azuay* and *Florida* and the residenciales *Charito, Familiar, San Marcos* and *Mayrita*, and the *Hotel Turistas* none of which look particularly enticing.

Even if you're on a tight budget it's worth checking out the clean *Hotel Imperial* by the river. The rooms all have private bathrooms (cold water) with soap and towel provided, and there are fans. Many of the rooms have river views (excellent view from the roof). It's very secure and you have to ring the bell to get in. They charge about US$2.25 per person. The *Hotel Condado* has rooms with private bathrooms for US$2.50 per person.

Places to Stay – middle

There are several slightly more expensive hotels. The *Hotel Ejecutivo Internacional* at 7 de Octubre and Quarta is quite good – all you international executive travellers can get spacious air-conditioned singles/doubles with private bath for a very reasonable US$5.50/9.50. The *Hotel Continental* at 7 de Octubre 713 charges US$4.50 per person but not all its rooms are air-conditioned.

Finally, on the eastern edge of town is the *Hotel Olimpico* on Calle 19 near Simón Bolívar. This is a tourist complex, complete with swimming pool, restaurant, bar etc and is the best place to stay. Rooms are around US$18 for a double with private bath.

Places to Eat

With its large Chinese community, Quevedo has plenty of chifas. There are several along Avenida 7 de Octubre.

Another cheap place to go is across the river. If you just keep going straight after the bridge, you'll be walking along Avenida Guayaquil which, after half a dozen blocks, makes a large Y. One arm goes to Latacunga and the other to Babahoyo. Between the bridge and the Y are dozens of restaurants, ranging from little street stands to bigger comedores and fish restaurants. There's a good choice of places, it's colourful, and it's worth a look.

The restaurant in the *Hotel Olimpico* has been recommended as the best in town.

Getting There & Away

Bus There is no central bus terminal so you have to roam the streets looking for the various terminals; the main ones are on the map. Quevedo is 180 km from Guayaquil by flat road and 235 km from Quito by mountainous road so it's not surprising that the bus situation heavily favours Guayaquil. In fact, there is only one company with direct buses to Quito (US$1.90; four hours). This is Transportes Macuchi at the north-western end of 7 de Octubre. Alternatively, stand at the town exit at the end of Avenida 7 de Octubre and wait for a bus *de paso* heading for Quito, or take one of the frequent Transportes Sucre buses to Santo Domingo where you can change to equally frequent buses to Quito.

Buses to Guayaquil (US$1.30) are very frequent and take from 2½ to four hours depending on the bus. All companies seem to have both large, slow buses and small, fast ones. Ask at Transportes Sucre, TIA and CIA companies, all on or near 7 de Octubre near Tercera and Quarta. These companies normally go via Daule. If you want to go via Babahoyo, you should go with FBI – which translates, inoffensively, into Flota Babahoyo Internacional and has an office at Simón Bolívar and Tercera.

Other bus companies you should know about are Transportes Cotopaxi and Flota Bolívar. The first runs seven buses a day to Latacunga, about seven hours by dirt road. The second has an 8 am and a 1 pm bus to Portoviejo, about five hours by dirt road. This route, from Latacunga via Quevedo to Portoviejo, is one of the least frequently travelled and also one of the prettiest highland-to-coast routes. The buses are old, crowded and uncomfortable but the journey more interesting than the standard routes.

Transportes Flor de los Ríos has local buses every hour to Mocache, a small agricultural community about 20 km south of Quevedo and off any main road.

Boat Although the Río Quevedo is wide and deep enough for boats and eventually runs into the Pacific at Guayaquil, there is little river traffic. It is much cheaper and more convenient to use the good road connections to the coast. A few dugouts chug up and down and there's usually a raft of bamboo logs floating through, but figure on using the bus to get anywhere.

SOUTH OF QUEVEDO

If your southbound bus crosses the Río Quevedo bridge, then you are going to Babahoyo; if it doesn't, then you are heading to Daule, which is the most frequent route to Guayaquil and described here.

About 20 km away from Quevedo you reach **Empalmé** – or Velasco Ibarra, as it's officially called. Here the road forks, westbound on a dirt road to Portoviejo and southbound on paved road to Guayaquil. Empalmé is a busy little junction town with several basic restaurants and pensiones. You're in the heart of banana country here and it continues that way to **Balzar**, another small market town with a basic hotel.

Near **Palestina** the banana plantations give way to rice paddies, and *piladoras* are frequently seen along the road. These are husking and drying factories with tons of rice spread out on huge concrete slabs to dry in the sun (assuming you're travelling in the dry season). Not everyone can afford the commercial piladoras and often you see a poor campesino spreading out his few bushels of rice to dry on the tarmac on the side of the road. In other areas, similar piladoras are used to dry various crops such as coffee.

About three quarters of the way to Guayaquil, you'll reach **Daule**. This is another small commercial and agricultural centre with basic hotels. You cross the Río Daule and though you can see a few outboard-powered dugouts, few people travel to Guayaquil that way, as it is prohibitively expensive compared to the bus. Three hours after leaving Quevedo, the bus gets to Guayaquil, Ecuador's major port and largest city, described in the chapter on the South Coast.

BABAHOYO

With about 45,000 inhabitants, Babahoyo is the capital of the flat agricultural province of Los Ríos. North of it lie banana and palm plantations, south of it are rice paddies and some cattle raising. The ride from Babahoyo to Guayaquil is often made very pretty with huge flocks of white cattle egrets.

Babahoyo, only seven metres above sea level and on the banks of the Río Babahoyo, was badly flooded during the 1982/83 El Niño. To get some idea of what the flood was like, go to the library at the edge of the river. The flood-retaining walls, some six metres high in the dry season, have been completely washed away in places. The water level reached the library entrance, which is on a small patio about half a metre higher than the surrounding streets – all of which were flooded for several weeks. The inhabitants waded knee deep from house to house or used canoes.

An interesting feature of the river is the floating houses which were there before the floods; they just rose and fell with the waters. A few drifted loose but most remained undamaged. You can cross the river for a few cents; there are frequent departures from the dock.

The church on the central plaza has a large modern mural of the Virgin and Child decorating the entire front. The otherwise pleasing effect is marred somewhat by the massive rusty iron doors, which look more like the doors of a maximum security prison than the entrance to a place of worship.

Although it's not exactly exciting, Babahoyo is a bustling and energetic town with much commercial activity. The downtown streets are very busy and, for some strange reason, I found myself liking the place.

Information

The post office is found in the government buildings on the central plaza. There is an IETEL office but no moneychanging facilities. Babahoyo was founded on 27 May 1869, and this is celebrated with parades.

Places to Stay – bottom end

There are several hotels to choose from – none very fancy or expensive. The *Mesón Popular* rents very basic boxes for US$1.20 per person, but at least it's locked up and looks secure. Similarly priced is the basic *Hotel Zaida*, which has a few rooms with river views. Even cheaper is the *Residencial Babahoyo* – liveable in for US$1. Other cheap places include the *Pensión Sanchez* (really basic little concrete boxes) and the *Hotel San Marcos*, with rooms starting around US$1.20 per person, though you'll pay twice that for rooms with a private bath. The *Residencial Ensueño* is about US$1.50 per person but is next to the FBI bus station and apt to be noisy. *Hotel Dorado Gigante* has fairly clean, spacious rooms with private bath for US$2 per person, but when I was there I was asked if I wanted the room for a while or for the night!

Better places include the *Hotel Riberas de Babahoyo* (☎ 730 907) which is on the Malecón at P Carbo. It is good value with clean rooms costing from US$2 to US$4.50 per person depending on whether you have a fan, air-conditioning, private bathroom, or river view. Also in this price range is the *Hotel Capitol* (☎ 730 907) on Sucre at García Moreno. It has been remodelled and looks quite good.

Places to Stay – middle

The fanciest place in town is the *Hotel Cachari* (☎ 730 749) at Bolívar 120 just up from the boat dock. They charge from US$4.50 to US$7 per person depending on whether you want air-conditioning, river views, etc. It looks pretty good if you want some comfort.

Places to Eat

There are many chifas in the town centre, especially on General Barona east of the central plaza. There is a corner café with

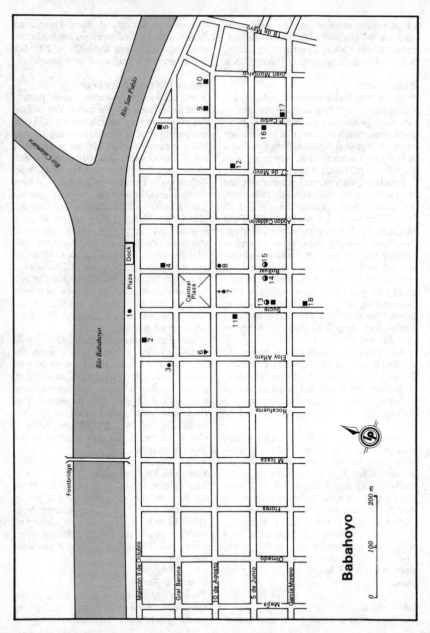

Babahoyo

0   100   200 m

1 Library
2 Hotel Zaida
3 Teatro Babahoyo
4 Hotels Cachari & Los Ríos
5 Hotel Riberas del Babahoyo
6 Restaurant Munich
7 Church
8 IETEL
9 Pensión Sanchez
10 Hotel San Marcos
11 Mesón Popular
12 Residencial Babahoyo
13 Residencial Ensueño & Bus
   companies
   (Flota Babahoyo, Interprovincial etc)
14 Transportes El Dorado
15 Flota Bolivar
16 Hotel Reina Maria
17 Hotel Dorado Gigante
18 Hotel Capitol

outdoor tables from which to watch the activity of the plaza.

A good cheap place for an outdoor (or indoor) lunch is the *Restaurant Munich*.

Getting There & Away

Bus There is no proper terminal terrestre but most companies have departures from or near the block bounded by 5 de Junio and Bolívar. Most companies have frequent services to Guayaquil (US$0.40; 1½ hours). You can also get buses to most towns in the province.

The North Coast

Unlike the coast of Peru to the south, Ecuador has warm water bathing its coast, and swimming is pleasant year round. There are beautiful, palm-fringed, sandy beaches which, unfortunately, suffered greatly during the 1982/83 El Niño floods. Many of the beaches were destroyed (palm trees uprooted, the sand washed away, and ocean-front buildings and streets damaged) but they are now beginning to recover.

According to Cárdenas & Greiner, who recently completed the noteworthy (if slightly mad) project of *Walking the Beaches of Ecuador* (see Books & Maps in the Facts for the Visitor chapter), the Ecuadorian coastline is approximately 2790 km in length, of which less than one third is beaches. The rest is a combination of man-groves, estuaries, river deltas and other geographic features.

There are two definite seasons on the coast. The rainy season is from December to June and the dry season during the rest of the year. The rainy season is hot and humid as well as wet and the climate in the lowlands is uncomfortable. At this time, strangely enough, people flock to the beaches. I suppose the rationale is that if it is hot, humid, wet and stickily uncomfortable, you may as well go to the beach and cool off in the sea. January to March seem to be popular months.

The biggest problem during the wet months is that the rain can make roads slow or impassable but generally the main roads remain open year round. During the dry season there are often fewer tourists than during the wet!

Travelling along the coast is varied and exciting. If you were to begin in the north and work your way southward, you would travel by motorised dugout, normal bus, ran-chero, poled dugout and on foot.

This chapter describes the north coastal provinces of Esmeraldas and Manabí. Esmeraldas is the most northerly province in

Ecuador, reaching a latitude of 1°25′ North. It is also the wettest and most humid of the coastal provinces, with tropical rainforest in the far north coastal areas and inland regions of the province. The south coastal areas of Esmeraldas and on into Manabí become drier and less humid. Here, there are some remnants of tropical dry forest.

SAN LORENZO

There are no roads to San Lorenzo and most travellers arrive by train or boat. The train ride down from Ibarra in the highlands is beautiful and takes all day. San Lorenzo itself is not very attractive as there are no beaches; most people use it just as an over-night stop before continuing to Esmeraldas.

San Lorenzo is a small town with a few streets centred around the railway tracks. A couple of the most central streets are paved but there are very few vehicles. The town is not very well laid out, but is small and most everyone knows where everything is. *Marimba* music can sometimes be heard in town but there are no special bars or night-clubs; ask around.

A road from the highlands is under con-struction and almost half of it has been at least partially cleared − all at the highland end. It will probably be the late 1990s before it reaches San Lorenzo. There are approxi-mately 20,000 inhabitants in the town and surrounding area.

Information

In San Lorenzo itself, there are no proper

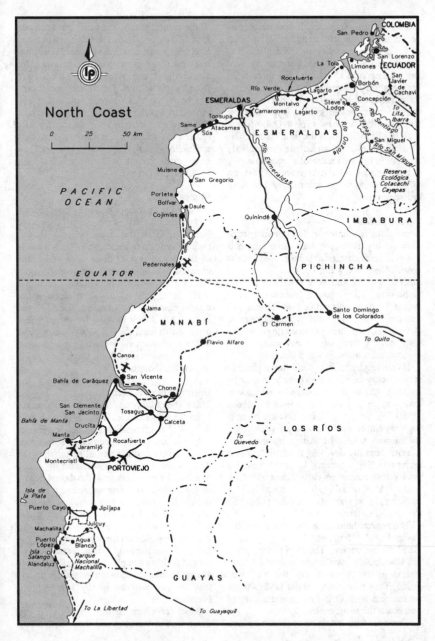

moneychanging facilities. If you ask around you'll find people will change small amounts of Colombian currency or US dollars. It is possible to arrive in San Lorenzo by boat from Tumaco in Colombia, but there is no immigration office and you have to go to Esmeraldas migración or Ibarra police station to see about getting your passport stamped. You may have to go to Quito. There is an IETEL office near the train station. The Catholic hospital in San Lorenzo is reputedly the best in the area north of Esmeraldas.

San Lorenzo celebrates its annual fiesta on 10 August and the town may be more crowded then.

Places to Stay

None of the few hotels in San Lorenzo are of high quality, so if you like some comforts you will be uncomfortable here. None of the rooms have hot water, air-conditioning or other amenities and very few have private bathrooms. They should, however, have a bed and a mosquito net or fan; the mosquitoes can be bad, especially in the wet months. Bring insect repellent or mosquito coils. The town suffers from occasional water shortages, so take showers when you can.

If arriving by train, try and find a place to stay quickly because everyone else will be looking. At the train station kids will ask to take you to a hotel (tip expected – about US$0.25). Several of these kids are becoming very entrepreneurial – they'll walk down the railway track to a station up from San Lorenzo and, by boarding the train before it arrives in San Lorenzo, begin to look for prospective customers early. Some travellers find the kids amusing, friendly, and helpful (which they are) whilst others feel put out by the kids' insistence.

The nearest hotel to the train station is the basic *Hotel Vilma* which charges about US$1.40 per person. The *Hotel Margaritas* is a 10-minute walk straight beyond the train station in the direction that the train was going. They also charge about US$1.40 per person and look OK. Five minutes further you reach the town centre.

There are four hotels on or within a block of the central plaza. The basic but adequate *Hotel Ecuador* is one of the cheapest at about US$1.30 per person. *Residencial Jhonny* has basic but clean rooms with mosquito nets for about the same price. The owners are friendly and helpful. The *Residencial Ibarra* has basic but clean rooms with a fan and mosquito netting for US$1.60 per person. The newest place in town is the friendly *Hotel Carondolet* where clean rooms with mosquito nets are US$2.30 per person. They have some rooms with private bath for US$2.80 per person.

Places to Eat

Food has to be transported in by boat or train and meals are pricier than most of the rest of Ecuador. Both the *Ecuador* and *Jhonny* hotels have decent restaurants. The set meals of the day at one of these is probably the cheapest safe bet for those on a tight budget. Eating à la carte anywhere in San Lorenzo is much more expensive and the food is not much better than the set menu. The *El Fogón* is a slightly fancy looking restaurant a few doors down from the Ecuador – it is popular with out-of-town visitors who pay a bit more for the 'ambience'. I don't think the food is any better, though.

Getting There & Away

Train The railway station is just over one km from the town centre. The autoferro leaves daily at 7 am from San Lorenzo for Ibarra. Services are often disrupted – sometimes trains run every other day, although they ran daily when I was in town recently. They won't sell you tickets until the day of departure. People start lining up around 6 am, the ticket office opens at 6.30 am, and the train usually leaves late. The fare is just under US$1. The train is almost always full and people often ride on the top. The scenery is great and the roof-top ride is recommended for good views and photography. Remember always to look ahead when the train is underway or you will be hit by low-hanging branches.

Most travellers do this trip from Ibarra down to San Lorenzo and then south along the coast as is described in this chapter. There are fewer people doing it the other way and so it is a little less crowded from San Lorenzo up to Ibarra. The first half of the journey is relatively flat, and a 30-minute lunch break is often made at **Lita** (at 450 metres above sea level) where there are a couple of simple restaurants by the train station and a basic place to stay on the main street. You may be asked to register your passport here, so be prepared.

North of Lita is the little known **Awa Ethnic & Forestry Preserve** which protects some of the lowland forests on the Ecuadorian-Colombian border. The preserve is managed by MAG and is the home of a few remaining Awa Indians.

The World Wildlife Fund was involved in the implementation of a management plan for the area and provided financial grants of US$119,000 in 1990 and US$70,000 in 1991 for this purpose. I do not know of any way to visit the preserve at this time.

Beyond Lita the train begins to climb noticeably, and there are many tunnels and gorgeous views of luxuriant forest – but watch those branches if riding on top!

Boat General enquiries about boat services are best directed at the Capitanía on the waterfront. They have lists of departing and arriving boats.

The most frequent travellers' destinations are Limones (officially called Valdéz, US$1.20; 1¼ hours), Borbón (US$1.80; 3½ hours) and La Tola (US$1.50; 2½ hours).

La Tola is the most frequent destination of most travellers and is served by two companies: Transportes San Lorenzo de Paila (also called Pailón and known locally as La Costeñita) and Turismo del Pacifico. Between them, they have departures almost every hour from 5.30 am to 3.30 pm daily. Most boats to La Tola stop at Limones en route but few travellers stop there. If you take an early morning boat to La Tola you can connect with a bus on to Esmeraldas. Tickets are sold in San Lorenzo for the complete journey or you can buy the bus portion when

you get to La Tola. The bus takes about four or five hours from La Tola to Esmeraldas, so the whole trip from San Lorenzo to Esmeraldas can be done in one day and costs about US$3.

Recently, a new route has opened to Esmeraldas from Borbón at the confluence of the ríos Cayapas and Santiago. Motorised dugouts go from San Lorenzo via Limones to Borbón from where there are buses going to Esmeraldas several times a day. Service from San Lorenzo to Borbón is at 7 am and 1 pm daily.

There are boats most days to Tumaco in Colombia, but make sure you have all the necessary visas (see Facts for the Visitor). Few people take this route; the journey is done in motorised dugouts, costs about US$7 and takes most of the day. It can get both very wet and sunny so protect yourself and your gear.

Border crossing facilities are not geared to foreign tourists and you may have difficulty in entering Colombia. Esmeraldas is probably the best place to get your exit stamp from Ecuador.

You can hire a motorised dugout to San Pedro which is a completely undeveloped beach on an island north of San Lorenzo. You can camp here if you bring everything you need – a trip for the adventurous and prepared traveller.

It is also possible to take a steamer all the way from San Lorenzo to Esmeraldas, but this isn't highly recommended. You don't see much of the countryside and the boats are cargo vessels that are dirty, hot and uncomfortable. Service is irregular – about twice a week.

The motorised dugout journey via Limones and on to Borbón or La Tola is much more pleasant. The dugouts are small enough to travel through the coastal mangrove swamps and you'll see much more scenery than you will from the larger steamer.

Keep your eyes open for the black scissor-tailed frigatebirds circling overhead, squadrons of pelicans gliding by, and schools of jellyfish floating past the boat.

LIMONES

Limones is a small town at the mouth of the deltas of the Santiago and Cayapas rivers. It has a population of about 7,000 and is economically more important than San Lorenzo, despite the latter's railway connections.

Timber is logged in this area and floated down the river to Limones, where there is a sawmill. There are few amenities in town and the two hotels are pretty rough.

The only way into Limones is by boat and you can sometimes see Cayapas Indians here, although more can be seen at Borbón and further up the Río Cayapas.

About twice a week a cargo steamer leaves Limones for Esmeraldas – ask the captain if you want to sail on it. Passengers are not normally carried, but the captain will allow you to go if you are interested. It's neither expensive nor very comfortable.

BORBÓN

This small river port on the Río Cayapas has a predominantly Black population of about 5000 inhabitants. The town now has road connections to Esmeraldas and it is also the best place from where to get boats up the Cayapas and to continue up the Río San Miguel to the Reserva Ecológica Cotacachi-Cayapas – an interesting trip to a remote area. Borbón is beginning to compete in importance with Limones. Market day is Sunday.

Tagua nut dolphin

A small local tagua nut industry is developing. Tagua nuts are also known as 'vegetable ivory' and come from a palm tree which grows in the local rainforest.

The nuts are extremely hard and can be carved into small ornaments, buttons, and other trinkets.

Harvesting the nuts is a sustainable and economically attractive alternative to harvesting the whole rainforest. With the help of Conservation International, the local industry has started finding buyers in North American clothing markets. If you shop in Canadian or US stores, you may find clothes labelled with a 'Tagua Initiative' tag, which explains to consumers how the buttons used on the clothing help make tropical forests worth more standing up than cut down.

You may also find tagua nut products for sale in the Borbón market, Esmeraldas, or even in Quito gift shops. I bought a beautiful tagua nut carving of a leaping dolphin – it was reminiscent of scrimshaw. The ornaments do make good souvenirs of the rainforest – and buying them helps to preserve that rainforest.

Information

Angel Ceron is the principal (headmaster) of the local school, 'Colegio Luz y Libertad'. He also runs the Pampa de Oro Hotel in Borbón. He is a good source of information about the area. He can tell you how to get to some of the local archaeological sites pertaining to the Tolita culture which existed here around 2000 years ago. There is not much to see – it is mainly of interest to professional archaeologists.

The US-run mission in Borbón can be of assistance to travellers. If you are driving, they may let you park your vehicle in their parking lot whilst you take river trips or whatever. Ask for directions in town – most people know the mission.

Places to Stay & Eat

The *Residencial Capri* charges US$1.40 per person in basic but clean rooms with mosquito nets – toilet facilities are primitive. The *Hotel Panama City* charges US$2.30 per person and is slightly better. The friendly *La Tolita Pampa de Oro* charges about US$2.50 per person and is a good source of visitor information. The *Residencial Anny Christina* is also a cheap place to stay.

There is a comfortable jungle lodge about an hour away by river (for more information see Nearby Excursions in the Getting There & Away section for Borbón).

Most restaurants don't bother with a menu

– ask them what they have. The *Restaurant Santiago* is on the waterfront by the dock. They serve simple but good meals for about US$1 each during day-light hours. There are several other basic comedores a block behind the waterfront, in the 'town centre'. Most places close by about 7.30 pm when they start running out of food.

Getting There & Away

Bus La Costeñita runs about six buses or rancheros a day to Esmeraldas (US$1.25; 4½ hours). The road is subject to temporary closures during the wet months (January to May).

Boat Passenger boats to San Lorenzo (via Limones) leave daily at 7 and 11 am. The fare is US$1.80 for the three hour trip. A daily passenger boat leaves at 11 am for San Miguel (US$3.75; five hours). This boat can drop you at any location on the Cayapas or San Miguel rivers (see Nearby Excursions later). There are boats to other destinations – ask around at the docks.

Fletes or private boats can be hired any time to take you anywhere if you have the money. These are not cheap – expect to pay about 15 times the fare that you would be charged in a passenger boat.

About twice a month there are cargo boats leaving Borbón for Esmeraldas or even Guayaquil. Although the boats don't have passenger cabins, you may be allowed to travel as a passenger if you ask the captain. The fares are low.

Nearby Excursions

Occasional passenger boats or fletes will take you up the Río Santiago, via the community of Maldonado, to the small village of **Concepción**. This is about a two-hour trip – a flete will cost about US$10 to US$12 if you bargain. In Concepción, villagers can show you the beginning of a well-beaten path through the forest to the San Lorenzo-Ibarra railroad, about a 12-km walk away. Turn left when you reach the tracks and, in about two km, you'll come to the little village of San Javier de Cachavi where you can wait for the train coming from Ibarra. The train passes through sometime in the mid to late afternoon, though there is also reportedly a local San Javier-San Lorenzo train leaving at 2 pm. If you left Borbón first thing in the morning, you should have no trouble in getting to the railway in time to catch a train to San Lorenzo that afternoon – an interesting and infrequently travelled route.

A few more travellers take the daily passenger boat to San Miguel. There are several possible stopping places along the way.

The first is **Steve's Lodge** at the mouth of the Río Onzole, about an hour from Borbón. Run by a friendly Hungarian, Steve Tarjanyi, the lodge has six comfortable double rooms with great river views. Rates are US$25 per person including meals, or US$150 per person for a three-night stay including meals and a guided boat tour up the Río Cayapas to the Reserva Ecológica Cotacachi-Cayapas (optional camping in reserve is possible). There are discounts for groups of four or more.

Reservations can be made in Quito with Antonio or Judy Nagy (☎ 431 555, 447 709) at Avenida 10 de Agosto 4341. Alternatively, write to Steve Tarjanyi, Casilla 187, Esmeraldas or the Nagys, Casilla 5148 CCI, Quito. All these people speak excellent English. If you just show up, you can sleep at the lodge or take a tour on a space available basis (space is available more often than not). The passenger canoe costs US$1 or a flete is about US$12 from Borbón.

Beyond Steve's Lodge there are a number of communities and missions where the boat stops. River travel is made interesting by passengers ranging from Catholic nuns to Cayapas Indians embarking or disembarking in the various tiny ports – usually no more than a few planks at the water's edge.

The first mission is the Catholic one at **Santa María**. Here, there is a clean dormitory which will sleep up to six people at US$1 per person. Ask for Señora Pastora who will show you where to sleep and cook meals if requested. The next mission is the Protestant one of **Zapallo Grande**. You can find a basic place to sleep here, too. Cayapas crafts are often for sale. Both missions have medical clinics. There are also a number of other communities such as Pichiyacu, Playa Grande, Atahualpa, and Telembi which are the homes of mainly Cayapas Indians or Black people.

Finally, San Miguel is reached.

SAN MIGUEL
This small, friendly village is the main base from which to visit the lowland sections of the Reserva Ecológica Cotacachi-Cayapas. There is a ranger station on a small hill overlooking the village – the view of the rainforest and river from here is quite spectacular. There are about 20 houses in the village, one of which is a small store selling soft drinks, crackers, sardines, candy, oatmeal, and little else. The inhabitants of the village are Black. Cayapas Indians' houses are scattered along the shores of the river nearby.

The grass in front of the ranger station has been macheted into a rough lawn – but it is a haven for chiggers. I forgot to put insect repellent on until a couple of hours after I arrived because there were so few mosquitoes. I didn't realise how bad the chiggers were until that evening, when I started itching. The next morning I counted over 100 bites just on one ankle. Put on repellent, especially around your ankles, before you disembark at San Miguel.

Places to Stay & Eat
The name of the *guardaparque* (park ranger) is Nelson Nazareno. He will let you stay in the ranger station for US$3 per person per night. There are four beds (with blankets and sheets) – larger groups can sleep on the floor or camp outside. The station has a cold shower, toilet, and kitchen facilities. You should bring food to cook. The stove may or may not have propane available, so either bring a small camping stove or be prepared to cook on a wood fire.

The head of the village is named Linden. His wife will cook for you and you can eat at his house. Meals cost about US$1.80 and

consist mainly of rice and fried bananas, with a little soup. The people are friendly.

Getting There & Away
The driver of the daily passenger canoe from Borbón spends the night about 15 minutes downriver from San Miguel. He will not come back to San Miguel unless he knows for sure that he has a passenger. It is essential to make arrangements with the boatman about the day you want to be picked up. The canoe leaves San Miguel around 5 am, when it is still dark. Dawn on the river makes this a nice trip.

RESERVA ECOLÓGICA COTACACHI-CAYAPAS
This 204,420-hectare reserve is by far the largest protected area of western Andean habitats in Ecuador. It covers an altitudinal range of from about 200 metres above sea level in the San Miguel area to 4939 metres above sea level at the summit of Cotacachi. Thus the type of habitat changes rapidly from lowland tropical wet forest to premontane and montane cloud forest to páramo, with many intermediate habitat types. This rapid change of habitat produces the so-called 'edge effect' which gives rise to an incredible diversity of flora & fauna.

These are the haunts of such rarely seen mammals as the giant anteater, Baird's tapir, jaguar, and, in the upper reaches of the reserve, the spectacled bear. The chances of seeing these are remote, however. You may see monkeys, squirrels, sloths, the nine-banded armadillo, bats, and a huge variety of bird species. It is certainly a great area for birding.

There are two principal ways to visit the reserve. You can go in from the highlands (as described in the North of Quito chapter) or you can go in from San Miguel, as described below. Whichever way you elect to go, you will find it extremely difficult to descend from the highlands to the lowlands or climb up in the opposite direction. The areas near the reserve boundaries can be visited in both the lowlands and the highlands; the steep and thickly vegetated western slopes of the

Andes in between are largely trackless and almost impenetrable. This is bad news for those who want to visit the interior of the reserve but good news for the species existing there – they will probably be left alone for a little while longer.

Conservation International is funding efforts to consolidate the protection afforded by this preserve.

Both the lower reaches of the reserve and the rivers leading into this area are the home of Cayapas Indians, of which about 5000 remain. The Cayapas are famous for their basket work and there are stores in Borbón, Limones, Esmeraldas and Quito selling these crafts. You can buy them far more cheaply direct from the Indians on the river – however, be warned that the baskets tend to be very large and so getting them home may be a minor problem. Many of the Cayapas live in traditional style in breezy, open-sided, thatched-roof houses built on stilts near the river. Fishing and subsistence agriculture is their main source of food, and many of the Indians speak only the Cayapas tongue. Some groups now live on or close to missions; others are largely beyond missionary influence. In these groups, both men and women go bare breasted.

Over the last few decades the Cayapas Indians have been swept by a form of river blindness that is supposedly carried by a blackfly which is particularly prevalent in April and May. Some 80% of the Indians have the disease to a greater or lesser extent. Insect repellent works to keep the insects off you, and taking chloroquine as a malarial prophylactic also works to prevent the disease.

The area is very rainy, with up to 5000 mm of rain being reported in some of the more inland areas, although it is somewhat less wet around San Miguel. The rainy season is December to May and the river levels are high then, which makes the local people consider it to be the best time to travel. It is also the season with the highest concentrations of mosquitoes, blackflies, and other insects, but they tend to be really bad only at dawn and dusk, so cover up then. Even during the rainy months, mornings are often clear.

Entrance into the reserve costs only a few cents, payable at the ranger station in San Miguel. Officially, it is US$2 for foreign visitors but the rangers charge the same fee to everyone, though they carefully note your nationality in their log book. When I was there in July of 1991, I was the 32nd visitor to have signed in that year – which gives an idea of how few visitors there are.

The rangers will act as guides. They charge about US$4 per day plus food. You also need to hire a dugout canoe which is about US$2 per day and will hold about three or four people. These canoes are paddled and poled – they don't have outboard engines. Not many people have engines out here.

It is about two or three hours by canoe to the park limits proper. A further one or two hours brings the visitor to a small but pretty waterfall in the jungle. There are a few poorly marked trails for which a guide is almost essential. There are places to camp if you have tents and all necessary gear. There are plans to build a hut by the waterfall and another somewhere within the reserve – ask the rangers about whether these plans have materialised.

LA TOLA

Most people travelling between San Lorenzo and Esmeraldas take the boat to La Tola and continue by bus to Esmeraldas. There is one very basic residencial in La Tola, and local people will find stranded travellers somewhere to sleep. There are a few stores where you can buy snacks. The annual fiesta is on 16 July. There is a Tolita archaeological site on the nearby island of Manta de Oro, but the gold ornaments found here are now in museums and there is not much to see unless you are an archaeologist. There is a small museum. A few people live on the island and can offer guiding services.

Getting There & Away

There are two transportation companies, both of which run buses to and from Esmeraldas and boats to and from San

Lorenzo. Although you can buy a single straight through ticket from San Lorenzo to Esmeraldas, it may be better to buy the sections separately so as to have a wider choice of buses in La Tola. La Costeñita tends to have more buses whilst Turismo del Pacifico tends to have more rancheros (flat-bed trucks mounted with excruciatingly narrow and uncomfortable benches). Try and get an end seat so you can at least stretch one leg. Buses take five hours to Esmeraldas and cost US$2. If you take a morning bus from Esmeraldas you will connect with a boat to San Lorenzo and vice versa, so there is no reason to stay in La Tola.

THE ROAD TO ESMERALDAS

The bus journey to Esmeraldas from either Borbón or La Tola is bumpy and uncomfortable. It is very dusty in the dry season and muddy in the wet. The first half of the road is very bad and may be impassable during the rainy season. The half way point is the Río Lagarto – if you are coming from Borbón you cross the river inland and if you are coming from La Tola you cross it close to the river mouth. In both cases, there is a village called **Lagarto** where there's a basic residencial and a restaurant. There is also a military checkpoint at the Río Lagarto on the Borbón-Esmeraldas route. The soldiers are a oafish bunch who have been known to search luggage and hold up women's underwear to the delight of their colleagues and disgust of the passengers. Have your passport available for these 'gentlemen'.

After crossing Río Lagarto the paved road begins and the routes from Borbón and La Tola unite. Beyond, the road passes through the village of **Montalvo** and on to the coastal village of **Rocafuerte** which has a very basic residencial and simple restaurants selling tasty fresh seafood. People from Esmeraldas drive out here at weekends for a good meal in a rural setting. Rocafuerte celebrates its annual fiesta on 31 August.

A few km further the road passes through the coastal village of **Río Verde**, again with a cheap hotel and restaurants. Almost 20 km beyond Río Verde is the village of **Camarones** which sells, as its name implies, delicious shrimp dishes in the simple beachfront restaurants. Ask around about cabins for rent if you want to stay by the beach – off the beaten track but close enough to the road that buses to Esmeraldas are easy to catch. A few km beyond Camarones, the road passes the Esmeraldas Airport on the east side of the Río Esmeraldas. The city is on the west side but there is no bridge until San Mateo, about 10 km upriver. It is a half-hour drive from the airport to Esmeraldas.

The drive gives good views of the coastal scenery and I persuaded the driver to let me ride on the roof of the bus, which was better than being squashed inside (there was no extra charge for the air-conditioning). I don't recommend this during the rainy season! Watch out for sunburn during the dry. The bird life along the coast is varied and spectacular; I enjoyed looking at trees filled with hundreds of roosting white cattle egrets.

ESMERALDAS

This important city of about 140,000 inhabitants is capital of Esmeraldas Province. It was near here that the Spanish conquistadors made their first landfall in Ecuador. Esmeraldas has been a major port throughout Ecuador's history. It is now the largest port in northern Ecuador. Although fishing and shipping are important, the recent construction of an oil refinery near the terminal of the trans-Andean oil pipeline has given Esmeraldas a new source of income and employment.

This is of little interest to most tourists who spend the night and continue south-west to the towns of Atacames, Súa and Muisne, where the best beaches are to be found. Esmeraldas also has beaches in the northern suburb of Las Palmas, but they are not as good and reportedly dirty.

Information

Tourist Office There is a tourist information office half a block from the main plaza. There is no sign or street number so you find it by going up the stairs of the nondescript office building marked on the map. The people at the office can answer direct questions like 'Where is the Post Office?' but are not much help if asked 'What is there to do around here?'

Money Moneychangers don't exist and last time I was in Esmeraldas the banks told me that it was 'illegal' for them to change money. This was, apparently, a temporary economic measure and has since been lifted. It is best to arrive with enough sucres, however, as the banks remain erratic with their foreign exchange policies.

Post & Telecommunications There is a post office at the corner of J Montalvo and the Malecón. The IETEL office is upstairs and there is a good view from the IETEL balcony of the Río Esmeraldas and the riverside market. The IETEL office was extraordinarily efficient when I was last there – they connected me with Quito in two minutes. Other travellers, however, have reported that telephone links are poor from Esmeraldas – the quality of communications obviously varies.

Immigration The immigration office is by the Capitanía, which is on the right-hand side of the road just before getting to the suburb of Las Palmas. You should have your passport stamped here if you are leaving or entering Ecuador via the little-used coastal route to Colombia.

Medical Services The public hospital (☎ 710 012) is on Avenida Libertad between Esmeraldas and Las Palmas.

Dangers & Annoyances Be careful in the market areas and away from the main streets. There are thievery and drug problems. Try to avoid arriving in Esmeraldas after dark and keep to the main well-lit streets to avoid these problems. Electricity and water supply are erratic. The incidence of malaria is high.

Things to See & Do
The **market** across from the IETEL office is open daily and sells Cayapas basketry among other things. Don't wander around with your camera and keep your money well hidden.

There is a **Banco Central Museum** with exhibits of the local Tolita culture. The museum was closed when I was there but may have reopened by now.

Bolívar's Birthday, the 24 July, is one of the more vigorously celebrated holidays in Esmeraldas.

Places to Stay
There are many hotels but the cheapest ones are not too good. Esmeraldas is definitely not the place to come looking for quaint or memorable hotels. Mosquitoes are a problem, particularly during the wet months, and you should have either a fan or mosquito net in your room to keep the insects off you.

There seem to be quite a few travellers in Esmeraldas (especially Ecuadorian holiday-makers and business people) and hotels are sometimes full. Single rooms can be especially hard to find. You may want to stay in Las Palmas or go directly to a coastal resort such as Atacames.

Places to Stay – bottom end
Many of the cheapest hotels are close to bus terminals and apt to be noisy. They are also not very well looked after. The following are among the very cheapest (less than US$1.50 per person) but otherwise have little to recommend them: *Pensión Elsita, Pensión 9 de Octubre, Hostal Miraflores* and *Hotel Suiza* (☎ 710 243). Slightly more expensive but not much better is the *Nuevo Hotel* at US$1.70.

There are several other cheap hotels. *Hotel Royal* (☎ 710 210), at Bolívar 724 and Rocafuerte, is US$2 per person but unfriendly – they wouldn't let me look at a room. 'Take it or leave it.' I left it. The *Hotel Asia*, on 9 de Octubre near the Malecón, is similarly priced and not too bad. The *Hotel Turismo* (☎ 714 416), on the corner of Montalvo and Bolívar, is also about US$2 per person and has basic rooms with private cold water bath.

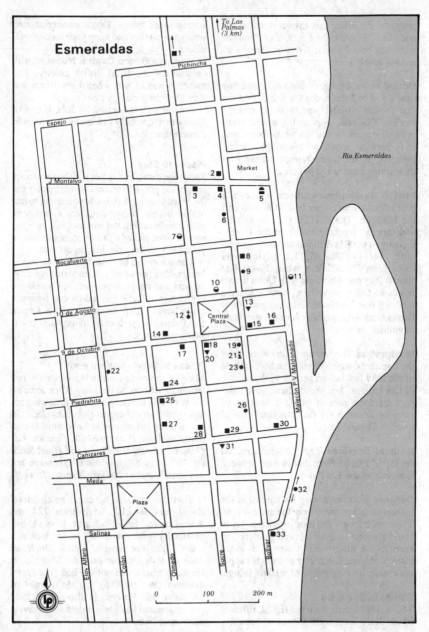

Esmeraldas

To Las
Palmas
(3 km)

Pichincha

Espejo

Market

Río Esmeraldas

J Montalvo

Rocafuerte

10 de Agosto

Central
Plaza

9 de Octubre

Piedrahita

Cañizares

Mejía

Plaza

Salinas

0   100   200 m

■ PLACES TO STAY

1	Two Blocks to Apart Hotel Esmeraldas
2	Hotel Chaberrin Internacional
3	Hotel Rita
4	Hotel Turismo
8	Hotel Royal
14	Pensión 9 de Octubre
15	Hostal Miraflores
16	Hotel Asia
18	Nuevo Hotel
24	Hotel Galeon
25	Hotel Roma
27	Residencial Sulema
28	Hotel Americano
29	Hotels Beatriz & Diana
30	Hotel Korea
33	Hotel Suiza

▼ PLACES TO EAT

13	Fuente de Soda Estrecho de Bering & Las Redes Restaurant
20	Restaurant Bo Derek
31	Chifa Asiatica

OTHER

5	IETEL & Post Office
6	Banco Central
7	Cita Buses
9	Cinema
10	Aero Taxi Buses & Transportes Esmeraldas
11	Transportes La Costeñita Buses
12	Church
16	Reina del Camino Buses
17	Transportes Occidentales Buses & Pensión Elsita
19	TAME
21	Tourist Office (2nd Floor)
22	Portón 26 Disco
23	Cine Bolívar
26	Filanbanco
32	Fish & Vegetable Market

Places to Stay – middle

There is a better selection if you can afford US$3 to US$4 each, but look at your room before paying for it, as the higher-priced hotels are sometimes no better than the cheapest. Most of the rooms in this section boast private bathrooms, mostly with cold water, but check to see if they are working.

The *Residencial Sulema* (☎ 711 789), on Olmedo near Cañizares, charges US$3.50 per person and is clean, well-lit and secure. There are fans in the rooms but its most commendable feature is the many plants decorating the place. The front yard is a popular evening venue for volleyball. The *Hotel Americano* (☎ 713 798/978), Sucre 709 and Cañizares, is clean and good value for US$3 a single and US$5 a double. They charge an extra dollar per person for air-conditioning. The *Hotel Diana* (☎ 710 333), on Cañizares near Sucre, has rooms for US$3.50 per person. The rooms have TV and telephone and the nice little old lady behind the reception desk told me to phone down if the water wasn't running. The place looks as if it has some character. Next door is the *Hotel Beatriz* (☎ 710 440) which looks quite good for US$3.50 per person or US$4 in rooms with private bath.

The *Hotel Korea*, on Cañizares near Bolívar, has good rooms with private bath, fan, and phone for US$4.50/8.50 for singles/doubles or cheaper rooms (no phone) for US$6 double. *Hotel Roma* (☎ 710 136), Olmedo 718 and Piedrahita, has some good rooms with private bath, TV and phone at US$6/10 for singles/doubles. *Hotel Galeon* (☎ 713 116/470), on the corner of Olmedo and Piedrahita, is well kept and charges about US$5.50 per person or an extra dollar for air-conditioning.

Hotel Chaberrin Internacional (☎ 712 438), on the corner of Montalvo and Bolívar, charges US$4 per person but is poor value. *Hotel Rita* (☎ 711 226), on Montalvo near Sucre, charges US$10 for a double room and looks sleazy.

Apart Hotel Esmeraldas (☎ 712 712/224, 713 713), at Libertad 407 and Tello, has singles/doubles for US$14/20 and is the best hotel in town.

Places to Stay – Las Palmas

Almost all of the hotels are on Avenida Kennedy which is the main street and parallels the beach. Most of the hotels in this beach suburb are mid-range. The exceptions are the clean, family-run *Residencial Mechita*, the *Hostal Familiar* and the *Residencial Chimborazo* which charge about US$1.50 per person for basic rooms.

The *Hotel del Mar* (☎ 713 910) is closest to the beach at the end of Avenida Kennedy. Rooms are about US$10 double but vary widely in quality – some have ocean views. Slightly more expensive places include the *Atahualpa Hotel* (☎ 713 204) in a large house with a flower garden and the *Hotel Cayapas* (☎ 711 022/77) which also has a pleasant garden. The *Hotel Estuario* (☎ 713 930/238) is half way between Esmeraldas and Las Palmas. Clean, modern rooms with air-conditioning and hot water are US$15/19 for singles/doubles.

Places to Eat

There are many dishes typical of the coast and sometimes found only in this province. Fish and other seafood are more common than meat and are usually served with a mountain of plain white rice, boiled beans and plantains. The plantains are sometimes boiled whole (very stodgy to my taste) or are sliced and fried to make patacones – very tasty. Raw seafood is often marinated to make ceviche, which is very good, and any seafood cocado is cooked with coconut to impart a delicate flavour. Camarones cocado or shrimp in a coconut sauce is a particularly typical dish of north coast. Cocadas, on the other hand, are sweet bars of grated coconut cooked in sugar and sold on bus journeys throughout the province.

The better hotels in Esmeraldas and Las Palmas have decent restaurants. The food in the many small and cheap pavement cafés and comedores is often very good – try the places along Olmedo between Mejía and Piedrahita. On the east side of the central plaza the *Las Redes Restaurant* is good for seafood and the nearby *Fuente de Soda Estrecho de Bering* is a good place for snacks and ice cream and watching the busy goings on in the plaza. The *Chifa Asiatica*, on Cañizares near Sucre, is the best place for Chinese food. The *Restaurant Bo Derek*, on

Sucre just south of the plaza, has been recommended for cheap meals.

In Las Palmas you can find cheap, no-name beach-hut restaurants which have limited menus because they only serve whatever was caught that day. The food is often delicious. There are a few more expensive and elegant restaurants near the Las Palmas hotels, such as the *Restaurant Atenas Tiffany* and *Bayardo's Restaurant*.

Entertainment

The coast is known for its lively African-influenced music. There are no particular places where you can go to listen to shows; you have to catch as catch can becə se impromptu gatherings are the norm. The best way is to make friends with the locals and ask them. There are a couple of cinemas, of which the *Ciné Bolívar* is the most comfortable. There are several discos, most away from the centre. One close to the centre is Portón 26 on Colón near 9 de Octubre.

Getting There & Away

Air There is a TAME flight from and to Quito every day except Sunday. It leaves Quito at 10.15 am and returns from Esmeraldas at 11.15 am. The one-way fare is US$11. Sometimes there is also a Friday afternoon flight. The TAME office (☎ 712 663) is on Bolívar just off the corner of the central plaza. You can also buy a ticket at the airport if the flight is not full. Make sure you get a seat assignment at the airport or you won't get on – there are different windows for ticket buying and seat assignments, so you have to wait in line twice. It's not very organised.

AECA (☎ 288 110 in Guayaquil) has small aircraft which are are based in Guayaquil. They have flights from there to Esmeraldas and back, subject to passenger demand. They leave Guayaquil most mornings at 8 am and return from Esmeraldas at 9.30 am, sometimes stopping in intermediate towns such as Pedernales, Bahía de Caráquez, or Manta. The fare is about US$18 to Guayaquil. If you have a large pack (over 10 kg) you may have to pay excess luggage charges or be denied boarding. The flight is repeated if there are enough passengers. There are no flights on Sunday. On other days, call Guayaquil or go to the airport and try your luck. At present, there is no office in Esmeraldas (though one may open).

The airport is about 25 km away from town across the Río Esmeraldas. Passengers and cab drivers gather in front of the TAME office a couple of hours before the flight and four or five passengers are crammed into each taxi at a cost of about US$2 per person. Incoming passengers get together to do the same thing at the airport. At the airport you can hire a taxi for US$10 to take you directly to Atacames, and thus avoid Esmeraldas completely.

To get to the airport cheaply, take a La Costeñita bus or ranchero heading for La Tola. They may not sell you a ticket at the office, so board without a ticket and pay the driver – about US$0.30 to the airport. If you leave Esmeraldas by 9 am you should get to the airport in good time to catch the flight at 11.15 am.

Bus There is no central bus terminal, although there are plans to build one during the 1990s. There is a direct road to Quito via Santo Domingo. The fastest service to Quito is with Aerotaxi (US$2.50; five hours) but they drive suicidally fast. Transportes Occidentales and Transportes Esmeraldas are slower and a few cents cheaper. Buses are frequent.

Transportes Occidentales also has frequent buses to Guayaquil (US$2.70; eight hours) and an early evening bus to Machala (US$3.60; 11 hours) if you want to go to Peru the next day. Guayaquil is also served by Transportes Esmeraldas. CITA has four buses a day to Ambato (US$2.30; eight hours). Reina del Camino has five buses a day to Manta (US$3.20; nine hours) and a couple to Bahía de Caráquez (US$2.90; eight hours).

For provincial buses go to Transportes La Costeñita. Buses for Atacames and Súa (US$0.30; less than an hour) leave every 45 minutes from 6.30 am to 8 pm. There are

eight buses a day to Muisne (US$0.90; 2½ hours). Buses to La Tola leave eight times a day and the US$3 ticket includes the boat to San Lorenzo. Take a morning bus to ensure that you don't have to overnight in La Tola. There are also several buses a day to Borbón (US$1.25; four hours). Buses also go to other small provincial villages.

Taxi A taxi will take you from Esmeraldas to Atacames for US$10.

Boat The Capitanía is on the right side of the road linking downtown with Las Palmas, just before you get to Las Palmas. They can give information about which boats are going where, and then you have to talk to the captain of the boat directly. Boats occasionally go to Guayaquil and other coastal ports but the most frequent sailings are for Limones. Boat travel from Esmeraldas is not particularly recommended because it is cheaper and more convenient to travel by land – besides, you see more.

There is an immigration office near the Capitanía should you be arriving from Colombia.

Getting Around
Take a bus signed 'Las Palmas' northbound along Avenida Bolívar to get to the port of Esmeraldas and beaches of Las Palmas. The fare is US$0.05.

TONSUPA
This small coastal village is just off the Esmeraldas-Atacames road, about 5 km before reaching the better known resort town of Atacames. It is a much quieter resort than Atacames.

Places to Stay
Most of the hotels have cabins renting for about US$30, usually sleeping three to six and geared to family groups. The hotels tend to be self-contained resorts, though there are a few simple restaurants near the beach.

Try *Hotel Club de Pacifico* (☎ 731 053),

Conjunto Vacacional Vista Azul (☎ 731 175) and *Hotel El Bosque* (☎ 731 032).

ATACAMES

This small resort town, about 30 km west of Esmeraldas, has built up a reputation among travellers as one of the best places to go for a relaxed and inexpensive beach vacation. It certainly is cheaper and less developed than the beaches in the Guayaquil area and is particularly popular with budget travellers.

Fairly inexpensive accommodation can be found right on the ocean front, so you can walk straight out of your room onto the beach. Atacames is also popular with visitors from Colombia and Quito and can get extremely crowded, particularly at weekends and national holidays.

Nightlife is variable. I've been here when nothing was happening and other times when every bar was hopping. I can't recommend anywhere in particular; if there's anything going on you'll hear it!

There is nothing to do in Atacames apart from sunbathe and swim, eat and drink, and hang out in bars and discos with new-found friends. Some travellers love it and stay for days or weeks. It's fine if that's what you want to do, but I get tired of Atacames very quickly. After a couple of days, all the discos sound the same, all the restaurants seem to have the same stuff on the menu, and I get bored. Ho hum. Bring a good novel.

Orientation & Information

The main road from Esmeraldas goes through the centre of town. The centre and the beach area are separated by the Río Atacames. To get to the ocean and beach hotels, you have to walk a few blocks to the right and cross the Río Atacames on a wooden footbridge. Buses do not go down to the beach.

There is no reason to go into the town centre except to catch a bus or go to the IETEL office to make a phone call.

There are no proper moneychanging facilities in Atacames, though you can usually negotiate cash dollars in some of the beach-front hotels and restaurants. It's best to bring enough sucres with you.

Warnings

There is a powerful undertow and no lifeguards. People get drowned every year, so keep within your limits.

Thieves thrive wherever there is a conglomeration of travellers. This is certainly true of beach areas, and Atacames is no exception. Camping is definitely not recommended because thieves cut through the tent material and rob you even if you're asleep inside the tent. Stay in a beach cabin or hotel room and make sure that it has secure locks on the doors and shutters on the windows.

Assaults have been reported by people walking the beaches at night. Stay in front of the hotel area – women have been raped and travellers have been mugged just a short distance away from the hotel area.

I have heard repeated reports from travellers of rape and theft by armed groups of men – though the local people deny it. It is safe if you stay in the lit areas in front of the hotels – it is definitely dangerous beyond the lit areas. Even during the day, you shouldn't walk the beaches alone or as a couple.

Bring insect repellent or mosquito coils, especially in the wet season. The cheapest hotels may have rats so stay in a medium-priced hotel to minimise the chance of seeing them if it worries you.

Although the chance of being bitten by a sea snake is remote, every once in a while they get washed up on the beaches. Don't pick them up, as they are venomous.

Places to Stay

Atacames can get rather full at weekends, especially holiday weekends, so you are advised to try and arrive mid-week. January through March is the high season, when prices tend to rise. At other times you can try bargaining, especially if you arrive mid-week and plan on staying a few days.

New hotels, or old hotels under new management and name, open frequently and there's always a wide choice of places to stay. There are about 20 or 30 hotels to choose from within an area of four or five blocks by the beach – I am not going to try and describe them all. Always check your room or cabin for security before you rent it.

Most showers have brackish water (which is quite salty) and only the more expensive hotels have fresh-water showers.

Places to Stay – bottom end

For the cheapest accommodation the best selection is to your right after you cross the footbridge. The *San Baye* is one of the cheapest places. They charge US$4 a double. Some rooms have a private bathroom for US$1 extra. A good choice is the *Hostal Jennifer* (☎ 710 482, 731 055) which has clean, spacious rooms for US$3 per person. Perhaps the best of the budget places, on the beach and often full, is the *Hotel Galerias Atacames* (☎ 731 149). The owners speak excellent English and the rooms are good value for about US$3/5 for singles/doubles with private bath.

Places to Stay – middle

The *Cabañas Los Bohios* (☎ 731 089, 525 228) has small but clean private cabins with brackish showers for about US$4/7.50 for singles/doubles – prices rise in the busy season. Similarly priced is the *Hotel Rodelu* (☎ 731 033, 712 244) which has basic but clean rooms with private bath. The *Hotel Chavalito* (☎ 731 113) is run by an ex-merchant marine who has a fund of good stories to keep you entertained. Rooms with private baths cost about US$7.50 a double. The two best rooms at the front of the hotel have ocean-view balconies.

For families or groups the following can be recommended. *Villas Arco Iris* (☎ 731 069) have clean and comfortable cabins with private bath and kitchen facilities. Rates are US$16 for four beds. *Residencial Jorgé's* (☎ 731 064) has clean rooms sleeping six for US$20. Each room has a balcony, refrigerator, and private bathroom. Other possibilities in this price range include the *Hotel Casa Blanca* (☎ 731 031), the *Cabañas Le'Castell* (☎ 731 289), and the *Casitas Familiares Marbella* (☎ 731 129).

The *Costa del Sol* is described as dirty and over-priced. The *Tahiti* has had robberies reported by travellers. One traveller wrote 'my wife and I were robbed by a night watchman who ran away dropping a gun and the hotel keys.' Another traveller wrote that the hotel is 'very friendly, cheap, clean, US$3.50 per person'. This illustrates one of the main difficulties of being a travel survival kit writer – every traveller has their own unique experiences and no description I give will be right for everybody.

Places to Eat

There are many simple comedores close to the beach near the footbridge. They all tend to serve the same thing – whatever was caught that morning. Make sure you ask the price before you get served or you may be overcharged. All the comedores seem to be much of a likeness, so wander around till you find one that you fancy. Many of them double as bars or dancing places in the evenings and their popularity changes with the seasons. Keep your ears open and you'll soon hear where it's happening.

Getting There & Away

Bus All buses stop on the main road near the road to the footbridge crossing the Río Atacames; there is no bus terminal. If leaving Atacames, you pay for your ticket after you board the bus. Buses for Esmeraldas (US$0.30; 45 minutes) normally begin from Súa and there are plenty of seats. Most buses from Esmeraldas to Atacames continue to Súa. Buses for Muisne (US$0.60; 1½ hours further down the coast) are often full when they come from Esmeraldas and you may find it easier to return to Esmeraldas and then retrace your route. Alternatively, be prepared to ride on the roof or stand the whole way.

Taxi Taxis from either Esmeraldas Airport or downtown Esmeraldas charge about US$10 to Atacames.

SÚA

This is a small fishing village and is rather more bustling than Atacames from a fisherperson's point of view. It's an interesting place to stay if you'd rather watch the boats and fishers at work than just hang out on the beach. The fishing industry brings its attendant frigatebirds, pelicans and other sea birds but also means that the small beach is dirtier than the one at Atacames. The general setting is attractive. There is an IETEL office with one phone.

Súa is about a six-km walk by road from Atacames. I've heard that you can walk along the beach at the lowest tides, but if you try this be careful not to get cut off by the tide and go with friends to avoid getting robbed.

Places to Stay & Eat

There's much less to choose from than in Atacames. The *Residencial Quito* is a basic hotel on the road into town which charges US$1.50 each. On the waterfront are several cheap places, of which the *Hotel Súa* and *Residencial Proaño* are the cheapest but aren't up to much. The *Residencial España* has a dance floor and is liable to be noisy if it's a party night on the weekend. They charge US$1.50 each. Slightly better is the *Residencial Mar y Sol* for US$2 each. They also have a couple of rooms with private showers for twice that price. The *Hotel Chagra Ramos* (☎ 713 202) is the best place in town and has singles/doubles with fan and private bath for US$4/6 in the off-season. There is a good restaurant here. Otherwise you can try the cheap comedores past the *Residencial España*.

Getting There & Away

Buses to and from Esmeraldas run about every 45 minutes and arrive and leave from in front of the Residencial Mar y Sol. It takes 10 minutes to Atacames (US$0.10) and about an hour to Esmeraldas (US$0.35). You pay on the bus.

If you want to go further along the coast to Muisne you have to wait out of town along the main road for a bus passing from Esmeraldas (often full).

SAME

This small village is a quiet beach resort

about five or six km south-west of Súa. Same lacks the hustle and bustle of Súa or Atacames and is slightly more expensive. The beach is palm-fringed and clean.

Places to Stay – bottom end

La Terraza near the beach charges US$3.50 per person. Their restaurant and bar is popular and the service reportedly slow. Other cheap places include *Cabañas Isla del Sol* at the end of the beach, with basic cabins sleeping four to six people for about US$20. The *Cabañas Canoas* is also in this price range and is OK.

Places to Stay – middle

El Acantilado (☎ 235 034, 550 535) is located on a cliff overlooking a small but private beach. They have cabins for four to eight people, each with kitchen facilities and daily maid service. Rates are about US$6 per person. The *Hotel Manila* charges US$26 for a cabin with four beds. The owners are friendly and discounts can be arranged for longer stays. Reservations can be made through Wagons-Lit Turismo in Quito (☎ 235 110, 560 472).

Places to Stay – top end

Hotel Club Casablanca is a first-class resort with swimming pool and games facilities. Reservations can be made through Wagons-Lit Turismo in Quito (☎ 235 110, 560 472).

TONCHIGÜE

This beach is a continuation of the Same beach (described earlier). The *El Acantilado* hotel is actually between Same and Tonchigüe. There is also the cheaper *Cabañas Luz del Mar* and other cheaper places to stay.

MUISNE

This small port is fairly important for banana shipping. It is on an island at the end of the road from Esmeraldas. I like Muisne because it is relatively remote and far fewer people come here than the more popular beaches like Atacames. You can sometimes ride on top of the bus and enjoy the views of rolling green countryside with tropical trees and birds.

Orientation & Information

At the end of the road you have to take a motorised dugout across the Río Muisne to the island. Boat owners will meet the bus and take you to their boat – just follow other passengers. The fare is about US$0.10 and boats leave every few minutes. When you disembark at Muisne you'll see the main road heading south-west directly away from the pier into the town 'centre'. There is an IETEL office here but it's often closed. It's best to continue on the main road, past the town square, and towards the ocean. The 'main road' deteriorates into a grassy lane and it's about 1½ km to the beach.

Some of the hotels will change or accept cash dollars – try the Ipanema or the Galápagos.

Warnings There have been reports of thefts from beach cabins, some of which are not very secure. Bring your own padlock and check the windows. Single travellers, particularly women, should not wander the beach away from the hotels and restaurants – rapes and muggings have been reported.

Note that water shortages occur frequently in Muisne.

Places to Stay

The basic *Residencial Nuevo Muisne* is on the mainland side of the river, near the dock and bus terminal. Most travellers elect to cross the river to the island. In the town centre the basic and unremarkable *Pensión Ginger* and *Residencial Muisne* charge about US$1.50 per person. The better *Pensión Sarita* charges about US$2 per person and has some rooms with private baths.

About 750 metres before arriving at the beach, and one block to the right of the 'main road', you pass the *Hotel Galápagos*. They are the most expensive in Muisne and charge US$3 per person in rooms with private bathroom. The rooms on the left hand side of the hotel (as you face it) are quieter. The

Galápagos is the best and most secure place to stay.

Closer to the beach are the *Cabinas Ipanema* which charge US$2.50 per person in basic cabins with private bath. On the beach itself, the *Hotel Delfín* is to the left and charges US$1.50 per person in clean but basic rooms. To the right are a set of cabins with no name, charging US$2/3 for singles/doubles with bath.

Places to Eat

The *Bambu Bar* on the corner of the main plaza has good, reasonably priced food. There are several inexpensive comedores on the beach – names, owners and popularity among travellers seem to change every year. There is a basic store by the beach where simple foodstuffs can be bought. There's a lot of driftwood on the beach and some travellers cook their own food.

Entertainment

The Disco Maitai on the beach is open on weekend evenings.

Getting There & Away

Bus La Costeñita has buses about every hour to Esmeraldas (US$0.90; 2½ hours) passing Same, Súa and Atacames en route.

Boat There are two or three boats a day to Cojimíes (US$3; 2 hours). They leave from the dock at the end of the road from Esmeraldas.

Nearby Excursions

You can take a boat trip up the Río Muisne to see the mangrove forests. There are passenger canoes going once or twice a day to **San Gregorio** (US$1; 1½ hours). At San Gregorio, the red house on the left side of the church on the main plaza is a place where you can get information about the area. To get back to Muisne, stand by the river and flag down any boat that is heading down river. You can hire your own boat for about US$8 per hour.

SOUTH OF MUISNE

There is no road south of Muisne, so if you want to travel further south you have to take a boat or walk. The boat trip takes you out past the mangroves of the Río Muisne and into the open ocean – crossing from the river mouth into the ocean can be tricky and exciting. The open section can get very wet because of spray, so be prepared. The boat rounds Punta Portete and heads in towards a protected river delta near Bolívar before continuing 'inland' past Daule and on to Cojimíes.

You can also head south on foot and get to Cojimíes in one day if you leave early. At low tide, pickup trucks sometimes act as buses on some sections and you may get a ride, but don't rely on them. There are several rivers to cross but you can find dugouts to ferry you for a few sucres. Bring change. Make sure you leave when the tide is falling to make sure you are not cut off by a high tide later in the day. From Muisne, walk south along the beach for about five km (this first section can be avoided by taking a boat to Las Manchas on the way to San Gregorio); take a dugout across the river and continue seven km along the beach past Mompiche (small store); follow a jeep track over the headland four km to Punta Suspiro; make the dugout crossing to Portete (small store); walk five km to Bolívar.

Although you can sometimes catch rides, be prepared to walk the whole distance if necessary. I've done this walk twice and seen sea snakes, a beached whale, crabs galore, jellyfish, seabirds and other sea creatures along the beach.

Bolívar has a little port and if you wait and ask around you can get a boat ride to Cojimíes for about US$1.50. It may take a few hours to get a passage so leave Muisne at dawn, as there are no hotels in Bolívar. You can rent a boat for about US$15 to take you to Cojimíes if you can't get a ride.

COJIMÍES

Cojimíes is a small port with road connections to the south. It is sometimes cut off by heavy rains. Because it is so isolated, food prices in Cojimíes tend to be expensive.

The village is on a headland which is constantly being washed away into the ocean. Consequently, the village has to keep moving inland and the houses closest to the sea get washed away every few years. The locals say that the cemetery, now near the shoreline, was once way at the back of the town.

Places to Stay & Eat

There are a few very basic (wash in a bucket) places to stay on or just off the one main street. These include the *Residencial Cojimíes* and *Residencial España*. The *Residencial Mi Descanso* is a little better and has one shower, which works intermittently. Basic rooms are US$1.25 per person. The newest and best place is *Hotel Costa Azul*.

There are a few basic restaurants with pricey meals. Ask around to eat in small comedores in people's houses – the meals are cheaper and often better.

The *Hotel Coco Solo* is 14 km south of Cojimíes – a hotel lost in the coconut groves. It's for lovers of deserted beaches and the noise of the wind clattering through the palm leaves. Rates are about US$6 per person in the cabins; there is a restaurant with a limited menu. Horseback riding can be arranged. Reservations can be made in Quito (☎ 565 504, 564 444).

Getting There & Away

Air There is a small airstrip with occasional flights to and from Pedernales during the wet season (see under Pedernales).

Bus The Costa del Norte bus office is on the main street and can give transportation information. Trucks to the next village of Pedernales cost US$1 and take about 1½ hours – they simply run along the beach for much of the way. Departures depend on low tide – if the tide is rising, you could be in town for 12 hours or more before the next vehicle can make it out. Buses sometimes go further, depending on the state of the 'road'. Cojimíes is occasionally cut off by road during the wet season (January to May).

Boat There is a shack by the beach which sells tickets for the boat to Muisne (US$3; 2 hours). Although there is a posted schedule listing four daily departures, boats don't stick to schedule. My boat left 1½ hours early because all the seats had already been sold. If a boat isn't full at departure time, the captain may hang around for an extra hour.

PEDERNALES

Pedernales is about 40 km south of Cojimíes and, with a population of some 10,000 inhabitants, it is the most important market town between Muisne and Bahía de Caráquez. Until recently, fishing and agriculture (especially bananas, cacao and coffee) were the main industries. Now the shrimp industry has expanded from the south, and there are many shrimp ponds and hatcheries in the area. This new industry has given Pedernales a free-wheeling, boom town and frontier atmosphere. The people are hard-working and friendly, but will cheerfully overcharge you if you give them half a chance.

Pedernales is about eight km north of the equator. There is a monument marking the equator near the beach at the appropriate spot.

Places to Stay

The best hotel in town is the *Hotel Playas* which is clean and friendly – but you have to bargain hard. Rooms with private bath and TV rent for US$4 per person for Ecuadorians – but gringos are often charged twice that! Being friendly and speaking Spanish is the best approach to avoid being overcharged.

There are several cheaper places which aren't as good but will be OK for most budget travellers. These include the *Residencial Hamacas, Hotel Turismo* and *Residencial Gitano* among others.

Getting There & Away

Air AECA (☎ 288 110 in Guayaquil) has flights from Guayaquil in the morning, returning to Guayaquil in the afternoon daily except Sunday. Fares are about US$17 one way. Stops are sometimes made at intermediate points such as Bahía de Caráquez and

Portoviejo. These flights are often subject to passenger demand.

NICA has flights in three or five passenger aircraft between Pedernales and Bahía de Caráquez several times a day, depending on passenger demand. This may mean one or two flights in the dry season but several more flights in the wet season when the roads may be impassable. The one-way fare is US$12. Flights may continue to Cojimíes on demand. These small aircraft have very limited luggage space – 10 kg is the usual maximum. These coastal flights give a good look at the coastline, shrimp hatcheries, banana plantations, and villages of the area.

Bus There is a Costa del Norte bus office on the main street where you can buy tickets for Cojimíes (northbound) or San Vicente (southbound; US$3; four hours). There are three or four departures a day. The buses (often trucks or rancheros) usually follow the beach and the ride is very fast on the hard-packed sand, especially between Pedernales and Cojimíes. There are some rougher stretches south of Pedernales. Bus travel depends on tides and road conditions and delays are frequent during the wet months of January to April.

There is an inland dirt road (between San Vicente and Pedernales and on to Cojimíes) which avoids the beach, but it is very rough and seldom used. There is also a rough road which heads inland to El Carmen and on to Santo Domingo de los Colorados. Now and then trucks take this road but there seems to be no regular bus service yet.

JAMA

This village is becoming more important since a shrimp hatchery was opened nearby. There are a couple of basic places to stay of which the *Hotel Jamaica* has showers and is as good as any.

Buses (trucks) between Pedernales and San Vicente pass through Jama in either direction, but may be full when they come through. If so, ride on the roof.

CANOA

This village is about 8 km north of San Vicente and has a quiet beach, a basic pensión, and a few beach-front comedores. It is fairly straightforward to get here by bus or truck going up the beach from San Vicente.

SAN VICENTE

This resort village is a short ferry ride across the Río Chone from the more important town of Bahía de Caráquez. There are beaches and a few hotels, a market, and the regional airport.

Places to Stay

If you turn right from the pier you'll find two cheap and basic places for US$1 each – the *Residencial San Vicente* and *Lilita*.

Closer to the pier is the more expensive but good *Hotel Vacaciones* (☎ 690 671), which charges US$8 a single and US$14 a double. They have a pool and decent restaurant. On the northern outskirts of town on the road to Pedernales there are the *Cabañas Alcatraz* (☎ 690 842) and *Hotel Las Hamacas* (☎ 690 889, ext 134, or 542 700 in Quito). Both have bungalows with private bathroom, a pool, a private beach, and charge about US$7.50 per person. Three km north of San Vicente on the beach is *Cabañas La Playa* (☎ 690 889, ext 148) with family bungalows costing about US$20. They have a restaurant.

Places to Eat

Behind the market there are some cheap and clean comedores such as the *Yessenia*. The best hotels have restaurants.

Getting There & Away

Air There is an airstrip for light aircraft behind the market. This is the main regional airport serving Bahía de Caráquez. The airline offices are in Bahía and further information is given under that town.

Bus San Vicente is the main office of the Costa del Norte company and they have three or four buses (trucks, rancheros) a day to Pedernales, one or two to Cojimíes and two inland to Chone. The bus office is close to the boat pier.

Boat Ferries take 10 minutes to reach Bahía de Caráquez and leave several times an hour all day long. The fare is US$0.10. After 9 pm it costs about US$1.25 to hire a boat to take you across (four passengers maximum). There is a car ferry. You can hire boats for trips anywhere you want for US$5 an hour.

BAHÍA DE CARÁQUEZ

This is a small (18,000 inhabitants) but nevertheless fairly important port and holiday resort. There are beaches both here and across the river in San Vicente. For some reason it is rarely visited by foreign travellers although the beaches are as good as elsewhere and the hotels adequate. The Río Chone entrance is quite busy and you can laze around at a riverside café and watch the boats go by, or go for a ferry ride.

Orientation & Information

The Banco Central (on the Malecón) sometimes changes US dollars or even travellers' cheques, but you can't rely on this. There are both IETEL and post offices and a cinema. To get to the best beaches go north on Avenida Montúfar for about 500 metres. The strange-looking corrugated tin church on the main plaza is worth a look if you've nothing better to do. The locals simply refer to the town as 'Bahía'.

Places to Stay – bottom end

Most of the cheapest places have singles/doubles for US$2/3.50. These include the friendly *Residencial Tamarindo* (☎ 690 513) at the west end of Ascazubi – they often have problems with water supply, as do other cheap hotels in town. Other basic places at this price include the *Residencial San José*, *Hotel Manabí*, *Pensión Victoria* and *Pensión Miriam*.

Slightly better places include the *Hotel Vera*, on Ante and Montúfar, which charges US$2 per person or US$3 per person in rooms with private bath – they have their

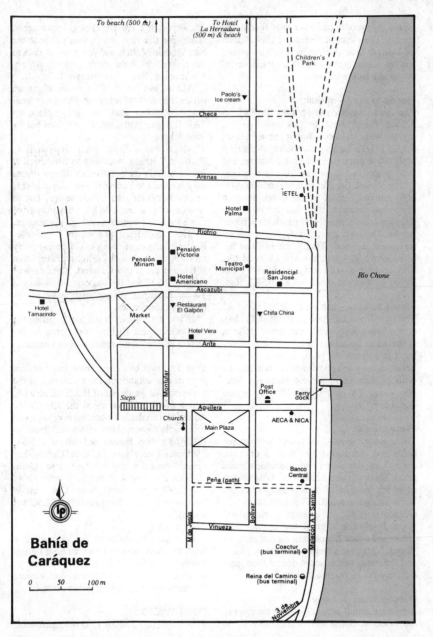

To beach (500 m)

To Hotel
La Herradura
(500 m) & beach

Children's
Park

Paolo's
Ice cream ▼

Checa

Arenas

IETEL ●

Hotel ■
Palma

Riofrio

Pensión ■
Victoria
Pensión
Miriam ■
Teatro
Municipal
Residencial
San José
■
Hotel ■
Americano

Ascazubi

Hotel ■
Tamarindo

Restaurant
▼ El Galpón

▼ Chifa China

Market

Hotel Vera ■

Ante

Río Chone

Post
Office ■
Ferry
dock

Steps

Aguilera

Church ✝
Main Plaza

AECA & NICA

Banco
Central ●

Peña (path)

Vinueza

Coactur ◉
(bus terminal)

Reina del Camino ◉
(bus terminal)

M de Jesús

Bolívar

Malecón A F Santos

3 de Noviembre

Bahía de Caráquez

0   50   100 m

own water supply but have very few single rooms. The clean and secure *Hotel Palma*, on Bolívar near Ríofrio, is similarly priced and has more singles available – but many of the rooms lack windows.

Places to Stay – middle

The *Hotel Americano* (☎ 690 524/94), on Ascazubi and Montúfar, has rooms with a private bath, air-conditioning and telephone for US$11/16 for singles/doubles – rather a prohibitive price jump from the bottom-end hotel prices, but there's nothing in between.

The *Hotel La Herradura* (☎ 690 446/266), on Bolívar out by the beach north of town, has been in operation for over two decades and is the oldest of Bahía's better hotels. The staff are friendly and the hotel restaurant is good. The beach is close by. Most rooms have telephone or TV available. Singles/doubles with fans are US$15/17 and rooms with air-conditioning are US$2 more.

Places to Stay – top end

The new *Hotel La Piedra* (☎ 690 780/154), on the beach just beyond the end of Bolívar, is the most luxurious hotel in Bahía. They have a swimming pool, a 'semi-private' beach, and a good restaurant and bar. Rooms with private bath, air-conditioning, telephone and TV cost US$25/28 for singles/doubles.

Places to Eat

There are some reasonable and inexpensive cafés and parrilladas by the river near the dock – wander down and see which looks good. There are also a couple of cheap chifas, of which the *Chifa China* is simple but has been recommended. The *Restaurant El Galpón* opposite the market is cheap and good. *Paolo's* is a good and popular ice-cream and snack bar on Bolívar just north of Checa. There are several other cheap places and the better hotels serve decent food, particularly the Herradura and La Piedra.

Getting There & Away

Air The regional airport is across the river in San Vicente. Some ferries cross directly to the airport if there are enough passengers; otherwise the ferry drops you off near the San Vicente Market and you have to walk to the right, behind the market, to the airport. It's about a 10 or 15-minute walk.

AECA and NICA Taxi Aereo share an office (☎ 690 377/32) on Montúfar near Ascazubi. They also have information on TAME flights (although TAME does not fly into Bahía).

AECA has a flight from Guayaquil to Bahía at 7.30 am, returning to Guayaquil at 8.45 am daily except Sunday. Some flights may continue to Pedernales or stop at Manta or Portoviejo en route. The one-way fare to Guayaquil is about US$13. They may have more flights if there are enough passengers.

NICA has light planes to Pedernales (occasionally continuing to Cojimíes) every morning except Sunday. Flights are repeated if there is passenger demand. The one-way fare is US$12 and the baggage allowance is 10 kg maximum. They also have planes available for charter.

If you are unable to get to the office the day before you fly, try just going to the airport before 7 am – space is often available.

Bus The two bus companies have offices next to one another on the south end of the malecón. All buses out of Bahía climb a hill which gives good views of the Río Chone estuary; sit on the left when leaving town and look back. Coactur have buses to Portoviejo (US$0.80; two hours) and Manta (US$1; 2½ hours) every hour. Reina del Camino has several buses a day to Portoviejo, Quito (US$3.20; eight hours), Esmeraldas (US$2.90; eight hours), Santo Domingo de los Colorados and Guayaquil (US$2.50; six hours).

Boat Passenger ferries to San Vicente leave from the dock several times an hour during daylight (US$0.10; 10 minutes). There is also a car ferry to San Vicente. San Vicente has more boats for hire to other areas.

PORTOVIEJO

This large city of about 110,000 inhabitants,

founded on 12 March 1535, is one of the oldest in Ecuador. It is the capital of Manabí Province, which is important for coffee and cattle. Portoviejo has a thriving agricultural processing industry and is an important commercial centre with good road connections with Quito and Guayaquil. It is a bustling town but not visited much by tourists who prefer to head to the coast, especially for the major resort and port of Manta some 37 km away.

Orientation
Most travellers arrive at the bus terminal which is 1 km west of downtown. The streets have both names and numbers but locals tend to use the names more frequently.

Information
The Banco Comercial de Manabí (☎ 653 888) or the Banco de Pichincha (☎ 651 900) are the most likely places to change money.

The post office (☎ 652 384) is in the government buildings on the main plaza and there is an IETEL office.

The public hospital (☎ 650 766) is out of town; take a taxi there or call the Red Cross ambulance (☎ 652 555)

Things to See
Despite the town's colonial history, there are few old buildings. There is a **Museo de Casa de Cultura** (☎ 651 753), on Sucre near García Moreno, with an exhibit of traditional musical instruments, but opening hours are erratic and unpredictable. You can wander down to the pleasant **Parque Eloy Alfaro**, where you'll find the starkest, barest modern **cathedral** I've seen in Ecuador. It takes the wind out of the sails of those people who complain that the Catholic church in Latin America spends all of its money on gold ornaments. Next to the cathedral you will find a **statue of Francisco Pacheco**, the founder of Portoviejo.

Places to Stay – bottom end
The basic *Pensión Cristal*, on Ricaurte and Pedro Gual, charges only US$1 per night but

is often full by mid-afternoon so it can't be too bad. The *Residencial Alfaro*, on Olmedo and F de Moreira, is basic but fairly clean and charges US$1.50 each. Many of its rooms are without windows. This seems to be a fairly common problem.

Many of the rooms at the *Residencial Pacheco* (☎ 651 788), 9 de Octubre 512 near Universitaria, are also without windows but they do at least have fans. They charge US$2 per person or US$3.60 in rooms with a private bath. *Hotel Portoviejo Plaza* (☎ 634 442), on Universitaria and Pedro Gual, has small but clean rooms for US$2 single or US$5 double with a private bath. Unfortunately its nicest rooms look out on the street and so are noisy.

The *Hotel Paris* (☎ 652 727), Sucre 513 and Olmedo, is a simple but good, clean, old and rather charming hotel. Rooms with private baths are US$2.50 per person and this is a recommended choice for budget travellers. The good, clean *Hotel Gregorio*, on Rocafuerte near Alajuela, charges US$3 per person in rooms with private baths and US$2.50 if you use the communal bath. *Hotel Madrid*, on Pedro Gual and García Moreno, has clean and spacious rooms with fans for US$3.50 per person, or US$4.50 per person with air-conditioning. The *Hotel Conquistador* (☎ 651 472, 633 259), 18 de Octubre 407 and 10 de Agosto has quite nice rooms with private bath, fan and telephone for US$4/7 for singles/doubles. The *Hostal Zucasa* is by the bus terminal, and charges about the same.

Places to Stay – middle
The *Hotel San Marcos* (☎ 650 650/1), on Olmedo and 9 de Octubre, has singles/doubles with phone, fan and private bath for US$6/10. Better rooms with air-conditioning cost a couple of dollars more. The *Hotel Cabrera Internacional* (☎ 633 199/200, 652 159), García Moreno 102 and Pedro Gual, charges US$5.50/10 in rooms with private bath and fan or US$8/13 with air-conditioning. Both hotels are OK, though nothing special.

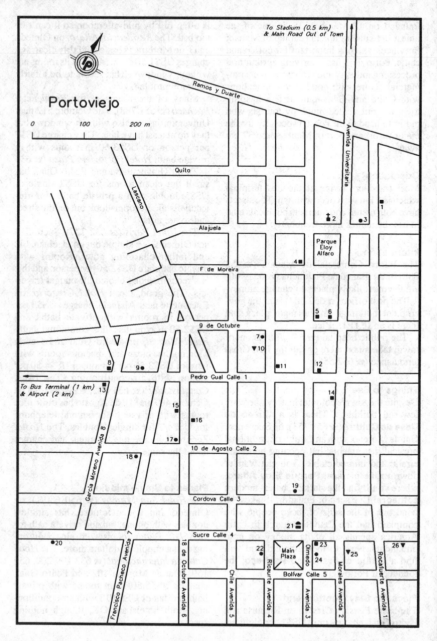

Portoviejo

0   100   200 m

To Stadium (0.5 km)
& Main Road Out of Town

Ramos y Duarte

Quito

Lascano

Alajuela

F de Moreira

9 de Octubre

Pedro Gual Calle 1

To Bus Terminal (1 km)
& Airport (2 km)

10 de Agosto Calle 2

Cordova Calle 3

Sucre Calle 4

Bolívar Calle 5

Main Plaza

Avenida Universitaria

Parque
Eloy
Alfaro

García Moreno Avenida 8

Francisco Pacheco Avenida 7

18 de Octubre Avenida 6

Chile Avenida 5

Ricaurte Avenida 4

Avenida 3

Olmedo

Morales Avenida 2

Rocafuerte Avenida 1

■ PLACES TO STAY

1   Hotel Gregorio
4   Residencial Alfaro
5   Hotel San Marcos
6   Residencial Pacheco
8   Hotel Madrid
11 Pensión Cristal
12 Hotel Comisario El Gato
13 Hotel Cabrera Internacional
14 Hotel Portoviejo Plaza
15 Hotel Conquistador
16 Hotel Ejecutivo
23 Hotel Paris & Chifa

▼ PLACES TO EAT

10 Restaurant Oasis
25 Restaurant Mariano & Chifa Luk
26 Heladería Venecia

    OTHER

2   Cathedral
3   Francisco Pacheco Statue
7   TAME
9   Cine Acapulco
17 Banco Comercial de Manabí
18 IETEL
19 Cine
20 Museo de Casa de Cultura
21 Post Office
22 Cine Central
24 Banco de Pichincha

Places to Stay – top end

The *Hotel Ejecutivo* (☎ 632 105/235/385, 652 108), on 18 de Octubre near 10 de Agosto, charges US$27/32 or US$38/44 for a single/double depending on whether you want a regular rooms or a suite. This is the best in town but the staff have been described as provincial snobs.

The *Hotel Comisario El Gato* is a new place on Pedro Gual and Olmedo which is also in the top-end price range.

Places to Eat

The *Restaurant Oasis* is a chifa on top of the shopping mall north of the corner of Pedro Gual and Chile. There is outside dining and views of the city. Inside dining is also an option and the prices are reasonable, even though it looks quite elegant and the food is good. Another good choice is the *Restaurant Mariano* at Morales and Sucre – the *Chifa Luk* is a couple of doors down. There is also an inexpensive chifa below the *Hotel Paris*. The *Heladería Venecia*, on Sucre near Rocafuerte, is clean and has the best ice cream in town

Getting There & Away

Air The TAME office (☎ 652 429, 650 000) is at Ricaurte 608 and 9 de Octubre. The airport (☎ 650 361) is about two km northwest of town (taxi US$0.60). TAME has flights from Quito at 4 pm, returning from Portoviejo to Quito at 5 pm, Monday to Friday. There used to be a Sunday flight but it has been suspended. The one-way fare is US$16. Although Portoviejo is the provincial capital, the beach resort of Manta, 35 km away, has more flights to Quito.

AECA (☎ 288 110 in Guayaquil) has flights from Guayaquil every day except Sunday at 7.15 am and 4.15 pm, returning to Guayaquil at 8 am and 5 pm. Fares are about US$12 and planes often stop at Manta en route.

Bus There is a new central bus terminal ('Terminal Terrestre') about one km west of town, beyond the Río Portoviejo. A taxi will take you downtown for about US$0.50.

Coactur has several buses an hour to Manta (US$0.50; 50 minutes). They also have buses for Bahía de Caráquez (US$0.80; two hours). CTM Aerotaxi also has buses for Manta. Rutas Ecuatorianas has frequent service to Guayaquil (US$2; 3½ hours). Carlos A Aray has many buses to Santo Domingo de los Colorados (US$2.70; five hours) with some buses continuing to Quito (US$3.80; eight hours) or going to Guayaquil. Reina del Camino has buses to Quito, Santo Domingo, Esmeraldas (US$3.30; nine hours), Bahía de Caráquez and Guayaquil. Flota Bolívar has two slow, old buses leaving at 8 am and 1 pm for Quevedo. Ciudad de Calceta has buses to Calceta.

Co-op 15 de Octubre and Co-op Jipijapa

have buses to Jipijapa about every 45 minutes. Other small nearby villages, including the beaches of San Clemente and Crucita in the Bahía de Manta region, are served by small bus companies which often use open-sided rancheros.

INLAND FROM PORTOVIEJO

Manabí is an important agricultural province and a relatively good road system links Portoviejo with a number of cantón capitals. These towns act as market centres for coffee, cattle, citrus, corn, cotton, yucca and bananas. The towns are colourful and bustling, and often quite large, but they are rarely visited by tourists. This region is quite easy to travel in using the small local buses and rancheros, and you can find cheap and basic hotels in the bigger towns. The people are hard working and friendly, and this area would provide a great glimpse of rural and provincial Ecuadorian life for those travellers who want to get off the beaten track.

Rocafuerte, approximately 20 km north of Portoviejo, is known for its confectionery made of coconuts and caramel. **Calceta**, 43 km north-east of Portoviejo, is known for sisal production. Sisal is the fibre gathered from the spiny-leaved agave plant which grows in the region. The sisal fibres are used for ropes and sandals, among other things.

From Calceta, a good road continues about 25 km north-east to the sizable town of **Chone**. From here, an important but not frequently travelled road continues northeast, linking the coastal lowlands with Santo Domingo, 155 km away. This road climbs to over 600 metres above sea level as it crosses the coastal mountains, then drops back down on the eastern side of these mountains to the cantón capitals and market towns of **Flavio Alfaro** and **El Carmen** en route to Santo Domingo.

MANTA

Manta, with about 140,000 inhabitants, is the major port along the central Ecuadorian coast and an important tourist resort and commercial centre. Despite its popularity among (mainly Ecuadorian) tourists, the

Above: Manteño stone seat or throne
Below: 'Mother and child' figure, Bahía culture

city's beaches are not very good, though there are better ones in nearby villages. Some of the beach-front restaurants, however, do serve good seafood.

Manta has a long history. It was founded by Francisco Pacheco on 2 March 1535, 10 days before he founded Portoviejo. But even before its Spanish foundation Manta, named Jocay by the local Indians, was an important port. The Manta culture thrived throughout the whole western peninsula from about 500 AD until the arrival of the conquistadors, and many artefacts made by these early inhabitants have been found.

The pottery of the Manta culture was well made and decorated with pictures of daily life. Through these pictorial decorations, archaeologists have learnt that the Manta people enhanced their appearance by skull deformation and tooth removal, thus increasing the backward slope of their foreheads and chins and emphasising their large, rounded, hooked noses. This facial structure is apparent in many of the local people even today.

Also evident in their pottery, as well as being recorded in detail by the early conquistadors, was the Mantas' astonishing skill in seamanship. They were able to navigate as far as Panama and Peru, and claims have been made that they reached the Galápagos. There are records claiming that the Manta seafarers sailed as far north as Mexico and as far south as Chile.

Capitán Bartolomé Ruiz captured a Manta balsa sailing raft in 1526 and recorded that of the 20 crew members, 11 jumped overboard in terror, and the remainder were captured for translating purposes and later freed. Similar but smaller balsa rafts can still be seen sailing the coasts today.

Not only their navigational and ceramic skills were well developed. The Mantas were also skilled stonemasons, weavers and metal workers. People wishing to learn more about the Manta culture should visit the museum in the town.

After the conquest, Manta had a history of attack and destruction by pirates from various European countries. Attacks in 1543,

1607 and 1628 left the city ruined and the survivors fleeing for inland areas, in particular Montecristi.

Orientation

The town is divided into two by an inlet. Manta is on the west side and Tarqui on the east. They are joined by a road bridge. Avenidas and calles in Manta are single or double digits; Avenidas or calles in Tarqui begin at Calle 101. Manta has the main offices and shopping areas, as well as the bus terminal. Tarqui has a bigger hotel selection and beaches. The main residential areas are to the south-west of Manta business district.

Information

Tourist Office In Manta there is a CETUR tourist information office (☎ 611 558) on Avenida 3 between Calle 10 and Calle 11. This whole block is a pedestrian precinct with no traffic allowed.

Money The Banco Pacifico (☎ 613 200), on Avenida 3 near Calle 12, changes money, as do the exchange houses nearby. Rates vary from day to day and place to place, so shop around. They are usually 2% to 5% lower than in Quito.

Post & Telecommunications There is an impressive modern IETEL building on the waterfront in Manta. The post office is on Calle 8. DHL International (☎ 612 155, 611 186) has air courier service from Manta.

Travel Agencies Principal travel agents include Metropolitan Touring (☎ 611 600), Avenida 3, 1149 and Calle 11, and Ecuadorian Tours (☎ 611 796), Avenida 2, 1342 and Calle 13.

Medical Services The public hospital (☎ 613 403) is on Avenida 24 and Calle 13. A physician who has been recommended is Dr Oscar Pico Santos (☎ 611 482/080). The Clinica Dental (☎ 610 163, 612 670) is at Avenida 3, 1023 and Calle 10. There are many pharmacies – a good one is Farmacia

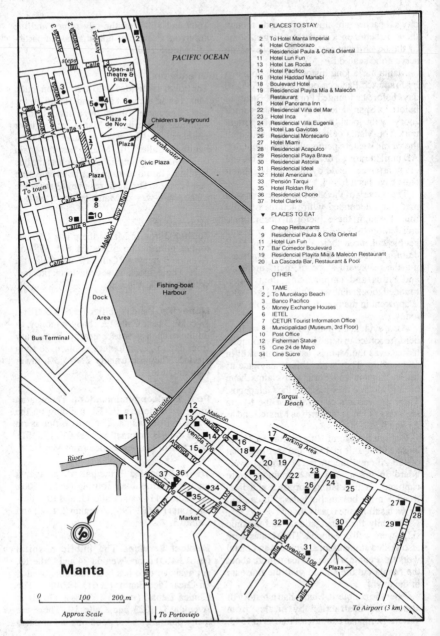

PACIFIC OCEAN

PLACES TO STAY

2   To Hotel Manta Imperial
4   Hotel Chimborazo
9   Residencial Paula & Chifa Oriental
11 Hotel Lun Fun
13 Hotel Las Rocas
14 Hotel Pacifico
16 Hotel Haddad Manabí
18 Boulevard Hotel
19 Residencial Playita Mía & Malecón
    Restaurant
21 Hotel Panorama Inn
22 Residencial Viña del Mar
23 Hotel Inca
24 Residencial Villa Eugenia
25 Hotel Las Gaviotas
26 Residencial Montecarlo
27 Hotel Miami
28 Residencial Acapulco
29 Residencial Playa Brava
30 Residencial Astoria
31 Residencial Ideal
32 Hotel Americana
33 Pensión Tarqui
35 Hotel Roldan Rol
36 Residencial Chone
37 Hotel Clarke

PLACES TO EAT

4   Cheap Restaurants
9   Residencial Paula & Chifa Oriental
11 Hotel Lun Fun
17 Bar Comedor Boulevard
19 Residencial Playita Mía & Malecón Restaurant
20 La Cascada Bar, Restaurant & Pool

OTHER

1   TAME
2   To Murciélago Beach
3   Banco Pacifico
5   Money Exchange Houses
6   IETEL
7   CETUR Tourist Information Office
8   Municipalidad (Museum, 3rd Floor)
10 Post Office
12 Fisherman Statue
15 Cine 24 de Mayo
34 Cine Sucre

Open-air theatre & plaza

steps

Calle 3

Avenida 3
Avenida 2
Avenida 1

Calle 1

Avenida 4
Avenida 5
Avenida 6

Plaza 4 de Nov

Children's Playground

Calle 11

Plaza

Calle 10

Breakwater

Civic Plaza

Plaza

To town

Calle 9

Calle 8

Malecón / Hoy Alfaro

Calle 7

Dock Area

Fishing-boat Harbour

Bus Terminal

Tarqui Beach

Breakwater

River

Malecón

Avenida 102
Avenida 104
Avenida 106

Parking Area

Avenida 105

Avenida 107

Calle 101

Calle 103

Market

Calle 105

Avenida 108

Avenida 106

Avenida 110

Calle 107

Calle 109

Plaza

Manta

0   100   200 m

Approx Scale

↓ To Portoviejo

To Airport (3 km)

Imperial (☎ 611 688, 612 982), Calle 104, 507 in Tarqui.

Emergency Contact the police on ☎ 610 900, the fire department on ☎ 610 200 and the Red Cross ambulance service on ☎ 613 904.

Things to See & Do

The **Municipal Museum** on the 3rd floor of the Municipalidad on Calle 9 is worth a visit to understand more of the Manta culture. The exhibit is small, but is well laid out and labelled in Spanish. Although it's officially open from 9 am to 3 pm Monday to Friday, but they sometimes close for lunch.

Manta's **fishing boat harbour** is busy and picturesque. To get over to Tarqui, don't follow the harbour around or you'll have to swim. Cross on the bridge set back from the harbour. In Tarqui there is a huge **statue of a Manabí fisherman** and beyond it the protected sandy **Tarqui Beach**. At the end of the beach there are many more fishing boats, which are interesting to watch in the early morning while they unload their cargo. There is a bustling market in Tarqui and a cinema nearby.

The **Playa Murciélago** (beach) in Manta is less protected and has bigger waves. There is a powerful undertow which can sweep swimmers away even when the beach appears fairly calm. It is a couple of km west of the town centre along the waterfront and is less visited than Tarqui Beach.

There is an outdoor theatre in Manta which occasionally has performances, especially during the annual agriculture, fishing & tourism exposition which is held from 14 to 18 October. Portoviejo has a similar event at the same time. You can get more information on what's going on then from the CETUR office in Manta.

Places to Stay – bottom end

Prices tend to rise during holiday weekends and during the December to March high season. At other times of the year, particularly mid-week in the low season, hotels can be almost empty and you can bargain for cheaper rates.

One of the cheapest places in Manta is the *Hotel Chimborazo* on Avenida 1 near the Plaza 4 de Noviembre. They charge about US$1.50 per person. Another cheap place in Manta is the basic *Residencial Paula*.

In Tarqui, a good choice for the budget traveller is the clean and secure *Residencial Villa Eugenia* on the Malecón near Calle 105. It's not very well signposted – but it's there. They charge US$2 per person, have hot water in the communal showers, and are recommended. Other cheap places in Tarqui include the *Residencial Playa Brava* which charges US$2 for basic boxes which do have private bathrooms. The *Residencial Viña del Mar* has basic rooms for US$2 per person or US$5 double with air-conditioning and private bathroom – its cleanliness has been criticised. Similarly priced is the student and youth-group-oriented *Boulevard Hotel* (☎ 613 812, 625 633), on Calle 103 near Avenida 105, which might be a good place to meet young Ecuadorian travellers. Its prices rise during the high season or weekends – basically, they'll charge whatever they can get! The *Residencial Chone*, on Avenida 109 and Calle 102, is reasonably clean and charges US$2 per person. Other cheap hotels are the *Residenciales Acapulco, Montecarlo, Astoria, Ideal* and the *Pensión Tarqui*.

Hotel Miami, on the east end of the Malecón in Tarqui, has simple rooms with private bathrooms and cockroaches for US$3 per person. Some rooms have good ocean views.

Places to Stay – middle

Hotel Clarke (☎ 614 367), on Calle 102 near Avenida 108, charges US$3.25 per person in clean rooms with private bath. It is simple but adequate. *Hotel Roldan Rol* charges US$3.50 per person in rooms with private bath but is near the market and likely to be noisy. *Hotel Americana*, Calle 105 and Avenida 106, is clean, and charges US$7.50 for a double room with a private bath and fan. Air-conditioning costs an extra US$1. Some of the upper rooms have good views. *Residencial Playita Mia*, on the Malecón near Calle 104, charges US$3.75 a single or US$4.50 a single with bath in clean and reasonable rooms. *Hotel Las Rocas* (☎ 612 856, 610 299, 620 607), on Calle 101 at Avenida 105, is a favourite of Ecuadorian tour groups. Singles/doubles are US$4.50/7.50 with bath, and about twice as much for rooms with air-conditioning. Their rooms are clean but their restaurant is nothing special. *Hotel Inca* (☎ 620 440, 610 986), on Calle 105 near the Malecón, charges US$5.50 for a single room with bath and fan, and has some pleasant rooms with air-conditioning, ocean views and private bathrooms for about US$12 a double. The *Hotel Pacifico* (☎ 613 584), on Avenida 106 near Calle 102, is also in this price range.

Hotel Panorama Inn (☎ 611 552/673), on Calle 103 near Avenida 105, has rooms from US$10 to US$16 a double depending on the amenities you choose. Rooms are rather worn but clean and spacious, all with private bathrooms, most with air-conditioning, and some with TV and good views. They give you pool privileges for La Cascada across the street.

Places to Stay – top end

These hotels are considered the best in Manta, although none of them are luxurious. In Manta, the *Hotel Lun Fun* (☎ 622 966, 612 400), on Calle 2 near the Malecón, is good and comfortable. It is the best hotel close to the bus terminal. Singles/doubles are US$13/16.50 in rooms with bathroom and hot water, air-conditioning, and telephone.

In Tarqui, the *Hotel Las Gaviotas* (☎ 610 140, 612 693), on the Malecón near Calle 106, has rooms for US$12 double with bath, or better rooms (with a sea view) for US$19 a double. Also in this price range is the *Hotel Haddad Manabl* (☎ 612 710), on Calle 102 near the Malecón, which dates from 1931 and is Manta's oldest good hotel.

The *Hotel Manta Imperial* (☎ 611 955, 613 016) is near Manta's Playa Murciélago (beach). It has air-conditioning, a swimming pool, a disco at weekends, and a somewhat mediocre restaurant. It charges US$24 a double or US$28 with air-conditioning.

Places to Eat

There are many cheap outdoor comedores on the east end of Tarqui Beach which serve fresh seafood. The market is also a centre for cheap food. There are several restaurants and bars along the Tarqui waterfront, of which the *Bar Comedor Boulevard* has large servings of good and inexpensive food. Opposite it is the slightly pricier but good *Malecón Restaurant* which has good seafood. Both places have outside dining and there are several other restaurants nearby, some of which are cheaper. For a night out you can have a slightly expensive but good meal in the more elegant *La Cascada* (which has a swimming pool).

In Manta, there is the cheap *Chifa Oriental* on Calle 8 at Avenida 4. There are also cheap restaurants near the Hotel Chimborazo by the Plaza 4 de Noviembre. The restaurant at the *Hotel Lun Fun* serves good Chinese and other food and is popular with the locals.

Getting There & Away

Air The TAME office (☎ 612 006) is on the Manta waterfront. TAME has flights from Quito at 8.15 am, returning from Manta to Quito at 9.05 am daily except Sunday. On Sunday, they have a flight from Quito at 3 pm, returning to Quito at 4 pm. The one-way fare is US$16. This service is, as always, subject to change. You can buy tickets at the airport on the morning of the flight but the planes tend to be full at weekends and holidays.

If you can't get on a flight to or from Manta, you could try flying from Portoviejo, 35 km away, where there are afternoon flights to Quito from Monday to Friday.

TAME no longer has flights to Guayaquil – these are now serviced by AECA (☎ 288 810 in Guayaquil). AECA has flights from Guayaquil every day except Sunday at 7.15 am and 4.15 pm, returning to Guayaquil at 8 am and 5.15 pm. Fares are about US$12. Flights may stop in Portoviejo en route.

The airport (☎ 610 450) is some three km

east of Tarqui and a taxi costs about US$1 if you bargain hard.

Bus There is a large central bus terminal in front of the fishing-boat harbour in Manta and almost all buses leave from here, which makes things easy. There are several companies with buses to most major Ecuadorian cities. Journey times and prices are similar to Portoviejo's. Some of the smaller companies running buses to nearby Manabí towns and villages don't have an office in the terminal but their buses leave from there anyway and you pay aboard the bus. An example of this is Coactur's service to Portoviejo.

BAHÍA DE MANTA

Although Manta itself does not have good beaches, several coastal villages on the large Bahía de Manta (Manta Bay), have pleasant beaches and are local resorts. You can get to these villages by local buses and rancheros which take the inland road to Portoviejo and then backtrack to the coast. During low tide, however, vehicles often drive north-east of Manta along the beach. This makes the journey less than half the distance and much quicker. Taxis can be hired to these destinations – the price depends on whether you have to go inland or can drive along the beach. Ecuadorian tourists often go to these villages on day trips, to bathe in the ocean and eat seafood, and then return to their hotel in Manta overnight. Gringo travellers, on the other hand, are seldom seen on these beaches.

About 8 km east of Manta by road is **Jaramijó**, a picturesque fishing village of about 7000 inhabitants. It is said to be one of the oldest fishing villages in Ecuador and was called Xamaxejo before the conquest. There are some cheap restaurants selling decent seafood, but no hotels. It is popular at Easter and Carnaval time and quiet for most of the rest of the year. They have an annual fiesta on 24 August.

Beyond Jaramijó the road stops, although vehicles often drive along the beach at low tide. The next fishing village is **Crucita**, about 16 km beyond Jaramijo. Here, there

are several restaurants, a very long beach, a basic pensión, and the *Hotel Hipocampo* which charges US$7 for a double room with private bath. It can take up to two hours to get here from Manta via Portoviejo by bus, or about 30 minutes along the beach by car.

The next villages are **San Jacinto**, about 13 km beyond Crucita and slightly inland, and **San Clemente** about three km beyond and on the coast. There are good sandy beaches between these villages, both of which have restaurants and cheap places to stay. In San Jacinto, try *Hotel San Jacinto*.

On the outskirts of San Clemente, there is the *Hostería San Clemente* with a swimming pool and the *Cabañas Tío Gerardo* which has cabins with sleeping space for from two to six people. Beyond San Clemente, a good new road (not marked on Ecuadorian road maps) continues north-east along the coast to Bahía de Caráquez, about 20 km away. Crucita, San Jacinto and San Clemente can all be easily reached from Portoviejo.

MONTECRISTI

This small, interesting village of some 8000 inhabitants can be reached in 15 minutes by frequent buses from the terminal terrestre in Manta. Buses cost US$0.10 and stop running at about 6 pm.

Montecristi is an important centre for both the panama hat industry and wickerwork. There are many stores along the main road and along the road leading into the town centre. If you go in towards the centre and ask around, you can see various stages in the manufacture of panama hats.

The town is an old colonial one founded around 1628, when many of the inhabitants of Manta fled inland to avoid the frequent pirate plundering to which the port was subjected. There are many unrestored colonial houses left which give the village a rather tumble-down and ghostly atmosphere.

The main plaza has a beautiful church dating back to the early part of the last century. It contains a famous statue of the Virgin to which miracles have been attributed, and is worth a visit. In the plaza is a statue of Eloy Alfaro, who was born in

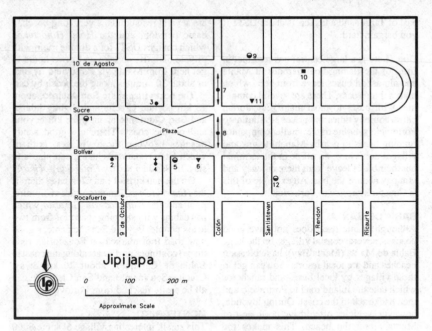

Jipijapa

0   100   200 m

Approximate Scale

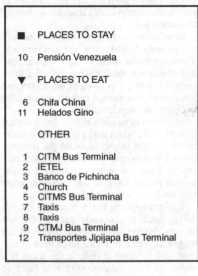

■ PLACES TO STAY

10 Pensión Venezuela

▼ PLACES TO EAT

6 Chifa China
11 Helados Gino

OTHER

1 CITM Bus Terminal
2 IETEL
3 Banco de Pichincha
4 Church
5 CITMS Bus Terminal
7 Taxis
8 Taxis
9 CTMJ Bus Terminal
12 Transportes Jipijapa Bus Terminal

Montecristi and was president of Ecuador at the beginning of the century. His tomb is in the town hall by the plaza.

There is reportedly one basic pensión near the church (though I didn't see it) and only a couple of basic comedores so it's best to stay in Manta and visit Montecristi on a day trip.

JIPIJAPA

The 'j' is pronounced as 'h' in Spanish, so this town's name is pronounced 'Hipihapa.' Jipijapa has a population of about 30,000, and is an important centre for the panama hat industry as well as for coffee and cotton. The town market is a good place to buy panama hats. Sunday is market day and the town is very busy – there are signs outside many merchants' stores reading 'Compro Café' (Coffee Bought Here).

Jipijapa is the main town on the good road linking Manta and Portoviejo with Guayaquil. This road crosses the coastal hills and

Jipijapa is at an elevation of about 350 metres above sea level in these hills. Manta is about 60 km to the north and Guayaquil is about 140 km to the south-east. Parque Nacional Machalilla is a short distance to the south-west.

Places to Stay & Eat

There are a couple of very basic pensiones; try the *Pensión Venezuela* on 10 de Agosto near V Rendon. They charge about US$2 per person.

The *Chifa China* on the main plaza looks like the best place for a meal. *Helados Gino* on Sucre, just east of the plaza, serves good ice cream.

Getting There & Away

Bus There is no central bus terminal. CTMJ, on 10 de Agosto near Santistevan, has frequent buses to Manta (US$0.45; 1¼ hours). CITMS, on the plaza by the church, has several buses a day for Puerto López (for Parque Nacional Machalilla). CITM, on Sucre a block west of the plaza, has several buses a day through Puerto López and on down the coast to La Libertad (three to four hours). Transportes Jipijapa, on Santistevan just south of Bolívar, has buses to Quito and Guayaquil.

Other companies have buses to Guayaquil passing through from Manta or Portoviejo – ask locals about which street corners are the best place to flag them down.

PARQUE NACIONAL MACHALILLA

This is the only coastal national park in Ecuador and so it is of particular importance in preserving a very small part of the rapidly disappearing coastal habitats of the country. The park was created in 1979 to protect about 50 km of beach (less than 2% of Ecuador's coastline), some 40,000 hectares of tropical dry forest and cloud forest, and about 20,000 hectares of ocean which includes two off-shore islands and the only coral formations found on the Ecuadorian mainland coast.

In addition, there are a number of archaeological sites within and near the park. These mainly date from the Manta period, from 500 AD to the conquest. There are also remains of the much older Machalilla and Chorrera cultures, dating from about 1500 to 500 BC, and the Salango culture from 3000 BC.

The tropical dry forest found in much of the inland sectors of the park forms a strange and wonderful landscape of characteristically bottle-shaped trees with small crowns and heavy spines – these last as a protection against herbivores. Some of the most common species include the leguminous algarrobo, *Prosopsis juliflora*, which has a green bark and is able to photosynthesise even when it loses its leaves.

The kapok tree, *Ceiba pentandra*, which has huge plank-like buttresses surrounding the base of the grey trunk, has fruits which yield a fibre with the property of floating and not becoming waterlogged. The kapok fibre was used in life-jackets before the advent of modern synthetics.

Figs *(Ficus* species) and laurels *(Cordia* species) and the palo santo, *Pursera graveolens* are also commonly seen trees.

The tall spindly cactus which grows profusely on some hillsides belongs to the genus *Armatocereus* and the prickly pear, of the genus *Opuntia*, is also common.

Within this strange-looking forest, a variety of bird and animal life is found. So far, a total of 119 species of birds have been recorded, including a variety of coastal parrots, parrotlets and parakeets, as well seabirds such as frigatebirds, pelicans and boobies, some of which nest in the offshore islands.

Other animals include deer, squirrels, howler monkeys, guantas, anteaters and a variety of lizards, snakes and iguanas.

This interesting and unusual tropical dry forest used to stretch along much of the Pacific coasts of Central and South America, but has suffered from human interference as much as or more than any other tropical forest type. It has now almost entirely disappeared and is one of the most threatened tropical forests in the world. It is particularly vulnerable to fire and to grazing by goats which eat young trees before they have developed their protective spines and full complement of chemicals which make the trees less palatable to herbivores.

The Nature Conservancy estimates that there are about 1000 cows and 1500 goats grazing within the mainland confines of the national park. Some of these animals belong to people living in small communities within the park and their grazing is, for the most part, relatively controlled. Many of the goats, however, belong to people living outside the park who illegally introduce their animals into hitherto ungrazed sectors of the park. Some of these people are poor campesinos who don't have other land to graze their animals on. This is typical of the management problems facing Parque Nacional Machalilla and the Ecuadorian national park system as a whole.

Fortunately, Machalilla has been identified as an area deserving of immediate and special protection because of its uniqueness. It has a staff of about 15 people, including a park superintendent and seasonal and full-time rangers, who are trying to work with the local people to establish better protection of the park. Locals work as tourist guides and in maintaining a museum and archaeological area. Also, alternative agricultural projects such as bee-keeping and pig-raising are being developed to replace goat grazing.

Orientation & Information

The national park is in the southernmost part of coastal Manabí Province. The coastal road goes through the park and provides the main access. It is also possible to enter the park from the inland side by taking the road south from Jipijapa.

The **park headquarters & museum** are in Puerto López, a coastal village on the south side of the park. The museum is open daily from 8 am to 4pm; entry is US$0.03. Here, there are informative exhibits and a good map of the park. Staff can answer questions and brochures and maps are available.

About six or seven km north of Puerto López you come to the **park entrance** on the right side of the road. There is a sign and an entrance booth where you pay the US$0.03 admission.

Officially, foreign visitors pay US$2, but, in common with many parks in Ecuador, the person at the gate charged the same rate for foreign or Ecuadorian visitors, even though I told him I was British.

A dirt road goes through tropical dry forest to **Agua Blanca**, five km from the entrance. This little village has an **archaeological museum** explaining the excavation of the Manta site which is about a half-hour walk away. The site can be visited. Only the bases of the buildings can be seen, but there are plans to restore some of the approximately 400 buildings excavated at the site, which was thought to be an important political capital of the Manta people.

From Agua Blanca, it is a four-hour hike to the south-east up through a transition zone and to a remnant area of cloud forest at **San Sebastián**, about 600 metres above sea level. Guides are available in Agua Blanca to take you to either the archaeological site or San Sebastián. Horses can be hired if you don't want to hike.

The dirt road to Agua Blanca continues up the Río Julcuy valley to the north-east. From the village, it is a six to seven-hour hike up this road through the park, coming out at the village of **Julcuy**, just beyond the park boundary. From Julcuy, it's about another three hours to the main Jipijapa-Guayaquil road.

About 10 km north of Puerto López, just before reaching the village of Machalilla, a poor dirt road goes three km to the coast at **Los Frailes**. There is a good beach here and sport fishing is a possibility.

Boats can be hired from several coastal villages, particularly Puerto López, to take you out to the offshore islands. The one most frequently visited is **Isla de la Plata** which is in the ocean about 40 km north-west of Puerto López. The island has nesting colonies of seabirds – blue-footed boobies are usually seen. Red-footed boobies, frigatebirds and pelicans have also been recorded as well as a variety of gulls, terns, petrels and other seabirds. There are a few

Top: Boats off Islas Plazas, Galápagos Islands (TW)
Bottom: Isla Bartolomé, Galápagos Islands (TW)

Top: Boat building in Puerto Ayora, Galápagos Islands (TW)
Bottom: Brachycereus cactus on pahoehoe lava, Isla San Salvador, Galápagos Islands (RR)

coral reefs as well, and you can snorkel if you bring gear. Whales and dolphins have been sighted on the trip over to the island, which has been locally dubbed as 'the poor person's Galápagos'. The island is used as a resting or overnighting place by the local fisherfolk. A closer island is **Isla Salango** which is about 1½ km west of Salango or about 8 km southwest of Puerto López.

From December to June it is sunny and hot, with rainstorms most days. From June to November it does not rain much and is cooler and usually overcast.

Places to Stay
You can camp almost anywhere within the park, but check with park authorities about the availability of water, particularly during the May to December dry season. Officially, there are camping areas at San Sebastian and Los Frailes.

It is also possible to camp on Isla de la Plata – there are no facilities at any of these places. The local fisherfolk may sell you fish on Isla de la Plata.

People in Agua Blanca will put you up in their houses if asked. Basic food is available on request, but it's best to bring some of your own. You can also camp near Agua Blanca.

Most people stay in hotels at Puerto López or at the nearby Alandaluz Ecological Tourist Centre.

Getting There & Away
Bus Every hour buses run up and down the coast between Puerto López and Jipijapa. You should have no difficulty, therefore, in getting a bus to drop you off at the national park entrance, and to find one to pick you up when you are ready to leave.

Trucks occasionally go from the main road to Agua Blanca and back; most likely, you'll have to walk or hire a taxi in Puerto López.

Buses south from Jipijapa can drop you at the settlement of San Dimas, about 11 km south of town. From here, the dirt road goes west to Guarango, three km away, and on through Julcuy to the park.

Boat You can arrange boat trips through the national park office in Puerto López, or you can bargain with the local fishers. Prices with the park tend to be fixed; the fisherfolk are open to bargaining but you have to be a pretty good bargainer to get a cheap deal.

The national park office will help you arrange a boat for about US$55 plus US$7.50 for a guide. The boat holds up to twelve, so it's not very expensive if you can get a group together. The ride out takes from 2½ to five hours one way, depending on the boat and the winds, tides and weather. Be prepared to get wet and take motion sickness pills if you are susceptible. The crossing can get very rough. ('Bath time!' one traveller exclaimed – or did she say 'Barf time!' I didn't press her on the subject.)

PUERTO LÓPEZ
This is a busy fishing village, with a population of about 10,000. You can watch the fishermen come in and unload their catch most mornings – the fish are gutted on the spot and the air is full of wheeling frigatebirds and vultures trying to grab the scraps. If you make friends with the local fishers, they may take you out on a fishing trip.

Buses running from La Libertad to Jipijapa often stop here for about 10 minutes while passengers buy snacks. Children get on the bus yelling 'Corviche Caliente!' This snack is encountered only in this region and consists of a dough which is made of flour and banana paste, stuffed with salty fish. Served hot, maybe with a dash of 'salsa', it will give your taste buds something new to think about.

Puerto López is the nearest town of any size to Parque Nacional Machalilla and houses the park headquarters.

Orientation & Information
The bus stops in the centre of town, about a block away from the IETEL office which is on the right side of the main road if you are northbound. The national park museum and administrative centre is a block behind the IETEL away from the main road. The ocean

is about five blocks to the left of the main road.

Places to Stay & Eat
There are two or three cheap pensiones in various states of disrepair. The owners are generally friendly, but the accommodation is poor. Rooms are about US$2 per person. You are better off staying at Alandaluz (see later description).

There are several restaurants, mostly on the waterfront and selling good seafood. *Carmita's* has been recommended, and the *Mayflower* is another choice.

Getting There & Away
Cooperativa Manglaralto and CITM has buses running between La Libertad and Jipijapa – they stop in Puerto López about every hour or two. It is about 2½ hours and US$1.30 to La Libertad and 1½ hours to Jipijapa. CITMS also has buses between Puerto López and Jipijapa. These buses will drop you off at any point you want along the coast.

MACHALILLA
This village is about 10 km north of Puerto López. There is reportedly a pricey hotel and good beach near here, but I missed it when I went through the area.

SALANGO
This little fishing village is about 5 km south of Puerto López. Isla Salango is less than two km out to sea – you could hire a fishing boat to take you out and see the seabirds, but they are not as numerous as on Isla de la Plata.

There is a small, modern and well laid out archaeological museum here. It was founded by the Banco Central and has exhibits about the local archaeological sites – a worthwhile stop. Admission is about US$0.30.

There is a decent seafood restaurant but no hotels in the village. A couple of km away, there is a new set of cabins at *Los Piqueros*. They charge about US$30 for cabins which will sleep up to six, and have private bathrooms with hot water.

ALANDALUZ
About five km south of Salango, the road passes through the village of Puerto Rico. About one km south of the village, the **Alandaluz Ecological Tourist Centre** is reached. This is an alternative Ecuadorian-run hotel, built entirely of local fast-growing and easily replenishable materials, such as bamboo and palm thatch. The result is an interesting looking building with grassy, overhanging eaves, and a slightly contorted appearance. Within, each room is different – twisted beams, uneven floors and rough wooden beds make for a truly rustic decor.

The main building is surrounded by organic gardens which produce many of the spices, herbs, fruits, and vegetables served at meal times. The lavatories are also organic and, by using sawdust, it is possible to convert human wastes to odour-free fertilisers. The idea is to create a hotel which is, as much as is possible, self sustaining and minimally impacting upon the environment.

There is a bar and dining room which serves delicious meals with a predominantly vegetarian menu. There is a volleyball area and a small games room. The beach is close by and you can swim undisturbed. Horses are available for rent at US$1.80 per hour.

The management is friendly and will try to help travellers organise trips to Machalilla, the museums, and the off-shore islands (though this depends on how many people are staying there). The ambience is very relaxed, and people end up staying for days as they unwind from a fast-paced travel schedule.

Communal showers are heated by the sun – you get a hot shower sometimes. Rooms inside the main building are US$4 per person; outside, in strangely shaped private cabins, beds are US$6.50 per person. Meals are US$1.80 for breakfast, US$2.50 for lunch or dinner. You can camp nearby if you have your own gear – arrange the price with the manager.

Reservations can be made by telephoning 450 992 in Quito. You need to pay half of the fee in advance – you can do this by paying into an account at any branch of the Banco de Pichincha (if you can't get to their Quito office). Often they have space available if you just show up at the hotel, although they are occasionally full. Try to get there early in the day.

Any bus going up or down the coast can drop you off in front of the hotel (see Puerto López for more details).

About five km south of Alandaluz, the provincial line between Manabí and Guayas is crossed. The south coastal provinces of Guayas and El Oro are described in the next chapter.

The South Coast

The south coast, consisting of the provinces of Guayas and El Oro, is generally much drier and more barren than the north coast. The weather pattern changes and the rainy season, which in the north lasts from December to May, lasts only from January to April in Guayaquil. Further west and south it becomes drier still and by the time the Peruvian border is reached the South American coastal desert begins.

The agriculturally important lowlands of Los Ríos Province continue into the provinces of Guayas and El Oro. Bananas are the most important crop and irrigation in the dry south means that plantations can continue beyond Machala. Rice, coffee, cacao and African palm are other important crops of the region.

West of Guayaquil is the dry, infertile and scrubby Santa Elena Peninsula with not enough rivers for irrigation. Archaeological investigation shows that the land used to be as wet and fertile as it is now in the northern coastal areas, but drought and deforestation over the last 5000 years have wrought severe changes. Pottery decorations and other remains indicate that early farmers living in the area from 3000 to 1500 BC cultivated maize (corn), manioc, avocados, beans, squash, chillies, papayas, pineapples, palms and the bottle gourd. Bananas, Ecuador's most important crop, were introduced after the Spanish conquest.

The heart of the south coast is Guayaquil, Ecuador's largest city. To the west are the popular beach resorts of Playas and Salinas and to the south another important port city, Machala, which is the normal gateway to Peru.

GUAYAQUIL
This is by far the most important port in Ecuador. More exports and imports pass through Guayaquil than through all the other ports combined. It is also the most populous city in the country.

Travellers to Ecuador tend to avoid Guayaquil. It has a reputation as a hot and humid port with too many inhabitants and little of interest. It certainly does have many inhabitants, about 1,700,000 of them, and it is oppressively hot, wet and humid from January to April.

I spent over two years travelling in Ecuador before I finally visited Guayaquil and I must admit to having been pleasantly surprised. It does have its attractions. There is a pleasant walk along the river front, shady plazas, colonial buildings, friendly people and interesting museums. It's worth spending a day or two.

The province of Guayas is named after the Puna Indian chief of the same name who fought bravely against first the Incas and then the Spanish. The capital of the province, Guayaquil, is named after the chief, Guayas, and his wife, Quill, whom he is said to have killed before drowning himself, rather than allowing her to be captured by the Spanish conquistadors.

Orientation
Most travellers stay in the city centre, which is organised in a grid-like fashion on the west bank of the Río Guayas. The main east-west street is Avenida 9 de Octubre, terminating at the river by 'La Rotonda', the famous statue of the liberators, Bolívar and San Martín.

The airport is about five km north of the centre, and the bus terminal is about two km north of the airport (seven km north of the

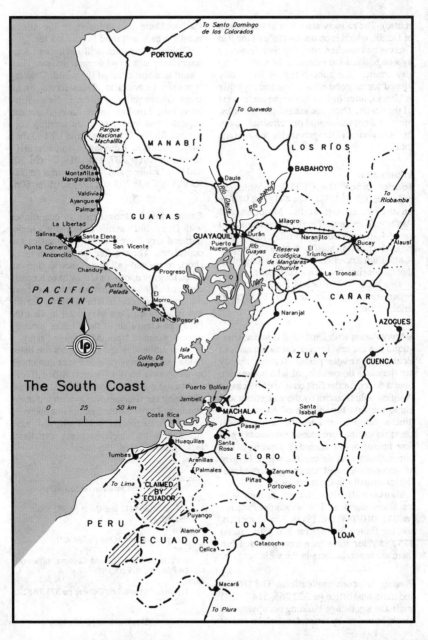

The South Coast

0   25   50 km

centre). The railway station is in the suburb of Durán, which is on the east side of the Río Guayas and reached either by river ferries or by a huge three-km bridge to the north of the city centre. One suburb that is frequently visited for its good restaurants and nightlife is Urdesa, three or four km to the north-west of the centre. There are many other suburbs, most of them residential or industrial, many of them poor and dangerous for the average tourist.

Information

Tourist Office The CETUR information office (☎ 328 312/964, 324 471, 518 926) is on the waterfront at the Malecón and Aguirre. They are officially open from 8.30 am to 4.30 pm Monday to Friday, have some English-speaking staff, and try to be helpful – although travellers sometimes complain that the tourist office is not very useful. There is also a CETUR office at the airport. The better travel agencies are also sources of information.

Money Along with Quito and Cuenca, Guayaquil has the best foreign exchange rates in Ecuador. The easiest places to change money are the casas de cambio, of which there are over a dozen on the first couple of blocks of Avenida 9 de Octubre by the waterfront and along the first few blocks of Avenida Pichincha. Shop around for the best rate. All casas de cambio are closed on Sunday and few are open on Saturday morning. The airport has a casa de cambio which is open at weekends to meet incoming international flights (usually in the morning).

Banks will also change money and travellers' cheques. The Banco del Pacífico (☎ 311 010/744) on Plaza San Francisco, and the Banco Popular (☎ 328 980), Carbo 555 and Vélez, have been recommended, but there are several others in the vicinity.

Post & Telecommunications The IETEL and main post office (☎ 322 265, 514 710/3) are in the same huge building occupying the block bounded by avenidas Ballén and P

Carbo. There are agencies in the streets nearby which will send faxes for a fee.

Courier companies will insure and send important packets and documents from Guayaquil to major cities of the world. Delivery is within 48 hours to places served by air from Guayaquil (eg Miami, New York, Frankfurt, London, most Latin American capitals) and longer to cities needing connecting flights. Costs are about US$40 for a small package. Companies include DHL International (☎ 287 044/101), Carchi 702 and 9 de Octubre, and World Courier (☎ 326 050/553), Chile 303 and Luque, office 806.

Embassies & Consulates In accordance with Guayaquil's status as Ecuador's major port and city, there are many embassies and consulates. Their office hours tend to be short, so try and call in advance to find out when they are open – or if they have recently changed addresses. Most countries also have diplomatic representatives in Quito. Travellers heading for Peru may want to visit the Peruvian Consulate – their hours recently were 8.30 am to 1 pm, Monday to Friday.

Most embassies and consulates are listed below – there may be a few more so check in the phone book or tourist office if you want to take the slow boat to China. To avoid cluttering the Guayaquil map with too many symbols, I have omitted embassies and consulates. Those marked below with an * have street addresses which are on my map; those lacking the * are off the map.

Argentina*
    Aguirre 104 and Malecón (☎ 513 367)
Austria*
    9 de Octubre 1411 and Quito (☎ 282 303, 392 307)
Belgium
    L García 301 and Vélez (☎ 364 429)
Bolivia*
    F Paula de Icaza 302 and Córdova, office 601 (☎ 304 260, 305 200)
Brazil
    L García 103 and 9 de Octubre (☎ 373 370/252, 362 772)
Britain*
    Córdova 623 and Solano (☎ 300 400)

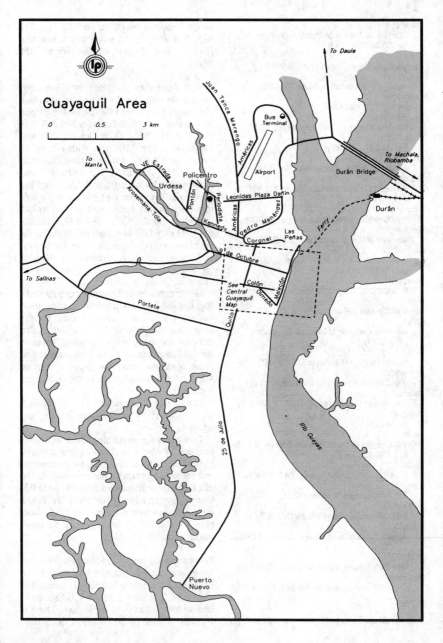

Guayaquil Area

Canada*
  Córdova 812 and V M Rendón, 4th floor
  (☎ 303 580, 313 747)
Chile
  Carchi 601 and Quisquis (☎ 285 995)
Colombia*
  Aguirre 116 and Pichincha (☎ 526 008)
Costa Rica
  (☎ 360 760, 400 300)
Denmark*
  Córdova 604 and Mendiburo (☎ 308 020)
El Salvador
  (☎ 341 849, 314 588)
Finland*
  Urdaneta 212 and Córdova (☎ 304 381)
France*
  Boyacá 1215 and 9 de Octubre (☎ 322 854,
  328 159)
Germany*
  9 de Octubre 109 and Malecón (☎ 512 700)
Greece*
  Machala 200 and Luque (☎ 517 220, 327 250)
Holland
  9 de Octubre 2309 and Tungurahua, 5th floor
  (☎ 374 551, 366 410)
Honduras*
  9 de Octubre 110 and Pichincha (☎ 302 695)
Israel*
  9 de Octubre 727 and Avilés (☎ 322 555)
Italy*
  Baquerizo Moreno 1120 and 9 de Octubre
  (312 522/3)
Mexico
  Tulcán 1600 and Colón (☎ 327 928, 305 499)
Norway*
  9 de Octubre 109 and Malecón (☎ 329 661)
Panama
  Trujillo and 6 de Marzo (☎ 442 877, 328 758)
Paraguay
  (☎ 303 191)
Peru*
  9 de Octubre 411 and Chile, 6th floor (☎ 322 538,
  512 738, 321 738)
Spain*
  V M Rendón 120 and Panamá (☎ 304 860)
Sweden
  Km 6.5 on Daule Road (☎ 352 111)
Switzerland
  9 de Octubre 2105 and Tulcán (363 607)
Uruguay*
  Aguirre 512 and Escobedo (☎ 320 658, 513 461,
  515 026)
USA*
  9 de Octubre and García Moreno (☎ 323 570)
Venezuela*
  Chile 331 and Aguirre (☎ 528 563, 517 053)

Immigration To extend your tourist card, go

to the immigration office (☎ 322 541, 514 925, 516 789) in the government building (Palacio de Gobierno) on Aguirre and the Malecón.

Travel Agencies Anybody who has anything to do with travel will try and sell you a Galápagos trip. One of the cheapest agencies is Galasam Economic Tours (☎ 306 289, 313 724, fax 313 351), 9 de Octubre 424 and Córdova, office 1106 (they also have an office in Quito). Metropolitan Touring (☎ 522 115, 326 815), Pichincha 415 and Aguirre, has its main office in Quito and has good middle to luxury-priced tours, including both small boats and cruise ships. Canodros (☎ 285 711, 280 143, fax 287 651), Urdaneta 1418 and Ejército, is the agent for the Galápagos Explorer, the newest and most expensive cruise ship. Coltur (☎ 306 711), Córdova 1011, with its main office in Quito, is another possibility. One reader recommends Diprotur (☎ 529 893), Aguirre 503 and Chimborazo, for low-budget tours, but I suspect they simply broker for the Galasam boats, which is also the case for many other agencies. Tours to the Galápagos are generally expensive and these agencies cover the price spectrum. More information is given in the Galápagos section.

Ecuadorian Tours (☎ 287 111, 394 984), 9 de Octubre 1900, is the American Express agent.

City tours are available. Tours to nearby beaches are also sold (but I suggest a bus or hiring a taxi for the day to be more economical for small groups). I have recently heard of a new tour to Babahoyo by boat up the Río Guayas, giving a look at the river life. Prices for a one-day tour start around US$50 per person – ask at the travel agencies for more information.

Bookshops If you want to buy English-language and other books, the best store is the Librería Científica (☎ 514 555) at Luque 223 and Chile. The Bookshop on V E Estrada in Urdesa also sells books in English. There is a public library (☎ 515 738) at the Museo

Municipal. Use the back entrance on Avenida 10 de Agosto for the library and the front entrance on Avenida Sucre for the museum.

Medical Services The best hospital in Guayaquil (and the whole coastal region) is reputedly the Clínica Kennedy (☎ 286 963), Avenida del Periodista (also known as San Jorge), by the Policentro shopping centre in the Nueva Kennedy suburb, near Urdesa. They have specialists for almost everything. Take a taxi if you're sick.

Recommended physicians in Guayaquil include Dr Carlos Albán Cárdenas (☎ 519 578), Boyacá 1215 and Vélez, office 15, Dr Alfonso León Guin (☎ 528 179, 517 793), Boyacá 1320 and Luque, and Dr Angel Serrano Sáenz (☎ 301 373), Boyacá 821 and Junín.

I have never had reason to visit a hospital or doctor in Guayaquil (there are limits to what I will do to research this book) but a resident of the city recommends that patients be prepared to pay at the time of treatment. For example, an X-ray and treatment for a simple fracture (no hospitalisation) might run US$30 to US$40.

Good dental care is available from Clínica Dental Urdesa Central (☎ 384 215), in Urdesa. Another choice is Clínica de Odontología Integral (☎ 398 791, 293 620) in Guayaquil.

There are many pharmacies. A good one is Farmacia Fybeca (☎ 510 584), Moncayo 938.

Emergency Contact the Red Cross ambulance on ☎ 300 674/744. The CEAMSA ambulance centre is contacted on ☎ 445 406.

The police are on ☎ 101, or 392 221/30. The fire department is on ☎ 102, or 526 666.

Dangers & Annoyances Problems with thefts continue to rise. Avoid walking in ill-lit areas at night. At all times, keep money and valuables well hidden. Avoid wearing expensive watches or jewellery and dress in simple clothing in public. If arriving or departing from the bus terminal or airport

with luggage, taxis are safer than public buses. Public buses are usually OK if you just have hand luggage which you can easily keep your eagle eye and firm handhold on, or if you are with a couple of other travellers.

Always be alert for pickpockets and bag snatchers – they are everywhere. Be especially alert near hotel entrances, particularly when arriving with baggage – well-dressed thieves may even enter hotel lobbies in search of poorly attended bags or bulging pockets.

Walking Tour
The majority of interesting sights are on or within a few blocks of the waterfront, locally called the Malecón Simón Bolívar, or the Malecón for short. It is a good idea to begin your sightseeing walk near the CETUR tourist information office at Olmedo and the waterfront. CETUR may be able to provide a guide to accompany you or a fee.

The whole walk as described in this section can be done in two or three hours, but if you want to inspect the sights thoroughly, you could spend all day, or even two. Keep your eyes open for plaques and signs. Guayaquil is full of them and they give interesting historic information (if you read Spanish).

The Malecón At the south end of the Malecón and Olmedo there is an imposing **statue** of José Joaquín Olmedo Maruri, an Ecuadorian poet and politician born in Guayaquil on 19 March 1789. He sits, bard-like, in a colonial armchair.

Heading north along the Malecón, with the Río Guayas to your right, you pass several **monuments**. One is to the UN, known in Spanish as the ONU (Organización de Naciones Unidas) and another is the famous Moorish-style **clocktower** which dates originally from 1770 but has been replaced several times. Occasionally, the tower is open to visitors who can climb the narrow spiral staircase inside.

Across the street from the clocktower is the **Palacio Municipal**, an ornate grey building which is separated from the simple and

Central Guayaquil

0   200 m

Cemetery

Tulcán
Los Ríos
Esmeraldas

Quisquis

Urdaneta

1

T de Mayo

2

9 de Octubre

Parque

Hurtado

3

4   5

6

7

Olympic
Pool

Parque del
Centenario

Vélez

27

28

Luque

50

51   49 48 47

Aguirre

Malecón
Eloy Alfaro
García Moreno
José de Antepara
Machala

Ballén

52   53   54

46

45

Parque
Victoria

56

55   57

Market   58

10 de Agosto

71

Sucre

72

Colón

73

Alcedo

Quito
P. Moncayo
Montúfar
6 de Marzo
Garaycoa

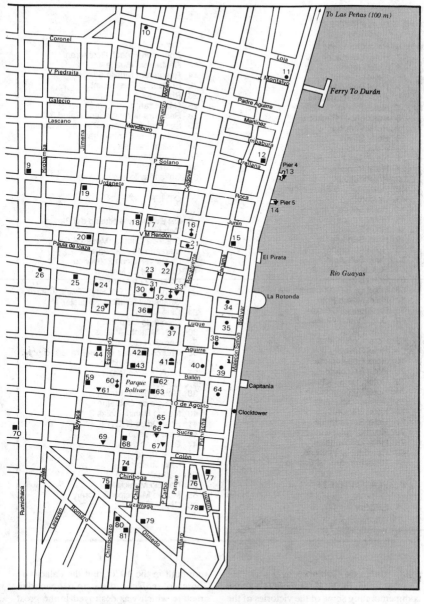

To Las Peñas (100 m)

Coronel

V Piedraíta

Galecio

Lascano

Loja

10

Moreno

Baquerizo

Montalvo

11

Padre Aguirre

Mendiburo

Martínez

Imbabura

12

P Solano

Córdova

Orellana

Pier 4

13

9

Urdaneta

19

Roca

Pier 5

14

18 17

16

Junín

El Pirata

V M Rendón

15

20

21

Paula de Icaza

Rocafuerte

Panamá

Río Guayas

26

23 22

La Rotonda

25

24

30 31

33

29 36

32

34

Luque

35

37

38

Aguirre

44

42

41 40

Malecón Simón Bolívar

Capitanía

Escobedo

43

i 39

59 60

62

Ballén

Parque Bolívar

61

63

64

1 de Agosto

Boyacá

65

Clocktower

66

Sucre

Pichincha

70

69

68

67

Colón

74

75

Chiriboga

Chile

P Carbo

Parque

76

77

Rumichaca

Avilés

Luzarraga

78

Lazayen

Romero

Chimborazo

80

81

79

Villamil

Olmedo

Alfaro

Ferry To Durán

■ PLACES TO STAY

4	Hotel Oro Verde
7	Hotel Libertador
8	Hotel Regina
9	Hotel Colonial
12	Hotel Ramada
15	Hotel Metropolitana
17	Hotel Tourist
18	Residencial Pauker
19	Hotel Venecia
20	Hotel Savoy
23	Hotel Boulevard
25	Hotel San Francisco
27	Hotel Centenario
36	Hotel Palace
42	Hotel Doral & Plaza Hotel
43	Unihotel
44	Hotel Sol del Oriente
45	Hotel de Los Andes
48	Hotel Ecuador
49	Hotel Sanders
50	Hotel Alexander
53	Hotel San Juan
54	Residencial Baños
55	Hotel Delicia
56	Hotel La Buena Esperanza
57	Hotel Marco Polo
58	Residencial Centro
59	Grand Hotel Guayaquil
62	Hotel Rizzo
63	Hotel Continental
68	Hotel Boston
70	Hotel Ecuatoriana
71	Hotel El Inca
72	Hotel Reina Victoria
74	Hotel María del Cisne
75	Residencial María
76	Hotel Nacional
77	Hotel Santa María
78	Hotel Orquidea Internacional
79	Hotel Los Angeles
80	Residencial El Cisne
81	Hotel Residencial Espejo

▼ PLACES TO EAT

1	El Taller
2	Caracol Azul
3	Anderson French Restaurant
13	Restaurant Muelle 4
14	Restaurant Muelle 5
22	El Camino Restaurant
23	Pizza Hut
25	Restaurant San Remo
28	Restaurant Vegetariano Salud Solar
29	La Palma & Cyrano Pavement Cafés
33	Submarine Sandwiches
61	Galleta Pecosa
66	Chifa Himalaya
67	Gran Chifa
69	Chifa Mayflower

OTHER

5	US Embassy & Museo del Banco Central
6	Casa de Cultura (Museo & Cine)
10	Mercado de Artesanía
11	La Peña Rincón Folklórico
16	Church of La Merced
21	Plaza de La Merced
23	TAME Airline, Galasam Tours, Teatro Guayaquil (Edificio Pasaje)
24	Cine Metro
26	Cine 9 de Octubre
30	SAN & Saeta Airlines
31	Peruvian Consulate
32	Church & Plaza of San Francisco
34	Ecuatoriana Airline
35	Bank of America
37	Librería Científica
38	Metropolitan Touring
39	Palacio de Gobierno
40	Museo Nahim Isaías B
41	Post Office & IETEL
46	Cine Imperio
47	Cine Presidente
51	Cine Tauro
52	Cine Quito
60	Cathedral
64	Palacio Municipal
65	Museo Municipal & Library
73	Cine Apollo

solid **Palacio de Gobierno** by a small but pleasant plaza. In the plaza there is a statue commemorating some of the victories of the liberator, General Sucre. Both buildings were built in the 1920s, but the Palacio de Gobierno replaces the original wooden structure which was destroyed in the great fire of 1917. The CETUR office is nearby.

Continuing along the Malecón, you soon come to the famous statue of **La Rotonda**, one of Guayaquil's more impressive monuments (particularly when it is illuminated at night). It shows the historic but enigmatic meeting between Bolívar and San Martín in 1822. Bolívar was the Venezuelan who liberated Venezuela, Colombia and Ecuador from Spanish colonial rule.

San Martín was the Argentinian liberator who defeated the Spanish in Chile and Peru. After their secret meeting in Guayaquil, San Martín returned to Argentina and exile to France, while Bolívar continued his triumphs in Bolivia.

From La Rotonda there are good views north, along the river front, of the colonial district of Las Peñas at the foot of Cerro El Carmen and, far beyond, the impressive Guayaquil-Durán bridge, the biggest in the country.

Many people like to continue along the waterfront to the picturesque colonial district of Las Peñas. Several piers are passed en route, some of which are working docks and others with restaurant boats. You can eat seafood and sip a beer while you watch the busy traffic of the Malecón on one side and Guayaquil's river traffic on the other. Fragile craft paddled by banana pedlars bob close inshore and huge ocean-going vessels lumber by in mid-channel. Pleasure craft and fishing trawlers abound, and frigatebirds, terns and seagulls fly by in a constant stream.

Soon after passing the **Durán ferry** pier you reach the end of the Malecón. This north end has a reputation for being a poor neighbourhood and tourists are advised to guard their belongings against pickpockets, especially those working the passenger exits from the Durán ferry. The ferry is used by tourists arriving every evening at the railway station in Durán. These baggage-laden travellers are the targets for thieves. The ferry across to Durán makes a very inexpensive and enjoyable sightseeing trip across the Río Guayas. A couple of hundred metres beyond the Durán ferry dock one enters the Las Peñas district.

Las Peñas At the end of the Malecón you'll see a short flight of stairs leading up to the small **Plaza Colón**, which has two cannons pointing out towards the river, commemorating a battle against Dutch pirates in 1624. The narrow, winding **Calle Numa Pompilo Llona**, named after the Guayaquileño (1832-1907) who wrote the national anthem, begins from the corner of the plaza. This street is one of my favourite sights in Las Peñas. Walking up this historic street, you'll see several unobtrusive plaques set into the walls of some houses. The plaques indicate the simple residences of past presidents. The colonial architecture has not been very much restored; rather, it has been well looked after and is interesting to see.

Several artists now live in the area and there are a few art galleries, of which the one at No 186 is the best known and belongs to the painter Hugo Luis Lara. Take your time – it's a short street. At the end of the street is the **National Brewery** which is open from 7 am to 12 noon and 2 to 5 pm Monday to Friday. Brewery tours can be arranged.

Calle Numa Pompillo Llona is a dead-end street, so you retrace your footsteps to the Plaza Colón and, instead of continuing back along the Malecón, you turn right and walk past a small plaza with a brightly painted statue of a fireman (there are two fire stations near by), and past a statue of the conquistador Orellana, to the open-air theatre Bogotá. Behind the theatre is the oldest church in Guayaquil, **Santo Domingo**, which was founded in 1548, restored in 1938, and is worth a visit.

You can continue by climbing the stairs to the right of the church and then heading left up the steep Calle Buitrón (the Street of the Vulture!) which will soon take you to the top of the hill, **Cerro El Carmen**. From here is a good view of the north section of the river and the impressive **Durán Bridge** which is almost four km long.

It is important to note, however, that Las Peñas is unfortunately not a safe district. A couple of readers sent me a letter describing how they were assaulted: 'Someone tried to assault us on Calle Numa Pompillo Llona, at midday on Sunday. Fortunately some locals came out with a shot-gun to protect us, or themselves, I'm not sure which. This halted the two men and we ran off down the street with only bruises. Further down the street, without prompting, we were advised by more than one local that the street was not safe'.

Despite this story, Ecuadorian guide publications continue to describe the Las Peñas area as a 'typical colonial section'. It's worth asking at the CETUR information office about the area's safety and also to go with a group of friends or on a guided tour.

In 1990, the government made a grant of US$750,000 to renovate the area. This may make it safer in the future. I hope so, because this is one of the more historically interesting and attractive districts in Guayaquil.

Downtown Area From Las Peñas walk back along Calle Rocafuerte to the downtown area. The colonial buildings blend into modern ones and after a few blocks you pass the church of **La Merced**. Although this building is comparatively modern (constructed in 1938), the original wooden church dated back to 1787 but, like most of Guayaquil's colonial buildings, was destroyed by fire. The modern version is worth seeing for its richly decorated golden altar. There's a pleasant plaza in front of the church.

Two blocks beyond La Merced you cross the busy Avenida 9 de Octubre, downtown Guayaquil's major thoroughfare. Here Calle Rocafuerte becomes Calle P Carbo and you find the church of **San Francisco**, originally built in the early 1700s, burnt in 1896, reconstructed in 1902, and now beautifully restored. The plaza in front is notable for containing Guayaquil's **first public monument**, unveiled on New Year's Day, 1880. It is a statue of the first Ecuadorian president, Vicente Rocafuerte, who held office from 1835-39 (Ecuador's first president, Juan Flores, was a Venezuelan).

A couple of blocks south on P Carbo and a block over to Pichincha brings you to the **Museo Nahim Isaías B**. This museum has a

small display of religious art and some archaeological pieces.

Museo Municipal A few blocks further along P Carbo (at Sucre) you find the Museo Municipal (☎ 516 391) and the municipal library. The museum is small but has varied exhibits. On the ground floor there is an archaeology room, a colonial room and a changing display of modern art. The archaeology room has mainly Inca and pre-Inca ceramics, with some particularly fine pieces from the Huancavilca period (circa 500 AD) and several figurines from the oldest culture in Ecuador, the Valdivia (circa 3200 BC). The colonial room has mainly religious paintings and a few household items from colonial times.

Upstairs there are modern art and ethnography rooms, inexplicably joined. Here you'll see five of the famous tsantsas, or shrunken heads. Other jungle artefacts include beadwork, featherwork, tools and weapons, but unfortunately very few labels. There are also regional costumes and handicrafts. Another room on this floor contains paintings of presidents and famous men, of which my favourite is a wild and eccentric-looking Theodor Wolf, the geologist after whom the highest active volcano in the Galápagos is named. All in all, a varied collection with which to pass the time.

The Museo Municipal is open 9 am to 12 noon and 3 to 6 pm Wednesday to Friday, 10 am to 3 pm on Saturday, and 10 am to 1 pm on Sunday. Admission is US$0.40.

Parque Bolívar A block north-west of the Municipal Museum is one of Guayaquil's most famous plazas, the Parque Bolívar (also known as the Parque Seminario). In its small but well laid out ornamental gardens live prehistoric-looking land iguanas of up to a metre in length, and of a species different from those found in the Galápagos. They're a surprising sight here, right in the centre of the city. Around Parque Bolívar are many of Guayaquil's first-class hotels.

Cathedral On the west side of the Parque

Bolívar is the Cathedral. The original building on this site dates from 1547 but, as is common with most of Guayaquil's original wooden buildings, it burnt down. The present structure was completed in 1948 and renovated in 1978. The front entrance is extremely ornately decorated but inside it is cool, simple, high vaulted and modern. High up on the white walls are some fine stained-glass windows.

Parque del Centenario From the Parque Bolívar you can head north a few blocks and then walk west along the modern Avenida 9 de Octubre to the huge Parque del Centenario, the city's largest plaza. A more colourful walk is along 10 de Agosto to the main **market** area, which is so crowded with street stalls, people and traffic that your pace slows to a crawl. Watch your belongings – pickpockets are common in market areas. In the Parque del Centenario, which covers four city blocks, there are many monuments. The most important is the great central column topped by Liberty and surrounded by the founding fathers of the country – a monument to patriotism.

Casa de Cultura Avenida 9 de Octubre continues beyond the Parque del Centenario. At its junction with the west side of the park is the archaeology museum of the Casa de Cultura (☎ 300 500). The main attraction at this museum was the gold collection, but the building was damaged by fire in 1987 and the museum was closed for some time. Recent reports indicate it has reopened – call or check with the tourist office for new hours of admission.

There is also a cinema on the premises which shows good movies on occasion. Recently, the cinema had a foreign film season, with different films showing at 6.30 pm every Tuesday and Friday. Foreign films are very popular and the cinema is small – get there early to get a ticket (about US$0.40).

Museo del Banco Central Three blocks west of the Parque del Centenario you reach the Museo del Banco Central (☎ 320 576, 327 402) at 9 de Octubre and José de Antepara (half a block from the US Embassy). This houses a good archaeology museum which is open from 10 am to 6 pm Monday to Friday, and 10 am to 1 pm on weekends. It is free, well laid out, and has a varied and changing display of ceramics, textiles, metallurgy (some gold) and ceremonial masks. The descriptions are good but are only in Spanish.

City Cemetery If you continue north of the Parque del Centenario along P Moncayo, you'll come to the City Cemetery, which is well worth a visit. It is a dazzling white and contains hundreds of tombs, monuments and huge mausoleums. A palm tree-lined walk leads to the impressive grave of President Vicente Rocafuerte.

A traveller writes that the area north of the Parque Central is becoming increasingly dangerous, so go with friends and be alert.

Festivals
All the national holidays are celebrated vigorously in Guayaquil, but one stands out as the major annual festival. This is, in fact, a combination of two holidays: Simón Bolívar's birthday on 24 July (1783) and the Founding of Guayaquil on 25 July (1538). The city goes wild with parades, art shows, beauty pageants, fireworks, and plenty of drinking and dancing – a carnival atmosphere. Hotels are booked up well in advance – the evening of 24 July is not a good time to arrive in Guayaquil without a hotel reservation. The festivities often begin on the 23 or even 22 July, depending on which day of the week the holiday falls in any particular year. Banking and other services are usually disrupted.

Other important dates are Guayaquil's Independence Day on 9 October (1820) which combines with Columbus Day celebrated on 12 October to create another long holiday, though much less exciting than the July festivities. New Year's Eve (31 December) is celebrated with bonfires. Life-sized puppets are made by stuffing old clothes –

these are called *viejos* (the old ones) and represent the old year. The viejos are displayed on the main streets of the city, especially the Malecón, and they are burnt in midnight bonfires – fun for all the family. Less fun is the annual carnival (a movable feast held on the days immediately preceding Ash Wednesday and Lent) which, in addition to the traditional throwing of water, is 'celebrated' by dousing passers-by with all manner of unpleasant liquids – no one is exempt.

Locals say that holidays, especially 24 & 25 July, are a good time to visit areas such as Las Peñas because of the sheer number of visitors. Generally, the locals are very friendly to foreign visitors during the holidays. Pickpockets still abound, but they are looking for easy targets like drunks. Leave your camera in your room and come out to enjoy yourself.

Places to Stay

The Guayaquil Tourist Board controls hotel prices and each hotel is required to post its approved prices near the entrance. Perhaps surprisingly, most hotels do have the price list prominently displayed. You may be charged up to 15% tax on the listed price, though some of the cheaper hotels don't bother.

During holiday periods finding a room can be problematical, especially in the better hotels, and prices are usually higher than the listed price. Most hotels, including the budget ones, are registered at the CETUR tourist office where you can complain if you get gouged. Hotel prices seem to change frequently.

For some reason there are not many single rooms to be had. In the cheaper hotels I usually had two or more beds in my room when I was travelling alone. If it's not the holiday season, you can persuade many hotel owners to give you a double or triple at the price of a single. During fiesta time, travel with a friend or be prepared to pay for a double.

Unfortunately, water shortages occur frequently. Most top-end hotels have fairly reliable water supplies (though unfortunately this is because they can afford to pay premium prices for water which is supposedly destined for the poor areas of town). The cheaper hotels may lack water at times, so grab a shower when you can.

Guayaquil has unfortunately begun the practice of having a two-tier pricing system in the better hotels. Foreign tourists are charged about twice as much as residents, particularly in the top-end hotels.

Places to Stay – bottom end

Bottom-end hotels in Guayaquil are generally of a higher price and lower standard when compared to other cities. One of the best cheap hotels is the *Hotel Delicia* (☎ 524 925) at Ballén 1105 and Montúfar. The hotel is secure and clean and charges about US$2 per person but is often full. Opposite is the *Residencial Baños* which charges about US$2.50 per person and is also often full.

Most hotels which charge less than US$2 per person are not as good. Among the cheapest are the *Hotel Residencial Espejo* and the *Residencial María* (US$2 per person), and the *Residencial El Cisne* (US$1.50 per person). All three are very basic hotels near the intersection of Olmedo and Chimborazo – a poor area of town, particularly at night. The nearby *Hotel Los Angeles*, on Olmedo near Chile, is fairly basic but has better rooms with private bathrooms and fans. They charge US$3 per person.

Hotel La Buena Esperanza is on the corner of the market at Ballén and 6 de Marzo and charges only US$1.50 per person. It is a very basic hotel. The *Hotel San Juan*, Quito and Ballén, has rather shabby rooms with double beds and private bathroom for US$3.50 (one or two people). The *Hotel Ecuatoriana* (☎ 518 105), Rumichaca 1502 and Sucre, charges US$4 double for the night, or US$2 'for a short while'. It is clean and fairly secure, despite the short-stay clients. Some of the cheap hotels near the market double as low-class brothels, and lone female travellers may be improperly treated or molested. The market area is also rife with pickpockets, so stay alert. One of the better-run cheap hotels in the market area is the *Hotel El Inca*, on 10 de Agosto and opposite the market. The hotel has many rooms, most with bathrooms. They charge about US$2 per person, but there are few singles. The *Hotel Ecuador* (☎ 514 450), P Moncayo 1117 and Aguirre, is close to the market area but is a decent and friendly hotel. Rooms are US$6/10 for doubles/triples with private bath and fan – there are no singles. Nearby, the *Hotel Marco Polo* is US$2.50 without and US$4 with bath per person, but I've heard that it's not recommended for single women. Another basic hotel in this price range is the *Residencial Centro*.

There are some basic but reasonably clean hotels on Villamil near the waterfront. The *Hotel Santa María*, at 102 Villamil, charges US$4/7 for shabby but clean singles/doubles with bath and fan. Opposite, the *Hotel Nacional* is similar, though some cheaper rooms lack private baths or don't have windows. This is the waterfront area, however, and when I stopped by the Hotel Nacional they asked me, 'All night or just a little while?' A few blocks away on Chimborazo, between Colón and Sucre, is the *Hotel Boston* which charges US$3 per person in rooms which are tiny, unattractive wooden boxes.

The *Residencial Pauker* (☎ 517 348), at Baquerizo Moreno 902 and Junín, is reasonably secure though rather run down, and has been fairly popular with travellers over the years. Basic rooms are about US$3 per person – the singles are very shabby. Across the street is the *Hotel Tourist*, which is a little better. They charge US$4/7 in rooms with private bath; rooms with air-conditioning are a little more. *Hotel Libertador*, on Garaycoa at the corner of Parque del Centenario, is a reasonable choice. They have clean rooms with bath and fan for about US$3.50 per person. The *Hotel Savoy*, V M Rendón and Boyacá, is similarly priced. The *Hotel Reina Victoria*, on Colón near P Moncayo, looks clean and has rooms for US$4.50/6.50 for singles/doubles with bath and fan.

A good, simple but clean hotel with air-conditioned rooms with private bath is the *Hotel Regina* (☎ 312 754), Garaycoa 421 and P Solano. Although the hotel itself is secure, I have received reports of theft on the street outside, so don't parade around with your camera. Rooms are a reasonable US$4.50/6.50. Nearby, the *Hotel Colonial*, at Rumichaca and Urdaneta, has been recommended as being a clean, secure and friendly hotel. Rooms are US$4.50/7.50 with private bath and fan – some rooms have balconies. A block away at Rumichaca and Junín is the *Hotel USA* (☎ 307 804) which is similarly priced but has received mixed reports – it looks OK to me.

The *Hotel Metropolitana* (☎ 305 250), V M Rendón 120 and Panamá, is very good value for US$8.50 a double (very few singles). Some rooms have river views, the private bathrooms are spotless, and the management is anxious to please. Don't be put off by the fact that it's on the top floor of an office block.

The *Hotel Venecia*, Urdaneta and Jimena, has rooms with private baths for US$7/10 with air-conditioning, a little less with fans. The *Hotel Centenario* (☎ 524 467), Vélez 726 and Garaycoa, charges US$8 for a double with one bed or US$10 for a double with two beds. These rooms have private bathrooms and air-conditioning – rooms with fans are a little cheaper. Despite its price, the hotel is pretty basic. For roughly similar prices but better value, try the *Hotel Sanders* (☎ 320 030, 510 030), P Moncayo and Luque. Rooms here vary in price depending on whether you have air-conditioning or a fan, two beds or one double bed, and window or interior.

Places to Stay – middle

The *Hotel Orquidea Internacional* (☎ 513 875, 515 696), Villamil 120, is adequate at US$9/12 for singles/doubles with private bath; rooms with balconies (noisy) are US$3 more. The newer *Hotel María del Cisne*, on Chiriboga between Chimborazo and Chile, has clean rooms with air-conditioning for US$10/14. Both these hotels are reasonable value, although the neighbourhood is not very good. A more central hotel is the comfortable *Hotel Alexander* (☎ 522 010), Luque 1107 and P Moncayo, which charges US$11/15 for air-conditioned rooms. Similar prices are charged at the *Hotel de Los Andes* (☎ 329 796, 529 793), Garaycoa 1233 and Ballén. It calls itself a first-class hotel – but is merely adequate.

The *Hotel San Francisco* (☎ 324 701, 514 701), 9 de Octubre 731 and Boyacá, has clean, air-conditioned rooms for about US$12/20 for singles/doubles. A good mid-priced choice is the *Hotel Doral* (☎ 327 133/75, 328 002), Chile 402 and Aguirre, PO Box 10938, Guayaquil. This hotel is clean and secure and has a restaurant. Rooms are about US$25 double.

The following hotels all charge about US$30-40 for a double room; singles are a little less. All of the rooms are clean and comfortable. Expect private baths, hot water, air-conditioning, telephone, TV, restaurants on the premises and similar amenities. A good choice in this price range is the *Hotel Sol del Oriente* (☎ 325 500, 405 500), Aguirre 603 and Escobedo. Rooms are spacious and the hotel has a decent Chinese restaurant. Other reasonable possibilities include the *Plaza Hotel* (☎ 327 140, 324 195), Chile 414 and Ballén, PO Box 10299, Guayaquil; the *Hotel Palace* (☎ 321 080, 511 080), Chile 216 and Luque; and the *Hotel Rizzo* (☎ 325 210, 511 210), Ballén 319 and Chile.

Places to Stay – top end

There seems to be a big jump in hotel prices between middle and top-end hotels. This is artificially created by the top-end hotels themselves, who consider themselves luxury class and charge nonresident tourists twice the rate for residents. I would not be surprised if some of the middle-category hotels jump on the two-tier pricing bandwagon – if this occurs, expect higher prices.

If you have any kind of residency status, use it. The prices I give below are for nonresidents and include the obligatory 20% tax. All these hotels have good restaurants.

Perhaps the least expensive of the top-end hotels is the *Hotel Boulevard* (☎ 306 101/700, 308 840), 9 de Octubre 432 and Chile, PO Box 7524, Guayaquil. The hotel is popular with business travellers because of its location by the financial district. There is a casino. Rooms are about US$60/80.

The following three hotels all charge about US$80/100 for singles/doubles. More expensive suites are often available.

The *Hotel Ramada* (☎ 312 200, 311 888, or toll-free in the USA 1-800 334 3782), on the Malecón at Orellana, PO Box 10964, Guayaquil, overlooks the Río Guayas. There is an indoor pool, a sauna, and a casino. If you stay here, bear in mind that the Malecón north of the hotel is not a good place to wander around at night.

The *Unihotel* (☎ 327 100, 519 077, or toll-free in the USA 1-800 223 5652, 1-800 882 4777), Ballén 406 and Chile, PO Box 563, Guayaquil, is centrally located. They have numerous facilities, including a sauna and gym, a games room for children, a shopping mall with scores of stores, and a casino. One of their restaurants has delightful views into the Parque Bolívar.

The *Grand Hotel Guayaquil* (☎ 329 690, 529 918, or toll-free in the USA and Canada 1-800 223 9868, or in the USA 1-800 528 5568), Boyacá and 10 de Agosto, PO Box 9282, Guayaquil, is behind the cathedral. This hotel has plenty of sporting facilities for the energetic: pool, squash court, gym, sauna. They have outdoor barbecues by the pool.

Finally, the following two hotels are considered the most luxurious and are the most expensive.

The *Hotel Continental* (☎ 329 270, or toll-free in the USA and Canada 1-800 333 1212, 1-800 223 0888), Chile and 10 de Agosto, PO Box 4510, Guayaquil, is right on the Parque Bolívar. It is the oldest of the city's luxury hotels. If you want to swim or work out, this is not the place for you. The hotel is known for its restaurants, one of which has won international gastronomy awards, another which specialises in Ecuadorian cuisine, and a third which is open 24 hours. Rooms are US$115/130 for singles/doubles.

The *Hotel Oro Verde* (☎ 327 999, 372 100, 329 358, or toll-free in the USA 1-800 223 1230), 9 de Octubre and García Moreno, PO Box 9636, Guayaquil, is the largest hotel in town. It is also considered the best place to stay. It is slightly away from the centre, out by the US Embassy. They have a pool, gym, sauna, casino, shops, and several restaurants. Rooms are US$120/155 for singles/doubles, and suites go up to US$300.

Places to Eat
Breakfast For breakfast I like the *La Palma* pavement café on Escobedo and Vélez. They sell good coffee and warm croissants, and it's a good place at which to wake up and ease into the day. This is also a good place for snacks and light meals throughout the day.

Next door, the *Cyrano* serves much the same, though the coffee is not as good. Many of the better hotels (see Hotel Restaurants later) do good breakfasts – even if you are on a budget, this might be the chance for a lovely breakfast in comfortable surroundings. Relax, read the newspaper, or catch up on your journal.

Chifas A chifa is often a reasonable choice for the hungry budget traveller and there are several on and around Avenida Colón. One of the very best – ornate and expensive-looking but in fact very reasonably priced – is the *Gran Chifa* (☎ 510 794, 512 488) on P Carbo 1016 near Sucre. Around the corner, on Sucre 308 and P Carbo, is the cheaper *Chifa Himalaya* (☎ 529 593) which is good and popular as is the nearby *Chifa Mayflower*, Colón and Chimborazo. There are many other chifas to choose from.

9 de Octubre There are many modern cafeterias, restaurants, and fast-food places on Avenida 9 de Octubre, but they are not very cheap. There's even an authentic *Burger King* at 9 de Octubre and Escobedo – the burgers are OK and the 'soft serve' chocolate ice cream has been recommended by none other than Betsy Wagenhauser, founder of the Quito office of the South American Explorers Club and self-professed dessert

expert. (Betsy also recommends the *Galleta Pecosa* bakery, at 10 de Agosto and Boyacá, for the best cookies and cakes in Ecuador. No, it's not on 9 de Octubre – just checking to see if you were paying attention.)

Other places on 9 de Octubre include the *Submarine* near the intersection with P Carbo – this restaurant is highly recommended for sandwiches. *Pizza Hut* (☎ 310 050) is at 9 de Octubre 404 and Córdova and serves what you might expect plus other Italian dishes. The *Restaurant San Remo* (☎ 510 620), 9 de Octubre 737 and Boyacá, is a popular spot for business lunches. There's good Italian and Ecuadorian food for about US$5 to US$8 for a full meal.

Riverboats One of my favourite places to eat or snack is on a boat moored on the riverbank. There are several piers along the Malecón where restaurant boats are moored and it is fun to spend some time watching the busy river traffic. A medium-priced place is *El Pirata*, a couple of blocks from the La Rotonda statue. They have an indoor section and an open top deck with sunshades for when the weather is good. North of El Pirata there are fancier and more expensive restaurants at *Muelle 4* and *Muelle 5* (Pier 4 and 5). These all serve good seafood.

Vegetarian The *Restaurant Vegetariano Salud Solar* at Luque and P Moncayo serves good, simple and cheap food. The *El Camino* restaurant at Paula de Icaza and Córdova used to be called El Camino Vegetariano, but it struggled as a purely vegetarian restaurant. Now it serves a wider variety of inexpensive dishes, including a few meatless ones. It is a good place for an inexpensive lunch but is often closed by supper time. Vegetarianism isn't big in Guayaquil.

Hotel Restaurants Many of the city's best restaurants are are in the better hotels (normally open to the public). The *Gran Hotel Guayaquil* has a continental breakfast (rolls and coffee) for about US$2.50. The coffee is excellent and coffee addicts can get many refills. Cheaper breakfasts with good coffee are served at the *Hotel Doral Cafeteria* which has a pleasant outside patio. All the best hotels serve decent, if pricey, breakfasts.

The *El Parque* restaurant (on the 4th floor of the Unicentro building – enter through Unihotel) overlooks the Parque Bolívar and is recommended for dinner – good value and good views but not cheap. They also have less expensive buffet lunches – help yourself to seconds and thirds... In the Hotel Continental, the expensive *Restaurant El Fortín* has won international gastronomic awards and the less expensive *Restaurant La Canoa* serves Ecuadorian specialities. The restaurants in the other top-end hotels are also very good.

Other The expensive *Caracol Azul* (☎ 280 461), 9 de Octubre 1918 and Los Ríos, has often been described as the best seafood restaurant in the city. I keep meaning to try the food but, inexplicably, have never made it out there. You'll have to decide for yourself whether it merits the description – I could think of worse ways to spend the evening. Meat dishes are also served.

The best French restaurant is the *Anderson* (☎ 369 138), Tulcán 810 and Hurtado. They are closed on Sunday.

A good Ecuadorian-style restaurant is *El Taller* (☎ 393 904), Quisquis 1313 and Los Ríos. They exhibit local antiques as well as serving typical food.

Urdesa This suburb, 6 or 7 km north-west of the city centre, is one of the best restaurant areas and worth the trip if you like to eat well. The main drag is V E Estrada and most of the restaurants, bars and nightlife are found along this street.

La Parrillada del Ñato (☎ 387 098), V E Estrada and Laureles, serves good Ecuadorian-style steaks, grills, and barbecues, as well as pizzas – prices are reasonable. A couple of blocks away, *Pizzería Ch'Enano* (☎ 388 333), V E Estrada 1320, also serves good pizzas. Other Italian restaurants include *Pizza Hut* (☎ 381 167), V E Estrada 472 and Ebanos, and *La Carbonara* (☎ 382 714), Bálsamos 108 and V E Estrada. *La Tablita* (☎ 388 162), Ebanos 126 and V E Estrada, has good Ecuadorian-style grills and steaks. For Mexican dinners try *Paco's* (☎ 442 112), Acacias 725 and Guayacanes. They sometimes have mariachi bands playing.

Los Ajos (☎ 382 831), V E Estrada 712 and Ficus, serves excellent if expensive Spanish cuisine. The *Mediterráneo* (☎ 387 671), Bálsamos 671 near Pasaje, also serves Spanish food at more moderate prices.

The Japanese restaurant *Tsuji* (☎ 387 091, 384 386), V E Estrada 816 and Guaycanes, is not cheap but serves excellent food. There are two excellent and expensive restaurants just off V E Estrada at the entrance to Urdesa. The *Barandua Inn* (☎ 389 407, 387 366), Circunvalación Norte 528B, serves delicious seafood and the *La Posada de las Garzas* (☎ 383 256), Circunvalación Norte 536 has international cuisine.

Entertainment

Read the local newspapers *El Telégrafo* and *El Universo* to find out more about what's going on. They give cinema listings for the approximately 18 cinemas in Guayaquil, of which about half are downtown and are listed below. If you're buying the newspaper for the cinema listings, make sure that the newspaper has them. Occasionally, even the best papers omit the listing if there's been no change. English-language movies with Spanish sub-titles are often shown.

Cine Apollo
    Colón and 6 de Marzo
Cine Casa de Cultura
    9 de Octubre and Parque del Centenario
Cine (Teatro) Guayaquil
    9 de Octubre 424 (☎ 305 367)
Cine Imperio
    6 de Marzo and Ballén
Cine Metro
    Boyacá 1217 and 9 de Octubre (☎ 322 301)
Cine Nueve de Octubre
    9 de Octubre 815 and Avilés (☎ 516 888)
Cine Presidente
    Luque 715 (☎ 325 180)
Cine Quito
    Aguirre and Quito

Cine Tauro
  Quito and Luque (☎ 323 381)
Policine Kennedy
  Policentro Shopping Centre, Kennedy suburb
  (☎ 288 312)

Friday newspapers advertise peñas (folk music evenings) which are normally held at weekends. They are rarely cheap and always start late. A good one is *La Peña Rincón Folklórico* at Malecón 208 and Montalvo (take a cab – it's not a very safe area at night). They open around 10 pm for food and drinks, and the show gets under way about midnight and continues until the early hours. Cover is US$3 and drinks aren't cheap. One reader recommends the *Peña Amnesia* – he had so much fun that he couldn't remember where it was.

V E Estrada in Urdesa is a good street to hang out on Friday and Saturday nights, along with the more affluent Guayaquileño kids. The *Infinity Club*, V E Estrada 505, is currently popular for disco dancing. It's reportedly best at weekends from midnight to 6 am (!) and there's a US$3 cover for men – women are not charged. There are two dance floors, one for American-style rock and disco, the other for Latin music. In Guayaquil, there are discos in some of the better hotels, especially the Oro Verde. Other places to dance include *Flashdance* at Aguirre 221.

Gamblers will want to try their luck at the casinos found at the Ramada, Unihotel, Boulevard, and Oro Verde Hotels. These top-end hotels will also help guests spend a day at a club with golf, tennis, or sailing.

If you're the athletic type, visit the *Olympic Pool*, which costs US$0.30 for a two-hour period. Enquire at the entrance for times.

Things to Buy

Guayaquileños like to shop at the outdoor black-market called La Bahía, located on P Carbo and Villamil between Olmedo and Colón. It's crowded, busy, and colourful. Anything from blue jeans to video cameras can be found here – some of it at bargain prices, much of it counterfeit. There are pickpockets, naturally, but the area has a high police profile and is not especially dangerous.

If you prefer a more sedate shopping atmosphere, try one of the several indoor shopping centres, styled like North American shopping malls. The Unicentro, downtown by the Parque Bolívar, is the smallest. The Policentro, in the Kennedy suburb at the end of the Avenida del Periodista (San Jorge), is one of the biggest and has many modern stores as well as restaurants and a movie theatre. The Central Comercial Urdesa is similar. Just outside Urdesa is the Centro Comercial Albán Borja.

On the first block of Chile off 9 de Octubre you'll find Otavaleños selling handicrafts and souvenirs, though the quality isn't high. Better quality can be found in the Mercado de Artesanía (Artesans' Market) in a warehouse at Loja and Escobedo. It's on the edge of the Las Peñas district, however, so go with a couple of friends for added security. Other crafts and souvenirs stores include the government-run OCEPA at V M Rendón 405 and Córdova and several on the first block of 9 de Octubre by the waterfront.

The shopping centres are mainly geared to general shopping, but usually have one or two souvenir shops. The better hotels have stores selling good quality and higher priced crafts.

Getting There & Away

Air Guayaquil's Simón Bolívar Airport is one of Ecuador's two international airports, and it is about as busy as Quito. There are three terminals. The international and main national terminals adjoin one another and are on the east side of Avenida de las Américas, about 5 km north of the city centre. The *Avioneta* (small aircraft) terminal is at the south end of the airport, about one km south of the main terminal. It can be reached by turning left out of the main terminal and walking south along the busy Avenida de las Américas.

The main national terminal deals with most internal TAME, SAN, and Saeta flights. Passengers for the Galápagos may go through the international terminal, however, particularly if they are changing in Guayaquil on a Quito-Guayaquil-Galápagos flight. The main terminal has a casa de cambio which pays about as much as the downtown rate. It is open for most incoming international flights. There are also the usual cafeteria, car rental, gift shop, and international telephone facilities.

International If you are leaving on an international flight, there is a US$25 departure tax, payable in sucres or dollars.

The following airlines have offices in Guayaquil. Those marked with an asterisk * have direct flights into and out of Ecuador. Some airlines fly to Quito but it is a simple matter to connect between Quito and Guayaquil on the many domestic flights.

Aerolineas Argentinas*
    P Moncayo and V M Rendón (☎ 302 141)
AeroPerú*
    Paula de Icaza 451 and Baquerizo Moreno
    (☎ 303 600)
Air France*
    Aguirre 106 and Malecón (☎ 320 313)
American Airlines* (USA)
    V M Rendón 401 (☎ 312 111)
Avianca* (Colombia)
    9 de Octubre 905 and Rumichaca
    (☎ 517 103/057)
British Airways
    Vélez 226 (☎ 325 080)
Continental Airlines* (USA)
    9 de Octubre 1911 and Esmeraldas, 11th floor
    (☎ 284 600)
Ecuatoriana*
    9 de Octubre 111 and Malecón (☎ 322 025,
    262 020)
Iberia* (Spain)
    9 de Octubre 101 and Malecón (☎ 320 664,
    329 558)
Icelandair
    Malecón 1203 and 9 de Octubre (☎ 522 110)
JAL Japan Airlines
    (☎ 310 818/21)
KLM* (Holland)
    Aguirre 411 (☎ 328 028)
Korean Air
    Córdova 1013 and 9 de Octubre, 3rd floor
    (☎ 320 908, 306 390)

Ladeco (Chile)
    Malecón 1400 and Illingworth (☎ 324 360,
    328 692)
Lufthansa* (Germany)
    Malecón 1400 and Illingworth (☎ 324 360,
    328 692)
Saeta Internacional* (Ecuador)
    Vélez 226 and Chile (☎ 329 855)
Swissair
    Martínez 102 and Malecón (303 333)
Varig* (Brazil)
    P Carbo and 9 de Octubre (☎ 307 876/90)
Viasa* (Venezuela)
    Avenida C L Plaza Dañín, by airport (☎ 393 971,
    392 126)

Domestic There are many internal flights to all parts of the country. The most frequent are to Quito with TAME, SAN, and Saeta. If you buy your ticket with cash, the companies will honour one another's tickets so you can arrive at the airport and leave on the next available flight if it isn't full. There are about 11 flights a day, Monday to Friday, 10 flights on Saturday, and seven flights on Sunday. Tickets cost about US$16. Sit on the right side when flying to Quito for the best views.

TAME has flights from Guayaquil to Cuenca at 10.45 am from Monday to Friday for US$13.50. There have been more frequent flights in the past, including some with SAN, so check the current situation. Only TAME operates flights between Guayaquil and Loja (Monday to Saturday at 7 am, US$12.50), Machala (Monday to Friday at 3.15 pm, US$10), Salinas (6 pm Friday and 3 pm Sunday during the holiday season subject to aircraft availability and passenger demand), and Macará at irregular intervals. Fares and departure times are subject to change. Flights sometimes leave early – this seems to be a problem with the Machala flight in particular. Get to the airport early.

TAME operates the only scheduled flights to Baltra Airport in the Galápagos. They leave daily at 10.30 am and cost US$330 for the round trip. Cheaper fares are available to Ecuadorian residents. SAN-Saeta operates the only scheduled flights to San Cristóbal Airport in the Galápagos. They leave daily except on Thursday and Sunday at 12 noon – same fare.

All the above flights (TAME, SAN and Saeta) leave from the main national terminal. Several small airlines have flights leaving from the Avioneta terminal, one km from the main terminal. These airlines use small aircraft to service various coastal towns. AECA flies to Manta (US$12), Portoviejo (US$12), Bahía de Caráquez (US$13), Pedernales (US$17) and Esmeraldas (US$18). Flights are subject to passenger demand but there is usually one flight a day (except Sunday) to each of these towns between 7 and 8 am and also a second flight to Manta and Portoviejo at 4.15 pm.

More flights may be available if there is passenger demand. CEDTA has four flights a day from Monday to Friday to Machala (US$10). Some flights go to Santa Rosa, which is a little closer to the Peruvian border than Machala. Other airlines – AvioPacifico, Edsan and LANSA – also operate from the Avioneta terminal to coastal destinations. Charters are possible. Bear in mind that some of these flights are in five passenger aircraft and baggage is limited to a small 10 kg bag.

AECA
    Avioneta terminal (☎ 286 640, 288 110)
AvioPacifico
    Avioneta terminal (☎ 283 304/5)
CEDTA
    Avioneta terminal (☎ 280 065)
    Escobedo 924 and V M Rendón (☎ 301 954/165)
EDSAN
    Avioneta terminal (☎ 915 138)
LANSA
    Avioneta terminal (☎ 280 898/665)
SAN & Saeta
    Vélez 206 and Chile (☎ 329 855, 326 466)
TAME
    9 de Octubre 424, Gran Pasaje (☎ 303 128, 302 277)

Bus The terminal terrestre opened in late 1986 just beyond the airport. It is modern and efficient and boasts many stores, restaurants, tourist information, a bank, hairdresser etc. There are scores of bus company offices and you can get just about anywhere. The following selection gives an idea of what's available – there are many more. Fares will almost certainly change but not drastically.

For the Santa Elena Peninsula you can take Transportes Villamil or Co-op Posorja, which have frequent buses to Playas (US$1.15; 1¾ hours) and Posorja (US$1.30, two hours). Co-op Libertad Peninsular and CICA have buses to Salinas (US$1.90; 2½ hours) every 15 minutes.

If you're headed southbound or to Peru, take CIFA, Transportes Rutas Orenses, Ecuatoriana Pullman or Co-op El Oro to Machala (US$2; 3½ hours) and Huaquillas (US$2.60; five hours). CIFA and Rutas Orenses run frequent small buses; the others run larger coaches. Transportes Loja has one bus at 6.30 pm to the border at Macará (US$4.50; 12 hours), and five buses to Loja (US$3.50; 10 hours).

Several companies run buses to Cuenca (US$2.30 to US$2.80; five to seven hours). Supertaxis Cuenca and Buses San Luis run faster small buses while Transportes Oriental run larger, slower and cheaper buses. All three companies have buses about every hour.

Babahoyo (US$0.50; 1½ hours) is served by Transportes Urdaneta and Flota Babahoyo Interprovincial (or FBI). Flota Bolívar has eight slow buses every day to Guaranda via Babahoyo.

For Riobamba and Ambato there are many companies taking as little as 3½ hours to Riobamba if the road is OK. These include: Transportes Andino, Transportes Patria, CITA, Transportes Gran Colombia and Transportes Santa. One of the fastest is probably Transportes Andino. Transportes Cotopaxi has slow buses to Latacunga via Quevedo.

Santo Domingo de los Colorados and Quevedo are served by Transportes Sucre, Transportes Zaracay and others.

Quito (US$2.70 to US$3; seven to nine hours) is served by frequent buses with Flota Imbabura, Transportes Ecuador and Transportes Panamericana. All three are close to one another so check around for what's best for you.

Transportes Esmeraldas and Transportes Occidental have about 10 buses a day to Esmeraldas (US$3; nine hours).

Rutas Ecuatorianas has many departures for Portoviejo (US$2.20; four hours), as does Reina del Camino, who also have buses to Manta and Bahía de Caráquez.

It's easy enough to buy tickets in advance if you want to assure yourself of a place. Otherwise, if you just show up at the terminal, you'll as often as not find a bus to your destination within an hour or so. Friday nights and holidays can get booked up – so think in advance if travelling then.

Train Trains leave from the Durán railway station, which is best reached by taking the Durán ferry from Guayaquil. Details are given under Durán.

Boat Cruise lines occasionally call at Guayaquil and passengers may make brief forays ashore. A few cargo boats will take passengers to and from North America or Europe (see the Getting There & Away chapter). Generally, sailing between Guayaquil and a foreign port is more expensive and less convenient than flying.

Ecuadorian cargo ships ply the coastal routes down to Puerto Bolívar (Machala) and up to Manta, Bahía de Caráquez and Esmeraldas. These working boats are not not very attractive and don't normally have passenger facilities – though occasionally a captain will take passengers. Hanging out by the waterfront and asking around for the captain may yield the opportunity of a fairly inexpensive coastal trip – very few people do this however. Most cargo boats work from the docks in the new port, about 12 km south of downtown.

Cargo boats steam for the Galápagos about two or three times a month. The round trip from Guayaquil takes about 12 to 20 days, of which about three to four days are spent crossing the ocean from Guayaquil to the islands and the rest is spent in the archipelago. The trips are designed to deliver and pick up cargo from various Galápagos ports and are not very comfortable. Passengers are accepted, however. It's possible to get off the boat for a few days in the Galápagos and do some sightseeing trips – the round trip from

Guayaquil is between US$200 and US$300, and this includes a bunk to sleep in and basic food. As far as I know, one-way fares are not available and you have to return with the ship you go out on. Bring a long book and seasickness medication for the ocean crossing.

You can try hanging around the waterfront near the Malecón looking for a boat, but your best bet is to check with some shipping agencies. Acotramar (**☎** 401 004/711, 402 371) at General Gómez 522 and Chimborazo is the agent for the *Piquero* which has five small cabins and has been used by travellers. TRAMSFA at Baquerizo Moreno 1119 and 9 de Octubre, 6th floor, is another agent to try – Sr Rafael Castro is supposedly the man to talk to. Or you can try a shorter trip with the Ecuadorian Navy which can be contacted at Transnave (**☎** 308 400) at 9 de Octubre 416 and Chile. The Capitanía on the Malecón have details of shipping traffic and may also be able to help.

Sailing dates are not guaranteed and late departures and cancellations are common. With only a couple of sailings a month, you may be stuck waiting for weeks. This is not for the traveller who is in a hurry but, if you have time and patience, you could give it a try. This is one trip that is very much a matter of luck – you may find a boat leaving tomorrow or you may lose many frustrating days.

Apart from the cargo boats, there are expensive cruise ships going out from Guayaquil to the Galápagos – talk to travel agents about these.

Getting Around
To/From the Airport The airport is on Avenida de las Américas, about four or five km north of the centre of town. A taxi from the airport to the centre will cost about US$2. Taxi drivers are supposed to use meters but many try to charge higher fares from the airport – bargain. If you cross the street in front of the airport, you can take a bus downtown, and from the centre of town the best bus to take to the airport is the No 2 Especial, which costs US$0.05 and takes about a half hour. It runs along the Malecón but is sometimes full, so you should leave yourself

plenty of time or take a taxi – often only about US$1 from downtown.

From the airport to the terminal terrestre is about two or three km. You can walk it if you want – turn right out of the airport terminal and head for the obvious huge terminal. Or take a bus or taxi.

Bus City buses are cheap (US$0.05) but are always crowded and the system is complicated. They are mainly designed to get workers and commuters from the housing districts to downtown and back again, and are not much use for riding around the city centre. They never seem to go exactly where you want to go, and what with waiting for them and battling the traffic, you'd be better off walking, which is what I always do. The downtown area is less than two sq km so it's easy to walk anywhere.

The CETUR information office can help you with bus information if you want to go out into the suburbs, though there isn't much to see there except for the suburb of Urdesa which has good restaurants. The No 52 Policentro bus goes along the Malecón and can drop you off at the beginning of Urdesa. The No 15 bus also goes to Urdesa.

Buses to the terminal terrestre leave from Parque Victoria (near 10 de Agosto and P Moncayo).

Taxi If you really must get somewhere in a hurry, you won't get there much quicker on a city bus than on foot. Take a taxi but make sure the meter is working because Guayaquil taxi drivers have the worst reputation in the country for overcharging. You should be able to get between any two points downtown for under US$1, and to the airport, the terminal terrestre or Urdesa for between US$1 and US$2.

If you need a taxi to pick you up at your door, call Radio Taxis Paraíso (☎ 204 232/549, 201 877).

Car Rental If you're feeling affluent, you can rent a car; if you're not, then forget it because it's not cheap. There are several car rental agencies at the airport. Expect to pay at least US$30 per day for a small car for a seven-day rental. Make sure that insurance, tax and mileage are included. If you find a cheaper deal, ensure that the car you get isn't about to break down. Read the Getting Around chapter for more details.

Avis
    Paula de Icaza 425 (☎ 302 815)
    Hotel Oro Verde (☎ 327 278)
    Airport (☎ 395 554)
Budget
    Airport (☎ 284 559, 288 510)
Dollar
    Chimborazo 418 and C Ballón (☎ 510 290, 306 983)
Hertz
    Airport (☎ 281 315, 202 565)

Boat The Durán ferry across the Río Guayas leaves three or four times an hour from 5.30 am to 7 or 8 pm daily. The crossing lasts 15 minutes and costs US$0.03 – a great sightseeing trip! The ferry dock is on the Malecon at the foot of Avenida J Montalvo. It makes a nice trip around sunset – but make sure you don't miss the last ferry back.

DURÁN

This suburb of Guayaquil is on the east bank of the Río Guayas and easily reached by ferry (see the previous reference). The main reasons for coming here are to enjoy the ferry ride across the river or to catch the train from Durán to the highlands.

It's a small town and you won't have any difficulty in finding your way around. Two blocks inland from the river is the main street of Loja on which you'll find a bank, a cinema, stores and a hotel.

Places to Stay & Eat

There are several places near the ferry dock serving seafood and beer – not fancy but certainly adequate. *Hotel Buenos Aires* at Loja 516 and Esmeraldas is a basic but friendly hotel charging about US$1.50 per person. There are a couple of other basic places.

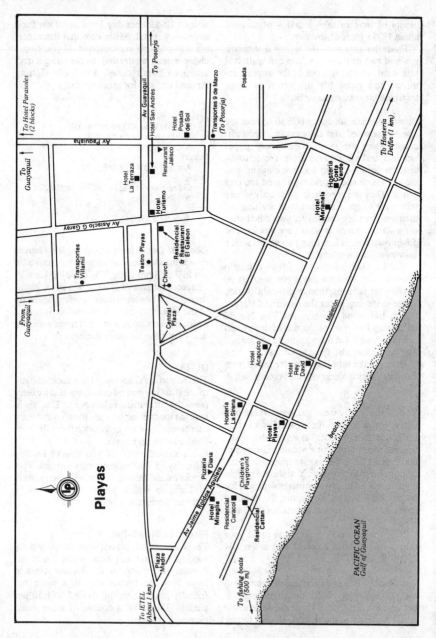

Playas

Getting There & Away

Most people get here by ferry or train – the dock is less than a block from the railway station so it's easy to get from one to the other. You can glimpse the railway station and ferry dock from the left of a bus just before crossing the huge bridge linking the east and west banks of the Río Guayas. Buses are not a good way to get to Durán however – the ferry is much cheaper and more convenient.

Train Services from Durán (Guayaquil) to Quito were disrupted by the 1982/83 El Niño disaster which closed the tracks for some years. Now, trains run from Durán as far as Alausí in the highlands but it is unlikely that the entire route to Quito will be reopened any time soon. The trip to Alausí does ascend the famous El Nariz del Diablo (the Devil's Nose) – a difficult ascent involving many switchbacks and tunnels. The trip is described in greater detail under Alausí.

The train leaves Durán daily, except Sunday, at 6.30 am. Sometimes there is also an autoferro leaving at 6 am – this is faster but not as colourful as the belching steam train. If you catch the first ferry from Guayaquil you can make the train without having to overnight in Durán. Many travellers ride on the roof for the 10 to 12-hour trip – you can buy a ticket for US$0.60 for a seat inside but if you don't have a ticket you can simply pay the conductor during the trip.

The first section to Bucay is mostly flat and not very interesting. It takes about five hours. You could take a bus from Guayaquil to Bucay in two hours and catch the train there for the ascent to Alausí, which is the most interesting part of the trip.

West of Guayaquil

This region is a fairly dry, barren and sparsely populated area, but one containing Guayaquileños' favourite beach resorts. It is busy during the high season (Christmas to April, especially weekends, and also July to September to a lesser extent) but is very quiet at other times. These beaches are infrequently visited by foreign travellers, who prefer the more northerly areas.

PROGRESO

Progreso is officially known as Gómez Rendón and is a village almost 70 km southeast of Guayaquil. Here the road forks and you head west to Salinas and the Santa Elena Peninsula or south to the resort of Playas. The road fork is Progreso's claim to fame; there's no reason to stop here except to change buses.

From Guayaquil to Progreso the paved road passes through very dry scrubland. It is amazing how quickly the land changes from the wet rice-growing areas in the regions north and east of Guayaquil to the dry lands of the west. Despite the dryness, the scenery is quite attractive and interesting, with strange bottle-shaped kapok trees and bright flowers dotting the hilly landscape.

PLAYAS

From Progreso the paved road heads due south for 30 km to Playas (called General Villamil on some maps), the beach resort nearest Guayaquil.

Playas is also an important fishing village. A generation ago, many of the fishing craft were small balsa rafts with one sail – similar in design to the boats used up and down the coast for many centuries before the Spanish conquest. Now, motor-driven dugouts and other more modern craft are most frequently used, but you can still see a few of the old balsa rafts in action. This is one of the most interesting things to look for in Playas. They usually come in at the west end of the beach but this depends on winds and tides. Large flocks of frigatebirds and pelicans hoping for scraps wheel spectacularly around the fishing fleet as it comes in to unload the catch.

Because of its proximity to Guayaquil, there are many holiday homes in Playas. It is quite a bustling little resort during the busy seasons but is very quiet at other times of year. Weekends are much busier than mid-week.

In the high season all the hotels are open and prices may rise a little; in other months many of the hotels, especially the cheaper ones, may close down. Those which are open have few guests and will sometimes lower their prices to have you stay there – try bargaining.

The Teatro Playas cinema is often closed in the low season too.

Places to Stay – bottom end

The cheapest places may lack running water on occasion and are pretty basic. Mosquitoes can be a problem in Playas, so try and get a room with mosquito netting or a fan. The best of the cheapies seems to be the *Hotel Marianela* which charges US$2.25 per person in rooms with a private bath. Other possibilities for about US$2 per person are the clean *Hostería Costa Verde*, the run-down looking *Hotel Turismo* and the *Hotel Posada del Sol*. The basic *Residencial Caracol* charges US$2.75 per person.

The *Residencial El Galeon* is clean, friendly and good value for US$3 per person. Rooms have private showers and mosquito nets are provided. The *Hotel San Andrés* is fairly new and charges US$5.50 for a double with bath. Also new is the *Hotel La Terraza* which charges US$3.75 per person, though they offered me a room for US$3 with almost no bargaining. Rooms are clean and with private bath, but lack mosquito nets.

For US$3.25 per person you can stay at the *Hotel Miraglia*. It's a sprawling old wooden building but the rooms are adequate – some have private bathrooms. There is a library of novels in English if you plan on spending a few days. The *Hostería La Sirena* has doubles with private bath for US$6.50, but their disco may be too loud at weekends. The *Hotel Acapulco* has clean rooms for US$4 per person.

Places to Stay – middle

Hotel Playas (☎ 760 121) on the Malecón has simple but clean rooms with private bathrooms for US$7 a single and US$11 a double, but the showers are reportedly brackish. They have a decent restaurant. *Residencial Cattan* (☎ 760 179) also on the Malecón provides a bed and three good meals a day for US$11 per person. The rooms have private baths and are clean but the showers have brackish water only. Accommodation without meals costs US$9/11 for a single/double with bath. Their restaurant is quite good.

The *Hotel Rey David* on the Malecón has some rooms with a view of the ocean. Rooms are plain but clean and cost US$7.50/9 for singles/doubles with bath. Also in this price range is the *Hotel Parasoles* a few blocks north of the town centre on Avenida Paquisha.

If you want to stay out of town you can head roughly east on Avenida Jaime Roldos Aguilera to the *Hostería Delfín* about a km away on the road to Data and Posorja. It's in a quiet location by the sea and rooms are about US$12 for a double with bath. Also near here is the similar *Hostería La Gaviota* (☎ 760 133). West of the town is the *Hotel Oro Azul* – there is a sign just before you enter Playas from Guayaquil. These are the best three hotels in the Playas area and have decent restaurants and pleasant rooms which cost a few dollars more than places in town.

Places to Eat

The better hotels have good restaurants; the one below the *Residencial Galeon* is recommended as being good, fairly cheap and open to the public. The *Hotel Acapulco* and *Hostería La Sirena* also have reasonably priced restaurants. For Italian food try *Pizzería Diana* – a friendly place run by a US-Ecuadorian couple. The *Restaurant Jalisco* has fairly good cheap meals.

Getting There & Away

Transportes Villamil and Posorja are the bus companies with services to Guayaquil (US$1.15; 1¾ hours). Buses leave every half hour with Transportes Villamil and they often pass the corner of Avenida Paquisha and Avenida Guayaquil.

Transportes Posorja picks up passengers

for Posorja if the bus from Guayaquil is continuing there. Transportes 9 de Marzo and other companies have frequent pickup trucks to Posorja (US$0.20; 30 minutes) leaving from Avenida Paquisha – see the map.

Services are normally to Guayaquil, though occasionally a bus may go to the Santa Elena Peninsula. The easiest way to get to Santa Elena is to go to Progreso and change, but buses from Guayaquil to Santa Elena are often full during holidays.

PUNTA PELADA

This is a long and fairly deserted beach stretching north-west from Playas. Salt flats, cliffs and cacti provide an interesting looking backdrop. There is a dirt road along the beach and it is a popular drive for those with their own vehicles – no public transport. Bring food and water.

POSORJA

Posorja is an attractive little fishing village with many working boats and hundreds of seabirds wheeling overhead but the beach is dirty and not good for swimming. Shrimping is becoming increasingly important. Posorja is best visited on a day trip – it is about 20 km south-east of Playas.

There are two roads between Playas and Posorja – one follows the coast and the other heads inland. The coastal road goes through the villages of Data de Villamil and Data de Posorja which are often collectively called Data. These places are known for boat building. The inland road passes through the old village of El Morro, which is less important than it used to be. There is a huge old wooden church with dilapidated bamboo walls and three white wooden towers; the place is falling into disrepair.

Places to Stay

There are two very basic pensiones. One is literally on the point of disintegrating and the other looks like a particularly sleazy whorehouse – neither are recommended.

Getting There & Away

Pickup trucks serve as a frequent public bus service between Playas and Posorja.

SANTA ELENA PENINSULA

As you continue westward from Progreso the land becomes increasingly dry and scrubby, the ceibal (kapok) trees giving way to interminable forests of five-metre-high cactus. Few people and little animal life is seen, though herds of tough, half-wild goats seem to thrive. Some of the few inhabitants scratch a living from burning the scrub to make charcoal and occasionally you see someone on the side of the road with bags of charcoal.

A little over half way between Progreso and Santa Elena a road to the left leads to the coastal village of **Chanduy**, some 15 km from the main road. Archaeological excavations nearby have led to the opening of a small museum on the outskirts of the village. This place is not easy to find or get to. You can get to Chanduy by bus from La Libertad.

About 15 km before reaching Santa Elena, a road to the right leads 7 km to **Baños de San Vicente** where there are thermal pools and mud baths. A government-operated tourist complex has been built here and visitors can enjoy therapeutic and rejuvenating mud packs or swims. Daily entrance to the complex is about US$0.50. There is one place to spend the night, the *Hotel Florida* (☎ 353 016, 352 221 for information and reservations) although the clientele is mostly upper-class Guayaqileños on day trips.

As you arrive in Santa Elena the landscape changes. Not that it becomes any less dry, it simply becomes built-up. There are three towns near the end of the peninsula and they all seem to run into one another, making the area almost one complete dusty urban zone with few open spaces.

Santa Elena itself is the least important of the towns from the traveller's point of view, though it does have a nearby oil refinery and is the home of the peninsula's radio station. *Residencial El Cisne* is a clean, basic hotel on the main square. The other towns on the peninsula are La Libertad and Salinas

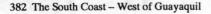

382 The South Coast – West of Guayaquil

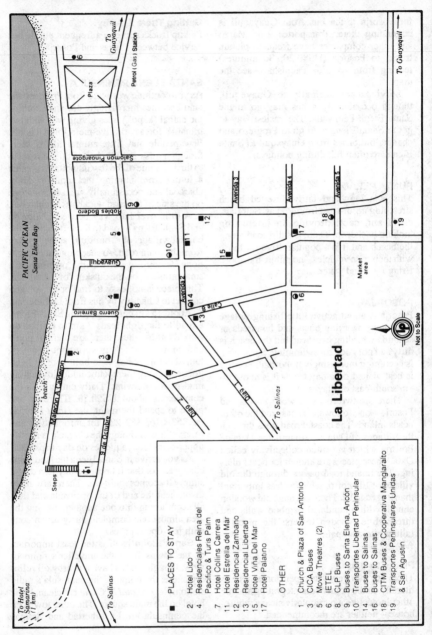

La Libertad

Not to Scale

PLACES TO STAY

2 Hotel Lido
4 Residenciales Reina del
   Pacifico & Turis Palm
7 Hotel Collins Carrera
11 Hotel Estrella del Mar
12 Residencial Zambano
13 Residencial Libertad
15 Hotel Viña Del Mar
17 Hotel Palatino

OTHER

1 Church & Plaza of San Antonio
3 CICA Buses
5 Movie Theatres (2)
6 IETEL
8 CLP Buses
9 Buses to Santa Elena, Ancón
10 Transportes Libertad Peninsular
14 Buses to Salinas
16 Buses to Salinas
18 CITM Buses & Cooperativa Mangaralto
19 Transportes Peninsulares Unidas
   & San Agustin

(which is the main resort town for Guayaquileños).

LA LIBERTAD

La Libertad, largest town on the peninsula, has almost 50,000 inhabitants. It is a fishing village and port of some importance as well as being the transportation hub for the area and it is more interesting to visit (especially in the low season) than Salinas. The El Niño floods caused severe damage to the waterfront and most of the Malecón has been washed away and the beach is mainly rubble. A plaza at the east end of the Malecón is where the modern IETEL office is found. There is a bustling market and a cinema.

Places to Stay – bottom end

One of the cheapest hotels on the whole peninsula is the basic but friendly *Residencial Libertad*, which costs US$1.50 per person. Another cheapie is the *Residencial Reina del Pacífico* which also costs US$1.50 but the rooms are rather horrible little boxes, though they do have a few better rooms with private bath for US$5. Next door is the *Turis Palm* with basic rooms at US$2 per person or US$3 with private bathroom.

Other possibilities in the US$1.50 to US$2 bracket include the *Hotel Lido* and the *Residencial Zambano*, neither of which look too prepossessing.

Places to Stay – middle

The *Hotel Viña del Mar* (☎ 785 979) at Guayaquil and Avenida 3 has rooms with balconies and private baths, and parking is available – a good deal for about US$7 a double. The *Hotel Collins Carrera*, also in this price range, is not as good. *Hotel Palatino* (☎ 786 770) on Guayaquil and Avenida 4 is reasonable value though nothing special. Rooms are US$7/11 for singles/doubles with private bathroom. The *Hotel Estrella del Mar* on Avenida 2 and Guayaquil was being completely remodelled in 1991 and looks like it may be a good mid-range choice when it is finished.

The best place in town is the *Hotel Samarina* (☎ 785 167) on 9 de Octubre at the waterfront about one km north-west of the town. They have a restaurant, a swimming pool and clean rooms and bungalows for about US$14/18 for singles/doubles. There is a clean but small beach in front of the hotel.

Places to Eat

Most restaurants are on Avenida 9 de Octubre or Guayaquil. There are several cheap chifas and comedores near the Residencial Reina del Pacífico and on the way up to the market.

Getting There & Away

La Libertad is the centre of bus services on the peninsula. For Guayaquil (US$1.10; 2½ to three hours) there are several choices. Transportes Libertad Peninsular has buses about every hour all day long. CICA at 9 de Octubre and Diagonal 2 has the fastest and most frequent service. Their buses often leave from opposite the Residencials Reina del Pacífico and Turis Palm on Avenida 9 de Octubre. The CICA buses from Guayaquil continue to Salinas and then return to Guayaquil from Salinas via La Libertad. CLP on the corner of 9 de Octubre and Guerro Barreiro also has buses to Guayaquil.

To get to Santa Elena you take one of the pickup trucks which depart frequently from Avenida Robles Bordero near Guayaquil. Frequent buses to Salinas run all day from Calle 8 and either Avenida 2 or 4.

To visit Punta Carnero, the fishing village of Anconcito, or the oil town of Ancón, take one of the frequent buses or pickup trucks leaving from near the market on Avenida Guayaquil and Avenida 5. Near here is Transportes San Agustín, which has open-sided rancheros or *chivas* running further east along the coast to the fishing village of Chanduy. Various small coastal villages are served by transport from the market area – ask around. Apart from at Punta Carnero there is no accommodation in these places.

For going north along the coast to the fishing villages of Palmar, Ayangue, Manglaralto (US$0.80; 1½ hours) and Puerto López (US$1.30; 2½ hours) you take rancheros, buses and trucks with Transportes

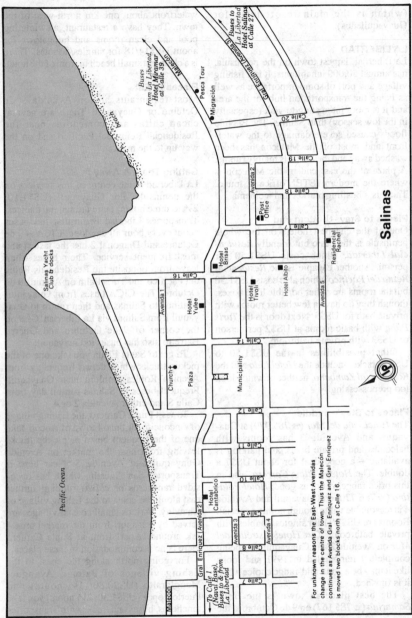

Salinas

For unknown reasons the East-West Avenidas change in the centre of town. Thus the Malecón continues as Avenida Gral Enriquez and Gral Enriquez is moved two blocks north at Calle 16.

Top: Male frigatebird with inflated neck pouch, Galápagos Islands (TW)
Bottom: Marine Iguana (RR)

Top: Climber descending from Chimborazo, (6310 metres), the paramo far below (JW)
Bottom: Chimborazo, with the climber's refuge in the foreground (JW)

Peninsulares Unidas, Cooperativa Manglaralto or CITM. The first one has departures about every half hour but few of the vehicles make it as far as Manglaralto. Most go as far as Palmar and some go to Ayangue. The other two companies have several buses a day that go through Puerto López and on to Jipijapa. Note that buses may be booked up in advance during weekends in the high season.

PUNTA CARNERO

This is a point of land in the middle of a wild and largely deserted beach, some 15 km in length. There is a resort hotel on the point, the *Punta Carnero Inn* (☎ 785 377) which overlooks the ocean. Comfortable, balconied rooms cost about US$30 for a double with bath and air-conditioning. There is a restaurant and swimming pool. Reservations can be made at the Plaza Hotel in Guayaquil.

The ocean in front of the hotel may be too wild for swimming but the beach is good for walks. The sea abounds with fish, and sport-fishing is a popular activity. Boats and equipment can be chartered from Salinas. The area has also been recommended for birdwatching – some unusual arid land birds and shorebirds like the Chilean flamingo have been reported from the area (see Green's *Birding Ecuador* for more details).

Buses from La Libertad will get you to Punta Carnero, but most visitors come with their own vehicle.

SALINAS

This important resort town with a permanent population of over 20,000 inhabitants is on the tip of the Santa Elena Peninsula. About 150 km west of Guayaquil, it is the most westerly town on the Ecuadorian mainland. Unfortunately you cannot go to the very furthest point as there is a naval base there.

Salinas is called the 'best' resort in Ecuador and its casino, expensive hotels and high-rise condos make it the haunt of affluent Ecuadorians. It's relatively expensive and quite busy during the season and still fairly expensive and dead in the off-season. The

water is warmest for swimming from January to March. The beaches are not spectacular and basically rather spoilt by the high-rise backdrop. I prefer the less-developed beaches of Playas or the north coast.

There is a Yacht Club and, should you arrive in your own boat, you'll find Migración on the waterfront. Foreign sailors say that the Yacht Club is not very accommodating and 'yachties' hang out in other places – a French café on the waterfront has recently been popular.

Also on the waterfront is Pesca Tour (☎ 443 365), who do deep-sea fishing trips and provide all the equipment. They have a fleet of several boats and have been recommended by people who enjoy sport-fishing. Charters run about US$800 per person per week, everything included from Guayaquil. Day charters can also be arranged. The continental shelf drops from about 400 metres, 13 km offshore, to over 3000 metres about 40 km offshore and so a short sail of an hour can take you out into really deep water. Swordfish, sailfish, tuna, dorados, and marlin are some of the fish to go after – the black marlin occasionally go over 600 kg. Black marlin are the world's third biggest sport fish, after a couple of shark species. The world black marlin record is 707 kg, set in 1953 in neighbouring Peru. Locals claim that there is an 800 kg black marlin on the Ecuadorian coast. Salinas occasionally hosts world fishing competitions.

Places to Stay

Many local tourists have holiday homes in which they stay rather than in the hotels. There is no very cheap accommodation and hotels may close down in the off-season.

The cheapest place is the old and tumble-down *Hotel Tivoli* which has rooms with private bathrooms at US$4 per person. Other hotels in the US$4 to US$7 per person range are the *Hotel Yulee* and *Hotel Albito* which are recommended, and the worse-looking *Hotel Brisas* and *Residencial Rachel*.

Hotel Cantabrico is good value if you eat all your meals there. They charge US$12 per person in basic but clean rooms with private bathrooms, and all three meals are included. If you don't want to eat here you pay US$9 for the room. They have a rather dusty garden with hammocks to lie around in.

The modern *Hotel Salinas* (☎ 774 268, 772 760) charges US$13 for good, comfortable double rooms with bathrooms. The most expensive place in town is the *Hotel Miramar* (☎ 772 115), which boasts air-conditioned rooms, a casino, swimming pool, bar and restaurant. They charge about US$26 for a double in the low season, a little more in the busy months.

Places to Eat

There are various restaurants, bars and discos along the waterfront between Calles 19 and 25 but they're mostly closed in the low season. Near the Hotel Miramar are the expensive but good *Mar y Tierra* and the cheaper and simpler *Flipper* both recommended for, what else, seafood. *Restaurant Caracol* on Calle 6 at the waterfront is good and medium priced – they have a discotheque attached. Another good place for nightlife is *Peña del Rey* by the town hall – taxi drivers all know it.

Getting There & Away

Buses enter town along the Malecón and continue to the naval base, where they turn around and head back to La Libertad along Gral Enriquez. During the low season, most buses go only as far as La Libertad. Those that continue to Guayaquil usually stop at La Libertad for up to an hour to pick up more passengers. During the high season there are direct buses and there may be flights to and from Guayaquil.

NORTH ALONG THE COAST

From La Libertad many buses run north along the coast. Some go only a short way but many make it as far as Puerto López and Jipijapa in the province of Manabí (see the North Coast chapter). The beaches en route are often very good and there are several fishing villages where Guayaquileños have holiday homes, but there are not many hotels. This area is not visited by foreign travellers as much as the better known beaches in Manabí and Esmeraldas. The season from Christmas to about May is hot, sunny, but wet – the scenery is lush and pretty between rain showers. The ocean is warmest during January to March. The rest of the year is dry, cooler, and cloudier. It can sometimes be grey and miserable during the dry months.

The coast views are good, so sit on the left or ocean side of the bus. The most interesting sight is the literally hundreds of local fishermen surf-fishing. They catch shrimp with hand nets stretched between a framework of two crossed poles, at the end of which a couple of floats are attached. Wading knee deep in the surf, they push these hand nets up and down the beach. It looks ridiculously like a lawn-mowing convention gone crazy.

The first place of particular interest is the **Valdivia** area, which is the site of Ecuador's oldest culture. There is a small museum in the little village of Valdivia, about 50 km north of La Libertad, but the best pieces of antiquity are in Guayaquil museums. About five km before reaching Valdivia, the fishing village of **Ayangue** is passed, and five km before that (40 km north of La Libertad), the village of **Palmar**. Both are close to pleasant beaches and have attracted Guayaquileños into buying holiday homes there. The area is fairly crowded with visitors during high season weekends, but only Ayangue has a small hotel.

North of Valdivia the dry landscape begins to get a little wetter. The cactus and scrub give way to stunted trees and the occasional banana plantation.

Manglaralto, about 60 km north of La Libertad, is the main village on the coast of Guayas Province north of La Libertad. There is a nice beach but little shade. There are a few simple pensiones, particularly near the north end of the beach, or ask around for accommodation. I managed to find a place to stay with a friendly local family for US$1.50. You can do this in the other villages too. There are a couple of basic comedores and an IETEL office on Manglaralto's main square.

Approximately four or five km north of Manglaralto is the village of **Montañita**. Like other places along the coast, it is a pleasant little fishing village with nice beaches. There are a couple of places to stay, of which *El Rincón del Amigo* has been recommended. It is run by an Irish-American who will provide penurious travellers with a bunk in the dormitory for about US$1. Nicer private rooms go for US$2 to US$3 per person depending on the room. Some rooms have beach views and all beds have mosquito nets – essential during the wet months. There is a decent restaurant. Montañita and Manglaralto have good waves and are popular hang-outs for surfers.

A few km further north is the coastal village of **Olón**. This too has a decent beach and a hotel which charges about US$4.50 per person. I haven't stayed here, but I'm told it's a good hotel.

Six or seven km north of Olón, the provincial line between Guayas and Manabí is crossed – see the North Coast for further travel.

You can easily do a round trip from La Libertad in a day if you just want to sightsee and swim at some beaches.

South of Guayaquil

Guayas Province south of Guayaquil is of little interest to Guayaquileño holiday-makers, compared to west of the city. For the most part, this route is taken by travellers on their way to Peru.

RESERVA ECOLÓGICA MANGLARES CHURUTE

This 35,000-hectare reserve protects an area of mangroves south-east of Guayaquil. Much of the coast used to be mangrove forest – an important and unique habitat (see the Facts about the Country chapter). This is one of the few remaining mangrove coastlands left – the rest have been destroyed by the shrimp industry.

I talked to people at MAG in Quito but they had no idea about how to visit Manglares Churute. I have never met anybody who has been there – it appears to be largely inaccessible and this is probably why it has remained intact until the present.

MACHALA

South of Guayaquil is the important city of Machala, with about 125,000 inhabitants and the capital of the province of El Oro. It lies in an important banana-growing area and during the 200-km drive from Guayaquil you pass many plantations of bananas, coffee, pineapple and citrus fruits. About halfway to Machala you go through Naranjal, an important agricultural centre but otherwise of little interest.

Despite its economic importance, Machala is not of great tourist interest. Most travellers on their way to and from Peru pass through here but few people stay more than a night.

It is not totally devoid of interest, however, as the local international port of Puerto Bolívar, only seven km away, is worth visiting. There are beaches nearby. Machala also has a highly touted International Banana & Agricultural Festival during the third week in September which the Ecuadorian tourist authorities assure me is of great interest to tourists. I'm afraid I missed it.

Information

Most streets in Machala are both named and numbered (I use names). The CETUR information office is next to the Hotel Mosquera on Guayas and Olmedo. It is open somewhat erratically on weekdays.

The IETEL office is several blocks away from the centre on 9 de Octubre. Casa de Cambio Illauri (☎ 921 342) at Páez 17-23 changes both US cash dollars and travellers' cheques at rates only a little lower than Guayaquil and Quito. There are a couple of cinemas, of which the Teatro Tauro is the best.

For those who need visas to enter Peru (such as Australians and New Zealanders, among others), there is a Peruvian Consulate (☎ 920 680), at Bolívar and Colón, open

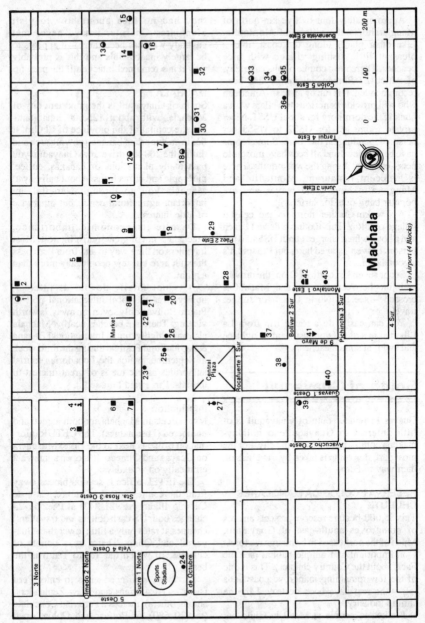

■ PLACES TO STAY

2 Hotel Ines
3 Hotel El Mosquero
5 Hotel La Delicia
6 Residencial La Internacional
7 Residencial Machala
8 Hotel Oro
9 Hotel Perla de Pacifico
11 Hostal Mercy
14 Hotel La Cueva de los Tayos
19 Hotel Suites Guayaquil
20 Hotel Reina Paccha
21 Residencial Almache
22 Residencial Pichincha
28 Gran Hotel Machala
30 Hotel Encalada
32 Hotel Ecuatoriana Pullman
37 Residencial El Oro
40 Rizzo Hotel

▼ PLACES TO EAT

10 El Jeff Pizzería
17 Restaurant Chifa Central
41 Bar Restaurant El Bosque

OTHER

1 Transportes Azuay Buses
4 CETUR Tourist Information
12 Transportes Pullman Sucre Buses
13 Transportes Occidentales Buses
15 Transportes Union Yantzaza Buses
16 Transportes Cooperativa Loja Buses
18 Rutas Orenses Buses
23 Cinema
24 IETEL
25 Ecuatoriana Airline
26 Cinema Central
27 Church
29 Casa de Cambio Illauri
31 CIFA Buses to Guayaquil
32 Ecuatoriana Buses
33 Cuidad de Piñas Buses
34 Transportes TAC Buses
35 Panamericana Buses
36 Peruvian Consulate
38 Travel Agencies
39 CIFA Buses to Huaquillas
42 Post Office
43 TAME Airline

from 8 am to 1 pm Monday through Friday. It is reportedly easier to get a visa in Quito or Guayaquil, because the Machala consul demands to see an onward ticket and may be closed more often than the indicated hours.

For more information about the **Puyango Petrified Forest** (more information is provided later) ask at the office of Comision Administradora de los Bosques Petrificados de Puyango (☎ 930 012) which has an office at the Fabrica de Cola in the Cuidadela Las Brisas – many cab drivers know where the Fabrica is.

On the main road into Machala, south-east of the city, there is a huge **statue of El Bananero** – a man carrying a large branch of bananas. This is Machalas's most important monument. Watch for it as you arrive into town.

Places to Stay
Machala has a better variety of hotels than does the border town of Huaquillas, so trav-

ellers are better off staying here. The border is not open until 8 am, so by taking a dawn bus you can still be in Huaquillas by the time the border opens.

Places to Stay – bottom end
Most of the cheap hotels have only cold water but the weather is hot enough that it's not a great hardship. Perhaps the best of the cheap and basic hotels is the *Hotel La Delicia*, on Olmedo near Páez, which charges US$2.50 per person and is friendly – but often full. Some of the most basic places (also about US$2.50) are the *Residencial Almache*, Sucre and Montalvo, which looks very dirty, the *Residencial El Oro*, 9 de Mayo near Bolívar, which looks very rundown, and the *Residencial Pichincha*, Sucre near 9 de Mayo, which looks a little better. Somewhat cleaner and better looking is the *Residencial La Internacional*, Guayas near Olmedo, which is friendly, and the *Residencial Machala*, Sucre and Guayas, for US$2

a single and US$3 for single with bath, although the toilets have been criticised as dirty. Another possibility is the clean *Hotel La Cueva de los Tayos*, Sucre near Buenavista, which charges US$3 per person.

Many budget travellers end up staying at the *Gran Hotel Machala* (☎ 920 530), Montalvo and Rocafuerte, which has simple rooms for US$3.75 per person or US$4.50 with private bathroom and fan. Most of the rooms are OK and some have air-conditioning but a few are not as good. Ask to see another if you don't like the first one you are shown.

Although the *Hotel Ecuatoriana Pullman* (☎ 921 164), 9 de Octubre 912 and Colón, is above the bus terminal, some rooms are surprisingly quiet and some have air-conditioning. It's a bit run down and has rather grubby private bathrooms in the rooms which cost about US$4 per person – but it's not too bad. A good choice is the small and clean *Hostal Mercy*, Junín 609 and Sucre, which charges US$4.50 per person in rooms with private bath and fan. This place is often full. Another fairly good possibility is the *Hotel Suites Guayaquil* (☎ 922 570), Páez and 9 de Octubre, which charges US$5.50/9.50 for singles/doubles with bath (some have air-conditioning).

Places to Stay – middle & top end
The *Hotel El Mosquero*, next to the tourist office on Olmedo and Guayas, has singles with private baths for US$5.50 and with air-conditioning for US$8. The *Hotel Encalada* (☎ 920 247) has clean rooms with private bath and fans for US$8/12 for singles/doubles.

The rest of the hotels in this price range have clean rooms with private bathrooms and air-conditioning. The *Hotel Ines* (☎ 922 301), Montalvo 1509 and Pasaje, charges US$9/14 for singles/doubles with TV. The *Hotel Perla de Pacifico* (☎ 921 472), Sucre 613 and Páez, charges US$13/17. The *Hotel Oro* (☎ 922 408), Sucre and Montalvo, charges US$15/19 in rooms with TV and telephone.

The best hotel in town, complete with

swimming pool and casino, is traditionally the *Rizzo Hotel* (☎ 921 511), Guayas near Pichincha, which charges about US$17/22. The new *Hotel Reina Paccha*, Montalvo near 9 de Octubre, is also good at US$21/28. All of these hotels have their own restaurants and the Encalada has a discotheque.

Places to Eat
There are many chifas, and the *Restaurant Chifa Central*, Tarqui near 9 de Octubre, is recommended as having a wide variety of good and reasonably priced meals.

Budget travellers should try the chaulafan which is a cheap but filling rice dish. There are a number of other cheap places along 9 de Octubre between the Chifa Central and IETEL, including chifas and chicken restaurants – take your pick.

For Italian food try *El Jeff Pizzería* at Junín and Sucre. For a pleasanter outdoor ambience try the *Bar Restaurant El Bosque* (☎ 924 344), 9 de Mayo near Bolívar, which has simple but decent meals for about US$2.

The best hotels have more expensive restaurants but the food is good. The *Hotel Perla del Pacifico* serves vegetarian food and the *Hotel Oro* reputedly has the best (and most expensive) restaurant in town. The *Hotel Rizzo* is good for breakfasts.

If you have some spare time, consider heading over to Puerto Bolívar for a seafood banquet.

Getting There & Away
Air TAME flights from Guayaquil to Machala and back leave Machala at 4 pm, Monday to Friday, subject to change. The fare is US$10. You can connect with a Guayaquil-Quito flight to be in the capital the same evening for about US$26. TAME has a downtown office (☎ 920 130) on Montalvo near Pichincha. The airport is barely one km from the town centre and a taxi will cost about US$0.60. If you are on foot, walk south-west along Montalvo.

CEDTA and LANSA also have an office at the airport and they have light aircraft for flights to Guayaquil.

There is an Ecuatoriana airline office on 9

de Mayo near 9 de Octubre if you need information about their international flights from Guayaquil or Quito. There are two or three travel agents on Bolívar between Guayas and 9 de Mayo.

Bus There is no central bus terminal. To get to the Peruvian border at Huaquillas (US$0.80; two hours) it's best to go with CIFA, who leave at very frequent intervals from the corner of Bolívar and Guayas. They go through Santa Rosa and Arenillas. Make sure your documents are in order and not packed deep in your luggage as there are two or three passport checks en route. You will be asked to leave the bus to register but the driver is used to this and will wait for you.

CIFA buses also go to Guayaquil (US$2; 3½ hours) from their depot on 9 de Octubre near Colón. There are several other companies in the area. Rutas Orenses, 9 de Octubre near Tarqui, has efficient and frequent services to Guayaquil in small buses and Ecuatoriana, 9 de Octubre near Colón, goes there in larger coaches.

Panamericana, Colon and Bolívar, has several large coaches a day to Quito (US$3; 10 to 12 hours). Transportes Occidentales, Buenavista and Olmedo, has two morning and two night buses to Quito, and a couple of morning buses to Esmeraldas.

Ciudad de Piñas, Colón and Rocafuerte, has nine buses a day to Piñas, a few of which continue to Loja. They also have one or two buses to Cuenca (US$2.20; five hours).

Transportes Azuay, Montalvo and 3 Norte, has many buses daily to Cuenca (US$1.75; four hours) and Transportes Pullman Sucre, Sucre near Tarqui, has eight buses daily to Cuenca. Transportes Union Yantzaza, Sucre near Buenavista, has a slow old daily bus leaving at 8.30 am for Yantzaza (US$3.25; 12 hours) in the Southern Oriente.

Transportes Cooperativa Loja, Sucre and Buenavista, goes to Loja – ask the driver to set you down at the Puente Nuevo de Alamor to connect with buses to Puyango. Transportes TAC, Colón near Bolívar, has several buses a day to Zaruma.

Getting Around
The most important local bus for travellers is the No 1 bus which goes north-west from the central plaza along 9 de Octubre to Puerto Bolívar (US$0.05; 15 minutes, crowded). A taxi will cost a little over US$1. The No 1 bus returns into town along Pichincha and goes south-east as far as the El Bananero Monument, almost two km from the centre.

PUERTO BOLIVAR
The international port, Puerto Bolívar, is about six km from Machala and is that city's maritime outlet for the south coast's banana and shrimp exports. There are some simple seafood restaurants by the waterfront where you can enjoy a beer among cooling sea breezes whilst watching seabirds wheeling overhead and ocean ships sailing by. I've heard claims that Puerto Bolívar has some coastal nightlife but I couldn't discover any.

The port is protected from the ocean by islands and mangroves. Motorised dugouts can be hired for a cruise among the mangroves to watch the birdlife or to go to the nearby island beach at Jambelí.

Places to Stay & Eat
There are a couple of cheap and basic hotels, though most people stay in Machala. The seafood restaurants on the pier are not fancy but are pleasant enough. If you are on a tight budget you'll find the same food to be cheaper in restaurants a block or two away from the waterfront.

Getting There & Around
Bus The No 1 bus from Machala's central plaza runs frequently. The last stop is about two blocks away from the pier and boat dock.

Boat Boats leave Puerto Bolívar for Jambelí at 10 am, 1, 3.45 and 6 pm from Monday to Friday. Boats return from Jambelí at 8 am, 12 noon, 3 and 5 pm. There are more frequent departures, dependent on passenger demand, at weekends and holidays. The fare for the half hour trip is about US$0.40 per person, or you can hire a boat carrying up to 20 passengers for about US$7.50 to take you from Puerto Bolívar to Jambelí anytime.

Boats can also be hired to other beaches, with the furthest being at Costa Rica near the Peruvian border (carry your passport). These beaches offer little shade and, with the exception of Jambelí, are undeveloped, so carry food, drink, sunscreen and insect repellent – the mosquitoes can be nasty.

JAMBELÍ
This long beach is on the ocean side of the island sheltering Puerto Bolívar. This is the favourite resort of holidaymakers from Machala and can be (relatively) busy at weekends – though it is not particularly well developed. There is little shade and abundant mosquitoes.

Places to Stay & Eat
There are a couple of basic but clean places to stay. The *Cabañas del Pescador* (☎ 923 710 in Machala, information at 9 de Mayo 1926 and Bolívar in Machala), has double rooms for about US$6. The *Hotel Maria y Sol* charges about the same. Meals for about US$2 are available.

Getting There & Away
See the information given for Puerto Bolívar.

PASAJE
This small town, about 25 km east of Machala, is the capital of its cantón and the centre of a banana-growing region. It is the last town of any size before the attractive road from Machala to Cuenca (see under Cuenca) begins to rise into the mountains.

Places to Stay
The *Hotel San Martín* (☎ 910 434) at Piedrahita and Olmedo has rooms with private bathrooms for about US$5/8 for single/doubles. Rooms with air-conditioning are about US$1 more. The *Hotel Pasaje* (☎ 910 118) at 10 de Agosto 629 and San Martín has cheaper rooms with private bath.

ZARUMA AREA
This old gold-mining town in the mountains

is to the south-east of Machala. Now, the gold is almost all worked out although visits to a mine can be arranged by asking for permission at the Municipalidad (town hall). Some archaeological ruins have been discovered in the area – people have probably been mining gold here for many centuries.

The town is a small one and the best reasons to visit are to see the turn-of-the-century architecture (quaint wooden buildings with elaborate balconies) and admire the mountainous views. The nearby towns of Piñas (15 km away) and Portovelo (7 km away) can also be visited.

Places to Stay
There are a couple of basic hotels in Zaruma. The best place to stay in town is probably the *Hotel Municipal* (☎ Zaruma 8179) which charges about US$2.50 per person. There is reportedly a country hotel, the *Pedregal*, about 3 km outside Zaruma which is better. Roughly 12 km north of Zaruma is a good country resort *Los Rosales de Machay* (☎ 921 898, 924 478 for reservations), information from Edificio Vasquéz-García, Office 4, Montalvo between Bolívar and Rocafuerte in Machala. This resort boasts a pool, pretty gardens, a decent restaurant and comfortable rooms for US$30 a double.

Getting There & Away
Transportes TAC has several buses a day between Machala and Zaruma.

PIÑAS
Piñas is known as a coffee producing area. It was near Piñas where, in 1980, a new bird species was discovered – the El Oro parakeet (see Green's *Birding Ecuador* for more details). Few travellers come here, however – this is off-the-beaten-track travel.

Places to Stay & Eat
There are a couple of basic hotels. The best place in Piñas is the *Residencial Dumari* in the town centre – clean rooms are about US$2.50 per person and hot water should be available.

There are several simple restaurants, and the *Restaurant El Tunel* is recommended.

Getting There & Away
Cuidad de Piñas bus company has buses between Machala and Piñas.

PUYANGO PETRIFIED FOREST
This small reserve was created in 1988 to protect the fossil remains and wildlife of the area. Despite its small size of 2659 hectares, Puyango is known for its birds and over 130 species have been listed since the recent creation of the reserve – there are undoubtedly more. FEPROTUR has published a booklet on the birds of Puyango, containing a bird checklist. The flora and geology is also of great interest and research is underway in the area. Fossilised Araucaria tree trunks, many millions of years old and up to 11 metres long and 1.6 metres in diameter, have been found. Various other fossilised trees, ferns and extinct plants are present.

Puyango is in a valley at about 360 metres above sea level, some 55 km directly inland from the coast. The valley is separated from the ocean by the Cordillera Larga which reaches over 900 metres above sea level. Despite the separation, the area experiences a coastal weather pattern, with warm temperatures and most of the annual 1000 mm of rainfall occurring from January to May.

Camping is allowed and a lookout point and trails have been constructed under the auspices of the Puyango Petrified Forest Commission, which has administrative and information offices in Machala. A visitor interpretation centre is planned.

The nearby village of Puyango is comprised of some 20 families. There is nowhere to stay (except to camp) although the villagers may give you floor space if asked. The Puyango Commission has encouraged and educated the local people to learn more about the reserve and some of the locals will act as guides – ask around. I recommend hiring a local as a guide. They'll show you where to see the fossilised trees and tell you about them, give you some ideas about where to look for the local wildlife etc. Even better,

they will tell you about themselves, their interests and their families.

Getting There & Away
If you are driving, head from Machala to Arenillas, and from there take a dirt road south through Palmales (22 km from Arenillas) and on to Puyango (38 km south of Palmales). Alternatively, a road heads west from the Loja-Macará (on the Peruvian border) highway, about half way between Macará and Catacocha (see the Cuenca & the Southern Highlands chapter). This road goes via Celica and Alamor to Puyango and is less frequently used.

Buses with Transportes Cooperativa Loja leave from Machala and Loja and will enable you to go through Puyango. The service is irregular but you should be able to get to Puyango from either city within a day if you start in the morning.

TO THE PERUVIAN BORDER
It is about an 80-km drive from Machala to the border town of Huaquillas – this is the route taken by most overland travellers to Peru. The bus from Machala passes through banana and palm plantations and the dusty market towns of **Santa Rosa** and **Arenillas** of which Santa Rosa is the most important. There are two or three passport checks en route but these take only a minute (assuming your passport is in order). Foreign travellers have to get off the bus and register their passports at a control booth – the drivers know the routine and will wait for you.

Places to Stay
There are a couple of fairly cheap and basic hotels in Santa Rosa. The *Hotel América* (☎ 915 130) at Colón and El Oro is probably the best. The *Residencial Dos Piños* (☎ 915 338) at Cuenca and Libertad is cheaper.

Getting There & Away
Santa Rosa is about 30 km closer to the border than Machala and there is an airport with light aircraft flying to Guayaquil – CEDTA and EDSAN are reportedly the companies doing this route at present. The fare is

about US$10 and baggage is limited to a small bag of under 10 kg. Most people coming from Peru continue on to Machala by bus and make connections there for onward transport. Buses to Huaquillas pass by frequently.

HUAQUILLAS

This dusty one-street town is of importance only because it is at Ecuador's border with Peru. It has a population of about 20,000 (though it doesn't look it). There is a busy street market by the border and the place is full of Peruvians shopping on day passes. It's a run-down and dirty town and not a particularly attractive introduction to Ecuador if you're arriving from Peru. Almost everything happens on the one long main street although the town is growing and civic amenities like a plaza and park are planned.

Huaquillas continues across the border into Peru where it becomes known as Aguas Verdes.

Money

Banks in Huaquillas or Aguas Verdes do not normally do foreign exchange, so you have to rely on street moneychangers. They may try to give you a very bad rate but will soon become more reasonable if you can show that you know what the real rate is. Check with other travellers going the opposite way for up-to-date exchange rates.

If you are leaving Ecuador for Peru, it is best to try and get rid of as many sucres as you can in Ecuador and arrive in Peru with US dollars. The Peruvian currency is frequently devalued and changes names every few years. If heading to Peru, ask travellers from Peru or at the South American Explorer's Club in Quito about the current situation. Some old notes may have values of a million or more so count carefully and make sure you know what you are getting into before crossing the border.

Peruvian moneychangers will give you better rates for dollars than you'll get in Ecuador and exchange rates should be almost as good as in Lima – but shortchanging is common. Count carefully and change

only what you need. There are 'official rates' and 'free exchange rates' in Peru. The official rate is used for international transactions such as buying an airline ticket. The free exchange rate is used to change tourist dollars and is usually about 25% higher than the official rate. So don't be fooled by the official rate.

If you're just arriving in Ecuador you can get within 2% of the Quito rate from street changers if you bargain hard. Again, it is best to use dollars. Other major foreign currencies can be exchanged, but less favourably, and fewer changers want to deal with them. Travellers' cheques can also be exchanged, though with some difficulty – usually cash is preferred and gets a better rate.

Places to Stay

There are several basic hotels on the main street near the Migraciones office. None of them are particularly good and I can't work up much enthusiasm for any of them. Hotels tend to be full by early afternoon and you may have to take whatever is available or go to Machala. Most travellers go on to Machala (or to Tumbes if heading to Peru – less than an hour from the border and with plenty of hotels).

The *Hotel Guayaquil* behind the Migraciones office has basic rooms with bath for about US$6 a double, less without bath. Nearby, the *Hotel Quito* is more basic and cheaper. Almost opposite the Migraciones building, next to the IETEL office, is the very basic and noisy *Residencial San Martín* with rooms for about US$2 per person. Further down the street (away from the border) is the *Hotel Continental* which charges about US$5.50 for basic double rooms with bath. Nearby is the *Hotel Lima* which has marginally better rooms for about US$4/6 for singles/double with bath. The *Residencial Mini* is also in this price range and is OK.

The government-run *Parador Turistico Huaquillas* (☎ 907 374) is about 1½ km away from the border on the right side of the main road out of town. You can take a taxi for about US$0.50 or walk. This is by far the best hotel in town. They charge about US$6/10 for singles/doubles – the rooms are simple but clean and have fans and private bathrooms. There is a restaurant and pool.

Places to Eat

There aren't any particularly good restaurants. There is a café behind the immigration office where travellers and moneychangers often hang out. Other places are along the main street. The restaurant in the *Residencial Mini* is OK but pricey – cheapest meals are over US$2. The nearby *Restaurant Chick* has cheaper chicken meals. The best food is at the *Parador Turistico*.

Getting There & Away

CIFA buses run seven times a day to Machala (US$0.80; two hours). There is no main bus office but you'll see buses on the main street a block or two away from the Migraciones office. Panamericana, behind Migraciones, has four buses a day to Quito (US$4.20; 13 hours). Ecuatoriana Pullman, a couple of blocks past Migraciones (walking away from the border) has buses to Guayaquil (US$2.20; 5½ hours), but it's often easier to go to Machala and change. A few buses go to Loja and Cuenca.

Crossing the Peruvian Border

The border is the Río Zarumilla, which is crossed by an international bridge. As you enter Ecuador from the bridge you'll find yourself on the main road, crowded with market stalls, that stretches out through Huaquillas.

The Ecuadorian Migraciones office is on the left side about 200 metres from the bridge and is identified by the yellow, blue and red-striped Ecuadorian flag. All entrance and exit formalities are carried out here. The Ecuadorian office is open daily from 8 am to 12 noon and 2 to 5 pm.

You won't have any difficulty in finding the office. Dozens of small boys will offer their services as luggage carriers and guides and the many moneychangers (identified by the ubiquitous black attaché case) will show you the way.

If you are arriving in Ecuador you first need an exit stamp in your passport from the Peruvian authorities. After walking across the international bridge, continue 200 metres to the Ecuadorian Migraciones office. Entrance formalities are usually straightforward. No tourists need visas but everyone needs a T3 tourist card, which are available free at the office. If you're not entering as a tourist, you need a student, resident, worker or business visa which must be obtained from an Ecuadorian embassy, usually the one that serves your home country.

Exit tickets from Ecuador and sufficient funds (US$20 per day) are legally required but are very rarely asked for. You will receive your T3 card (keep it for when you leave) and an identical stamp in your passport allowing you up to 90 days' stay. Usually, only 30 days are given but it is easy to obtain a renewal in Quito or Guayaquil.

Note that you are allowed only 90 days per year in Ecuador. If you've already been in the country for 90 days and try and return, you will be refused entry. If you have an exit ticket from Quito or Guayaquil international airports, you can usually get a 72-hour transit visa just to get you to the airport and out of the country.

If you are leaving Ecuador, the procedure is as follows. Go to the Ecuadorian Migraciones office and present your passport and T3 tourist card (the duplicate copy of the small document you filled out on arrival). You will receive an exit stamp in your passport and the immigration authorities will keep your T3 card. You must have an exit stamp to legally leave (and later re-enter) Ecuador. There are no costs involved. If you have lost your T3 card, you should be able to get a free replacement at the border, assuming that the stamp in your passport has not expired.

If you have overstayed your permitted time by a few days you can sometimes persuade the immigration official to charge you a fine right there and then – expect to pay no more than US$10. If you get sent back to Guayaquil you will still have to pay a fine, so it's best to get it over with. You can usually get away with a few days over the limit by telling the official how much you loved Ecuador and that you didn't realise how much time had passed.

As you cross the international bridge you will be asked to show the exit stamp in your passport to the Ecuadorian bridge guard. On the Peruvian side (now called Aguas Verdes instead of Huaquillas) you normally have to show your passport to the bridge guard, but full entrance formalities are carried out in the immigration building about 100 metres from the border on the left.

Most European nationalities don't need a visa for Peru, neither do North Americans but Australians and New Zealanders do. Visas are not obtainable in either Aguas

Verdes or Huaquillas and you have to go back to the Peruvian Consulate in Machala if you haven't got one. Other nationalities normally just need a tourist card, available at the Peruvian immigration office.

Although an exit ticket out of Peru is officially required, gringo travellers are rarely asked for this unless they look thoroughly disreputable. Other Latin American travellers are often asked for an exit ticket, however, so if you're a non-Peruvian Latin American (or travelling with one) be prepared for this eventuality. There is a bus office in Aguas Verdes which sells (nonrefundable) bus tickets out of Peru. The immigration official will tell you where it is.

The Galápagos Islands

The Galápagos Archipelago is world famous for its incredibly fearless and unique wildlife. Here, you can swim with sea lions, float eye-to-eye with a penguin, stand next to a blue-footed booby feeding its young, watch a giant 200-kg tortoise lumbering through a cactus forest, and try to avoid stepping on iguanas scurrying over the lava. The wildlife is truly phenomenal. The scenery is barren and volcanic and has its own haunting beauty – though some people find it bare and ugly. A visit to the Galápagos is for the wilderness and wildlife enthusiast, not for the average sun-seeker.

Compared to the rest of your travels in Ecuador, the Galápagos are very expensive to visit. Flying from Quito and spending a week cruising the islands will cost a minimum of US$800 for even the most thrifty of budget travellers travelling in cramped, uncomfortable boats. You can pay over three times that for the most expensive of the top-end tours. Even in the expensive boats, conditions are comfortable, but not luxurious. Therefore the trip is not recommended unless you are really interested in wildlife. The environment is a fragile one, and the islands don't need bored visitors tramping around wondering why they are spending hundreds of dollars to sit on a rocky piece of lava under a searing equatorial sun to watch some squawking seabirds. If you are interested in natural history, however, then visiting the Galápagos will be the highlight of your trip to Ecuador.

This chapter is essentially divided into three sections. The first introduces you to the archipelago, gives background information and describes the individual islands and visitor sites. The second section gives you the practical details you will need to know in order to visit the Galápagos. The third section is an illustrated Wildlife Guide to help you identify and learn something about the animals you see.

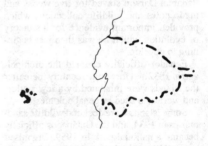

Introduction to the Galápagos

HISTORY

The Galápagos Archipelago was discovered by accident in 1535, when Tomás de Berlanga, the Bishop of Panama, drifted off course while sailing from Panama to Peru. The bishop reported his discovery to King Charles V of Spain and included in his report a description of the *galápago* or 'giant tortoise' from which the islands received their name.

It is possible that the Indian inhabitants of South America were aware of the islands' existence before 1535, but we have no definite record of this.

For over three centuries after their discovery, the Galápagos were used as a base by a succession of pirates, buccaneers, sealers and whalers. The islands provided sheltered anchorage, firewood, water and an abundance of fresh food in the form of the giant Galápagos tortoises, which were caught by the thousands and stacked, alive, in ships' holds. The tortoises could survive for a year or more and thus provided fresh meat for the sailors long after they had left the islands.

The first rough charts of the archipelago were made by buccaneers in the late 1600s and scientific exploration began in the late 1700s. The Galápagos' most famous visitor was Charles Darwin, who arrived in 1835, exactly 300 years after the Bishop of Panama. Darwin stayed for five weeks and made notes and wildlife collections which provided important evidence for his theory of evolution which he was then just beginning to develop.

Ecuador officially claimed the archipelago in 1832 and for about a century thereafter the islands were inhabited by a few settlers and were also used as penal colonies.

Some islands were declared wildlife sanctuaries in 1934, and the Galápagos officially became a national park in 1959. Organised tourism began in the late 1960s and an estimated 60,000 people visited the islands in 1991.

GEOGRAPHY

The Galápagos are an isolated group of volcanic islands which lie in the Pacific Ocean on the equator about 90° west of Greenwich. The nearest mainland is Ecuador, some 1000 km to the east, and Guatemala, some 1600 km to the north. The land mass of the archipelago covers 7882 sq km of which well over half consists of Isabela, the largest island in the archipelago and the 12th largest in the South Pacific Ocean. There are 13 major islands (from 14 to 4588 sq km), six small islands (from one to five sq km) and scores of islets of which only some are named. The islands are spread over roughly 50,000 sq km of ocean. The highest point in the Galápagos is Volcán Wolf (1707 metres) on Isabela.

Five of the islands are inhabited; the total population reached about 14,000 people in 1991 and was reported to be growing at about 12% annually. They make a living mainly from tourism, fishing and farming. About half the residents live in Puerto Ayora.

Most of the islands have two – and sometimes three – names. The earliest charts gave the islands both Spanish and English names, and the Ecuadorian government assigned official names in 1892. Thus an island can have a Spanish, English and official name. The official names are used here in most cases; the few exceptions will be indicated where appropriate.

GEOLOGY

The earliest of the islands were formed roughly four to five million years ago by underwater volcanoes erupting and rising above the ocean's surface (the islands were never connected to the mainland). The Galápagos region is volcanically very active and over 50 eruptions have been recorded since their discovery in 1535. In 1991, the infrequently visited northern island of Marchena was erupting. Thus the formation of the islands is an ongoing process and the archipelago is a relatively young one compared to the age of the earth (four and a half billion years old – a billion is a 1000 million).

Geologists generally agree that two relatively new geological theories explain the islands' formation. The theory of plate tectonics holds that the earth's crust consists of several rigid plates which, over geological time, move relative to one another over the surface of the earth. The Galápagos lie on the northern edge of the Nazca Plate close to its junction with the Cocos Plate. These two plates are spreading apart at a rate of about a km every 14,000 years and thus the Galápagos Islands are slowly moving southeast. How fast is one km every 14,000 years? It's about the same rate at which your finger nails grow – which is pretty fast by plate tectonic standards.

The hot spot theory states that deep within the earth (below the moving tectonic plates) are certain superheated areas which remain stationary. At frequent intervals (measured in geological time) the heat from these hot spots increases enough to melt the earth's crust and produce a volcanic eruption of sufficient magnitude to cause molten lava to rise above the ocean floor and eventually above the ocean surface.

The Galápagos are moving slowly to the south-east over a stationary hot spot, so one would expect the south-eastern islands to have been formed first and the north-western islands to have been formed most recently. This has proved to be the case. The most ancient rocks known in the islands are about three and a quarter million years old and come from Española in the south-east. In comparison, the oldest rocks on the western islands of Fernandina and Isabela are less than three quarters of a million years old. The north-western islands are still in the process of formation and contain active volcanoes such as Volcán Cerro Azul on Isabela, which erupted in 1979 and 1982. The northern island of Marchena is currently erupting.

Most of the Galápagos are surrounded by very deep ocean. Less than 20 km off the coasts of the western islands the ocean is over 3000 metres deep. When visitors cruise around the islands, they can see only about the top third of the volcanoes – the rest is underwater. Some of the oldest volcanoes are, in fact, completely underwater. Recent research by Christie et al published in 1992 in the British scientific journal *Nature* shows that the Carnegie Ridge, which is a submerged mountain range stretching to the east of the Galápagos, has the remnants of previous volcanic islands, some of which were as much as nine million years old. These have been completely eroded away and now lie 2000 metres beneath the ocean surface and stretch about half the distance between the Galápagos and the mainland.

Most of the volcanic rock forming the Galápagos is basalt. Molten basalt has the property of being more fluid than other types of volcanic rock and so when an eruption occurs, basalt tends to form lava flows rather than explosive eruptions. Hence the volcanoes of the Galápagos Islands are gently rounded 'shield volcanoes' rather than the Fuji-like ice-cream cone shape popularly associated with volcanoes.

Whilst not every visitor has the time or energy to climb a volcano, a visit to one of the lava flows is within everyone's reach. There are several which can be visited but the one at Sullivan Bay on the east end of San Salvador (also known as Santiago or James Island) is especially rewarding. This lava flow is almost a century old and remains uneroded.

Here you can see *pahoehoe* or 'ropy' lava, formed by the cooling of the molten surface and the wrinkling of the skin into ropy shapes by the continued flow of the molten

lava beneath. Impressions of trees can be found in the solidified lava, and some of the first colonising plants – the *Brachycereus* cactus and the *Mollugo* carpetweed – can be seen beginning the slow conversion of a lava field to soil.

COLONISATION & EVOLUTION

When the Galápagos were formed they were barren volcanic islands, devoid of all life. Because the islands were never connected with the mainland, all the species present there now must have somehow crossed about 1000 km of open ocean. Those that could fly or swim long distances had the best chance of reaching the islands but other methods of colonisation were possible, though more difficult.

These methods include being brought over in animals' stomach contents, or attached to the feathers and feet of birds (as may have happened to plant seeds or insect eggs and larvae), or floating across on vegetation rafts (as may have happened to small mammals, land birds and reptiles as well as plants and insects).

Thus the wildlife is dominated by birds (especially seabirds), sea mammals and reptiles. There are no amphibians because their moist skin is unable to withstand the dehydrating effect of salt water. There are, of course, plenty of tropical fish and marine invertebrates.

Compared to the mainland there are few small land mammals and insects. Large predators never colonised the Galápagos (until the arrival of man). This suggests that the reason the animals of the islands exhibit their well-known fearlessness is because they had no large predators to fear until pigs, goats, cats, donkeys, etc were introduced by man. Escaped domestic animals found little competition and became successful, and now these feral animals create a major problem in the islands.

When the first colonising species arrived millions of years ago they found that the islands were different from the mainland in two important ways. The first was that the islands were physically different from the

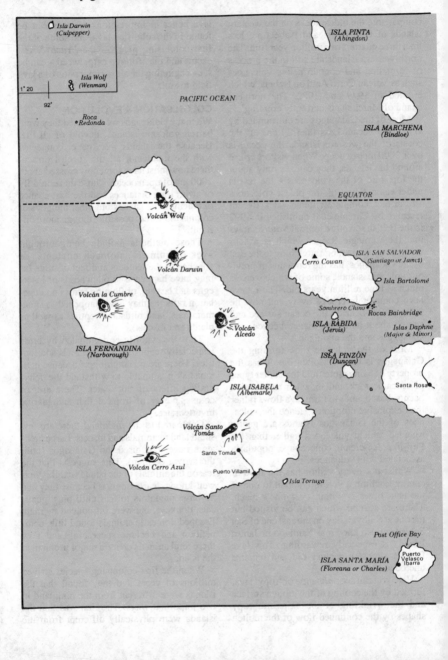

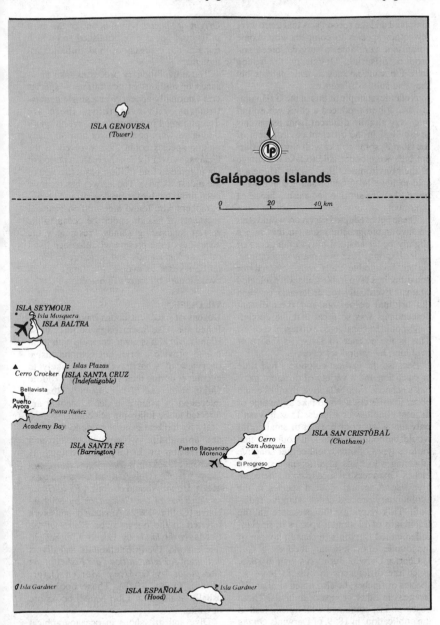

mainland and the second was that there were few other species to compete with. Some colonisers were able to survive, breed and produce offspring. Obviously, the young were the same species as their parents but they had subtle differences.

A classic example of this in the Galápagos is when a bird produced a chick whose bill was very slightly different from its parents or siblings. In the different environment of the islands, some chicks with slightly different bills were better able to take advantage of their environment than others. These are said to have been better adapted and were more likely to survive and raise a brood of their own.

These better adapted survivors would pass on favourable genetic traits (in this case a slightly better adapted bill) to the genes of their offspring. Thus over many generations, certain favourable traits were selected for and other less favourable traits were selected against. Eventually the difference between the original colonisers and their distant descendants was so great that the descendants could be considered a different species. This is the essence of Darwin's theory of evolution by natural selection.

Because the earliest colonisers had little competition and a variety of different habitats to choose from, adaptive changes could occur in different ways to take advantage of different habitats or islands. Thus it wasn't only that a longer or broader or smaller bill would be better adapted – it could be that various types of bills could confer adaptive advantages to birds in different ecological niches. One ancestral species could therefore give rise to several modern species in the evolutionary process called adaptive radiation. This explains the presence in the Galápagos of 13 similar species of finches, called called Darwin's finches in honour of the founder of evolutionary theory.

Charles Darwin, during his visit in 1835, noted the differences in bills in these 13 species of finches; he also noted similar differences in other groups of animals. These observations, combined with others, lead to the publication, in 1859, of Darwin's *On the Origin of Species* which is one of the most influential books ever published and which remains the mainstay of modern biological thought.

These evolutionary processes take thousands or millions of generations – species don't normally appear over a single generation (as with everything, there are exceptions). For many years, evolutionary biologists were puzzled over how so many unique species could have evolved in the Galápagos over the relatively short period of about three to four million years (the age of the oldest islands). The answer has recently been provided by the geologists and oceanographers who found nine-million-year-old remnants of islands under the ocean to the east of the existing islands. Presumably, the ancestors of the present wildlife once lived on these lost islands, and therefore had nine million years to evolve – a figure which evolutionary biologists find acceptable.

WILDLIFE

Dozens of excellent books have been published about the fascinating wildlife of these islands. My aim is not to compete with them but to provide a brief but comprehensive overview of what travellers are likely to encounter during their visit (see the Wildlife Guide at the end of this chapter). Readers interested in a more in depth account are directed to the following selection.

By far the best general guide to the plant and animal life, with much background information on history and geology, is Michael H Jackson's *Galápagos: A Natural History Guide* (University of Calgary Press, 1985). Birders should consult *A Field Guide to the Birds of the Galápagos* by Michael Harris (Collins, 1982). Amateur botanists are referred to the pocket-sized *Plants of the Galápagos Islands* by Eileen K Schofield (New York, 1984). Snorkellers and divers will want *A Field Guide to the Fishes of the Galapagos* by Godfrey Merlen (Libri Mundi, Quito, 1988). These books are usually available at Libri Mundi bookstore in Quito.

Dive and gift shops in oceanographical

aquariums and museums in the United States sell plastic waterproof cards illustrating common fish of the Pacific (from Hawaii and the Sea of Cortez, Mexico). These can be taken underwater and help in identifying some of the Galápagos species. Unfortunately, these cards are not available in Ecuador.

Maps of the Galápagos are available from the IGM in Ecuador. The best map, full of useful information about wildlife, history and tourism, was published in 1985 by Bradt Publications, 41 Nortoft Rd, Chalfont St Peter, Bucks SL9 OLA, England. A colourful brochure *Galapagos: Guide in Brief*, by Tui de Roy & Mark Jones, is sold in Puerto Ayora.

CONSERVATION & TOURISM

As early as 1934, the Ecuadorian government set aside some of the islands as wildlife sanctuaries, but it was not until 1959 that the Galápagos was declared a national park. The construction of the Charles Darwin Research Station on Isla Santa Cruz began soon after, and the station began operating in 1962. In 1986 the Ecuadorian government granted further protection to the islands by creating the Galápagos Marine Resources Reserve.

The national park covers approximately 90% of the islands' 7882-sq-km land mass – the rest is taken up by urban areas and farms which existed prior to the creation of the park. The Marine Resources Reserve covers the 50,000 sq km of ocean and sea bed within which the islands are located plus a further 20,000-sq-km buffer zone. The function of the park and reserve is to protect and conserve the islands and surrounding ocean and

to encourage educational and scientific research.

Few tourists had visited the islands before the station opened, but by the mid-1960s organised tourism had begun with a little over 1000 visitors a year. This figure soon increased dramatically. In 1970 an estimated 4500 tourists arrived and in 1971 there were six small boats and one large cruise ship operating in the islands. In less than two decades, the number of visitors had increased tenfold and 1991 saw an estimated 60,000 visitors. Roughly half the visitors are mainland Ecuadorians.

To cope with the increased demands of tourism, a second airport with regular flights to the mainland was opened in the mid-1980s and a third is being talked about. The number of hotels in Puerto Ayora and Puerto Baquerizo Moreno doubled from 15 in 1981 to about 30 in 1991. There are now two large and one medium-sized cruise ship (carrying 90 and 34 passengers respectively) and several dozen smaller boats (carrying from four to 20 passengers). The resident population of the islands is growing at 12% annually to provide labour for the booming tourism industry.

This is all well and good for the economy of Ecuador but inevitable problems have resulted. Among the more serious are entrepreneurial proposals of building luxurious high-rise hotels and introducing as many more cruise ships into the islands as possible. Fortunately, the Ecuadorian government has seen the sense of preventing these projects, at least until a comprehensive and enlightened tourism policy has been developed.

The increased numbers of tourists has led to trail erosion and litter, to feeding and frightening the animals. Most tourists are concerned enough to avoid disturbing the wildlife or spoiling the scenery, but with tens of thousands of visitors, there is inevitable degradation. Resort hotels compound the problem by attracting many more tourists, with a greater proportion of people who care little for the wildlife. Thus it is important that tourism is sensibly regulated. The numbers of visitors is not the real issue – education and environmental awareness is. One thoughtless or uncaring visitor can cause more damage than a hundred people who are aware of their potential impact on the fragile resources and work on minimising that impact.

The wildlife of the Galápagos is, literally, unique. The islands have been called 'a laboratory of evolution' and are of immense importance to our understanding of the natural world. The incredible assemblage of wildlife is being threatened not only by tourism, but also by the increased colonisation that accompanies the booming tourist industry.

Earlier colonisation created problems with the introduction of domestic species such as goats, pigs and rats which can easily cause the extinction of an island species in a matter of years. For example, three goats were introduced to Isla Pinta by colonists as a source of food in 1959; by 1973 the goat population had increased to 30,000 animals who were destroying the vegetation of the island. A determined hunting program managed to eradicate the feral goats and today Pinta is goat free. But Pinta is one of the smaller islands – eradication programs on larger islands like Santiago are more difficult. Santiago is estimated to have about 50,000 goats, roughly half of what was there a decade ago. The numbers can be controlled but probably not eliminated. In addition, about 1000 wild pigs (down from 5000 in the 1980s) cause serious problems by eating bird and reptile eggs.

One of the most recent animal immigrants has been the wasp, which arrived on Isla Floreana in the late 1980s, probably with some food items brought in by visitors or residents. Now, the wasps are all over the island and control seems impossible.

There are various solutions to these problems. One is to prohibit all colonisation and tourism – this is an extreme view which few people want. The tourist industry is an important one for Ecuador's economy. The best solution is an enlightened mixture of environmental education for both residents and visitors and a program of responsible

tourism. Unfortunately, the number of park rangers fell from 75 to 46 during the 1980s and essential equipment, such as patrol boats, was lacking.

The situation is improving slowly and there is optimism that the islands and their wildlife will survive the human onslaught. More rangers are being trained and all tour boats, by law, must be accompanied by certified guides. On the better boats, these are bilingual, university-educated biologists with a very real interest in preserving and explaining the wildlife. On the cheapest boats, auxiliary guides are provided who know relatively little about the wildlife but will, at least in principle, keep visitors from littering or molesting the wildlife and be able to identify what is seen.

There are basically two types of tours around the islands. One is to go from island to island, sleeping aboard a boat or occasionally in a hotel. The other is hotel-based and goes out to visitor sites on day trips. The first system staggers the times of visits to islands over different times of day, allowing dawn and dusk visits. In addition, more outlying islands can be reached. The day trips, on the other hand, tend to cram large numbers of tourists onto a few nearby destinations around the middle of the day. These trips are the ones which tend to cause the greatest amount of erosion, litter, and pressure on the wildlife.

Training guides and rangers costs money, and all foreign visitors must pay a US$80 park entrance fee upon arrival – some of this goes to the Ecuadorian government, some to protecting other parks in the Ecuadorian mainland but at least a portion is used to aid the park service in the Galápagos. Visitors to the Charles Darwin Research Station are invited and encouraged to make donations to that worthwhile organisation's efforts to carry out research in the islands and advise government and tourist agencies on how to cause minimum impact on the islands. The Smithsonian Institution's Galápagos Support Project, Dept 0553, Washington DC 20073-0053, USA will send the journal *Noticias de Galápagos* (with articles on island research and conservation) to anyone sending US$25 or more to the Smithsonian with a request to use the money in Galápagos conservation and research projects.

Upon paying their US$80 entrance fees, visitors are given a full set of park rules and other informative leaflets. The rules are for the protection of the wildlife and environment, and are mostly a matter of courtesy and common sense. Don't feed or handle the animals; don't litter; don't remove any natural object, whether living or dead; do not bring pets; do not buy objects made of sea lion teeth, black coral, tortoise, or turtle shells or other artefacts made from plants and animals; show a conservationist attitude. You are not allowed to enter the visitor sites after dark or without a qualified guide, and a guide will accompany every boat. On all shore trips, the guide will be there to answer your questions and show you the best sites, and also to ensure that you stay on the trails and don't molest the animals.

With 60,000 tourists visiting the islands annually, it is essential to have a system of protection for the islands. The rules are sensible and necessary – they do not infringe on your enjoyment of the Galápagos. Staying on the trails is a good rule unless a sea lion goes to sleep in the middle of the trail and you are then forced to go off trail to avoid the animal! The wildlife is so prolific that you'll see just as much on the trail as anywhere else, and staying on the trails means other areas are properly protected.

VISITOR SITES

To protect the islands from haphazard tourism, the national park service restricts access to about 50 visitor sites, in addition to the towns and public areas. These visitor sites are found in places where the most interesting features and most varied wildlife can be seen. Almost all of the visitor sites are reached by boat and normally landings are made in a small dinghy (*panga*) that every boat carries for shore trips (the larger boats carry several pangas).

Most landing sites are sandy or rocky beaches – there are few docks. Landings are

called 'wet' or 'dry'. During a wet landing you will have to climb out of the panga onto a beach and wade ashore in shallow water, sometimes up to your knees. Dry landings are made onto rocky outcrops or jetties and you'll probably not get wet, unless a rogue wave comes up and splashes you or you slip on some seaweed and fall into the ocean (I've seen it happen). Boat captains will not take groups to places other than designated visitor sites. Occasionally, a new site is added to the list.

Here follows a brief description of all the islands and their visitor sites. Further information about the towns is given later. More detailed site descriptions and maps are to be found in the *Guide to the Visitor Sites of Galápagos National Park* by Alan & Tui Moore (Galápagos National Park Service, 1980). This book is not easy to find outside of the Galápagos.

Isla Santa Cruz

This island is rarely referred to by its lesser known English name of Indefatigable, and most people call it Santa Cruz. With an area of 986 sq km it is the second largest island in the archipelago. A road crosses Santa Cruz from north to south and gives the visitor the easiest opportunity of seeing some of the highland interior of an island. The highest point is Cerro Crocker, 864 metres.

This island has the highest population and the greatest number of tourist facilities. The main town is Puerto Ayora on the south coast and most visitors either stay here whilst arranging a boat, or anchor in the town's famous harbour, Academy Bay, sometime during their cruise. In addition to the tourist facilities, there are nine national park visitor sites and one privately owned visitor site on Santa Cruz. Two more park visitor sites are planned.

The **Charles Darwin Research Station** is about a 20-minute walk by road north-east of Puerto Ayora and can be reached on foot or by dry landing from Academy Bay. It contains a National Park Information Centre, an informative museum in the Van Straelen Exhibition Centre, a baby tortoise house where you can see hatchlings and young tortoises, and a walk-in adult tortoise enclosure where you can meet these Galápagos giants face to face.

This is the only place in the islands where you are permitted to touch the wildlife and many visitors get to tickle a giant tortoise's neck, which seems to entertain both human and reptile. Several of the eleven remaining subspecies of tortoise can be seen here. Lonesome George, the only surviving member of the Isla Pinta subspecies, is also here but can be viewed only by special request. There is apparently a US$10,000 reward for finding a Pinta female, but before you go rushing off to try and find one, remember that Isla Pinta is off-limits to visitors (except scientists and researchers). George is still fairly young as tortoises go (about 50 or 60 yrs old) and although the chances of finding a Pinta female are remote, he may be allowed to breed with a female from a closely related subspecies on a neighbouring island.

Other attractions include paths through arid zone vegetation such as prickly pear and other cacti, salt bush, and mangroves. A variety of land birds, including Darwin's finches, can be seen. T-shirts are sold to support the research station.

A three-km trail takes you to **Turtle Bay**, south-west of Puerto Ayora. There is a very fine white sand beach and a spit of land giving protected swimming (there are strong currents on the exposed side of the spit). There are sharks as well as marine iguanas, and a variety of water birds, including pelicans and occasional flamingos. There are mangroves.

This is one of the few visitor sites where you can go without a guide, and camping has been permitted in the past although there is no drinking water or other facilities (a recent report says that camping is no longer permitted here). To get there, find the trail which goes from behind the IETEL office and hike out for about half an hour. Alternatively, walk north-west of Puerto Ayora on the trans-island road for about a km, and then follow a six-km footpath to the left to the

beach (this longer and older trail is now the lesser used one and may be overgrown – ask locally). The beach can also be reached by boat. Ask at the park headquarters for up-to-date information.

There are several sites of interest in the highlands of Santa Cruz and they can be reached from the trans-island road. Access to the sites is through colonised areas so respect private property. These sites can also be visited without guides. From the village of Bellavista, seven km north of Puerto Ayora by road, one can turn either west on the main road or east on a road leading in about two km to the **Lava Tubes**. These are underground tunnels of over a km in length, formed by the solidifying of the outside skin of a molten lava flow. When the lava flow ceased, the molten lava inside the flow kept going, emptying out of the solidified skin and thus leaving tunnels. They lie on private property and are not administered by the national park authorities. The owners of the land are happy to let you visit if you pay an entrance fee of about US$2, and provide information, guides and a flashlight if you want (bring your own flashlight to be sure).

To the north of Bellavista lie **The Highlands** which are national park land. A footpath from Bellavista leads towards Cerro Crocker and other hills and extinct volcanoes. This is a good chance to see the vegetation of the Scalesia, Miconia and fernsedge zones, and to look for the vermilion flycatcher or the elusive Galápagos rail and paint-billed crake. It is about five km from Bellavista to the crescent-shaped hill of Media Luna and a further three km to the base of Cerro Crocker.

A part of the highlands which can be visited from the road is the twin craters called **Los Gemelos**. These are actually sink holes rather than volcanic craters and they are surrounded by Scalesia forest. Vermilion flycatchers are often seen here, and shorteared owls on occasion. Los Gemelos is reached by taking the road to the village of Santa Rosa, about 12 km west of Bellavista, and continuing about two km beyond Santa Rosa on the trans-island road. Although the

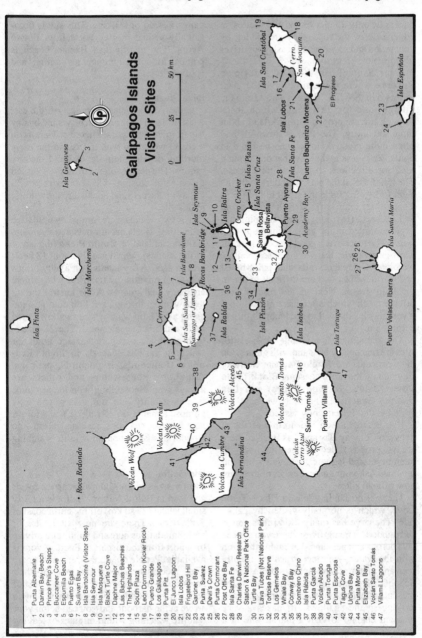

Galápagos Islands Visitor Sites

1 Punta Albemarie
2 Darwin Bay Beach
3 Prince Philip's Steps
4 Buccaneer Cove
5 Espumilla Beach
6 Puerto Egas
7 Sullivan Bay
8 Isla Bartolomé (Visitor Sites)
9 Isla Seymour
10 Isla Mosquera
11 Black Turtle Cove
12 Daphne Major
13 Las Bachas Beaches
14 The Highlands
15 South Plaza
16 Leon Dormido (Kicker Rock)
17 Puerto Grande
18 Los Galápagos
19 Punta Pitt
20 El Junco Lagoon
21 Isla Lobos
22 Frigatebird Hill
23 Gardner Bay
24 Punta Suarez
25 Devil's Crown
26 Punta Cormorant
27 Post Office Bay
28 Isla Santa Fe
29 Charles Darwin Research
   Station & National Park Office
30 Turtle Bay
31 Lava Tubes (Not National Park)
32 Tortoise Reserve
33 Los Gemelos
34 Whale Bay
35 Conway Bay
36 Sombrero Chino
37 Isla Rábida
38 Punta García
39 Volcán Alcedo
40 Punta Tortuga
41 Punta Espinosa
42 Tagus Cove
43 Urbina Bay
44 Punta Moreno
45 Elizabeth Bay
46 Volcán Santo Tomás
47 Villamil Lagoons

craters lie only 25 metres and 125 metres on either side of the road, they are hidden by vegetation and so you should ask your driver to stop at the short trailhead.

Near Santa Rosa there is a **Tortoise Reserve** where you can observe the giant tortoises in the wild. There is a trail from the village (ask for directions) which leads through private property to park land about three km away. The trail is downhill and often quite muddy. Horses can be hired in Santa Rosa – ask at the store/bar on the main road for directions to the outfitters house. The trail forks at the park boundary, with the right fork going up to the small hill of Cerro Chato (three more km) and the left fork going to La Caseta (two km) where camping has been permitted in the past. Bring your own water. The reserve is a good place to look for short-eared owls, Darwin's finches, yellow warblers, Galápagos rails and paint-billed crakes (these last two are difficult to see in the long grass). Next to the reserve is a private ranch which often has tortoises on it – you may be allowed to see them if you ask permission.

The remaining four Santa Cruz visitor sites are reached by boat and with guides. On the west coast are **Whale Bay** and **Conway Bay** and on the north coast are **Black Turtle Cove (Caleta Tortuga Negra)** and **Las Bachas Beaches**. The first two bays are attractive but infrequently visited.

I've heard that on the north-west coast between Conway Bay and Las Bachas, there are two proposed new visitor sites, one with mangroves and lagoons, the other with land iguanas. Ask your guide if either of these are now official sites.

There is no landing site in Black Turtle Cove, which is normally visited by panga ride. The cove has many little inlets and is surrounded by mangroves where you can see lava herons and pelicans. The main attraction is in the water – marine turtles are usually seen and mating can sometimes be observed. Schools of golden mustard rays are often present and white-tipped sharks may be seen basking in the shallows. It makes a very pleasant change to visit a marine site in a panga instead of walking. This site is occasionally visited by day boats from Puerto Ayora. The nearby Las Bachas beach is popular for sunbathing and swimming, and is often deserted.

Islas Plazas

These two small islands are just off the east coast of Santa Cruz and can be visited by day trip from Puerto Ayora. Therefore visitors on a cruise would do well to visit in the early morning or late afternoon to avoid the day groups. The heavy volume of visitors has led to some trail erosion – please be extra careful to stay on the path and not disturb the wildlife at this site.

The two islands were formed by uplift due to faulting. Boats anchor between them and visitors can land on **South Plaza** (the larger of the islands), which is only about 13 hectares in area. A dry landing on a jetty brings you to an opuntia cactus forest where there are many land iguanas. A one-km trail circuit leads visitors through sea lion colonies and along a cliff top walk where swallow-tailed gulls and other species nest. The 25-metre-high cliffs are a superb vantage point for watching various seabirds in flight. Red-billed tropicbirds, frigatebirds, pelicans, Audubon's shearwaters and others are always seen. Snorkelling with the sea lions is a possibility and out to sea you may glimpse a manta ray 'flying'. Cactus forest, land iguanas, sea lions, seabirds galore – no wonder this is a favourite wildlife watching site.

Isla Baltra

Most visitors to the Galápagos arrive by air and land at Baltra Airport. Baltra is a fairly small island (27 sq km) off the north coast of Santa Cruz. There are no visitor sites or accommodations here and public and private transport from the airport to Puerto Ayora is available. People on a pre-arranged tour are often met at the airport and taken to their boats a few minutes' drive away – a host of pelicans and noddies will greet you as you arrive at the harbour and you can begin your wildlife watching within minutes of leaving

the airport. Public transport is described under Puerto Ayora.

Isla Seymour

Separated from Baltra by a channel, Isla Seymour is a small 1.9-sq-km uplifted island with a dry landing. There is a circular trail (about 1¼ km) leading through some of the largest and most active seabird breeding colonies in the islands. Magnificent frigatebirds and blue-footed boobies are the main attractions. There is always some kind of observable activity going on – such as courtship, mating, nesting, or chick rearing – whatever time of year you come. You can get close to the nests – there is always at least one pair of boobies who decide that the middle of the trail is the best place to build their nest.

Swallow-tailed gulls also nest here and other birds are often seen. Sea lions and marine iguanas are common and occasional fur seals are seen as well as lava lizards. I saw a Galápagos snake here on my last visit.

Isla Mosquera

This tiny sandy island (about 120 metres wide by 600 metres long) lies in the channel between Baltra and Seymour. There is no trail but visitors can land on the sandy beach to see the sea lion colony. Swimming and snorkelling with the sea lions is a popular activity.

Islas Daphne

These are two islands of obviously volcanic origin which are seen roughly 10 km west of Seymour. Daphne Minor is the one which is

very eroded and **Daphne Major** is less eroded, retaining most of its typically volcanic shape which is called a tuff cone. There is a visitor landing site here – a rough scramble onto almost vertical rocks. A short but steep trail leads to the 120-metre-high summit of this ⅓-sq-km island.

There are two small craters at the top of the cone and these contain hundreds of blue-footed booby nests. Masked boobies nest on the crater rims and a few red-billed tropicbirds nest in rocky crevices in the steep sides of the islands.

The island is difficult to visit because of the acrobatic landing. In addition, the steep slopes are fragile and susceptible to erosion which has lead the national park authorities to limit visits to one per boat per month. Either you have to be lucky or arrange your visit well in advance.

Isla Santa Fe

This 24-sq-km island lies about 20 km southeast of Santa Cruz and so is popular for day trips. Its infrequently used English name is Barrington. There is a good anchorage in an attractive bay on the north-east coast and a wet landing gives the visitor a choice of two trails. A short 300-metre trail takes you to one of the tallest stands of opuntia cactus in the islands – some of the cacti are over 10 metres high. A somewhat more strenuous and rough 1½-km trail takes the visitor up into the highlands where the Santa Fe land iguana may be seen – if you are lucky. This species of iguana is found on no other island in the world. Other attractions include a sea lion colony, excellent snorkelling, marine iguanas, and, of course, birds.

Isla San Cristóbal

Also known as Chatham, this island of 558 sq km is the fifth largest in the archipelago and has the second largest population. The provincial capital of Puerto Baquerizo Moreno is found on the south-west point. Despite being the capital, little tourist activity was found here until the recent introduction of regular flights from the mainland which resulted in an increase in boats and hotels. Nevertheless, most people still use Puerto Ayora as a base.

There are six visitor sites on or near San Cristóbal, but they are not frequently visited by boats from Santa Cruz. The Chatham mockingbird, a species not found elsewhere, is common throughout the island.

Frigatebird Hill is about 1½ km east of Puerto Baquerizo Moreno and can be reached via foot trail without a guide. There is a national park information office en route. From the hill there is a beautiful view of a bay below and the town behind. Both species of frigatebirds nest here and lava lizards can be seen.

A road leads from the capital to the village of El Progreso, about eight km to the east and at the base of the 896-metre-high Cerro San Joaquín, the highest point on San Cristóbal (buses go here several times a day from Puerto Baquerizo Moreno). Jeeps can be hired or you can walk on a dirt road going about 10 km further east to **El Junco Lagoon**, a freshwater lake at about 700 metres above sea level and one of the few permanent freshwater bodies in the Galápagos. Here you can see white-cheeked pintails and common gallinules and observe the typical highland Miconia vegetation and endemic tree ferns.

Puerto Grande is smaller than its name suggests. It is also known as Bahía Stephens or Caleta Sappho and is a well protected little cove on San Cristóbal's north-western coast. There is a good sandy beach suitable for swimming and the island's fishermen sometimes beach their boats here to work on the hulls. Various seabirds can be seen, but the site is not known for any special colonies.

About an hour north-east of Puerto Baquerizo Moreno by boat is the rocky and tiny **Isla Lobos** which is the main sea lion and blue-footed booby colony for visitors to San Cristóbal. There is a 300-metre-long trail and lava lizards are seen. Both the boat crossing and the trail tend to be rough and there are better wildlife colonies elsewhere.

About two hours north-east of Puerto Baquerizo Moreno by boat is another little rocky island which, because of a fanciful resemblance to a sleeping lion, is named **León Dormido**. The English name, however, is Kicker Rock. The island is a sheer-walled tuff cone which has been eroded into two – smaller boats can sail between the two rocks. Because the sheer walls provide no place to land, this is not an official visitor site.

At the north end of the island is the **Los Galápagos** visitor site which is one of the newest areas to have been opened to visitors. Here, one can often see the giant Galápagos tortoises in the wild, but it takes some effort to get to the highland area where they live. One way is to land in a bay at the north end of the island and hike up – there is a trail and it takes about two hours to reach the tortoise area. I have heard reports from people saying that there were no tortoises to be seen; on my last visit, however, I saw about three dozen animals, so they are definitely there. The road from Puerto Baquerizo Moreno through El Progreso and on to El Junco Lagoon is slowly being pushed further north-east. It may be possible to get to the Galápagos tortoise area by taking this road to the end and hiking in – ask in town.

The most north-easterly point on the island is **Punta Pitt**, another new visitor site. The volcanic tuff formations are of interest to geologists (and attractive in their own right) but the unique feature of this site is that it is the only one on which you can see all three Galápagos booby species nesting. The walk is a little strenuous, but rewarding.

Isla Española

This island, often called by its English name of Hood, is the most southerly in the archipelago. It is a medium sized island of 61 sq km and there are two visitor sites. Because Española is somewhat outlying (about 90 km south-east of Santa Cruz), reaching it requires a fairly long sea passage and captains of some of the smallest boats may be reluctant to go this far. The better boats will often do the long crossing as an overnight passage. The island is well worth visiting from late March to December because it has the only colony of the waved albatross, one of the Galápagos' most spectacular seabirds.

The best visitor site on Española is **Punta Suarez** at the western end of the island. A wet landing is necessary. There is a trail of about two km in length which takes the visitor through masked and blue-footed booby colonies and past a beach full of marine iguanas before reaching the main attraction, the waved albatross colony.

Just beyond the colony is a blow hole through which the waves force water spouts about 20 metres into the air. Sitting on top of the cliffs between the waved albatrosses and the blow hole, you can watch seabirds performing their aerial ballets and their less elegant attempts to land and take off.

Other birds to look for are the Hood mockingbird, found nowhere else, swallow-tailed gulls, red-billed tropicbirds, and oystercatchers. The large cactus finch can also be seen, and is found on few other islands. This is one of my favourite visitor sites in the Galápagos.

Gardner Bay is a beautiful white sand beach at the east end of Española. It is reached with a wet landing and there is good swimming and a sea lion colony. An island a short distance offshore provides good snorkelling – there's one rock that often has white-tipped reef sharks basking under it.

Isla Santa María

Officially known as Santa María but more often called Floreana or Charles, this, at 173 sq km, is the sixth largest of the islands. It has had an interesting history. The first resident of the Galápagos was Patrick Watkins, an Irishman who was marooned on Floreana in 1807 and spent two years living there, growing vegetables and trading his produce for rum from passing boats. The story goes that he managed to remain drunk for most of his stay until he stole a ship's boat and set out for Guayaquil accompanied by five slaves. No one knows what happened to the slaves – only Watkins reached the mainland.

After Watkin's departure, the island became an Ecuadorian penal colony for

some years. In the 1930s, three groups of German settlers arrived on Floreana and strange stories have been told about them ever since.

The most colourful of the settlers was a baroness who arrived with three lovers. There was also an eccentric vegetarian, Dr Friedrich Ritter, who had all his teeth removed before arriving so as to avoid dental problems. He was accompanied by his mistress. The third group was a couple from Cologne, the Wittmers.

Despite their similar nationality, there was a great deal of friction between the groups and mysteriously, one by one, the settlers died. The baroness and a lover simply disappeared and another lover died in a boating accident. The vegetarian Dr Ritter died of food poisoning after eating chicken.

The only ones to survive were the Wittmers, and now Margaret Wittmer, one of the original settlers, continues to live on Floreana with her children and grandchildren. Although several books and articles have been written about the strange happenings on Floreana, no one is really sure of what happened.

The Wittmers live in the tiny village of Puerto Velasco Ibarra on the west coast of Floreana where they run a small hotel and restaurant. The village can be visited and a road runs inland for a few km to an area where the endemic medium tree finch can be seen (this finch exists only on Floreana). Nearby are some caves used by early settlers.

It is an all-day hike up there and back – I went with local biologist Felipe Cruz who hired the town's dump truck for the trip. There are no taxis!

There are three visitor sites on the north coast of Floreana. **Post Office Bay** used to have a barrel where whalers left mail. Any captain of a boat which was heading to where the mail was addressed would deliver it. The site continues to be used, though obviously the barrel has been changed many times. About 300 metres behind the barrel is a lava cave which can be descended with the aid of a short piece of rope. Nearby, there are the remains of a canning factory. There is a pleasant swimming beach. A wet landing is necessary. I have heard talk of building a trail from here to the baroness' old house – you might ask about this.

Punta Cormorant is also reached with a wet landing. There is a greenish beach; green because it contains crystals of the mineral olivine. There are often sea lions, and swimming and snorkelling are both good.

A 400-metre trail leads across an isthmus to a white sand beach where turtles sometimes lay their eggs. The white beach is also good for swimming, but beware of stingrays and shuffle your feet when entering the water.

Between the two beaches is a flamingo lagoon and this is probably the main attraction of this visitor site. Several dozen flamingos are normally seen, and this is also a good place to see other wading birds such as the black-necked stilt, oystercatchers, willets and whimbrels. White-cheeked pintail ducks are often seen in the lagoon and Galápagos hawks wheel overhead.

The third Floreana visitor site is the remains of a half submerged volcanic cone, poking up out of the ocean a few hundred metres from Punta Cormorant. Aptly named the **Devil's Crown**, this ragged semicircle of rocks forms one of the most outstanding marine sites in the Galápagos.

A panga ride around the cone will give views of red-billed tropicbirds, pelicans, herons and lava gulls nesting on the rocks, but the greater attraction is snorkelling in and around the crater. There are thousands of bright tropical fish, a small coral formation, sea lions and, if you are lucky, sharks.

I've heard rumours of a fourth visitor site proposed for the east coast of the island – this site features a green sand beach, caves and a blue-footed booby colony.

Isla San Salvador

The official name is used less often than the old Spanish name Santiago, or the English name James. Santiago is the fourth largest of the islands and has four excellent visitor sites within its 585 sq km. The best site is **Puerto**

Egas on James Bay on the west side of Santiago.

Here, there is a long, flat, black lava shoreline where eroded shapes form lava pools, caves, and inlets which house a great variety of wildlife. This is a great place to see colonies of marine iguanas basking in the sun. The tide pools contain hundreds of red sally lightfoot crabs which attract hunting herons of all the commonly found species.

The inlets are favourite haunts of the Galápagos fur seal and this is one of the best places in the islands to see them. You can snorkel with the fur seals and there are also many species of tropical fish. I have seen moray eels, sharks, and octopuses during snorkels here – you never know what might show up.

Behind the black lava shoreline is Sugarloaf Volcano which can be reached via a two-km footpath. Lava lizards, Darwin's finches and Galápagos doves are often seen on this path. It peters out near the top of the 395-metre summit but from here the views are tremendous. There is an extinct crater in which feral goats are often seen (the wild goats are a major problem on Santiago) and Galápagos hawks often hover a few metres above the top of the volcano. North of the volcano is a crater where a salt mine used to be; its remains can be visited by walking along a three-km trail from the coast.

At the north end of James Bay, about five km from Puerto Egas, is the brown sand **Espumilla Beach** which can be reached with a wet landing. Swimming is good. There is a small lagoon behind the beach where various wading birds are often seen, including flamingos at times. A two-km trail leads inland through transitional vegetation where there are various finches and the Galápagos flycatcher.

At the north-western end of Santiago there is a site which is normally visited by cruising past it. This is **Buccaneer Cove**, so called because it was a popular place for 17th and 18th-century buccaneers to careen their vessels. Its main attraction today is the beautiful cliffs and pinnacles which are used as nesting areas by several species of seabirds.

This is best appreciated from the sea, but it is possible to land in the cove where there are beaches.

Sullivan Bay is on Santiago's east coast. Here, a huge black lava flow from the turn of the century has solidified into a sheet which reaches to the edge of the sea. A dry landing enables the visitor to step onto the flow and follow a trail of white posts in a two-km circuit on the lava. You can see uneroded volcanic formations such as pahoehoe lava, lava bubbles, and tree trunk moulds in the surface. A few pioneer colonising plants such as *Brachycereus* cactus and *Mollugo* carpetweed can be seen. This site is of particular interest to those interested in volcanology or geology.

As with several of the other islands, there have been proposals for new visitor sites to be opened in the 1990s – ask your guide.

Isla Bartolomé

Just off Sullivan Bay is Isla Bartolomé with an area of 1.2 sq km from where you can see the most frequently photographed and hence most famous vista in the islands. There are two visitor sites and footpaths. One begins from a jetty (dry landing) from where it is about 600 metres to the 114-metre summit of the island. This is a good but sandy trail which leads through a wild and unearthly looking lava landscape; wooden stairs have been built on the last (steepest) section, both to aid visitors and to protect the trail from erosion. There are a few pioneering plants on either side of the trail but the main attraction is the view towards Santiago which is as dramatic as the photographs suggest.

The other visitor site is a small sandy beach in a cove (wet landing). Here there is good snorkelling and swimming and the opportunity to swim with the endemic Galápagos penguins which frequent this cove. Marine turtles and a gaudy variety of tropical fish are also frequent visitors.

The best way to see and photograph the penguins is by taking a panga ride close to the rocks on either side of the cove and particularly around the aptly named Pinnacle Rock to the right of the cove from the seaward side. You can often get within a few metres of the penguins. This is the closest point to Puerto Ayora where you can frequently see these fascinating birds. It avoids the long voyage to the other penguin colonies which are mainly on the west side of Isabela.

From the beach there is a short 100-metre trail leading across the narrowest part of Bartolomé to another sandy beach on the opposite side of the island. The main attraction of this beach is that the marine turtles may nest here between January and March. Both beaches are clearly seen from the viewpoint at the first visitor site described.

Sombrero Chino

This tiny island is less than a quarter of one sq km in size and found just off the southeastern tip of Santiago. It is a fairly recent volcanic cone which accounts for its descriptive name which means 'Chinese Hat'. The hat shape is best appreciated from the north. There is a small sea lion cove on the north shore where you can anchor and land at the visitor site. Opposite Sombrero Chino, on the rocky shoreline of nearby Isla Santiago, penguins are often seen.

There is a 400-metre trail around the cove and through a sea lion colony – marine iguanas scurry everywhere. The volcanic landscape is attractive and there are good views of the cone which gives the island its name. There are snorkelling and swimming opportunities in the cove.

Isla Rábida

Also known as Jervis, this approximately five-sq-km island lies five km south of Santiago. There is a wet landing onto a dark red beach where sea lions haul out, and where pelicans nest. This is one of the best places for seeing these birds nesting.

Behind the beach there is a salt-water lagoon where flamingos and white-cheeked pintails are sometimes seen. This lagoon is also the site of a sea lion bachelor colony where the *solteros*, deposed by the most dominant bull, while away their day.

There is a ¾-km-long trail with good

views of the 367-metre-high volcanic peak covered with palo santo trees. At the end of this there is a great snorkelling spot.

Isla Genovesa

This island is known more often by its English name of Tower. It is 14-sq-km and the most north-easterly of the Galápagos islands. It is rather an outlying island and so is infrequently included on a one-week itinerary. If you have the time, however, and are interested in seabirds, this island is well worth the long trip. It is the best place to see a red-footed booby colony, as well as giving the opportunity to visit colonies of masked boobies, great frigatebirds, red-billed tropicbirds, swallow-tailed gulls, and many thousands of storm petrels. Other bird attractions include Galápagos doves and short-eared owls. Both sea lions and fur seals are present and there are exciting snorkelling opportunities – I have seen hammerhead sharks here.

The island is fairly flat and round, with a large, almost landlocked cove named Darwin Bay on the south side. There are two visitor sites, both on Darwin Bay. **Prince Philip's Steps** is on the eastern arm of the bay and can be reached with a dry landing. A steep and rocky path leads to the top of 25 metre-high cliffs and nesting seabirds are sometimes found right on the narrow path.

At the top of the cliffs the one-km long trail leads inland, past dry forest vegetation and various seabird colonies, to a cracked expanse of lava where thousands of storm petrels make their nests and wheel overhead. Short-eared owls are often seen here and it is an excellent hike for the bird enthusiast.

The second visitor site is **Darwin Bay Beach** which is a coral beach reached by a wet landing. There is a ¾ -km trail along the beach which passes through more seabird colonies.

A pleasant panga ride can be taken along the cliffs. The panga is often followed by playful sea lions. This recommended excursion gives a good view from the seaward side of the cliffs and of the birds nesting on them.

Finally, this is the only regularly visited island which lies entirely north of the equator (the northernmost part of Isabela also pokes above the line). Cruises to Tower may well involve various crossing-the-line ceremonies for those passengers who have never crossed the equator at sea before.

Isla Marchena

This island is also known as Bindloe. At 130 sq km, this is the seventh largest island in the archipelago, and is the largest one not to have any official visitor sites. There are some good scuba diving sites, however, so you may get to see the island up close if you are on a dive trip. There are landing sites.

The 343-metre-high volcano in the middle of the island has been very active during 1991 – ask your guide whether it continues to be active. You may be able to see the eruptions from a distance as you cruise in the northern part of the islands.

Isla Pinta

This is the original home of Lonesome George (the tortoise described in the Isla Santa Cruz section). Pinta is the ninth largest of the islands and further north than any of the bigger islands. Its English name is Abingdon. There are landing sites but no visitor sites and researchers require a permit to visit.

Isla Isabela

The largest island in the archipelago is the 4588-sq-km Isabela (occasionally called Albemarle) which occupies over 58% of the entire land mass of the Galápagos. It is a relatively recent island and consists of a chain of five fairly young and intermittently active volcanoes, one of which, Volcán Wolf, is the highest point in the Galápagos at 1707 metres (some sources claim 1646 metres). There is also one small older volcano.

Although Isabela's volcanoes dominate the westward view during passages to the west of Santa Cruz, the island itself is not frequently visited by smaller boats because most of the best visitor sites are on the west side of the island. The reverse 'C' shape of the island means that the visitor sites on the west side are reached only after a very long passage (over 200 km) from Santa Cruz and so either you have to make a two-week cruise or you visit Isabela without seeing many of the other islands.

I've heard of a proposal to open a visitor site on Bahía Cartago on the eastern side of Isabela, which would make it a little more accessible to shorter cruises.

There are 10 visitor sites on Isabela. One of these is the summit of **Volcán Alcedo** (1128 metres) which is famous for its seven-km-wide caldera with steaming fumaroles where hundreds of giant tortoises can be seen, especially from June to December. The view is fantastic.

Reaching this site is quite an undertaking, however, and needs some preparation and effort. A wet landing at Shipton Cove brings you to the start of a steep, rocky, and strenuous 10-km trail to the edge of the caldera, and then it is a further six km to the fumarole. All food and water must be carried. There is a camp site at the beach, another half way up the volcano, and three more on the caldera rim. One of these is at the point where the trail first reaches the caldera, another is at the fumarole, and the third is in between.

You should enquire in the national park office for up-to-date information and a camping permit. This is a most rewarding trip if you can afford the time, and well worth the hassle and hard work. At the very least it is an overnight trip and two nights are better still.

Day trips are offered – but spending six or seven strenuous hours to get there and then having to return almost immediately is not a good idea – you really need to spend a night near the rim to appreciate it properly.

A few km north of the landing for Alcedo is the **Punta García** visitor site. This consists mainly of very rough *aa* lava and there are no proper trails though you can land if you want to. Until recently, this was the only place where you could see the endemic flightless cormorant without having to take the long passage around to the west side.

Recently, however, these birds have been present only intermittently and visits to this site have declined.

At the northern tip of Isabela is the **Punta Albemarle** visitor site which used to be a US radar base during WW II. There are no trails and the site is known for the flightless cormorants which normally are not found further to the east.

Further west there are several points where flightless cormorants, Galápagos penguins, and other seabirds can be seen, but there are no visitor sites to land in. You can see the birds from your boat, however.

At the west end of the northern arm of Isabela is the small old Volcán Ecuador (610 metres) which comes down almost to the sea. Punta Vicente Roca, at the volcano's base, is a rocky point with a good snorkelling area.

The first official visitor site on the western side of Isabela is **Punta Tortuga** which is a beach at the base of Volcán Darwin (1280 metres). Part of the land here was formed through a recent uplift. Locals report that one day in 1975 the uplift just appeared – no one saw it happen. One day there was nothing and the next day there was an uplifted ledge.

Although there is no trail, you can land on the beach and explore the mangroves for the mangrove finch which is present here, though not always easy to see. This finch is found only on Isabela and Fernandina Islands.

Just south of the point is the visitor site of **Tagus Cove** where early sailors frequently anchored. You can still see some of the names of the vessels scratched on to the cliffs around the cove.

A dry landing will bring you to a trail which you follow for two km past a salt-water lagoon and onto the lower lava slopes of Volcán Darwin, where various volcanic formations can be observed. There are some steep sections on this trail. A panga ride along the cliffs will enable you to see the historical graffiti and various seabirds, usually including the Galápagos penguin and flightless cormorant. There are snorkelling opportunities in the cove.

Urbina Bay lies around the middle of the

western shore of Isabela and is a flat area formed by an uplift from the sea in 1954. Evidence of the uplift includes a coral reef on the land. Flightless cormorants, pelicans and marine iguanas can be observed. Rays and turtles can be seen in the bay and a wet landing onto a beach brings you to a one-km-long trail leading to the corals. There is a good view of Volcán Alcedo.

Near where the western shoreline of Isabela bends sharply towards the lower 'arm' of the island there is a visitor site known for its marine life. **Elizabeth Bay** is best visited by a panga ride and there are no landing sites. The Mariela Islands are at the entrance of the bay and they are frequented by penguins. The end of the bay itself is a long, narrow and convoluted arm of the sea surrounded by three species of mangroves. Marine turtles and rays are usually seen in the water and various sea and shore birds are present.

West of Elizabeth Bay is the **Punta Moreno** visitor site where you can make a dry landing onto a lava flow where there are some brackish pools. Flamingos, white-cheeked pintails and common gallinules are sometimes seen and various pioneer plants and insects are found in the area. There is a rough trail.

On the south-eastern corner of Isabela there is the small village of Puerto Villamil. Behind and to the west of the village there are the **Villamil Lagoons**. This visitor site is known for its migrant birds, especially waders. Harris writes that over 20 species of migrant waders have been reported here and the lagoons are by far the best water-bird area in the Galápagos. The vegetation around the lagoons is dense and there are no trails, although the road to the highlands and the open beach do give reasonable access to the lagoons.

The massive **Volcán Santo Tomás** (1490 metres, also known as Volcán Sierra Negra) lies to the north-west. The tiny settlement of Santo Tomás is on the lower flanks of the volcano and 18 km by road from Puerto Villamil. Trucks or jeeps can be hired for the ride. From Santo Tomás it is nine km further up a steep trail to the rim of the volcano – horses can be hired in the village.

The caldera is roughly 10 km in diameter and is a spectacular site with magnificent views. An eight-km trail leads around the east side of the volcano to some active fumaroles. It is possible to walk all the way around the caldera but the trail peters out. You should carry all your food and water or hire horses. Camping is allowed on the rim. Galápagos hawks, short-eared owls, finches and flycatchers are among the common birds seen on this trip. The summit is often foggy, especially during the June to December garúa season, and it is easy to get lost – stay in a group. Nearby is **Volcán Chico** where you can see more fumaroles.

Isla Fernandina

At 642 sq km, Fernandina (infrequently called Narborough) is the third-largest island and the most westerly of the normally visited ones. It is considered the youngest of the main islands and the recently formed volcanic landscapes are most impressive. At least 10 eruptions have been recorded since 1813, the most recent being 1988.

There is one visitor site at **Punta Espinosa**, just across from Tagus Cove on Isabela. The point is known for one of the greatest concentrations of the endemic marine iguanas which are found in their thousands. Also, flightless cormorants, Galápagos penguins and sea lions are common here.

A dry landing brings one to two trails – a short ¼-km one to the point and a longer ¾-km one out to recently formed lava fields. Here you can see various pioneering plants, such as the *Brachycereus* cactus, as well as pahoehoe and aa lava formations.

Other Islands

The one sizeable island in the central part of the archipelago which has no visitor sites is **Isla Pinzón**, also called Duncan. It is a cliff-bound island, which makes landing difficult, and a permit is required to visit (usually reserved for scientists and researchers).

The northernmost islands are the two tiny islands of **Isla Wolf** (Wenman) and **Isla Darwin** (Culpepper). They are about 100 km north-east of the rest of the archipelago and very seldom visited, except on occasional scuba diving trips. Both have nearly vertical cliffs making landing difficult – Darwin was first visited in 1964 when a helicopter expedition landed on the summit. Various other rocks and islets are present in the archipelago but all are extremely small.

ACTIVITIES
Snorkelling

You don't have to be a great swimmer to be able to snorkel. Donning a mask and snorkel will literally open up a completely new world for you. Baby sea lions may come up and stare at you through your mask, various species of rays come slowly undulating by, and penguins dart past you in a stream of bubbles. The hundreds of species of fish are spectacularly colourful and you can watch the round, flapping shapes of sea turtles as they circle you. This won't, of course, happen immediately you enter the water, but you have a good chance of seeing most of these things if you spend, say, half an hour per day in the water during a week of cruising the islands.

A mask and snorkel also let you observe more sedentary forms of life. Sea urchins, starfish, sea anemones, algae and crustaceans all colourfully combine in an exotic display of underwater life. If I were to give only one piece of advice to someone visiting the Galápagos, I would say, 'Bring a snorkel and mask.' You may be able to buy them in sporting goods stores in Quito or Guayaquil, and they can sometimes be borrowed in the Galápagos, but if you definitely plan on visiting the islands, you should bring a mask from home to ensure a good fit and to enable you to snorkel when you feel like it.

The water temperature is generally around 21°C from January to April and about 19°C during the rest of the year. If you plan on spending a lot of time in the water you may want to bring a wet suit top with you.

Scuba Diving

Scuba diving is available in the Galápagos but you must have all your own equipment and book a tour in advance, usually through a dive company. Compressed air and tanks are supplied on boats which run dive tours. Learning to dive is not an option offered in the Galápagos – all divers must be certified.

Photography

Any kind of camera will enable an amateur photographer to get satisfying pictures – the animals will stay near the trails and can often be approached within two or three metres.

Advanced photographers will already have their own favourite lenses and equipment. A few suggestions: First, I have seen non-professional photographers use two 36 exposure rolls of film per day in the Galápagos – and then complain that they didn't really bring enough film. Film is not available on the boats and hard to come by in the Galápagos towns; make sure you bring enough. If you happen to have some left over towards the end of your trip, selling film will be very easy.

Don't forget spare batteries for camera and flash unit. If your camera battery goes dead, you won't find another in the islands. Also bring plastic ziplock bags for wet panga rides. Specially designed waterproof camera bags are available from photography stores, but plastic bags are an adequate and much cheaper alternative. Lead foil bags are a good idea to protect your film from airport X-ray machines.

A zoom lens is very useful. You can change from a wide angle landscape shot to a telephoto opportunity of a pelican flying over your head without having to change lenses – by which time the bird has flown!

Finally, remember to note down what you photographed after each island excursion and label each film. Otherwise, when you get home, you'll find you can't remember which island is which. You'll know the difference between your red-footed and blue-footed booby shots, but you'll have a hard time telling the difference between the four endemic mockingbirds.

Visiting the Galápagos

PUERTO AYORA

This town is on the central island of Santa Cruz and is the town that most visitors stay in or visit. The population is some 6000 and growing fast. There are the usual amenities – hotels, bars and restaurants, stores, an IETEL and post office, tourist information, a TAME office, a basic hospital, churches, a movie theatre, and a radio station.

The town's harbour is named Academy Bay after the boat *Academy* which arrived here in 1905 carrying an expedition sent by the California Academy of Sciences. Recently, the town imposed a US$2 per person port tax on passengers using Academy Bay – this may or may not be included in the cost of your tour.

Note that the nearest airport, Baltra, is three hours away by bus and ferry.

Tourist Information

There is a CETUR tourist information on the waterfront a short walk from the docks. There are several self-styled 'information centres' nearby which will give you information about their day trips and boat charters.

The Charles Darwin Research Station and national park office is about a km east of town. There is an exhibition hall, an information kiosk, a scientific library, tortoise-raising pens, and a self-guided walk but tours are not organised.

INGALA (Instituto Nacional Galápagos) can give you information about inter-island ferries and the Capitanía can give you information about boats to the mainland.

The TAME office is open from 8 am to 12 noon Monday to Thursday and on Saturday. It is also open from 2 to 4 pm Monday to Friday. Reconfirming your departures is essential. Flights are often full and there is sometimes difficulty in changing your reservation or buying a ticket. Be persistent.

Recently, electricity was turned off at 11 pm (though some places have generators and stay open later). Carry a flashlight on late night forays.

See the description of Isla Santa Cruz earlier in this chapter for information of places to visit on the island.

Money Moneychanging facilities are not very good and you should change travellers' cheques on the mainland. It is easier to change cash than travellers' cheques but rates are generally poor. The bank usually does not exchange money. A store which changes travellers' cheques (at a poor rate) is shown on the map. Other stores will sometimes also exchange money, and some hotels and restaurants will do so if you are a client. Ask around for the best rates – better still, bring sucres (especially if you are organising your own island tour).

Time The Galápagos are one hour behind mainland Ecuador.

Post & Telecommunications The IETEL office is often out of service for phone calls. When it is working, international calls are rarely possible. They can send telegrams, however. In an emergency, radio messages are sent from the INGALA office.

The post office is slow in sending mail out of the islands. Make sure your letters are stamped and franked – I once sent a dozen postcards and not one got delivered. The larcenous post mistress took my money but kept the stamps.

Rental Bicycles can be rented from La Garrapata Restaurant & Bar and also from a place marked on the map. Rentals are about US$1.25 per hour. Henri's Bar has snorkelling gear for rent.

Shopping You can buy the famous Galápagos T-shirts in most of the souvenir shops; the profits from the ones sold at the Charles Darwin Research Station go to support that worthwhile institution. Other souvenirs available include objects made from black coral, turtle and tortoise shell. These threatened animals are protected and it is illegal to use these animal products for the manufacture of novelties. The practice still continues, unfortunately, and the most effective way of stamping it out is to avoid buying these things.

Most other things (T-shirts excepted) are either expensive or unavailable and you are strongly advised to stock up on suntan lotion, insect repellent, toiletries, film and medications on the mainland. Food and drink are available but the choice is limited and comparatively expensive.

A good selection of postcards is available at the post office. Many of these are photographs or drawings by local resident Tui de Roy, famous for her beautifully illustrated books on the wildlife of the islands. Her books are also for sale in various stores and at the Libri Mundi bookstore in Quito. Her mother, Jacqueline de Roy, makes exquisite silver jewellery of the Galápagos animals. The work is not cheap but well worth the money. Tui's brother, Gil, has a store named Inti Joyería – ask here about his mother's jewellery.

Studying & Working The Charles Darwin Research Station runs guide courses lasting about six weeks every September. It is necessary to take and pass this course before you can work as a tour guide on the boats. Information on the course is available from Estación Científica Charles Darwin, Puerto Ayora, Santa Cruz, Galápagos, Ecuador.

Some of the main tourist companies, especially Metropolitan Touring in Quito, sponsor English-speaking biology graduates to take the course in return for a year's paid work guiding their boats. You should also be able to speak Spanish. If you qualify, Metropolitan will obtain visas and work permits for you.

If you are a biologist, it is possible to work as a volunteer with one of the ongoing projects in the islands. Send resumes and work/project suggestions or requests to the director of the research station. If you are working or studying in the islands you normally qualify for the discounted Ecuadorian airfare to the Galápagos.

Places to Stay
A good range of hotels is available in Puerto Ayora, ranging from cheap and basic to first class, by Galápagos standards at least. There are no luxury hotels. Prices tend to rise with demand and during the heaviest tourist season (December to January and June to August) prices may be higher if the town is full.

It cannot be over-emphasised that a cheap 'tour' based at a hotel and visiting other islands on day trips gives you only a superficial look at the Galápagos. Stay in Puerto Ayora by all means, but make every effort to visit the islands by taking a cruise of at least several days and preferably a full week or more.

Places to Stay – bottom end
It used to be possible to camp next to the cemetery near the Charles Darwin Research Station – the fee was about a dollar and facilities were almost non-existent. It may no longer be permitted to camp here. Ask at the research station for information about this and other camp sites (which are generally difficult to get to and require that you pack in your own water.)

There are several cheap and basic hotels some of which are good value. They are clean and friendly, and better value than some of the more expensive places. Although facilities are basic, the following four are all recommended for the friendly service and chances of meeting other budget travellers trying to arrange a tour.

Just behind the TAME office is *Residencial Los Amigos* which charges US$2.50/4.50 for singles/doubles; this place has recently been very popular and recommended among budget travellers. A block inland is the good and clean *Residencial Flamingo* which charges US$2.50 per person in rooms with private bath.

Two other places are a km north of downtown on the way to the Charles Darwin Research Station. *Pensión Gloria* is a small hotel run by Señora Gloria, whose husband is a guide. They are friendly and will help you organise a tour boat group. They charge

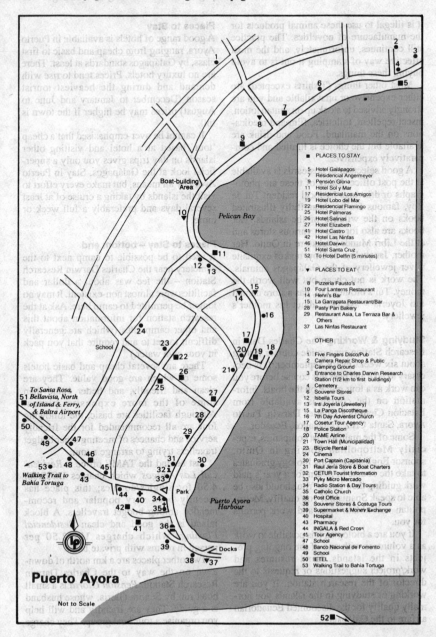

US$2 per person and serve a good bread and jam, eggs, juice and coffee breakfast for about US$1.

The bigger *Residencial Angermeyer* is run by members of the family who were among the earliest permanent residents. They are a mine of information and the hotel is in a pleasant garden. It is also popular with budget travellers, but I have received reports that the management is rather eccentric! Rooms are about US$3 per person and they help with putting you in contact with boats.

The *Lobo del Mar Hotel* is popular with Ecuadorian tour groups and tends to be noisy. Most of their rooms are basic but reasonably clean and with private showers. They charge US$6/9 for singles/doubles and have some triple and quadruples which are not much more. For about US$4 more per person they include three meals a day. The hotel organises day trips to various islands for about US$35 to US$40 per passenger.

The *Hotel Las Palmeras* is quite good but often full. Prices are around US$5/7 for clean singles/doubles with private bath. Similarly priced and also clean and modern looking is the *Hotel Salinas*, opposite. *Hotel Elizabeth* is about the same price, though is reportedly open to bargaining. They have improved since my negative comments in the last edition. In this price range are the *Hotel Darwin* and *Hotel Santa Cruz*, which are both on the road out of town.

Places to Stay – middle

The *Hotel Ninfas* charges about US$10 per person without and US$16 with meals and has private baths in all rooms. They arrange tours. The *Hotel Castro* is usually used by tour groups booked with Señor Miguel Castro but you can always try it if you have no luck elsewhere.

The *Hotel Sol y Mar* is very pleasantly situated right on the waterfront and marine iguanas sunbathe with the guests on the deck or walk over your feet while you're having breakfast. The owner is Señor Jimmy Perez, a rather colourful character who speaks English and runs Trans-Galápagos Tourism. He can also help you get a boat. Clean rooms

with private bath are US$12/18 for singles/ doubles; extra people are about US$4 per person. Good meals are available for US$1.50 (breakfast), US$3.50 (lunch) and US$5 (supper).

Places to Stay – top end

The best hotel in Puerto Ayora is the well recommended *Hotel Galápagos*, which charges US$48/US$84/US$105 (including tax) for comfortable single/double/triple cabins with private bath and ocean view. They serve excellent meals (about US$6.50, US$8 and US$12 for breakfast, lunch and supper). A pleasant bar and a paperback book library are on the premises. They are represented in Quito by the Coltur Agency (☎ 545 777, 548 219, fax 502 449), Robles and Páez. Mail to PO Box 2771, Quito.

Across the bay from Puerto Ayora is the *Hotel Delfín* with a private beach. All rooms have a beach view, private bathrooms and hot shower and are almost as much as the Hotel Galápagos. There is a good restaurant. This is a very private location – you need a boat to get to this hotel from Puerto Ayora. The hotel is used as a base for day tours organised by Metropolitan Touring in Quito – they can make reservations for you.

Places to Eat, Drink & Dance

There are a number of restaurants and bars in Puerto Ayora and they are good places to meet people. Some of them change hands or names quite often, as places frequented by seasonal influxes of people tend to do. Most of the following have been around for a few years.

Las Ninfas Restaurant by the dock has been the standard meeting place during the day for years – it hasn't changed much in a decade and has been eclipsed somewhat by newer places. Nevertheless, you can grab a beer, snack or meal here while waiting for your panga.

Heading into town from the dock along the main street soon brings you to *Restaurant Asia* which is the best chifa in town. A few doors away is the *Pasty Pan* bakery – good for baked goods and also for boat contacts.

There are several other places on the same block, including the upstairs bar at *La Terraza* which gets pretty rowdy (a recent report tells me it's closed – maybe they were just having an off-day. La Terraza has been around for a while).

Further along the main ocean-front street is *La Garrapata Bar/Restaurant* which is popular and serves good, though not particularly cheap, meals. The bar often stays open until the early hours and is a favourite with locals and visitors alike. The Garrapata is often closed in the afternoons and all day Sunday. Next door is the *La Panga* discotheque which was the place to dance in the early 1990s – local guides assure me that this is where 'the landings are always wet'. Opposite is *Henri's Bar* which is German-run (they speak English and Spanish) and has recently been a popular meeting place for gringo travellers. They sell good breakfasts, rather pricey beer, have a notice board and rent snorkelling equipment.

Further along you'll find *Four Lanterns Restaurant* which has been recommended for good pizzas, sandwiches, other snacks and coffee. *Fausto's Pizzería* is also good for pizzas. They used to have a book exchange and screen videos in the evenings for a fee. I don't know if they still do. A couple of blocks inland is the *Five Fingers Disco Pub* which is an alternative to La Panga.

The restaurant at the *Hotel Galápagos* is good and open to the public, though you should make advance reservations, particularly if there is a group of you. This is the only place in Puerto Ayora where all the drinking water is properly filtered and safe. They prepare safe salads and their bar is very pleasant and relaxed.

For the cheapest meals, ask around and eat where the locals go. There are a bunch of inexpensive comedors which come and go; *El Pescador, El Pirata* and *Las Peñas* have been recommended to me by travellers (but are not on the map).

Getting There & Away

You can either go by boat or by air from the Ecuadorian mainland. If you go by boat you will normally waste a lot of time in Guayaquil getting one of the infrequent passages. The money you spend on hotels and food in Guayaquil, plus the hassles involved, means that you really end up saving very little money, if any at all – unless you are lucky.

Air Rather than spend frustrating days and weeks looking for a ship in Guayaquil, I recommend that you just get on a plane and have done with it. TAME operates morning flights daily (except Sunday) from both Quito and Guayaquil to Isla Baltra Airport, about three to four hours away from Puerto Ayora by public transport (see the Getting Around section). SAN flies daily (except Thursday and Sunday) from Quito and Guayaquil around 12 noon for San Cristóbal.

Flights from Guayaquil cost US$330 for the round trip and take 1½ hours to the Galápagos. From Quito flights costs US$374 for the round trip and you have to check in again in Guayaquil and usually board another aircraft.

If you buy tickets to the Galápagos in the US with Ecuatoriana or Saeta, you can save US$100 on this price. You have to fly with these airlines from Miami. Ecuatoriana connects you with TAME (for Baltra and Puerto Ayora), whilst Saeta connects you with SAN (for San Cristóbal and Puerto Baquerizo Moreno).

It is important to realise TAME and SAN will not usually honour one another's tickets so you must know which airport you want to fly in and out of before you buy these discounted international tickets. It is possible to go from one island to the other but this takes time and is not reliable – boats are infrequent and often full. These tickets, for the most part, are an incentive for buying an organised tour out of one or the other of these islands. If you do buy these tickets in advance, make sure that you check that your name is on the computer when you get to Ecuador – it usually is but you never know till you check.

Ecuadorian nationals can fly from Guayaquil for about US$80 round trip; Galápagos residents pay half that. Some foreign residents of Ecuador or workers in the islands are also eligible so if you have a residence visa you should make enquiries.

Cheap flights to the islands are very difficult to get unless you are a resident. Nevertheless, rumours and stories about these 'good deals' float around periodically – therefore, none of the following possibilities are recommended as being reliable.

There is a military logistic flight on Saturday which occasionally has room for passengers. Ecuadorians are given priority, but they get cheap flights with TAME anyway and so there are sometimes seats available for foreigners. Make inquiries at the Ministry of Defense in Quito (ask for Departamento de Operaciones, Fuerza Aerea del Ecuador).

Travellers with official looking letters from universities, embassies, presidents etc will have the best chance. I have never met anyone who has done this but I keep hearing that it is possible – especially if you know someone high-up in the airforce.

Other possibilities for cheap flights are that students with international student ID can get a discount (variously reported as 20% and 25% with TAME and 25% with SAN). If you have a bona-fide student card, ask at the airlines. Finally, researchers, biologists etc, affiliated with a university can also get discounts – don't leave this to the last minute but work on it in advance if you are a bona-fide biologist.

I suppose that as long as the flights are expensive there will be people who will happily waste a month of their time trying to beat the system; if you're not eligible for cheap flights and you think the airfare is too expensive, then maybe you shouldn't be visiting the islands anyway.

Flights to the Galápagos are sometimes booked up well in advance but if you go to the airport you'll often find that there are many no-shows. Travel agencies book up blocks of seats for their all-inclusive Galápagos tours. First they sell them to people taking their tours but will release the seats on the day of the flight when there is no longer any hope of selling their tour. If you are tied into a definite itinerary, you should make a reservation; if you're flexible, you can buy your ticket at the airport when you want to fly. You have a better-than-even chance of getting a ticket and it's unlikely that you'll be turned away two days in a row.

Some travel agencies will offer you a 'discount' on an airline ticket if you buy their tour of the Galápagos, which is OK if their tour happens to be what you want. Sometimes you can persuade an agency to sell you a discount ticket because they can't fill their tour space.

There are no air connections between Baltra and other islands.

Boat If you really insist on avoiding air transport, there are four ways to get to the islands by boat: with the navy, on a cargo boat, on a cruise ship or on your own vessel.

The navy runs the *Calicuchima*, which leaves Guayaquil about twice a month for an 11-day trip. Only about half this time is available for visiting the islands, some naval bases are visited en route, and the accommodation, crew, guides and food have been criticised. On the other hand, some people enjoyed the trip. The tour costs about US$330 and you can find out more from their office at Transnave on 9 de Octubre and Chile in Guayaquil.

Cargo ships leave irregularly and charge about US$100 for a one-way trip, which are hard to get. Most passengers get round trips, lasting about 15 to 20 days. Conditions are tolerable but basic. The journey out takes about 3½ days and you should be prepared to bring a sleeping bag or hammock, though a bunk in a cabin may well be available. These ships normally do round trips and are mainly for cargo purposes, not for wildlife viewing. Sandra, writing from Holland, tells me she enjoyed her 20-day round trip from Guayaquil in the *Piquero* – she paid US$300 in 1991, and saw a fair amount of wildlife. She found the crew helpful and was given a cabin to sleep in. More information can be found in the Guayaquil section of The South Coast chapter.

The 'best' boats to the islands are the cruise ships which are more comfortable, have a regular schedule, offer better food and guide service, and are much more expensive. They accommodate 90 passengers in comfortable double cabins (see the cruise ship descriptions under Tours later). These seven-day tours usually cost US$200 or more per day and go one way by boat and return by air. Note that the cruise from or to Guayaquil is not offered frequently – the boats spend most of their time in the Galápagos.

You can travel to the Galápagos in your own boat, but the Ecuadorian authorities give only a 72-hour transit pass to non-Galápagos boats, so you can't normally cruise the islands in your own boat unless you arrange it in advance – a difficult and time-consuming process. If you succeed in getting a permit, you must hire a licensed guide to accompany you in the islands.

There is a US$35 port entrance fee (subject to increase) charged to visiting yachts. You can moor the boat in Puerto Ayora and hire a Galápagos boat to visit the islands. If you do this you'll also have to pay a US$80 national park fee as well as the boat hire.

Getting Around

To/From the Airport Most visitors arrive by air and land on Isla Baltra. Have your passport and US$80 visitor fee ready – you won't get out of the airport otherwise. Outside the airport you will be met by a boat representative (if you are on a prearranged tour) and taken by bus on a five-minute drive to the boat dock.

If you are an independent traveller heading to Puerto Ayora, do not take the bus to the boat dock. Instead, take the bus to the ferry dock for Isla Santa Cruz. This is a 10 to 15-minute drive. A 10-minute ferry boat ride will take you across to Santa Cruz where you will be met by a bus to take you to Puerto Ayora, almost two hours away. This drive gives you a good look at the interior and highlands of Santa Cruz – dusty and dry in the north and greener and wetter in the highlands and on the south slopes. The ferry and second bus are scheduled to coincide with the departure of the first bus from the airport

so there isn't much waiting involved. You should be in Puerto Ayora within three or four hours of your arrival in Baltra.

The combined bus/ferry/bus trip costs about US$2.50. There is a ticket booth at the airport in the departure lounge, to your left as you leave the arrival area. You should buy your ticket as soon as you arrive as there is normally only one bus (although a second bus may run if there is enough passenger demand). The journey is often very crowded and passengers sometimes ride on the roof.

Bus Buses from Puerto Ayora to Baltra (via the ferry) leave at 8 or 8.30 am, every morning that there are flights (Monday to Saturday), from in front of the Hotel Colón and Raul Jería Store. The fare is about US$2.50, including the ferry. They return in the afternoon after the plane from the mainland has landed. A second and third bus will run if there is passenger demand. (The flight from Baltra to Guayaquil leaves at 1 pm.)

You can use these buses to be dropped off at the villages of Bellavista or Santa Rosa to explore some of the interior. Neither of these villages have hotels and sometimes the return bus is full with passengers from the airport. The most convenient way of seeing the interior and ensuring that you don't get stuck is to hire a bus or truck for the day with a group of other travellers. Ask at your hotel about this. Or hitchhike if you have the time.

Boat INGALA can give you up-to-date details of their inter-island passenger boat services. You should buy the tickets a day in advance. Priority is given to islanders and Ecuadorians, so it may take some days to be able to get on a boat. Departure days change frequently and are not reliable. Recently, there were two passenger services were in operation from Puerto Ayora.

Firstly, to San Cristóbal, US$11, Tuesday and Saturday, returning on Wednesday and Monday. Also, to Isabela, Monday, US$11, continuing on Tuesday to Santa María and on Wednesday returning to Puerto Ayora.

All these voyages take about four hours. Most inter-island transport is by private boat.

Ask around for fishing-boat owners etc who may be able to give you a ride. Marcos Martínez in Puerto Ayora arranges trips to Isabela. Tourist boats typically charge about US$30 to go to San Cristóbal.

At time of writing, it is not a good idea to rely on inter-island boats to get you to San Cristóbal for a particular date, as for a flight. There has been talk, however, of organising an efficient and reliable system of inter-island boats to those islands with settlements. This may be the case by the time you get there, ask about it.

PUERTO BAQUERIZO MORENO

This is the political capital of the Galápagos and is on Isla San Cristóbal. Few travellers came here until recently, when SAN started operating a regular jet service. Although it is the second largest town in the islands, with a population of about 3000, many of the inhabitants work in government-related jobs or fishing and the town is still a long way behind Puerto Ayora for tourism. Facilities are improving, however, and aggressive marketing by SAN is steadily making this an increasingly important tourist town.

Information

There are no official tourist offices as yet. Moneychanging is possible for cash dollars but the exchange is poor – ask around. It's best to bring sucres with you.

There is a small museum and a statue of Darwin. There is a small hospital and a post office. Frigatebird Hill is a short walk from town and other visitor sites are described under Isla San Cristóbal earlier in this chapter.

Places to Stay & Eat

The cheapest hotels include the *Hotel San Francisco* which is reportedly clean and good value for US$6 a double. The *Pension Monica* and the *Residencial Delfín* are among the cheapest at about US$2 per person. One of the best of the cheaper hotels is the *Pensión Laurita* which charges US$7/11 for singles/doubles with bath.

Other cheaper places include the *Northia Hotel* and the *Cabañas Don Jorge*.

The best and most expensive hotel is run in conjunction with SAN airline. This is the *Grand Hotel* which faces a beach at the east end of town. Until recently double rooms with private bath were about US$25 – I have received reports that prices have now doubled.

With the new airline services, more hotels are being opened.

There are basic restaurants and comedores in town. The best food is at the *Grand Hotel*. *Pensión Laurita* also has good (and cheaper) meals, the *Cafetería Tagu* is popular but pricey, and *Rositas Restaurant* serves tasty bacalao (a local fish). The *Restaurante Iris* has also been recommended.

Getting There & Away

SAN flights to Puerto Baquerizo Moreno cost the same as the TAME flights to Baltra. Departures from Quito via Guayaquil are daily except Thursday and Sunday – further information is given under Puerto Ayora. The airport is within walking distance of the town.

Getting Around

Bus There are a few buses a day from the capital to the farming centre of El Progreso, about eight km up into the highlands. From here it is possible to rent jeeps for the further 10 km to the visitor site of El Junco Lagoon. The road is being pushed eastwards and some buses go further than El Progreso.

Boat INGALA runs a twice weekly passenger boat service to Puerto Ayora, costing US$11 and leaving on Monday and Wednesday. The trip takes about four hours. Departure days are subject to frequent change and preference is given to islanders and Ecuadorians – therefore this is not a reliable way to get to Puerto Ayora if you are in a hurry. You can sometimes get a ride in fishing boats for about the same price. Tourist boats charging about US$30 to US$40 are also available; ask around.

Tours There are a few private boats in Puerto Baquerizo Moreno which can be hired for day trips and overnight trips, but there aren't too many travellers looking to share costs. Galasam is now operating many of its departures from Puerto Baquerizo Moreno. The 90-berth *Galápagos Explorer* is also based at Puerto Baquerizo Moreno. See the general section on Tours & Charters later.

PUERTO VELASCO IBARRA

This port is the only settlement on Isla Santa María (Floreana). There is not much to do in this tiny town – the population is about 100. There is a black beach nearby where there is a sea lion colony and there's a flamingo lagoon within walking distance. A road goes into the highlands – very little traffic but easy walking. See the earlier description of Isla Santa María for further information.

Places to Stay & Eat

There is a small hotel and restaurant run by the famous Margaret Wittmer and her family. They also have a small gift shop and post office. You can write for reservations (Señora Wittmer, Puerto Velasco Ibarra, Santa María, Galápagos – allow a couple of months) or just show up. They are rarely full, and even if they were, you could ask them to show you somewhere to crash. Rates are about US$20 per person per day including meals. There is nowhere else.

Getting There & Away

INGALA runs a boat every week on Monday, Tuesday and Wednesday making the triangular passage Puerto Ayora to Puerto Villamil, Isabela (Monday), Puerto Villamil to Puerto Velasco Ibarra (Tuesday) and back to Puerto Ayora (Wednesday). This schedule is liable to frequent change and preference is given to Ecuadorians – don't rely on this boat. Fishing boats and tourist boats also go there.

PUERTO VILLAMIL

This is a small port on Isabela, the largest island. There are a few hotels and basic restaurants but they are not visited much by

travellers, although some tours do stop here. This island is a marvellous one, with several active volcanoes and large numbers of Galápagos tortoises, and it looks like Isabela is going to become more important in Galápagos tourism in years to come. From Puerto Villamil, there is an 18-km road to the even tinier village of Santo Tomás where horses can be hired to continue up Volcán Santo Tomás. There are a couple of men in Puerto Villamil who work as guides – I don't know their names.

Places to Stay & Eat

The *Hotel Ballena Azul* in town is recommended for budget travellers. It charges about US$3.50 per person. Down on the beach is the *Hotel Alexander* which is roughly the same price and the *El Rincón del Bucanero* which is more expensive. There is also the *Tero Real* which has been recommended – I don't know the price but it's bottom to middle. The *Hotel Loja* on the road up to the highlands is fairly cheap, friendly and has been recommended.

The *Hotel Loja* has a good restaurant. The *Costa Azul* restaurant near the *Tero Real* has also been recommended. There are some cheap comedores in the port, but you need to ask them in advance to cook a meal for you – that gives you an idea of how few visitors there are.

Getting There & Away

INGALA runs a boat service from Puerto Ayora on Monday and on to Puerto Velasco Ibarra on Tuesday, but this cannot be relied upon.

Marcos Martínez in Puerto Ayora organises tours to Isabela, and fishing boats and tourist boats go there occasionally.

TOURS & CHARTERS

There are basically three kinds of tours to the Galápagos: day trips returning to the same hotel each night; hotel-based trips staying on different islands; and boat-based trips with nights spent aboard. Once you have decided on what kind of tour you want, you can either fly to the islands and find a tour there, or make reservations in advance on the mainland or through a travel agent in your home country. Public transport around the islands is very limited and so visiting the islands without taking a tour is a waste of time and money.

For detailed listings of boats, tours, Ecuadorian and US agencies, read *A Traveler's Guide to the Galápagos Islands*, by Barry Boyce, himself a tour operator. This book is very useful for those looking at more up-market tours but of little interest to the budget traveller.

Day trips

These are most often based in Puerto Ayora, although there are now a few day trip operators out of Puerto Baquerizo Moreno but the latter are reportedly more expensive. A typical day begins at dawn, with either a walk down to the dock or a bus ride across the island to meet a boat at the north side of Santa Cruz. Several hours are spent sailing to the visitor site(s), and the island is visited during the middle of the day with a large group. Only a few central islands are close enough to be visited on day trips.

Because a lot of time is spent going back and forth and because you don't have the chance to visit the islands early or late in the day, I do not enjoy these types of tours. The cheapest boats may be slow and over-crowded. Their visits to the islands may be too brief, the guides poorly informed and the crew lacking an adequate conservationist attitude. Therefore I do not recommend the cheapest day trips. Nevertheless, day trips are useful for some people who cannot stand the idea of sleeping in a small rocking boat at night.

There are plenty of day-trip operators in Puerto Ayora who charge around US$40 per person per day. The one you choose will depend on which destinations they offer. Talk to other travellers about how good the guide and boat are with any particular agency.

Better and more expensive day trips, using fast boats with knowledgeable guides and staying in good hotels, can be arranged in the mainland. These day trips are normally booked as a series of trips lasting a week, give a greater choice of islands to visit and are OK if you insist on day trips. Prices range from US$600 to US$1000 per week, including guided trips, hotel, meals, but not airfare and park fee. Book through Metropolitan Touring, which uses the Hotel Delfin in Puerto Ayora or Coltur which uses the Hotel Galápagos. Both agencies are listed under Quito. In Guayaquil, Isbella Agency (☎ 390 658, 396 393), Leonidas Plaza Dañín 802 (near the airport), uses several variously priced hotels. SAN airlines does day trips using the Hotel Grand in Puerto Baquerizo Moreno.

Hotel-based trips

These tours go from island to island and you sleep in hotels on three or four different islands (Santa Cruz, San Cristóbal, Floreana, Isabela). Tours typically last a week and cost US$600 to US$1000 per person, plus airfare and park fee. Personally, I find this preferable to day trips offered out of one hotel – but fewer companies offer this kind of tour. This kind of tour may be possible to arrange in Puerto Ayora more cheaply, but is usually arranged in advance. Coltur and Isbella agencies (mentioned under day trips) both are recommended. Also, Playa de Oro (☎ 543 221), 6 de Diciembre 2396 and La Niña, 5th floor, Quito, has recently began offering four-island tours.

Boat tours

Far more visitors (particularly non-Ecuadorians) tour the Galápagos on boat tours, sleeping aboard, than go on any kind of hotel-based tours. Tours can be from three days to three weeks; generally, though, tours from four to eight days are the most common. I don't think you can do the Galápagos justice on a tour lasting less than five days, and a full week is preferable. If you want to visit the outlying islands of Isabela and Fernandina, a two-week cruise is recommended. On the first day of a tour, you arrive from the mainland by air at about lunch time and so this is only half a day in the Galápagos; on the last day you have to be in the airport in the morning. Thus a five-day tour gives only three full days in the islands.

Boats used for tours range from small yachts to large cruise ships. By far the most common type of boat, however, is the motor sailer which carries about six to 12 passengers. Most people arrive in the islands with a pre-arranged tour; some people come hoping to hook up with a tour when they get there.

Tours when you get there It is cheaper to arrange a tour for yourself in Puerto Ayora than to pay for a pre-arranged tour from the mainland. The only exception to this is for the very few people who elect to look for a cargo or similar boat coming from Guayaquil – see under Getting There & Away in the Puerto Ayora section. Only the cheapest boats are available in the Galápagos. The better boats are almost always full with pre-arranged tours bought on the mainland. Therefore you shouldn't fly to the Galápagos hoping to get on a really good boat for less money – it rarely works that way.

Flying to the Galápagos and arranging a tour is frequently done but is not as straightforward as it sounds. It can take several days, or a week or more – though you may get very lucky and find a suitable boat leaving the next day. Therefore this is not an option for people with a limited amount of time, nor for people wanting a comfortable boat.

The best place to organise a tour for yourself is from Puerto Ayora. It is possible to do this in Puerto Baquerizo Moreno as well but there are few boats available and it is easier to try in Puerto Ayora.

Once you arrive in Puerto Ayora, first find somewhere to sleep (especially during the high season when the choice of rooms may be limited) and then you can start looking for a boat. If you are alone or with a friend, you'll need to find some more people as even the smallest boats take four passengers. There are usually people in Puerto Ayora

looking for boats and you should be able to get a group together in a few days.

The busiest times are June to August, December to January and around Easter – more travellers are looking but many of the boats are already full with pre-arranged groups. Finding boats in August and around Christmas and Easter is especially difficult.

The less busy months have fewer travellers on the islands but boats are most often being repaired or overhauled then, particularly in October.

Getting a group together and finding a boat involves checking the hotels and restaurants for other travellers and asking around for boats. If they have no business lined up, captains will be looking for passengers. Your hotel manager can often introduce you to someone. After all, almost everyone knows everybody else so word will quickly get around.

The cheapest and most basic boats are available for about US$50 per day per person and this should include everything. The cheaper the boat, the more rice and fish you can expect to eat, and the more crowded the accommodation.

Boats won't sail unless all passenger berths are taken – empty spots add to group space and comfort but must be paid for. Bargaining over the price is acceptable and sometimes necessary.

The most important thing is to find a boat whose crew you get along with and which has a good and enthusiastic naturalist guide who will be able to point out and explain the wildlife and other items of interest. It is worth paying a little more for a good guide. The cheapest boats may have Spanish-speaking 'auxiliary guides' whose function is to fulfil the legal obligation that every boat has a certified guide aboard. Some of these auxiliary guides know very little about the wildlife and simply act as rangers, making sure that groups stay together on the trails and don't molest the wildlife. (You cannot land without a guide and you must always walk around in more or less of a group.)

Owners, captains, guides, cooks, etc change frequently and, in addition, many boats make changes and improvements from year to year. Generally speaking, a boat is only as good as its crew. You should be able to meet the naturalist guide and captain and inspect the boat before you leave, and you should have an itinerary agreed upon with the boat owner or captain. You can deal with a crew member or boat representative during your search, but don't hand over any money until you have an agreed itinerary and then pay only the captain.

It is recommended that you have the itinerary in writing to avoid disagreements between you and other passengers and the crew during the cruise. Even with a written agreement, the itinerary may sometimes be changed, but at least it does give you some measure of bargaining power. The South American Explorers Club in Quito has a Galápagos information packet which is updated every year and includes a detailed contract, in Spanish/English, which is suitable.

Conditions can be cramped and primitive. Washing facilities vary from a bucket of sea water on the very cheapest boats to freshwater deck hoses or showers on the better boats. If you don't want to stay salty for a week, ask about washing facilities. You should also inquire about drinking water. I'd recommend treating the water on most of the cheaper boats or, alternatively, bring your own large containers of fresh water. Bottled drinks are carried but cost extra – agree on the price before you leave port and make sure that enough beer and coke is loaded aboard if you don't want to run out of your favourite refreshments.

Because a boat is only as good as the crew running it, it is difficult to make foolproof recommendations. However, two or more travellers have sent me recommendations for the following boats, though there are many others which are also good: *Cormorant, Española, Golondrina, Elizabeth II* and *San Juan*.

I have also received single recommendations for *Daphne, Aida Maria, Angelito* and *San Antonio*. The *Fenix* has received several good reports and a couple of bad ones. The *Flamingo* has also received mixed reports. No boats received consistently poor reports.

This is just a small selection. If you have a particularly good or bad experience with a boat, please write.

Pre-arranged tours If you don't have the time or patience then you can arrange tours from your home country (expensive but efficient) or from Quito or Guayaquil (cheaper but you sometimes have to wait several days or weeks during the high season).

If you are trying to economise, you may find that you can get a substantial discount by checking various agencies and seeing if they have any spaces to fill on departures leaving in the next day or two. This applies both to the cheaper and some of the more expensive tours. Particularly out of the high season, agencies may well let you travel cheaply at the last minute rather than leave berths unfilled. This depends on luck and your skill at bargaining.

The cheapest prearranged tours that I know of are sold by César Gavela at the Gran Casino Hotel in Quito. Departures are on limited dates and getting something suitable is largely a matter of luck – don't expect any luxury. The boats used are similar to those run by Galasam.

A little more expensive and with more frequent departure dates are the economy tours run by Galasam (Economic Galápagos Tours) and they will often sell you just an air ticket even if you don't want a tour. Galasam are in Quito and Guayaquil (see these sections for addresses). Their economy tours are suitable for budget travellers who don't want to organise their own tour once they get to the islands. Galasam have three levels of tours: economy, tourist and luxury.

Seven-day economy tours are aboard small boats with six to 12 bunks in double, triple and quadruple cabins. All bedding is provided and the accommodation is clean but spartan, with little privacy. Plenty of simple but fresh food and juice is served at all meals and an auxiliary guide accompanies the boat (few guides in the economy tours speak English).

There are toilets, and fresh water is available for washing of faces and drinking. Bathing facilities may be buckets of sea water, though showers are available on some boats. There are pre-set itineraries which visit most of the central islands and give enough time to see the wildlife.

I have received several letters criticising both the Gran Casino trips and the economy-class Galasam tours. Things go wrong occasionally, and when they do a refund is extremely difficult to obtain. Two friends from Canada wrote:

The first evening, our boat (the *Albatros*) just about sunk. We woke up to three feet of water in our cabins. Everything, luggage etc was floating around and the boat was beginning to tilt. We got onto a life boat and waited for them to pump out the *Albatros* and fix the hole. The next morning we continued on our five-day voyage in the same boat. We requested a new boat but to no avail. We were never given an explanation on why our boat just about sunk and the crew and guide would not just take us to Baltra as no one wanted to continue with the tour. They said the itinerary must go on. So no one, not even the crew, slept at night and the ocean was horribly rough. They were quite perverted, very unseaworthy and very unprofessional. The guide did not know anything and would take us to an island, we'd sit on the beach for an hour and then get back on the boat.

Since receiving this report, I have heard that the *Albatros* has been refitted – but I don't know for sure. Generally speaking, the cheaper the tour the less comfortable the boat and the less knowledgeable the guide. On the other hand, for every letter I get saying a tour was poor, I get another letter saying that they had a great trip which was good value.

One-week (eight days) economy tours cost about US$500 per person. There are weekly departures. Shorter and cheaper tours are available – four days for US$300 and five days for US$350. The US$80 park fee, airfare and bottled drinks are not included.

If you add up the cost of the cheapest one-week tour plus airfare and park fees, you get almost no change out of US$1000. Sorry, budget travellers, that's the way it is. My feeling is that if you're going to spend that much, the Galápagos are probably an important destination for you and you want to get as much out of it as possible. The economy-class boats are usually OK, but if something is going to go wrong, it's more likely to happen on the cheaper boats. If this is all you can afford and you really want to see the Galápagos, go! It'll probably be the adventure of a lifetime. But you might consider spending an extra few hundred dollars and go on a more comfortable, reliable boat and get a decent guide (though more expensive boats have their problems too!)

For about US$800 for eight days, you can take a tourist-class tour with Galasam or several other companies – the usual extra costs apply. Other companies with tours at about this price are Turgal (☎ 524 878, 553 658), Robles 653, Quito; Soleil Turismo (☎ 524 805, 553 658), Pinto 427, Quito; and Etnotur (☎ 230 552, 564 565), Cordero 1313, Quito. Etnotur's cheapest cruises have been criticised.

More luxurious tours are also available with other agencies which advertise in Quito and Guayaquil. These typically cost US$1000 or more per person per week, plus the usual extras. The most expensive boats are reasonably comfortable, have superb food and excellent crews. Many of these boats run pre-arranged tours with foreign groups and you are not likely to find these available for budget or independent travel. If you want this kind of luxury, then a good travel agent in Ecuador or at home will be able to help you with information. Normally, you can book a first-class trip in Quito or Guayaquil, particularly in the low season.

Galasam, Soleil Turismo, Etnotur and Metropolitan Touring all have some of the better boats.

Other recommended companies in Quito are Nuevo Mundo (☎ 552 617), Amazonas 2468; Samoa Turismo (☎ 239 892, 524 135), J L Mera 1140; and Turismo Galápagos (☎ 433 902, 235 841), Reina Victoria 100. In Guayaquil, try Trans Galápagos (☎ 326 517, 320 151), Colón 309.

Boats which are very good and recommended, but usually sold by charter only (ie you have to provide a whole group of eight to 12 passengers) include the *Sulidae* (☎ 201 376), PO Box 260, Guayaquil, and the *Andando* and *Cachalote*, Angermeyer's Enchanted Excursions (☎ 569 960, 231 713), Foch 769, Quito. I can personally attest to the excellence of these three boats.

There are two large cruise ships carrying 90 passengers. They have the advantage of having comfortable double cabins with private showers and are spacious and more stable than the smaller boats.

These cruise ships often appeal to older travellers. Each ship carries four expert naturalist guides and passengers divide into four groups landing on the islands at approximately half-hour intervals, thus avoiding the horrendous idea of trooping around a visitor site with 90 other people. Tours can be for three, four or seven nights.

The best known ship is the *Santa Cruz* which costs US$140 to US$240 per person per night, depending on your cabin and whether or not you share it. Information and reservations are available from Metropolitan Touring.

The newer *Galápagos Explorer* is operated by Canodros in Guayaquil and costs about the same. This boat has a pool and live entertainment in the lounge – one traveller reports that the naturalist guides were good but 'the atmosphere on board was a failed attempt at the *Love Boat*. A group of 50 bored European tourists didn't help – costume balls and 'lounge lizard' singers didn't quite make for the atmosphere we expected'. Both these boats can be booked via any good travel agent in most countries.

If you prefer to book a guided tour from the US I can personally recommend the Galápagos cruises run by Wilderness Travel (☎ (415) 548 0420, or toll-free (800) 247 6700), 801 Allston Way, Berkeley, CA 94710. Wildland Adventures (☎ (206) 365 0686, (800) 345 4453), 3516 NE 155th, Seattle, WA 98155 are also good. Other companies advertise in travel and nature-oriented magazines.

In Britain, a recommended choice is Galápagos Adventure Tours (☎ (01) 460

7908), 29 Palace View, Bromley, Kent BR1 3EJ which is run by David Horwell, who has written about the Galápagos and worked there as a naturalist guide.

When booking a tour, make absolutely sure that your cruise is not a hotel-based one with day trips to various islands (unless that is what you want). These tours are sometimes offered and it is not clear from the information that the itinerary involves overnights in Puerto Ayora – ask.

Finally, tipping. It is customary to tip the crew at the end of a trip. A tip may be anywhere between about US$20 and US$40 per passenger per week depending on the quality and cost of the tour. On an exceptionally good boat, you could tip more than US$40; on some of the cheapest boats passengers might tip less than US$20.

The total tip is divided among the crew; the guide (if an experienced bilingual naturalist) may get as much as half (definitely less for Spanish-speaking auxiliary guides who know little natural history). The cook and captain both get larger portions than the other crew members. It is best for the passengers to do the dividing – giving the money to one crew member and having that person deal with it is asking for complaints from other crew members.

Cruise Itineraries

You can go almost anywhere but it takes time to reach the more outlying islands. It is best to visit a few central islands and inspect them closely rather than trying to cram as many ports of call as possible into your cruise. Inter-island cruising will take up valuable hours of your time and you don't see very much while at sea. If you want to visit the largest island, Isabela, you'll have to allow two weeks.

Assuming you go for a cruise of four to seven days, the islands you should make an effort to visit so that you can see the most are the following: South Plaza, off the east coast of Santa Cruz, has sea lion, land iguana and swallow-tailed gull colonies, a cactus forest and good snorkelling. Isla Seymour, just north of Baltra, has both blue-footed booby and magnificent frigatebird nesting colonies. Black Turtle Cove, on the north shore of Santa Cruz, has marine turtles and white-tipped reef sharks.

Isla Bartolomé, on the east side of San Salvador, has a small volcanic cone which you can easily climb for one of the best views of the islands. Also there are penguins, sea lions and good snorkelling on Bartolomé.

On San Salvador (often known as Santiago or James) you can walk on a lava flow by Sullivan Bay on the east, and see marine iguanas, sea lions, fur seals, Galápagos hawks and many kinds of seabirds near Puerto Egas on the west. Rábida has a sea lion 'bachelor' colony as well as a small flamingo colony.

In addition to the species mentioned, you'll see common species almost everywhere. Masked and blue-footed boobies, pelicans, mockingbirds, finches, Galápagos doves, frigatebirds, lava lizards and red sally lightfoot crabs are so frequently seen that they'll become part of the normal surroundings to you.

If you have more time (say a full week) you could visit some of the other islands. The red-footed booby is found only on the more outlying islands such as Genovesa (Tower), San Cristóbal and the small islets surrounding Santa María (Floreana).

The waved albatross breeds only on Española (Hood) and the flightless Galápagos cormorant is found on the western islands of Isabela and Fernandina, which require a two-week trip.

Time to Go

The Galápagos can and are visited year-round (peak tourist periods have been discussed earlier). The wildlife is always there, and birds breed at different times so even within a single species you can see courting behaviour or young in nests in any month.

The big exception is the waved albatross as these birds leave en masse in mid-December and spend until late March at sea – avoid that period if seeing the albatrosses is important to you.

There are two seasons. The rainy season is from January to about June; the dry season is June to December. The rainy season has many warm sunny periods interspersed by rain showers and occasional heavy downpours – it is generally pleasant. February is the hottest month; March and April are milder.

Water temperatures are a balmy 23°C or 24°C and are great for snorkelling. The water is usually fairly calm. By May, water temperatures begin to drop and can be 20°C or even cooler by July.

The dry season is generally cooler and often misty. A warm sweater or jacket is needed at night. The ocean tends to get choppy in July and is often at its roughest from August to October.

Things to Bring

You can get most things in Puerto Ayora, but at a price. Little or nothing is available aboard the boats. You should bring all the film, sun tan lotion, insect repellent, books and medical supplies (including motion sickness medication) that you need. Sunglasses and a shade hat are recommended.

If you plan on doing a lot of snorkelling, it is best to have your own mask. Avid birders should bring binoculars. Shipboard life is casual and clothes should also be so. Be prepared to get wet during landings – shorts are a good idea because your legs dry faster than trousers (at least my legs do). Trails can be very rocky and the lava is extremely rough – sturdy shoes which can get wet are important (old tennis shoes are ideal). Bring a spare pair of footwear to keep dry and wear on the boat.

Galápagos Islands
Wildlife Guide

Galápagos Wildlife Guide

BIRDS

There are 58 resident bird species on the Galápagos, of which 28 are endemic. A further half a dozen regular migrants are frequently seen and about 25 other migratory species are regularly but not frequently recorded. Several dozen other species are accidental and rarely recorded. Many people are confused between a migrant, resident and endemic species. A resident lives and breeds in the island year round, but the species is also found in other parts of the world. A migrant is found in the island for only part of the year. An endemic species is a resident which does not normally breed anywhere else in the world (except in captivity or by accident).

Seabirds are the birds that make the most lasting impression on most visitors. Highly in evidence, spectacular and amusing, the seabirds of the Galápagos will turn everyone into a birdwatcher.

During a week of touring the islands, most careful observers will see about 40 species of birds. If two weeks are spent and some of the more outlying islands are visited, over 50 birds can be recorded, particularly during the northern winter when migrants are present. Even the most casual visitor will see 20 to 30 species. Enjoy your observations!

The birds described below are listed by family in standard taxonomic order. Latin family names can be recognised because they always end in -idae. Uncommon migrants and accidentals are mentioned in passing but not described. A checklist of the 58 resident birds plus six common migrants is provided at the end for you to record the species you see.

PENGUINS (SPHENISCIDAE)

The penguin family is found exclusively in the southern hemisphere. The single Galápagos species is therefore the most northerly penguin in the world.

Galápagos Penguin

Scientific name: *Spheniscus mendiculus*
Spanish name: *Pingüino de Galápagos*

Most penguins are associated with the colder regions of the southern hemisphere but the cool Humboldt current flowing from Antarctica along the South American coast enables the Galápagos penguin to live here – the most northerly penguin in the world. Although they normally breed on the western part of Isabela and Fernandina, a small colony is often seen by visitors to Bartolomé. They are occasionally present in Floreana or on Santiago (across from the visitor site on Sombrero Chino).

Breeding can occur year-round – two broods a

Galápagos Penguin (RR)

year are possible under good conditions. Colonies are small and not tightly packed with nests.

This flightless bird is one of five endemic seabirds in the islands. Penguins' clumsiness on land belies their skill and speed underwater. The best way to appreciate this is to snorkel with them – it is great fun but don't even think about trying to keep up with an underwater penguin!

ALBATROSSES (DIOMEDEIDAE)
One member of this family is a Galápagos resident but a couple of other species have been recorded.

Waved Albatross
Scientific name: *Diomedea irrorata*
Spanish name: *Albatros Ondulado*

One of the world's most magnificently graceful flying birds is the waved albatross which can spend years at sea without touching land. It is the largest bird in the islands, averaging 86 cm in length, up to a 240-cm wingspan, and reaching up to five kg in weight. Apart from a few pairs which have bred on the Isla de la Plata off the Ecuadorian coast, the entire world population of some 12,000 pairs nests on Española. Egg laying occurs from mid-April to late June and the colonies are active with parents feeding their single young through December. When the fledged bird finally leaves the nest, it does not return for four or five years. From January to March, all the birds are at sea.

The waved albatross engages in one of the most spectacular ritualised courtship displays of any bird. Courtship tends to occur in the second half of the breeding season, with October being the busiest month, but you may see it anytime that the colony is occupied. The display involves a perfectly choreographed 'dance' of up to 20 minutes of bowing, bill clicking, bill circling, swaying and freezing, honking and whistling. This is one of the most memorable of Galápagos sights.

TRUE PETRELS & SHEARWATERS (PROCELLARIIDAE)
Eight members of this family have been recorded in the Galápagos; the following two are the only residents and frequently seen.

Dark-rumped Petrel
Scientific name: *Pterodroma phaeopygia*
Spanish names: *Petrel Lomioscuro; Pata Pegada*

Audubon's Shearwater
Scientific name: *Puffinus lherminieri*
Spanish name: *Pardela de Audubon*

Waved Albatross pair grooming (RR)

Left: Audubon's Shearwater
Right: Hawaiian Petrel

The dark-rumped petrel is also called the Hawaiian petrel – in Hawaii it is in danger of extinction because of introduced predators. It is also endangered in the Galápagos but is better protected here. The Audubon's shearwater is widespread in tropical waters around the globe. Both species breed in the Galápagos, but are most frequently seen feeding at sea.

The birds are quite similar at first glance – black upperparts and white underparts. The dark-rumped petrel is 43 cm long and has a wingspan of over 90 cm – it is much larger than the commoner shearwater with a length of 30 cm and wingspan of less than 70 cm. Also, the petrel has a white cap whilst the shearwater is entirely black on top. These features are difficult to pick out when the birds fly by 100 metres away from your boat.

The best way to tell these birds apart when you see them at sea is by their flight. The petrel characteristically glides over the ocean in a series of swoops and banks, displaying the contrasting black and white body surfaces. It is more likely to be seen far out at sea, where it feeds on fish and squid. Shearwaters skim the waves much more directly, without the diagnostic swoops and banks of the petrel. The shearwaters are most likely seen closer to shore feeding on small crustaceans and fish larvae.

STORM PETRELS (HYDROBATIDAE)

The Galápagos has eight recorded and three commonly-seen species of storm petrels which are among the smallest of seabirds. The largest is only 20 cm long with a wingspan of 30 cm, or about the size of a swallow. Their diminutive size distinguishes storm petrels from the true petrels and shearwaters. They are locally called *golondrinas del mar*.

White-vented (Elliot's) Storm Petrel
Scientific name: *Oceanites gracilis*
Spanish name: *Paíño Gracil*

Wedge-rumped (Galápagos) Storm Petrel
Scientific name: *Oceanodroma tethys*
Spanish name: *Paíño de Galápagos*

Band-rumped (Madeiran) Storm Petrel
Scientific name: *Oceanodroma castro*
Spanish name: *Paíño Lomibandeado*

Storm petrels are dark with a white rump. The three species are distinguished by the differences in the shape of the white area – a job for an experienced birder or a good naturalist guide. They feed by grabbing scraps from the surface of the sea, which makes them look as if they are walking on water. The white-vented storm petrel, in particular, is often seen hanging around boats at anchor, looking for food.

Left: Band-rumped (Madeiran) Storm Petrel
Right: Wedge-rumped (Galápagos) Storm Petrel
Below: White-vented (Elliot's) Storm Petrel

The wedge-rumped and band-rumped storm petrels breed in huge colonies on Genovesa (Tower). These colonies are estimated to number hundreds of thousands but not much is known about them. Breeding colonies of the Elliot's white-vented storm petrel have yet to be discovered.

TROPICBIRDS (PHAETHONTIDAE)

Red-billed Tropicbird
Scientific name: *Phaethon aethereus*
Spanish names: *Rabijunco Piquirrojo, Piloto*

The unmistakeable red-billed tropicbird is one of the most spectacular of Galápagos seabirds. The most noticeable feature of this splendid white bird is its pair of long tail streamers – two elongated feathers often as long as the rest of the body. The birds are 76 cm long (including the tail feathers) and have a wingspan of just over one metre. They are extremely graceful in the air and often fly by in small groups, uttering a distinctive and piercing shriek. The coral-red bill and black eye stripe are noticeable at closer range. The birds nest in crevices and holes in cliffs or rock piles on most of the islands, but are most frequently seen from trails that follow cliff tops, such as on South Plaza, Genovesa (Tower) and Española (Hood). They feed far out to sea, plunge diving for fish and squid.

Red-billed Tropicbird on nest (RR)

PELICANS (PELECANIDAE)

Brown Pelican
Scientific name: *Pelecanus occidentalis*
Spanish name: *Pelícano Pardo*

The brown pelican is instantly recognisable with its huge pouched bill and large size (122 cm long and with a two-metre wingspan) and is often the first bird the visitor identifies. It feeds by shallow plunge diving and scoops up as much as 10 litres of water in its distendable pouch. The water rapidly drains out through the bill and the trapped fish are swallowed. It sounds straightforward but apparently it isn't. Although parents raise frequent broods of two or three chicks, many of the fledged young are unable to learn the scoop-fishing technique quickly enough and so starve to death.

As the name suggests, these pelicans are generally brownish in colour. During the breeding season, however, the adults gain bright white and chestnut markings on their heads and necks. They nest year-round in most of the islands.

The pelicans have wide fingered wings and are good gliders. They are often seen flying in a squadron-like formation, flapping and gliding in unison to create an elegant aerial ballet.

Brown Pelican on nest (RR)

BOOBIES (SULIDAE)

Four species of booby have been recorded and three of them breed in the islands. Although they are not endemic, they are still among the most popular birds visitors want to see. It is easy to understand why – their appearance is amusing and their colonies are among the most approachable in the islands. You can often get within a few feet of an active nest which will provide you with great photographs.

The boobies are in the same family as the gannets and look very much like them; they are fast fliers and exceptional plunge divers. Punta Pitt on San Cristóbal is the only visitor site where all three species are seen together.

Blue-footed Booby

Scientific name: *Sula nebouxii*
Spanish name: *Piquero Patas Azules*

Blue-footed Boobies (female with larger
pupil on right) (RR)

The blue-footed booby is perhaps the most famous Galápagos bird and is often the first booby seen by visitors. Large active colonies on Seymour and Española (Hood) are occupied throughout the year.

This large, whitish-brown seabird (length, 74 to 89 cm; wingspan, about 1½ metres) really does have bright blue feet which it picks up in a slow, most dignified fashion when performing a courtship display. Bowing, wing spreading, and sky pointing (with the neck, head, and bill stretched straight upwards) are also features of courtship. Watching this clownish behaviour is one of the highlights of any trip to the Galápagos.

At first glance, the males and females are almost identical but you can tell them apart: the larger females have a slightly bigger pupil and honk, whereas the males whistle. Courtship, mating and nesting occur year round – although nesting is a euphemism for a scrape on the ground surrounded by a ring of guano. The young, of which there may be one, two or three, are covered with fluffy white down which can make them look larger than their parents. In a good year, all three young may survive – otherwise the strongest one or two will outcompete the youngest, which dies of starvation.

Masked Booby

Scientific name: *Sula dactylatra*
Spanish names: *Piquero Enmascarado; Piquero Blanco*

Masked Boobies courtship display (JW)

The masked (white) booby is pure white with a black band at the edges of the wings and the end of the tail. The face mask which gives the bird its name is formed by a blackish area of bare skin surrounding the bill, which can be yellow or pinkish. It is the biggest of the Galápagos boobies (76 to 89 cm long; 152 to 183-cm wingspan). This booby is found on most of the islands.

Breeding is on an annual cycle (unlike the other boobies) but the cycle varies from island to island. On Genovesa (Tower), the birds arrive in May, courtship, mating and nest building ensue and eggs are laid from August to November. Most of the young have fledged by February and the colony is out at sea until May. On Española (Hood), the colony is present from September to May, with egg-laying occurring from November to February.

Males and females look the same but their calls differ – the smaller males whistle whilst the females utter a trumpeting quack. They often nest near cliff tops to give themselves an advantage when taking off – they are large birds. Two eggs are laid but the older sibling ejects the younger from the nest and only one survives, even in a good year with plenty of food.

Red-footed Booby
Scientific name: *Sula sula*
Spanish name: *Piquero Patas Rojas*

Red-footed Booby (RR)

The red-footed booby is the smallest of the Galápagos boobies (74 cm long; 137-cm wingspan) and is readily distinguished by its red feet and blue bill with red base. Most adults are brown, but about 5% are white – this is a different colour phase and does not represent a new, different or hybrid species. The red-footed is the most numerous of the Galápagos boobies but also the least frequently seen; this is because it is found only on the more outlying islands, such as Genovesa (Tower) where there is a sizable colony estimated at 140,000 pairs. It feeds far out to sea and thus avoids competing with the blue-footed booby which feeds close inshore and the masked booby which feeds intermediately.

The nesting behaviour of this booby is quite different from the others. It builds rudimentary nests in trees (as opposed to the guano-ringed scrapes on the ground of the other boobies) and lays only one egg. This usually happens when food is plentiful, and can occur at any time of year.

CORMORANTS (PHALACROCORACIDAE)

Flightless Cormorant
Scientific name: *Nannopterum harrisi*
Spanish name: *Cormorán No Volador*

Apart from the penguins, there is only one other flightless seabird found in the world. This is the flightless cormorant, which is endemic to the Galápagos. At about 90 cm long it is the tallest of the world's 29 species of cormorant and the only one which has lost its ability to fly. It is found only on the coasts of Isabela and Fernandina.

Flightless Cormorant

Male Frigatebird displaying colourful pouch

Great Frigatebird (female) (RR)

To see this unique bird, you should plan on a two-week tour. If you think that is a long time, consider the time it must have taken for flightlessness to evolve in this cormorant. Its ancestors were almost certainly able to fly, but when they reached the Galápagos, they found no predators in the rocky inshore shallows where they fed. Therefore they didn't need wings to flee, and the cormorants that survived the best were the streamlined ones which could swim and dive strongly in the surf of the shallows. Thus birds with small wings and strong legs were selected for and eventually the flightless cormorant evolved.

Flightless cormorants nest in small colonies and there are only about 700 to 800 pairs of birds in existence. That number dropped to 400 to 500 pairs after the disastrous El Niño year of 1982/83, though they have recovered since. Flightless cormorants are not endangered, but could become so if predatory feral animals (especially wild dogs) are introduced into the islands where they breed.

The birds can breed year-round, though March to September is favoured for egg-laying. Unlike most seabirds, the adults do not mate for life. Indeed, a female may well leave a brood to be raised by the father whilst she mates with another male; thus a female may have two broods a year.

FRIGATEBIRDS (FREGATIDAE)

Magnificent Frigatebird
Scientific name: *Fregata magnificens*
Spanish name: *Fragata Magna*

Great Frigatebird
Scientific name: *Fregata minor*
Spanish name: *Fragata Grande*

The two frigatebird species in the Galápagos are not easy to tell apart. Both are large, elegant and stream-lined black seabirds with long forked tails. They make an acrobatic living by aerial piracy, often harassing smaller birds into dropping or regurgitating their catch and then swooping to catch their stolen meal in midair. This occurs because frigatebirds have a very small preening gland and are not able to secrete enough oils to waterproof their feathers – therefore they cannot dive underwater to catch prey. They are, however, able to catch fish on the surface by snatch-ing them up with their hooked beaks. With their 230 cm wingspan, the birds are magnificent fliers and have the largest wingspan to weight ratio of any bird.

As with many Galápagos seabirds, frigatebird courtship display is quite spectacular. The males have flaps of bright red skin hanging under their necks and these are inflated into football-sized bal-loons to attract females. It takes about 20 minutes to fully inflate the pouch and the male normally sits on a tree and displays skywards to passing females.

Occasionally, a male is seen flying overhead with his pouch still distended – a strange sight.

North Seymour Island has a constantly active magnificent frigatebird colony and is the place where most people get a good look at these birds. There are colonies on many of the other islands. Great frigatebirds tend to go further out to sea and are found more often on the outer islands; recommended locations are Isla Genovesa (Tower) and Punta Pitt, Isla San Cristóbal. Telling the all-black males apart is problematical – the magnificent frigatebird, at 107 cm in length, is about 5 cm longer than the great frigatebird. This is almost impossible to tell in the field. Also, the male magnificent has a metallic purplish sheen to its black plumage while the great has a greenish sheen – again, it takes an experienced eye to tell the difference.

Great Frigatebird Colony, male adult with young (RR)

Females are easier to tell apart. Magnificent females have white underparts with a black throat and also have a thin blue eye-ring. Great females have white underparts, including the throat, and have a reddish eye-ring. Once you identify the females, you can assume that their mates are of the same species. Immature birds of both species, in addition to white underparts, also have white heads.

HERONS & EGRETS (ARDEIDAE)

This family has five species resident in the islands and three other species have been recorded. There is controversy among ornithologists about naming and classifying some of these birds.

Great Blue Heron

Scientific name: *Ardea herodias*
Spanish names: *Garzón Azulado, Garza Morena*

This is the largest heron in the Galápagos (138 cm long; almost two-metre wingspan) and will be familiar to visitors from North and Central America. Despite its name, it is a mostly grey bird but is easily recognised with its long legs and great size. Like many members of this family, it often stands with its head hunched into its shoulders – it always flies this way, with the legs trailing behind.

Great blue herons are found along the rocky coasts of most of the islands, often standing motionless as they wait for a fish to swim by, although they also will take lizards, young marine iguanas and birds for food. They tend to be solitary or in pairs, but occasionally form a small colony of up to six nests. They breed year round and often nest in mangroves.

Great Blue Heron (RR)

Common Egret

Scientific name: *Casmerodius albus*
Spanish names: *Garceta Grande, Garza Blanca*

Common Egret (RR)

Lava Heron (RR)

Yellow-crowned Night Heron (RR)

This bird is also known as the Great Egret or the American Egret. The scientific name of *Egretta alba* has also been assigned to this bird. It is a large (102 cm long; 137-cm wingspan) all-white heron with a yellow bill and black legs and feet. It is less common than the great blue heron but found in similar habitats, and occasionally inland.

Cattle Egret
Scientific name: *Bubulcus ibis*
Spanish names: *Garcilla (Garza) Bueyera*

This small white heron (51 cm long; 91-cm wingspan) is distinguished from the common egret at a distance by its shorter neck and stockier appearance. Closer up, the yellow legs and feet can be seen. This bird came originally from Africa and southern Eurasia and was unknown in the Americas until the 1800s. It was first recorded in the Galápagos in 1965 and is now common in pasturelands, especially in the highlands of Santa Cruz where the birds are most often seen.

Lava Heron
Scientific name: *Butorides sundevalli*
Spanish names: *Garcilla de Lava, Garza Verde*

This small (41 cm long; 64-cm wingspan) dark heron is the only endemic one in the Galápagos. Its dark green plumage camouflages it well against the lava shorelines where it stealthily hunts for prey. It has yellow/orange legs. They breed year round, although September to March is the preferred time. Immature birds are brown and streaked. Their nests are usually solitary (occasionally in twos and threes) and found under a lava outcrop or in mangrove trees. They are common on the rocky shores of all the islands, but because of their camouflage and solitary nature, are a little difficult to see – your naturalist guide should be able to show you one with no problem.

The striated heron *(Butorides striatus)* is about the same size but paler than the lava heron. Ornithologists are uncertain if the lava heron is simply a variety of the striated heron, or whether the two can hybridise, or whether they are distinct species.

Yellow-crowned Night Heron
Scientific name: *Nyctanassa violacea*
Spanish names: *Garza Nocturna, Garcilla Coroniamarilla*

This common heron tends to feed at night, but can often be seen during the day in shaded areas along the coasts of all the islands. It is a stocky, grey heron with a black and white head and yellow crown. Because of its nocturnal habits, its eyes are larger than other herons. It is 61 cm long and has a 117-cm wingspan. They breed in single pairs and build nests year round in mangroves or under rocks.

FLAMINGOS (PHOENICOPTERIDAE)

Greater Flamingo
Scientific name: *Phoenicopterus ruber*
Spanish name: *Flamenco*

These large (122 cm long; 152-cm wingspan), long-necked, pink shorebirds are immediately recognisable. Their wing feathers are black and the birds look spectacular in flight with their long necks stretched out, legs trailing, and black and pink markings flapping contrastingly. They are nervous birds, however, particularly when nesting, and visitors should act quietly when viewing flamingos or they may desert their nests. This is one bird for which a long telephoto lens is very useful in photography.

Flamingos breed in small colonies in salty lagoons. They build cone-shaped nests out of mud and lay a single egg in a depression at the top of the nest. They can breed year-round but prefer moist conditions and so most breeding takes place in the wet season (January to May). There are commonly-visited flamingo lagoons on Santa María (Floreana), Rábida and Santiago (James) islands.

Flamingo feeding behaviour is mildly bizarre – they feed by dangling their long necks into the water and swinging their upside down heads from side to side. Water is sucked in through the front of the highly specialised bill and filtered through sieves before being expelled through the sides of the bill. Food consists of insects, small crabs, shrimps and other crustaceans – the pinkish colour of the shrimps maintains the colour of the birds' plumage.

Greater Flamingo (RR)

DUCKS & GEESE (ANATIDAE)
Three species of ducks have been recorded in the Galápagos; only one breeds here.

White-cheeked Pintail
Scientific name: *Anas bahamensis*
Spanish names: *Patillo, Anade Cariblanco*

If you see a duck in the Galápagos it is usually the white-cheeked pintail which breeds in small numbers on salt lagoons and ponds on most of the major islands. It can be seen year-round.

White-cheeked Pintails (RR)

HAWKS (ACCIPITRIDAE)
Apart from the hawks, ospreys (Pandionidae) and peregrine falcons (Falconidae) visit occasionally.

Galápagos Hawk (RR)

Galápagos Hawk
Scientific name: *Buteo galapagoensis*
Spanish name: *Gavilán de Galápagos*

This endemic hawk is the only raptor which breeds in the islands. It is 56 cm long and has a 122-cm wing-span, and has much broader wings than similarly-sized seabirds. The birds are dark brown with yellow legs, feet and ceres (the fleshy area at the base of the bill). Immature birds are lighter and heavily mottled.

These predatory birds have no natural enemies and are relatively fearless. This has led to their extinction by hunters on several islands, including Santa María (Floreana), San Cristóbal, Seymour, Baltra, Genovesa (Tower) and Daphne. They have been severely reduced on Santa Cruz and just over 100 pairs are estimated to remain in the Galápagos. Santiago (James), Bartolomé, Española (Hood), Santa Fe, Fernandina and Isabela are the best islands on which to see them.

Breeding occurs year-round but is most frequent from May to July. The birds practice cooperative polyandry, where a single female has two or more mates and all the adults help in raising the young. It is not easy to separate the sexes, but the female is generally larger than the males.

RAILS, CRAKES & GALLINULES (RALLIDAE)
The three Galápagos species are common but are rarely seen because they are small and secretive. Brief descriptions of these are given.

Galápagos Rail
Scientific name: *Laterallus spilonotus*
Spanish names: *Pachay, Polluela de Galápagos*

This tiny (15 cm long) dark, endemic bird scurries around in the vegetation of the highlands, particularly Santa Cruz and Santiago (James). It has white spots on its wings. It rarely flies and escapes by running.

Paint-billed Crake
Scientific name: *Neocrex erythrops*
Spanish names: *Gallareta, Pollula Pinta*

Slightly larger (20 cm), this dark bird is similar to the rail but lacks the white wing spots and has red legs and a red and yellow bill. The crake, too, dislikes flying. It is associated with farmlands, particularly on Santa Cruz and Santa María (Floreana). It was first recorded in the islands in 1953.

Common Gallinule
Scientific name: *Gallinula chloropus*
Spanish names: *Gallinula, Gallareta Común*

Paint-billed Crake

This chicken-like waterbird (also called the common moorhen) is 35 cm long and is quite cosmopolitan. It is black, with a red and yellow bill, yellow legs, and a white patch under the tail. It lives on a few ponds and brackish areas of water in all the larger islands except Santiago (James). When swimming, it pumps its head back and forth in a characteristic way.

OYSTERCATCHERS (HAEMATOPODIDAE)

American Oystercatcher
Scientific name: *Haematopus palliatus*
Spanish names: *Ostrero Americano, Cangrejero*

This 46-cm-long black and white shorebird has a stout, red, eight-cm long bill, pink feet and yellow eyes, making it quite unmistakeable. Although there are only between 100 and 200 pairs in the islands, they are spread out along the rocky coasts and you are likely to see them on many of the islands. The first sign of their presence is often their repetitive, high-pitched call, described as 'kleep' in some books.

They nest mainly from October to March and are solitary nesters. One or two precocial young are hatched which join their parents within a few minutes.

PLOVERS (CHARADRIIDAE)
Plovers are small, compact, wading shorebirds which tend to run in short bursts. Their bills are generally small and pigeon-like. Six or seven species

American Oystercatcher (RR)

have been recorded in the Galápagos, all migrants. The two most common ones may remain year-round in small numbers and are described below.

Semi-palmated Plover
Scientific name: *Charadrius semipalmatus*
Spanish name: *Chorlitejo semipalmado*

This 18-cm-long shorebird is mainly brown above except for a white collar, forehead and stripe above the eye. Most of the underneath is white except for a brown chest band. Breeding birds may have a black band and head. The base of the bill is orange and the legs are yellowish. It is most commonly seen on sandy beaches from August to April.

Semi-palmated Plover

Ruddy Turnstone
Scientific name: *Arenaria interpres*
Spanish name: *Vuelvepiedras Rojizo*

This 23-cm-long shorebird is found on rocky coasts where it feeds, as its name suggests, by turning over small stones in search of prey. It is common from August to March and has a brown back, white chin and throat, and white underparts with a brownish breast patch. In breeding plumage (not often seen in the Galápagos) it has a black and white patterned head and chest, bright russet back, and white underparts. The legs are orange. Some authorities suggest that the turnstones are sandpipers, not plovers.

SANDPIPERS (SCOLOPACIDAE)
Sandpipers are an extremely varied family of shorebirds. Most are waders and generally have longer necks and beaks and are slimmer than the plovers. Some 22 species have been recorded from the Galápagos, all migrants which breed in the northern hemisphere. The four species described below are commonly seen from August to April; a few individuals remain year-round.

Wandering Tattler
Scientific name:*Heteroscelus incanus*
Spanish name: *Correlimos Vagabundo*

This 25-cm-long shorebird is the most frequently seen migrant but is rather nondescript. It has dark brownish-grey upperparts and breast, white belly and yellowish-green legs. It prefers rocky shores.

Sanderling
Scientific name: *Calidris alba*
Spanish name: *Correlimos Arenero*

Sanderlings (RR)

These common 20-cm-long shorebirds are the palest of the small Galápagos waders. They prefer sandy beaches where they run along the wave fronts like a flock of clockwork toys. They have light grey backs, dark wing tips, and white underparts. The legs and bill are dark. In breeding plumage, the head and upperparts are a rusty brown.

Whimbrel

Scientific name: *Numenius phaeopus*
Spanish name: *Zarapito Trinador*

This common wader is about 43 cm long and has a characteristic down-curved bill which is as much as 10 cm long. The dark legs are also long – long is the operative word in identifying this shorebird. It has a mottled grey-brown plumage, and light and dark stripes through the head. Unlike most other waders, it shows no wing patterns in flight.

Northern Phalarope

Scientific name: *Phalaropus lobatus*
Spanish name: *Falaropo Picofino*

These birds (also called red-necked phalaropes) swim rather than wade and may be seen some way out at sea in 'rafts' of hundreds of birds. These 18-cm-long birds have a blackish back with a pair of whitish longitudinal streaks, and white underparts. There is a conspicuous white wing-bar in flight. The bill is very thin.

STILTS (RECURVIROSTRIDAE)

Black-necked Stilt

Scientific name: *Himantopus himantopus*
Spanish names: *Tero Real, Cigüeñuela Cuellinegra*

This elegant black and white wader is also called the common stilt. It is slightly smaller (38 cm) than the oystercatcher, from which it is easily distinguished by its very slim shape, long red legs, and slim black bill.

It is most frequently seen alone or in pairs, wading in lagoons. Stilts are solitary breeders and lay four eggs in a scrape at lagoon edges during the wet season. They are noisy, especially in flight.

GULLS, TERNS & SKUAS (LARIDAE)

There are two resident gull species, both endemic to the Galápagos, and two resident terns, neither of which are endemic. In addition, three other gull, four other tern and four skua species have been occasionally or rarely recorded.

Swallow-tailed Gull

Scientific name: *Creagrus furcatus*
Spanish name: *Gaviota Blanca, Gaviota Tijereta*

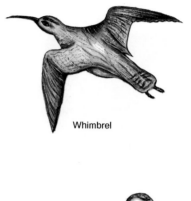

Whimbrel

Northern Phalarope

Swallow-tailed Gulls (RR)

The lovely swallow-tailed gull is grey and white with bright red feet and legs and a crimson eye-ring. It is 51 cm long and has a 114-cm wingspan. This bird feeds at night and is the only nocturnal gull in the world – its eyes are larger than in most other gulls. It is frequently seen perched on cliff tops during the day. Although a few pairs nest on an island off Colombia, almost the entire world population nests in the Galápagos and therefore the swallow-tailed gull is considered endemic.

Swallow-tailed gulls nest in colonies near small cliffs and beaches and can be seen on most major islands except the far western ones. Their breeding cycle lasts about nine or 10 months and so nesting can be seen at any time of year. There are about 10,000 to 15,000 pairs in the islands.

Lava Gull (RR)

Lava Gull

Scientific name: *Larus fuliginosus*
Spanish names: *Gaviota Morena, Gaviota de Lava*

The lava gull is the rarest gull in the world – only about 400 pairs are estimated to exist. Despite this, you have a very good chance of seeing one because they are widely distributed in the Galápagos. They are about 53 cm long and are generally dark grey to black with white eyelids. They are solitary nesters and breed throughout the year.

Brown Noddy

Scientific name: *Anous stolidus*
Spanish names: *Nodi, Charrán Pardo*

Brown Noddy Tern (RR)

The brown noddy tern is, as its name suggests, generally dark brown with a whitish forehead and is often seen feeding with pelicans. It may catch fish scraps from the water draining out of a pelican's bill and even perch on the pelican's head to better enable it to reach the food. This bird is 38 cm long and has a 76-cm wingspan. It nests in small colonies on cliffs and in caves at any time of year.

Sooty Tern

Scientific name: *Sterna fuscata*
Spanish name: *Gaviotín Sombrió*

The black and white sooty tern also breeds in the Galápagos, but is restricted to Isla Darwin in the far north and so is rarely seen.

PIGEONS (COLUMBIDAE)

Galápagos Dove

Scientific name: *Zenaida galapagoensis*
Spanish names: *Paloma, Tórtola de Galápagos*

This pretty little 20-cm-long dove is endemic. The underneath is reddish, the upperparts are brownish, and there are green neck patches, blue eye rings, and red legs and feet – a colourful bird.

Breeding occurs year-round. Two eggs are laid in a haphazard nest of grass and twigs under a rock or in an abandoned nest of another species. When incubating, adults may walk away from a nest feigning injury, to lure predators away from the nest – this behaviour evolved long before doves arrived in the Galápagos and has been retained, even though it was of little advantage in the islands.

CUCKOOS & ANIS (CUCULIDAE)
Two species of cuckoos and two of anis have been recorded; one of each is common.

Dark-billed Cuckoo
Scientific name: *Coccyzus melacoryphus*
Spanish names: *Cuclillo Piquioscuro, Aguatero*

About half of this 28-cm-long bird is tail – long tails are characteristic of this family. It is a dark brown-grey bird with a light underside with a yellowish wash, white tail tips, and black beak and legs. The cuckoo is reasonably common but secretive – therefore its low, chuckling call is heard more often than the bird is seen. It is commonly found only on Santa Cruz, San Cristóbal, Santa María (Floreana), Isabela and Fernandina. The nesting season is January to May.

Groove-billed Ani
Scientific name: *Crotophaga sulcirostris*
Spanish name: *Garrapatero Piquiestriado*

The groove-billed ani was introduced to the islands in the 1960s and it is now seen regularly in the Santa Cruz highlands where it probably breeds. The similar looking smooth-billed ani *(C. ani)* was recorded in the same area during the 1980s. Both birds are all black, about 30 cm long, and with a distinctively long, floppy tail. Telling them apart is not easy.

OWLS (TYTONIDAE & STRIGIDAE)
The two families of owls are each represented by one species in the Galápagos.

Barn Owl
Scientific name: *Tyto alba*
Spanish names: *Lechuza Campanaria, Lechuza Blanca*

This small (25 cm long) owl is found all over the world. The almost white, heart-shaped facial disk is the most striking feature of this pale owl which, because of its nocturnal habits, is rarely seen. It is most common on

Galápagos Dove (RR)

Short-eared Owl (RR)

Vermilion Flycatcher (RR)

Fernandina but also has been recorded from Santa Cruz, Isabela, Santiago (James) and San Cristóbal.

Short-eared Owl
Scientific name: *Asio flammeus*
Spanish names: *Lechuza de Campo, Buho Orejicorto*

This owl is much larger (36 cm long; 94-cm wing-span) and darker than the barn owl. Also, it is diurnal and so is seen much more often. It is found on all the main islands but is least common on Fernandina and most common on Santa Cruz and Genovesa (Tower) where it is frequently seen hunting in the storm petrel colonies. Owls have specialised feathers which enable them to fly and glide soundlessly – a great advantage when hunting small birds, rodents and lizards. They can breed year round but prefer the wet season. They nest on the ground in heavy vegetation and are territorial.

TYRANT FLYCATCHERS (TYRANNIDAE)

Vermilion Flycatcher
Scientific name: *Pyrocephalus rubinus*
Spanish names: *Mosquero Bermellón, Brujo*

This adult male is tiny (about 13 cm long) but quite unmistakeable with its bright red crown and under-parts. The upperparts, tail and eye stripe are almost black. Females are brown above and yellowish beneath; the chest is almost white and lightly streaked.

The vermilion flycatcher is widespread in the high-lands of most islands, though it is occasionally seen by the coast. The trees and shrubs around the col-lapsed calderas of Los Gemelos, in the Santa Cruz highlands, is a good place to see this bird.

They are territorial and like to breed during the rainy season. Small nests are built in trees in the highlands.

Large-billed (Galápagos) Flycatcher
Scientific name: *Myiarchus magnirostris*
Spanish names: *Papa Moscas, Copetón Piquigrande*

This endemic bird is seen more frequently than the vermilion flycatcher. It is about 15 cm long, and is grey and brown with a yellowish belly, although less yellow than the female vermilion flycatcher. The large-billed flycatcher is found in drier and lower areas than the vermilion flycatcher and is widespread on all the main islands except Genovesa (Tower).

SWALLOWS & MARTINS (HIRUNDINIDAE)
Five species of this family have been recorded, but only one is resident.

Galápagos (Southern) Martin
Scientific name: *Progne modesta*
Spanish names: *Martín Sureño, Golondrina*

This 16-cm-long bird is very dark, with a shallowly forked tail and pointed wings. The female is dark brown; the male is glossy black. They have a characteristic flight of a few quick flaps followed by a glide. The dark plumage, small size, typical flight, and pointed silhouette identify this martin. Martins are less common in the northern islands but are distributed throughout the Galápagos. They hunt for insects on the updrafts from cliffs and highlands.

MOCKINGBIRDS (MIMIDAE)
The fearless and endemic mockingbirds are often seen on all the islands except Pinzón (which has no mockers). These birds are a classic example of adaptive radiation – there are four species descended from a common ancestor which look very similar to one another, except for their bills which differ in size and shape. The mockingbirds are 25 to 30 cm long, streaked grey and brown, with a long tail and curved bill. So how do you tell them apart? Very easily, it turns out. They are most easily separated by their geographic distribution.

The mockingbirds lay from two to four eggs from October to April – two broods may be raised during this period. The birds are territorial and build nests of twigs in trees, shrubs or cacti. Occasionally, they are cooperative breeders, with three or more adults raising a brood.

Galápagos Mockingbird
Scientific name: *Neosomimus parvulus*
Spanish name: *Sinsonte de Galápagos*

This bird is found on all the central and western islands except the ones mentioned later.

Charles Mockingbird
Scientific name: *Nesomimus trifasciatus*
Spanish name: *Sinsonte de Floreana*

This bird was originally found on Santa María (Floreana, Charles) but is now extinct on that island. About 150 birds are left on the nearby islets of Champion and Gardner-near-Floreana.

Hood Mockingbird
Scientific name: *Nesomimus macdonaldi*
Spanish name: *Sinsonte de Española*

Large-billed (Galápagos) Flycatcher (RR)

Galápagos Mockingbird (RR)

Hood Mockingbird (RR)

Yellow Warbler (RR)

One of Darwin's Finches (RR)

Sharp-beaked Ground Finch

This mocker is the largest of the four species and has a noticeably heavier bill than the others. It is easily found, but only on Española (Hood) and the nearby islet of Gardner-near-Hood.

Chatham Mockingbird
Scientific name: *Nesomimus melanotis*
Spanish name: *Sinsonte de San Cristóbal*

This species is endemic to San Cristóbal (Chatham) where it is common.

WOOD WARBLERS, TANAGERS, BLACKBIRDS etc (EMBERIZIDAE)
There are at least four species of emberizids recorded from the Galápagos, of which only one is resident or commonly seen.

Yellow Warbler
Scientific name: *Dendroica petechia*
Spanish names: *Canario, Reinita Amarillo*

This tiny (only 13 cm long) warbler is the only bright yellow bird in the Galápagos. It is yellow below and greenish olive above; the male has fine reddish streaks on the chest. It occurs throughout the Galápagos, from the coasts to the highlands.

Although they lay eggs only from December to April, they defend territories throughout the year.

FINCHES (FRINGILLIDAE)
The 13 Darwin's finches are the most famous and biologically important birds of the Galápagos. Some visitors find them disappointing; they certainly are not very spectacular to look at.

Darwin's finches are all endemic and everyone will see some of them – although it takes an expert to be able to tell them apart. All 13 species are thought to have descended from a common ancestor and their present differences in distribution, body size, plumage, beak size and shape, and feeding habits helped Darwin formulate his evolutionary theories.

The best islands to separate three of the species is Española (Hood). Here, you'll find only the warbler finch (with its tiny warbler-like bill), the small ground finch (with its small finch-like bill) and the large cactus finch (with a massive bill). After that, the going gets more difficult. There are tree finches which are seen on the ground, ground finches which are seen in the trees, and cactus finches which may be seen in all sorts of places apart from cacti.

If you want to see all thirteen species, you'll need to do some travelling. The medium tree finch is found only in the highlands of Santa María (Floreana). The mangrove finch is found only on Isabela and Fernandina. The large cactus finch is found only on Genovesa (Tower) and Española (Hood) of the islands with visitor sites. The other finches are more widely distributed.

The most famous of these birds is the woodpecker finch, which sometimes grasps a twig in its bill and pokes this 'tool' into holes and cracks in dead trees or bark. With some perseverance, the bird may extract a grub or other prey which it would otherwise not have been able to reach. This remarkable example of tool use is very rare among birds. Mangrove finches have also been recorded to do this.

It is beyond the scope of this guide to describe individually all 13 finches adequately enough to enable you to identify them. If your tour guide is a very good naturalist, she or he will help you. Otherwise, get Harris' field guide – he has about 25 pages on the finches alone. And remember what Harris writes: 'It is only a very wise man or a fool who thinks he is able to identify all the finches which he sees.'

Large Cactus Finch (RR)

Small Ground Finch
Scientific name: *Geospiza fuliginosa*
Spanish name: *Pinzón Terrestre Chico*

Medium Ground Finch
Scientific name: *Geospiza fortis*
Spanish name: *Pinzón Terrestre Mediano*

Large Ground Finch
Scientific name: *Geospiza magnirostris*
Spanish name: *Pinzón Terrestre Grande*

Cactus Finch on prickly pear cactus flower (RR)

Sharp-beaked Ground Finch
Scientific name: *Geospiza difficilis*
Spanish name: *Pinzón Terrestre Piquiagudo*

Cactus Finch
Scientific name: *Geospiza scandens*
Spanish name: *Pinzón Cactero Chico*

Large Cactus Finch
Scientific name: *Geospiza conirostris*
Spanish name: *Pinzón Cactero Grande*

Vegetarian Finch
Scientific name: *Platyspiza crassirostris*
Spanish name: *Pinzón Vegetariano*

Small Tree Finch
Scientific name: *Camarhynchus parvulus*
Spanish name: *Pinzón Arbóreo Chico*

Vegetarian Finch

Small Tree Finch

Warbler Finch (RR)

Medium Tree Finch
Scientific name: *Camarhynchus pauper*
Spanish name: *Pinzón Arbóreo Mediano*

Large Tree Finch
Scientific name: *Camarhynchus psittacula*
Spanish name: *Pinzón Arbóreo Grande*

Woodpecker Finch
Scientific name: *Camarhynchus pallidus*
Spanish name: *Pinzón Artesano*

Mangrove Finch
Scientific name: *Camarhynchus heliobates*
Spanish name: *Pinzón Manglero*

Warbler Finch
Scientific name: *Certhidea olivacea*
Spanish name: *Pinzón Reinita*

REPTILES

The prehistoric-looking reptiles found all over the islands are easily approached and observed. There are 22 species, belonging to five families. Of these, all but three species are endemic.

TORTOISES (TESTUDINIDAE)

Giant Tortoise
Scientific name: *Geochelone elephantopus*
Spanish name: *Tortuga Gigante, Galápagos*

The most famous of the reptiles is, of course, the endemic giant tortoise for which the islands are named. There is only one species which has been divided into 14 subspecies – three of these are extinct. One of the best ways to distinguish them (apart from geographic distribution) is by differences in the shape of their carapaces (shells). These differences contributed to Darwin's thoughts whilst he was developing his theory of evolution.

Many thousands of tortoises were killed by whalers and sealers, particularly in the 18th and 19th centuries, and now only some 15,000 remain. A breeding project at the Charles Darwin Research Station appears to be successful and it is hoped to begin re-introduction of animals into the wild. The easiest way to see both tiny yearlings and full-grown adults is at the research station. Although they are in enclosures, visitors are permitted to enter and get a close look at these giants, some of which can reach a weight of 250 kg – or 3000 times more than newborn hatchlings, which weigh only about 80 g. The Research Station is one of the few places where you can actually touch the animals. To see tortoises in the wild you can go to the tortoise reserve on Santa Cruz, visit the Los Galápagos visitor site on San Cristóbal, or climb Volcán Alcedo on Isabela.

The tortoises are vegetarians and have slow digestive systems – a meal can take up to three weeks to pass through. Scientists guess that the tortoises' life span is about 150 years, but records have not been kept for long enough to know for certain. Sexual maturity is reached at about 40 years of age (now you know why they say 'Life begins at forty!') Mating usually occurs towards the end of the rainy season. The males posture and shove other males in contests of dominance and then try to seek out a suitable mate – unsuccessful males have been known to attempt to mate with other males or even with appropriately shaped boulders!

Once mated, the females look for dry and sandy areas in which to make a nest. They dig a hole about 30 cm deep with their hind legs – this may take several days. Anywhere from two to 16 eggs are laid, and covered with a protective layer of mud made from soil mixed with urine. The eggs take about four to five months to develop and hatchlings usually emerge between December and April.

Giant Tortoise (JW)

MARINE TURTLES (CHELONIIDAE)
Leatherback and hawksbill turtles have been occasionally recorded in the Galápagos but only the green sea turtle is a resident breeder.

Pacific Green Sea Turtle
Scientific name: *Chelonia mydas*
Spanish name: *Tortuga Marina*

This marine turtle breeds and lays eggs in the Galápagos, but it is not endemic to the islands. Green sea turtles are quite promiscuous and during the breeding season, especially November to January, much mating activity can be observed in the water.

Nesting occurs at night on many of the sandy beaches of the islands and occurs mainly from December to June, with a peak around February. The females dig a hole in the sand above the high tide mark and deposit several dozen eggs – a process which takes about three hours. Once the eggs hatch, the hatchlings are very vulnerable to predation. They try and get to the ocean and then swim off for years – almost nothing is known about this period of their lives. Turtles seem to have great navigational skills – they return to nest at the same beach where they were hatched. Tagged adults have been recovered as far away as Costa Rica.

Pacific Green Sea Turtle (RR)

The adult turtles are huge and may reach 150 kg in weight. Snorkellers sometimes see them swimming underwater and it is an exciting sight to watch such a large animal come flapping serenely by.

IGUANAS & LIZARDS (IGUANIDAE)

The most frequently seen reptiles are the iguanas, of which there are three species, all endemic. There are seven endemic species of lizards.

Marine Iguana

Scientific name: *Amblyrhynchus cristatus*
Spanish name: *Iguana Marina*

The marine iguana is the only sea-going lizard in the world and is found on the rocky shores of most islands. This iguana has a blackish skin, which in the males can change to startling blues and reds during the breeding season. Breeding occurs at different times on different islands; the males on Española (Hood) are colourful year-round. Marine iguanas are colonial (often piling up one on top of the other) but when breeding, the larger males become territorial and aggressive, butting and pushing their rivals. Mated females lay two to four eggs in a sandy nest – these nests are guarded by the mothers although the hatchlings, which emerge after three or four months, are not given much parental protection.

Marine iguanas feed mainly on intertidal sea-weeds, although mature males have been recorded offshore at depths to 12 metres and can remain

Marine Iguana (RR)

submerged for an hour or more. The row of spines along the entire length of their backs, their scaly skins, their habit of occasionally snorting little clouds of salt spray into the air, and their length – which can reach almost a metre – makes them look like veritable little dragons.

Galápagos Land Iguana
Scientific name: *Conolophus subcristatus*
Spanish name: *Iguana Terrestre*

Santa Fe Land Iguana
Scientific name: *Conolophus pallidus*
Spanish name: *Iguana Terrestre de Santa Fe*

The two species of land iguanas look almost alike. They are yellowish in colour and bigger than their marine relatives – adults weighing six kg have been recorded. The Galápagos land iguana is found on Isabela, Santa Cruz, Fernandina, Seymour and South Plaza islands, with South Plaza being the best place to see them. They were formerly found on most of the other islands but hunting and competition with introduced animals (goats, rats, pigs, dogs), which prey on the eggs, has caused their demise on many islands. The similar looking Santa Fe land iguana is limited to that island only. It is slightly bigger, on average, than the Galápagos land iguana and is somewhat yellower with more pronounced spines. They can exceed a metre in length.

Galápagos Land Iguana under prickly pear cactus (RR)

The preferred food of both species is the prickly pear cactus and the iguanas are sometimes seen standing on their rear legs in efforts to reach the succulent pads and yellow flowers. Their mouths are incredibly leathery, enabling them to eat the cactus pads whole without removing the spines.

Land iguanas are known to live for at least sixty years. They reach sexual maturity between six and ten years of age. Mated females lay from five to 15 eggs and, as in the marine iguana, they defend their nests until hatching occurs. Land iguanas breed in different months on different islands.

Santa Fe Land Iguana (JW)

Lava Lizard
Scientific name: *Tropidurus spp*
Spanish name: *Lagartija de Lava*

Less spectacular than the iguanas, but also endemic, are the seven species of lava lizard which are frequently seen scurrying around. They can reach 30 cm in length but are usually smaller. Their most distinctive behavioural patterns are rapid head-bobbing and push-up stances to defend their territories and assert dominance. The male is larger and strongly patterned with yellow, black, and brown. The female is less strongly patterned but makes up for this by a flaming red throat.

Male Lava Lizard (RR)

It is easy to separate the seven species of lava lizard by geographical distribution. Six islands have their own endemic species that are found nowhere else in the world. These are *T. bivittatus* on San Cristóbal, *T. grayi* on Santa María (Floreana), *T. habellii* on Marchena, *T. delanonis* on Española (Hood), *T. pacificus* on Pinta and *T. duncanensis* on Pinzón. *T. albemarlensis* is found on most of the other islands except for Genovesa (Tower), Wolf, and Darwin which have no lava lizards.

GECKOS (GEKKONIDAE)

Less often seen are the small, harmless, nocturnal lizards called geckos, of which there are seven species (five endemic). They are often associated with human habitations and may be seen near houses at night. Geckos have adhesive pads on their digits and can climb vertical walls and even walk upside down on ceilings. Again, geographical distribution helps with separating the species. *Phyllodactylus bauri* is limited to Santa María (Floreana) and Española (Hood); *P. galapagoensis* is on Santa Cruz, Isabela, Santiago (James) and Daphne Major; *P. barringtonensis* is only on Santa Fe; *P. gilberti* is only on Wolf. All four are endemic. There are three other species of gecko on San Cristóbal, but only one is endemic. These three are *P. tuberculosis, P. leei* and *Gonatodes collari* – this last often lives in houses and has recently been introduced.

SNAKES (COLUBRIDAE)

Finally, you may see the Galápagos snake, which is small, drab and non-poisonous. There are three species, all of the genus *Dromicus*, all endemic, all of the constrictor type, and they are difficult to tell apart. The adults reach a length of one metre and they are not dangerous. Many visitors spend a week touring the islands without even glimpsing one.

Galápagos Snake (RR)

MAMMALS

In the Galápagos, the mammals are poorly represented because they had greater difficulty in surviving a long ocean crossing. There are but six native mammals, of which two are seals, two are bats, and two are rice rats. Other land mammals are introduced species gone wild and they create a major nuisance to the native species by preying on them and by competing for food resources. They include feral goats, pigs, burros, cats, dogs, rats and mice.

PLAINNOSE BATS (VESPERTILIONIDAE)

There are two bat species, which probably flew across or were blown over in a storm. The hoary bat *(Lasiurus cinereus)* is well-known in North America but the endemic Galápagos bat *(Lasiurus brachyotis*) has been little studied. Bats are occasionally seen flying around lampposts in the island towns. The Spanish for bat is *murciélago*.

MICE & RATS (CRICETIDAE)
Two endemic species of rice rat are found in the Galápagos. *Nesoryzomys narboroughii* is on Fernandina and *Oryzomys bauri* is on Santa Fe. Visitors occasionally catch a glimpse of these small rodents running around the trails of the appropriate island. These mammals probably floated across on vegetation rafts. It's thought that there were once seven species of rice rat, but five have become extinct since humans introduced the black rat.

EARED SEALS (OTARIIDAE)
Members of this family have external ears, use their front flippers for swimming, and can turn the hind flippers forward to enable them to 'walk' on land (true seals, Phocidae, can't do this). Both seal species found in the islands are members of the Otariidae.

Galápagos Sea Lion
Scientific name: *Zalophus californianus*
Spanish name: *Lobo Marino*

The native mammal you'll see the most of is the Galápagos sea lion, which is a subspecies of the Californian sea lion and found on most islands. There are an estimated 50,000 individuals in the Galápagos. The territorial bulls, which can reach 250 kg, are quite aggressive and sometimes chase swimmers out of the water. They have been known to bite if harassed so don't approach them too closely. The females and young, on the other hand, are extremely playful and you can often watch them swimming around you if you bring a mask and snorkel.

Sea lions live up to 20 years. Females are sexually mature at five years; males are capable of mating then, too, but don't do so until they are older. Dominant males patrol and guard particularly attractive beaches – these territories may contain up to 30 females. The dominant male has mating access to these females, but only for as long as he is able to keep other males away. Defending a territory is very demanding work and males may go for days without getting much food or sleep. After several weeks of this, a fresh new male may challenge and beat a harem-master and take over his position.

Females become sexually receptive once a year. Gestation lasts nine months and the (usually) single pup is born around the beginning of the dry season. The mother nurses the pup for almost a week before returning to the water to feed; thereafter, she will continue to nurse the pup after fishing trips until the pup is five or six months old, when it will begin to learn to fish for itself. Even then, pups will continue to

Sea Lion and pup (RR)

Sea Lion and pup on Sombrero Chino
(RR)

Galápagos Fur Seals (RR)

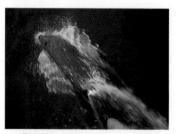

Dolphin surfing bow wave (JW)

supplement their diet with milk, and some females may nurse two pups from different years.

Galápagos Fur Seal
Scientific name: *Arctocephalus galapagoensis*
Spanish name: *Foca Peletera, Lobo de Dos Pelos*

The endemic fur seals are less commonly seen than the sea lions, which superficially they resemble. On closer inspection, however, fur seals are quite different from sea lions. Fur seals are smaller, and have a broader, shorter shape of the head which supposedly resembles a bear's, hence the scientific name. (Arcto means bearlike and cephalus means head in Greek.) Fur seals' ears are a little more prominent and they have larger front flippers than sea lions.

Their fur is very dense and luxuriant, being made of two layers of hair. This attracted the attention of sealers who decimated the population in the 1800s whilst hunting for the valuable skins. Because of their thick fur, the animals like to hide out in cool caves during the heat of the day and hunt at night. This secretive behaviour helped the species survive the sealers depredations. Today, fur seals are fully protected and have recovered – there are almost as many fur seals as sea lions but the more secretive habits of the former explains why fur seals are seen less frequently by visitors.

Fur seals' social and breeding behaviour is quite similar to sea lions' – one difference is that fur seal males tend to defend territory from the land whilst sea lion males defend from the water.

The best place to see fur seals is Puerto Egas on Isla Santiago.

WHALES & DOLPHINS (Order CETACEA)
Other marine mammals you may see when cruising between the islands are whales and dolphins. There are seven whale species regularly recorded in the archipelago but they are difficult to tell apart because they are normally glimpsed only momentarily and from a distance. The seven species are the finback, sei, humpback, minke, sperm, killer, and pilot whales.

Bottle-nosed dolphins *(Tursiops truncatus)* are often seen surfing the bow waves of the boats. If seen at night, the dolphins cause the ocean to glow with bioluminescence as they stir up thousands of tiny phosphorescent creatures which glow when disturbed. Less frequently seen are the common *(Delphinus delphis)* and spinner *(Stenella caerulleoalba)* dolphins.

FISH

Scientists have recorded 307 species of fish from 92 families in the Galápagos and it is expected that more will be discovered. Over 180 of these fish are found in much of the tropical eastern Pacific and about 50 are endemic. Merlen's *Field Guide to the Fishes of Galapagos* is available in Quito and recommended for snorkellers. This booklet describes and illustrates 107 of the most frequently seen species.

It is interesting that many species of tropical fish change their colour and shape as they age and a few can even change their sex midway through life. This certainly makes identification confusing!

Snorkelling in the Galápagos is a rewarding experience and schools containing thousands of tropical fish are routinely seen. Some of the naturalist guides working on the boats can help identify the more common species. These include blue-eyed damselfish, white-banded angelfish, yellow-tailed surgeonfish, moorish idols, blue parrotfish, concentric puffer fish, yellow-bellied triggerfish and hieroglyphic hawkfish – to name but a few and to give you some idea of the variety in form and colour.

The one type of fish that swimmers are often the most interested in is the **shark** (in Spanish, tiburón). There are several species found here and the most common are the white-tipped reef shark *(Triaenodon obesus)* and the Galápagos shark *(Carcharhinus galapagensis)*. Hammerheads *(Sphyrna lewini)* are also occasionally seen. For some reason, the sharks of the Galápagos have never been known to attack and injure a human swimmer.

They are often seen by snorkellers and their speed and grace underwater is almost otherworldly. In fact, one of the best reasons to snorkel in the Galápagos is the chance of seeing these magnificent animals in reasonable safety. Despite this reassurance, you should leave the water if you cut or graze yourself.

Another kind of fish which provides the snorkeller with a real thrill is the **ray.** Again, there are several species; all harmless with the exception of the stingray *(Urotrygon spp)*, which sometimes basks on the sandy bottoms of the shallows and can inflict an extremely painful wound to waders and paddlers. It is a good idea to enter the water by shuffling your feet along the sandy bottom – this gives stingrays the chance to swim away before you step on them.

Other rays are found in slightly deeper water and are often camouflaged on the sandy bottom. My first ray sighting was of a spotted eagle ray *(Aetobatus narinari)* which lay on the bottom motionless and almost invisible. As I swam over it, the fish suddenly broke loose of the sand and flapped away giving me a real shock. The sight of a metre-wide ray gently undulating through the water is quite mesmerising. Sizable schools of beautiful golden coloured mustard

Moorish Idol

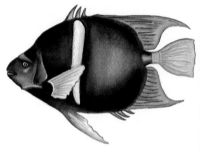

White-banded Angelfish

rays *(Rhinoptera steindachneri)* are also seen quite regularly.

Less frequently seen is the giant manta ray *(Manta hamiltoni)* which is found in deeper offshore waters. You are most likely to catch sight of one as it leaps out of the water and falls back with a loud slap – with a maximum spread of six metres they make a huge splash as they hit the water.

INVERTEBRATES

The remaining animals encountered in the Galápagos do not possess a backbone and are hence collectively called invertebrates. The most common phyla include the Poriferans (sponges), Coelenterates or Cnidarians (jellyfish, sea anemones and corals), Molluscs (snails, chitons, shellfish, and octopuses), Arthropods (insects, spiders, barnacles, crabs, and lobsters), and Echinoderms (starfish, sea urchins, and sea cucumbers). There are other phyla which are less frequently encountered.

The first invertebrate which most visitors notice is the **Sally Lightfoot crab** *(Grapsus grapsus)*. This small crab is bright red above and blue below and ubiquitous on almost every rock beach.

Also present on rock beaches is a small black crab which blends well with the lava background. These well camouflaged small black crabs are young Sally Lightfoots. The adults are far from camouflaged and rely on their alertness to escape predators. If you try and approach them, they will run away and are even capable of running across the surface of the water in tide pools. The crabs will, however, approach you if you sit as still as a rock. This is the strategy of the herons which prey on the Sally Lightfoots. Often you'll see a lava heron standing motionless on rocky beach. When a crab comes within reach, the bird will lunge forward and, if successful in capturing a crab, will then proceed to shake it and bang it against rocks until the legs fall off before devouring the animal.

Other crabs are found on sandy beaches. These are the pale coloured **ghost crabs** *(Ocypode spp)* which stare at you with unusual eyes at the end of long eye stalks. They leave the characteristic pattern of sand balls which are seen on most sandy beaches. In tide pools, you may see the **hermit crab** *(Calcinus explorator)* which lives in an empty sea shell which it carries around. As a young crab outgrows its protective shell, it finds a larger one to grow into. This 'moving house' occurs several times before the hermit crab reaches adult size.

At low tides, **tide pools** offer a good opportunity to study marine invertebrates. Starfish, sea anemones, sea urchins, marine snails, barnacles, chitons, and limpets are often found.

As you go further into the water with a mask and

Sally Lightfoot Crab (RR)

snorkel, you can see many more species including sea cucumbers, octopuses, and corals and, if you care to poke around some of the rocky underwater crevices, lobster.

Be careful where you poke though, because you may encounter the **sea urchin**, *Diadema mexicana*, which has beautiful iridescent black spines which are long, brittle and needle sharp.

Less painful encounters with sea urchins can be had with *Eucidaris thouarsii* which has blunt pencil-like spines which often break off and are washed ashore, sometimes forming a large part of a beach.

The endemic green *Lytechnicus semituberculatus* urchin is also common and despite its prickly appearance, can be held quite easily and its tiny tube feet examined.

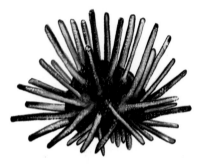

Sea Urchin

Sea urchins' prickly ball appearance belies their taxonomic grouping. They are in fact radially symmetrical in five or more planes and are hence members of the same phylum as the starfish and the sand dollar – the **Echinoderms.** The sand dollar looks like a flattened disc which has a starfish pattern on it. The starfish themselves are immediately recognisable but come in a fascinating array of sizes, colours, shapes, and numbers of arms ranging from five to many. The sea cucumbers are also Echinoderms. They lie on the bottom and look unfortunately similar to turds.

The phyla **Coelenterates** are represented by **sea anemones** which are stationary creatures which capture their food by waving stinging tentacles in the water. These tentacles do not create enough sting to hurt you, should you brush against one in a tide pool or shallow area.

Because of their appearance and the fact that they don't move from place to place, they are sometimes nicknamed 'sea-flowers'.

Swimming Coelenterates are represented in the islands by **jellyfish** which also capture prey using stinging tentacles. These can be quite painful should you come into contact with them, but fortunately, jellyfish aren't often seen in the main swimming spots.

Corals are also Coelenterates but there are not many in the Galápagos. The Devil's Crown off Isla Santa María is one of the best places to see living coral.

Sea Biscuit or Sand Dollar

Dead coral is often found washed up ashore and sometimes forms a large part of a beach.

Insects are the most numerous animals in the world and literally millions of species are found in the tropics. A little over 1000 species are described from the Galápagos, and this comparatively small number reflects the difficulty that insects had in crossing almost 1000 km of ocean to colonise the islands.

There are not many colourful insect species. There are a few species of butterflies, ants, grasshoppers, and wasps, and many more representatives of the beetle and moth groups.

There is one species of bee, one preying mantis,

and two scorpions in the Galápagos. The scorpions (which are more closely related to spiders than insects but like them are in the Arthropod phyla) are rarely encountered and though their sting can be painful, they are not normally dangerous.

Of the other biting insects, mosquitoes, horse flies, and midges are found and can sometimes make beach sunbathing unpleasant. Fortunately, these insects do not fly far and nights spent aboard a boat anchored several hundred metres off shore will usually be insect free. And if they're not, just anchor a few hundred metres further off.

PLANTS

Between 700 and 800 species of vascular plants have been recorded in the Galápagos, of which over 250 species are endemic. In addition, about 500 non-vascular plants (mosses, lichens, and liverworts) have been described. There are six different vegetation zones, beginning with the shore and ending with the highlands. These zones are the Littoral, Arid, Transition, Scalesia, Miconia, and Fern-Sedge. Each zone supports different and distinctive plant species.

The **littoral zone** contains species such as mangroves, saltbush and sesuvium. These plants are characterised by their ability to tolerate relatively high quantities of salt in their environment.

Immediately beyond the littoral zone is the **arid zone** where many of the islands' cactus species are found, including forests of the giant prickly pear cactus. Trees such as the ghostly looking palo santo, the palo verde, and the spiny acacias are found here as well as the yellow cordia shrub (with yellow flowers).

The **transition zone** has decreasing numbers of the arid zone trees and increasing numbers of lichens, perennial herbs, and smaller shrubs. The vegetation is both varied and thick and no particular plants are dominant.

In the higher islands, the transition zone gives way to a cloud forest type vegetation where the dominant tree is the endemic **Scalesia.** The trees are covered with smaller plants such as mosses, bromeliads, liverworts, ferns, and orchids.

Next is a treeless high altitude layer characterised by dense endemic **Miconia** shrub, liverworts, and ferns. This Miconia zone is found only on the south slopes of Santa Cruz and San Cristóbal.

Finally, the **fern-sedge zone** is the highest and contains mainly ferns and grasses, including the Galápagos tree fern which grows to three metres in height.

It is beyond the scope of this book to delve more deeply into the many hundreds of plant species and the reader is referred to Schofield (1984), Jackson (1985), and Wiggins & Porter (1971).

BIRD SPECIES IN THE GALÁPAGOS

	Species	Sighted	Date	Notes
*	Galápagos Penguin	☐		
*	Waved Albatross	☐		
R	Dark-rumped Petrel	☐		
R	Audubon's Shearwater	☐		
R	White-vented Storm Petrel	☐		
R	Band-rumped Storm Petrel	☐		
R	Wedge-rumped Storm Petrel	☐		
R	Red-billed Tropicbird	☐		
R	Brown Pelican	☐		
R	Blue-footed Booby	☐		
R	Masked Booby	☐		
R	Red-footed Booby	☐		
*	Flightless Cormorant	☐		
R	Great Frigatebird	☐		
R	Magnificent Frigatebird	☐		
R	Great Blue Heron	☐		
R	Common Egret	☐		
R	Cattle Egret	☐		
*	Lava Heron	☐		
R	Yellow-crowned Night Heron	☐		
R	Greater Flamingo	☐		
R	White-cheeked Pintail	☐		
*	Galápagos Hawk	☐		
*	Galápagos Rail	☐		
R	Paint-billed Crake	☐		
R	Common Gallinule	☐		
R	American Oystercatcher	☐		
M	Semi-palmated Plover	☐		
M	Ruddy Turnstone	☐		
M	Wandering Tattler	☐		
M	Sanderling	☐		
M	Whimbrel	☐		
M	Northern Phalarope	☐		
R	Black-necked Stilt	☐		
*	Swallow-tailed Gull	☐		
*	Lava Gull	☐		
R	Brown Noddy	☐		
R	Sooty Tern	☐		
*	Galápagos Dove	☐		
R	Dark-billed Cuckoo	☐		
R?	Groove-billed Ani	☐		
R	Barn Owl	☐		
R	Short-eared Owl	☐		
R	Vermilion Flycatcher	☐		

*	Galápagos Flycatcher	☐			
*	Galápagos Martin	☐			
*	Galápagos Mockingbird	☐			
*	Charles Mockingbird	☐			
*	Hood Mockingbird	☐			
*	Chatham Mockingbird	☐			
R	Yellow Warbler	☐			
*	Small Ground Finch	☐			
*	Medium Ground Finch	☐			
*	Large Ground Finch	☐			
*	Sharp-beaked Ground Finch	☐			
*	Cactus Finch	☐			
*	Large Cactus Finch	☐			
*	Vegetarian Finch	☐			
*	Small Tree Finch	☐			
*	Medium Tree Finch	☐			
*	Large Tree Finch	☐			
*	Woodpecker Finch	☐			
*	Mangrove Finch	☐			
*	Warbler Finch	☐			

REPTILE SPECIES IN THE GALÁPAGOS

	Species	Sighted	Date	Notes
*	Giant Tortoise	☐		
R	Pacific Green Sea Turtle	☐		
*	Marine Iguana	☐		
*	Galápagos Land Iguana	☐		
*	Santa Fe Land Iguana	☐		
*	Lava Lizard (7 species)	☐		
*	Gecko (5 species)	☐		
R	Gecko (2 species)	☐		
*	Galápagos Snake (3 species)	☐		

MAMMAL SPECIES IN THE GALAPÁGOS

	Species	Sighted	Date	Notes
R	Hoary Bat	☐		
*	Galápagos Bat	☐		
*	Santa Fe Rice Rat	☐		
*	Fernandina Rice Rat	☐		
R	Sea Lion	☐		
*	Galápagos Fur Seal	☐		
R	Whales (7 species)	☐		
R	Dolphins (3 species)	☐		

Key: * Endemic
      R Resident
      M Migrant

Index

MAPS

Ambato 184
Azogues 238
Baños 190
Babahoyo 316
Bahía de Caráquez 339
Catamayo 252
Coca 285
Cuenca & the Southern
    Highlands 218
Cuenca
    Centre 220
    Cuenca Area 232
Ecuador 12-13
    Internal Air Services 86
    Locator 9
Esmeraldas 328
Galápagos Islands 400-401
    Visitor Sites 407
Gualaceo 235
Guaranda 202

Guayaquil
    Centre 362-363
    Guayaquil Area 359
Ibarra 158
Jipijapa 350
La Libertad 382
Lago Agrio 292
Latacunga 176
Loja 244
Macará 254
Macas 265
Machala 388
Manta 346
North Coast, The 319
North of Quito 142
Northern Oriente, The 269
Otavalo 144
    Otavalo Area 153
Playas 378
Portoviejo 342

Puerto Ayora 420
Puyo 272
Quevedo 312
Quito
    New Town 98-99
    Old Town 106
    Quito Area 134
Riobamba 206
Salinas 384
Santo Domingo de los
    Colorados 308
South Coast, The 357
South of Quito 172
Southern Oriente, The 257
Tena 274
Tulcán 166
Western Lowlands 303
Zamora 259

TEXT

Map references in **bold** type

(Gal) - Galápagos Islands

Academy Bay (Gal) 418
Achupallas 215-216
Agato 152-154
Agoyan Falls 199
Agua Blanca 352
Aguas Verdes, Peru 396
Ahuano 282-284
Alandaluz 354
Alausí 213-215
Alluriquín 306
Ambato 182-188, **184**
Angamarca 181
Apuela 156
Arapicos 267
Archidona 277
Area Nacional de Recreación
    (National Recreation Area):
    Boliche 174
    Cajas 231-234
    Yamburaro 250
Arenillas 393
Atacames 332-333
Awa Ethnic & Forestry Preserve
    321

Ayangue 386
Azogues 236-239, **238**

Babahoyo 315-317, **316**
Baeza 300-301
Bahía de Caráquez 338-340, **339**
Bahía de Manta 349
Balzar 314
Baños 189-199, **190**
Baños de San Vicente 381
Baños, Cuenca 231
Bellavista (Gal) 406
Black Turtle Cove (see Caleta
    Tortuga Negra)
Bolívar 336
Bomboiza 261
Borbón 322-324
Bucay 215
Buccaneer Cove (Gal) 412

Cajabamba 212
Calceta 344
Calderón 137
Caleta Tortuga Negra (Gal) 408
Camarones 326
Cañar 239
Canoa 338
Catacocha 253

Catamayo 251-252, **252**
Cayambe 141
Cerro Crocker (Gal) 406
Chanduy 381
Charles Darwin Research Station
    (Gal) 405, 418, 454
Chical 169, 170
Chimborazo 211-212
Chone 344
Chordeleg 235-236
Chota 164
Chugchilán 181
Coca 284-287, **285**
Cochasquí 140-141
Cojimíes 336-337
Colombian Border 295
Concepción 323
Conway Bay (Gal) 408
Cornejo Astorga 306
Cotacachi 155
Crucita 349
Cuenca 217-231, **220**, **232**
Cueva de los Tayos 262-263

Darwin Bay Beach (Gal) 414
Devil's Crown (Gal) 412, 463
Durán 377-379
Dureno 296-297

Ecuador-Colombia Border 168
El Altar 200
El Carmen 344
El Chaco 300
El Cisne 252-253
El Junco Lagoon (Gal) 410
El Pangui 261
Elizabeth Bay (Gal) 416
Empalmé 314
Esmeraldas 326-331, **328**
Espumilla Beach (Gal) 412

Fauna (see Wildlife
    (Galápagos))
Flavio Alfaro 344
Flora (see Wildlife (Galápagos))
Flotel Orellana 297
Frigatebird Hill (Gal) 410

Galápagos Islands 397-466, **400-
    401, 407**
Galápagos Wildlife Guide 433-
    466
Gardner Bay (Gal) 411
Girón 241
Guagua Pichincha 139
Gualaceo 234-235, **235**
Gualaquiza 261-262
Guamote 213
Guano 212
Guaranda 201-204, **202**
Guayaquil 356-377, **359, 362-363**
Guayllabamba 140

Hacienda Primavera 287-288
Huaquillas 394-395

Ibarra 156-162, **158**
Ilinizas 171-173
Ilumán 152, 154
Ingapirca 239-241
Intag Cloud Forest Reserve
    154
Ipiales, Colombia 168
Islas (Islands):
    Abingdon (see Isla Pinta)
    Albemarle (see Isla Isabela)
    Baltra (Gal) 408-409
    Barrington (see Isla Santa Fe)
    Bartolomé (Gal) 413, 432
    Bindloe (see Isla Marchena)
    Champion (Gal) 453
    Charles (see Isla Santa María)
    Chatham (see Isla San
        Cristóbal)
    Culpepper (see Isla Darwin)
    Darwin (Gal) 417
    De la Plata 352
    Duncan (see Isla Pinzón)

Española (Gal) 410-411, 432
Fernandina (Gal) 416, 432
Floreana (see Isla Santa
    María)
Genovesa (Gal) 414, 432,
    437, 439, 441, 444, 450,
    452
Hood (see Isla Española)
Indefatigable (see Isla Santa
    Cruz)
Isabela (Gal) 414-416, 426,
    432
James (see Isla San Salvador)
Jervis (see Isla Rábida)
Lobos (Gal) 410
Marchena (Gal) 414, 458
Mosquera 409
Narborough (see Isla
    Fernandina)
Pinta (Gal) 406, 414
Pinzón (Gal) 41
Rábida (Gal) 413-14, 432
Salango 355
San Cristóbal (Gal) 409-410,
    425-426, 432
San Salvador (Gal) 412-413,
    432
Santa Cruz (Gal) 405-408,
    418-425
Santa Fe (Gal) 409
Santa María (Gal) 411-412,
    426, 432
Santiago (see also James and
    Isla San Salvador)
Seymour (Gal) 409, 432
Sombrero Chino (Gal) 413,
    432
South Plaza (Gal) 408, 432
Tower (see Isla Genovesa)
Wenman (see Isla Wolf)
Wolf (Gal) 417, 458
Islas Daphne (Gal) 409
Islas Plazas (Gal) 408, 432

Jama 337
Jambelí 392
Jaramijó 349
Jatun Sacha 284
Jipijapa 350-351, **350**
Julcuy 352

Kicker Rock (see León
    Dormido, Galápagos)

La Balbanera 213
La Ciénega 173
La Esperanza 163

La Libertad 383-385, **382**
La Paz 164
La Selva Jungle Lodge 288-289
La Tola 325-326
Lagarto 326
Lago Agrio 291-295, **292**
Laguna de Colta 213
Laguna de Cuicocha 155-156
Laguna San Pablo 143, 154
Laguna Yaguarcocha 164
Lagunas de Mojanda 154
Las Bachas Beaches (Gal) 408
Latacunga 175-180, **176**
Lava Tubes (Gal) 406
León Dormido (Gal) 410
Limón 262
Limoncocha 288
Limones 322
Loja 242-248, **244**
Los Frailes 352
Los Galápagos (Gal) 410, 455
Los Gemelos (Gal) 406, 450

Macará 253-254, **254**
Macas 264-266, **265**
Machachi 171
Machala 387-391, **388**
Machalilla 354
Malacatos 250
Maldonado 170
Manglaralto 386
Manta 344-349, **346**
Méndez 262
Mindo 302-304
Misahuallí 277-282
Mitad del Mundo 135-136
Montalvo 326
Montañita 387
Montecristi 349-350
Morona 262
Muisne 334-335
    South of Muisne 336

Nambija 260-261
North Coast, The 318-355, **319**
North of Quito 140-170, **142**
North Seymour Island (Gal) 409
Northern Oriente, The 269-301,
    269
Nuevo Rocafuerte 289

Olón 387
Oña 241
Otavalo 141, 143-152, **144, 153**

Palestina 314
Palmar 386
Palora 267
Pañacocha 289

Papallacta 301
Parques Nacionales (National
  Parks):
  Cotopaxi 173-175
  Machalilla 351-353
  Podocarpus 248-250, 260
  Sangay 199-201, 266-267
  Yasuní 290-291
Pasaje 392
Pasochoa Forest Reserve 137-138
Patate 188
Paute 236
Pedernales 337
Peguche 152
Pelileo 189
Peruvian Border 254-255, 393-
  396
Picaigua 188
Píllaro 188
Piñas 392-393
Pinllo 188
Playas 379-381, **378**
Pomasqui 137
Pompeya 288
Portoviejo 340-344, **342**
  Inland from Portoviejo 344
Posorja 381
Post Office Bay (Gal) 411
Prince Philip's Steps (Gal) 414
Progreso 379
Puerto Ayora (Gal) 405, 418-425,
  420
Puerto Baquerizo Moreno (Gal)
  409, 425-426
Puerto Bolívar 391-392
Puerto Egas (Gal) 412, 432
Puerto Grande (Gal) 410
Puerto López 353-354
Puerto Napo 273-275
Puerto Velasco Ibarra (Gal) 426
Puerto Villamil (Gal) 426
Pujilí 181
Punta Albemarle (Gal) 415
Punta Carnero 385
Punta Cormorant (Gal) 412
Punta Espinosa (Gal) 416
Punta García (Gal) 415
Punta Moreno (Gal) 416
Punta Pelada 381
Punta Pitt (Gal) 410
Punta Suarez (Gal) 411
Punta Tortuga (Gal) 415
Puyango Petrified Forest 393
Puyo 271-273, **272**

Quevedo 311-314, **312**
Quilotoa 181
Quinche 2
Quindigua 181

Quito 95-133, 139, **98, 106, 134**

Reserva Biológica Maquipucuna
  304-305
Reservas Ecológicas (Ecological
  Reserves):
  Cotacachi-Cayapas 155-156,
    324-325
  Manglares Churute 387
Reserva Geobotánica Pululahua
  136-137
Reserva Producción Faunísta
  Cuyabeno 298-299
Río Palenque Science Center
  310-311
Río Tigua Valley 181
Río Tiputini 291
Río Verde 2, 326
Riobamba 205-211, **206**
Rocafuerte 326, 344
Rucu Pichincha 139
Rumicucho 136

Salango 354
Salasaca 188-189
Salinas (South Coast) 385-386,
  384
Salinas (South of Quito) 204-205
Same 334
San Antonio de Ibarra 162-163
San Clemente 349
San Gabriel 164
San Gregorio 335
San Jacinto 349
San Lorenzo 169, 318-321
San Lorenzo-Ibarra Railroad 323
San Miguel 324
San Miguelde Salcedo 182
San Rafael Falls 299-300
San Sebastian 352
San Vicente 338
Sangay 200-201
Sangolquí 137
Santa Elena 381
Santa Elena Peninsula 381-383
Santa Isabel 241
Santa María 323
Santa Rosa 393
Santa Rosa (Gal) 406
Santa Teresita 212
Santo Domingo de los
  Colorados 306-310, **308**
Saquisilí 180-181
Saraguro 241-242
Shell 270
Sigchos 181
Sígsig 236
Sombrero Chino (Gal) 413

South American Explorers Club
  46, 96
South Coast, The 356-396, **357**
South of Quito 171-216, **172**
South Plaza (Gal) 408
Southern Oriente, The 256-267
Súa 333-334
Sucúa 263-264
Sullivan Bay (Gal) 413, 432

Tabacundo 2
Tagus Cove (Gal) 415
Taisha 267
Tarapoa 297-298
Tena 275-277, **274**
Tinalandia 306
Tonchigüe 334
Tonsupa 331-332
Tortoise Reserve (Gal) 408
Tufiño 169
Tulcán 164-168, **166**
Tungurahua 199-200
Turtle Bay (Gal) 406

Urbina Bay (Gal) 415

Valdivia 386
Vilcabamba 250-251
Villamil Lagoons (Gal) 416
Volcanes (volcanoes):
  Alcedo (Gal) 415
  Cayambe 142, 143
  Cerro Azul (Gal) 399
  Chico (Gal) 416
  Chimborazo 211-212
  Chiles, Colombia 170
  Pichincha 138-139
  Reventador 299
  Santo Tomás (Gal) 416
  Sierra Negra (see Volcán
    Santo Tomás)
  Wolf (Gal) 398, 414

Western Lowlands, The 302-
  317, **303**
Whale Bay (Gal) 408
Wildlife (Galápagos):
  American Oystercatcher 445
  Audubon's Shearwater 435-
    436
  Band-rumped (Madeiran)
    Storm Petrel 436-437
  Barn Owl 449-450
  Black-necked Stilt 447
  Blue-footed Booby 438
  Brown Noddy 448
  Brown Pelican 437
  Cactus Finch 453
  Cattle Egret 442

Charles Mockingbird 451
Chatham Mockingbird 452
Common Egret 441-442
Coelenterates 463
Common Gallinule 444-445
Corals 463
Dark-billed Cuckoo 449
Dark-rumped Petrel 435-436
Dolphins 460
Echinoderms 463
Fish 461
Flightless Cormorant 439-440
Galápagos (Southern) Martin 451
Galápagos Dove 448-449
Galápagos Fur Seal 460
Galápagos Hawk 444
Galápagos Land Iguana 457
Galápagos Mockingbird 451
Galápagos Penguin 434-435
Galápagos Rail 444
Galápagos Sea Lion 459-460
Geckos 458
Ghost Crabs 462
Giant Tortoise 454-455
Great Blue Heron 441
Great Frigatebird 440-441
Greater Flamingo 443
Groove-billed Ani 449
Hermit Crab 462
Hood Mockingbird 451-452
Insects 463
Invertebrates 462-463
Jellyfish 463

Large Cactus Finch 453
Large Ground Finch 453
Large Tree Finch 454
Large-billed (Galápagos) Flycatcher 450-451
Lava Gull 448
Lava Heron 442
Lava Lizard 457-458
Magnificent Frigatebird 440-441
Mangrove Finch 454
Marine Iguana 456-457
Masked Booby 438
Medium Ground Finch 453
Medium Tree Finch 454
Mice 459
Northern Phalarope 447
Pacific Green Sea Turtle 455-456
Paint-billed Crake 444
Plainnose Bats 458-459
Plants 464
Rats 459
Rays 461
Red-billed Tropicbird 437
Red-footed Booby 439
Ruddy Turnstone 446
Sally Lightfoot Crab 462
Sanderling 446-447
Santa Fe Land Iguana 457
Sea Anemones 463
Sea Urchin 463
Semi-palmated Plover 446
Sharks 461

Sharp-beaked Ground Finch 453
Short-eared Owl 450
Small Ground Finch 453
Small Tree Finch 453
Snakes 458
Sooty Tern 448
Swallow-tailed Gull 447-448
Vegetarian Finch 453
Vermilion Flycatcher 450
Wandering Tattler 446
Warbler Finch 454
Waved Albatross 435
Wedge-rumped (Galápagos) Storm Petrel 436-437
Whales 460
Whimbrel 447
White-cheeked Pintail 443
White-vented (Elliot's) Storm Petrel 436-437
Woodpecker Finch 454
Yellow Warbler 452
Yellow-crowned Night Heron 442-443

Yantzaza 261

Zabalo 297
Zamora 258-260, **259**
Zapallo Grande 323
Zaruma 392
Zumba 251
Zumbagua 181

Thanks

Thanks must go to the travellers who used the second edition of this book and wrote to Lonely Planet with information, comments and suggestions.

Agee Jr, Phil (USA), Allum, Claire (C), Amador, Fernando, Andrew, Christine (UK), Anmuth, Rick (USA), Atulyo & Preyasi (no last names); Sailing Vessel *S/V Wailana*, USA), August, Steve & Seger, Carol (USA), Badner, Robert H (USA), Bahr, Aniko (Ecu), Bailey, Michael (?), Bartaletti, Fabrizio (I), Bauer, Gayle (USA), Bechtel, Jim (?), Bendorff, Mona (Uru), Blankenship, Judy (Ecu), Boettcher, Mark J (G), Bohman, Ulrika & Larsson, Helén, (S), Breitkreutz, Cindy (C), Burden, Michael (UK), Camarra, Craig (USA), Cameron, David (USA), Carmean, Kim (C), Cheetham, Steve (UK), Christie, Judith A (F), Coberly, Steven (USA), Cornell, Greg (C), Corral, Patricia (Ecu), Cotton, Nick (UK), Cronin, David (UK), Cross, John (USA), Davis, Deborah (USA), Davis, Jenny (USA), Dendy, Margaret & Huiban, Monique (AUS), Devine, Kieram & Jillian (UK), Dineen, Jacqueline (C), Doroghy, Dave (USA), Dorssers, Wim & Koster, Anita (NL), Dunbar-Rees, R J (UK), Dunphy, Roberta (AUS), Dursch, Gretchen & Smith, Steve (USA), Dyk, Sandra A van (NL), Edesa, José Ramón (Ecu), Evans, Humphrey (UK), Eynde, Wim van (B), Fleming, Kelly (USA), Francis, Jonathan P (UK), Franke, Jolie (NL), Frederick, David C (USA), Freeman, M & R (USA), Fuller, Kathryn (UK), Gaby, Don C (USA), Galan, Etienne (F), Galen, Solana, & Sandoval, Maria (USA), Galas, June (USA), Geert, Cromphout (B), Gifford, Clive (UK), Gilbert, Douglas J (CH), Gilman, Steven (USA), Giovanni, Elena (I), Goldstone, Rachel & Young, Joe (USA), Gregersen, Per & Graversen, Tine S (DK), Gurn, Paul H, & Synnott, Eileen M (USA), Hack, Garrett (USA), Hall, Vanessa (UK), Hamilton, Elder John (USA), Haratani, Amy (USA), Harrison, Andrew (UK), Haas, Jörg (Ecu), Hatt, Kiersten (C), Hazewinkel, Marjolyn (NL), Hein, Terry (USA), Hession Jr, Leo J (USA in West Malaysia), Hilty, J W (USA), Hloch, Herbert (D), Hoffman-Riem, Holger (D), Huggan, Mrs Mary (UK), Hupjé, Robert (NL) & Cook, Lisa (UK), Hutchinson, Tracy (C), Huxley, Joyce & Chris (St Lucia), Hyman, Randall (USA), Irby, Dennis (USA Peace Corps in Ecu), Irving, Kim (Peru), Isgar, Tom & Susan (USA), Jackson, Michael (C), Jager, Inge (NL), Jenny, Andrea (CH), Jones, Roslyn (UK), Kaegel, Mary Ellen (?), Kauffman, Phil (USA), Kaufmann, Mark J & Porret, Etienne (CH), Killefer, Gail (USA), Kinson, Victor (USA), Klapper, Janet (USA), Knight, Darryl (AUS), Koppen, Karl van (NL), Kraybill, Nancy & Blair, Joan (USA), Landeborg, Monica & Alunquist, Lars (S), Lathrop, Eva (USA), Lawrence, Hanna (USA), Leifer, Anders (DK), Lerner, Raissa (USA), Liefert, Patricia (USA in Ecu), Liker, Keith A (USA), Lomosse, Christine (S), Mahler, Richard (USA), Maitland, Toby (UK), March, Robert (Ecu), Mathieu, L G (USA), McClaskey, M (C), McFadden, Peter (UK), Medhora, Rohinton (C), Merrill, Bruce (USA), Millhouse, Nick (USA), Milton, Lindsay (C), Minear, Beth (USA), Monique (F), Mora, Rodrigo M (Ecu), Morales, Carlos E (Ecu), Morman, Shelba Jean (USA), Morrow, Glenn (USA), Moyse, Chris (UK), Myers, Laura (USA in Ecu), Nemeth, Katalin & Bender, Gabriel (CH), Norman, Sue (C), Nunan, Mary Pat (USA), O'Sullivan, Ros (IRL), Olsen, Eigil (N), Packman, Meriel (UK), Parkinson, Laura (C), Pfeiffer, Ton (NL), Pichault, François (B), Pichler, Robert (A in Colombia), Pommer, Heinz (D), Pommier, Yvonne (C), Porta, Gianna & Guido (I), Porter, Tim (UK), Puvilland, Annick (F), Raguso, Robert A (USA), Raider, Faith (USA), Ramsay, Mr John Wm (USA), Rana, Dev (UK), Rehm, Kathy M (USA), Rengifo, Mary & Clarke, Douglas (Ecu), Rivadeneira, Carlos Mora (Ecu), Russell, Ruth Ogden (Tucson Audubon Society in USA), Samuelson, Mark (UK), Schechter, Danny (USA), Schmidt, Elizabeth B (USA), Schnurpfeil, Herbert (A), Schultheis, Alexandra (USA), Seltman, Charles (USA), Seltzer, Mark (C), Shiner, Mary & Walsh, Martin (UK), Silk, John & Hayden, Therese (UK), Simon, Harlan (USA), Slagt, Erik (NL), Smith, Brenda (USA), Smith, Lesley & Elston, Tony (UK), Smith, Roy (USA in Ecu), Sohrt, Christiane (D), Sørensen, Birtemarie & Jespersen, Paul Erik (DK), Sørensen, Merete & Christensen, Jakob (DK), Soteriades, Mr S (UK), Spence, Richard & Kreitman, Julia (UK), Spencer, Matthew (UK in Ecu), Staite, Jill (UK), Stoft, Judy (USA), Synnevåog, Helga (N), Tamblyn, Joe (USA), Tavella, Steve & Janet (USA), Tillotson, Guy Steven (USA), Trounce, Russell (AUS), Van Rompaey-Schuermans, Lydia & Erik (B), Wagenhauser, Betsy (USA in Ecu), Warren, Peter (AUS), Webber, B (USA), Wikeley, Adrian & Battersby, André (UK), Wilkinson, Robert (USA), Willey, Walter (USA), Williams, Jeff & Alison (AUS), Wirth, Hanspeter (CH), Wyatt, Anne & Jeffrey (UK), Wyatt, S (Ecu), Yates, Barbara (UK), Zettl, Helmut (A), Ziarno, Ray (USA), Zimmerman, Tony (NZ), Zorilla, Carlos (Ecu)

A – Austria, AUS – Australia, B – Belgium, C – Canada, CH – Switzerland, D – Germany, DK – Denmark, Ecu – Ecuador, F – France, IRL – Ireland, I – Italy, N – Norway, NL – Netherlands, NZ – New Zealand, S – Sweden, UK – United Kingdom, Uru – Uruguay, USA – United States of America

Keep in touch!

We love hearing from you and think you'd like to hear from us.

The Lonely Planet Newsletter covers the when, where, how and what of travel. (AND it's free!)

When...is the right time to see reindeer in Finland?
Where...can you hear the best palm-wine music in Ghana?
How...do you get from Asunción to Areguá by steam train?
What...should you leave behind to avoid hassles with customs in Iran?

To join our mailing list just contact us at any of our offices. (details below)

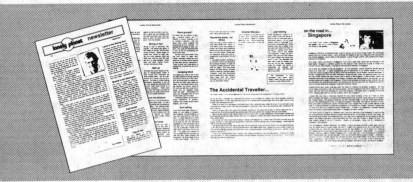

Every issue includes:

- *a letter from Lonely Planet founders Tony and Maureen Wheeler*
- *travel diary from a Lonely Planet author - find out what it's really like out on the road*
- *feature article on an important and topical travel issue*
- *a selection of recent letters from our readers*
- *the latest travel news from all over the world*
- *details on Lonely Planet's new and forthcoming releases*

Also available Lonely Planet T-shirts. 100% heavy weight cotton (S, M, L, XL)

LONELY PLANET PUBLICATIONS
Australia: PO Box 617, Hawthorn, 3122, Victoria (tel: 03-819 1877)
USA: Embarcadero West, 155 Filbert Street, Suite 251, Oakland, CA 94607 (tel: 510-893 8555)
UK: Devonshire House, 12 Barley Mow Passage, Chiswick, London W4 4PH (tel: 081-742 3161)

Guides to the Americas

Alaska – a travel survival kit
Jim DuFresne has travelled extensively through Alaska by foot, road, rail, barge and kayak. This guide has all the information you'll need to make the most of one of the world's great wilderness areas.

Argentina, Uruguay & Paraguay – a travel survival kit
This guide gives independent travellers all the essential information on three of South America's lesser known countries. Discover some of South America's most spectacular natural attractions in Argentina; friendly people and beautiful handicrafts in Paraguay; and Uruguay's wonderful beaches.

Baja California – a travel survival kit
For centuries, Mexico's Baja peninsula – with its beautiful coastline, raucous border towns and crumbling Spanish missions – has been a land of escapes and escapades. This book describes how and where to escape in Baja.

Bolivia – a travel survival kit
From lonely villages in the Andes to ancient ruined cities and the spectacular city of La Paz, Bolivia is a magnificent blend of everything that inspires travellers. Discover safe and intriguing travel options in this comprehensive guide.

Brazil – a travel survival kit
From the mad passion of Carnival to the Amazon – home of the richest and most diverse ecosystem on earth – Brazil is a country of mythical proportions. This guide has all the essential travel information.

Canada – a travel survival kit
This comprehensive guidebook has all the facts on the USA's huge neighbour – the Rocky Mountains, Niagara Falls, ultramodern Toronto, remote villages in Nova Scotia, and much more.

Central America on a shoestring
Practical information on travel in Belize, Guatemala, Costa Rica, Honduras, El Salvador, Nicaragua and Panama. A team of experienced Lonely Planet authors reveals the secrets of this culturally rich, geographically diverse and breathtakingly beautiful region.

Chile & Easter Island – a travel survival kit
Travel in Chile is easy and safe, with possibilities as varied as the countryside. This guide also gives detailed coverage of Chile's Pacific outpost, mysterious Easter Island.

Colombia – a travel survival kit
Colombia is a land of myths – from the ancient legends of El Dorado to the modern tales of Gabriel Garcia Marquez. The reality is beauty and violence, wealth and poverty, tradition and change. This guide shows how to travel independently and safely in this exotic country.

Costa Rica – a travel survival kit
This practical guide gives the low down on exceptional opportunities for fishing and water sports, and the best ways to experience Costa Rica's vivid natural beauty.

Hawaii – a travel survival kit
Share in the delights of this island paradise – and avoid its high prices – both on and off the beaten track. Full details on Hawaii's best-known attractions, plus plenty of uncrowded sights and activities.

La Ruta Maya: Yucatán, Guatemala & Belize – a travel survival kit
Invaluable background information on the cultural and environmental riches of La Ruta Maya (The Mayan Route), plus practical advice on how best to minimise the impact of travellers on this sensitive region.

Mexico – a travel survival kit
A unique blend of Indian and Spanish culture, fascinating history, and hospitable people, make Mexico a travellers' paradise.

Peru – a travel survival kit
The lost city of Machu Picchu, the Andean altiplano and the magnificent Amazon rainforests are just some of Peru's many attractions. All the travel facts you'll need can be found in this comprehensive guide.

South America on a shoestring
This practical guide provides concise information for budget travellers and covers South America from the Darien Gap to Tierra del Fuego. The *New York Times* dubbed the author 'the patron saint of travellers in the third world'.

Trekking in the Patagonian Andes
The first detailed guide to this region gives complete information on 28 walks, and lists a number of other possibilities extending from the Araucanía and Lake District regions of Argentina and Chile to the remote icy of South America in Tierra del Fuego.

Also available:
Brazilian phrasebook, **Latin American Spanish** phrasebook and **Quechua** phrasebook.

Lonely Planet Guidebooks

Lonely Planet guidebooks cover every accessible part of Asia as well as Australia, the Pacific, South America, Africa, the Middle East, Europe and parts of North America. There are five series: *travel survival kits*, covering a country for a range of budgets; *shoestring guides* with compact information for low-budget travel in a major region; *walking guides*; *city guides* and *phrasebooks*.

Australia & the Pacific
Australia
Bushwalking in Australia
Islands of Australia's Great Barrier Reef
Fiji
Melbourne city guide
Micronesia
New Caledonia
New Zealand
Tramping in New Zealand
Papua New Guinea
Bushwalking in Papua New Guinea
Papua New Guinea phrasebook
Rarotonga & the Cook Islands
Samoa
Solomon Islands
Sydney city guide
Tahiti & French Polynesia
Tonga
Vanuatu
Victoria

South-East Asia
Bali & Lombok
Bangkok city guide
Cambodia
Indonesia
Indonesia phrasebook
Laos
Malaysia, Singapore & Brunei
Myanmar (Burma)
Burmese phrasebook
Philippines
Pilipino phrasebook
Singapore city guide
South-East Asia on a shoestring
Thailand
Thai phrasebook
Vietnam
Vietnamese phrasebook

North-East Asia
China
Beijing city guide
Mandarin Chinese phrasebook
Hong Kong, Macau & Canton
Japan
Japanese phrasebook
Korea
Korean phrasebook
Mongolia
North-East Asia on a shoestring
Seoul city guide
Taiwan
Tibet
Tibet phrasebook
Tokyo city guide

West Asia
Trekking in Turkey
Turkey
Turkish phrasebook
West Asia on a shoestring

Middle East
Arab Gulf States
Egypt & the Sudan
Arabic (Egyptian) phrasebook
Iran
Israel
Jordan & Syria
Yemen

Indian Ocean
Madagascar & Comoros
Maldives & Islands of the East Indian Ocean
Mauritius, Réunion & Seychelles